THE SEAS OF L

THE SEAS OF LANGUAGE

Michael Dummett

CLARENDON PRESS · OXFORD

Oxford University Press, Great Clarendon Street, Oxford OX2 6DP
Oxford New York
Athens Auckland Bangkok Bogota Bombay
Buenos Aires Calcutta Cape Town Dar es Salaam
Delhi Florence Hong Kong Istanbul Karachi
Kuala Lumpur Madras Madrid Melbourne
Mexico City Nairobi Paris Singapore
Taipei Tokyo Toronto Warsaw
and associated companies in
Berlin Ibadan

Oxford is a trade mark of Oxford University Press

Published in the United States by
Oxford University Press Inc., New York

First published 1993
First issued as paperback 1996
Reprinted as paperback 1997

British Library Cataloguing in Publication Data
Data available

Library of Congress Cataloging in Publication Data
Dummett, Michael A. E.
The seas of language/Michael Dummett.
Includes index.
1. Language and languages—Philosophy. 2. Metaphysics.
I. Title.
P106.D86 1993 121'.68—dc20 93-933
ISBN 0-19-824011-2
ISBN 0-19-823621-2 (Pbk.)

Printed in Great Britain
on acid-free paper by
Biddles Ltd, Guildford and King's Lynn

To
Paul, Virginia, Charlotte, Hannah, and Esther

See how high the seas of language run here!

(Wittgenstein, *Philosophical Investigations* I. 194)

Preface

This book contains almost all my articles and essays on metaphysics and the philosophy of language—two branches of philosophy that I regard as closely intertwined—that have been published or are shortly to be published and were not contained in *Truth and Other Enigmas* (London, 1978) or in *Frege and Other Philosophers* (Oxford, 1991). It also contains one essay, 'Could there be Unicorns?', not previously published in English, and two neither forthcoming nor previously published in any language. Of these, 'Truth and Meaning' was written for publication; the other is my valedictory lecture 'Realism and Anti-Realism'.

Apart from the publication of matter not published previously, the chief purpose of such a collection as this is the convenience of readers, who no longer have to strive to remember in which journal or book a given article or essay was published, nor to go from one to another if they are wishing to read more than one of them at a time. (It is also a great convenience to the author, who no longer has to keep messy and incomplete piles of offprints; but that is obviously an inadequate justification for publishing such a book.) A further purpose is to introduce readers to some articles or essays they had previously missed; the author hopes, moreover, that they will be prompted to reread some that they had not missed but have now largely forgotten.

Among the earliest of the items in this collection to be written are 'Does Quantification Involve Identity?' and 'Mood, Force, and Convention', both composed in 1976 and intended for Festschrifts, the former for one in honour of Peter Geach and the latter for one in honour of Donald Davidson. Those that were *published* earliest are the two—a lecture and an essay—entitled 'What is a Theory of Meaning?', both of which appeared before the compilation of *Truth and Other Enigmas*. They were excluded from that book because at the time I intended to make them the first two chapters of a short book, with, perhaps, only one other chapter. That project was never carried out, because, by the time that I might have started work on the third chapter, 'What is a Theory of Meaning? (II)' no longer seemed to me satisfactory. Some evidences of this dissatisfaction appear in other essays included here, for instance in 'What do I Know when I Know a Language?' It is to the two essays called 'What is a Theory of Meaning?' that I shall principally direct my comments in this Preface.

From the start, I have felt an awkwardness about the first of the pair, for the following reason. My memory was, and is, that I experienced great illumination from listening to a discussion after a lecture of Donald Davidson's which I attended when on a visit to the United States. In the course of this discussion, as I remember it, Davidson answered an objector by saying that, according to his conception of a theory of meaning, such a theory was not intended to convey the concepts expressible in the object-language, but to convey an understanding of that language to one who already had those concepts. This struck me as a luminous way of expressing his idea of what he was after in his discussions of a theory of meaning, and also as focusing very precisely on the difference between the ways he and I conceived of such a theory. The two of us each contributed to a series of Wolfson Lectures held in Oxford in 1974 (and published as *Mind and Language*, edited by Samuel Guttenplan, Oxford, 1975); by an odd coincidence, out of the six lecturers, all but the two Americans were Catholics, although you could not have inferred that from their lectures. When I came to compose my lecture, I decided to treat of the conception of a theory of meaning I remembered Davidson to have expressed with such clarity, and borrowed that formulation for my characterization of what I called a 'modest' theory of meaning: but I was embarrassed whether or not to acknowledge the source of the formulation. On the one hand, I surely owed it to Davidson to do so; on the other, it is unfair to saddle people in public, and particularly in print, with things they said in discussion, which may well not have expressed their considered view. In the event, I decided, with some uneasiness, not to make any acknowledgement. I was later relieved, but at the same time greatly surprised, when Davidson, in informal conversation, declared that he had never intended a theory of meaning, as he conceived it, to be modest in my sense, and had never asserted it to be. My memory is extremely unreliable; in particular, I have often discovered that people never said what I thought I remembered them as saying. One possibility, therefore, is that Davidson had not said what I remembered as having afforded me so much illumination, and that I misunderstood him at the time or misremembered him later. Another, of course, is that *he* had forgotten saying something by which he would not wish to stand. Either way, I am glad that I made no acknowledgement to him in the lecture. I nevertheless retain an uneasy feeling that I failed to avow a debt; I take this opportunity to thank him for saying whatever it was he said that prompted me, by one means or another, to frame an idea which I believe to be fruitful.

The formulation, as I gave it in the lecture, was faulty; the error was corrected in 'What is a Theory of Meaning? (II)'. It plainly cannot be demanded of a 'full-blooded' theory of meaning that it should be so framed as to convey every concept expressed by a word in the language to one who does not possess it; some concepts must be taken as basic, and others cannot by their nature be conveyed by means of a verbal explanation, and hence by any statement that can be incorporated in a theory of meaning. The most that can be generally demanded of such a theory, therefore, is that, in the course of specifying what is required for a speaker to grasp the sense of a given word, it should explain what it is for him to possess the concept it expresses. I do not believe, however, that this means that conceptual analysis has no contribution to make to a theory of meaning. A speaker, to be credited with an understanding of the expressions of a language, must manifest his grasp of connections between them; it is those connections that conceptual analysis aims to make explicit. When the concept expressed by some word of the language can be wholly or partly conveyed by verbal explanation, such an explanation may reasonably be expected to be incorporated into a full-blooded meaning-theory.

After giving the lecture, I thought of a way of construing Davidson's conception of a theory of meaning as not being modest, by giving full weight to the holistic component in his thinking, which I had ignored in the lecture. This is expounded in the Appendix to the lecture, which was written for the published version in *Mind and Language*.

Before this, however, Davidson had, with the greatest mildness, voiced, again in private conversation, a complaint I had not anticipated, that it had been he who introduced the notion of a theory of meaning for a specific language, whereas, in the lecture, I had treated it as a notion in common currency, on which he had put a particular interpretation. The phrase "theory of meaning" is, of course, quite old, in that use in which it denotes a branch of philosophy, in analogy with "theory of knowledge"; this differs sharply from the conception of a detailed theory relating to a particular language and giving the meanings of all words and sentences of the language. Davidson has operated with that conception since the earliest of his published papers on the philosophy of language (that is, since 1967). If I have borrowed it and used it without proper acknowledgement, I hereby express my thanks and my apologies. I find it impossible to be sure whether this is so, or whether there is merely a partial convergence of ideas. Davidson's earliest relevant essays antedate my first book, *Frege: Philosophy of Language* (London, 1973), in the preface to which I acknowledged Davidson's general influence on me; so an examination of it does not settle the matter. Looking through it, I find the phrase "theory of meaning" used repeatedly, and with no care to distinguish different senses of it. Sometimes it is used in the old sense; more often as denoting a comprehensive theory describing the workings of 'language', with all its component expressions, and thereby explaining what constitutes the possession by those expressions of the meanings that they have, but as if there was only a single human language; but sometimes (e.g. pp. 106, 397, 413–17, 452–6, 460–1) as denoting a theory of this kind relating to a single specific language. So I certainly had that concept then, without keeping it at all sharply in focus; but that does not show that I did not derive it from Davidson. For any injustice or ungraciousness of which I may have been unintentionally guilty, I hereby sincerely apologize.

'What is a Theory of Meaning? (II)' was meant, when it was written, to be a definitive statement of my views upon the topic; that, indeed, was what Gareth

Evans and John McDowell, the editors of the volume *Truth and Meaning* (Oxford, 1976), in which it appeared, had asked me for. Not long after *Truth and Other Enigmas* came out, however, I began to have doubts about its treatment of the notion of a speaker's knowledge of a language: it offered two incompatible conceptions of that notion, neither of them satisfactory. One is that knowledge of a language is simply a practical ability, like knowing how to swim, save for being immeasurably more complex: this view is expressed in the characterization of a theory of meaning as a theoretical representation of a practical ability, and its articulation as corresponding to the articulation of that complex ability. I now think that a knowledge of a language has a substantial theoretical component; better expressed, that the classification of knowledge into theoretical and practical (knowledge-that and knowledge-how) is far too crude to allow knowledge of a language to be located within it. For one thing, a ground for taking seriously the attribution of *knowledge* to someone able to speak a language is that his linguistic utterances are (usually) rational acts, concerning which we may ask after the motives and intentions underlying them; it is in fact essential to an account of the practice of using language that the hearer may ask himself, or the speaker, why he said what he did—not only his ground for saying it, but his point in saying it. An intention or motive in performing an action is always based upon knowledge: it cannot relate to anything the agent did not know about the character, significance, or likely effects of the action. In the same way, our interpretation of a speaker is strongly affected by our awareness of imperfections in his knowledge of the language—if he is a child or a foreigner, for example. A mere practical ability does not, however, provide sufficient grounding for a purpose or intention, because one may be able to do something without knowing how one does it. In endeavouring to follow what someone is saying, the hearer has frequently to estimate his point in expressing himself in one way rather than another, on the presumption that he knew the other way of expressing it and was aware that it was the more natural; but if his knowledge amounted to no more than the mere ability to express himself in the language, such questions would lapse. Secondly, the classic examples of pure practical abilities, like the ability to swim, are those in which it is possible, before acquiring the ability, to have a fully adequate conception of what it is an ability to do. By contrast, there is a clear sense in which it is only by learning a language that one can come by a knowledge of what it is to speak that language, just as it is only by learning how to play chess that one can come by a knowledge of what it is to play chess. Knowledge of a language is therefore not a pure example of a practical ability.

It would be preposterous to be propelled by these considerations into attributing to speakers of a language an explicit knowledge of a theory of meaning for that language: obviously, they have no such knowledge. Knowing a language is a species of knowledge intermediate between pure practical knowledge and pure theoretical knowledge: it is the salient illustration of the crudity of the practical/theoretical dichotomy. 'What is a Theory of Meaning? (II)' offers another characterization of linguistic knowledge, however, namely as implicit or tacit (theoretical) knowledge. Implicit knowledge is explained as possessed by a subject who cannot himself formulate the content of the knowledge, but can recognize as correct a formulation that is offered him. This is not compatible with the characterization of linguistic knowledge as a form of practical ability: implicit knowledge in this sense is quite irrelevant to possession of a practical ability, because, as already remarked, I can know how to do something without knowing how I do it. Someone shows me how to do something; I try to copy him, but get it wrong, without being able to see wherein what I did differed from what my instructor did. After repeated trials, I get it right. I repeat my success: now I have got the knack. I *may* now have implicit knowledge of how I do it. But I may not: offered an accurate description of what I do, I may say, "You may be right" or "Is *that* what I do?"; the implicit knowledge, if it exists, is quite inessential to my acquisition of the practical ability.

Furthermore, attribution of implicit knowledge, in the sense explained, is unexplanatory. A speaker's employment of his language rests upon his knowledge of it: his knowledge of what the words and sentences of the language mean is an essential part of the explanation of his saying what he does. What matters about knowledge, for philosophy, is not how it is stored but in what form it is delivered. Hence, however psychology may evaluate it, Chomsky's characterization of mastery of a language as unconscious knowledge contributes nothing to philosophical understanding. Presumably the qualification of the knowledge as unconscious implies that it cannot be brought into consciousness, at least readily or assuredly, or otherwise it would not differ from explicit knowledge; presumably, also, its possessor will not in general even be able to recognize as correct a formulation of it offered to him. But this merely rules out one way in which the knowledge might be delivered to him: it does nothing to explain how it is delivered—how possession of the unconcious knowledge operates to guide, prompt, or control the speaker's utterances. The same, however, is true of implicit knowledge, explained as comprising an ability to recognize a formulation of its content when presented with one. That definition tells us nothing about how the knowledge is applied when the occasion for its application arises: it therefore fails to explain what the philosopher seeks an explanation for. Take the case of an uncontroversial rule, one of orthography. A writer habitually writes "deferred" and "proffered", and in all other cases conforms to the rule governing when you should and when you should not double the final consonant of a verb in forming the past tense or past or present participle. He cannot state the rule, however: in what sense can he be said to know it? He may or may not be able to recognize a formulation of the rule when it is offered to him; but what does it matter whether or not he can? When he is writing, no formulation of the rule is before him; in what sense, then, and by what mechanism, is he guided by the rule to spell correctly? Talking about unconscious knowledge does not solve this problem; nor does talking about implicit knowledge.

If I do not think that 'What is a Theory of Meaning? (II)' is right, why am I reprinting it? Well, in the first place, I do not think that it is wrong from beginning to end, as the Caterpillar severely said to Alice of her rendering of 'You are old, Father William'. Much in it still seems to me right. I continue to believe that any knowledge attributed to a speaker as constituting a component of his knowledge of a language must be manifested in his employment of that language, including his reactions to things said to him in that language by others. I continue to think, furthermore, that this constraint poses a grave difficulty for the proponents of truth-conditional theories of meaning. And, secondly, I do not see that anyone is an authority on whether his present views are closer to the truth than his earlier views. Of course, he must *think* that they are, because otherwise he would not hold his present views; but he cannot maintain that there is any strong objective probability that later views will be an improvement on earlier ones. After all, I feel no great confidence that the views I shall hold in ten years' time will be nearer the truth than those I hold now, although I shall, of necessity, think so in ten years' time. Of course, there has to be *some* reasonable chance that one's later views on a given topic will be an improvement on the earlier ones, or there would be no point in continuing to think about the topic having once expressed oneself upon it. The chance is, however, seldom so high that one should want to suppress the earlier writings; and the behaviour of philosophical authors confirms this. Wittgenstein, for example, did not wish the *Tractatus* to go out of print: on the contrary, he wanted it reprinted together with the *Philosophical Investigations*.

The five following essays (3 to 7) all embody attempts at improving some of the formulations of 'What is a Theory of Meaning? (II)'. Indigestion is therefore likely to result from reading them consecutively; I recommend interspersing some of the later essays.

My insistence that linguistic knowledge must be *fully* manifested in linguistic practice has opened the way for objections by my critics. How can this be so, they have asked, when a speaker says only finitely many things? However aptly his utterances so far may have been consistent with his attaching a certain meaning to a word, for example, it always remains possible that his next use of it may fail to fit an interpretation of him as understanding it in that way. How, the critics ask, could the finitely many uses a speaker makes of an expression, and the finitely many responses he makes to its use by others, *fully* manifest the meaning he attaches to it, which is in a certain sense infinite?

A realistic first response to this challenge is that it is overblown. There is no requirement that all the uses a speaker makes of an expression throughout his lifetime should admit of some uniform interpretation: he may come to attach a different meaning to it, whether or not he is aware of having done so, or he may consciously use it with different senses in different contexts. If on one occasion his use of it appears to deviate from previous uses, we may have the opportunity to ask him if he is using it in the same sense as before. If he affirms that he is, but can offer no coherent account of this supposedly constant sense, and if we cannot perceive any interpretation that would make the new use consistent with the old, we may conclude that it was an aberration, and judge that he did not know what he was saying, as we judge of utterances of someone half-asleep, in great pain, drunk, or in the grip of passionate emotion. The fact is that we do often judge, from a finite amount of evidence, if sufficiently varied, that a speaker attaches a particular meaning to a word or expression, and treat our judgements as immune from overthrow by any instance of subsequent use inconsistent with them.

There is some substance to the criticism, all the same. It may be that the totality of things some speaker has said does not provide the basis for such a judgement; and then it can happen that some later utterance of his causes us to revise our former interpretation of the expression as he uses it, and substitute a new but coherent, uniform interpretation. In such a case, what he had said previously plainly did *not* fully manifest his understanding of the expression; and it might have been that nothing he said or did throughout his life would have done so. In the light of this, more than one commentator has suggested weakening the requirement thus: any difference in the meanings attached to an expression by two speakers must be *capable* of being manifested by some differences in the uses they make of it. That is to say, there are things they *might* say that will manifest the difference; but there is not in general any guarantee that they *will* say them, in which case the difference in their understanding of the expression will never come to light.

My reason for requiring a complete manifestation was not that this weakened requirement had not occurred to me, but that I did not consider it adequate. This is best illustrated by the conception, which I take to be spurious, of an understanding of statements of a mathematical theory as resting on an intuitive grasp, unmediated by language, of a model for the theory. The conception was combated in 'The Philosophical Significance of Gödel's Theorem', reprinted in *Truth and Other Enigmas*. Suppose someone who applies this conception to the understanding of first-order arithmetic, but is willing to restrict a manifestation of the use made of arithmetical statements to the progressive enunciation of true statements and of principles for deriving true statements, in such a way that, at any one time, the set of statements asserted as true or derivable from those so asserted by the principles enunciated is recursively enumerable. Then he must admit that no specific way of understanding statements of first-order arithmetic can ever be fully manifested, since it follows from Gödel's theorem that, for any recursively enumerable set of such statements, there will be models satisfying all the members of the set but differing over the truth or falsity of statements not belonging to the set. Now it would be idle to attribute to anyone a grasp of a particular model of arithmetic and yet hold that his capacity ever to recognize an arithmetical statement as true was confined to some recursively enumerable set of them (such as could be captured by a formal system). The attribution has content only if, although the set of statements he recognizes, explicitly or implicitly, as true at any given time must be recursively enumerable, he is always capable of recognizing as true statements not in that set; indeed, Gödel's theorem may itself be cited in favour of such a belief. Now suppose that two individuals have each an intuitive grasp of a different model of first-order arithmetic, and that there are statements true in one model but false in the other. Then the difference in their understanding may show up in a difference of use: there will be a statement that one is capable of coming to recognize as true on his understanding of it and the other is capable of recognizing as false on his. The weak requirement is then satisfied. It appears to me, however, that to make understanding rest upon an inner mental grasp of a mathematical structure that can never be made fully explicit is to render it incommunicable in just that way objected to by Frege in psychologistic accounts of understanding: that is why I made the stronger claim that understanding must be capable of being *fully* manifested in use.

It is plain that it cannot be demanded that every aspect of a speaker's understanding of an expression should in fact be manifested by something he says or does; the most that can be required is that there is something he would say or do, should the occasion arise, that would manifest it. It is not enough, however, to require, of every aspect of his understanding, that it be capable of being manifested. Rather, we are entitled to require that it be possible that every aspect of his understanding should have been manifested; for, if not, there can never be conclusive evidence for the attribution to him of any specific understanding of the expression. This will be controverted by those who insist on the infinite character of meaning—of the meaning of *any* expression. The meaning a speaker attaches to the word "chair", for example, depends upon his classification, as a chair or not a chair, of any actual or hypothetical piece of furniture or putative piece of furniture; and it is not possible that the actual uses he has made up to any given time should reveal how he would classify every conceivable borderline case. Does he treat it as essential, for example, that a chair be movable? Certainly most chairs are movable, and, indeed, the French and Italian words for "piece of furniture" simply *mean* 'movable'; but would the speaker think that, if a chair were clamped to the floor, it would cease to be a chair and become a mere seat? Even if he has encountered chairs clamped to the floor, and allowed that they *were* chairs, he has probably never met with a chair welded to a (metal) floor, or a chair carved out of the same piece of wood as the part of the floor on which it stands; so nothing he has ever said will show whether he would grant or withhold the title of "chair" to it. But to demand that the meaning someone attaches to a word should determine in advance the application he will make of it in every future case, or would make of it in every hypothetical case, however bizarre, is to demand too much: meanings, however precise, are almost always to some degree indeterminate. In some unanticipated case, he would probably say something (though he might confess that he did not know what to say). It does not follow that there is now something that he would say in such a case; the meaning he now attaches to the word may simply not determine what he would say.

A Wittgensteinian may object that that is how it is even in the most ordinary case. Every new application of the word, even to something resembling in every way things to which he has applied it before, will, the objector thinks, demand a decision, in a logical, though doubtless not in a phenomenological, sense. That is to say, there is nothing in whatever constituted his attaching a certain meaning to the word that logically entails that, if he fails to apply it to some one or another object, he will be attaching a different meaning to it. Certainly there is nothing that entails that he will regard himself as using the word with a different meaning; but there is no more to the question whether he is *actually* using it in accordance with the meaning he attached to it before than whether he would generally be judged to be doing so. How should we decide? If, for instance, he refuses to apply the word "chair" to something just like the standard examples of chairs to which he has applied it before, we may ask him why he will not call it a 'chair'. He might give some principled (if eccentric) answer, and we might then agree that he was using the word with the meaning he had always attached to it, though not that which we attach to it; the evidence of his past uses had not, after all, been sufficiently varied to justify our assumption that he understood the word in the same way as everyone else. If, on the other hand, he simply says, "*I* don't regard it as a chair", or proffers some wildly irrelevant consideration, such as that none of the things he had formerly called 'chairs' had first been seen by him at a time when the clock was striking, we shall judge that he is *not* being faithful to the understanding of the word "chair" that he formerly evinced. It may be retorted that everything still rests upon spontaneous communal agreement in judgements. This is no doubt true; but it is not what is at issue. What is at issue is whether it makes sense to speak of someone's having manifested every aspect of the meaning that he attaches to an expression. If it does make sense, then it is a constraint upon any legitimate conception of meaning that it should be possible for any speaker to have done so; Wittgensteinian considerations do not have the power to demonstrate that it does not make sense.

'Could there be Unicorns?' is an attempt to correct a puzzling anomaly. A great advance occurred in the formal investigation of modal logics at the end of the 1950s, by the application to them of possible-world semantic theories. Somewhat later, there was a great vogue among philosophers for the use of possible-worlds semantics for interpreting statements involving modality; this became the basis for introducing into philosophical discourse a supposedly new kind of necessity, metaphysical necessity. In both developments, Saul Kripke played a salient part.

At first sight, this was a natural sequence of events: a technique that had proved highly successful in formal logic was found to be equally successful in the philosophy of language and its attendant metaphysics. But, at a second glance, it is perplexing. The advance in logic was due to the realization that, for all modal logics, the semantic values of (closed) formulas should be taken not, as in the traditional manner, merely as truth-values in a system of many truth-values, but specifically as subsets of an underlying set; the ordinary sentential operators would then correspond to Boolean operations on these sets, and the modal operators to non-Boolean ones. Interpreted, the elements of the underlying space were possible worlds; a closed formula was to be taken as true or false with respect to each world, and the standard operators being interpreted, relatively to each world, by the two-valued truth-tables: only the modal operators were to be understood as yielding a formula whose truth-value, with respect to a given world, depended on the truth-values of the immediate subformula at other worlds.

The discovery was, however, that this could be done for *all* modal logics. The technique had been familiar from the very beginning of the 1950s as applied to the modal logic S5, ever since the completeness proof for that system by S. J. Scroggs ('Extensions of the Lewis System S5', *Journal of Symbolic Logic*, 16 (1951), 112–20). The new discovery was that it could be adapted for weaker modal logics by putting a structure on the underlying set; intuitively, by relativizing the notion of a possible world, so that one world might be possible relatively to a second, but not to a third. But the application of the Leibnizian notion of possible worlds that became fashionable amongst philosophers took no account of this relativization: the possible-worlds semantics adopted by them was simply that yielding the modal logic S5, of which logicians interested in the subject had known for years before the significant advance was made. Thus the idea that gained a vogue among philosophers was not that which had enabled the advance to be made in logic, but one long available; and the idea underlying the advance in logic was made no use of in philosophy.

My article was an attempt to find a use for it: to devise, within a generally Kripkean framework, an application for a semantics yielding S4. It may possibly not be watertight, and, in any case, I do not attach much importance to it, because I believe that the use by philosophers of possible-worlds semantics has done, on balance, more harm than good. I offer it, however, as a challenge to those who believe otherwise to make philosophical use of a version of that semantics that yields an S4 logic, or some other more interesting than, because not as strong as, S5.

Even though I should not now endorse every word in the remaining essays, all of course of a later date than the two entitled 'What is a Theory of Meaning?', it appears to me quite unnecessary to comment on them here: they stand as attempts I have made at various times to handle particular philosophical problems, to be judged on their merits. I hope only that readers may enjoy them, and be stimulated to new thoughts of their own: I do not, of course, expect agreement.

Oxford, October 1992

Contents

Acknowledgements   xx

1. What is a Theory of Meaning? (I)   1
2. What is a Theory of Meaning? (II)   34
3. What do I Know when I Know a Language?   94
4. What does the Appeal to Use Do for the Theory of
   Meaning?   106
5. Language and Truth   117
6. Truth and Meaning   147
7. Language and Communication   166
8. The Source of the Concept of Truth   188
9. Mood, Force, and Convention   202
10. Frege and Husserl on Reference   224
11. Realism   230
12. Existence   277
13. Does Quantification Involve Identity?   308
14. Could there be Unicorns?   328
15. Causal Loops   349
16. Common Sense and Physics   376
17. Testimony and Memory   411
18. What is Mathematics About?   429
19. Wittgenstein on Necessity: Some Reflections   446
20. Realism and Anti-Realism   462

Index   479

Acknowledgements

The author is grateful to the following for permission to reprint copyright material:

Oxford University Press for Essays 1 and 2 in this collection;
Stockholms Universitet for Essay 3;
Kluwer Academic Publishers for Essays 4, 11, and 13;
Pergamon Press Ltd. for Essay 5;
Basil Blackwell Publishers for Essays 7, 15, and 19;
Cambridge University Press for Essay 8;
Macmillan India Ltd. for Essay 12;
Macmillan London Ltd. for Essay 16.

1

What is a Theory of Meaning?
(I)

According to one well-known view, the best method of formulating the philosophical problems surrounding the concept of meaning and related notions is by asking what form that should be taken by what is called 'a theory of meaning' for any one entire language; that is, a detailed specification of the meanings of all the words and sentence-forming operations of the language, yielding a specification of the meaning of every expression and sentence of the language. It is not that the construction of a theory of meaning, in this sense, for any one language is viewed as a practical project; but it is thought that, when once we can enunciate the general principles in accordance with which such a construction could be carried out, we shall have arrived at a solution of the problems concerning meaning by which philosophers are perplexed.

I share the belief that this is the most fruitful approach to the problems within this area of philosophy, although I should not feel capable of giving a demonstration that this was so to someone who denied it: but we can see some reasons for it if we contrast certain other cases. So far as I know, no one has ever suggested a parallel approach to the problems of epistemology: no one has proposed that the right way to go about tackling the philosophical problems relating to the concept of knowledge would be by considering how one might construct a theory of knowledge in the sense of a detailed specification of everything that any one individual, or community, can be said to know. The reason is, I think, that our grasp on the concept of knowledge is rather more secure than our grasp on the concept of meaning. We are in doubt about what ought to count as knowledge; we are even more in doubt about how to formulate the principles we tacitly apply for deciding whether or not something is to count as knowledge; we also have some uncertainty about the semantic analysis of a sentence attributing knowledge of something to somebody: but at least we are quite certain *which* are the sentences whose logical form and whose truth-conditions we are seeking to analyse. By contrast, while most of us, myself included, would agree that the concept of meaning is a fundamental and indispensable one, we are unclear even about the surface structure of statements involving that concept. What kind of sentence, of natural language, should be taken as the characteristic form for an

First published in Samuel Guttenplan (ed.), *Mind and Language*, Wolfson Lectures, 1974 (Oxford, 1975).

attribution of a particular meaning to some given word or expression? Not only do we not know the answer to this: we do not even know whether it is the right question to ask. Perhaps it is impossible, in general, to *state* the meaning of an expression: perhaps we ought, rather, to enquire by what linguistic means, or possibly even non-linguistic means, it is possible to *convey* the meaning of an expression, otherwise than by explicitly stating it. Or perhaps even that is wrong: perhaps the question should be, not how we express that a particular expression has a certain meaning, but how we should analyse sentences which involve the concept of meaning in some different way. It is precisely because, in this area of philosophy, we know even less what it is that we are talking about than we do in other areas, that the proposal to approach our problems by considering how we might attempt to specify the meanings of the expressions of an entire language does not appear the waste of time that an analogous proposal would seem to be within epistemology.

As is well known, some, pre-eminently Quine, have preferred to circumvent this difficulty by investigating the principles underlying the construction not of a theory of meaning for a language, but of a translation manual from it into some known language. The advantage is that we know exactly what form a translation manual has to take, namely an effective set of rules for mapping sentences of the translated language into sentences of the language into which the translation is being made: we can therefore concentrate entirely upon the questions how we are to arrive at a system of translation as embodied in such a manual, and what conditions must be satisfied for such a system to be acceptable. The disadvantage is that, while the interest of such an enquiry must lie in the light it throws on the concept of meaning, we are unable to be certain what consequences the results of the enquiry into translation do have for the notion of meaning, just because they are stated without direct appeal to that notion. To grasp the meaning of an expression is to understand its role in the language: a complete theory of meaning for a language is, therefore, a complete theory of how the language functions as a language. Our interest in meaning, as a general concept, is, thus, an interest in how language works; a direct description of the way a language works—of all that someone has to learn to do when he learns the language—would, accordingly, resolve our perplexities in a way in which an indirect account, by means of a translation, cannot. It will quite rightly be said that the interest in the enquiry into translation attaches, not to the translation itself, but to the criteria proposed for judging the acceptability of a scheme of translation, and that these must relate to what can be observed of the working of the language to be translated. Indeed, it might plausibly be maintained that nothing short of a complete theory of meaning for the language—a complete account of the way it works— could be an adequate basis for judging the correctness of a proposed scheme of translation. I shall not attempt to adjudicate the soundness of this claim. If it is sound, then the apparent advantage of the approach via translation, rather than by asking outright what form a theory of meaning for the language should take, is wholly illusory. If it is unsound—and certainly the actual procedure of the principal practitioner of the approach via translation suggests that he takes it as unsound—then it follows that there is no immediate inference from results concerning translation to conclusions concerning meaning.

I have said that it is the job of a theory of meaning for a language to give an account of how that language works, that is, of how its speakers communicate by means of it: here "communicate" has no more precise signification than "do whatever may be done by the utterance of one or more sentences of the language". And here I will repeat what I have maintained elsewhere, that a theory of meaning is a theory of understanding; that is, what a theory of meaning has to give an account of is what it is that someone knows when he knows the language, that is, when he knows the meanings of the expressions and sentences of the language. One question about the form which a theory of meaning should take is whether it should issue in direct ascriptions of meaning, that is, in propositions of the form "The meaning of the word/sentence X is . . ." or of the form "The word/sentence X means . . ." If the answer to this question is affirmative, then it may seem that such a theory of meaning will have no need to advert explicitly to the notion of knowledge: if the theory allows us to say that the meaning of a given word or sentence is something or other, say Q, then, presumably, we shall likewise want to say that someone knows the meaning of that word or sentence if he knows that Q is what that word or sentence means. We shall later see reason to doubt this; but for the present let us suspend judgement. If the theory of meaning allows us to derive such direct ascriptions of meaning, and if these direct ascriptions are such as to lead in this simple way to a characterization of what it is to know the meaning of each word or sentence in the language, then, indeed, my claim that a theory of meaning must be a theory of understanding is not intended in so strong a sense as to rule out such a theory, merely on the ground that it did not itself employ the notion of knowledge: it would be proper to accept such a theory as being a theory of understanding. If, on the other hand, although the theory of meaning allows the derivation of direct ascriptions of meaning, these ascriptions are so framed as not to permit an immediate characterization of what it is that a person knows when he knows the meaning of a given word or sentence, then, by hypothesis, the theory is inadequate to account for one extremely important type of context in which we are disposed to use the word "meaning". If, however, the theory of meaning does not issue in such direct ascriptions of meaning at all; and if, further, it does not contain within itself any overt account of what someone has to know in order to know or grasp the meaning of each expression of the language, but merely provides an explanation of other contexts in which we use the word "meaning", such as "X means the same as Y" or "X has a meaning": then, it appears to me, it will again be inadequate for the construction out of it of any theory of understanding. That is, if it were possible to give an account of, for example, when two expressions have the same meaning, which did not overtly rely on an account of what it was to know the meaning of an expression, then it would not be possible to derive an account of knowledge of meaning from it. There is, indeed, good reason to suppose it impossible to give an account of synonymy save via an account of understanding, since it is a requirement on the former that whoever knows the meanings of two synonymous expressions must also know that they are synonymous: but I am saying merely that, if such an account of synonymy were possible, there would be no route from it to an account of understanding.

Any theory of meaning which was not, or did not immediately yield, a theory of understanding, would not satisfy the purpose for which, philosophically, we require a theory of meaning. For I have argued that a theory of meaning is required to make the workings of language open to our view. To know a language is to be able to employ a language; hence, once we have an explicit account of that in which the knowledge of a language consists, we thereby have an account of the workings of that language; and nothing short of that can give us what we are after. Conversely, it also appears to me that once we can say what it is for someone to know a language, in the sense of knowing the meanings of all expressions of the language, then we have essentially solved every problem that can arise concerning meaning. For instance, once we are clear about what it is to know the meaning of an expression, then questions about whether, in such-and-such a case, the meaning of a word has changed can be resolved by asking whether someone who understood the word previously has to acquire new knowledge in order to understand it now.

If a theory of meaning gives an account of the working of the language to which it relates, then, it seems, it must embody an explanation of all the concepts expressible in that language, at least by unitary expressions. We need not stop to enquire whether, or in what cases, someone who does not possess the linguistic means to express a concept, or who lacks a language altogether, may yet be said to grasp that concept: it is sufficient to acknowledge that the prototypical case of grasping a concept is that in which this grasp consists in the understanding of a certain word or expression, or range of expressions, in some language. Hence, if a theory of meaning is a theory of understanding, as I have claimed, it would appear to follow that such a theory of meaning must, in explaining what one must know in order to know the meaning of each expression in the language, simultaneously explain what it is to have the concepts expressible by means of that language.

The theory of meaning will, of course, do more than this: it plainly cannot merely explain the concepts expressible in the language, since these concepts may be grasped by someone who is quite ignorant of that particular language, but who knows another language in which they are expressible. Hence the theory of meaning must also associate concepts with words of the language—show or state which concepts are expressed by which words. And an alternative view will be that it is only this latter task which properly belongs to the theory of meaning: that to demand of the theory of meaning that it should serve to explain new concepts to someone who does not already have them is to place too heavy a burden upon it, and that all that we can require of such a theory is that it give the interpretation of the language to someone who already has the concepts required. Let us call a theory of meaning which purports to accomplish only this restricted task a *modest* theory of meaning, and one which seeks actually to explain the concepts expressed by primitive terms of the language a *full-blooded* theory. One question which I wish to try to answer is whether a modest theory of meaning is possible at all, or whether anything to be ranked as a theory of meaning must be full-blooded.

If a well-known conception, propounded by Davidson, of the form which a theory of meaning ought to take be accepted, then, I think, it must be maintained that a modest theory of meaning is all that we have a right to ask for. On this conception, the core of the theory of meaning will be a theory of truth, framed on the model of a truth-definition of Tarski's kind (the object-language not, in general, being assumed to be a fragment of the metalanguage): such a theory of truth will, however, lack the apparatus required for converting it into an explicit definition, and will not be serving to explicate the concept of truth in any way, but, taking it as already known, to give the interpretation of the object-language. The theory of truth will yield a T-sentence for each sentence of the object-language, namely either a biconditional whose left-hand side is of the form "The sentence S is true" or the universal closure of a biconditional whose left-hand side is of the form "An utterance of the sentence S by a speaker x at a time t is true". The notion of translation is not, however, appealed to in judging whether the T-sentences which the theory yields are the correct ones; rather, there are constraints which the theory must satisfy, to be acceptable, relating to the sentences held true by the speakers of the language (it being supposed that we can frame adequate criteria for whether a speaker holds a given sentence to be true): in the first place, that, by and large, the T-sentences derivable in the theory of truth state, on their right-hand sides, the conditions under which in fact the speakers hold true the sentences named on their left-hand sides.

The axioms of the theory of truth, when it forms part of the theory of meaning for a language under such a conception, will state the denotations of the proper names of the language, give the conditions for the satisfaction of the primitive predicates, etc. If a primitive predicate of the language expresses a certain concept, it would seem quite out of place to claim that a theory of meaning of this kind, or, in particular, the axiom of the theory of truth which governed that predicate, provided any explanation of that concept. Rather, the theory would be intelligible only to someone who had already grasped the concept. A Davidsonian theory of meaning is a modest theory.

I have already observed that a translation manual is to be contrasted with a theory of meaning, and cannot itself claim to be one. A theory of meaning describes directly the way in which the language functions; a translation manual merely projects that language on to another one, whose functioning must, if the translation is to be of practical use, be taken as already known. This point has equally been insisted upon by Davidson, who has put it by saying that the translation manual tells us only that certain expressions of the one language mean the same as certain expressions of the other, without telling us what, specifically, the expressions of either language mean; it would, he says, be in principle possible to know, of each sentence of a given language, that it meant the same as some particular sentence of another language, without knowing at all what meaning any of these sentences had. This objection to regarding a translation manual as itself constituting a theory of meaning is evidently just: but we may wonder why so heavy an emphasis is laid upon the distinction between a translation manual and a theory of meaning when the theory of meaning is required to be, not full-blooded, but only modest. A translation manual leads to an understanding of the translated language only via an understanding of the language into which the translation is made, an understanding which it does not itself supply; hence, we may say, it does not directly display in what an understanding of the translated language consists. But a modest theory of meaning, likewise, leads to an understanding of the object-language only via a grasp of the concepts expressed by its primitive expressions, which it does not itself explain; it seems, therefore, that we should similarly say that such a theory of meaning does not fully display in what an understanding of the object-language consists. Especially is this so since our best model—and, in many cases, our only model—for the grasp of a concept is provided by the mastery of a certain expression or range of expressions in some language. Thus a translation manual presupposes a mastery of some one other language—that into which the translation is made—if we are to derive from it an understanding of the translated language; but a modest theory of meaning presupposes a mastery of *some*, though unspecified, language, if we are to derive from it an understanding of the object-language. The significant contrast would, however, appear to be not between a theory which (like a translation manual) makes a specific presupposition and one which (like a modest theory of meaning) makes as heavy a presupposition, though less specific; but between theories which (like both of these) rely on extraneous presuppositions and those which (like full-blooded theories of meaning) involve no such presupposition at all.

Let us return to the question: Should a theory of meaning issue in direct ascriptions of meaning? A theory of meaning should, of course, tell us, for each expression of the language, what it means: but it would be very superficial to conclude from this that it must therefore be possible to derive from the theory statements beginning "The expression X means ...". To give a trifling example, a successful theory of a crime, say a murder, should tell us the identity of the murderer: that does not entail that we should be able to derive from the theory a statement beginning "The identity of the murderer is ..."; indeed (where "is" is the sign of identity) there are no well-formed statements beginning that way. As a more serious example, we may note that "chemistry" is not itself a concept of chemical theory. We do indeed require, of chemical theory, that it enable us to say which properties of a substance are chemical properties, which interactions are chemical ones, etc.; likewise, it may be required of a theory of meaning that it enable us to say which properties of an expression are semantic ones, that is, depend on and only on its meaning: but we cannot require that "meaning" itself be a concept of the theory of meaning, at least if this is taken as entailing that we are enabled by it to characterize the semantic properties of an expression by means of a statement beginning "The meaning of the expression is ..." or "The expression means ...".

For expressions smaller than sentences, and particularly for connectives, prepositions, etc., there is some difficulty in framing even a grammatically correct form for a direct ascription of meaning (where, of course, we do not want to employ as the object of the verb "means" a term denoting an expression, so that "means" would become replaceable by "means the same as"). However, it is not to my purpose to enquire how, or even whether, such difficulties may be resolved: we may restrict our attention to the case of sentences, for which the difficulty does not arise. Davidson himself allows that, from a theory of meaning of the kind he favours, a direct ascription of meaning will be derivable, at least for sentences. Given a T-sentence derivable from a theory of truth satisfying the required constraints, for instance the sentence " 'La terra si muove' is true if and only if the Earth moves", we may legitimately convert it into what we may call an M-sentence, in this instance " 'La terra si muove' means that the Earth moves". Now, earlier, we considered the question whether a theory of meaning which made no overt allusion to knowledge could nevertheless enable us to derive from it an account, for each expression, of what knowledge of the meaning of that expression consisted in; and, in particular, we supposed it argued that, if the theory allowed the derivation, for each expression, of a direct ascription of meaning, then it must also provide us with an account of what it was to know the meaning of a given expression, namely that this would be to know what was stated by the direct ascription of the meaning of the expression. But, now, if we are asked whether the M-sentence " 'La terra si muove' means that the Earth moves" expresses what someone has to know in order to know what the Italian sentence "La terra si muove" means, we can hardly do other than answer affirmatively: to know that "La terra si muove" means that the Earth moves *is* just to know what "La terra si muove" means, for that is precisely what it does mean. If, on the other hand, we are asked whether an adequate account of what a knowledge of the meaning of "La terra si muove" consists in is given by saying that one must know what is stated by the relevant M-sentence, then, equally, we are impelled to answer negatively: for the M-sentence, taken by itself, is, though by no means uninformative, signally unexplanatory. If these reactions are correct, then it follows that the fact that a theory of meaning issues in direct ascriptions of meaning is not in itself a sufficient ground for claiming that it gives an adequate account of what knowledge of meaning consists in.

One of our as yet unresolved problems was to discover what advantage a modest theory of meaning could have over a mere translation manual. A translation manual will inform us, for example, that "La terra si muove" means the same as "The Earth moves": but the inadequacy of this was said to lie in the fact that someone could know the two sentences to be synonymous without knowing what either of them meant. In order to derive, from a knowledge that the two sentences are synonymous, a knowledge of what the Italian sentence means, what someone has to know in addition is, obviously, what the English sentence means. Equally obviously, what, in addition to knowing the two sentences to be synonymous, has to be known in order to know that the Italian sentence means that the Earth moves, is that that is what the English sentence means. It follows that if we were to hold that a knowledge of the meaning of the Italian sentence consisted in knowing that it means that the Earth moves, we must also hold that knowing what the English sentence "The Earth moves" means consists in knowing that *it* means that the Earth moves. An M-sentence such as " 'The Earth moves' means that the Earth moves", for an object-language which is part of the metalanguage, appears totally unexplanatory because, this time, quite uninformative; although it still seems impossible to deny that someone knows what "The Earth moves" means just in case he knows that it means that the Earth moves.

In this context, it is important to observe a distinction which, in many contexts, can be neglected: that between knowing, of a sentence, that it is true, and knowing the proposition expressed by the sentence. In using the phrase "to know the proposition expressed by a sentence", I am intending no acknowledgement of propositions as entities, no commitment to an ontology of propositions: I employ the phrase simply as a convenient means of expressing the generalization of the distinction between, for example, saying of someone that he knows that the sentence "19 is prime" is true, and saying of him that he knows that 19 is prime. The reason why the M-sentence " 'The Earth moves' means that the Earth moves" appears quite uninformative is that it could not possibly be maintained that a knowledge of the meaning of "The Earth moves" consisted in the knowledge that that M-sentence was true; for anyone who has grasped the simplest principles governing the use of the verb "to mean", and who knows that "The Earth moves" is an English sentence, must know that that M-sentence is true, even though he may not know what, in particular, "The Earth moves" means. The case is analogous with Kripke's example of the sentence "Horses are called 'horses' ". Kripke says that anyone who knows the use of "is called" in English must know that that sentence expresses a truth, irrespective of whether he knows what horses are: plainly, all he needs to know is that "horse" is a meaningful general term of English, and, equally plainly, the relevant sense of "knowing what horses are" is that in which it is synonymous with "knowing what 'horse' means". Kripke allows, however, that someone who does not know what horses are will not know *which* truth. "Horses are called 'horses' " expresses. It seems reasonable to suppose that, by this concession, Kripke intends to deny that we could say of such a person that he knew that horses are called 'horses', although he is not explicit about this: that is, in my terminology, such a person may know that the sentence "Horses are called 'horses' " is true, without knowing the proposition expressed by that sentence.

It might be objected that someone who knows a sentence to be true must also know the proposition expressed by the sentence, on the ground that if he knows enough about the meaning of the word "true" to be credited with the knowledge that the sentence is true, he must know the connection between knowing something and knowing it to be true (and between believing it and believing it to be true, etc.); a connection which is displayed by the T-sentences. For instance, he must know that "Horses are called 'horses' " is true if and only if horses are called 'horses': hence, since by assumption he knows that "Horses are called 'horses' " is true, he will, if he is capable of performing a simple inference, also be capable of knowing that horses are called 'horses'. But this objection derives its plausibility from ignoring in its premiss the distinction which it purported to demonstrate to be without substance, that, namely, between knowing that a sentence is true and knowing the proposition it expresses. We may justifiably credit someone who does not know what "horse" means, but who knows that it is a meaningful general term, with the knowledge that the T-sentence " 'Horses are called "horses" ' is true if and only if horses are called 'horses' " is true: but to assume, as the argument requires, that he knows that "Horses are called 'horses' " is true if and only if horses are called 'horses' is to beg the question.

To say of someone who does not know what "The Earth moves" means that he does not know that "The Earth moves" means that the Earth moves, but only knows that the M-sentence is true, is not at all to say that he is not prepared to utter that M-sentence assertorically, but only the sentence "The sentence ' "The Earth moves" means that the Earth moves' is true". It is not even to say that he could not give excellent grounds for the former utterance: on the contrary, he can give quite conclusive grounds, namely an appeal to the use of "means" in English. But we have learned from Gettier's paradox that not every sound justification for a true belief is sufficient to entitle the holder of the belief to claim knowledge; the justification must be suitably related to what makes the belief true. A justification of an utterance of the M-sentence which would ground the ascription to the speaker of knowledge of the proposition expressed by that M-sentence would have to be one depending upon the specific meaning of the sentence of which the M-sentence treated, in our case the sentence "The Earth moves", even though, in ordinary circumstances, no one would think of justifying such an utterance in so complicated a way.

All this shows that we were entirely right in our first inclination, to regard it as a necessary and sufficient condition of someone's knowing what "The Earth moves" means that he know that it means that the Earth moves, that is, that he know the proposition expressed by the corresponding M-sentence. But it shows equally that we were also right to regard the M-sentence as being quite unexplanatory of what it is to know the meaning of the sentence "The Earth moves". The simplest way we have to state its unexplanatory character is by observing that we have so far found no independent characterization of what more someone who knows that the M-sentence is true must know in order to know the proposition it expresses, save that he must know what "The Earth moves" means: knowledge of that proposition cannot, therefore, play any part in an account of that in which an understanding of that sentence consists. And, if an M-sentence for which the metalanguage contains the object-language is unexplanatory, then an M-sentence for an object-language disjoint from the metalanguage is equally unexplanatory. In the latter case, the M-sentence does indeed provide some information: but the knowledge of the truth of such an M-sentence (as opposed to a knowledge of the proposition it expresses) does not require the possession of any information not also contained in the corresponding sentence from a translation manual.

The considerations about the connection between knowledge and justification which we saw to underlie the distinction between knowing the truth of a sentence and knowing the proposition expressed by it can be generalized to cases where it is not precisely this distinction which is in question. The expression "knows that" is, of course, frequently used in everyday discourse, and in philosophical contexts in which attention is not focused on the concept of knowledge, merely as synonymous with "is aware that". Where "knowledge" is used in a stricter sense, however, knowledge of a fact transcends mere awareness of it in that it involves that the awareness of it was arrived at in some canonical fashion, that is, that it was *derived* in some special way. If, then, we attempt to explain in what some capacity consists by saying that it consists in having a certain piece of knowledge, and if the plausibility of this account depends upon taking "knowledge" in the strict sense, rather than as mere awareness, the attempted representation of the capacity will remain inadequate so long as it stops short at simply stating the *object* of knowledge—what it is that must be known, in the strict sense of "know", for someone to have that capacity. To give an adequate explanation of the capacity in question, the account must do more than simply specify the fact that must be known: it must indicate how, in particular, awareness of that fact must have been attained, that is, what process of derivation is required for it to count as *knowledge*, in the strict sense.

It may be objected that no one has ever supposed that an adequate explanation of the meaning, or the understanding, of a sentence could be given by alluding merely to the M-sentence relating to it. In the terms in which I have just discussed the matter, the whole point of the theory of meaning is that it displays the canonical means by which the M-sentence is to be derived: only someone who was capable of so deriving it could be said to know it, in the strict sense, or, as I earlier expressed it, could be said to know the proposition it expresses. Such an objection is entirely just: my purpose in discussing M-sentences at such length was not to refute a thesis which no one has held, but to analyse the intuitive reasons we all share for rejecting such a thesis, in order to bring out some general points which we may apply elsewhere.

In order, then, to see in what, on a Davidsonian account, the knowledge of the meaning of a sentence consists, we must look to the way in which the M-sentence relating to it is derived in the theory of meaning. The M-sentence is, as we noted, obtained by replacing "is true if and only if" in the corresponding T-sentence by "means that": and the T-sentence is, in turn, derived from the axioms of the theory of truth governing the constituent words of the sentence and those governing the methods of sentence-formation exemplified by it. This, of course, entirely accords with our intuitive conviction that a speaker derives his understanding of a sentence from his understanding of the words composing it and of the way they are put together. What plays the role, within a theory of meaning of Davidson's kind, of a grasp of the meanings of the words is a knowledge of the axioms governing those words: in our example, these may be stated as " 'The Earth' denotes the Earth" and "It is true to say of something 'It moves' if and only if that thing moves". (This latter formulation of the axiom governing "moves" eschews appeal to the technical device of satisfaction by an infinite sequence, and is only an approximate indication of what is wanted: but, if we are intending a serious representation of what is known by anyone able to speak English, we cannot literally credit him with an understanding of that technical device.)

It is not sufficient, for someone to know what the sentence "The Earth moves" means, for him to know the M-sentence relating to it to be true; he must know the proposition expressed by that M-sentence. And the natural way to characterize what, in addition, someone who knows the truth of the M-sentence has to know in order to know the proposition it expresses is: the meanings of the component words. If, now, we explain an understanding of the component words as consisting in a knowledge of the axioms of the theory of truth which govern those words, the same question arises: is it sufficient for him to know those axioms to be true, or must he know the propositions which they express? The objection to requiring only that he know the axioms to be true is parallel to that we allowed in the case of the M-sentence: anyone who knows the use of "denotes", and who knows that "the Earth" is a singular term of English, must know that the sentence " 'The Earth' denotes the Earth" is true, even if he does not know what, specifically, the phrase "the Earth" means or what it denotes.

This might be objected to, however, on the ground that if we were to change the example from "The Earth moves" to "Homer was blind", it would become apparent that, in order to know that " 'Homer' denotes Homer" is true, one must know more than that "Homer" is a proper name: one must know also that it is not an empty name. Such an objection is ill taken, because, for any language in which the possibility that "Homer" is an empty name is open, the relevant axiom of the theory of truth will not take the simple form " 'Homer' denotes Homer"; at least, it will not do so if the name's being empty would deprive the sentence " 'Homer' denotes Homer" of truth. It is only in a theory of truth for a language of a Fregean type, in which all singular terms are so understood as to be guaranteed a denotation, that the axiom governing each proper name will take that simple form. For languages of other types, the axiom governing such a name as "Homer" will have to take a different form. For instance, for any language in which the predicate ". . . is Homer" was taken as true of the referent of "Homer", if any, and false of everyone and everything else, the axiom could take the form "For every x, 'Homer' denotes x if and only if x is Homer". If, now, the language was Russellian, so that the presence of an empty name in an atomic sentence rendered that sentence false, suitable further axioms would yield the T-sentence " 'Homer was blind' is true if and only if Homer was blind". If, on the other hand, the language was such that the presence of an empty name in a sentence, save when it followed the sign of identity, rendered that sentence neither true nor false, then we should not want that T-sentence to be derivable, since, if "Homer" were an empty name, the left-hand side would be false while the right-hand side was not false. One would want, instead, the non-standard T-sentence " 'Homer was blind' is true if and only if, for some x, x is Homer and x was blind". Hence the demand that, in order to be able to derive the T-sentence relating to "Homer was blind", one would first have to know whether or not "Homer" was an empty name is quite unjustified.

This could be denied only if it were held that in order to know the meaning of "Homer", one must know whether or not there was in fact such a man as Homer: for the theory of truth is a part of the theory of meaning for the language, and can embody only what is required for an understanding of the language. But, clearly, in order to know the use of the name "Homer" in our language, it is not necessary to know whether or not it has a denotation: the most that could be required is that one should know whether or not it is known whether the name has a denotation. That is, it might be held that for a name for which it is known that it has a denotation, this knowledge enters into the understanding of the name: if so, then, for such a name, say "London", the axiom governing it will take the simple form " 'London' denotes London". The knowledge whether "Homer" has a denotation or not, on the other hand, cannot be part of what is involved in knowing the use of that name, for the obvious reason that this knowledge is not possessed by the speakers of the language.

If it is supposed that anyone attempting a serious inquiry whether there was such a place as London would thereby show that he was not in command of the accepted use of the name "London", then it will be true that someone who knows of the word "London" only that it is a proper name cannot yet recognize the axiom governing it to be true: he must also know that it is a name of which we are certain that it is not empty. But, plainly, one could be informed of this fact, and hence conclude to the truth of the sentence " 'London' denotes London", without knowing what, precisely, "London" meant; and so we must still conclude that a knowledge of the truth of the axiom is insufficient for an understanding of the name. It would be wrong to argue against this that merely to be informed that "London" is a name known for certain not to be empty is not to *know* that fact, but that to know it, in the strict sense, involves knowing specifically how the name "London" is used. If such an argument were correct, then Davidson's objection to considering a translation manual as a theory of meaning, that one could, for example, know that "la terra" means the same as "the Earth" without knowing what either of them meant, would be unsound: for one could, in the same way, argue that while someone might be informed of their synonymy, he could not, in the strict sense, *know* it without knowing what both words meant. The objection would run foul of the methodological principle we have adopted, namely not to accept as part of an explanation a requirement that someone know something, where "knowledge" is taken in the strict sense, as transcending mere awareness, but no account is given of what would constitute such knowledge.

It is essential to observe this principle if we are to avoid null or circular explanations. Suppose it true—doubtful as it seems to me—that one could not know, in the strict sense, that a name denotes a well-known object still in existence, without knowing the precise use of the name. This must be because, in order to count as *knowledge*, an awareness of the fact must be derived in a particular way. It is one of the merits of a theory of meaning which represents mastery of a language as the knowledge not of isolated, but of deductively connected, propositions, that it makes due acknowledgement of the undoubted fact that a process of derivation of some kind is involved in the understanding of a sentence. Where such a theory makes no appeal to any process of derivation is, naturally, in the recognition of the truth of the axioms. An insistence that such recognition amount to knowledge in the strict sense would, however, make a tacit appeal to a process by which their truth was derived, a process which the theory would fail to make explicit. It would, for example, be simply circular to say that an understanding of the name "London" consisted in a knowledge, in the strict sense, of the truth of the sentence " 'London' denotes London", and then go on to say that a condition for having such knowledge was a grasp of the precise use of the name: what we were seeking was a characterization of what constituted a grasp of the use of such a name.

There is thus no possibility of holding that an understanding of the component words of a sentence consists just in an awareness of the truth of the axioms governing them: one would have to know the propositions expressed by those axioms. The theory of meaning must therefore be capable of explaining what differentiates a knowledge of the propositions expressed by those axioms from a mere awareness of their truth. Now Davidson himself has fully recognized the obligation upon a theory of meaning to yield a theory of understanding: he has been quite explicit about what, on his view, an understanding of a sentence consists in, namely in a knowledge both of the relevant T-sentence and of the fact that that T-sentence was derived from a theory of truth for the language which satisfies the constraints imposed upon such a theory for it to be acceptable. The analogue, for the understanding of a word, would presumably be a knowledge of the axiom governing it and also of the fact that that sentence was an axiom of a theory of truth satisfying those constraints. This time, therefore, the suggestion is that we may represent a knowledge of the propositions expressed by the sentences which serve as axioms as consisting in an awareness of their truth supplemented by certain background knowledge about those sentences.

It appears to me that only a very little consideration is needed to recognize that this appeal to background information cannot supply what we need. If someone does not know what "the Earth" means, he will learn something from being told that the sentence " 'The Earth' denotes the Earth" is true, provided that he understands the verb "denotes": he will learn, namely, that "the Earth" is a singular term and is not empty. But if, now, he asks to be told the specific meaning of the term, he will not be helped in the least by being told that the sentence in question is an axiom in a theory of truth for English satisfying certain particular constraints. Obviously, what tells him what, specifically, "London" denotes is the *sentence* " 'London' denotes London" itself, and, in particular, the object of the verb "denotes" in that sentence, and not any extraneous information *about* that sentence. What is being attributed to one who knows English is not merely the awareness that that sentence (and others like it) is true, but that awareness taken together with an understanding of the sentence; in other words, a knowledge of the proposition expressed by the sentence. Of course, when we consider the degenerate case in which the metalanguage is an extension of the object-language, the requirement that the metalanguage be understood becomes circular; in order to derive from the axiom a knowledge of what "London" denotes, one would have already to understand the name "London". But there is no requirement that the theory of truth be expressed in an extension of the object-language: if the axiom ran " 'London' denota Londra", then it would be an understanding of the term "Londra" that was needed in order to learn the denotation of "London", and there would be no circularity.

This is reasonable enough in itself, but it does not help us to understand what significant difference there is between a modest theory of meaning of this kind and a translation manual. It now appears clearly that we must ascribe to anyone able to use the theory of truth in order to obtain an interpretation of the object-language that he have a prior understanding of the metalanguage. This is even more apparent when we attribute to him an awareness that the theory of truth satisfies the required constraints, since these constraints allude to the conditions *stated* on the right-hand sides of the T-sentences, a notion which cannot be explained in terms of the formal theory, but presupposes an interpretation of it. Hence a theory of meaning of this kind merely exhibits what it is to arrive at an interpretation of one language via an understanding of another, which is just what a translation manual does: it does not explain what it is to have a mastery of a language, say one's mother tongue, independently of a knowledge of any other.

This conclusion could be avoided only if we could ascribe to a speaker of the object-language a knowledge of the propositions expressed by the sentences of the theory of truth, independently of any language in which those propositions might be expressed. If this is the intention of such a theory of meaning, it appears deeply dissatisfying, since we have no model, and the theory provides none, for what an apprehension of such propositions might consist in, otherwise than in an ability to enunciate them linguistically.

It may be replied that the apprehension of these propositions cannot be explained piecemeal, for each sentence of the theory of truth taken separately; but that a knowledge of the theory of truth as a whole issues, precisely, in an ability to speak and understand the object-language, so that there is no lacuna. What we are being given is a theoretical model of a practical ability, the ability to use the language. Since it is a theoretical model, the representation is in terms of the knowledge of a deductively connected system of propositions; and, since we can express propositions only in sentences, the model has to be described in terms of a deductively connected system of sentences. No presumption is intended that a speaker of the object-language actually has a prior understanding of the language in which those sentences are framed— that is why it is harmless to frame them in a language which is actually an extension of the object-language; but, equally, there is no undischarged obligation to say in what a grasp of the propositions expressed by the theory consists: it consists in that practical ability of which we are giving a theoretical model.

It is just here that the connection becomes apparent between a theory of meaning that proceeds via a theory of truth and a holistic view of language, a connection at first sight puzzling. A semantics which issues in a statement of truth-conditions for each sentence, derived from finitely many axioms, each governing a single word or construction, appears at first as a realization of an atomistic conception of language, under which each word has an individual meaning and each sentence an individual content: the T-sentence for a given sentence of the language is derived from just those axioms which govern the words and constructions occurring in that sentence. But the connection between such a conception and the holistic view of language lies in the fact that nothing is specified about what a knowledge of the propositions expressed by the axioms, or by the T-sentences, consists in: the only constraints on the theory are global ones, relating to the language as a whole. On such an account, there can be no answer to the question what constitutes a speaker's understanding of any one word or sentence: one can say only that the knowledge of the entire theory of truth issues in an ability to speak the language, and, in particular, in a propensity to recognize sentences of it as true under conditions corresponding, by and large, with those stated by the T-sentences.

Thus the appeal to the knowledge that the theory of truth satisfies the external constraints does not serve to explain a speaker's understanding of any individual word or sentence, to bridge the gap between his knowing an axiom or theorem of the theory of truth to be true and his knowing the proposition expressed by it: it mediates merely between his knowledge of the theory as a whole and his mastery of the entire language. Now the allure of a theory of meaning of this type is that it appears to refute the suspicion that a holistic view of language must be anti-systematic; since to speak a language is to have the capacity to utter sentences of it in accordance with their conventional significance, there appears no hope of any systematic account of the use of a whole language which does not yield an account of the significance of individual utterances. A Davidsonian theory of meaning, on the other hand, combines the basic tenet of holism with what purports to be an account of the way in which the meaning of each individual sentence is determined from the meanings of its constituent words. This appearance is, however, an illusion. The articulation of the theory of truth is not taken as corresponding to any articulation of the practical ability the possession of which is the manifestation of that knowledge of which the theory is presented as a theoretical model. A speaker's knowledge of the meaning of an individual sentence is represented as consisting in his grasp of a part of a deductive theory, and this is connected with his actual utterances only by the fact that a grasp of the whole theory is supposed to issue, in some manner of which no explanation is given, in his command of the language in its entirety; but no way is provided, even in principle, of segmenting his ability to use the language as a whole into distinct component abilities which manifest his understanding of individual words, sentences, or types of sentence. To effect any such segmentation, it would be necessary to give a detailed account of the practical ability in which the understanding of a particular word or sentence consisted, whereas, on the holistic view, not only cannot a speaker's command of his language be so segmented, but no detailed description of what it consists in can be given at all. Hence the articulation of the theory plays no genuine role in the account of what constitutes a speaker's mastery of his language.

Against this it may be objected that the theory of truth does tell us something about the use of each individual sentence: for it states conditions under which a speaker will probably hold it to be true. Now it is certainly the case that a theory of meaning based on a theory of truth would reflect a molecular, rather than a holistic, view of language, if we could take the right-hand sides of the T-sentences as stating conditions under which speakers of the language invariably held true the sentences named on the left-hand sides. This is not a possible way of construing the theory, for two reasons. First, for any natural language, the conditions stated on the right-hand sides of the T-sentences will not, in general, be ones which we are capable of recognizing as obtaining whenever they obtain. A molecular theory of meaning based on the notion of truth-conditions must attribute to one who understands a sentence a knowledge of the condition which must obtain for it to be true, not a capacity to recognize that sentence as true just in case that condition holds. Secondly, such an account would leave no room for mistakes. In order to leave room for them, we must claim that an acceptable theory of truth will give the *best possible* fit between the conditions for the truth of a sentence and the conditions under which it is held to be true, not a *perfect* fit: it follows that a speaker's understanding of a sentence cannot be judged save in relation to his employment of the entire language. (Indeed, it is somewhat dubious whether an individual speaker's mastery of the language can be judged at all. If we have identified a linguistic community from the outside, then a Davidsonian theory of meaning will give us a fairly good, though necessarily imperfect, guide to which sentences its members will hold to be true. There will be divergences on the part of the entire community—cases when we shall say, on the basis of that theory of meaning, that the community shares a mistaken belief. There will also be disagreements between individual speakers. How are we to discriminate between such a disagreement as may occur between two speakers who both tacitly accept the same theory of meaning for their common language, and one which reflects differing interpretations of that language? Presumably, if a member of the linguistic community holds a divergent theory of truth for the language, he will tend to diverge more in his judgements than most speakers do from the majority. But, since no finite set of such divergences will, in itself, reveal his reliance on a non-standard theory of truth, it is hard to see how either he or the other speakers or we as observers could ever detect this, or how, once discovered, it could be corrected. The difficulty arises precisely because there is no way of determining, within such a theory, the individual content with which any speaker endows a sentence.)

Davidson makes a virtue of necessity, and uses the gap between the truth-condition of a sentence and the condition under which it is held true to explain the genesis of the concept of belief.[1] This is, however, an abnegation of what we are entitled to expect from a theory of meaning: such a theory ought to be able to distinguish between disagreements stemming from difference of interpretation and disagreements of substance (disagreements about the facts); it ought to be able to explain how it is possible for disagreement over the truth-value of sentences to occur even when there is agreement over their meaning. We have, of course, been taught by Quine to regard this distinction with suspicion; and it is undeniably the case that the meanings of expressions of natural language are frequently fuzzy, and that the distinction becomes in consequence blurred. It is equally true that, as Davidson says,[2] we ought not lightly to assume that every disagreement over truth-value, for instance of the sentence "The Earth is round", should be regarded as one of substance rather than of interpretation. But a theory of meaning which denies in principle the viability of the distinction runs the risk of becoming solipsistic. A disagreement between individual speakers of the same language at the same time either cannot be accounted for at all, or should be explained by attributing to them divergent theories of truth for the language: and the same applies to a change of mind on the part of one individual. If the latter course is taken, we lose the conception of the linguistic community: a language, considered as determined by a theory of meaning, becomes something spoken by a single individual at a certain period.

The obvious fact of the matter is that the judgements which we make are not directly correlated with the states of affairs which render them true or false. Even if the correct theory of meaning for our language would represent our grasp of the meaning of each sentence as consisting in our knowledge of the condition which must hold for it to be true, we do not, in general, arrive at our evaluation of the truth of a sentence by direct recognition that the appropriate condition obtains, since, for the most part, that condition is not one we are capable of so recognizing. Should we therefore say that an adequate theory of meaning must be able to give an account not merely of what determines our judgements as correct or incorrect, but also of how we arrive at them, since this also depends upon the meanings we assign to the sentences whose truth-value we are judging; and that this account must be able to show how, in the process, we are capable of going astray, even when we share with other speakers a common interpretation of the sentence? Whether we say this or not is partly a matter of taste, of how much we wish to reckon as belonging to a theory of meaning; such an account certainly belongs within a complete description of

---

[1] See D. Davidson, 'Thought and Talk', in Guttenplan (ed.), *Mind and Language*, 20.
[2] Ibid. 21.

the workings of language. If a theory of meaning, based on a molecular view of language, enables a clear content to be given to an individual's associating a certain meaning with a sentence, a meaning which determines when that sentence may rightly be judged to be true, then we also have a clear criterion for when a judgement represents a mistake of fact; if we then choose to decree that an account of the processes leading to such mistakes does not belong to the theory of meaning, only a demarcation dispute is involved. But a theory of meaning based on a holistic view, which has no criterion for a speaker's associating a specific meaning with any one sentence, save his inclination to hold it true or false, and does not therefore purport to give an account of his understanding of that sentence, but only of the entire language, can give no determinate content to the notion of a mistake, which it invokes only to account for the lack of fit between the theory of truth and the judgements actually made by speakers. It would be absurd to expect a theory of meaning to ascribe to every expression a completely sharp meaning; I am arguing, however, that it is required that a place be left for a distinction between a disagreement of substance and a disagreement over meaning, a distinction which was not, after all, invented by misguided theorists, but is actually employed within our language. Any theory which associates sentences merely with truth-conditions, without either attempting any account of the means by which we recognize or judge those truth-conditions to be fulfilled, or providing any means of determining that an individual speaker, or even the whole community, associates a particular truth-condition with a particular sentence, save a rough agreement between the truth-conditions of all sentences under a given theory and the judgements made concerning them, is incapable of providing any place for such a distinction.

Now it could be replied that I am quite wrong in denying that Davidson can represent an individual speaker's grasp of the meaning of a particular sentence: he has stated, after all, that an individual's understanding of a sentence consisted in his knowing, of the relevant T-sentence, that it was derivable from some theory of truth, satisfying the required constraints, for the language, without his having actually to know that theory of truth.[3] But how is it to be judged that an individual knows this? What, indeed, is he to do with the information if he has it? It might be claimed that he will manifest this knowledge by judging that sentence to be true just in case the condition stated in the T-sentence obtains. But why should he do this? Well, it may be said, he knows that the theory of truth which yields that T-sentence achieves the best fit with the judgements made by other speakers, and he wants to maximize the agreement of his judgements with theirs. It is true, by hypothesis, that this theory of truth will achieve the best fit possible *for a theory of truth*: but since it will not achieve a perfect fit, he would do better, in maximizing agreement, not to be guided exclusively by any theory of truth. How can he know that he

---

[3] Ibid. 13.

would not achieve a better agreement by disregarding the theory of truth in this instance? After all, it cannot be the case that other speakers all follow the policy of judging the truth-values of sentences only in accordance with the given theory of truth, otherwise the fit *would* be perfect: so why should he? To this it can only be replied that the other speakers do try to follow that policy, but make mistakes in doing so. We have now come round once more to the question: What is a mistake? In attributing to the speakers a policy of conforming their judgements to a theory of truth, we have surreptitiously ascribed to them a capacity for judging whether the truth-conditions of sentences are fulfilled—judgements which will not always be correct; but we have given no content to the notion of such a judgement, as distinct from a judgement as to the truth-value of a sentence.

That we should appeal to the notion of a mistake in order to explain the lack of fit between a theory of truth and the actual judgements made by speakers of the language sounds plausible only because we find the notion of such a mistake already intelligible: we are familiar enough with the idea that someone may assign a determinate meaning to a sentence, and yet wrongly judge it to be true. But a theory which offers no explanation of how such mistakes occur has no right to appeal to this notion. We can see this plainly if we consider any theory which does not have language as its subject-matter, for instance, a physical theory. It would not be tolerable, for example, to say that a theory of the motions of the planets was one that achieved the best possible fit with their observed movements, any discrepancy being due to mistakes on the part of the planets. If all we had to go on, in constructing a theory of meaning, were judgements of speakers as to the truth or falsity of sentences, and the conditions prevailing when those judgements were made, then we should be entitled to demand, of any theory we were asked to accept, that the fit be perfect, save for small discrepancies assignable to errors of observation. Fortunately, this is not all that we have to go on.

The upshot of our discussion, therefore, is this. If a theory of meaning of this type is taken literally, as relating to a theory of truth framed in actual sentences, it has no advantage over a translation manual, since it has to presuppose an understanding of the metalanguage. If, on the other hand, it is construed as attributing to a speaker an unverbalized knowledge of the propositions expressed by the sentences of the theory, its explanatory force evaporates, since it provides no means whereby we can explain the ascription to an individual of a knowledge of the various distinct propositions and their deductive interconnection. That is to say: a modest theory of meaning either accomplishes no more than a translation manual, and hence fails to explain what, in general, someone knows when he knows a language; or it must be construed holistically, in which case its claim to give a systematic account of the mastery of a language is spurious, since a holistic view of language precludes the possibility of any such account.

We have noted that a theory of meaning, if it represents an understanding of an expression as consisting in the possession of a certain piece of knowledge, cannot rest content with specifying the object of this knowledge, and insisting that "knowledge" must be taken in a strict sense; it must also display the way in which that knowledge had to be derived in order to qualify as knowledge. But our more recent considerations have related to a different point. In many contexts, we may take as unproblematic the ascription to someone of awareness of some fact, since we may credit him with an understanding of language, and the manifestation of his awareness will consist primarily in his ability to state the fact or his propensity to assent to a statement of it. But, where we are concerned with a representation in terms of propositional knowledge of some practical ability, and, in particular, where that practical ability is precisely the mastery of a language, it is incumbent upon us, if our account is to be explanatory, not only to specify what someone has to know for him to have that ability, but also what it is for him to have that knowledge, that is, what we are taking as constituting a manifestation of a knowledge of those propositions; if we fail to do this, then the connection will not be made between the theoretical representation and the practical ability it is intended to represent. I am not objecting to the idea of a theoretical representation of a practical ability as such, and certainly not to the representation of a mastery of a language by means of a deductive theory: I am saying only that such a representation is devoid of explanatory power unless a grasp of the individual propositions of the theory is explained in terms of a specific practical capacity of the speaker. I do not know whether this is possible; I do not know that holism is an incorrect conception of language. But I am asserting that the acceptance of holism should lead to the conclusion that any systematic theory of meaning is impossible, and that the attempt to resist this conclusion can lead only to the construction of pseudo-theories; my own preference is, therefore, to assume as a methodological principle that holism is false.

The next question that naturally arises is whether a full-blooded theory of meaning could be given in terms of the notion of the truth-conditions of a sentence: you will be relieved to hear that I shall spare you the extended discussion that an answer would demand. But we are in a position to deal briefly with another question about the form which a theory of meaning should take, namely whether, in terminology which I borrow from McDowell, it should be rich or austere. If the theory of meaning is given in terms of truth-conditions, then, where a proper name is concerned, a rich theory will attribute to a speaker who understands the name a knowledge of the condition which must be satisfied by any object for it to be the bearer of the name, while an austere theory will simply represent him as knowing, of the object for which the name in fact stands, that it is the bearer. For this case at least, namely where the theory is framed in terms of truth-conditions, the distinction appears to coincide with that between a full-blooded and a modest theory, although it is differently formulated. For a more verificationist type of theory, an austere theory will credit anyone who understands a name with a capacity to recognize its bearer when encountered, whereas a rich theory will, instead, represent him as ready to acknowledge whatever is taken as establishing, for any given object, that it is the bearer. In favour of the rich theory, it might be said: "We don't *simply* recognize objects: we recognize them *by* some feature." It might be replied, on behalf of the austere theory, that *how* we recognize an object is a psychological matter, irrelevant to a theory of meaning, and that, in any case, there does not have to be a means by which we recognize them; no one could give much of an account, for example, of the means by which he recognizes the predicate ". . . is red" as applying to something. So let us suppose that we encounter some rational but non-human creatures who have a language which contains what appear to be names of rivers: though they identify rivers under these names with remarkable accuracy, we cannot discover the means by which they make such identifications, nor can they give any account of this. It nevertheless remains that if one of these creatures has identified two distinct stretches of water by the same river-name, and it is subsequently proved, by tracing their courses, that there is no flow of water from one to the other, then he must withdraw one or other identification; at least, if these creatures do not acknowledge this necessity, then their words cannot be taken as names *of rivers*. So-called theories of reference are theories about what, in problematic cases, we should take as establishing which object, if any, was the bearer of a given proper name, and hence should more accurately be called theories of sense for proper names: the fact that they are so disputable shows how inexplicit our grasp of our own use of proper names is. But if our imaginary creatures use names in such a way that, in a case of disagreement, they would not accept as settling the question which object was the bearer whatever we should in fact so accept, then they do not understand these names in the way that we understand ours. Such examples bring out sharply the merit of the idea that what determines the meaning of a word is not so much what in practice normally prompts its application as what is agreed on as conclusively establishing its correct application in cases of dispute: to argue that we do not need to rely, on ordinary occasions of use, on any principle guiding us to apply it, is to miss the point of this familiar idea.

I conclude, therefore, that a theory of meaning, if one is to be possible at all, must accord with an atomistic, or at least a molecular, conception of language, not a holistic one; that it must be full-blooded, not modest, and rich, not austere. It need not issue in any direct ascriptions of meaning; but it must give an explicit account, not only of what anyone must know in order to know the meaning of any given expression, but of what constitutes having such knowledge. As I remarked, the next step would be to ask whether such a theory of meaning should be based upon the notion of truth-conditions or upon some other notion. When I began composing this essay, I had the absurd idea that I should have the time to go on to discuss not only that, but also the question raised by Strawson in his inaugural lecture,[4] concerning the relation between theories of meaning as we have been discussing them and the account of meaning given by Grice, and so to conclude by examining the notion of a linguistic act and the relation between such acts and their interiorizations, for example between assertion and judgement. Only by treating of these topics could one claim to have answered the question I have taken as my title: but I have thought it best not to try to complete the answer now.

APPENDIX

It is helpful to view a Davidsonian theory of meaning by contrasting it with Frege's theory of sense and reference. Frege had two kinds of argument for the necessity of a notion of sense alongside the notion of reference. The first relates to the knowledge of a language by a speaker, and consists, fundamentally, in the observation that it is unintelligible to attribute to anyone a piece of knowledge of which the *whole* account is that he knows the reference of a given expression; if someone knows what the referent of an expression is, then this referent must be given to him in some particular way, and the way in which it is given constitutes the sense which he attaches to the expression. The way to understand this argument is as follows. To attribute to someone a knowledge of the reference of, say, the name "Oxford" is to say of him that he knows, of the city of Oxford, that it is the referent of that name. To say of him that he knows the reference of the name, without attaching any particular sense to it, is to say that the *complete* account of his possessing this piece of knowledge is given by saying that he knows, of the city, that it is the referent of the name; and this amounts to saying that this piece of knowledge cannot be further characterized by saying of him something of the form "He knows that the city which . . . is the referent of 'Oxford' ". Likewise, to attribute to someone a knowledge of the reference (extension) of, say, the predicate "x is supple" is to say of him that he knows, of those things which are supple, that the predicate is true of them: while to say that he knows the reference of the predicate, without attaching any particular sense to it, is to say that this attribution constitutes a *complete* account of this particular piece of knowledge; and this amounts to denying that that piece of knowledge can be further characterized by saying of him anything of the form "He knows that 'x is supple' is true of any object which . . .".

That is to say, an attribution to someone of a knowledge of the reference of an expression is to be understood as a statement of the form ⌜X knows, of a, that it is F⌝, or of the form ⌜X knows, of the Gs, that they are F⌝, that is, a statement in which the subject of the "that"-clause stands, in a transparent context, outside the "that"-clause; let us call such a statement an "attribution of knowledge about an object or objects". And the assertion that someone knows the reference of an expression without attaching to it any particular sense amounts to attributing to him knowledge about an object, or objects, while denying that there is any further characterization of that piece of knowledge by

---

[4] P. F. Strawson, 'Meaning and Truth', *Logico-Linguistic Papers* (London, 1971).

means of a statement of the form ⌜*X* knows that *b* is *F*⌝, or ⌜*X* knows that the *G*s are *F*⌝, that is, one in which the subject of the "that"-clause appears within it and hence in an opaque context; let us call such a statement an "attribution of propositional knowledge". But, according to the Fregean argument, an attribution of knowledge about an object or objects is unintelligible if accompanied by the claim that no further characterization, in terms of propositional knowledge, is possible. For, on this view, propositional knowledge is basic: whenever an attribution of knowledge about an object or objects is correct, there must be some correct attribution of propositional knowledge from which it follows. Hence there can never be such a thing as *bare* knowledge of the reference of an expression, that is, knowledge of the reference unmediated by any sense which is attached to the expression.

It should be noted that this argument, as stated, does *not* entail the so-called "description theory of names", which its opponents tendentiously ascribe to Frege. The "causal theory of names", for instance, itself proffers an account of the condition which an object must satisfy to be the bearer of a name. The crucial disagreement between the causal theory and the description theory is not over whether any such condition exists, but over whether it is possible to state it without essential reference to the name itself. (The attribution of the description theory to Frege is tendentious because there is no argument which he advanced which purported to show that this is always possible.)

For all that this line of argument can show, the sense which each speaker attaches to an expression might be different, even though each must attach *some* sense to it. Frege's second line of argument concerns the contribution which is made to our non-linguistic knowledge, at the time when we first recognize it as true, by a sentence which we understand. This argument is most familiar in application to identity-statements: if, in order to understand a proper name, a speaker has to know, of the referent, that it is the referent, then it is incomprehensible how a true identity-statement ⌜*a* = *b*⌝ can convey new knowledge to him, since he must already know, of the object which is the referent of the two names, that it is the referent of each of them. Actually, the argument works just as well for any atomic statement: on the above assumption about names, and on the corresponding assumption that, in order to understand a predicate, a speaker must know, of each object of which the predicate is true, that the predicate is true of it, it is equally incomprehensible how a true statement formed by inserting a name in the argument-place of a predicate can convey new information to him. If we suppose that an account of the use of language in communication demands that each sentence possess a common cognitive content for all speakers, then this argument does provide a ground for ascribing to each expression a sense constant from speaker to speaker.

The conclusion of the first argument is, in effect, that we need to ascribe to a speaker *more* than just a bare knowledge of the reference of each expression, whereas the conclusion of the second argument is that if sentences are to be informative, we cannot, in general, attribute to speakers *as much as* a knowledge of the reference of expressions. There is no real tension here. If we merely require, for someone to be said to know of an object *x* that it is the referent of the name *N*, that there be some term *t* which stands for *x* and is such that it is true to say of that person ⌜He knows that *t* is the referent of *N*⌝, then it does *not* follow that someone who knows, of a certain object, both that it is the referent of one name and that it is the referent of another, that he knows that the names have the same referent; on the contrary, we have here in schematic form precisely the account in terms of sense which Frege proposes as the solution of the problem. The supposition which the second argument seeks to reduce to absurdity is, rather, that an understanding of an expression consists in a *bare* knowledge of the reference. What it adds to the first argument is just a ground for thinking that sense must be common to different speakers.

Now at first sight Davidson's theory is one which explains everything in terms of reference, without bringing in sense; but this first appearance is quite misleading. Davidson's attribution to a speaker of an (implicit) knowledge of the proposition expressed by the axiom governing the name "Oxford" does not consist in holding that that speaker knows, of the city of Oxford, that the name "Oxford" denotes it, but, rather, that he knows that "Oxford" denotes the city of Oxford. Thus Davidson is certainly not attributing to each speaker a *bare* knowledge of the reference of each expression that he understands, in the sense in which Frege's arguments tell against such an attribution. (I did, in the lecture, interpret McDowell's notion of an austere theory of meaning as involving a bare knowledge of the reference. This was probably a misinterpretation of McDowell's intention.)

The question indeed arises exactly *what* knowledge we attribute to a speaker when we represent him as knowing that "Oxford" denotes Oxford, given that we want to attribute more to him than just the trivial knowledge of the truth of the sentence " 'Oxford' denotes Oxford": and here we are inclined to say that Davidson's theory is modest in that, while it does not fall foul of Frege's arguments by ascribing to speakers a bare knowledge of reference, but allows that they attach particular senses to expressions, it does not attempt to explain what these senses are. This is essentially the line which I took in the lecture when I was criticizing the notion of a modest theory of meaning; although, when I came to consider Davidson's holism, I was inclined to take it as entailing that no account of sense could be supplied.

Subsequent reflection has, however, suggested to me that this may not have been the right line to take. What is a modest theory of meaning? Is it one which leaves room for an account of the senses which speakers attach to their words (the concepts they associate with them), but which does not itself provide such an account? Or is it a theory which denies in principle the possibility of giving any such account? If we take Davidson's theory as modest in the former sense, then the possibility remains open of filling it out with an account of the specific senses speakers attach to the words of the language, and thus converting the theory into a full-blooded, atomistic one: but, in that case, what becomes of the holistic aspect of the theory? Such holism as remained would relate only to the description of the way in which a theory of meaning for a language which, initially, one did not know might be arrived at from an observation of the linguistic and other behaviour of the speakers: in devising a theory of meaning, one would have to fit the theory to all the evidence provided by the judgements of speakers as to the truth and falsity of their sentences. Holism in respect of the evidence for a theory of meaning is, however, a quite different thing from the holistic view of language of which I spoke in the lecture. The latter concerns the theory of meaning itself, not the way in which a non-speaker might arrive at it; specifically, it relates to the account that is given of the way in which an implicit grasp of the theory of meaning, which is attributed to a speaker, issues in his employment of the language, and hence, as I argued, in the content of that theory. Holism merely in respect of how one might, starting from scratch, arrive at a theory of meaning for a language, on the other hand, has, in itself, no such implications, and is, so far as I can see, unobjectionable and almost banal. It is certain that Davidson intends his holism as a doctrine with more bite than this.

Davidson might subscribe personally to a tendentious doctrine of holism, even though his conception of a theory of meaning was, in itself, neutral as between a holistic, a molecular, and an atomistic view of language; but it is unlikely that there is no more organic a connection between the different features of his philosophy of language. If, on the other hand, we take his theory of meaning as being modest in the second of the two senses indicated above, it becomes difficult to see how it differs from a theory which repudiates the notion of sense altogether, and ascribes to the speakers a bare knowledge of the references of their words. The conclusion to which I am driven is that it is, after all, a mistake to view a Davidsonian theory of meaning as a modest one in any sense. Let us see how this can be.

There are many different kinds of consideration which have been adduced in favour of linguistic holism: the most relevant for our purpose is that which generalizes Wittgenstein's observations about the name "Moses". Wittgenstein's thesis is that there are a number of things which we ordinarily believe to be true of Moses—that he was brought up in a royal palace, that he led his people out of slavery, that he delivered the Law to them, etc., etc. No one of these has to continue to be held true, on pain of our losing the use of the name "Moses": provided that we continue to believe that there was just one man of whom a large number of those things are true, we may reject the rest. Here it may be allowed that we attach more weight to some things we believe about Moses than to others; as far as the determination of the bearer of the name is concerned, we may attach no weight at all to some of them. Wittgenstein treated only of the case in which we are concerned with determining the referent of a single name; but it is plain that we may adapt it to that in which we are concerned with the simultaneous determination of the referents of two names, say "Moses" and "Aaron". There are a number of sentences containing one name or the other which we regard as true, some of which, such as "Moses and Aaron were brothers", contain both. We may now make some such stipulation as the following. If there exists a unique pair of individuals, m and a, such that, when these are taken as the respective referents of "Moses" and of "Aaron", a (weighted) majority of the sentences containing "Moses" come out true, and also a (weighted) majority of the sentences containing "Aaron" come out true, then these individuals are the actual referents of the names. If there is no such pair, or more than one such pair, but there is a unique individual m such that, when m is taken as the referent of "Moses" and all sentences containing "Aaron" are taken as false, a (weighted) majority of the sentences containing "Moses" come out true, then m is the actual referent of "Moses", while "Aaron" lacks a referent; and correspondingly for the case in which "Aaron" has a referent but "Moses" is empty. If none of these cases obtains, both names lack a referent.

I am not advocating such a doctrine; but it is readily intelligible, and has an obvious plausibility. On this account, the sense of a proper name is such that we have provided in advance that any one of the things which we regard as partially determinative of the referent may prove false, without the name's being deprived of reference. That does not, of course, mean that when we repudiate as false something that we had formerly regarded as true and as in part determinative of the reference, the sense of the name undergoes no alteration; on the contrary, it does so, because we no longer count the rejected statement among those a majority of which must be true of the bearer of the name.

The plausibility of Wittgenstein's account is not restricted to personal proper names; it is natural to apply it also to words of other kinds, for example mass terms. We arrive at a form of holism if we generalize the thesis simultaneously to all words in the language, including predicates, with the sole exception of the logical constants and perhaps prepositions and the like. Suppose that we have some large class (T) of sentences considered as true and as jointly determinative of the references of our words (names and predicates). Suppose also, as a large simplification, that we are given a determinate universe of objects over which the predicates may be taken as defined and within which the denotations of the names will fall. We now consider all possible *total assignments* of references to the names and predicates of the language: each such total assignment will constitute an interpretation of the language, relative to the given universe, in the sense of the standard semantics for a classical first-order language, save that a total assignment may allow that one or more names have no referents; it will assign referents to the other names, and extensions to the predicates. Any one total assignment will determine truth-values for the atomic sentences of the language, and the valuation will be extended to all sentences via those axioms of the theory of truth which govern the sentence-forming operators. We may now specify the actual referents of the names and the actual extensions of the predicates to be those which they have under the *preferred* or *correct* total assignment, this latter notion being in turn explained in some suitable manner in terms of the class T. The simplest explanation, and the one which a holist would be most likely to favour, would be to say that the preferred total assignment is that unique one (if any) which brings out true a maximum number of sentences of T.[5]

If we now interpret Davidson's theory of meaning as incorporating a holistic account, along these lines, of how the references of the primitive non-logical words of the language are determined, we can no longer regard it as lacking an account of a speaker's grasp of the senses of those words: on the contrary, what a speaker implicitly knows is that reference is determined in this holistic manner. Such knowledge enters

[5] An explanation more faithful to the original Wittgensteinian model would have to be rather complicated. We could say that a total assignment was *admissible* if, for each word to which it assigns a referent, it brings out true a majority of the sentences in T which contain that word, and call the *degree* of an assignment the number of names to which it assigns a referent; the preferred total assignment could then be stipulated to be that unique admissible assignment, if any, which is of maximal degree among admissible assignments. The complexity of this formulation seems to be unavoidable, if the pattern set by the case of just two interconnected proper names, such as "Moses" and "Aaron", is to be followed. For consider a case in which we have two such proper names, "a" and "b", and just five sentences contain them which we hold true, "Fa", "Ga", "Rab", "Hb", and "Kb"; I assume the extensions of the predicates fixed. Suppose that there are just four individuals, i, j, m, and n, which are candidates to be the referents of these names, that i and m are in the extension of "F", m alone in the extension of "G", j and n in the extension of "H", and n alone in the extension of "K", while the pair $\langle i, j \rangle$ is the only one standing in the relation denoted by "R". Then if we assign i to "a" and j to "b", two of the three sentences containing "a" come out true, and two of the three containing "b" come out true; but exactly the same result is obtained by assigning m to "a" and n to "b". We should want, in this case, I suppose, to say that the indeterminacy deprived the names "a" and "b" of reference; there would be no ground for ruling that just *one* lacked a reference, since we should have no basis for deciding which.

into the speaker's knowledge of the propositions expressed by the axioms of the theory of truth. For instance, what a speaker knows when he knows that "Oxford" denotes Oxford is, on this account, that "Oxford" denotes that object which is assigned to the name "Oxford" under the preferred total assignment to the names and predicates of English; what he knows when he knows that "*x* is supple" is true of an object if and only if that object is supple is that "*x* is supple" is true of an object if and only if that object belongs to that set of objects which is assigned as the extension of "*x* is supple" under the preferred total assignment; what he knows when he knows that "The Earth moves" is true if and only if the Earth moves is that "The Earth moves" is true if and only if that object which is assigned to "the Earth" under the preferred total assignment is a member of that set which is assigned to the predicate "*x* moves" under that assignment.

Looked at in this way, a Davidsonian theory appears as ineradicably holistic, but no longer as in any sense a modest theory: so regarded, it goes unscathed by complaints, such as I made in the lecture, that the theory gives no account of what the knowledge that is attributed to the speakers of the language consists in. I should still argue that the whole conception of a modest theory of meaning is misbegotten; but I think that the impression which not only I but, I believe, a number of Davidson's supporters had, that a theory of meaning of his kind is to be interpreted as a modest one, is to be rejected. A large part of the reason for so interpreting it lies in the fact that Davidson has always represented the collection of data about the judgements actually made by speakers as to the truth and falsity of sentences as standing in a relation of *evidence* to the resulting theory of truth; whereas, on the holistic conception of sense which I sketched above, they do not provide external support to the theory, but are integral to it. For consider the model from which we started, Wittgenstein's account of the name "Moses". Someone who has no idea *which* sentences containing the name "Moses" are generally held to be true, but who knows merely that the name denotes that unique individual, if any, of whom a majority of those sentences, whatever they are, are true, would not be said by Wittgenstein to grasp the use of the name "Moses": he merely has a correct schematic account of the form which a specification of its use—or that of any other name—must take. In order to know the specific use of the name "Moses", he must know which particular sentences involving the name are generally held true. Admittedly, individual speakers frequently exploit the existence of an established use for a name or other word, holding themselves responsible to the established means for determining the application of the word without themselves having a complete mastery of it; this often applies strikingly to place-names. This is a consequence of the fact that a language is a social phenomenon rather than a family of similar idiolects, and does not affect the fundamental point. To be able to use a name, or other word, at all, otherwise than in the fashion of a recording apparatus, a speaker must know something specific about the way its reference is determined, even if he does not know everything relevant; and the fact that there is a socially established application to which he holds himself responsible depends upon there being a means of discovering what governs that application.

In the same way, on a holistic theory, a man cannot be said to know the axiom governing "the Earth", that is, to know that "the Earth" denotes the Earth, if he merely knows that the expression denotes that object which is assigned to "the Earth" under that total assignment to the primitive expressions of English which brings out true the maximum number of sentences generally held true by English speakers, whatever those sentences may be. In knowing that, he knows only the general schema in accordance with which the particular explanation of the use of any singular term, in any language, must be given, and, in addition, no more than that "the Earth" is a singular term of English; he could have that knowledge without knowing anything more about the English language whatever, and could hardly, in such a case, be said to know what "the Earth" meant, or, therefore, the proposition expressed by " 'The Earth' denotes the Earth". In order to know the specific meaning of "the Earth", to know the proposition expressed by that axiom, he must know which particular sentences make up the class *T*, relative to which it is determined which total assignment is the preferred one. (The holism comes out in the fact that it is the same specific piece of knowledge which is required for a grasp of the senses of all names and predicates of the given language.) Thus what Davidson calls the 'evidence' for the theory of truth is actually internal to it. The theory is not something that we base upon the 'evidence', but which can be understood without knowing what the evidence for it may be: we cannot grasp or convey the content of the theory without explicit mention, in detail, of the sentences which jointly determine the references of our words; for without such mention, we cannot tell what references the theory of truth asserts those words to have.

My primary interest, in the lecture, was to arrive at certain basic principles regulating the construction of a viable theory of meaning; and most of those conclusions stand, even if I was mistaken in construing Davidson's conception of a theory of meaning as a modest one. One important conclusion, however, requires reconsideration, namely that the adoption of a holistic view of language renders the construction of a systematic theory of meaning impossible. That now depends upon whether a Davidsonian theory, interpreted in the holistic manner sketched above, is or is not credible. The first impression, which is, I believe, a correct one, is that even if it is in principle coherent, it simply is not credible. We saw that to state the principles underlying the simultaneous determination of the references of two proper names in a Wittgensteinian manner was fairly complex: but in that context, the senses of the other words occurring in the various sentences containing those names were being taken as already known; and, because of the assumed fixity of the applications of general terms, the results of an enquiry as to the referents of the proper names, and, accordingly, the truth-values of the sentences containing them, could be thought of as able to be *stated* by the use of general terms. But when we try to take seriously the idea that the references of all names and predicates of the language are determined simultaneously, it becomes plain that we are thereby attributing to a speaker a task quite beyond human capacities. In such a simultaneous determination, there is no reason why the reference of any one word should prove to be such as to bring out true the maximum number of sentences of *T* containing that word; but, even if it were so, the speaker would derive little guidance from the thought that the referent of a name was that individual of whom the majority of the predicates extracted from such sentences were true. This would afford him little guidance, because he could not take it as already given what it was for any one such predicate to be true of any particular individual: on the contrary, that would be up for determination at the same time, via the determination of the extensions of the primitive predicates occurring in those sentences, and, ultimately, of all those in the language. For the same reason, the outcome of the process of determining the reference of any word could never be stated verbally, except perhaps when the referent was a possible object of ostension, since the words that might be used for stating it could not be taken as having an application given in advance of the determination of the reference of the word in question. Admittedly, while a conclusive demonstration of the truth of any one sentence would require that the task of discovering the referents of its constituent words under the preferred total assignment should actually be accomplished, the making of a single judgement as to truth-value need not wait upon that task, any more than a judgement concerning Moses has to wait upon a definitive decision as to which of the things we normally believe about him are true; one might indeed infer from the holistic theory that no conclusive demonstration of truth could ever be provided. The fact remains that just as, on Wittgenstein's theory, one must know both how the referent of "Moses" is determined, and the particular things we believe concerning Moses, in order to know the content of any sentence containing that name; so, on the holistic theory, one must both know the composition of the entire totality *T*, and have the conception of a simultaneous determination of the references of our words in relation to it, in order to grasp the content of any single sentence.

The difficulty of making the holistic account plausible becomes more apparent when we enquire into the composition of the base totality *T*. It would be somewhat contrary to the spirit of holism to admit that there exists a special class of privileged sentences, among all those generally considered true, which we might call 'quasi-analytic': sentences which are not individually immune to revision (although the rejection of any of them will effect a change in the senses of our words), but which play a special role, which other sentences acknowledged as true do not, in the determination of the references of our words. The holist nevertheless faces a choice, in the exact formulation of his doctrine, over whether or not he is to allow for disagreements between speakers. If he does not, then he must regard *T* as comprising just those sentences which all speakers accept as true, or, at least, which many accept as true and none rejects as false, and, therefore, as including only sentences having no significant indexical feature. But in this case it becomes implausible that *T* will be adequate to determine the application of many predicates, for instance of ". . . is supple": although most English speakers would agree on any one particular application of such a predicate, there are just too few actual sentences containing the word, whose truth most speakers would acknowledge, to determine its extension. In the face of this difficulty, the holist is more likely to make the other choice, and regard the base totality T as consisting not of sentences, but, rather, of individual judgements of truth-value made by particular speakers. In this case, *T* will contain not only divergent judgements concerning non-indexical sentences, but also judgements relating to sentences with indexical elements, or, more accurately, to statements (where a statement is taken as a triple of a sentence, a speaker, and a time). This choice, however, involves a different implausibility: where *T* is taken as the totality of all judgements actually made by speakers of the language, no one speaker will come anywhere near having a grasp of the correct theory of meaning for that language, since the vast majority of those judgements will be unknown to him.

In order to escape this absurdity, the holist is subject to a strong temptation to shrink the notion of a language down to that of an idiolect; each individual speaker is now to be conceived of as having his personal theory of truth for the language as he speaks it, a theory which incorporates, in its base totality *T*, all the judgements which he personally makes, but none of other speakers, since they are irrelevant to his idiolect. Such a conception inverts the true relation between the notion of an idiolect and that of a language, in the everyday sense of "language". A language, in the everyday sense, is something essentially social, a practice in which many people engage; and it is this notion, rather than that of an idiolect, which ought to be taken as primary. We cannot, indeed, dispense with the notion of an idiolect, representing an individual's always partial, and often in part incorrect, understanding of his language; but it needs to be explained in terms of the notion of a shared language, and not conversely. One among many reasons for holding this is the phenomenon called by Putnam the 'linguistic division of labour'; but it is unnecessary here to pursue the point in detail, since the shift from a common language to an idiolect does not extricate the holist from his difficulty.

If a speaker's mastery of his language consists in an implicit grasp of a theory of meaning for that language, then, if the theory is holistic, he must be aware of the judgements which comprise the base totality. Even when the language is his own personal idiolect, therefore, that totality cannot contain a multitude of casual judgements which he has made but has subsequently forgotten; it can, at any given time, contain only such judgements as can be elicited from him at that time. This still makes it grossly improbable that the totality can be sufficiently extensive to determine the references of all the words in his language.

Of certain words, it is perfectly reasonable to maintain the thesis that the reference of each of them is determined by the requirement that one or more sentences containing it should come out true. Wherever it can be held that there is an essentially unique way of defining a word, this fact can be expressed by applying that thesis to a single sentence incorporating the definition; and the thesis may be applied to any other word which must, or even may, be introduced by means of a verbal explanation, whether or not that explanation amounts to an actual definition. The description theory of proper names derives the considerable plausibility that it possesses precisely from the fact that proper names may be, and often are, introduced to someone who does not know them by means of a verbal explanation; and this fact also underlies Wittgenstein's account of the name "Moses", which, as Kripke has observed, is a modification of the description theory. The modification has two features: first, it allows for the fact that there is usually more than one legitimate way of introducing a proper name, and that these different ways, taken together, supply more than is needed in order to determine its reference; and, secondly, it provides in advance for the resolution of any conflict that may emerge between the alternative means of fixing the referent. This account may, again, be represented by the thesis that the reference of such a name is determined by the requirement that a weighted majority of the sentences which might be used in introducing it should be rendered true. Among general terms, some behave in this respect like proper names, while, for some others, there are no multiple criteria for their application which could come into conflict, but, rather, essentially only one correct way of explaining them. Others, again, occupy an intermediate position: their explanation is complex, in the sense that one could represent their extension as being determined by the requirement that a number of different sentences should come out true; but the conflict which would be provoked by the discovery that it was impossible to maintain all these sentences, hitherto taken as constitutive of their meaning, would be much more severe than in the case of a name like "Moses", and the means we should adopt for resolving such a conflict is not provided for in advance.

It is, undoubtedly, a fallacy to suppose that one may always simply equate the sense of what is said in explanation of a word with the sense of that word; and, whatever may be thought in detail of Kripke's views on proper names, they serve to underline the fallacy: to the extent that there is a generally understood difference in the employment of a definite description and of a proper name, the hearer will make a tacit allowance for that difference when a proper name is introduced to him by means of a definite description. Such a concession does not, however, invalidate the idea that the means we should employ for conveying to someone the sense of a word he did not previously understand displays the sense which it bears in the language, where grasping the sense of a word is equated with understanding its accepted use. If, for instance, there exists an established means of fixing the reference of a name, it will necessarily be integral to the sense of that name.

The thesis that reference is determined by the requirement that all, or most, sentences in a certain set should come out true may thus be sustained in respect of a large number of words. It loses its plausibility, however, when it is generalized by the holist to apply to all the words of the language simultaneously. This is because it was, in the first place, a particular way of representing the sense of a word which it is possible to introduce by means of a verbal explanation: its plausibility therefore extends so far as it is applied only to words which may be so introduced, and maintained only in relation to those sentences which could legitimately be used in giving such an explanation. If a speaker's grasp of the sense of a word is to be represented as consisting in his knowledge that its reference is determined by a set of sentences containing that word, then those sentences must be ones that might actually be elicited from him in explaining the word; and, if we are considering the word as part of a common language, then they must be sentences generally accepted as true and also as determinative of the sense of the word, that is, as legitimate to cite in explanation of its sense. The holist is therefore wrong to include, in his base totality *T*, judgements particular to individual speakers, or ones which an individual speaker does not remember making or would not allude to in explaining a word to someone who did not understand it. It follows that the thesis that the references of our words are determined by the requirement that certain sentences be true cannot be generalized, as the holist wishes to generalize it, to provide an account of how the references of *all* words in the language are fixed: there are many words in the language which are not, and cannot be, introduced by means of purely verbal explanations, and to these the thesis simply does not apply. Our language is a many-storeyed structure, and the possibility of introducing new expressions—into the language or into the vocabulary of a particular speaker—by means of linguistic explanations depends upon our first constructing the lower storeys by different means; notoriously holism is at its weakest in the account that it gives of the progressive acquisition of language. But a correct theory of meaning is required to give an account of what it is to have a mastery of a language *at all*: a model which gives a representation only of how, by the use of a fundamental part of the language, one may come to grasp the senses of expressions at higher levels is a bad general model to employ in constructing such a theory.

As we have already seen, the judgements made by individual speakers play a dual role on Davidson's account: on the one hand, they form the evidence which might be used by someone with no prior knowledge of the language who was wishing to construct a theory of meaning for it; on the other, they become an ingredient of the theory itself, as making up the totality *T* which determines the references of the words. In the former role, no objection can be levelled against the appeal which is made to them: if we are trying to discover, from observation of someone's linguistic behaviour, the sense which he attaches to a certain word, we shall naturally pay attention to all the judgements of truth-value which he makes in regard to sentences containing that word, since such judgements obviously display the propensity which he has to employ that word in a certain manner. But the idea that we can then, by reference to the totality of all judgements made by speakers, obtain a single uniform representation of the manner in which the bearers of all the names and the extensions of all the predicates of the language are determined, overlooks the diversity of the many types of expression our language contains, and the gradations of level at which they lie. This may seem a hard saying, in face of the fact that it was Quine, the principal modern exponent of linguistic holism, who advanced the celebrated image of language as an articulated structure, whose sentences lie at differing depths from the periphery; but the fact is that that image in no way represents an essentially holistic view of language, and, indeed, accords rather badly with such a view. For holism, language is not a many-storeyed structure, but, rather, a vast single-storeyed complex; its difficulties in accounting for our piece-meal acquisition of language result from the fact that it can make no sense of the idea of knowing part of a language. As in the present case, the insights which provide the starting-points for arguments to a holistic view are perfectly genuine; holism results from succumbing to the temptation to generalize them beyond their range of application, in order to arrive at a single formula to cover every case.

2

What is a Theory of Meaning? (II)

1

Does the meaning of a sentence consist in its truth-condition? Does the meaning of a word consist in the contribution it makes to determining the truth-condition of any sentence in which it occurs?

It is unnecessary to labour the observation that an affirmative answer to these questions represents by far the most popular approach, among those philosophers who would not jettison the concept of meaning altogether, to an account of that concept, and that it has been explicitly contended for by Frege, by the Wittgenstein of the *Tractatus*, and by Davidson. I am far from being certain that an affirmative answer is wrong. I am quite certain, however, that such an answer faces formidable difficulties, and that we have no right to assume it correct until we have shown how it is possible to overcome them. It is, to my mind, very far from obvious why we should need, or how we can use, the notion of truth (or, rather, the twin notions of truth and falsity) in this connection, that is to say, as the basic concept, or pair of concepts, in the theory of meaning: a case needs to be made out that it is either necessary or possible to do so before we have any title to presume that meaning and truth are connected in anything like the way Frege supposed them to be.

Because more philosophers have favoured an affirmative answer to the above question than a negative one, and because Frege, in particular, was so great a genius, we have more grasp on what a theory of meaning given in terms of truth-conditions looks like than on the general form of a theory of meaning of any rival kind; indeed, the retort that equally formidable difficulties face the construction of any rival theory is entirely just. However, the difficulties are of different kinds. Thanks to the work of Frege, Tarski, and many others, the difficulties that face the construction of a theory of meaning in terms of truth-conditions are not difficulties of *detail*: they are difficulties of *principle*, which

This essay was first published in Gareth Evans and John McDowell (eds.), *Truth and Meaning* (Oxford, 1976). It is intended as a sequel to 'What is a Theory of Meaning? (I)' (Essay 1). It can, however, be read independently.

In a discussion of this sort, it is hard to retain lucidity while making due allowance, in one's formulations, for the phenomenon of indexicality, and I have preferred to aim at lucidity; thus my use of "sentence" and "statement" is very inexact. I do not think that this has vitiated the thought or obscured its expression, if the reader will grant me a little licence.

face us at the very outset of the enterprise. We know well enough how to build the machine: but we have no grounds for confidence that we can set it in operation. There are some problems of detail, of course, concerning the adaptation to natural language of the techniques devised by Frege and Tarski for formalized languages; but we may reasonably feel optimistic about finding solutions to problems of this kind. By contrast, theories of meaning of alternative types, in which the central concept is not taken to be that of truth, do not face an objection of principle before their construction is even undertaken; but, just because no serious attempt has ever been made to work out such a theory, even as applied to a formalized version of natural language (i.e. a quantificational language for everyday use), we encounter difficulties of detail as soon as we start to think how such a construction might proceed. I do not in the least rule out the possibility that a thorough investigation would reveal these difficulties to be, after all, difficulties of principle, blocking the construction of any such theory of meaning; the discovery that such difficulties existed for any such theory of meaning would enable us to give grounds for regarding it as necessary to employ the concept of truth as our basic notion in explaining meaning, and it is because I think that there may be such grounds to be discovered that I conceded at the outset that I am not certain that meaning is not to be explained in terms of truth-conditions. A proof that it is *necessary* to use the concept of truth for this purpose would not, in itself, show how it is *possible* for it to play this role; it would not of itself overcome the initial objections to a theory of meaning in terms of truth-conditions, but it would guarantee that there was a way of overcoming them to be found. But, at present, we do not have any proof that it is necessary to take the concept of truth as the basic notion for the theory of meaning, and hence we ought to treat the objections to the possibility of doing so with more respect; and, if we are to discover any such proof, we shall most probably do so by investigating the construction of rival theories of meaning.

Before we can look at this topic any more closely, we have to be clearer about what it means to say that the meaning of a sentence consists in its truth-condition: for it is, I believe, a common experience that this idea, though luminous at first glance, is maddeningly difficult to state coherently. A step in the right direction is taken by conforming to what is, I believe, the correct observation that philosophical questions about meaning are best interpreted as questions about understanding: a dictum about what the meaning of an expression consists in must be construed as a thesis about what it is to *know* its meaning. So construed, the thesis becomes: to know the meaning of a sentence is to know the condition for it to be true. This is a step to elucidation, but only a small step: the really elusive notion is that of truth-conditions itself. What *is* it to know the truth-condition of a sentence?

We can make no progress with this question without taking account of the fact that we want that knowledge of the truth-condition of a sentence which is to constitute an understanding of that sentence to be derived from an understanding of the words which compose the sentence and the way they are put together. It is obvious that we do not want to say that, whenever it is the case that a certain sentence is true if and only if certain circumstances obtain, anyone who knows that fact is to be credited with an understanding of the sentence; the condition is much too weak. What we are after is an account of the sort of understanding which a speaker of the language has. It may be that, for someone to be said to know the meaning of a sentence, including one from a language which he does not know, it is too strong a requirement that he should know the meanings of all the individual words in the sentence; or it may be that there is no definite answer to this question. That does not matter—the question is unimportant. What we need to have is an account of what it is to know a language; and a speaker of a language derives his understanding of any sentence of that language from his knowledge of the meanings of the words.

Our problem is, therefore: What is it that a speaker knows when he knows a language, and what, in particular, does he thereby know about any given sentence of the language? Of course, what he has when he knows the language is practical knowledge, knowledge how to speak the language: but this is no objection to its representation as propositional knowledge; mastery of a procedure, of a conventional practice, can always be so represented, and, whenever the practice is complex, such a representation often provides the only convenient mode of analysis of it. Thus what we seek is a theoretical representation of a practical ability. Such a theoretical representation of the mastery of an entire language is what is called by Davidson, and will be called here, 'a theory of meaning' for the language; Davidson was, perhaps, the first to propose explicitly that the philosophical problems concerning meaning ought to be investigated by enquiring after the form which such a theory of meaning for a language should take.

A theory of meaning will, then, represent the practical ability possessed by a speaker as consisting in his grasp of a set of propositions; since the speaker derives his understanding of a sentence from the meanings of its component words, these propositions will most naturally form a deductively connected system. The knowledge of these propositions that is attributed to a speaker can only be an implicit knowledge. In general, it cannot be demanded of someone who has any given practical ability that he have more than an implicit knowledge of those propositions by means of which we give a theoretical representation of that ability. But, in the particular case when the ability is the ability to speak a language, it would be self-defeating to require that the speaker's knowledge of the propositions constituting the theory of meaning for the language should be manifested in an ability to formulate them verbally, since the fundamental aim of the theoretical representation is to explain what it is that someone who does not yet know any language has to acquire in order to come to know the given language. It would, moreover, be palpably incorrect to hold that, once someone had mastered a language, he could give, in that language or any other, an explicit formulation of a theory of meaning for the language.

A theory of meaning of this kind is not intended as a psychological hypothesis. Its function is solely to present an analysis of the complex skill which constitutes mastery of a language, to display, in terms of what he may be said to know, just what it is that someone who possesses that mastery is able to do; it is not concerned to describe any inner psychological mechanisms which may account for his having those abilities. If a Martian could learn to speak a human language, or a robot be devised to behave in just the ways that are essential to a language-speaker, an implicit knowledge of the correct theory of meaning for the language could be attributed to the Martian or the robot with as much right as to a human speaker, even though their internal mechanisms were entirely different. At the same time, since what is being ascribed to a speaker is *implicit* knowledge, the theory of meaning must specify not merely what it is that the speaker must know, but in what his having that knowledge consists, i.e. what counts as a manifestation of that knowledge. Without this, not only are we left in the dark about the content of ascribing such knowledge to a speaker, but the theory of meaning is left unconnected with the practical ability of which it was supposed to be a theoretical representation. It is not enough that a knowledge of the theory of meaning as a whole be said to issue in a general ability to speak the language: for the whole point of constructing the theory was to give an analysis of this complex ability into its interrelated components. Rather, certain individual propositions of the theory must be correlated with specific practical abilities, the possession of which constitutes a knowledge of those propositions. The demand that every proposition of the theory be correlated with some practical ability would, indeed, be far too strong. For example, a knowledge of a language involves a knowledge of its syntax, and this requires a classification of words and phrases into syntactic categories, so that we may attribute to one who has the capacity to speak grammatically a tacit knowledge that a given word is for example, a noun. There is obviously no single ability which manifests this piece of knowledge, taken in isolation: the capacity to recognize certain sentences containing that word as well formed, and others as ill formed, depends upon knowing the syntactic categories of other words and the complex rules of sentence-formation which may be expressed in terms of those categories. Here, an implicit grasp of certain general principles, naturally represented by axioms of the theory, has issued in a capacity to recognize, for each sentence in a large, perhaps infinite, range, whether or not it is well formed, a capacity naturally represented as the tacit derivation of certain theorems of the theory. To each of these theorems corresponds a specific practical ability, i.e. the ability to recognize of a particular sentence whether it is well formed or not; but this is not true of the axioms. A knowledge of certain axioms, taken together, issues in a general capacity, in this case to recognize of any sentence whether or not it is well formed; and the ascription to the speaker of an implicit knowledge of those axioms is based on the confidence that he has a general capacity which embraces all the specific abilities which correspond to theorems derivable from that set of axioms. An axiom earns its place in the theory, however, only to the extent that it is required for the derivation of theorems the ascription of an implicit knowledge of which to a speaker is explained in terms of specific linguistic abilities which manifest that knowledge.

What holds good at the syntactic level also holds good for the semantic part of the theory. A theory of meaning will contain axioms governing individual words, and other axioms governing the formation of sentences: together these will yield theorems relating to particular sentences. If a theory correlates a specific practical capacity with the knowledge of each axiom governing an individual word, that is, if it represents the possession of that capacity as constituting a knowledge of the meaning of that word, I shall call it *atomistic*; if it correlates such a capacity only with the theorems which relate to whole sentences, I shall call it *molecular*. I know of no demonstration that an atomistic theory of meaning is in principle impossible; but since, with unimportant exceptions, the unit of discourse (the shortest expression whose utterance effects a significant linguistic act) is the sentence, there can be no general requirement, of a theory of meaning, that it be atomistic. What a speaker knows, in knowing the language, is how to use the language to say things, i.e. to effect linguistic acts of various kinds. We may therefore require that the implicit knowledge which he has of the theorems of the theory of meaning which relate to whole sentences be explained in terms of his ability to employ those sentences in particular ways, that is, that the theory be molecular. But his employment of words consists only in his employment of various sentences containing those words, and hence there need not be any direct correlation of that knowledge which is taken as constituting his understanding of any one word with any specific linguistic ability. The ascription to him of a grasp of the axioms governing the words is a means of representing his derivation of the meaning of each sentence from the meanings of its component words, but his knowledge of the axioms need not be manifested in anything but the employment of the sentences.

We should not have the least idea how such a theory of meaning might be constructed if we were not familiar with the distinction, introduced by Frege, between sense and force. Without such a distinction, a speaker's understanding of any given sentence would have to be taken to consist in nothing less than his awareness of every feature of the use of that sentence, that is, of the entire significance of any possible utterance of the sentence. Wittgenstein's celebrated slogan "Meaning is use" can be interpreted in many ways, most of which probably tally with some aspect of his understanding of it. One very radical way of interpreting it is as repudiating altogether any distinction between sense and force; but the fact is that we have no conception of how to set about describing the employment of any one particular sentence without the help of any general machinery which would involve making a distinction of that kind, and hence we should have to despair of constructing any systematic account of language whatever. A distinction between sense and force is implicit in any thesis such as the one which we are considering, that to know the meaning of a sentence is to know its truth-condition. Someone who knows, of a given sentence, what condition must obtain for it to be true does not yet know all that he needs to know in order to grasp the significance of an utterance of that sentence. If we suppose that he does, we are surreptitiously attributing to him an understanding of the way in which the truth-condition of a sentence determines the conventional significance of an utterance of it: but, since the theory of meaning is intended to display explicitly all that a speaker must implicitly know in order to be able to speak the language, the presumed connection between the truth-condition of a sentence and the character of the linguistic act effected by uttering it must be made explicit in the theory. This is made apparent by the phenomenon of mood (which need not actually be signalized by the inflection of the verb): in most languages, there are many sentences whose utterance would not normally be described as saying anything that could be true or false, although they bear a systematic syntactic relation to sentences the utterance of which would be so described. The theory of meaning may be formulated so as not to attribute truth or falsity to such sentences but to associate with them conditions of a parallel kind, e.g. obedience-conditions in the case of imperatives; in that case, it must make explicit what may be done by uttering a sentence which has a truth-condition, and what other things may be done by uttering a sentence which has a condition of some other kind. Alternatively, the theory may be formulated so as to associate truth-conditions with all sentences: but, in that case, the theory must include an explicit explanation of the significance of the various moods, that is, it must explain the different relations which the truth-condition of a sentence has to the act of uttering it, according to the mood of the sentence. Even if we considered a language without mood, it would hold good that the conventional significance of a given utterance was not uniform—one and the same sentence could be used to do different things; and the theory would still have to give an account of the different ways in which the truth-condition of a sentence might, according to context, be related to the significance attached to an utterance of it.

The simplest way to put the point is this. If we suppose that, by knowing the condition for a sentence to be true, a speaker thereby knows the whole use of the sentence, this can only be because of his grasp of the concept of truth. That part of the theory of meaning which stipulates the truth-conditions of the sentences of the language merely specifies the extension of the concept: it therefore does not display those features of it which allow the whole use of a sentence to be derived from its truth-condition. If, in place of the term "true", taken as already understood, the theory had employed some primitive technical term which had no existence outside the theory, it would be impossible to maintain that, by knowing only the principles governing the application of this predicate, a speaker thereby knew the use of each sentence: rather, there would have to be a supplementary part of the theory which stated, by the use of this term, the connection between its application to any sentence and the use of that sentence. This supplementary part of the theory of meaning would embody those principles relating to the concept of truth which someone would have to grasp if he were to be able to derive the use of a sentence from a specification of the condition for it to be true.

A theory of meaning which takes the concept of truth as its central notion will, therefore, consist of two parts. The core of the theory will be a theory of truth, that is, an inductive specification of the truth-conditions of sentences of the language. This core would be better called 'the theory of reference', since, while among its theorems are those stating the conditions under which a given sentence, or utterance of it by a given speaker at a given time, is true, the axioms, which govern individual words, assign references of appropriate kinds to those words. Surrounding the theory of reference will be a shell, forming the theory of sense: this will lay down in what a speaker's knowledge of any part of the theory of reference is to be taken to consist, by correlating specific practical abilities of the speaker to certain propositions of the theory. The theory of reference and the theory of sense together form one part of the theory of meaning: the other, supplementary, part is the theory of force. The theory of force will give an account of the various types of conventional significance which the utterance of a sentence may have, that is, the various kinds of linguistic act which may be effected by such an utterance, such as making an assertion, giving a command, making a request, etc. Such an account will take the truth-condition of the sentence as given: for each type of linguistic act, it will present a uniform account of the act of that type which may be effected by the utterance of an arbitrary sentence whose truth-condition is presupposed as known.

It is only against such a background that it makes any sense to say that to know the meaning of a sentence is to know the condition for its truth; what is intended is not that to know the condition for the application of the predicate "true" to the sentence is, in itself, *all* that a speaker has to know in order to be able to use that sentence or understand the utterance of it by another, but that it is all that has to be known that is *specific* to that sentence; all else that has to be known is of a general character—a set of general principles by means of which we can determine uniformly, from the truth-condition of any arbitrary sentence, every feature of its use. And the same holds good for any other thesis according to which there is some one property of a word or sentence an awareness of which constitutes a grasp of its meaning, for instance that the meaning of a sentence is the method of its verification. In this latter case, what is being proposed as constituting the meaning of a sentence is, unlike the truth-condition of the sentence, a feature of its use; but it is only one particular feature. If the sole activity in which our use of language consisted were the verification of sentences, then the thesis would be a platitude; but plainly it is not. Learning to use language involves learning to do many other things: to act on, or respond verbally to, the assertions of others; to make assertions on grounds which fall short of being conclusive; to offer grounds for our assertions; to draw inferences; to ask and answer questions; to give, obey, or flout commands; and so on. The thesis that the meaning of a sentence is the method of its verification is not a denial that there are all these different aspects of the use of language, but a claim that there is some uniform means of deriving all the other features of the use of any sentence from this one feature, so that knowledge of that one feature of a sentence is the only specific piece of knowledge about it that we need to know its meaning. Such a claim involves, precisely, an acknowledgement of a distinction between sense and force: a conception of the correct theory of meaning as falling into two parts, a central part giving the theory of sense and reference (here conceived of as an inductive specification, for each sentence, of the method of its verification), and a supplementary part giving a uniform means of deriving, from that feature of any sentence determined by the central part, every aspect of its use.

As I have said, we have no idea how to construct a systematic theory of meaning which does not embody a sense/force distinction. The question before us is whether the concept of truth is the right choice for the central notion of a theory of meaning, that in terms of which its core theory is stated, or whether we need to employ some other notion in this role. One large question concerning this choice is whether a viable supplementary theory (theory of force) can be constructed in terms of the notion chosen as central; whether there really is a uniform means of describing our whole linguistic practice in terms of it. So far, we have very little conception of what such a supplementary theory, formulated without appeal to a prior understanding of notions, such as assertion, relating to linguistic behaviour, would look like: attention has been concentrated more on the form of the core theory. It is because the core theory represents a grasp of the sense of an expression, not as the mastery of its entire use, but as the apprehension of one particular property of it, that we have no general argument to show the impossibility of an atomistic theory of meaning, any more than we have one to show the necessity of a theory of that type. To know the sense of a sentence is to know one particular thing about it—the condition for its truth, or the method of verifying it, or the like, according to what is taken as the central notion for the given theory of meaning; or, more accurately, it is to have derived that knowledge from the way the sentence is put together out of its component words. I have argued that an acceptable theory of meaning must be at least molecular; its theory of sense must state how a speaker's knowledge of the meaning of any sentence is manifested. But because the supplementary part of the theory is available to explain how he derives, from his grasp of its sense, a complete understanding of its use, it is quite unnecessary that what is stipulated as constituting his knowledge of its meaning should cover every aspect of his ability to use that sentence as it is used in the language: it may, rather, be some quite restricted ingredient of that ability (for instance, an ability to carry out a verification of the sentence). By the same token, therefore, there is no reason why the theory of sense should not identify a speaker's grasp of the sense of each individual word with some specific ability of his relating to that word, say his grasp of the senses of some very specialized range of sentences containing that word.

2

The question "Does the meaning of a sentence consist in the condition which must obtain for it to be true?" thus amounts to this: Is the choice of the notion of truth as the central notion for a theory of meaning which admits a distinction between sense and force the right one?

One of the reasons for the great popularity of the conception that the meaning of a sentence is given by its truth-condition is its intuitive obviousness. If we take the notion of truth for granted, if we credit ourselves with a grasp of that notion, but do not stop to ask how it should be analysed, it appears evident that no other notion but that of truth can be adequate to explain our understanding of a sentence, and, equally, that nothing more is needed. This impression is in large part due to the equivalence principle, i.e. the principle that any sentence A is equivalent in content to the sentence $\ulcorner$It is true that $A\urcorner$. This seems to show that truth *must* be the right notion to use to explain meaning: we could not say, for example, that to know the meaning of a sentence A is to know what has to hold good for A to be known to be true, for $\ulcorner$It is known that $A\urcorner$ is much stronger than A itself; nor could we say that it is to know when there are adequate grounds for asserting A, since these could exist even though A was false.

The equivalence principle provides a basis for an acceptable explanation of the role of the word "true" *within* the language. If someone already understands a language L, and L is then extended, to a language L^+, by the introduction of the predicate "true", regarded as applicable to sentences of L and as subject to the equivalence principle, such a stipulation makes it quite intelligible that the speaker will be equipped to understand sentences of L^+. (The stipulation would actually have to be made more complex, to take account of indexicality, but these complications need not detain us.) We can even see why the extension would be useful; if the word "true" is treated as an ordinary predicate, not confined to contexts of the form "It is true that . . .", but allowed also in such contexts as "He said something to me which was not true", then it will not always be eliminable, but its extension will be determinate. Of course, such an account will not serve to explain the word "true" when it is used to give the semantics of a language, in particular when it is used as the central notion of a theory of meaning for the language, since it depends upon supposing that the speaker has a prior understanding of those sentences of the language which did not contain the word "true". It will also not do for an account of the word "true" as it actually functions in natural language, since such a language aspires to be what Tarski called 'semantically closed', i.e. to contain its own semantics. This is not merely a matter of the extension's being impredicative, i.e. of our allowing the predicate "true" to be applied also to sentences of the extended language; we also use the word "true", and many other words, to enunciate propositions belonging to a theory of meaning for the language, that is, we attempt to use the language as its own metalanguage, and, in so doing, admit as principles governing the use of the word "true" ones which are not covered by the stipulation of the equivalence principle. For the most part, however, we continue to require that the equivalence principle be maintained.

As long as we take the notion of truth for granted, then it seems obvious that it is in terms of it that meaning must be explained. The moment that we cease to take it for granted, however, and start to enquire into the correct analysis of the notion, to ask where we get it from, this obviousness evaporates. To ask such questions is to ask where, in the process of acquiring a mastery of language, an implicit grasp of the notion of truth comes in. If the notion of truth is to serve as the basic notion of a theory of meaning for the language, then we cannot think of it as introduced by a stipulation of the equivalence principle, for that, as we have seen, is in effect to suppose that we may acquire a mastery of the greater part of our language in advance of having any apprehension of the concept of truth: if we want to maintain that what we learn, as we learn the language, is, primarily, what it is for each of the sentences that we understand to be true, then we must be able, for any given sentence, to give an account of what it is to know this which does not depend upon a presumed prior understanding of the sentence; otherwise our theory of meaning is circular and explains nothing.

If the notion of truth is to serve as one belonging to our theory of meaning, which serves to display in what our knowledge of the language consists, the equivalence principle cannot fulfil an explanatory role; but, as already remarked, it may still play a very important part in our grasp of the concept of truth, in that we continue to require that the concept be so understood that the equivalence principle remains correct. Now any acceptable theory of meaning must give recognition to the interconnectedness of language. Since words cannot be used on their own, but only in sentences, there cannot be such a thing as a grasp of the sense of any one word which does not involve at least a partial grasp of the senses of some other words. Equally, an understanding of some one sentence will usually depend on an understanding not merely of the words which compose that sentence, and of other sentences that can be constructed from them, but of a certain sector of the language, often a very extensive one. The difference between a molecular and a holistic view of language is not that, on a molecular view, each sentence could, in principle, be understood in isolation, but that, on a holistic view, it is impossible fully to understand any sentence without knowing the entire language, whereas, on a molecular view, there is, for each sentence, a determinate fragment of the language a knowledge of which will suffice for a complete understanding of that sentence. Such a conception allows for the arrangement of sentences and expressions of the language in a partial ordering, according as the understanding of one expression is or is not dependent upon the prior understanding of another. (That it be, or approximate to being, a partial ordering, with minimal elements, seems to be required if we are to allow for the progressive acquisition of a language. On a holistic view, on the other hand, the relation of dependence is not asymmetric, and in fact obtains between any one expression and any other: there can be nothing between not knowing the language at all and knowing it completely.)

In particular, it is evident that, in practice, once we have reached a certain stage in learning our language, much of the rest of the language is introduced to us by means of purely verbal explanations; and it is reasonable, as well as traditional, to suppose that such explanations frequently display connections between expressions of the language a grasp of which is actually essential to an understanding of the words so introduced. That is to say, in effect, that the possibility of explaining certain expressions by purely verbal means is an essential characteristic of the meaning they possess; if so, this must be reflected in any correct theory of meaning for the language. Now if we want to offer a purely verbal explanation of a certain form of sentence, we cannot do better—indeed, we cannot do other—than state the conditions under which a sentence of that form is *true*: for, in virtue of the equivalence principle, to do that will be precisely to state the content of a sentence of that form, and there is no other property a statement of the condition for the possession of which by such a sentence would serve that purpose. Here, again, therefore, is another reason, once more traceable to the equivalence principle, why the idea that to give the meaning of a sentence is to give its truth-condition should be so compelling; moreover, it indicates a respect in which any correct theory of meaning must conform to that idea.

A theory of meaning which takes truth as its central notion has to supply an explanation of what it is to ascribe to someone a knowledge of the condition which must obtain for a sentence to be true. If the sentence is of a form which a speaker can come to understand by means of a verbal explanation, then there is no problem: his knowledge of the truth-condition of the sentence is explicit knowledge, knowledge which is manifested by his ability to state that condition. An explanation of this form obviously presupposes that the speaker already knows a fairly extensive fragment of the language, by means of which he can state the condition for the truth of the given sentence, and in terms of which he came to understand it. It follows that, however large the range of sentences of the language his understanding of which can be explained in this way, this form of explanation will not suffice generally. Since, in virtue of the equivalence principle, to state the condition for the truth of a sentence is simply to give the content of that sentence in other words, an explicit knowledge of the truth-condition of a sentence can constitute a speaker's grasp of its meaning only for sentences introduced by means of purely verbal explanations in the course of his progressive acquisition of the language: it would, notoriously, be circular to maintain that a speaker's understanding of his language consisted, in general, of his ability to express every sentence in other words, i.e. by means of a distinct equivalent sentence of the same language. His understanding of the most primitive part of the language, its lower levels, cannot be explained in this way: if that understanding consists in a knowledge of the truth-conditions of sentences, such knowledge must be implicit knowledge, and hence the theory of meaning must supply us with an account of how that knowledge is manifested.

The difficulty of giving a suitable explanation of that in which a speaker's knowledge of the truth-condition of a sentence consists does not lie in deciding what to count as displaying his recognition that that condition is satisfied. It is true that there is no single universal and unmistakable sign of acknowledgement of the truth of a given sentence, nor any absolutely standard means of eliciting such a signal: but it is reasonable enough to suppose that, in relation to the speakers of any one language, we can devise a criterion for a speaker's recognition of the fulfilment of the condition which establishes any given sentence as true. If we allow this, then we have no difficulty in stating what constitutes a speaker's knowledge of the condition for the truth of a sentence, provided that the condition in question is one which he can be credited with recognizing whenever it obtains: that knowledge will consist in his capacity, perhaps in response to suitable prompting, to evince recognition of the truth of the sentence when and only when the relevant condition is fulfilled. Plainly, however, an explanation of this form covers at best a very restricted range of cases; there are very few sentences the condition for whose truth cannot obtain without its being recognized as obtaining. Such a form of explanation may be generalized to cover any sentences which are, in practice or even in principle, decidable, that is, for which a speaker has some effective procedure which will, in a finite time, put him into a position in which he can recognize whether or not the condition for the truth of the sentence is satisfied. For any such sentence, we may say that the speaker's knowledge of the condition for it to be true consists in his mastery of the procedure for deciding it, that is, his ability, under suitable prompting, to carry out the procedure and display, at the end of it, his recognition that the condition does, or does not, obtain. (Of course, this characterization contains a number of general terms which would not occur in an actual theory of meaning, which would mention only the specific decision procedures involved and the particular means by which the speaker displayed his recognition that the condition for the truth of a sentence was satisfied: the general characterization is intended only to show that there is no difficulty in principle in doing that.)

The difficulty arises because natural language is full of sentences which are not effectively decidable, ones for which there exists no effective procedure for determining whether or not their truth-conditions are fulfilled. The existence of such sentences cannot be due solely to the occurrence of expressions introduced by purely verbal explanations: a language all of whose sentences were decidable would continue to have this property when enriched by expressions so introduced. Many features of natural language contribute to the formation of sentences not in principle decidable: the use of quantification over an infinite or unsurveyable domain (e.g. over all future times); the use of the subjunctive conditional, or of expressions explainable only by means of it; the possibility of referring to regions of space-time in principle inaccessible to us. Of course, for any given undecidable sentence, the possibility may well be open that we may find ourselves in a position to recognize that the condition for its truth is satisfied, or that it is not. But, for such a sentence, we cannot equate a capacity to recognize the satisfaction or non-satisfaction of the condition for the sentence to be true with a knowledge of what that condition is. We cannot make such an equation because, by hypothesis, either the condition is one which may obtain in some cases in which we are incapable of recognizing the fact, or it is one which may fail to obtain in some cases in which we are incapable of recognizing that fact, or both: hence a knowledge of what it is for that condition to hold or not to hold, while it may demand an ability to recognize one or other state of affairs whenever we are in a position to do so, cannot be exhaustively explained in terms of that ability. In fact, whenever the condition for the truth of a sentence is one that we have no way of bringing ourselves to recognize as obtaining whenever it obtains, it seems plain that there is no content to an ascription of an *implicit* knowledge of what that condition is, since there is no practical ability by means of which such knowledge may be manifested. An ascription of the knowledge of such a condition can only be construed as *explicit* knowledge, consisting in a capacity to *state* the condition in some non-circular manner; and that, as we have seen, is of no use to us here.

The problem which here confronts the attempt to construct a theory of meaning which uses the notion of truth as its central notion does not relate to the supplementary part of the theory, to which I have given the title "the theory of force". That part of the theory is concerned with displaying the connection between the truth-condition of a sentence and the actual practice of using it in discourse; unless it proves possible to devise such a theory of force in a convincing way, the whole enterprise of constructing a theory of meaning of this type collapses. But it would be rash at the present time to base any predictions on the feasibility of this task; we know as yet hardly anything about how to go about it. The problem which I am here discussing relates to the theory of sense, which I depicted as a shell about the core theory. The core theory states the way in which the references of the component words of each sentence determine its truth-condition; or, better, how the application to each sentence of the predicate "true" depends upon the references of its component words. The shell—the theory of sense—relates this theory of truth (or of reference) to the speaker's mastery of his language; it correlates his knowledge of the propositions of the theory of truth with practical linguistic abilities which he displays. Now when someone learns a language, what he learns is a practice; he learns to respond, verbally and non-verbally, to utterances and to make utterances of his own. Acknowledging sentences as true or as false is among the things which he learns to do; more precisely, he learns to say and do various things as expressions of such acknowledgement. But knowing the condition which has to obtain for a sentence to be true is not anything which he *does*, nor something of which anything that he does is the direct manifestation. We have seen that, in some cases, we can explain acceptably enough, in terms of what he says and does, what it amounts to to ascribe such knowledge to him. But in other, crucial, cases, no such explanation appears to be available: and so we fail to attain a genuinely explanatory account of what the practice that he acquires consists in.

Where does the concept of truth come from? Its most primitive connection is plainly with the linguistic act of assertion, as is seen from the fact that we naturally call assertions 'true' or 'false', but not questions, commands, requests, bets, etc. If we apply a Fregean sense/force analysis to our sentences, we see the sentence as falling into two parts, that which conveys the sense of the sentence (the thought), and that which indicates the force which is being attached to it, assertoric, interrogative, imperatival, etc. It is the thought alone which is, from this standpoint, properly said to be true or false, whether we are asserting it to be true, asking whether it is true, commanding that it be made true, or whatever else. On such a view, therefore, someone who asks a (sentential) question or gives a command can be said to be saying something true or false with as much right as one who makes an assertion; and it is as much of a solecism to call the *assertion* 'true' or 'false' as it is so to call a question or command. However attractive this way of speaking may be, it is a revision of our natural mode of expression; and this is not due solely to the fact that we lack an assertoric mood corresponding to the interrogative and imperatival ones, but use the same form of words in a co-ordinate clause, or, in

English, in a subordinate one, as we do when the sentence is used on its own assertorically. To say something true is to say something correct, to say something false is to say something incorrect. Any workable account of assertion must recognize that an assertion is judged by objective standards of correctness, and that, in making an assertion, a speaker lays claim, rightly or wrongly, to have satisfied those standards. It is from these primitive conceptions of the correctness or incorrectness of an assertion that the notions of truth and falsity take their origin.

An utterance may be criticized in different ways. Certain kinds of criticism—as that a remark was impolite, a breach of confidence, or in bad taste—are directed, not at what is said, but at the saying of it. This intuitively clear distinction is difficult to draw without invoking problematic concepts. We might say, for instance, that what is criticized is the external utterance rather than the interior act, e.g. of judgement; but the fact that certain linguistic acts, such as assertion, can be internalized is itself a puzzling one which we should expect a theory of meaning to throw light on, not to take for granted. Perhaps the least question-begging way to draw the distinction between the two types of criticism is as follows. Any linguistic act can be cancelled, at least if the cancellation is sufficiently prompt: a speaker may withdraw an assertion, a command, a request, or a question. A criticism which is directed solely at what is said—as that an assertion is untrue, a command unjust or a question unfair—no longer stands if the utterance is cancelled. A criticism which is levelled at the act of saying, on the other hand, may be weakened, but is not wholly met, by its cancellation: if someone, by his utterance, broke a confidence or wounded his hearer's feelings, his withdrawal of the utterance mitigates, but does not wipe out, the offence. The distinction thus drawn does not fully coincide with that we should obtain by reference to the speaker's interior state: if we object to a question as being unfair, the objection is wholly met if the question is withdrawn, so that, on this principle, the objection is to what is said rather than to the saying of it; but we are not objecting to the speaker's desire to know the answer, but only denying his right to ask. I think, however, that the distinction as I have drawn it is closer to what we want in this context than one drawn by reference to interior states.

The notion of an assertion's being incorrect or correct relates only to the existence or non-existence of valid criticisms directed against what is said, rather than against the saying of it: I think it is important to filter out the possibility of criticisms of the latter kind; an undifferentiated concept of the acceptability of an utterance—of an utterance's not being open to criticism of *any* kind—would be of little use for our purposes. The notion of truth takes its rise from the more primitive notion of the correctness of an assertion; but it does not coincide with it. It is integral to the notion of truth that we can draw a distinction between the truth of what someone says and the grounds which he has for thinking it true; the idea that an assertion is judged by standards of correctness or incorrectness does not yet supply a basis for this distinction. An assertion which is made on inadequate grounds is open to criticism, criticism which is directed against what is said rather than against the saying of it, and hence is incorrect: the question is why we want to introduce a distinction between different ways in which an assertion may be incorrect, and on what basis we draw this distinction. Once we are supplied with a conception of the condition for the truth of the sentence used to make the assertion, then we know how to draw this distinction; but the question is where we got that conception from. We cannot suppose it given with the most primitive employment of assertoric sentences: for this, we require only a general distinction between the cases when a sentence may correctly be uttered assertorically and when it may not. This may be clearly seen when we consider sentences, such as the indicative conditionals of natural language, to which we are not ordinarily accustomed to apply the predicates "true" and "false". Philosophers dispute over the proper criteria for applying these predicates to such sentences: and they do so precisely because they are in disagreement about how much is to be reckoned to the condition for the truth of such a sentence, and how much to the grounds which a speaker may have for considering it true. Such disputes reflect no ambiguity in the everyday use of indicative conditionals. All parties to the dispute are agreed on the circumstances in which an assertion made by means of an indicative conditional is warranted, that is, when a speaker is entitled to make such an assertion; and this is all that we need to know in order to interpret an assertion of this type when it occurs in everyday discourse. In consequence of such knowledge, we know when to make such an assertion, how to support it when challenged, what makes it reasonable to accept it or reject it, how to act on it or to draw conclusions from it if we do accept it. What the philosophers argue about is the further question what makes an indicative conditional sentence *true*. Some hold that it is true just in case the corresponding material conditional is true; others that, when the antecedent is true, the conditional is true or false according as the consequent is true or false, but that, when the antecedent is false, the conditional is true or false according as the corresponding counterfactual conditional is true or false, further argument relating to the truth-conditions of counterfactuals; others, again, would accept the first part of this, but hold that, when the antecedent is false, the indicative conditional is neither true nor false; and yet others demand that, irrespective of the truth or falsity of the antecedent, the truth of the conditional demands the existence of some connection between antecedent and consequent. These disputes leave the ordinary understanding of the indicative conditional untouched: a grasp of the use of such conditionals in everyday discourse does not appear to turn on our having any conception of the truth-conditions of conditional sentences as opposed to the condition for the correctness of a conditional assertion. But, if this holds good in this case, why does it not hold good in every case? Why cannot we make do in all cases with the more primitive notion of the correctness of an assertion, without invoking the notion of the truth of a sentence, with its concomitant distinction between saying something false and saying something on inadequate grounds?

At least part of the answer lies in the formation of compound sentences. This comes out very clearly with the future tense. If our use of the future tense were confined to atomic sentences, there would be no saying how the line should be drawn between the condition for the truth of such a sentence and the grounds upon which it might reasonably be asserted; we should need no such distinction in order to understand future-tense assertoric utterances. Indeed, it would not only be that we should have no basis for denying that conditions prevailing at the time of utterance, including the speaker's intentions, were part of the truth-condition of the sentence; we should not be compelled to allow that what subsequently happened, when it belied the tendencies prevailing at the time of utterance, had any direct bearing on the truth of the sentence, since we should not have to regard a subsequent utterance of the negation of the sentence, or of its present-tense form, as a contradiction of the original assertion. What forces us to distinguish between the truth of the sentence and the speaker's warrant for its assertion is the behaviour of the sentence as a clause in a compound sentence, and, more particularly, when it figures as the antecedent in a conditional, as well as the use of compound tenses, in particular the past future ("was going to . . ."). In explaining the use of indicative conditionals, we do not need the notion of the truth-value of the conditional, as opposed to the circumstances which warrant its assertion; but we do need that of the truth of its antecedent.

The behaviour of future-tense sentences as constituents in compound sentences forces on us a distinction between their truth-conditions and the conditions which warrant their assertion, and therefore allows a differentiation between the genuine future tense, which yields a sentence true or false according to what subsequently happens, and the future tense used to express present tendencies, which yields one which is true or false according to the conditions prevalent at the time of utterance. The recognition of the truth-conditions of sentences involving the genuine future tense is also prompted by the use of future-tense sentences to effect certain linguistic acts other than assertion, e.g. commands, requests, and bets. The existence of these linguistic acts depends upon there being certain conventional consequences which follow on their being made, consequences determined solely from the content of the sentence used in making them; the understanding of the force attached to the sentence in these cases therefore itself provides a basis for separating the speaker's grounds for his utterance from the content of the utterance itself. Thus, although the notion of truth originates in connection with the making of assertions, we are assisted in disentangling it from the more general notion of the correctness of an assertion by our understanding of certain types of utterance which carry a non-assertoric force. This does not mean that the notion of truth can be satisfactorily explained solely in terms of commands, bets, etc. The behaviour of a form of sentence when it carries one kind of force may be quite different from its behaviour when it carries another: the interpretation of conditional commands and bets is a useless analogy for the explanation of conditional assertions; disjunctive questions behave quite differently from disjunctive statements. Unless we had a reason for appealing to a notion of truth-conditions for future-tense assertoric sentences which coincides with that required for commands relating to the future, we should not import the notion from one context to the other.

There is thus built into the concept of truth from the outset a contrast between the semantic and pragmatic aspects of an assertion; truth is an objective property of what the speaker says, determined independently of his knowledge or his grounds for or motives in saying it. Naturally, some such distinction arises as soon as enough language has been learned for a speaker to be capable of making mistaken assertions, where the mistake does not lie in an erroneous grasp of the language: but the contrast is greatly heightened by our need to discriminate between failure to say what is true and failure to say what is warranted.

To explain why we need the concept of truth, for semantic purposes, is not in itself to explain how the concept is to be applied. It is apparent from the foregoing that, in acquiring our mastery of language, we make a tacit appeal to the notion of the truth of a sentence in learning to form compound sentences and to construe assertions made by means of them, and that this process is assisted by our simultaneous learning of the use of certain sentences carrying non-assertoric force. The notion of truth thus tacitly acquired must be capable, in turn, of yielding the more primitive notion of the correctness of an assertion: this means that whatever further conditions, beyond the truth of the sentence, are in fact required for an assertion to be justified must be able to be explained as conditions for the speaker to have reasonable grounds for supposing the sentence to satisfy the condition for its truth; if that were not so, we should not be able to take the content of the sentence as being determined by its truth-condition. That is not to deny that there is an element of convention governing the claim which we take to be made by an assertion. It is, for example, a conventional matter that a mathematical assertion is construed as a claim that a proof of the statement is known (not necessarily to the speaker); our understanding of mathematical statements themselves would be quite unaffected if it were normal practice to make an unqualified assertion of such a statement on the basis only of plausible reasoning (in Polya's sense). But it is a requirement on the notion of truth—i.e. on what we take the truth-condition of any sentence to be—that whatever else is conveyed by an assertion effected by means of that sentence, beyond the satisfaction of its truth-condition, e.g. in the mathematical case the existence of a proof, can be represented as a ground for taking it to be true (or, as with Grice's principles of conversational implicature, a reason for uttering that sentence rather than a simpler and stronger one): all that remains for convention to determine, for assertions of different kinds, is how strong the ground is required to be if the assertion is to be justified.

None of this, however, does anything to resolve the difficulty about a theory of meaning based on the notion of truth which arises from the fact that the truth of many sentences of our language appears to transcend our powers of recognition. The case of future-tense sentences is instructive, because the truth-conditions we are forced to associate with such sentences in order to account for their behaviour as constituents of compound sentences are such as to make it impossible for a speaker to have conclusively established the truth of such a sentence at the time of utterance, and this compels us to make the sharpest possible distinction between the condition for the truth of a sentence and that which entitles a speaker to make an assertion. But, so long as we consider a future-tense sentence whose present-tense form remains decidable, we are still concerned with truth-conditions a knowledge of which can be directly manifested by the speaker, since, at a time subsequent to the utterance, he can display his recognition of whether or not the condition for its truth is satisfied. We are still no further towards explaining the content of an ascription to a speaker of a knowledge of the condition for the truth of a sentence, when that condition is not one which he is, in any circumstances, capable of directly recognizing.

3

In order to get clearer about what is involved in the ascription of truth to a statement, we need a fresh start, and this is provided by considering the principle: If a statement is true, there must be something in virtue of which it is true. This principle underlies the philosophical attempts to explain truth as a correspondence between a statement and some component of reality, and I shall accordingly refer to it as the principle C. The principle C is certainly in part constitutive of our notion of truth, but is not one which can be directly applied. It is, rather, regulative in character: that is to say, it is not so much that we first determine what there is in the world, and then decide, on the basis of that, what is required to make each given statement true, as that, having first settled on the appropriate notion of truth for various types of statement, we conclude from that to the constitution of reality.

Because it is a regulative principle, the principle C may at first strike one as empty. We feel its force only when we consider something which appears a violation of it. The most obvious such violation is provided by a counterfactual conditional alleged to be true even though there is nothing which, if we knew of it, we should accept as a ground for its truth: for instance, those counterfactuals asserted by one school of theologians to be the objects of God's *scientia media*, relating to the behaviour, had they been created, of beings endowed with free will whom, on the basis of such knowledge, God decided not to create. Most people naturally feel a strong objection to such a conception, precisely on the ground that, in such a case, there would be nothing to *make* the counterfactual true. This objection is based upon the thesis that a counterfactual cannot be, as I shall say, *barely true*, that is, that a counterfactual cannot be true unless there is some statement, not involving the subjunctive conditional, whose truth renders the counterfactual true; in other words, there must, for any true counterfactual, be a non-trivial answer to the question "What makes it true?"

Here the principle C yields substantial information, but only because combined with a more specific thesis, the thesis that a counterfactual cannot be barely true. In general, we can learn something by applying the principle C to a specific type of statement only when we have already decided something about the sort of thing in virtue of which a statement of that type can be true; and, in particular, this requires a basis on which to determine which types of statement can be barely true and which cannot. However, even in the case of counterfactuals, we have not yet obtained a very sharp conclusion until we know which statements are to be classified as involving the subjunctive conditional.

Our present considerations link up with our previous discussion just because, as then observed, the subjunctive conditional is one of the sentence-forming operations which allow us to construct sentences which are not effectively decidable. Why should anyone think that a counterfactual may be barely true? His only possible ground can be that he supposes it to be a matter of logical necessity that either that counterfactual or its opposite should be true (the opposite of a conditional being that conditional which has the same antecedent and the contradictory consequent), but does not think that there is necessarily any ground for the truth of either, of the sort on which we usually base assertions of such counterfactuals. Now no one could rationally take it as a quite general logical necessity that, of any pair of opposite counterfactual conditionals, one or other should be true: but we are strongly disposed to make this assumption of certain such pairs. The reason is that we readily equate the truth of certain statements, not overtly involving the subjunctive conditional, with the truth of certain subjunctive conditionals, and their falsity with the truth of the opposite subjunctive conditionals. If, then, we assume the law of bivalence for the statements of the first kind, we are forced into granting that, for any subjunctive conditional corresponding to such a statement, either it or its opposite must be true.

A clear case of a type of statement thus correlated with conditionals is provided by statements ascribing abilities to people. A statement like "*X* is good at learning languages" is, of course, normally tested by observing how quickly the subject acquires fluency in a foreign language. If, now, we consider the statement applied to someone who has never had any contact with a language other than his mother tongue, we are confronted by three possible attitudes to the question "Must this statement be either true or false?" (1) It is not necessarily either; there just does not have to be any determinate answer to the question whether or not this individual would learn a foreign language quickly if he were to attempt to learn one. (2) Linguistic ability must be correlated with, or consist in, some feature of brain structure, not at present known to us; the brain of this individual must either exhibit this feature or not; hence the statement must be determinately either true or false, whether or not we ever find out which. (3) Linguistic ability need not be correlated with any physiological feature, but, nevertheless, any one person either has it or lacks it; hence the statement must be either true or false.

That the truth of "*X* is good at learning languages" stands or falls with the truth of "If *X* were to attempt to learn a language, he would quickly succeed", and its falsity with the truth of the opposite conditional, is not at issue between the upholders of these three positions: it must be granted by anyone who understands the phrase "good at learning languages". Hence the question whether it is a matter of necessity that one or the other of the two opposite subjunctive conditionals is true coincides with the question whether the law of bivalence holds for the overtly categorical statement "*X* is good at learning languages". The upholder of position (3), recognizing that there is no necessity by which, when the antecedent of the conditional remains unfulfilled, we could, if we knew enough, recognize the truth either of that conditional or its opposite, frankly allows, in effect, that one or other of these conditionals may be barely true. The upholder of position (2) feels impelled to maintain the law of bivalence for the overtly categorical statement, but, since he finds the idea of a counterfactual conditional's being barely true repugnant, makes it a matter of necessity that the truth or falsity of the statement which ascribes the ability to the given individual should depend upon the truth or falsity of a statement of another type, namely about physiology. The upholder of position (1) shares with the proponent of (3) the conviction that there need be nothing which would enable us to determine the categorical statement as true or as false, however much we knew; but, since he also shares with the proponent of (2) a distaste for allowing as a possibility the bare truth of a counterfactual, he escapes the dilemma by rejecting the law of bivalence.

Of course, someone who takes up position (3) is not compelled to admit that a counterfactual conditional may be barely true. He may, if he likes, deny this, and claim that what makes the statement "If *X* were to attempt to learn a language, he would quickly succeed" true (if it is true) is the truth of the statement "*X* is good at learning languages". If this claim is to qualify as a denial that the counterfactual can be barely true, then he must hold that a statement like "X is good at learning languages" does not involve the subjunctive conditional. This may seem a futile contention, reducing the thesis that counterfactual conditionals of this kind cannot be barely true to utter triviality: for it is hardly to be disputed that we actually learn to apply such a predicate as "good at learning languages" to one who performs in a certain way under certain conditions, or to one who we have reason to think would perform in that way if those conditions were to be fulfilled, so that this seems to be a prime case of an expression which is introduced by means of the (subjunctive) conditional. He must, therefore, concede that the sentence "X is good at learning languages" does indeed *involve* the subjunctive conditional "If X were to attempt to learn a language, he would quickly succeed" in the sense that we come to understand the former by means of the latter, and that any ground for the truth of either is a ground for the truth of the other. But he may also retort that it does not follow that the overtly categorical sentence *reduces to* the subjunctive conditional, and that the criterion for a counterfactual conditional's being barely true ought to be that there is no statement the truth of which renders the counterfactual true and which does not actually itself *reduce to* a subjunctive conditional. His ground for denying that "X is good at learning languages" reduces to the corresponding subjunctive conditional, i.e. that the meaning of the one is to be strictly equated with that of the other, is precisely that "X is good at learning languages" can, according to him, be barely true, while a subjunctive conditional cannot. We cannot in general assume, of any random pair of opposite subjunctive conditionals, that one or other must be true: but of certain such pairs we do make precisely this assumption, and we do so because we regard them as reflecting some permanent feature of reality which we cannot directly observe. In allowing the transition from the conditional form of sentence to the categorical form, such as "X is good at learning languages", we are, on his view, giving expression to just this conviction. That is why the categorical form of sentence does not simply reduce to the conditional form: it embodies the assumption that a man's facility in learning a language reflects a permanent but not directly observable condition. That form of sentence can be correctly understood only when it is seen as embodying such an assumption, an assumption which does not underlie the use of the merely conditional form of sentence.

This version of position (3) must not be dismissed as a mere attempt, by juggling with words, to render nugatory the thesis that a subjunctive conditional cannot be barely true, while conforming to it. On the contrary, it distinguishes between cases in which the application of that thesis forces us to allow that neither of two opposite counterfactuals may be true, and cases in which, if we maintain the law of bivalence for certain overtly categorical statements, we need make no such concession. What it does not do is to delineate any principle upon which the two kinds of case may be distinguished, save by appeal to our customary linguistic practice; it therefore supplies no justification of that practice. That we are obliged to draw some such distinction cannot be denied; for the range of expressions within our language which may be said to be introduced by appeal to a conditional of some sort is vast. It includes every term for a property the possession of which is determined by a test, or for a quantity the degree of which is determined by measurement. We interpret some such tests and measurement procedures as revealing states of affairs which existed antecedently to and independently of the execution of the test or measurement; and we proceed to make the assumption that a sentence ascribing the property to something, or assigning to something a specific degree of the quantity, is determinately true or false independently of whether the test or measurement was or could be carried out.

In making such an assumption, we are adopting a realistic attitude towards the property or quantity in question; and it should now be apparent how it is that, as was claimed at the beginning of this section, the notion of truth which we take as governing our statements determines, via the principle C, how we regard reality as constituted. We may, in fact, characterize realism concerning a given class of statements as the assumption that each statement of that class is determinately either true or false.[1] Thus positions (2) and (3) amount to different versions of a realistic view of statements about human abilities, whereas position (1) is a rejection of realism concerning those statements. Position (2) is, however, a reductionist one: assuming that any statement ascribing a specific ability to a particular individual must be determinately true or false, its proponent concludes that there must be some physiological fact which renders it true or false. Reductionism does not, of course, have to take the strong form of asserting the translatability of statements of one class into statements of another; it is fundamentally concerned with the sort of thing which makes a statement of a given class true, when it is true. The thesis that statements of a class M are reducible, in this sense, to statements of another class R takes the general form of saying that, for any statement A in M, there is some family $\bar{A}$ of sets of statements of R such that, for A to be true, it

---

[1] This embraces the principle of bivalence for statements of that class; but it amounts to a little more than that, since the word "determinately" is not included merely for rhetorical effect. The formulation also embraces that semantic principle which is related to the distributive law as the principle of bivalence is related to the law of excluded middle; let us call it the principle of dissection. From the principle of bivalence, we know that, in relation to a single statement A, there are just two possibilities: that A is true, and that A is false. But we need to invoke also the principle of dissection if we are to conclude that, in relation to two statements A and B, there are just four possibilities: that A and B are both true, that A is true and B false, that A is false and B true, and that A and B are both false. I owe this point to Hilary Putnam, although he would not, I think, agree that the assumption either of the principle of bivalence or of the principle of dissection was required for a realistic interpretation. For the purposes of the present discussion, however, we may inaccurately identify realism concerning a class of statements with the assumption, for them, of the principle of bivalence.

is necessary and sufficient that all the statements in some set belonging to $\bar{A}$ be true; a translation is guaranteed only if $\bar{A}$ itself, and all the sets it contains, are finite. In such a case we may say that any statement of M, if true, must be true in virtue of the truth of certain, possibly infinitely many, statements in R.

Armed with this notion of reducibility, we may now say generally that a statement is barely true if it is true but there is no class of statements, not containing it or trivial variants of it, to which any class containing it can be reduced. While position (2) represents a reductionist form of realism concerning human abilities, position (3) embodies a naïve realism concerning them: naïve realism about statements of some class D consists in a combination of realism concerning that class with the thesis that statements of that class are capable of being barely true, i.e. that there is no class of statements to which they can be reduced. This amounts to holding that we cannot expect a non-trivial answer to the question "In virtue of what is a statement of the class D true when it is true?" Our view of the constitution of reality—our metaphysical position—depends in part on which are the classes of statements of which we take a realistic view, i.e. for which we assume the principle of bivalence, and in part on which are those which we admit as capable of being barely true.

We are now in a better position to understand what is involved in the ascription to a speaker of the knowledge of the truth-condition of a sentence. If a sentence S is such that statements made by uttering it are not capable of being barely true, then there will be some class R of statements such that an utterance of S can be true only if the statements in some suitable subset of R are all true; and a grasp of the truth-condition of S will consist in an implicit grasp of the way in which its truth depends upon the truth of statements in R. It may be that this dependence may actually be displayed within the theory of truth itself, so that, if we conceive of this theory as expressed in a metalanguage which is an extension of the object-language, the T-sentence for S will be non-trivial, i.e. will not have S itself on its right-hand side. It may be, alternatively, that the obstacle (if there is one) to giving an actual translation of S within the object-language will also prevent the construction of such a non-trivial T-sentence; in that case, the theory of sense, which explains in what a speaker's grasp of the propositions of the theory of truth consists, will have to make explicit the relation between S and the class R. In either case, the notion of a grasp of the truth-condition of S is not problematic.

Matters stand differently when S is understood as a sentence used to make a statement capable of being barely true. In this case, the corresponding T-sentence cannot but be of the trivial form. The explanation of what it is for a speaker to know the truth-condition of S must, therefore, in this instance, fall wholly to the theory of sense. Our model for such knowledge, in the case of a sentence capable of being barely true, is the capacity to use the sentence to give a report of observation. Thus if someone is able to tell, by looking, that one tree is taller than another, then he knows what it is for a tree to be taller than another tree, and hence knows the condition that must be satisfied for the sentence "This tree is taller than that one" to be true.

The notion of a report of observation is a very loose one. Without attempting to go into all the problems which arise if one wishes to make it sharper, we are here concerned to pick out those cases in which an ability to use a given sentence in order to give a report of observation may reasonably be taken as knowledge of what has to be the case for that sentence to be true; bearing in mind that this criterion is intended to apply only when the sentence is one for which we have no non-trivial way of *saying* what has to be the case for it to be true. The following conditions appear to be required. First, the making of the observation-report must not rest upon any extraneous inference (must not represent 'a conclusion of the witness'), as, for example, in "I see that the Smiths forgot to cancel their newspapers". Secondly, in every case in which the sentence is true, it must be in principle possible that it should be observed to be true. And, thirdly, the possibility of observing it to be true cannot involve any operation which effects a transformation of the constitution or situation of any object referred to in the sentence. It is the last of these three conditions which is the delicate one; I am unsure whether there is any precise intuitive principle, let alone whether I have stated it accurately. The point can, however, be illustrated from our example of human abilities. Everyday discourse will certainly permit the use of a sentence like "I observed that he was good at languages". But, if we take a naïvely realistic view of sentences ascribing abilities to people, we can hardly accept a capacity to observe manifestations of such abilities as sufficient to guarantee a knowledge of what it is, in general, that makes such a sentence true. If each individual determinately either possesses or lacks any one given ability, regardless of whether an occasion ever arises for his possession or lack of it to be manifested, then the possession of such an ability cannot *consist* in its manifestations. It cannot even consist in whatever renders true the appropriate subjunctive conditional, when this is considered as understood antecedently to the use of the vocabulary of permanent abilities, for otherwise an individual might neither possess nor lack the ability. Rather, in a particular case it may be the mere possession of the ability which renders the corresponding subjunctive conditional true, in the absence of anything else which would show that conditional to be true, or, therefore, that the ability was present. Hence, given a naïvely realistic view of human abilities, we ought not to count observing that someone learns a language quickly as an observation of the ability itself, but only as an observation of a manifestation of it, from which his possession of it is inferred; the ability itself must be regarded as something not directly observable by us. Now it may be said that the second of our two principles is enough to yield this result, since, of a man now dead, who had lived his whole life in a totally monolingual environment, it would be in principle impossible to observe whether or not he had linguistic ability; and a similar difficulty would attend making such observations before the building of the Tower of Babel. However, this would be to appeal to rather special features of our particular example. What seems of more significance is the fact that, if one tests out a person's linguistic ability by creating an incentive and an opportunity for him to learn a foreign language, and then observing the outcome, one has materially altered the situation; and it is for this reason that we should be reluctant to say that an understanding of how to carry out such a test amounted to a knowledge of what it is for someone to have linguistic ability even though it is never called into play; reluctant, that is, to say this in the context of a naïvely realistic view of human abilities. It was in order to sanction such reluctance that the third requirement was included above, unsatisfactory as its formulation undoubtedly is. We should contrast this case with that of observation of, say, shape. Although, as is well known, some philosophers have gone down this path, it would seem quite unreasonable to deny that someone who was capable of telling, by looking or feeling, whether or not a stick is straight knew what it was for a stick to be straight, on the ground that he would not thereby show that he knew what it was for a stick which no one had seen or touched to be straight; and the best way that occurs to me to explain the intuitive difference between the two kinds of case is to say that looking at or feeling the stick effects no alteration in it. It is not, indeed, that the modification effected by the test is in respect of the property being tested: by testing somebody's linguistic ability, we are supposed to establish the degree of ability he would have had even if it had not been tested; it is not only the case in which the test affects the relevant property that is being excluded. It may be said, with some justice, that it is again a matter for metaphysical decision which observation procedures are reckoned as effecting some modification in the object; but that is another matter.

We may, on the other hand, legitimately extend the notion of a report of observation to include assertions based upon the execution of the sort of operation of which counting is the prototype, something which does not operate upon the object observed, but serves to impose an order on the observations. Statements of number might be ranked among sentences whose truth-conditions can be informatively stated; but perhaps statements of equality of number might be regarded as ones the knowledge of whose truth-conditions consists in a capacity for reporting the result, not of passive observation, but of observation accompanied by an intellectual operation. Sentences which record the outcome of measurement or observations effected by instruments form an intermediate case, or rather a spectrum of intermediate cases, which approach, at the further end, those registering the result of a test of just that kind which we have tried to rule out. I do not know how to draw a sharp line, nor whether any can be drawn. It is not, indeed, part of my case that it is imperative to draw one, for I do not believe that, in the end, the conception of meaning as truth-conditions can be defended. All that I feel sure of is that we have just two basic models for what it is to know the condition for the truth of a sentence. One is explicit knowledge—the ability to state the condition; this, as we have seen, is unproblematic, and, moreover, is the model that we actually need in a large range of cases; but, as we have also seen, it is not a model that can be used if we want the notion of a grasp of truth-conditions to serve as our general form of explanation of a knowledge of meaning. The other is the capacity to observe whether or not the sentence is true. This notion may legitimately be stretched a certain way. It is not important to determine exactly how far it may be stretched: the important fact is that it cannot be stretched as far as we need.

It was argued earlier that the notion of a grasp of truth-conditions is problematic only when it is applied to a sentence not in principle decidable. This is actually more generous than the immediately foregoing discussion, since it would credit a speaker with a grasp of the truth-conditions of a sentence whenever there is some test which can in principle always be applied. The point is of relatively minor importance, however. It was also maintained earlier that there are three principal sentence-forming operations which are responsible for our capacity to frame undecidable sentences: the subjunctive conditional; the past tense (or, more generally, reference to inaccessible regions of space-time); and quantification over unsurveyable or infinite totalities. Now the claim that we tend to appeal to the mastery of observational sentences as a model for the knowledge of the truth-conditions of a sentence is borne out by our surreptitious, or sometimes explicit, appeal to such a model when sentences involving these operations are in question. Since the sentences in question are not in principle decidable, the observations which we imagine as being made are not ones of which we are capable: they are observations which might be made by some being with a different spatio-temporal perspective, or whose observational and intellectual powers transcend our own, such powers being modelled on those which we possess, but extended by analogy. Thus, for example, a naïve realist about mental abilities is disposed to appeal to a picture of the mind as an immaterial substance, whose constitution we can know about only indirectly, by inference, but which could be directly inspected by a being on whom spiritual substance made an impact like that made on us by material reality. Again, we are inclined to think of statements in the past tense as being rendered true or false by a reality no longer directly accessible to us, or, perhaps, only fragmentarily so, in memory, but which nevertheless is in some sense still there; for if there were, as it were, nothing whatever left of the past, then there would be nothing to make a true statement about the past true, nothing in virtue of which it would be true. On such a picture, we are for the most part forced to rely on inference in order to ground our statements about the past, that is, on indirect evidence; but our knowledge of what it is that actually makes such statements true or false involves our understanding of what it would be to apprehend their truth directly, i.e. by that which actually rendered them true. To be able to do this would be to be capable of observing the past as we observe the present, that is, to be able to survey the whole of reality, or, at least, any temporal cross-section of it at choice, from a position outside the time-sequence. The most celebrated example of this way of thinking relates to quantification over an infinite domain. We gain our understanding of quantification over finite, surveyable domains by learning the procedure of conducting a complete survey, establishing the truth-value of every instance of the quantified statement. The assumption that the understanding so gained may be extended without further explanation to quantification over infinite domains rests on the idea that it is only a practical difficulty which impedes our determining the truth-values of sentences involving such quantification in a similar way; and, when challenged, is defended by appeal to a hypothetical being who could survey infinite domains in the same manner as we survey finite ones. Thus Russell spoke of our incapacity to do this as 'a mere medical impossibility'.

In this way, we try to convince ourselves that our understanding of what it is for undecidable sentences to be true consists in our grasp of what it would be to be able to use such sentences to give direct reports of observation. We cannot do this; but we know just what powers a superhuman observer would have to have in order to be able to do it—a hypothetical being for whom the sentences in question would *not* be undecidable. And we tacitly suppose that it is in our conception of the powers which such a superhuman observer would have to have, and how he would determine the truth-values of the sentences, that our understanding of their truth-conditions consists. This line of thought is related to a second regulative principle governing the notion of truth: If a statement is true, it must be in principle possible to know that it is true. This principle is closely connected with the first one: for, if it were in principle impossible to know the truth of some true statement, how could there be anything which *made* that statement true? I shall call this second principle the principle K: its application depends heavily upon the way in which "in principle possible" is construed. One who adopts a realistic view of any problematic class of statements will have to interpret "in principle possible" in a fairly generous way. He will not hold that, whenever a statement is true, it must be possible, even in principle, for *us* to know that it is true, that is, for beings with our particular restricted observational and intellectual faculties and spatio-temporal viewpoint; it may be possible only for beings with greater powers or a different perspective or scale. But even the most thoroughgoing realist must grant that we could hardly be said to grasp what it is for a statement to be true if we had no conception whatever of how it might be known to be true; there would, in such a case, be no substance to our conception of its truth-condition. Moreover, he would further grant that it would be useless to specify in a purely trivial manner the additional powers which a hypothetical being would have to have if he were to be capable of observing directly the truth or falsity of statements of some given class. We could not, for example, explain that a being who had a direct insight into counterfactual reality would be able to determine by direct observation the truth or falsity of any counterfactual conditional, because the expression "a direct insight into counterfactual reality" provides no picture of what these powers consist in. Even the realist will concede that the picture of the required superhuman powers must always bear a recognizable relation to the powers which we in fact possess; they must be analogous to, or an extension of, our actual powers. It is precisely for this reason that the thesis that counterfactuals cannot be barely true is so compelling, since we cannot form any conception of what a faculty for direct recognition of counterfactual reality would be like.

The foregoing account is offered as a diagnosis, not as a defence. It gives, I believe, an accurate psychological account of how we come to suppose so readily that, for the sentences belonging to the less primitive strata of our language, we possess such a thing as a knowledge of what has to be the case for them to be true: but it provides no justification of this supposition. There is, so far as I can see, no possible alternative account of that in which our grasp of the truth-conditions of such sentences consists: but this one works only by imputing to us an apprehension of the way in which those sentences might be used by beings very unlike ourselves, and, in so doing, fails to answer the question how we come to be able to assign to our sentences a meaning which is dependent upon a use to which we are unable to put them. This difficulty faces any explanation of the meanings of certain expressions which consists solely of saying that we understand those expressions by analogy with or extrapolation from other expressions whose meanings we have come to grasp in some more direct way. There is no way of distinguishing such an account from the thesis that we treat certain of our sentences as if their use resembled that of other sentences in certain respects in which it in fact does not; that is, that we systematically misunderstand our own language.

4

What is the way out of this impasse? To find this, we must first ask what led us into it. The plain answer is that our difficulties all arise because of our propensity to assume a realistic interpretation of all sentences of our language, that is, to suppose that the notion of truth applicable to statements made by means of them is such that every statement of this kind is determinately either true or false, independently of our knowledge or means of knowing. For decidable statements, the assumption of the principle of bivalence does little or no harm, since, by hypothesis, we can at will determine the truth-value of those statements. It is when the principle of bivalence is applied to undecidable statements that we find ourselves in the position of being unable to equate an ability to recognize when a statement has been established as true or as false with a knowledge of its truth-condition, since it may be true in cases when we lack the means to recognize it as true or false when we lack the means to recognize it as false. When we are in this position, we can explain the attribution to a speaker of a knowledge of the truth-condition of the statement only when this can be represented as explicit knowledge, i.e. when that truth-condition can be informatively stated, and an understanding of the statement may be represented as consisting in an ability to state it. When this is not the case, we are at a loss to explain in what a speaker's implicit knowledge of the truth-condition of the statement can consist, since it apparently cannot be exhaustively explained in terms of the actual use which he has learned to make of the sentence.

If the realism which we adopt in regard to some class M of statements is of a reductionist type, then we have a means of enquiring whether or not the principle of bivalence holds good for statements in M. There will be a class R of statements to which the reduction is made, and the question will be comparatively easy to settle if we take a realist view of the class R itself. In that case, for any statement A in M, there either will or will not be some set, belonging to the family $\bar{A}$ of sets of statements of R, all the members of which are true, and hence A itself will either be or not be true. Whether or not this is sufficient to guarantee the principle of bivalence for the class M will depend upon how we interpret the notion of falsity in respect of that class. If we interpret "false" as meaning simply 'not true', then the principle of bivalence will hold trivially; but we are more often disposed to interpret "false" so that "A is false" is to be equated with "The negation of A is true", where the negation of a statement of the kind in question is to be identified by straightforward syntactic criteria. If the class M is closed under negation, the enquiry whether any statement A of M must be either true or false reduces to the question whether, if there is no set belonging to $\bar{A}$ all of whose members are true, there will always be some set belonging to $\overline{\text{Not } A}$ all of whose members are true; even if the answer is negative, the situation will be unproblematic. There will then be statements of M which are neither true nor false, and, provided that we wish to represent the operation of negation as the result of applying a genuine sentential operator, we shall require a many-valued semantics for statements of the class M; but there will be no particular obstacle to the construction of such a semantics.

The case which gives rise to our difficulties is that of a class M of statements which are not in principle decidable and our view of which is that of naïve realism: we assume the principle of bivalence for the members of M, but do not think that there is any non-trivial way of specifying what it is that makes a statement of M true when it is true. In any such case, we are bereft of any means of justifying our assumption of the principle of bivalence, save by appeal to the conception, discarded in the foregoing discussion, of a being with powers superior to ours for whom the statements of *M* would be decidable. It may, indeed, be the case that accepted linguistic practice is to treat as valid, in application to such statements, forms of inference which hold in classical two-valued logic; and it is this fact which impels us to suppose that we do in fact possess a notion of truth, applicable to those statements, according to which each statement is determinately either true or false. But a mere training in the acceptance of certain forms of inference cannot, by itself, endow us with a grasp of such a notion of truth, if we did not have it already, or, at least, if it is impossible to explain what it is to have such a notion of truth without reference to our acceptance of those forms of inference. Classical two-valued logic depends, for its justification, upon our having notions of truth and falsity which license the assumption that each statement has, determinately, just one of those truth-values; it cannot, of itself, generate those notions. It is true enough that classical logic can be justified in terms of a different semantics, specifically any in which the truth-values, whether finite or infinite in number, form a Boolean algebra. This is of no particular help, however, since the use of any semantics based upon some range of truth-values always presupposes that each statement has some one determinate truth-value in that range; and this assumption presents just the same difficulties as the assumption of bivalence (which is simply a special case of it).

In such a case, there is no possibility of constructing a workable theory of meaning which will apply to the sentences in this class unless we first abandon the assumption of bivalence. Without doing so, we are committed to attributing to ourselves, as speakers, a grasp of a notion of truth which, in application to these sentences, is transcendental, that is, which goes beyond any knowledge which we might manifest by our actual employment of the language, since the condition for the truth of such sentences is one which we are not, in general, capable of recognizing as obtaining when it obtains. If we abandon the assumption of bivalence, we must construct a semantics for these sentences which is not formulated in terms of truth-values; and it is probable, though not certain, that the outcome will be that we can no longer acknowledge classical logic as governing them. In so far as our ordinary unreflective practice is to accept all classical forms of inference as valid for such sentences, this will mean that our theory of meaning is no longer purely descriptive of our actual practice in the use of our language, but, on the contrary, has compelled us to propose a revision in that practice, namely the rejection of certain classically valid forms of argument. However, this development provides no ground of objection against that theory of meaning, for the possibility was present from the outset. Obviously, of any two viable theories of meaning, that which justifies our actual linguistic practice is always to be preferred to that which demands a revision of it; but we have no ground to assume in advance that our language is in every respect perfectly in order. Frege supposed that various features of natural language—the presence of vague expressions and of predicates undefined for certain arguments, and the possibility of forming singular terms lacking a reference—made it impossible to construct a coherent semantics for it as it stood; Tarski likewise asserted that the semantically closed character of natural language rendered it inconsistent. Such views may or may not be correct, but they cannot be ruled out a priori as absurd. The possibility that a language may stand in need of adjustment, that, in particular, the principles of inference conventionally recognized may require reassessment, is implicit in the idea that a language ought to be capable of systematization by a theory of meaning which determines the use given to each sentence from the internal structure of that sentence, that is, by an atomistic or molecular theory of meaning; for there can be no guarantee that a complex of linguistic practices which has grown up by piecemeal historical evolution in response to needs felt in practical communication will conform to any systematic theory.

This is, indeed, especially obvious when the theory of meaning is taken to have, as its core, a specification of the truth-conditions of sentences. If such a theory is to be adequate for a language containing counterfactual conditionals, to take them once more as our example, the truth-conditions assigned to those counterfactuals must allow us to determine the content of an assertion of any such counterfactual. What is given in linguistic practice is the content of a counterfactual assertion: the sort of grounds which a speaker may have for such an assertion, and the understanding which a hearer thereby has of what prompts the speaker to make such an assertion. Whatever is selected as providing the condition for a counterfactual conditional to be true must accord with this practice: the theory of force—the supplementary part of the theory of meaning which determines, from the truth-condition of a sentence, the content of an utterance of that sentence when endowed with assertoric (or other specific types of) force—must enable us to derive from the truth-condition of the counterfactual, as specified by the theory of truth, the content of an assertion made by uttering it. Now suppose that the speakers of the language accept as a valid principle of inference the alternation of opposite counterfactuals, mentioned earlier as a principle which we should reject: whatever follows both from some counterfactual conditional and from the opposite conditional is to be accepted as true. It is very likely that the truth-conditions determined for counterfactual conditionals will not justify this principle, i.e. will not yield the result that, of any pair of opposite counterfactuals, one or other must be true; likely, that is, if the content of counterfactual assertions in this language coincides with that of such assertions in our language. Now it is possible that there may be some way of rectifying this so as to provide a justification for the acceptance by the speakers of this language of the principle of the alternation of opposite counterfactuals.

That is, it is possible that there is some way of broadening the truth-conditions of counterfactuals, of allowing them to be true in cases in which, under the original specification, they were not true, so as after all to guarantee that one out of each pair of opposite counterfactuals must be true, without conferring on counterfactual assertions a content weaker than that which, in the actual practice of using the language, they in fact bear. But it is more likely that there is not: that we are driven to the conclusion that the speakers of this language are the victims of an error in permitting reasoning which depends upon the assumption that one of each pair of opposite counterfactuals must be true, and that they ought, in consistency, to reject such forms of argument. The idea, which Wittgenstein had, that acceptance of any principle of inference contributes to determining the meanings of the words involved, and that therefore, since the speakers of a language may confer on their words whatever meanings they choose, forms of inference generally accepted are unassailable by philosophical criticism, has its home only within a holistic view of language. If a language ought to be capable of systematization by means of an atomistic or molecular theory of meaning, we are not free to choose any logic that we like, but only one for which it is possible to provide a semantics which also accords with the other uses to which our sentences are put; in accepting or rejecting any particular form of inference, we are responsible to the meanings of the logical constants, thought of as given in some uniform manner (e.g. by two- or many-valued truth-tables).

We are thus in the position of having to abandon, for certain classes of statements, the principle of bivalence, or any analogous principle of multivalence. We cannot, therefore, employ as our general representation of a grasp of the meaning of a sentence a knowledge of the condition under which it possesses, independently of our knowledge, a particular one out of two, or any larger number of, truth-values. Instead, we shall have to construct a semantics which does not take, as its basic notion, that of an objectively determined truth-value at all.

One well-known prototype for such a semantics already exists: the intuitionistic account of the meanings of mathematical statements. This is most easily thought about, in the first instance, in application only to statements of elementary arithmetic. In this case, there is no problem about the meanings of atomic statements, namely, in this context, numerical equations, since these are decidable: a grasp of their meaning may be taken as consisting in a knowledge of the computation procedure which decides their truth or falsity. The whole difference between the classical or platonistic and the intuitionistic interpretation of arithmetical statements therefore turns upon the way in which we are given the meanings of the logical constants—the sentential operators and the quantifiers.

At this point some remarks are needed about the way that I have handled the phrase "true in virtue of". As explained above, a true statement is barely true only if there is no set of true statements, none of them trivial variants of the original statement, the truth of all of which determines the original statement as true. Whenever a sentence is capable of being barely true, the T-sentence relating to it in the theory of truth will, when the metalanguage is an extension of the object language, be of the trivial Tarskian form, i.e. the sentence occurring on the right-hand side of the biconditional will be the same as that named on the left-hand side. When it is not capable of being barely true, the T-sentence may or may not be trivial, according to the resources of the metalanguage. Now on the explanation given, no conjunctive, disjunctive, universal, or existential statement can be barely true. A conjunctive statement, when true, will be true in virtue of the truth of both its conjuncts. A disjunctive statement, when true, will be true in virtue of one of its disjuncts; we must allow that a given statement may be true in virtue of each of two or more distinct things. A true universal statement will be true in virtue of the truth of all its instances, and a true existential statement in virtue of the truth of any one of its true instances. This way of speaking accords with what has prompted philosophers to say such things as that there are no disjunctive facts; but the principal reason for adopting it is that it falls out as a by-product of the most convenient way of characterizing the notion of reducing one class of statements to another. It is plainly not a convenient way of speaking, however, when our interest is concentrated on the meanings of the logical constants themselves; it involves that the class of classical truth-functional combinations of sentences reduces to the class of atomic sentences and their negations, and, likewise, that the class of EA sentences (Σ_2^0 sentences) reduces to the class of quantifier-free sentences, and thus simply sweeps the problem of accounting for the meanings of the logical constants out of sight.

It is sometimes claimed that, while a theory of truth of the type envisaged in a Davidsonian theory of meaning does not itself give the meanings of the non-logical primitives of the language, it does give the meanings of the logical constants. In order to understand the meanings of the non-logical primitives, we have to look outside the theory of truth itself (presumably because the axioms governing those primitives are of a trivial form, such as " 'London' denotes London"), to the evidence, taken from the linguistic behaviour of the speakers, on which the theory of truth is based; or, as I should prefer to say, to the theory of sense, which explains what it is for a speaker to know the propositions expressed by the axioms. But, in order to understand the meanings of the logical constants, we need look to nothing but the axioms governing them within the theory of truth.

Presumably this claim is based on the notion that if, for example, the sentential operators of the language are classical, the theory of truth will embody the truth-table explanations of those operators. It is, however, entirely misguided. The question whether an axiom of the theory of truth itself displays that in which an understanding of the expression which it governs consists, or whether we have to look for that to the theory of sense, is the question whether or not that axiom is trivial. A trivial axiom is one which, when rendered in a metalanguage which is an extension of the object-language, will yield, in combination with suitable axioms for the other expressions, a trivial T-sentence for each sentence of the object-language containing the expressions which it governs. Now, notoriously, the axioms governing the classical logical constants are trivial in this sense: they take such forms as "For every sentence S and T, $\ulcorner S$ or $T \urcorner$ is true if and only if S is true or T is true" and "For every finite sequence of objects $\vec{b}$ having the same length as the sequence $\vec{y}$ of variables, $\vec{b}$ satisfies $\ulcorner$For some x, A $(x, \vec{y}) \urcorner$ if and only if, for some object a, $\langle a \rangle * \vec{b}$ satisfies A $(x, \vec{y})$".

Now it is indeed true that the use as the core theory of a theory of truth, that is, of a theory which issues in T-sentences for the sentences of the object-language, does not compel us to assign classical meanings to the logical constants. If we wish to impose upon the logical constants of the object-language some non-classical meanings, and are prepared to presume that the logical constants of the metalanguage are interpreted in a similar non-classical manner, then we can often endow the logical constants of the object-language with these non-classical meanings by adopting trivial axioms of just the same kind as in the classical case. This will be so whenever the relevant notion of truth distributes over the logical constants, as, for example, in the intuitionistic case. At first sight, truth will not distribute over the logical constants within the many-valued logics; for instance, in a three-valued logic, when B is false but A is neither true nor false, the statement "If A is true, then B is true" will be true although the statement $\ulcorner$If A, then $B \urcorner$ is not. However, this is so only because we are assuming, as can hardly be disputed, that the statement "A is true" is false when A is neither true nor false: for the purpose of constructing a theory of truth in which we may derive trivial T-sentences, we shall not want to use the predicate ". . . is true", construed as meaning ". . . has the value *true*", but a different predicate, say ". . . is True", which satisfies the requirement that, for any atomic sentence A, "A is True" has the same truth-value as A. If we can devise axioms for the primitive terms and predicates, and for the condition for an atomic sentence to be True, which satisfy this requirement, then the property of being True will distribute over the sentential operators, and hence the requirement will be satisfied for complex sentences also.

There will be difficulties in various cases: for instance, in a many-valued logic which has more than one designated truth-value; or when a logical constant, such as the modal operators, induces a context in which the variables of quantification must be taken as having a domain distinct from that which they have in other contexts. But there is certainly a large range of non-classical logics for which it would be possible to construct a theory of truth which yielded trivial T-sentences.

Whenever this can be done, however, the situation is exactly the reverse of what is claimed for a Davidsonian theory of truth. A trivial axiom for any expression, whether a logical constant or an expression of any other kind, does not, in itself, display in what an understanding of the expression consists, but throws the whole task of explaining this upon the theory of sense, which specifies what is to be taken as constituting a grasp of the proposition expressed by that axiom. An axiom of the form "$\vec{b}$ satisfies ⌜S or T⌝ if and only if $\vec{b}$ satisfies S or $\vec{b}$ satisfies T" (e.g. "$\vec{b}$ satisfies ⌜If it had been the case that S, then it would have been the case that T⌝ if and only if, if it had been the case that $\vec{b}$ satisfied S, then it would have been the case that $\vec{b}$ satisfied T") is no more explanatory of the meaning of the logical constant which it governs than is " 'London' denotes London" explanatory of the meaning of the word "London"; in either case, if there is to be any explanation at all, it will have to be found in the account of what a knowledge of the axiom consists in.

What is significant about a logical constant is not whether it is possible to construct a theory of truth so as to adopt a trivial axiom governing it, but, on the contrary, whether it is possible to devise a *non*-trivial axiom for it. If only a trivial form of axiom is possible, then the next significant question is whether the theory of sense can provide a non-circular account of what it is for a speaker to grasp its meaning, i.e. to have implicit knowledge of the trivial axiom governing the constant. Now, while it is possible to adopt trivial axioms for the intuitionistic constants, the standard explanations of these constants yield axioms of a different kind, stated not in terms of truth, but in terms of proof. The meaning of a logical operator is given by specifying what is to count as a proof of a mathematical statement in which it is the principal operator, where it is taken as already known what counts as a proof of any of the constituent sentences (any of the instances, where the operator is a quantifier). In so far as the logical operator being explained is itself used in the explanation, the circularity is harmless, since it is a fundamental assumption that we can effectively recognize, of any mathematical construction, whether or not it is a proof of a given statement; thus, when it is explained that a construction is a proof of ⌜A or B⌝ if and only if it is either a proof of A or a proof of B, the "or" on the right-hand side stands between two decidable statements, and is therefore unproblematic; we are explaining the general use of "or" in terms of this special use. To put the matter differently, such an explanation of disjunction can be taken as a representation of implicit knowledge possessed by the speaker, knowledge which is fully manifested by his practice in the use of mathematical statements: he displays his understanding of the operator "or" by acknowledging a construction as a proof of a disjunctive statement when and only when it is a proof of one or other disjunct. By contrast, the explanation in terms of truth-conditions is irremediably circular if the statements to which the disjunction operator is applied are not decidable, that is, if the condition for the truth of such a statement is not effectively recognizable; for then we have no way of explaining what it amounts to to ascribe to someone a knowledge that ⌜A or B⌝ is true if and only if either A is true or B is true. This is just how matters stand with the quantifiers, when they are understood classically and the domain of quantification is infinite. The truth-conditions of quantified statements are stated by the use of quantification over the same domain; and, because we have no effective means of recognizing in every case whether or not they are satisfied, we cannot find in a description of our linguistic practice a means of escaping that circularity.

The intuitionistic explanations of the logical constants provide a prototype for a theory of meaning in which truth and falsity are not the central notions. The fundamental idea is that a grasp of the meaning of a mathematical statement consists, not in a knowledge of what has to be the case, independently of our means of knowing whether it is so, for the statement to be true, but in an ability to recognize, for any mathematical construction, whether or not it constitutes a proof of the statement; an assertion of such a statement is to be construed, not as a claim that it is true, but as a claim that a proof of it exists or can be constructed. The understanding of any mathematical expression consists in a knowledge of the way in which it contributes to determining what is to count as a proof of any statement in which it occurs. In this way, a grasp of the meaning of a mathematical sentence or expression is guaranteed to be something which is fully displayed in a mastery of the use of mathematical language, for it is directly connected with that practice. It is not in the least required, on such a theory of meaning, that every intelligible statement be effectively decidable. We understand a given statement when we know how to recognize a proof of it when one is presented to us. We understand the negation of that statement when we know how to recognize a proof of *it*; and a proof of the negation of a statement will be anything which demonstrates the impossibility of finding a proof of that statement. In special cases, we shall possess an effective means of discovering, for a given statement, either a proof of it or a proof that it can never be proved; then the statement will be decidable, and we shall be entitled to assert in advance the relevant instance of the law of excluded middle. In general, however, the intelligibility of a statement in no way guarantees that we have any such decision procedure, and hence the law of excluded middle is not in general valid: our understanding of a statement consists in a capacity, not necessarily to find a proof, but only to recognize one when found.

Such a theory of meaning generalizes readily to the non-mathematical case. Proof is the sole means which exists in mathematics for establishing a statement as true: the required general notion is, therefore, that of verification. On this account, an understanding of a statement consists in a capacity to recognize whatever is counted as verifying it, i.e. as conclusively establishing it as true. It is not necessary that we should have any means of deciding the truth or falsity of the statement, only that we be capable of recognizing when its truth has been established. The advantage of this conception is that the condition for a statement's being verified, unlike the condition for its truth under the assumption of bivalence, is one which we must be credited with the capacity for effectively recognizing when it obtains; hence there is no difficulty in stating what an implicit knowledge of such a condition consists in—once again, it is directly displayed by our linguistic practice.

This characterization of a type of theory of meaning alternative to that which takes truth as its central notion requires one caveat and two reservations. The caveat is this: that, if a theory of meaning of this type is to be made plausible at all, it must take account of the interlocking or articulated character of language, as emphasized by Quine's 'Two Dogmas of Empiricism'. The great contribution of that essay was that it offered an essentially verificationist account of language without committing the logical positivist error of supposing that the verification of every sentence could be represented as the mere occurrence of a sequence of sense-experiences. Such a representation is approximately correct only for a restricted class of sentences, those which, in Quine's image, lie on the periphery; for other sentences, the actual process which we have learned to treat as leading to their being conclusively established will, in general, involve some inferential procedure; in the limiting case, e.g. for mathematical theorems, it will involve *only* this. For any non-peripheral sentence, our grasp of its meaning will take the form, not of a capacity to recognize which bare sense-experiences verify or falsify it, but of an apprehension of its inferential connections with other sentences linked to it in the articulated structure formed by the sentences of the language. A generalization of the intuitionistic theory of meaning for the language of mathematics must follow Quine in treating the verification of a sentence as consisting in the actual process whereby in practice we might come to accept it as having been conclusively established as true, a process which will usually involve the tacit or explicit use, in inference, of other sentences; proof, which is verification by inference alone, thus becomes merely a limiting case, not a distinct species.

The first of the two reservations is this. In the mathematical case, it is unnecessary to take the understanding of a statement as consisting both in the ability to recognize a proof of it and in the ability to recognize a refutation of it, since there is a uniform way to explain negation, i.e. to explain how to recognize a disproof of a statement. More exactly, we might regard the meanings of negations of numerical equations as being given directly in terms of the computation procedures by which those equations are verified or falsified: a proof of the negation of any arbitrary statement then consists of an effective method for transforming any proof of that statement into a proof of some false numerical equation. Such an explanation relies on the underlying presumption that, given a proof of a false numerical equation, we can construct a proof of any statement whatsoever. It is not obvious that, when we extend these conceptions to empirical statements, there exists any class of decidable atomic statements for which a similar presumption holds good; and it is therefore not obvious that we have, for the general case, any similar uniform way of explaining negation for arbitrary statements. It would therefore remain well within the spirit of a theory of meaning of this type that we should regard the meaning of each statement as being given by the simultaneous provision of a means for recognizing a verification of it and a means for recognizing a falsification of it, where the only general requirement is that these should be specified in such a way as to make it impossible for any statement to be both verified and falsified.

The second reservation is more far-reaching. In a theory of meaning in which truth plays the central role, the content of any assertion is fully determined by the condition that the sentence uttered be true. In this sense, we know the meaning of any sentence when we simply know what has to be the case for it to be true: provided with this knowledge, we know the content of any utterance of that sentence with assertoric force, and, equally, with imperatival, interrogative, optative force, etc. There is, however, no a priori reason why we should thereby know enough to know the meaning of any complex sentence into which the given sentence enters as a constituent; that is to say, there is no a priori reason why the truth-condition of a complex sentence should depend only on the truth-conditions of its constituent sentences. If we are able to represent the sentential operators of the language truth-functionally at all, we may be able to do so only by distinguishing different ways in which a sentence may be false, that is to say, different undesignated 'truth-values' that it may have, or, perhaps, different ways in which it may be true, that is, different designated 'truth-values'. These distinctions are irrelevant to the understanding of an utterance of the sentence on its own, with whatever variety of linguistic force the utterance is made: they are needed for a grasp of the way in which a sentence may contribute to determining the truth-condition of a complex sentence of which it is a constituent (i.e. the condition for such a sentence to have a designated 'truth-value').

Now, in a theory of meaning in which the central notions are those of verification and falsification, rather than those of truth and falsity, the same thing applies. In intuitionistic logic, a sentence serving as a constituent of a complex sentence contributes to determining what is to count as a proof of that complex sentence solely through the definition of what counts as a proof of *it*, that is to say, solely through its meaning considered as a sentence capable of being used on its own. In this respect, intuitionistic logic resembles two-valued logic as opposed to a many-valued logic, since in two-valued logic a sentence contributes to determining the truth-condition of a complex sentence of which it is a constituent solely through its own truth-condition, whereas in many-valued logic this is not so (if, as is intuitively natural, we identify the condition for a sentence to be true with the condition for it to have a designated value). But, just as the general conception of a theory of meaning in terms of truth-conditions carries with it no presumption that the truth-condition of a complex sentence can be determined solely from the truth-conditions of its constituents, i.e. that the semantics of the theory will not require the use of more than two 'truth-values', so, likewise, the general conception of a theory of meaning in terms of the conditions for the verification and falsification of a sentence carries no presumption that the meanings of the sentential operators will be able to be explained in the comparatively simple way that they are in intuitionistic logic. It may well be that, when we generalize the conception of such a theory of meaning to our language as a whole, we shall be unable to explain the meanings of the logical constants uniformly in terms of whatever constitutes a verification of each of the constituent sentences. The resulting logic will not be classical logic, and it therefore will not hang together with a realistic interpretation of all the sentences of our language: we shall have abandoned the assumption that every statement which has a definite sense is determinately either true or false, independently of our knowledge. But it will not necessarily very closely resemble intuitionistic logic either. The principal difference between the language of mathematics and our language as a whole lies in the fact that, within the former, the property of decidability is stable. A statement to the effect that some particular large number is prime can in principle be decided, and it is therefore legitimate to assert the disjunction of that statement and its negation, or any other statement which can be shown to follow both from the statement and from its negation, since at any time we wished we could, at least in theory, determine the statement as true or as false. But the decidability of an empirical statement is not in the same way an enduring feature: if we regard the statement "There is now either an odd or an even number of ducks on the pond" as assertable on the ground that we could, if we chose, determine one or other disjunct as true, we cannot offer the *same* ground for the assertability of "There was either an odd or an even number of geese which cackled on the Capitol"; and if, nevertheless, we want to regard the latter statement as assertable, then either the assertion has to be explained as making a claim weaker than that the statement asserted is even in principle verifiable, or the specification of what counts as verifying a complex statement cannot be given uniformly in terms of what counts as verifying the constituents. For instance, we may wish to lay down that a disjunctive statement is conclusively established by a demonstration that an effective procedure would, if it were or had been applied at a suitable time, yield or have yielded a verification of one or other disjunct. This would be contrary to the intuitionistic meaning of disjunction, since it would involve that a disjunctive statement might be verified by something which not merely did not verify either disjunct, but did not guarantee that either disjunct could be verified at all. If this interpretation of "or" were admitted, many instances ⌜*A* or not *A*⌝ of the law of excluded middle would be assertable when *A* could not be decided. (The effect of this, in achieving a greater *rapprochement* with classical reasoning than any permitted by a strictly intuitionistic interpretation of the logical constants, would probably be mitigated by the fact that, in such a case, a certain number of conditionals ⌜If *A*, then *B*⌝, whose antecedents were subject to the law of excluded middle, and which would be plausible on a realistic interpretation, would not be assertable on the appropriate verificationist interpretation of "if".) All will, however, remain within the spirit of a verificationist theory of meaning, so long as the meaning of each sentence is given by specifying what is to be taken as conclusively establishing a statement made by means of it, and what as conclusively falsifying such a statement, and so long as this is done systematically in terms only of conditions which a speaker is capable of recognizing.

5

I have argued that a theory of meaning in terms of truth-conditions cannot give an intelligible account of a speaker's mastery of his language; and I have sketched one possible alternative, a generalization of the intuitionistic theory of meaning for the language of mathematics, which takes verification and falsification as its central notions in place of those of truth and falsity. This does not mean that the notion of truth will play no role, or only a trivial one, in such a theory of meaning. On the contrary, it will continue to play an important role, because it is only in terms of it that we can give an account of deductive inference; to recognize an inference as valid is to recognize it as truth-preserving. If, in the context of such a theory of meaning, the truth of a statement were to be identified with that statement's having been explicitly recognized as having been verified, deductive inference which proceeded from premisses which had been conclusively established could never lead to new information. More accurately stated, it could lead to new information only when it represented the most direct route to the establishment of the conclusion of the inference; for, as we have noted, any adequate theory of meaning must recognize that the sense of many statements is such that inference must play a part in any process which leads to their verification. Within any theory of meaning, the way in which the sense of a sentence is determined in accordance with its structure will display what we may regard as the most *direct* means of establishing it as true. This applies to a theory of meaning in terms of truth-conditions as much as to one in terms of verification: the difference is that, in the former case, the most direct means of establishing the sentence will sometimes be one that is not available to us. For example, the classical representation of a universally quantified sentence as having a truth-value which is the product of the truth-values of the instances displays, as the most direct means of determining its truth-value, a process of determining the truth-values of all the instances in turn, a process which we cannot carry out when there are infinitely many of them. Any adequate theory of meaning must, however, account for the fact, not merely that we base many of our assertions upon evidence that falls short of being conclusive, but also that there exist ways of conclusively establishing the truth of statements which do not proceed by the direct route which is determined by the way in which their senses are given; one case of this is when we arrive at the truth of a statement as the conclusion of a deductive argument. In order to account for the possibility of establishing a statement conclusively but indirectly, it is essential to appeal to some notion of the *truth* of a statement, which, evidently, cannot be equated merely with the statement's having been directly verified. This holds good as much for the intuitionistic account of mathematics as for the generalization of this account to empirical statements; it would be plainly contrary to the facts of the matter to maintain that mathematical reasoning, even within constructive mathematics, always proceeds along the most direct possible path: that would involve, for example, that we never in practice concluded to the truth of a statement by universal instantiation or by *modus ponens*. The most that can be plausibly maintained is that any valid proof provides us with an effective means whereby we could construct a proof of the conclusion of the most direct possible kind. Hence, even in intuitionistic mathematics, a notion of the truth of a statement is required which does not coincide merely with our actually possessing a proof of the kind which is specified by the explanation of the sense of the statement in accordance with its composition out of primitive symbols. It is far from being a trivial matter how the notion of truth, within a theory of meaning in terms of verification, should be explained. What differentiates such a theory from one in which truth is the central notion is, first, that meaning is not directly given in terms of the condition for a sentence to be true, but for it to be verified; and, secondly, that the notion of truth, when it is introduced, must be explained, in some manner, in terms of our capacity to recognize statements as true, and not in terms of a condition which transcends human capacities.

A theory of meaning in terms of verification is bound to yield a notion of truth for which bivalence fails to hold for many sentences which we are unreflectively disposed to interpret in a realistic manner. It will therefore compel us to accept certain departures from classical logic, and hence a certain revision of our habitual linguistic practice. Obviously, the theory would lose plausibility if this revision was too extensive; although, as I have argued, we cannot rule out a priori the possibility that the adoption of a correct theory of meaning may lead to some revision, the principal purpose of a theory of meaning is to explain existing practice rather than to criticize it. Whether a plausible theory of meaning in terms of verification can be constructed, I do not know; there are many problems which there is no space in this general discussion to investigate. But such a theory of meaning is not the only conceivable alternative to one in terms of truth-conditions; I shall devote a little space to describing a quite different possibility.

What is the content of an assertion? According to a theory of meaning in terms of truth-conditions, the content is, simply, that the statement asserted is true. It may be that we are able to recognize it as true only in certain cases, and to recognize it as false only in certain cases; there may be states of affairs under which it is true, although we shall never know that it is true, and other states of affairs under which it is false, although we shall never know that it is false: but what the speaker is *saying* is that it is true. We have considered the difficulties—insuperable difficulties, if I am right—of explaining what it is for the speaker, or the hearer, to know what it is for the sentence to be true, in the general case; and there will be an equal difficulty in explaining what it is for the hearer, or the speaker, to act on the truth of the assertion. There is a general difficulty in explaining this notion, on any theory of meaning, namely that how one's actions are affected by a statement that one accepts depends upon what one wants. But, on a theory of meaning in terms of truth-conditions, there is an additional difficulty: even given the desires of the hearer, what is it for him to conform his actions to the obtaining of a condition which he cannot, in general, recognize as obtaining? The supplementary part of a theory of meaning, its theory of force, must, in giving an account of the linguistic activity of assertion, be able to explain what it is to act on an assertion, as part of an explanation of what it is to accept an assertion: and, within a theory of meaning in terms of truth-conditions, this explanation will be very difficult to construct.

According to a theory of meaning in terms of verification, the content of an assertion is that the statement asserted has been, or is capable of being, verified. It was conceded above that such a theory may have to allow that what is taken to constitute the falsification of a statement must be separately stipulated for each form of sentence. But, if so, this can only be for the purpose of laying down the sense of the negation of each sentence, no uniform explanation of negation being available: it cannot be for the purpose of fixing the sense of a sentence, considered as being used on its own. For, if we supposed otherwise, we should have to say that the content of an assertion was that the sentence asserted was capable of being verified, and, further, that it was incapable of being falsified. It may be said that this complication is quite unnecessary, since the stipulations are always required to be such that no statement can be both verified and falsified; hence the correctness of an assertion will always guarantee the weaker claim that the sentence cannot be falsified, which will be expressed by the double negation of the sentence. This retort is fully justified if the determination of what counts as falsifying the sentence need not be considered as affecting the sense of that sentence when used on its own; but, when it is so considered, it must play some role in fixing the content of an assertion made by means of the sentence. It would then follow that a speaker might be neither right nor wrong in making an assertion: not wrong, because it could be shown that the sentence could not be falsified; but not right either, because no way was known of verifying the sentence. This consequence would be fatal to the account, since an assertion is not an act which admits of an intermediate outcome; if an assertion is not correct, it is incorrect. A bet may have conditions; if they are unfulfilled, the better neither wins or loses. But there is nothing corresponding for an assertion; it is a *reductio ad absurdum* of any theory of meaning if it entails that there is.

It may be said that, even if the condition for a sentence's being falsified does not enter into the determination of the sense of that sentence as used on its own, a verificationist theory of meaning must leave open the possibility of an assertion's being neither right nor wrong: for the speaker's claim to be able to verify the statement may be unjustified, even though there is nothing to rule out the possibility of its coming to be verified at some future time. This situation, however, is one which cannot be ruled out by appeal to our understanding of the linguistic practice of assertion, though how it is described depends upon our background theory of meaning. If we hold a theory of meaning in terms of truth-conditions, then we shall describe such a situation as one in which the speaker was not entitled to make the assertion, but in which it has not yet been shown whether the speaker was right or wrong. Admittedly, some explanation is required of our having a place for such a distinction: on the face of it, if assertion is simply a linguistic act governed by objective conditions of correctness, and these are not fulfilled, then the assertion was simply wrong, without more ado. This point was discussed earlier: it is due to our understanding of sentences as constituents of more complex sentences, and of their use with, for example, imperatival force, that we are led to distinguish between the truth of an assertion and the speaker's entitlement to make it. Under a theory of meaning in terms of verification, we cannot say that every assertion is either right or wrong, but we can draw a similar distinction between a speaker's having the means to verify his assertion and his saying something a means of verifying which later became available. Such a distinction is indeed forced on us in exactly the same way as under a theory of meaning in terms of truth-conditions: given that notion of the verification of a sentence which is required for explaining its role in complex sentences, we cannot, in general, consider an assertion as a claim already to have a means of verifying the statement asserted, but only as a claim that such a means will be arrived at; for example, when the statement is in the future tense. Thus to say in *this* sense that an assertion may be neither right nor wrong is in full harmony with the nature of assertion as a type of linguistic act.

The sense which we have been discussing, in which it can legitimately be said that an assertion may be neither right nor wrong is, as we have seen, that which relates to the distinction between a speaker's entitlement to make the assertion and the truth of what he says, i.e. between *his* being justified in saying it and there being a justification not known to him at the time. We may say that the *speaker* is right if he is, at the time of speaking, able to verify what he says, but that his *assertion* is correct if there is some means of verifying it, a knowledge of which by the speaker at the time of utterance would have made him right. The sense in which it is false to the nature of assertion to say that an assertion may be neither right nor wrong is that in which, in this terminology, the assertion itself is neither correct nor incorrect. That is, there cannot be a piece of knowledge the possession of which by any speaker would show both that he would not be right to make a certain assertion and that he would not be wrong to make it. If someone makes a conditional bet, someone else, by knowing that the condition is unfulfilled, may know that he will neither win nor lose his bet: there is no piece of knowledge which is related in this way to an assertion.

Now, certainly, a verificationist theory of meaning rules out the possibility that an assertion may be both correct and incorrect, just because no statement can be both verified and falsified. But, even if the specification of what falsifies a sentence does not go to determine the sense of the sentence as used on its own, such a theory of meaning does come dangerously close to allowing that an assertion may be neither correct nor incorrect. If our logic at all resembles intuitionistic logic, there is indeed no possibility of discovering, for any statement, that it can neither be verified nor falsified, since whatever would serve to show that it could not be verified would *ipso facto* verify its negation. But, for any statement which is not stable in Brouwer's sense (which is not equivalent to its double negation), there is a possibility of our discovering that it can never be falsified without our yet having a verification of it. In such a case, we may say that we know that an assertion of the statement would not be incorrect, without knowing that it was correct. Admittedly, the possibility of verifying the statement would always remain open, so that this could never become a case of knowing the assertion to be neither correct nor incorrect; but it points to an obscurity in the representation, within such a theory, of the force of an assertion. What more is someone saying, when he makes an assertion, than that his statement is not incorrect? What more does he say, when he affirms a statement, than when he simply denies its negation? In so far as we are considering his assertion as a claim to have verified a statement, these questions are not hard to answer, since, in general, more is needed in order to verify a statement than is needed to verify its double negation; and so, in the mathematical case, when assertion always amounts to a claim that the statement asserted has actually been proved, no problem arises. But we have seen that, in the general case, we have to consider as primary, in determining the content of an assertion, not the speaker's personal entitlement to make the assertion, but the condition for its objective correctness; and, in connection with that, it is impossible to distinguish between the supposedly stronger content and the supposedly weaker one. If a speaker claims to have verified a statement, and we find that he has verified merely its double negation, his claim fails: but our present question is not this, but what we are doing if we accept his assertion as objectively correct, regardless of his personal entitlement to make it. To acknowledge it as not incorrect is, obviously, to rule out the possibility of its ever being falsified; what more is involved in accepting it as correct must, therefore, be to expect it at some time to be verified, or at least to hold the possibility open. Holding the possibility open adds nothing whatever to recognizing that it can never be falsified; if we have recognized this, then the possibility of its at some time being verified just *is* open; since we can never close it, we do not have to *hold* it open. But even expecting that it will at some time be verified amounts to nothing substantive, when there is no bound on the time within which this will happen; in knowing that the statement can never be falsified, we already know that that expectation can never be disappointed; and, given that the expectation will never be disappointed, the supposition that it will at some time be realized is consistent with *any* sequence of events over any finite interval, however long, and therefore adds nothing.

It is a well-known fact that some philosophers have wished to consider assertion as a linguistic act which may have an intermediate outcome, in a sense analogous to that in which a conditional bet has an intermediate outcome when the condition is not fulfilled. That is, they have wanted to hold that certain sentences will, under certain determinate conditions, be neither true nor false; and they have wanted to make a direct connection between the notions of truth and falsity here employed and the correctness and incorrectness of assertions, so that someone making an assertion by the utterance of a sentence which proves to be neither true nor false will have made an assertion which is neither correct nor incorrect. (Sometimes this is expressed by saying that he has made no assertion at all; but this form of expression cannot disguise the fact that he has made a significant utterance, that he has performed a linguistic act.) I have elsewhere argued against this that we can attach no sense to the notion of an assertion's being neither correct nor incorrect, except in so far as it is vague or ambiguous, and that the proper interpretation of a sentence's being neither true nor false is that it has an undesignated truth-value distinct from that which we label 'falsity', or else a designated truth-value distinct from that which we label 'truth'; and, accordingly, that the state of being neither true nor false is of significance only in connection with the behaviour of the sentence as a constituent in complex sentences, for which we wish to employ a many-valued semantics, and not with the use of the sentence on its own to make an assertion, for which we need to know only the distinction between its having a designated and an undesignated truth-value.

Now what is the proper way to argue for this? One approach might be to say the following. If the content of an assertion is specific, then it must be determinate, for any recognizable state of affairs, whether or not that state of affairs shows the assertion to have been correct. If some recognizable state of affairs does not suffice to show the assertion to have been correct, there are two alternative cases. One is that this state of affairs serves to rule out the possibility of a situation's coming about in which the assertion can be recognized as having been correct: in this case, the state of affairs must be taken as showing the assertion to have been incorrect. The other is that the given state of affairs, while not showing the assertion to have been correct, does not rule out the possibility of its later being shown to have been so: in this case, the correctness of the assertion has simply not yet been determined. What is not possible is that any recognizable state of affairs could serve to show both that the assertion was not correct and that it was not incorrect, since the content of the assertion is wholly determined by which recognizable states of affairs count as establishing it as correct: so any state of affairs which can be recognized as ruling out the correctness of the assertion must be reckoned as showing it to be incorrect. Hence, if a sentence is held to be neither true nor false in certain recognizable circumstances, this cannot be explained by saying that an assertion made by uttering the sentence would, in those circumstances, be neither correct nor incorrect.

This argument is not intended, as some have taken it, as a demonstration that every assertion must be either correct or incorrect. It allows the possibility that an assertion may never be recognized either as being one or as being the other; and a realistic metaphysics—or better, a realistic theory of meaning— needs to be invoked if we wish to claim that, nevertheless, it must actually *be* one or the other. It is therefore certainly not an argument to the conclusion that only those sentences can be used to make assertions for which the principle of bivalence holds good, or a derivation of the principle of bivalence from the nature of assertion. It is merely an argument that there can be no circumstances in which an assertion can be recognized to be neither correct nor incorrect. It would be consistent with this to hold that there were some assertions which were neither correct nor incorrect, although we are incapable of recognizing the fact for any particular assertion. However, I should repudiate such a view as an indefensible hybrid. If we are able to understand a description of a state of affairs which we are incapable of recognizing as obtaining, and to entertain the supposition that it *does* obtain, then there is no reason not to conceive of meaning as given in terms of truth-conditions which we cannot in general recognize, and for which the principle of bivalence holds good. In this case, the content of an assertion will be able to be given in terms of conceivable, though not necessarily recognizable, states of affairs, i.e. by which among such states of affairs render it correct, and the above argument goes through if the states of affairs considered are no longer restricted to recognizable ones. It would follow that, not only can an assertion not be recognized as being neither correct nor incorrect, but it could not in fact *be* neither correct nor incorrect. Indeed, since, on this realistic conception, the non-occurrence of any state of affairs which rendered the assertion correct would again be a state of affairs (which is not so if we restrict ourselves to recognizable states of affairs), every assertion would be either correct or incorrect. If, on the other hand, we are not able to form the conception of a state of affairs which we cannot recognize as obtaining, then we cannot attach any content to the notion of an assertion's *being* correct or incorrect other than our being able to recognize it as one or the other, in which case the fact that an assertion cannot be recognized to be neither correct nor incorrect is sufficient to show that it cannot be neither. Only on a realistic assumption, therefore, which the argument does not invoke, does the argument lead to the principle of bivalence. By itself, it establishes only the weaker conclusion that a statement cannot be neither true nor false, where the notions of truth and falsity are those directly connected with the correctness and incorrectness of assertions, so that a sentence is true if an assertion made by means of it is correct, and false if such an assertion is incorrect.[2] It requires classical logic to allow us to pass from saying that no statement is neither true nor false to saying that each statement is either true or false; and the argument does not presuppose the validity of classical logic.

The argument, as presented above, leads directly to a verificationist theory of meaning; at least, it does so if the restriction to recognizable states of affairs is justified. But *is* that the proper way to present it? Suppose that we are considering some assertoric sentence which we understand perfectly well in practice—that is, we have no uncertainty about the content of an assertion made by means of it—but the application to which of the notions of truth and falsity is intuitively obscure. How do we decide whether or not any given state of affairs shows an assertion made by means of the sentence to be correct? For instance, the sentence is an indicative conditional, and the state of affairs is one in which the antecedent is recognizably false. To make a fair test, we must of course take a sentence to which the application of the predicate "true" is obscure, since otherwise we shall simply (perhaps quite rightly) identify the correctness of the assertion with the truth of the sentence, whereas we are here concerned with whether an understanding of the content of the assertion alone determines what is to be taken as showing it to have been correct. The answer is, I think, that we have no clear direct guide to what should be regarded as showing the assertion to have been correct; and the reason is that it is not the *correctness* of an assertion which should be taken as the fundamental notion

[2] By this, I do not mean notions of truth and falsity so crude that we cannot distinguish a man's saying something false from his saying what he had no right to say on the evidence available, but only those notions of truth and falsity which correspond, in a many-valued logic, to the possession of a designated and of an undesignated value.

needed in explaining assertion as a linguistic act. An assertion is not, normally, like an answer in a quiz programme; the speaker gets no prize for being right. It is, primarily, a guide to action on the part of the hearers (an interior judgement being a guide to action on the part of the thinker); a guide which operates by inducing in them certain expectations. And the content of an expectation is determined by what will surprise us; that is, by what it is that is *not* in accord with the expectation rather than by what corroborates it. The expectation formed by someone who accepts an assertion is not, in the first place, characterized by his supposing that one of those recognizable states of affairs which render the assertion correct will come to obtain; for in the general case there is no bound upon the length of time which may elapse before the assertion is shown to have been correct, and then such a supposition will have, by itself, no substance. It is, rather, to be characterized by his *not* allowing for the occurrence of any state of affairs which would show the assertion to have been incorrect; a negative expectation of this kind has substance, for it can be disappointed. The fundamental notion for an account of the linguistic act of assertion is, thus, that of the *incorrectness* of an assertion: the notion of its correctness is derivative from that of its incorrectness, in that an assertion is to be judged correct whenever something happens which precludes the occurrence of a state of affairs showing it to be incorrect. (In just the same way, as I have argued elsewhere, the fundamental notion in an account of the linguistic act of giving a command is that of *disobedience*, the notion of obedience being derivative from it.)

This comes out very clearly when we ask, of some sentence the assertoric content of which we understand in practice, but to which the application of "true" and "false" is obscure, which states of affairs we should take as showing an assertion made by uttering it to have been incorrect. By making an assertion, a speaker *rules out* certain possibilities; if the assertion is unambiguous, it must be clear which states of affairs he is ruling out and which he is not. From our practical understanding of the assertoric sentence, we can answer at once whether, by such an assertion, a speaker is to be taken as ruling out this or that state of affairs. In answering such a question, we do not need to seek guidance from the intuitive application of the predicate "false" to the sentence, and our answer may even run counter to this; nor do we have to think whether we should *consider* the assertion to be incorrect in this or that case (as we have to think whether we should *consider* a conditional assertion to be shown to have been correct when the antecedent proves false). We know at once, for example, that the maker of a conditional assertion is *not* ruling out the possibility that the antecedent is false, and that therefore its falsity does not render the assertion incorrect, and, indeed, precludes the occurrence of the case which he *is* ruling out; and we know this independently of any decision as to whether the conditional sentence which he uses is to be called 'true' in this case. Likewise, we know at once that a speaker who makes an assertion by means of an atomic sentence containing a proper name or definite description *is* meaning to rule out the possibility that the name or description lacks a reference; and, again, we know this quite independently of any decision as to whether, when a reference is lacking, the sentence should or should not be called 'false'.

Thus, in the order of explanation, the notion of the incorrectness of an assertion is prior to that of its correctness. Why has this fact been so persistently overlooked? Partly because of the tendency to concentrate on the decidable case: an expectation as to the outcome of a test may indifferently be described as an expectation that the result will be favourable or as an expectation that it will not be unfavourable. Even, perhaps, in part because of a tendency to think particularly of future-tense assertions which predict the occurrence of an observable state of affairs within or at a specified time; for then the positive expectation has a bound, and hence has substance—if it is not satisfied within the given time, it will be disappointed. But principally, I think, because of the tacit assumption of a realistic theory of meaning in terms of non-effective truth-conditions. If the conditions in terms of which the content of an assertion is given are ones which we can recognize, then it makes a very substantial difference whether we take the notion of correctness or that of incorrectness as primary: it gives quite a different effect to say that an assertion is shown to be correct if something occurs which excludes the possibility of its being shown incorrect, from that yielded by saying that it is shown to be incorrect if something occurs which precludes the possibility of its being shown correct. But, if the conditions in terms of which the content is given are ones which we can grasp without, in general, being able to recognize, then it makes no effective difference, since the condition for the incorrectness of the assertion will obtain whenever that for its correctness does *not* obtain, and vice versa. That is not to say that, in the context of a realistic theory of meaning, the point is devoid of significance: even in this context, it remains true that, in the order of explanation, the notion of the incorrectness of an assertion is primary.

These considerations prompt the construction of a different theory of meaning, one which agrees with the verificationist theory in making use only of effective rather than transcendental notions, but which replaces verification by falsification as the central notion of the theory: we know the meaning of a sentence when we know how to recognize that it has been falsified. Such a theory of meaning will yield a logic which is neither classical nor intuitionistic.[3] In one respect, it stands on the other side of a theory of meaning

---

[3] Let us write f_A for the set of recognizable states of affairs in which A is falsified, and $\bar{f}$ for the set of recognizable states of affairs which preclude the occurrence of any state of affairs in f. Plainly, $f \cap \bar{f} = \emptyset$, $f \subseteq \bar{\bar{f}}$ and, if $f \subseteq g$, then $\bar{g} \subseteq \bar{f}$; hence $\bar{f} = \bar{\bar{\bar{f}}}$. We may also assume that $\overline{f \cup g} = \bar{f} \cap \bar{g}$ and that $\bar{f} \cup \bar{g} \subseteq \overline{f \cap g}$. It seems reasonable to take $f_{\neg A} = \bar{f}_A$, $f_{A \vee B} = f_A \cap f_B$, $f_{A \& B} = f_A \cup f_B$ and $f_{A \to B} = f_B \cap \bar{f}_A$, and to define $A_1, \ldots, A_n \vdash B$ as holding when $f_B \subseteq f_{A_1} \cup \ldots \cup f_{A_n}$, so that $\vdash B$ holds just in case $f_B = \emptyset$; on this definition, however, $\vdash A \to B$ may hold when $A \vdash B$ does not. On this basis, we have

84 *What is a Theory of Meaning? (II)*

in terms of truth-conditions from a verificationist theory. A verificationist theory comes as close as any plausible theory of meaning can do to explaining the meaning of a sentence in terms of the grounds on which it may be asserted; it must of course distinguish a speaker's actual grounds, which may not be conclusive, or may be indirect, from the kind of direct, conclusive grounds in terms of which the meaning is given, particularly for sentences, like those in the future tense, for which the speaker cannot have grounds of the latter kind at the time of utterance. But a falsificationist theory does not relate the meaning of a sentence directly to the grounds of an assertion made by means of it at all. Instead, it links the content of an assertion with the commitment that a speaker undertakes in making that assertion; an assertion is a kind of gamble that the speaker will not be proved wrong. Such a theory therefore has obvious affinities, not only with Popper's account of science, but also with the language-game type of semantics developed by Hintikka and others.

6

Any theory of meaning was earlier seen as falling into three parts: first, the core theory, or theory of reference; secondly, its shell, the theory of sense; and thirdly, the supplementary part of the theory of meaning, the theory of force. The theory of force establishes the connection between the meanings of sentences, as assigned by the theories of reference and of sense, and the actual practice of speaking the language. The theory of reference determines recursively the application to each sentence of that notion which is taken as central in the given theory of meaning: if truth is the central notion, it issues in a specification for each sentence of the condition under which it is true; if verification is the central notion, it specifies, for each sentence, the condition under which it is verified; and similarly when falsification is the central notion. It does this, for each of the infinitely many sentences of the language, by assigning to each minimal significant sentence-constituent (each word) a reference, which takes whatever form is required in order that the references of the components of any sentence shall jointly determine the application to that sentence of the central notion. Thus, when the central notion is that of truth, the referent of a one-place predicate is a set of objects (or function from objects to truth-values); when it is that of verification, it is an effective means of recognizing, for any given object, a conclusive demonstration that the predicate applies to that object; or that it does *not* apply, when the central notion is that of falsification.

The theory of sense specifies what is involved in attributing to a speaker a knowledge of the theory of reference. When the theory of reference takes the

¬ ¬ $A \vdash A$ and $\vdash A \rightarrow$ ¬ ¬ A, but not $A \vdash$ ¬ ¬ A. We also have $\vdash A \lor$ ¬ A, $\vdash$ ¬ $(A \& $ ¬ $A)$, ¬ $(A \& B) \dashv\vdash$ ¬ $A \lor$ ¬ B and ¬ $(A \lor B) \vdash$ ¬ $A \&$ ¬ B, but not ¬ $A \&$ ¬ $B \vdash$ ¬ $(A \lor B)$. However, I do not feel at all sure that this approach is correct.

form of a theory or truth, this is necessary whenever an axiom or T-sentence assumes a trivial form, and therefore fails to display in what the speaker's implicit knowledge of it consists. When, however, the central notion is an effective one—one the conditions for the application of which a speaker can recognize as obtaining whenever they obtain, like the notions of verification and of falsification—then there appears to be no need for a theory of sense to round out the theory of reference; we could say that, in a theory of meaning of such a type, the theories of reference and of sense merge. In a verificationist or falsificationist theory of meaning, the theory of reference specifies the application to each sentence of the central notion of the theory in such a way that a speaker will directly manifest his knowledge of the condition for its application by his actual use of the language.

The distinction between sense and reference derives, of course, from Frege, who gave two quite different arguments for making it. One was that it is unintelligible to attribute to a speaker a bare knowledge of the reference of an expression; for example, to say that the speaker knows, of a certain object, that it is the bearer of a given proper name, and to add that this is a *complete* characterization of that item of the speaker's knowledge. On Frege's view, such a piece of knowledge must always take the form of knowing that the object, considered as identified in a particular way, is the referent of the name; and that mode of identification of the object which enters into the characterization of what it is that the speaker knows constitutes the sense of the proper name. Exactly parallel considerations apply to expressions of other semantic categories.

This argument goes half-way in the same direction as the argument used in the present paper, to the effect that a theory of sense is needed to characterize that in which a speaker's knowledge of the meanings of expressions of the language, as determined by the theory of reference, consists. Frege's argument is that the theory of reference does not fully display what it is that a speaker knows when he understands an expression—what proposition is the object of his knowledge. I have here endorsed that argument, but have, in addition, gone one step beyond it, by maintaining that, since the speaker's knowledge is for the most part implicit knowledge, the theory of sense has not only to specify *what* the speaker knows, but also how his knowledge is manifested; this ingredient in the argument here used for the necessity of a theory of sense is not to be found in Frege.

Frege's other argument for the sense/reference distinction also concerns knowledge, but, this time, the knowledge that is acquired when a sentence comes to be accepted as true by one who already knows its meaning, rather than the knowledge of its meaning; it relates, therefore, to the use of language to convey information. Frege is not, of course, interested in the information that may be communicated to an individual by means of an assertion, for that will vary according to the information already possessed by that individual: he is interested in the informational content of the sentence in itself, which we might explain as the information which would be acquired, on coming to learn the truth of the sentence, by someone who previously knew nothing save the meaning of that sentence. Now it is obvious that the informational content of a sentence depends upon its meaning: a man can acquire no further information from learning the truth of a sentence of whose meaning he is unaware, and what information he does acquire will vary according to the particular meaning he attaches to it. Frege's argument is that a plausible account of the informational content of a sentence is impossible if the hearer's understanding of the sentence is represented as consisting, for each of the constituent words, in a bare knowledge of its reference (as this was characterized above). The celebrated example used by Frege is that of an identity-statement, the truth-value of which would already be known by anyone to whom it was—*per impossibile*—correct to ascribe a bare knowledge of the references of the terms on either side of the identity-sign (assuming, of course, that he also understood the identity-sign); such a statement would therefore have no informational content whatever, if a knowledge of meaning consisted in a bare knowledge of reference. Actually, a parallel argument works for *any* atomic statement.

The notion of sense is thus connected, from the outset, with that of knowledge. Now a very extensive body of theory is required to carry us from a knowledge of the meanings of sentences of the language, as specified jointly, in terms of the central notion of the given theory of meaning, by the theories of reference and of sense, to an understanding of the actual practice of speaking the language. We seldom think explicitly about the theory which effects this transition; as language-users, we have had an implicit grasp of it from early years, and, because it is so fundamental, philosophers find it elusive and do not contrive to say much about it. But we can recognize how extensive it would be if made explicit if we try to imagine how a Martian might be instructed in the use of human language. Martians are highly intelligent, and communicate with one another, but by a means so different from any human language that it is a practical impossibility to set up any translation from a human language into the Martian medium of communication. The only means, therefore, by which a Martian can come to learn a human language is by studying a fully explicit theory of meaning for that language (compare a speaker's mastery of the grammar of his mother tongue and his learning that of a foreign language by means of a grammar book). The Martian first masters the theories of reference and of sense for some one of our languages; but, since his ultimate objective is to visit earth as an alien spy, disguised as a human being, he needs to acquire a practical ability to speak the language, not just a theoretical understanding of it; he needs to know, not only what he may say, and when, without betraying his alien origin, but also, within these constraints, how he can use the language as an instrument to further his own ends of gaining knowledge and of influencing the actions of the human beings around him.

Obviously, having mastered the theories of reference and of sense, he has a great deal more to learn; he has to be provided with an explicit description of our linguistic practice, in terms of our utterances of sentences whose meanings (conceived of as given in terms, for example, of their truth-conditions) are taken as already known, and of our responses to such utterances on the part of others.

All of this additional information, which is required if one is to pass from a knowledge of meanings as given in terms of the central notion to a complete practical mastery of the use of the language, I have promiscuously gathered into the supplementary part of the theory of meaning; and it may be a valid criticism that I have thereby lumped together under the single title of the "theory of force" multifarious propositions concerning the language of very disparate kinds. Following a proposal of Donald Davidson's, we may distinguish two stages in the passage from the theory of reference to the actual employment of the language. The first takes us to the actual judgements which we make concerning the truth and falsity of sentences. At least, that is how Davidson expresses it. He is, however, more concerned with the stages in the process of constructing a theory of reference for a language which we do not originally know, but the use of which we observe; we begin with the raw data provided by our observations of the actual utterances of the speakers, and an intermediate stage in the construction of a theory of truth for the language will consist in our assigning to particular speakers particular judgements about the truth-values of sentences at various times. I have been concerned, on the other hand, not with the upward process of constructing a theory of reference from the records of initially uninterpreted utterances, but with the downward process of deriving, from the theory of reference, the practice of using the language, this process of derivation itself to be incorporated into a theory which forms part of the total theory of meaning for the language; if the claim that a given theory of reference is the correct one, i.e. can serve as the core of a viable theory of meaning for the language, is to be substantiated, such a downward process of derivation must be possible. We do not expect, nor should we want, to achieve a deterministic theory of meaning for a language, even one which is deterministic only in principle: we should not expect to be able to give a theory from which, together with all other relevant conditions (the physical environment of a speaker, the utterances of other speakers, etc.), we could predict the exact utterances of any one speaker, any more than, by a study of the rules and strategy of a game, we expect to be able to predict actual play. Hence what is to be derived, in accordance with the supplementary part of the theory of meaning, is not a detailed account of the utterances which will actually be made in given circumstances, but only general principles governing the utterance of sentences of the language, those principles a tacit grasp of which enables someone to take part in converse in that language. From our point of view, therefore, the intermediate stage in the downward process of derivation will yield, not actual individual judgements of the truth or falsity of sentences, but the general principles which govern our making such judgements.

The second stage in the downward process of derivation carries us from the judgements that we make, under given conditions, concerning the truth and falsity of sentences, to our actual utterances, assertoric, interrogative, imperatival, etc.; here, again, we can expect to obtain no more than a formulation of the general principles in accordance with which the language-games of assertion, question, command, request, etc. are played. It is this second stage which may be said to constitute the theory of force properly so called.

What, then, of the first stage, which determines, from the meaning of a sentence, the principles governing the conditions under which we judge it to be true or false? To what part of the theory of meaning do those principles belong? It can hardly be denied that there *are* such principles: what but the meaning of a sentence can determine what we count as a ground for accepting it as true? Admittedly, when the grounds fall short of being conclusive—and also when we cannot recognize with certainty that we have conclusive grounds (as with a very complex mathematical proof or computation)—there is an element of choice over whether or not we accept the sentence as true; the term "judgement", in its technical use, is well chosen. But the meaning alone determines whether or not something *is* a ground for accepting the sentence, independently of whether we decide to treat that ground as sufficiently strong. That might be because the specification of what counted as a ground for the truth of the sentence was an integral part of fixing its meaning; but none of the three types of theory of meaning at which we have looked has allowed this to be so. According to a theory of meaning in terms of truth-conditions, we know the meaning of a sentence when we know what it is for it to be true; to know that is not, in itself, expressly to know what counts as evidence for its truth. A verificationist theory represents an understanding of a sentence as consisting in a knowledge of what counts as conclusive evidence for its truth. Even on such a theory, that understanding does not immediately involve a capacity to recognize evidence which is less than conclusive. Indeed, as we have seen, it does not even take the meaning of the sentence as relating directly to everything that could serve as conclusive evidence for its truth, but only, as it were, to a canonical method of establishing the truth of the sentence—what we called its 'direct' verification; I argued that, even in the context of a verificationist theory, an adequate account of deductive inference must acknowledge the possibility of establishing the truth of a sentence conclusively but indirectly, that is, by a route distinct from that immediately provided for by the way in which the meaning of the sentence is given. Hence, within any theory of meaning of the types we have considered, the principles which govern what counts as evidence for the truth of a sentence must be systematically derivable from its meaning, since they are not immediately given with it, but are determined by it. By means of what part of the theory of meaning is this derivation effected?

In the previous discussion, I assigned it vaguely to that part of the theory of force which treats of the linguistic act of assertion. Now there is here a distinction to be made. It is certainly part of the conventions governing the assertoric use of language what kind of claim we take a speaker who makes an unqualified assertion to be advancing, i.e. what kind of ground or warrant is required for the assertion not to be misleading. This is something *not* uniformly determined by the meaning of the sentence used to make the assertion, and may vary from one area of discourse to another, and also from one context to another. We already noted, for example, that our convention requires the unqualified assertion of a mathematical statement to be backed by the existence of an actual proof, and that this convention, quite different from that governing assertions of other kinds, could be changed without altering in any way the meanings of mathematical sentences. The enunciation of these conventions does indeed belong to the theory of assertoric force. This is, however, an entirely separate matter from that with which we are here concerned. What we are concerned with is what determines that something is evidence of a certain strength for the truth of a given sentence, not with whether the existence of evidence of a particular strength is sufficient reason for accepting the sentence as true (that is a matter of personal strategy), nor yet with whether it warrants an assertion of the sentence (that is a matter of independent commonly agreed linguistic convention).

Now since, as we have seen, sense is a cognitive notion, it may seem that this epistemological component of the theory of meaning should belong to the theory of sense rather than to the theory of force. Even if the theory of reference merely states what has to be the case for a sentence to be true, should not the theory of sense state, not merely how we know the truth-condition of the sentence, but also how we can know, or on what basis we may judge, the sentence to be true? Does this not follow if Frege was right in thinking that the notion of sense can be employed not only to make the theory of meaning at the same time a theory of understanding, i.e. to give a representation of our grasp of the meanings of our expressions, but also to give an account of the use of language for the communication of information, since information is a cognitive notion, and the amount of information conveyed must depend upon what steps the original informant needed to take to obtain it?

Frege would certainly have answered "No" to these questions. For him, the sense of a sentence gives its cognitive value (informational content) only inasmuch as it determines *what* someone who understands the sentence knows when he knows it to be true, not *how* he might come to know it of his own knowledge, still less what might lead him to think it true without knowing it. In knowing the sense of the sentence, he knows that it expresses a certain thought, i.e. he knows that the sentence is true if and only if a certain condition obtains; so, in coming to accept the sentence as true, the thought which he takes it as expressing represents the information he has acquired, the information, namely, that the condition for the truth of the sentence is satisfied; *how* that information was obtained in the first place is an altogether different matter, which belongs to epistemology and not to the theory of meaning at all.

At first sight, this doctrine appears clear and sharp; but a little investigation disturbs this impression. If the sense of a sentence is not related to our methods of determining its truth, why does Frege refuse to allow that two analytically equivalent sentences have the same sense? The doctrine that in modal contexts a sentence stands for its sense would not be violated by such a concession, since, of two such sentences, it would not be possible for one to be true and the other false; and the concession is tempting, since Frege had a well-developed theory of analyticity, whereas, if two analytically equivalent sentences may differ in sense, no obvious criterion for identity of sense is forthcoming. Of course, if the concession were granted, it could not be maintained that the senses of sentences (thoughts) were the objects of belief and knowledge, i.e. that the referent of a sentence is its sense when it forms a clause governed by a verb for a 'propositional attitude': but this doctrine itself requires that sense be connected with the mode of knowledge or ground of belief.

Our question is: Can we say that sense determines only the *object* of knowledge or belief—*what* is known or believed, rather than *how* it is known or *why* it is believed? The difficulty is that the two things, at first sight so distinct, are bound together too tightly to be prised apart. Why cannot two sentences, *A* and *B*, have the same sense? It may be that the only argument against their doing so is that ⌜*X* believes (knows) that *A*⌝may be true, while ⌜*X* believes (knows) that *B*⌝ is not. What makes *this* possible is that a ground of belief in the truth of *A* is not a ground of belief in that of *B*; and the conclusion is that, since in these oblique contexts *A* and *B* stand for their respective senses, those senses must be distinct, otherwise the truth-values of the compound sentences would coincide. It follows that a difference in the possible grounds for one and the other belief, or in the mode of this and that item of knowledge, entails a difference in the objects of belief or of knowledge; and this corroborates our original contention that, in apprehending a possible object of belief or knowledge, i.e. in grasping the sense of a sentence, we must thereby know what grounds that belief may have or how that knowledge may be arrived at. Frege's conception of a thought as a possible object of knowledge or belief did not have to be surrounded by doctrines which forced this conclusion on us; but it was.

Two analytically equivalent sentences cannot, in general, have the same informational content, nor, therefore, the same sense, because one could know the one to be true without knowing the other to be true; someone knowing the one to be true would consequently acquire information by coming to learn the truth of the other, and hence the information conveyed by each must be different. It follows that the means by which a sentence can be recognized as true bears on the sense of that sentence. It might be argued that all that is shown is that, if the information conveyed by one sentence can be acquired without acquiring that conveyed by another, the two pieces of information must differ, since different things are true of them, without its following that to specify what they are involves specifying how they can be acquired. But, against that, the fact stands that, for Frege, the notion of analyticity and the more general notion of aprioricity are defined in terms of the way in which a sentence can be known to be true; and surely the sense of a sentence is sufficient to determine whether it is analytic or synthetic, a priori or a posteriori. And yet there is little indication in Frege's account of how the way in which the sense of a sentence is given connects with the grounds on which we may base a judgement as to its truth.

I think that the defect in Frege's account of sense which is responsible for this hiatus lies in Frege's failure to insist that the theory of sense must explain in what a speaker's grasp of sense is manifested; and this failure is due to the exigencies of constructing a theory of sense within the framework of a realistic theory of meaning in terms of truth-conditions. Sense is supposed by Frege to be something objective; that is, it can be definitely ascertained whether two speakers are using an expression in the same sense, and one speaker can effectively convey to another the sense which he attaches to any expression. This is possible only if the sense of a word is uniquely determined by the observable features of its linguistic employment (i.e. only if sense is use); it follows that a grasp of its sense is fully manifested by the manner in which the speaker employs it. If it were necessary to represent a speaker's grasp of the sense of a word as his knowledge of some proposition an awareness of which transcended all mere practical knowledge, that is, could not be exhaustively accounted for in terms of the ability to use in a particular way sentences containing the word, then sense would not be intrinsically fully communicable: we could never be sure that, by teaching someone to adopt a certain linguistic practice, we had really induced him to attach the right sense to the word. Frege's thesis that sense is objective is thus implicitly an anticipation (in respect of that aspect of meaning which constitutes sense) of Wittgenstein's doctrine that meaning is use (or of one of the family of doctrines so expressed): yet Frege never drew the consequences of this for the form which the sense of a word may take. Thus, in the case of proper names, the crudest picture of a speaker's grasp of the sense of a name would be as consisting in an ability to determine effectively, for any given object, whether or not it is the bearer of the name. On any credible theory of meaning, this account must be generalized. On either a verificationist or falsificationist theory, we should have to say that a grasp of the sense of a name consisted in a capacity to recognize whatever is to be taken as conclusively establishing, of a given object, that it is the bearer of the name. On a realistic theory, however, even this is too restricted an account: we must say, rather, that a grasp of the sense of a name consists in a knowledge of what has to be true of any given object for it to be the bearer of the name; and, since the condition to be satisfied by the object may be one our apprehension of which will transcend our capacity to recognize, in special cases, whether or not it obtains, an understanding of the name, as so conceived, will not, in general, be something that can be fully manifested by the use of the name. Similarly, Frege's insistence that a predicate ought to be everywhere defined is expressed by him as the demand that it be determinate, for every object, whether the predicate applies to it or not; but he explicitly allows that *we* may not be able to determine this. Our recognition that it is, nevertheless, determinate must therefore depend upon our attaching to the predicate such a sense that we can tell that there is a definite condition for its application without knowing how to tell whether that condition is satisfied or not; once more, it follows that our grasp of the sense of the predicate cannot be fully manifested by the use which we make of it. One might maintain that certain features of that use, for example our willingness to assert certain instances of the law of excluded middle involving it, manifest our conviction *that* the predicate stands for some condition which is determinately either satisfied or not satisfied by each object; but our use of it can never fully display *which* the condition that we associate with the predicate is. The first of Frege's two arguments for the sense/reference distinction is to the effect that one cannot attribute to a speaker the knowledge, about the referent of an expression, that it is the referent, without going further and attributing to him the knowledge of a specific proposition; but he failed to face the problem how an explanation of a speaker's understanding of an expression in terms of his knowledge of a proposition can avoid circularity if knowledge of that proposition cannot in turn be explained save by an ability to enunciate it. It is precisely because of this failure that he failed to give a convincing account of the connection between sense and knowledge.

To replace a realistic theory of meaning by a verificationist one is to take a first step towards meeting the requirement that we incorporate into our theory of sense an account of the basis on which we judge the truth-values of our sentences, since it does explain meanings in terms of actual human capacities for the recognition of truth. I have, however, already pointed out that this step does not, in itself, take us all the way towards meeting this requirement, and I have no clear idea how it may be met. It is a natural reaction to regard the requirement as excessive, as asking the theory of meaning to take over the functions of a theory of knowledge. If we were convinced that we understood in principle how the sense of a sentence determined what we took as being evidence for its truth, and that the problems in this area, however intricate, were ones of detail, then it might be satisfactory to relegate them to a different philosophical discipline: but the difficulty is that we have no right to be satisfied of this. A conception of meaning—that is, a choice of a central notion for the theory of meaning—is adequate only if there exists a general method of deriving, from the meaning of a sentence as so given, every feature of its use, that is, everything that must be known by a speaker if he is to be able to use that sentence correctly; unquestionably, among the things that he must know is what counts as a ground for the truth of the sentence. Most of us serenely assume that a theory of meaning in terms of truth-conditions is capable of fulfilling this role, without stopping to scrutinize the difficulties of devising a workable theory of this type. On our present exceedingly imperfect comprehension of these matters, reflection should make us admit that a verificationist theory of meaning is a better bet than a thoroughgoing realistic one, and, probably, a falsificationist theory a better bet still. But until we have, for some one choice of a central notion for the theory of meaning, a convincing outline of the manner in which every feature of the use of a sentence can be given in terms of its meaning as specified by a recursive stipulation of the application to it of that central notion, we remain unprovided with a firm foundation for a claim to know what meaning essentially is. And, so long as we remain in this shaky philosophical condition, any problem the possibility of solving which, given a choice of a central notion for the theory of meaning, will help to decide the correctness of that choice, must be regarded as the business of the philosophy of language.

3

What do I Know when I Know a Language?

Our usual ways of thinking about the mastery of a language, or of this and that element of it, are permeated by the conception that this mastery consists in *knowledge*. To understand an expression is to know its meaning; we speak of knowing what an ostrich is, of knowing what "credulous" means, and, above all, of knowing Swedish or Spanish. Are we to take seriously the use of the verb "to know" in this connection? Is an ability to speak a language really a case of knowledge?

The verb "to know" is used in connection with many practical abilities: in English we speak of "*knowing* how to swim/ride a bicycle" and in French, for example, one says "Il *sait* nager" rather than "il *peut* nager". But does the knowledge—the practical knowledge—involved in these cases *explain* the practical ability, or is it, rather, that the practical ability is all there is to the practical knowledge, that our appeal in these cases to the concept of knowledge is a mere manner of speaking, not to be taken seriously? And, if the latter view is correct, does not the same hold of the mastery of the language, which is also a practical ability?

A character in one of the novels of the English humourist P. G. Wodehouse, asked whether she can speak Spanish, replies, "I don't know: I've never tried". Where does the absurdity of this lie? Would there be the same absurdity in giving that answer to the question. "Can you swim?" The suggestion that the absurdity would be the same in both cases amounts to the proposal that our use of the verb "to know" in these two connections—"knowing Spanish", "knowing how to swim"—is due to the empirical fact that speaking Spanish and swimming are things no one can do unless he has been taught, that is, has been subjected to a certain training; "to know", in these cases, means "to have learned". But is this right? It is *only* an empirical fact that we cannot swim unless we have been taught. It would not be magic if someone were, instinctively as we should say, to make the right movements the first time he found himself in water, and, indeed, I have heard it said that this is just what happens when very small infants are put in water. But it seems natural to think that it would be magic if someone who had not been brought up to speak Spanish and

First published as a paper presented at the Centenary Celebrations, Stockholm University, 24 May 1978.

had never learned it since were suddenly to start speaking it. If asked for an explanation of the difference, we should be inclined to say that, if you are to speak Spanish, there are a great many things that you have to *know*, just as there are many things that you have to know if you are to play chess.

The difference lies in the fact that speaking a language is a conscious process. We can conceive that someone, put in the water for the first time, might simply find himself swimming. He need not, in any sense, know what he is doing; he need not even know that he is swimming. But what are we imagining when we imagine that someone, arriving for the first time in his life in a Spanish-speaking country, should find himself speaking Spanish? There are two different cases, according as we suppose that he knows what he is saying or that he just hears the words coming out of his mouth without knowing what they mean. In either case, it is magic, but, in the latter case, although, miraculously, he *can* speak Spanish, he still does not *know* Spanish. Knowing Spanish, or knowing how to speak Spanish, is not, after all, to be compared with knowing how to swim. Both may be called practical capacities: but practical capacities are not all of one kind.

What do you not know if you have not learned to swim? You know what swimming is; you just do not know *how* to do it. And, if you found yourself in water, you might do it all the same, without knowing how you did it. You know what it is to swim; you can, for example, tell whether or not someone else is swimming: that is why, if you had to, you might try to swim, and you might find out that you could. But, if you have not learned Spanish, you do not even know what it is to speak Spanish; you could not tell (at least for sure) whether someone else was speaking it or not: and that is why you could not even try to speak Spanish. Indeed, when you learn Spanish, you do not learn a technique for accomplishing the already known end of speaking Spanish. There is no gap between knowing what it is to speak Spanish and knowing how to do so (save in special cases of a psychological inhibition or the like): you do not first learn what speaking Spanish is and then learn a means by which this feat can be executed.

There are degrees of consciousness with which a person may perform a skilled operation. At one extreme, he will formulate to himself the action to be carried out at each step and the manner in which it is to be done, as when someone unaccustomed to such tasks has memorized instructions how to cook a certain dish, or how to assemble a machine. This is the case in which a person has explicit knowledge how to perform the operation, and appeals to that knowledge in the course of performing it. At the other extreme, someone may simply be unable to say what it is that he does, even on reflection or when he tries to observe himself very closely; notoriously, those who have acquired physical skills may be quite unable to explain to others how to perform those feats. This is the case in which, if we speak of him as knowing how to perform the operation (say swimming or riding a bicycle), the expression "knows how to do it" has only the force of "can do it as the result of having learned to do it". But there are also intermediate cases. In these, someone may be unable to formulate for himself the principles according to which he acts, but may nevertheless be capable of acknowledging, and willing to acknowledge, the correctness of a statement of those principles when it is offered to him.

In cases of this intermediate kind, it seems to me, we have to take more seriously the ascription of knowledge to someone who possesses the practical ability in question: "knows how to do it" is not here a mere idiomatic equivalent of "can do it". Rather, we may say of the agent that he knows *that* certain things are the case, that he knows certain propositions about how the operation is to be performed; but we need to qualify this by conceding that his knowledge is not *explicit* knowledge, that is, knowledge which may be immediately elicited on request. It is, rather, *implicit* knowledge: knowledge which shows itself partly by manifestation of the practical ability, and partly by a readiness to acknowledge as correct a formulation of that which is known when it is presented. Consider, as an example, the knowledge of how to play chess. As a matter of fact, no one ever learns chess without being given some explicit information, such as that no piece except the knight may leap over another. Nevertheless, I can see no reason why it should be in principle unthinkable that someone should learn the game without ever being *told* anything, and without even framing rules to himself, simply by being corrected whenever he made an illegal move. Now, if we said, of such a person, that he knew how to play chess, should we be using the verb "to know" solely in that sense which is involved in saying that someone knows how to swim? It appears to me that we should not. The reason is that it *would* be unthinkable that, having learned to obey the rules of chess, he should not then be able and willing to acknowledge those rules as correct when they were put to him, for example, to agree, perhaps after a little reflection, that only the knight could leap over another piece. Someone who had learned the game in this way could properly be said to know the rules *implicitly*. We might put the point by saying that he does not merely follow the rules, without knowing what he is doing: he is *guided* by them.

There now arises a further question, not so easy to answer or even to state. The central task of the philosopher of language is to explain what *meaning* is, that is, what makes a language *language*. Consider two speakers engaged in conversation. To immediate inspection, all that is happening is that sounds of a certain kind issue from the mouths of each alternately. But we know that there is a deeper significance: they are expressing thoughts, putting forward arguments, stating conjectures, asking questions, etc. What the philosophy of language has to explain is what gives this character to the sounds they utter: what makes their utterances expressions of thought and all these other things?

The natural answer is that what makes the difference is the fact that both speakers *understand* or *know* the language. Each has, so to speak, the same piece of internal (mental) equipment, which enables each to interpret the utterances of the other as an expression of thought, and to convert his own thoughts into sentences that the other can likewise understand. It thus seems as though the key to the explanation of the expressive power which makes a language a language is an individual speaker's mastery of the language; and this mastery, as we saw, requires the notion of knowledge for its explication.

This, then, becomes our second question: Is the significance of language to be explained in terms of a speaker's knowledge of his language? Philosophers before Frege assumed that it is; and they assumed, further, that what a speaker knows is a kind of code. Concepts are coded into words and thoughts, which are compounded out of concepts, into sentences, whose structure mirrors, by and large, the complexity of the thoughts. We need language, on this view, only because we happen to lack the faculty of telepathy, that is, of the direct transmission of thoughts. Communication is thus essentially like the use of a telephone: the speaker codes his thought in a transmissible medium, which is then decoded by the hearer.

The whole analytical school of philosophy is founded on the rejection of this conception, first clearly repudiated by Frege. The conception of language as a code requires that we may ascribe concepts and thoughts to people independently of their knowledge of language; and one strand of objection is that, for any but the simplest concepts, we cannot explain what it is to grasp them independently of the ability to express them in language. As Frege said, a dog will no doubt notice a difference between being set on by several dogs and being set on by only one, but he is unlikely to have even the dimmest consciousness of anything in common between being bitten by one larger dog and chasing one cat, which he would have to do were we to be able to ascribe to him a grasp of the concept we express by the word "one". Or, again, as Wittgenstein remarked, a dog can expect his master to come home, but he cannot expect him to come home next week; and the reason is that there is nothing the dog could do to *manifest* an expectation that his master will come home next week. It makes no sense to attribute to a creature without language a grasp of the concept expressed by the words "next week".

It is, however, a serious mistake to suppose this to be the principal objection to the conception of language as a code. That conception involves comparing someone's mastery of his mother tongue with his mastery of a second language. His mastery of a second language may be represented as a grasp of a scheme of translation between it and his mother tongue: by appeal to this, he can associate expressions of the second language with expressions of his mother tongue. In a similar way, his mastery of his mother tongue is viewed, on this conception, as an ability to associate with each of its words the corresponding concept, and thus with each sentence of the language a thought compounded of such concepts.

The fundamental objection to this conception of language is that the analogy it uses breaks down. If we explain someone's knowledge of a second language as consisting in his grasp of a scheme of translation between it and his mother tongue, we tacitly presuppose that he understands his mother tongue; it then remains to be explained in what his understanding of his mother tongue consists. We can, in this way, proceed to explain his understanding of the second language in two stages—first, his ability to translate it into his mother tongue, and, secondly, his understanding of his mother tongue—precisely because, in principle, the ability to translate does not involve the ability to understand. In principle, we can imagine a person—or a very skilfully programmed computer—able to translate between two languages without understanding either. That is why, when we explain someone's knowledge of a second language as an ability to translate it into his mother tongue, we are not giving a circular account: the ability to translate does not, in itself, presuppose an understanding of the second language like the understanding someone has of his mother tongue. It is quite otherwise when we try to explain someone's understanding of his mother tongue after the same model, namely as consisting in his associating certain concepts with the words. For the question arises what it *is* to 'associate a concept with a word'. We know what it is to associate a word of one language with a word of another: asked to translate the one word, he utters, or writes down, the other. But the concept has no representation intermediate between it and its verbal expression. Or, if it does, we still have the question what makes it a representation of *that* concept. We cannot say that someone's association of a particular concept with a given word consists in the fact that, when he hears that word, that concept comes into his mind, for there is really no sense to speaking of a concept's coming into someone's mind. All that we can think of is some image's coming to mind which we take as in some way representing the concept, and this gets us no further forward, since we still have to ask in what his associating that concept with that image consists.

Rather, any account of what it is to associate a concept with a word would have to provide an explanation of one thing which might constitute a grasp of the concept. What is it to grasp the concept *square*, say? At the very least, it is to be able to discriminate between things that are square and those that are not. Such an ability can be ascribed only to one who will, on occasion, treat square things differently from things that are not square; one way, among many other possible ways, of doing this is to apply the word "square" to square things and not to others. And it can only be by reference to some such use of the word "square", or at least of some knowledge *about* the word "square" which would warrant such a use of it, that we can explain what it is to associate the concept *square* with that word. An ability to use the word in such a way, or a suitable piece of knowledge about the word, would, by itself, *suffice* as a manifestation of a grasp of the concept. Even if we grant that there is no difficulty in supposing someone to have, and to manifest, a grasp of the concept antecedently to an understanding of the word, we can make no *use* of this assumption in explaining what it is to understand the word: we cannot appeal to the speaker's prior grasp of the concept in explaining what it is for him to associate that concept with that word. The question whether a grasp of the concepts expressible in language could precede a knowledge of any language thus falls away as irrelevant.

We have, therefore, to replace the conception of language as a code for thought by some account of the understanding of a language that makes no appeal to the prior grasp of the concepts that can be expressed in it. Such an account presents language, not just as a means of expressing thought, but as a *vehicle* for thought. The idea of a language as a code became untenable because a concept's coming to mind was not, by itself, an intelligible description of a mental event: thought *requires* a vehicle. And for this reason, the philosophical study of language assumes a far greater importance as being, not just a branch of philosophy, but the foundation of the entire subject, since it has to be, simultaneously, a study of *thought*. Only if we take language to be a code can we hope to strip off the linguistic clothing and penetrate to the pure naked thought beneath: the only effective means of studying thought is by the study of language, which is its vehicle.

The observation that there is no such mental event as a concept's coming to mind is paralleled by Wittgenstein's remark that understanding is not a mental process. One of the advantages of the approach to language as a vehicle of thought is that we do not need to look for any *occurrence* save the expression of the thought. Suppose that I am walking along the street with my wife, and suddenly stop dead and say (in English), "I have left the address behind". What constitutes my having at that moment had the thought I expressed need be no more than just the fact that I know English and said those words; there does not have to have been anything else that went on within me simultaneously with my utterance of the sentence. Wittgenstein said, "To understand the sentence is to understand the language". He did not mean that (as some American philosophers believe) you would not understand the sentence in the same way if you knew only a fragment of the language to which it belonged. He meant, rather, that, given you understand the *language*, that you are, as it were, in that *state* of understanding, nothing need happen, in which your understanding of the sentence consists, no *act* of understanding, other than your hearing that sentence.

This consideration only reinforces our initial idea, that the key to an account of language—and now, it seems, of thought itself—is the explanation of an individual speaker's mastery of his language. According to the conception of language as a vehicle of thought, this explanation must embody an account of what it is to have the concepts expressible in the language; and Frege, who originated this new approach, gave the outlines of an explanation of this kind. Naturally, I cannot here do more than gesture towards his theory: it involves distinguishing three different types of ingredient in meaning, sense (*Sinn*), force (*Kraft*) and colour (*Färbung*). The fundamental conception is that of the primacy of sentences. To a fair degree of approximation, we may say that what a speaker does by uttering a sequence of sentences is the sum of what he could do by uttering each sentence on its own. Nothing of the kind, however, holds good of the words that make up a single sentence: save in special contexts, nothing at all is conveyed by uttering a single word. The words do not make up the sentence in the same way that the sentences make up the paragraph. We indeed understand new sentences that we have never heard before because we already understand the words that compose them and the principles of sentence-construction in accordance with which they are combined. But we cannot explain the meanings of words independently of their occurrence in sentences, and then explain the understanding of a sentence as the successive apprehension of the meanings of the words. Rather, we have to have first a conception of what, in general, constitutes the meaning of a sentence, and then to explain the meaning of each particular word as the contribution it makes to determining the meaning of any sentence in which it may occur. As regards that ingredient of meaning which Frege called *sense*, which is that which determines the specific content of a sentence, Frege proposed that to grasp the sense of a sentence is to know the condition for it to be true; the sense of a word consists in the contribution it makes to determining the truth-condition of any sentence of which it forms part; and he went on to give a detailed theory concerning the manner in which the senses of words of different categories are given, so as jointly to determine the truth-condition of any given sentence, the whole theory thus displaying the way in which the sense of a sentence is determined in accordance with its composition out of its component words.

I am not here concerned with the particular features of Frege's theory, but only with the general line of approach to the philosophy of language of which it was the earliest example. Frege's theory was the first instance of a conception that continues to dominate the philosophy of language, that of a *theory of meaning* for a specific language. Such a theory of meaning displays all that is involved in the investment of the words and sentences of the language with the meanings that they bear. The expression "a theory of meaning" may be used in a quite general way to apply to any theory which purports to do this for a particular language: but I shall here use the phrase in a more specific sense. As I have here presented Frege's ideas, and as, I think, it is natural to conceive the matter from what he said about it, a theory of meaning is not a description from the outside of the practice of using the language, but is thought of as an object of *knowledge* on the part of the speakers. A speaker's mastery of his language consists, on this view, in his knowing a theory of meaning for it: it is this that confers on his utterances the senses that they bear, and it is because two speakers take the language as governed by the same, or nearly the same, theory of meaning that they can communicate with one another by means of that language. I shall reserve the phrase "a theory of meaning" for a theory thus conceived as something known by the speakers. Such knowledge cannot be taken as explicit knowledge, for two reasons. First, it is obvious that the speakers do not in general have explicit knowledge of a theory of meaning for their language; if they did, there would be no problem about how to construct such a theory. Secondly, even if we could attribute to a speaker an explicit knowledge of a theory of meaning for a language, we should not have completed the philosophical task of explaining in what his mastery of the language consisted by stating the theory of meaning and ascribing an explicit knowledge of it to him. Explicit knowledge is manifested by the ability to *state* the content of the knowledge. This is a sufficient condition for someone's being said to have that knowledge only if it is assumed that he fully understands the statement that he is making; and, even if we make this assumption, his ability to say what he knows can be invoked as an adequate explanation of what it is for him to have that knowledge only when we can take his understanding of the statement of its content as unproblematic. In many philosophical contexts, we are entitled to do this: but when our task is precisely to explain in what, in general, an understanding of a language consists, it is obviously circular. If we say that it consists in the knowledge of a theory of meaning for the language, we cannot then explain the possession of such knowledge in terms of an ability to state it, presupposing an understanding of the language in which the theory is stated. For this reason, the philosophical task of explaining in what a mastery of a language consists is not completed when we have set out the theory of meaning for the language. Whether the speaker's knowledge of that theory is taken to be explicit or merely implicit, we have to go on to give an account of what it is to have such knowledge. This account can only be given in terms of the practical ability which the speaker displays in using sentences of the language; and, in general, the knowledge of which that practical ability is taken as a manifestation may be, and should be, regarded as only implicit knowledge. I have already defended the conception of implicit knowledge, and argued that we need to invoke it in-explaining certain, but not all, types of practical ability.

The conception of mastery of a language as consisting in the implicit knowledge of a theory of meaning is just as much in accordance with our original notion that what makes the utterances of a speaker to be expressions of thought is a piece of internal equipment that he has, namely his general understanding of the language, as was the conception of language as a code. Anyone who knows the writings of Frege will object that I have either misrepresented him or, at best, have expounded only half his thought on this subject: for when Frege writes, not in detail, but on the general principles governing the notion of sense, he strenuously combats what he calls 'psychologism', that is, the explanation of sense in terms of some inner psychological mechanism possessed by the speakers; and this seems in flat contradiction to the conception of a theory of meaning as I have expounded it.

The principle which Frege opposes to psychologism is that of the communicability of sense. Of some inner experience of mine, a sensation or a mental image, I can tell you what it is like. But, in the case of thought, I do not have to confine myself to telling you what it is like to have a thought that I have had: I can communicate to you that very thought. I do this by uttering a sentence which expresses that thought, whose sense is that thought, without any auxiliary contact between mind and mind by any non-linguistic medium. Moreover, what enables me to express my thought by means of that sentence, and you to grasp the thought so expressed, lies open to view, as much so as the utterance of the sentence itself. The objection to the idea that our understanding of each other depends upon the occurrence in me of certain inner processes which prompted my utterance, the hearing of which then evokes corresponding inner processes within you, is that, if this were so, it would be no more than a *hypothesis* that the sense you attached to my utterance was the sense I intended it to bear, the hypothesis, namely, that the same inner processes went on within both of us. If such a hypothesis could not be established conclusively, if it were in the end an act of faith, then thought would not be in principle communicable: it would remain a possibility, which you could never rule out, save by faith, that I systematically attached different senses to my words from those you associated with them, and hence that the thoughts you took me to be expressing were not those I understood myself to be expressing. If, on the other hand, the hypothesis were one that could be conclusively established, either by asking me to elucidate my words or by attending to the uses I made of them on other occasions, then the hypothesis would not be needed. It would, in that case, amount to no more than the assumption, which is, indeed, required if we are to be able to communicate by means of our utterances, that we are talking the same language, a language that we both understand: but that in which our understanding of the language consisted would lie open to view, as Frege maintained that it does, in our use of the language, in our participation in a common practice.

This argument can be directed against the idea of a theory of meaning, conceived as the object of implicit knowledge by the speakers, as much as against an account in terms of psychological processes of the kind that was the immediate target of Frege's criticism. However, I have already answered such an argument: for I said earlier that implicit knowledge ascribed to the speakers must be manifested in their *use* of the language, and that it is part of the business of a philosopher of language to explain in what specific feature of this use a speaker's knowledge of each particular part of the theory of meaning is so manifested. There is no need for any act of faith.

But now it seems that the objection can be put in another way. If the speaker's implicit knowledge must be manifested by his actual use of the language, why not describe that use directly? Let us here make the well-known and often fruitful comparison of a language with a board-game. To immediate inspection, all that happens when two people play chess is that they alternately move pieces around the board, and sometimes remove them. Nevertheless, a move in chess has a significance not apparent to immediate inspection, a significance grasped by the players in virtue of their knowledge of the rules. It is a legitimate philosophical enquiry in what an individual player's mastery of the rule consists. Can it be a mere practical ability, or must it rest on knowledge, and, if on knowledge, must that knowledge be explicit or can it be only implicit? For all that, we do not attempt to explain the significance of a move, that is, the character of the game as a game, by reference to the individual player's mastery of the rules: rather, we simply state the rules, that is, we describe the *practice* of playing the game. And, according to this objection, this is what we should do in the case of language. What an individual speaker's understanding of his language consists in is a legitimate philosophical enquiry; and it may be that, to explain this, we must invoke the notion of implicit knowledge. But to answer the central question of the philosophy of language, we do not need, on this view, to appeal to the notion of an individual speaker's mastery of the language: we simply describe the social practice in which that mastery enables him to participate, and so need not invoke the notion of knowledge at all.

We could express this argument in the following way. Suppose that someone wishes to represent a practical ability, say that of riding a bicycle, as consisting in practical knowledge: so he says, for example, that the bicycle-rider knows that, when he goes round a bend, he must incline at an angle that is such-and-such a function of his speed and of the radius of curvature. This is, of course, one of the cases about which I said that we do *not* need to invoke the idea of implicit knowledge. But at least the representation of the ability as a piece of knowledge is unperplexing, because we can so easily convert the account of what the bicycle-rider is supposed to know into a description of what he *does*; for example, when he goes round a bend, he does incline at such-and-such an angle. Now we can represent the objection to the conception of a theory of meaning by means of the following dilemma. If the theory of meaning can be converted into a direct description of actual linguistic practice, then it is better so converted; and we have then eliminated any appeal to the notion of knowledge. If, on the other hand, it cannot be converted into such a description, it ceases to be plausible that, by ascribing an implicit knowledge of that theory to a speaker, we have given an adequate representation of his practical ability in speaking the language. The appeal to the notion of knowledge is therefore either redundant or positively incorrect.

I believe this objection, though very powerful, to be mistaken. We can best see this by considering again the analogy with a game. The mistake in our discussion of this analogy lay in taking for granted the notion of the *rules* of the game. What these rules are is also not given to immediate inspection: they do not, for instance, exhaust the observable regularities in play. Suppose that a Martian observes human beings playing a particular board-game, chess or some other. And suppose that he does not recognize the game to be a rational activity, nor the players to be rational creatures: he may perhaps lack the concept of a game. He may develop a powerful scientific theory of the game as a particular aspect of human behaviour: perhaps, after carrying out certain tests on the players, he is able to predict in detail the moves which each will make. He now knows a great deal more than anyone needs to know in order to be able to play the game. But he also knows *less*, because he cannot say what are the rules of the game or what is its object; he does not so much as have the conception of a lawful move or of winning and losing. He could simulate the play of a human player, but, for all the superior intelligence I am attributing to him, he could not play the game better than a human player, because he knows neither what is a lawful move nor what is a good move.

Any adequate philosophical account of language must describe it as a rational activity on the part of creatures to whom can be ascribed *intention* and *purpose*. The use of language is, indeed, the primary manifestation of our rationality: it is *the* rational activity *par excellence*. In asking for an explanation of what gives to a particular activity the character of a game, we are putting ourselves in the position of one who is trying to understand an unfamiliar game, and for some reason, cannot communicate with the players: he does not demand a theory that will enable him to predict the move that each player will make, even if there is such a theory to be had; he needs only so much as to comprehend the playing of the game as a rational activity. He wants, that is, to know just so much as anyone needs to know if he is to know how to play the game, and so to know what playing the game consists in. An account of language by means of a causal theory such as Quine appears to envisage, representing it as a complex of conditioned responses, is not the sort of theory that we need or should be seeking, even if we knew how to construct such a theory. To represent speech as a rational activity, we must describe it as something on to which the ordinary procedures of estimating overt motive and intention are brought to bear. This requires a place, for which a purely causal theory allows no room, for the distinction, essential to the comphrehension of an utterance, between why a speaker says what he does and what it is that he says, that is, what his words mean, as determined by the linguistic conventions that have to be specially learned. The concept of intention can in turn be applied only against the background of a distinction between those regularities of which a language speaker, acting as a rational agent engaged in conscious, voluntary action, *makes use* from those that may be hidden from him and might be uncovered by a psychologist or neurologist; only those regularities of which, in speaking, he makes use characterize the language as a language. He can make use only of those regularities of which he may be said to be in some degree aware; those, namely, of which he has at least implicit knowledge.

If this is right, it follows that the notion of knowledge cannot, after all, be extruded from the philosophy of language. It has also a further consequence for the criterion of suceess in constructing a theory of meaning for a language. For it follows that such a theory is not open to assessment in the same way as an ordinary empirical theory; it is not to be judged correct merely on the ground that it tallies satisfactorily with observed linguistic behaviour. Rather, the only conclusive criterion for its correctness is that the speakers of the language are, upon reflection, prepared to acknowledge it as correct that is, as embodying those principles by which they are in fact guided. Such a theory cannot be arrived at by observation alone, but requires reflection; and it is by reflection that it must be decided whether it succeeds or fails.

4

What does the Appeal to Use Do for the Theory of Meaning?

Consider the following style of argument. What would one say "Either he *is* your brother or he *isn't*" (for example) *for*? Well, it is tantamount to saying. "There must be a definite answer: there are no two ways about it". We say this when someone is shilly-shallying, behaving as if it were no more right to say the one thing than the other: so the utterance of that instance of the law of excluded middle is an expression of the conviction that the sentence "He is your brother" has a *definite* sense. That, therefore, is the meaning of the sentence "Either he is your brother or he isn't": that is its *use* in the language.

No doubt everyone here would agree that that is a bad argument: but why is it a bad argument? A superficial answer might be "It does not take account of other uses that exist for uttering an instance of the law of excluded middle, for example in the course of a deductive argument. Thus Littlewood proved a theorem by showing that it followed both from the Riemann hypothesis and from the negation of that hypothesis: so his proof might have started, 'Either the Riemann hypothesis is true or it is false'." This is a superficial answer, because, although it is quite true that people do use instances of the law of excluded middle in this way, they might, given classical logic, perfectly well not do so, and still be able to carry out all the deductive arguments that they wanted to; and yet the philosophical argument with which I started would still be a bad argument. The following explanation of this fact is a great improvement. The recognition of the law of excluded middle as valid hangs together with the admission of certain forms of inference as valid, in particular, the dilemma or argument by cases:

$$\frac{\text{If } A, \text{ then } B \qquad \text{If not-}A, \text{ then } B}{\text{Therefore, } B}$$

which underlies the proof of Littlewood's that was mentioned. It hangs together with it in the sense that any reasonable general formulation of these rules of inference, together with a few others that strike us as inescapable, will result in our being able to deduce each sentence of the form "*A* or not-*A*" from no hypotheses at all (for instance, by an argument whose last step is the dilemma, as above, with "*B*" replaced by "*A* or not-*A*"). The notion of truth is,

First published in A. Margalit (ed.), *Meaning and Use* (Dordrecht, 1979).

of course, connected with that of a valid inference by the fact that whatever follows by valid inferences from true premises must be true: so we are committed, if we accept the dilemma and related forms of argument, to regarding a sentence "*A* or not-*A*" as true. Now the meaning of a sentence is more closely connected with what, if anything, does or would render it true than with what would prompt an actual utterance of it. Hence, an understanding of a sentence of that form is to be sought by explaining those meanings of the logical constants "or" and "not" which permit of its derivation from the null set of hypotheses.

The second argument does not, like the first, tamely accept that the use of a sentence, in the sense of the point that an utterance of it might have, determines its meaning, and then claim that some such uses have been overlooked. Rather, it challenges that principle by giving reasons for thinking that we must have a prior understanding of the *sentence* before we can be in a position to ask what the point of a particular utterance of it may be. The argument, as stated, appeals to an already understood notion of truth, with a known connection with our recognition of any given principle of inference. The proponent of the argument that is being criticized may feel that such a notion of truth is spurious, and he has available a well-known device for countering an appeal to it: he declares that the whole explanation of "true", in its only intelligible sense, is given by the principle that "*A*" is equivalent to "It is true that *A*", or by a definition that is just sufficient to yield this equivalence for each case; the use, or meaning, of an assertion that a sentence is true will then be precisely the same as that of an utterance of that sentence, and the notion of truth will be impotent to yield any results about meaning not previously obtained by enquiring into use. But the sense of "true" required for the second counter-argument is shown by that argument itself: what is needed of a true sentence is that there should exist means of justifying an assertion of it of a kind we are accustomed to accept elsewhere; and so the word "true" can be dropped from the argument, and a direct appeal made to this notion. This is, indeed, to assume that we recognize certain general principles for the justification of our assertions; but so we obviously do, otherwise there would be no such thing as deductive argument. It is now open to the proponent of the second counter-argument to concede that, given classical logic, an instance of the law of excluded middle is so obvious that the point of an assertion of it is scarcely ever to call attention to the fact that it can be justified, without calling in question his own thesis that it is the possibility of justification to which our primary understanding of the sentence relates; indeed, he can even maintain that "*A* or not-*A*" would be true in some, or all, cases in which the sense of "*A*" is *not* definite, so that an assertion of it, intended to have the point which the proponent of the original argument rightly said that such assertions often have, would go awry otherwise than by failing to be true.

Now I do not for one moment suggest that an argument of the style with which we started out and with which some of us were made, during a period now passed, wearisomely familiar, represents faithfully the notion of use which Wittgenstein had in mind when he coined the slogan "Meaning is use". On the contrary, Wittgenstein's notion was a much more general one: it comprised anything that could be counted as belonging to the role of the sentence in the language-game, which certainly included, not only the communicatory function of an utterance of the sentence itself, but also that of an utterance of a complex sentence of which it was a constituent, and, as well, such other features as were appealed to in the counter-argument I set out. To say this, however, is to make the conception of meaning as use totally programmatic: any feature of our linguistic practice that relates to the sentence may be cited as bearing on its meaning. There is, however, a reason why Wittgenstein's later philosophy of language should have led to this misapplication of the identification of meaning with use. This lies in Wittgenstein's repudiation of the Fregean distinction between sense and force and, particularly, of Frege's idea that there is such a thing as assertoric force in general. There are, on this conception of Frege's, three grades in understanding an assertoric utterance. First comes the grasp we have of the sense of the sentence, of the thought expressed; and this consists in an understanding, which is derived in accordance with our apprehension of the construction of the sentence out of its linguistic elements (let us say, inexactly, its component words), of the condition which must obtain for the sentence to be true. Secondly, there is our knowledge of the practice of assertion: the speaker is not merely uttering a sentence with which is associated a certain truth-condition, that is, expressing a certain thought, but saying (that is, asserting) that that thought is true, as opposed to asking whether it is true, supposing it to be true for the purposes of argument, declaring himself unwilling to deny that it is true, advising his hearer to make it true, expressing the wish that it were true, or the like. (Whether or not there is a non-circular account of what it is to assert that a thought is true, that is, of what is effected by an assertoric utterance of a sentence expressing that thought, is another matter.) And, finally, there is the divination of the speaker's particular intention in asserting that thought to be true on that particular occasion. Wittgenstein rejected this conception, on the ground that there is no such thing as 'the practice of assertion', or as, in his terminology, the language-game of assertion, considered as effected by the utterance, in assertoric mode, of any sentence syntactically fitted to be used assertorically and to which we may ascribe conditions for it (or a specific utterance of it) to be true or false.

Something happens—and then I make a noise. What for? Presumably in order to tell what happens.—But how is *telling* done? When are we said to *tell* anything?—What is the language-game of telling?—I should like to say: you regard it much too much as a matter of course that one can tell anything to anyone. That is to say: we are so much accustomed to communication [*Mitteilung*—the abstract noun cognate with the verb used for "to tell"] through language, in conversation, that it looks to us as if the whole point of communication lay in this: someone else grasps the sense of my words—which is something mental: he as it were takes it into his own mind. If he then does something further with it as well, that is no part of the immediate purpose of language. (*Philosophical Investigations*, I. 363)

Now the fact is that it is difficult to obliterate the distinction between the first grade of understanding and the second without thereby also obliterating that between the second and the third. This is because our concept of truth gets a large part of its point from the contrast that we wish to draw between a statement's being true and any more primitive, or at least undifferentiated, conception of its being appropriate: for instance, between its being true and the speaker's having a sufficient warrant to take it as true, or between its being true and the intention that the speaker had in asserting it to be true just then being a just one, his having had a legitimate point in making it. Of course, once we have any given conception of a particular sentence's being determined, in some objective manner, as true or as false, then these distinctions arise naturally, indeed inevitably: the questions of interest are why we introduce the notion of truth at all, and why, in doing so, we draw the line between the condition for a statement to be true and the condition for a speaker's being in the right in making it in these more general ways at just the place we do, and not somewhere else. There are various correct answers to these questions, one being the necessity of explaining the role of the sentence when it figures as a constituent in more complex sentences; but this is not our present concern. Another partial answer is, obviously, the dependence of a speaker's point in making a statement on the context, something which, if we are to attain a conception of the meaning of the sentence as a type, we must either filter out or reduce to a definite rule (as we can explain indexical expressions systematically). But this is not an important feature of the objection to the account with which I started of sentences like "Either he is your brother or he isn't", an utterance of which was claimed as only ever having one kind of point; as I remarked, the account would be wrong even if the claim were sound. Rather, in that case, what we appealed to was the existence in the practice of the speakers of certain generally accepted procedures for justifying statements, procedures which would always yield a justification of an instance of the law of excluded middle even if it was never in fact invoked in such a case. This looks circular, since such procedures are for the purpose of justifying a statement *as true*, rather than as making a sound point. So it comes down to this: that our linguistic practice—the language-games in which we participate—involves the process whereby those utterances which we call assertions (and perhaps some others) are subject to challenge by our hearers and the process of responding to such challenges; and, if we were to try to give any account of these practices, a mastery of which is certainly essential for the ability to engage in converse with others, we shall be forced to distinguish between different types of such challenges, according to the kind of response that is appropriate; and among these are challenges as to the truth of what is said and challenges as to its point (the latter of which doubtless further subdivide into challenges as to relevance, as to implicature in Grice's sense, etc.). Here a challenge as to truth is to be distinguished by the fact that, if successfully met, the challenger will himself give assent to the statement (though he need not be prepared himself to make that statement, since it may be objectionable in other ways, e.g. as breaking a confidence or being insulting); hence Quine's properly placed emphasis upon the notions of assent and dissent. (A suspicion of circularity arises here also, since an expression of assent is surely an expression of a willingness to make the statement so far as its truth is concerned, that is, but for possible objections to it which are not objections as to truth; but I will not push the enquiry further. Of course, as I said, these distinctions are easy to draw once we have the notion of truth and know its application to a given sentence; but I have been concerned with what we need the notion for and why we give it the application that we do.) This is not to say that the notion of truth so arrived at will serve all the purposes for which we need it, for instance to explain the behaviour of a sentence when it is a constituent of a more complex sentence.

Once we have the notion of truth and so can distinguish between the second and the third grade of understanding, the distinction between the first and second grade is all but inevitable. If all utterances were assertoric, and no sentence ever occurred as a constituent of another sentence, there would indeed be no place for it, but this would make no difference to the present argument: so long as we appealed to the notion of the truth-conditions of a sentence as determining its particular content, we should, in explaining what is effected by an utterance of a sentence, have to give a general description of the linguistic practice of making assertions. But the notion of truth is precisely what we need, or, rather, what is forced on us, if we wish to distinguish between the second and third grades of understanding. Hence, if there is no such thing as the general practice of making assertions—or, at least, as a uniform description of what this practice consists in, for a sentence with an arbitrarily given individual content—then there can be no distinction, at any rate no general distinction, between the second and third grades of understanding either. And what this appears to mean is that any account of the meaning of a given sentence must simultaneously explain every feature of the significance of any possible utterance of it. This, indeed, is not particularly difficult to do for any one sentence, at least if we ignore utterances the point of which depends heavily upon context. What seems impossibly hard is to construct a systematic theory of meaning for a language along these lines, that is, one which would show the derivation of the significance of the sentence in accordance with its composition: as soon as we begin to think about the construction of such a theory, we at once start to segment the task it has to accomplish, along the lines of the repudiated distinctions between truth-conditions, force, and point.

Wittgenstein's repudiation of these distinctions is expressed by his adherence to the redundancy theory of truth (expressed in a characteristically sloppy manner in the *Remarks on the Foundations of Mathematics*, I, app. 1. 6— "For what does a proposition's *'being true'* mean? *'p' is true* = *p*. (That is the answer.)"). If the equivalence of " 'Snow is white' is true" with "Snow is white", and so on, constitutes the *whole* explanation of the concept of truth, then the concept is useless in giving a theory of meaning. It is because of his rejection of the concepts of assertion and of truth as capable of playing any role in an account of how language functions that Wittgenstein's identification of meaning with use lent itself to the kind of misapplication with which I began.

In an earlier period, however, Wittgenstein had seized on the notion of the justification of a statement as the key to an explanation of sense: "It is what is regarded as the justification of an assertion that constitutes the sense of the assertion" (*Philosophical Grammar*, I. 40).

It is natural to contrast the idea that meaning is given by determining what justifies us in using a sentence to make an assertion with the idea that it is given by determining the conditions under which the sentence is true; and Wittgenstein certainly meant to convey a very sharp divergence from the theory of meaning in terms of truth-conditions set out in the *Tractatus*. But to say that, on the view of meaning Wittgenstein held in the intermediate period, the meaning of a sentence is *not* determined by its truth-conditions is liable to misconstruction. If one holds that the meaning of a sentence is given in terms of what has to hold for it to be true, it is open to one to say that someone may understand a sentence although he has not yet learned by what means we may recognize it as true, nor, therefore, what justifies an assertion of it. But there is an asymmetry here: thinking that the meaning of a sentence is given by what justifies asserting it does not entitle one to suggest that someone might understand a sentence without yet knowing the condition that must obtain for it to be true. Rather, from such a standpoint one would say that the only legitimate notion of truth is one that is to be explained in terms of what justifies an assertion: a sentence is true if an assertion made by means of it would be justified (or, possibly, if there is some recognizable state of affairs such that, if a speaker knew of it, he would be justified in making that assertion). There is therefore a sense in which, even on the theory of meaning which is opposed to that of the *Tractatus*, it remains the case that the sense of a sentence is determined by its truth-conditions: the question is, What is the relation between the notion of truth and that of the justification of an assertion?

The theory of meaning expressed by the remark I have quoted from the *Philosophical Grammar* stands in opposition to any conception of meaning under which the sense of a sentence is given in terms of a notion of truth taken as objectively and determinately either attaching or not attaching to each sentence independently of our knowledge, or capacity to know, whether or not that sentence is true, a notion of truth which is therefore taken to be grasped without reference, in all cases, to the means available to us for judging a sentence to be true. This conception plainly informs the *Tractatus*. That work carries a fundamental commitment to the principle of bivalence, integral to the conception of meaning I have just characterized, since, if bivalence did not hold, the truth-tables would not have the kind of importance allotted to them in the *Tractatus*. Since the *Tractatus* also contends that our understanding of our sentences involves the grasp of infinitary truth-operations, it is equally plain that a grasp of the meaning of a sentence is not held to be in all cases related to, or given in terms of, the means available to us for recognizing it as true. Wittgenstein came to repudiate this conception for a multitude of reasons. First, a theory of meaning of this kind is powerless to explain how we come by our knowledge of the conditions which warrant us in asserting a statement, the means by which we can establish a statement as true. Granted that the meaning of a sentence is not, in the first place, given in terms of how we recognize it as true, still our grasp of what is to count for us as showing that it is true must be *derived* in some way from our knowledge of its meaning: for, if not, then, even when the meaning of a sentence has been fixed by determining its truth-conditions, there will still remain room for decision as to what we shall choose to count as showing it to be true, and this is counter-intuitive. But, once we have allowed the two notions, that of truth and that of the means by which truth is recognized, to be sundered at the outset, we shall never find a means to connect them up again, to explain how the one is derived from the other. More generally, the theory violates the intuitive connection between meaning and knowledge: two sentences may, according to the *Tractatus* theory, express the same sense (because they make the same division in logical space) without our perceiving that their senses are the same; this is because sense has been thought of as given in terms of what *makes* a sentence true, rather than in terms of how it is recognized as true. But, on the contrary, we ought to say that the meaning of any expression is determined by what a speaker must know if he is to be said to understand that expression; it follows that, if someone understands two expressions that have the same meaning, he must know that their meaning is the same. (It could be argued—and has been argued by me—that this is in part a consequence of Wittgenstein's abandonment of the distinction between sense and reference as drawn by Frege, and therefore not a necessary result of holding a conception of meaning as given by truth-conditions, under a notion of truth subject to bivalence and not directly connected, in all cases, with our means of recognizing truth. That is not to say that the more restricted form of the objection, that such a conception of meaning will not always allow an explanation of how we derive the means of recognizing the truth of a sentence from the condition for it to be true, is met by appealing to a Fregean distinction between sense and reference.)

Secondly, the *Tractatus* conception leaves us unable to state informatively the conditions for the truth of many of our sentences: an essential circularity appears in any attempt to do this, a circularity which does not appear in a characterisation of what *justifies* us in asserting a sentence. This circularity then leads us to attribute to a speaker a capacity for immediate *recognition* of certain qualities, objects, processes, or states (the private ostensive definition), which capacity can be no further explained. But now it is evident that this attribution is idle: all would go on in just the same way if the speaker misrecognized the entity every time, or if there were nothing there to be recognized; at least, it would do so provided that, whenever recognition by two or more speakers was called for, they tended to make the same mistakes. The conception of our apprehension of the truth-condition of a sentence, with its attendant capacity for immediate recognition of the presence of the referents of certain terms, therefore fails to be explanatory: what, ultimately, actually justifies us in the assertions we make is the fact of agreement between speakers, which need not be taken as resting on anything more basic. As for the notion of truth, the circularity disappears when we cease to think of it, as the *Tractatus* insists, as that in terms of which the meanings of our sentences are given, and, instead, regard its application to a sentence as explicable only after the sense of that sentence is known.

Thirdly, this same circularity attends our attempts to state the truth-conditions of those sentences our alleged grasp of which transcends our means of recognizing them as true: our grasp of the condition for such a sentence to be true cannot consist in our ability, in certain special cases, to recognize it as true, just because it involves our awareness that it may still be true even when we are unable to recognize it as such. But then to attribute to us a grasp of the condition for a sentence to be true, under such a transcendental notion of truth, violates the principle that meaning is use: for a knowledge of the condition for the truth of the sentence of this kind cannot be fully manifested by the use the speaker makes of it, that is, by the linguistic and non-linguistic behaviour on his part that is connected with the utterance of the sentence.

These arguments are all of a negative kind: in so far as they are cogent, they show the conception of meaning as given by truth-conditions, as found in Frege, and, in a different form, in the *Tractatus*, to be inadmissible; but they do not show the conception of it as given in terms of what justifies an assertion, rather than of some other feature of the use of a sentence, to be correct. In so far as they are merely negative arguments, they survive into Wittgenstein's later period: but I have suggested that he came to adopt a still more radical view, one involving a repudiation of the sense/force distinction in a way in which the idea of meaning as given in terms of the justification of an assertion does not. (Indeed, it is of importance that the formulation I quoted from the *Philosophical Grammar* employs the notion of assertion.) I cannot here attempt an evaluation of the negative arguments I have just sketched. Instead, I want to argue that the thesis that what constitutes a justification of an assertion determines, or shows, the sense of the sentence asserted indicates very precisely the constraints which the identification of meaning with use puts, and those it does not put, upon a theory of meaning.

First, the constraints it does not impose. If someone has the idea that the justification for an assertion is the key to its content, he is allowing himself a much richer set of data to which to appeal than those which either Quine or Davidson permits himself. For Quine, the relevant data consist solely of the correlations between the sensory stimuli to which a speaker is subjected and his readiness to assent to or dissent from a sentence. Davidson is more generous in allowing correlations between a speaker's holding a sentence true and prevailing conditions of any kind. Both, however, propose to construct a translation manual or meaning-theory by appeal solely to data of the form of answers to the question "When do the speakers hold, or acknowledge, sentences as true or as false?" The reason for this limitation is made very explicit by Quine, less so by Davidson. For both, the problem is of constructing a translation manual, or meaning-theory, for a language whose speakers one may observe and perhaps even interact with, but which is previously quite unknown. All that one has to go on is what one can see and hear of the speakers' utterances and associated behaviour. Now perhaps one can make a plausible identification, in behavioural terms, of the speakers' mode of expressing assent and dissent. But to go any further would be illegitimate. The notion of justification, as used by Wittgenstein, does not refer only to the process of justifying an assertion, when challenged, as this takes place within the language, since various things are involved in a full account of what justifies certain assertions that the speakers tacitly take for granted and would never explicitly cite. Nevertheless, it does involve all that would be appealed to in justifying an assertion, as this occurs between speakers. But, from the standpoint of Quine and Davidson, if I have understood them aright, to appeal to such a complicated thing as the justifications which speakers give of their assertions is out of the question, since, to become aware of that, or even to recognize what constituted a demand for justification and what a response to it, one would have already to understand a large part of the language.

Philosophers, unlike historians, do not have to solve problems that are clearly demarcated in advance; and so they make up their own problems—set themselves tasks, and then try to perform them. Disputes over philosophical methodology are largely about which are the right problems to set. One can hardly prove that this or that is the right problem: that would be possible only if, behind the problems philosophers try to solve, lay further clearly defined problems, and the solution to the former were a means to the solution of the latter. The question is only the vague one: By solving which problems shall we gain philosophical illumination? Now what is the point of posing the problem: How we should arrive at an interpretation of a language hitherto quite unknown to us? It is, surely, to exclude from the description of the interpretation or of the process of arriving at it any appeals to concepts which covertly presuppose an understanding of the language. But the consequence of so posing the problem is that we fasten on some feature of the speakers' linguistic behaviour which can be described at the outset, before any understanding of the language has been gained, and try to use it as the basis for the entire interpretation. Language is, however, an enormously complicated thing, and it is highly unlikely that a satisfactory interpretation of it is accessible if we so restrict ourselves. Certainly our actual acquisition of our mother tongue proceeds by stages: some features of our linguistic practice can be mastered only after others have already been mastered. We are, at any rate, not now in the position of having to interpret some radically foreign language: that is a practical problem, the solution to which is not obviously necessary or sufficient for the kind of understanding of how language functions which we, as philosophers, wish to attain. We already have, in our language, expressions for various concepts which relate to our use of language, among them that of the justification of an assertion. What we want to arrive at is a model of that in which our understanding of our language consists, a model which will be adequate to explain the entire practice of speaking the language. Certainly that model must itself be described in terms which do not presuppose a tacit understanding of terms, such as "assertion", "justification", "true", etc., which relate to the practice of which the model aims to provide an account, or it will, to that extent, fail to be explanatory. But that does not mean that, in groping our way towards such a model, we must eschew appeal to any of those concepts which are not to be used in giving the model itself. It does not matter whether or not an outside observer—a Martian, say, who communicated by means so different from our own that he would not for a long time recognize human language as a medium of communication—could ever arrive at the model we hope to give: all that matters is whether, once he had it, it would serve to make our language intelligible to him.

Now for the constraints which the identification of meaning with use does impose. Having expressed a point of basic methodological disagreement with Quine, let me now record one of strong agreement with him. In his lecture 'Mind and Verbal Dispositions',[1] Quine says, "when I define the understanding of a sentence as knowledge of its truth conditions I am certainly not offering a definition to rest with; my term 'knowledge' is as poor a resting-point as the term 'understanding' itself", and goes on to ask, "In what behavioural disposition . . . does a man's knowledge of the truth conditions of the sentence . . . consist?" This is in full consonance with what I have myself repeatedly insisted on, that a meaning-theory, being a theoretical representation of a practical ability, must not only say *what* a speaker must know in order to know the language, but in what his having that knowledge consists, that is,

---

[1] In Samuel Guttenplan (ed.), *Mind and Language*, Wolfson Lectures, 1974 (Oxford, 1975).

what constitutes a manifestation of it. (I disagree with Quine only if, as I suspect, he wants to *eliminate* the notion of knowledge from the theory of meaning altogether.) But, now, this requirement calls in question the feasibility of any model of understanding, any theory of meaning, according to which the understanding of a sentence consists, in general, of a knowledge of its truth-conditions, when the notion of truth is construed as satisfying the principle of bivalence and as, in general, given independently of our means of recognizing truth. Of the three arguments which I cited as contained in middle and late Wittgenstein, it is the third I wish to stress here. Our language contains many sentences for which we know no procedure, even in principle, which will put us in a position to assert or deny that sentence, at least with full justification. Indeed, for many such sentences, we have no ground for supposing that there necessarily exists any means whereby we could recognize the sentence as true or as false, even means of which we have no effective method of availing ourselves. Hence a notion of truth for such a sentence, taken as subject to the principle of bivalence, cannot be equated with the existence of a means of justifying an assertion of it—an equation which sufficed for the distinction between the meaning of a sentence, as a type, and the point of a particular assertion of it. More importantly, a speaker's knowledge of the condition which must, in general, hold for the sentence to be true cannot be taken to consist in his ability to recognize it as true whenever those conditions obtain under which it may be so recognized, and as false when it may be recognized as false, since, by hypothesis, it may be true even in the absence of any such conditions, and he must know the condition for it to be true in those cases also. Therefore, if meaning is use, that is, if the knowledge in which a speaker's understanding of a sentence consists must be capable of being fully manifested by his linguistic practice, it appears that a model of meaning in terms of a knowledge of truth-conditions is possible only if we construe truth in such a way that the principle of bivalence fails; and this means, in effect, some notion of truth under which the truth of a sentence implies the possibility, in principle, of *our* recognizing its truth. It is hard to swallow such a conclusion, because it has profound metaphysical repercussions: it means that we cannot operate, in general, with a picture of our language as bearing a sense that enables us to talk about a determinate, objective reality which renders what we say determinately true or false independently of whether we have the means to recognize its truth or falsity. On the other hand, if the identification of meaning with use does not impose on a theory of meaning the constraints I have suggested, I for one find it difficult to see how it can impose any constraints whatever.

5

Language and Truth

In the early years of this century, the notion of truth was the subject of vigorous philosophical dispute. The two principal philosophical theories of truth were known as the "correspondence theory" and the "coherence theory". According to the correspondence theory, a proposition is true provided that it corresponds to reality; more exactly, if there is a fact to which it precisely corresponds. This appears at first sight little more than a platitude: it captures the intuitive idea that our thoughts relate to a reality which is independent of them, that the language in which we express our thoughts describes such a reality, and that what we think or say is true provided that external reality is as we think or say that it is. But an account along these lines was rejected by the supporters of the coherence theory on the ground that a proposition cannot be compared with, or found to correspond or not to correspond with, anything so unlike itself as an objective fact. When, according to them, we establish the truth or the falsity of a proposition, we always do so on the basis of other propositions which we accept as true; we can relate a proposition only to other propositions, and therefore the truth of a proposition should be taken as consisting in its coherence with some overall system of propositions.

An argument very popular with the linguistic philosophers of the 1950s and 1960s purported to demonstrate the absurdity of any philosophical theory of truth which, like the correspondence and coherence theories, offered a general characterization of what it is for a proposition to be true. According to this argument, to attempt to say what it is for an arbitrary proposition to be true is absurd in the same way as to attempt to say what it is to win an arbitrary game. If a general characterization of what it is to win any game were possible, then one would be able to apply this characterization to a particular game, say chess, to determine what, specifically, constituted winning that game. In order to do this, one would of course have to know what the game in question was; and now the absurdity of the project becomes apparent. Knowing in what winning the game consists is an essential *part* of knowing what the game *is*. There is no way in which one could derive, from a description of the game that omitted to state what counted as winning it, a knowledge of how that omission ought to be rectified. This is apparent from the fact that it is possible to have two games whose rules agree in everything except what counts as winning—

First published in Roy Harris (ed.), *Approaches to Language*, Language and Communication Library, iv (Oxford, 1983).

what counts as winning in the second game may even be precisely that which counts as losing in the first one. Thus, if you know what the game is, you do not need any criterion for determining what counts as winning it, and, if you do not know what the game is, you cannot possibly decide what counts as winning it. In the same way, according to this argument, you cannot possibly determine in what circumstances a sentence states the truth unless you know what it means; and, in order to learn what it means, that is, what proposition it expresses, you have to be told explicitly in what circumstances we count it as true. Hence, just as before, if you know what the sentence means, you do not need any criterion for its truth, and, if you do not know what it means, you cannot possibly apply any such criterion.

This argument does not, as its original propounders believed, demonstrate that there is no philosophical problem of truth, or that no philosophical theory of truth is required. It does, however, point rather accurately to what was wrong with the classical theories of truth such as the correspondence and coherence theories. What the argument shows is that the concept of truth is intricately bound up with the concept of meaning; no philosophical elucidation of either concept is to be had which does not at the same time provide an elucidation of the other one. The classical theories of truth were at fault in taking the notion of meaning for granted, as if we could first know what it was for a sentence to have the meaning that it does and then go on further to enquire what it is for it to be true. The classical theories did not, of course, purport to explain the condition for an arbitrary sentence to be true, independently of its meaning. The characterizations of truth which they offered applied, not to sentences, but to propositions; a proposition being what a sentence expresses, indeed what can be expressed in different ways by sentences of different languages. To start with an arbitrary proposition and seek to say what it is for it to be true is, in effect, to assume that we know, of some arbitrary sentence, what it means, in advance of raising the question what counts as its being true. This is indeed a fruitless procedure; if we approach our task in this way, the best that we can hope for is a characterization both banal and unexplanatory. In order to arrive at any genuine elucidation of the concept of truth, we must make our enquiry part of an attempt to elucidate the concept of meaning. We must find an answer to the perplexing question what it is for a sentence to bear the meaning that it does and, therefore, what a language is. It will be a condition upon a successful outcome of this enquiry that the terms in which we answer it also enable us to frame an answer to the question what it is for a sentence to be true.

The analogy between language and play, or between sentences and games, is illuminating but not exact. Even if it were exact, it would show that there can be no informative general characterization of the condition for a sentence to be true, but it would not show that there is nothing to be said in a philosophical elucidation of the concept of truth. In order to know what it is to win a game, that is, what it means to say of someone that he has won particular game, it is by no means *necessary* to know, for each particular game, what counts under the rules as winning it; more importantly, it is not *sufficient* either. When someone reads the rules of a game hitherto unfamiliar to him, his understanding of the rule which states under what conditions a player or side has won the game depends upon his prior understanding of what it is, in general, to win a game. If, for example, in a statement of the rules of chess the word "win" was not used, but it was merely stated that in such-and-such a position a player was said to have checkmated his opponent and that the game then terminates, that would not be enough to convey in what playing a game of chess consisted. To grasp the general concept of winning a game is to understand the role that that concept plays in a general account of the activity of playing games; crudely stated, that each player undertakes to attempt to play in such a way that he or his side wins. (We are so familiar with games-playing that we often fail to notice how complex a notion it is. The presence of a player who is merely observing the rules but making no attempt to win will render it impossible for the other players to play the game in anything but a purely formal sense. On the other hand, one does not yet fully grasp the concept of playing a game if one thinks, as I have heard a young child say, that "There is no point in my playing if I don't win".)

Exactly the same applies to the concept of truth. If to grasp the meaning of a sentence involves knowing when it, or a particular utterance of it, is true, then this knowledge must involve knowing what it is, in general, for a sentence or an utterance to be true. To know this it is neither necessary nor sufficient to know, of every particular sentence, under what conditions it is true. It must, rather, involve knowing how in all cases the concept of truth is related to that of meaning. To be more exact, we ought here to speak of an implicit grasp of the connection between the concepts of truth and of meaning, rather than of a knowledge of it. For we all recognize that a difference between the conditions for the truth of two sentences must reflect a difference between their meanings, and this recognition rests upon our apprehension of a connection between the two notions; but we should be hard put to it to state what the relation between them is, this being a typical case in which it is the task of philosophers to bring to light and render explicit a conceptual connection which formerly was no more than implicit. This involves, therefore, precisely what was stated before: an elucidation of the concept of truth requires a detailed account of what it is for a sentence to have a meaning, an account against the background of which it would be possible to state explicitly how the concept of truth is related to that of meaning.

So much would be evident even were the analogy between games and language exact; but, as already remarked, it is far from being exact. To understand how a game is played, you have to have an explicit statement of the rules, which indeed will include a statement of the conditions for winning the game; but, to understand a sentence, you do not normally have to have any explicit statement of the meaning of that sentence. On the comparatively rare occasions when we are concerned to give the meaning of an entire sentence, we usually do so by offering a paraphrase; but, in case of a more ordinary kind, if someone says that he does not understand a sentence, it is legitimate to ask him what in that sentence he does not understand. It may then appear that he does not understand some particular word, or, perhaps, some construction; and the meaning of the whole sentence will become apparent to him when that particular word or construction is explained. If you understand the words contained, and the grammatical constructions employed, in a meaningful sentence, then you will normally understand the sentence; there is no need for a separate explanation of its meaning. Moreover, there is an evident sense in which you cannot be said genuinely to understand the sentence unless you know the meanings of the individual words and understand the grammatical constructions according to which they are put together. If I hear someone utter a sentence in a language of which I am wholly ignorant, say Burmese, and ask a companion who understands that language, "What did he say?", I shall be given an equivalent sentence in English. In one sense, I now know what the sentence that I heard means; if I remember the sentence phonetically, I may be said, in this sense, to know the meaning of a specific Burmese sentence. But I do not know it of my own knowledge, as the lawyers say; to know it in that way I should have to grasp the articulation of the sentence, how it splits up into words, what the meanings of those words are, and how they are put together to form the sentence, and only by knowing that should I have a genuine understanding of the sentence. It thus does not appear to be in any way literally true that, in order to understand a sentence, I have to have been told what it means; still less that, in the course of having its meaning explained to me, I must expressly have been told under what conditions an utterance of it would be true.

Nevertheless, there is a sense in which sentences, not words, may be said to be the primary bearers of meaning. To understand a paragraph or a speech, in the sense of a continuous utterance by one speaker, is, to a first approximation, to understand in succession the sentences composing it. This is true only to a first approximation: it must be qualified in two distinct ways. First, there are the manifold respects in which an understanding of what is being referred to depends upon what has been said previously. This, though a pervasive and practically important feature, is a relatively superficial one. It would be easy to transform any given speech in such a way that the content of each sentence was rendered independent of its linguistic context; the result would be stylistically intolerable, and the transformation would therefore make a significant rhetorical difference, but the content of the speech would remain unaltered.

The second qualification concerns our apprehension of the relationship between the different sentences composing the speech. Some statements are made by way of illustration or example of what has preceded or is immediately to follow; some by way of concession or qualification to the principal contention; some are advanced as following logically from, or rendered probable by, those preceding it. To take in the contents of the individual sentences without perceiving any of these relationships would be to fail to understand the speech as a whole. Nevertheless, the thesis that an understanding of the speech consists of the successive understanding of the sentences composing it remains true as a first approximation, precisely because the question how the speaker was presenting the different statements that he made as related to one another arises only if an understanding of the individual sentences he uttered is attainable in advance of settling that question.

By contrast, it is not true, even as the roughest approximation, that to understand a sentence is to understand in succession the words that compose it. One can extract a sentence from a speech, and, after supplying whatever is necessary to determine what the speaker was referring to, one can assert that he said *that*. The result may be misleading, in that it gives a quite false impression of his drift, but the assertion is none the less true. One cannot in the same way extract a word, phrase, or clause from a sentence that someone uttered, and assert, in the same sense, that he said *that*. In the relevant sense, one does not, by the utterance of a mere word or phrase, say anything at all; one does not, in Wittgenstein's phrase, "make a move in the language-game". Though a clause of a certain kind may convey something that it would be possible, in this sense, to say, the mere utterance of the clause does not constitute saying it; the clause might be being uttered as one half of a disjunctive sentence, or as the antecedent of a conditional sentence.

To understand a word is to grasp its potential contribution to the meaning of any sentence in which it may occur. This is not to say that one cannot explain the meaning of any individual word without explicit reference to sentences containing it. It is to say that any explanation of its meaning rests upon a tacit understanding of the way in which a word whose meaning has been so explained can be used in sentences. For example, the meaning of a proper name can be given by saying that it is the name of a particular object; but such an explanation rests upon a prior understanding of what it is for a word to be a name, that is, how it can be used in a sentence in order to say something about the object for which it stands. In a similar way, one can state what a bishop's move in chess is without overt reference to its occurrence as part of a whole game of chess; but the explanation is significant only because it is understood against the background knowledge that a game of chess consists of alternate moves by the two players. Although the meaning of a particular word can be stated without overt reference to its occurrence in sentences, the adequacy and correctness of any such explanation can be judged only in terms of whether it gives a satisfactory account of the contribution of the word to the meaning of any sentence in which it may occur; if it does, no more can be asked of an explanation of the word's meaning, and if it does not, the explanation fails. For this reason also, we cannot say what it is, in general, for a word to have a meaning save by explicit reference to sentences containing it.

Any general account of meaning must therefore take as its fundamental notion some feature possessed by sentences and intuitively connected with their meanings. At first sight, the great variety of our sentences—by means of which we ask questions, give commands, make requests, offer advice, voice our hopes, and do many other things—makes such a programme appear impracticable. It appears less so if we follow the great majority of philosophers in believing the assertoric use of language to be primary; if we can once explain in what the meanings of assertoric sentences consist, we shall, they think, be able to explain the meanings of sentences by which we perform these other types of linguistic act in terms dependent upon our prior explanations of the meanings of assertoric ones. A variation on this approach is to distinguish, within the overall meaning of any sentence, its *sense* and its *force*: the sense of the sentence yields a description of a state of affairs, its force constitutes the conventional significance we wish to attach to our giving such a description. Thus an assertoric, an interrogative, and an imperative sentence may have the same sense in common; they differ in that the first is used to say that that state of affairs obtains, the second to ask whether it obtains, and the third to command that it be made to obtain. The task of providing a systematic account of meaning thus splits into two: that of explaining the sense, or, as we may say, the specific content, of each sentence, and that of explaining the different kinds of force that a sentence may carry. Most words are neutral as to force; a word like "sheep" can occur indifferently in an assertoric, an interrogative, or an imperative sentence, and bears the same meaning in whichever type of sentence it occurs. Such a word therefore contributes to the sense or the content of the sentence, and does not in any way determine its force. Force, on the other hand, relates only to the sentence taken as a whole. It is therefore within the theory of sense that we shall find the explanation of how the meaning of the sentence is determined from its composition out of individual words; the explanation of each particular kind of force must be such as to apply uniformly to an arbitrary sentence expressing a given sense. That is not to say that the theory of sense is required to be intelligible in isolation from the theory of force.

The distinction between sense and force is often criticized on the basis of a misunderstanding, namely that the proponents of the distinction believe that there can be such a thing as simply expressing a sense, devoid of any force, or even an entire language whose speakers utter sentences which carry certain senses without having any particular force attached to them. Such critics make observations of the kind "When I say, 'It is going to rain', I am not doing *two* things, expressing the thought that it will rain *and* asserting that that thought is true: I am doing only *one* thing". Since there is no general criterion for counting "things that I do", they support their dictum by psychological considerations: I am not giving external expression to two distinct mental acts, that of conceiving a thought and that of judging it to be true. We had better refrain at this point from remarking that there is no rule for counting mental acts, either: even if there were, it would not matter, since the distinction between sense and force is not intended as a contribution to any psychological theory, but as a strategy for giving an account of what it is for a sentence to have a meaning, and hence for it to be an utterance in a *language*. The whole point of the theory is that, for an utterance to effect a linguistic act, or to constitute a 'move in the language-game', or, in the appropriate sense, for it to be an instance of *saying* something, it must carry some force or other: for this very reason, there can be no such thing as simply expressing a sense without any force attached to the utterance. The ground of distinction lies, not in discerning two things that the speaker does, but in recognizing two types of ways in which he might be misunderstood. If, when a policeman says, "Come along with me", I were to reply, "Thank you very much, but I'm afraid I don't have the time", I should have mistaken an order for an invitation; but a foreigner might very well understand that he was being given an order, without knowing what he was being ordered to do. The strategy of making this distinction seems fruitful, indeed unavoidable, precisely because the specific content may be common to utterances of different types: if it were not possible for one person to invite me to do what another orders me to do, it would not be possible to mistake an order for an invitation.

The distinction between sense and force appears valuable just because there are so many different kinds of utterance we make, or of linguistic acts that we perform: we make assertions, ask questions, give orders, advice, instructions, make requests, express wishes. There could hardly be a language adapted to human beings by means of which it was possible to do only one of these things: but perhaps there could be beings very different from ourselves who employed such a language, something to which, however defective, we should not deny the title "language", as Wittgenstein imagined people who used language only to give commands. Apropos of such an impoverished language, would the distinction between sense and force be otiose? In an obvious respect, it would be: utterances would differ in meaning only along one dimension. For this very reason, however, an account of the practice of using that language would fall into two distinguishable parts, that which explained how various sentences differed in meaning and that which explained the common ingredient in the significance of all sentences. Consider a language used only to give commands. It would be part of the tacit understanding of the language by the speakers that, when any of them heard a sentence uttered by one in authority over him, he had to take appropriate action in accordance with the particular sentence uttered. One part of any account of the use of the language would therefore consist in a specification of the dependence of the action to be performed by the hearer on the composition of the sentence; but another part would explain the general background. It would state the relationships of authority recognized in the community, spell out the correlation between an utterance and the response of the hearer, and say whether this response was invariable or not, and, if not, what were the consequences of disobedience.

This more general part of an account of the functioning of such a language might be said to explain the force uniformly attached to all sentences. The meaning of a sentence does not reside solely in that which differentiates its meaning from that of other sentences of the language to which it belongs, but also in that complex of linguistic and non-linguistic behaviour which renders it significant at all. The meaning of any sentence may be said to consist in the potential difference made by any utterance of it to what subsequently happens; and a full account of a language must spell this out. Since we have the concept of a command, we could give an account of the language in which all utterances are commands by saying just that: having stated that every sentence has the force of a command, we could then go on to the other part of the account, in which the specific content of each such command is shown to depend upon the composition of the sentence. Such an account would be correct, but it would fail to *display* that in which the significance of each utterance consisted: what is needed, in order to do so, is an account which would be intelligible even to people who were previously unfamiliar with the institution of giving commands.

The notion of a command is not altogether clear-cut. "Get out of my room" and "Take your hands off me" may be allowed among us to be commands, because we recognize everyone as having a certain authority over who may enter his room and who may touch him; but "Look where you are going" and "Stop making such a horrible noise" are not properly called commands and yet are not phrased as requests. Despite such uncertainties, it does not seem deeply problematic to give an account of the practice of giving commands, precisely because they are utterances which call for a quite specific response and because their failure to elicit that response has fairly well-defined consequences. The assertoric use of language stands in the sharpest contrast to this. We hardly know how to begin to characterize the use of sentences to make assertions without employing the verb "to assert" or some synonym, such as "to say" or "to tell", used in the appropriate sense. This has little to do with the fact that, in order successfully to convey to someone that a certain utterance was assertoric in character, we should have to give him to understand what we were saying as being itself assertoric, so that he would have already to have an implicit concept of assertion. We experience no similar difficulty in saying what it is for someone to apprehend (hear or read) a sentence, even though, to communicate our formulation to anyone, we should have to bring him to hear or read it. Our difficulty is, rather, that we do not know how to say what it is that anyone must believe about the significance of an utterance if he is to take it as assertoric; and this means that we do not know how to say what it is to have the concept of assertion. It is for this reason that we are so prone, when it is the assertoric use of language that we have in mind, to appeal to the notion of truth in order to characterize meaning.

It was Frege who first drew the distinction between sense and force, and it was he who first made the notion of truth central to the explanation of sense. That is not to say that Frege had a theory of truth of the same kind as the correspondence and coherence theories. On the contrary, he argued that such a theory was impossible in principle, a thesis he expressed by saying that truth is indefinable. There is some obscurity in the claim that truth is indefinable. There is a persistent dispute over what sort of thing we should take the predicate "is true" as applying to, if, indeed, we ought to take it as a *predicate* at all. Now whatever it is that is properly said to be true or false, it certainly cannot, in general, be a sentence, since many sentences can be used now to say something true, now to say something false—such a sentence as "It is raining", for example. We ought, therefore, to speak in this connection of particular utterances of sentences. The dispute may then be phrased thus: should "true" be applied to utterances, or to what utterances express, or to what they stand for? Frege was well aware of the existence of sentences like "It is raining", but preferred, as have many other philosophers when discussing these issues, to write as if all sentences resembled "Water is a compound" in being true on all occasions of utterance if true on any. This proves highly convenient in avoiding long-winded formulations, and is usually harmless provided that we remember that it is strictly incorrect; we may therefore follow Frege's example, and ask whether it is of a sentence, or of what it expresses, or of what it stands for, that we should say that it is or is not true.

What a sentence expresses is a thought or proposition: it is that which is in common to all sentences, in the same or in another language, which have the same meaning. At first sight, it is odd to speak of what a sentence stands for, as if it were related to anything as the phrase "the capital of Denmark" is related to the city of Copenhagen. Frege, in his mature period, believed exactly that about sentences; but it is not necessary to adopt that view in order to admit the expression "what a sentence stands for". If we regard an expression as standing for whatever it is both necessary and sufficient to associate with it in order to determine every sentence in which it occurs as true or otherwise, then, if we set aside certain occurrences of it as deviant, "the capital of Denmark" indeed comes out as standing for Copenhagen; but, since sentences can occur as parts of more complex sentences, they too will stand for something. In Frege's own formalized language, and in any for which a classical two-valued semantic theory holds good, sentences stand for truth-values, that is, either for truth or for falsity.

It lies to hand to say that the dispute over what "true" applies to is of no significance. A sentence cannot be called 'true' unless it is understood as having a certain meaning. If, then, we regard "true" as applying primarily to sentences, there will be a derivative sense in which the thoughts they express may be called 'true', since, if a sentence is true, any other sentence that expresses the same thought must also be true. Conversely, if we take "true" as applying primarily to thoughts, there will be a derivative sense in which a sentence can be called 'true' if it expresses a true thought. Moreover, whether we adopt classical semantics or not, it is evident that, on the interpretation given of the phrase "to stand for", what a sentence stands for must be sufficient to determine whether or not it is true: for a sentence can certainly occur as part of a more complex sentence in such a way that, if it were replaced by another sentence with a different truth-value, the truth-value of the complex sentence would thereby be altered. Hence, if we have a sense, primary or derivative, in which a sentence can be called 'true', there will also be a further, derivative, sense in which what it stands for can be called 'true'. Conversely, if we take "true" as applying primarily to that for which sentences stand, there will be derivative senses in which sentences themselves, and the thoughts they express, can be called 'true'. In something of the same way, the predicate "human" applies to what, say, "Charles the Fat" stands for, and not to that expression or to its sense; but there are corresponding predicates, "personal name" and "sense of a personal name", which apply to the phrase and to its sense.

It does not follow from this that nothing is really at issue in this dispute. What follows is that what is at issue is not: Given that "true" is a predicate, to what sort of thing may it *legitimately* be applied? It is, rather: Given that "true" is a predicate, to what sort of thing ought we, in the order of explanation, to take it as *primarily* applying? Frege held strong, and slightly confusing, views on this question. He repeatedly said that it is a thought which is, in the first instance, said to be true or false, and that it is only in a derivative sense that we can say of a sentence expressing that thought that it is true or false. One of his reasons was that he regarded thoughts as existing timelessly and independently of whether we have any means of expressing them and of whether they are grasped by us or any other rational creatures; and part of his reason for *that* was that truth itself is timeless, since whatever is properly said to be true must be true or false absolutely, rather than true at any particular time. If it were sentences that were, in the primary sense, true or false, then we could not say of a natural law that it was true before it was formulated, whereas, Frege argued, it would still have been true even if it had never been formulated. All this appears to rank Frege with those who hold that "true" primarily applies to what sentences express; but this is only part of his view. He argued, further, that truth is not a property of thoughts, but, rather, stands in the same relation to them as that in which the city of Copenhagen stands to the sense of the phrase "the capital of Denmark". His ultimate view was, then, that truth primarily attaches to what sentences stand for; more accurately, in the light of his semantic theory, that truth just *is* what certain sentences stand for (the true ones), while falsity is what others stand for.

It is a peculiarity of Frege's mature theory that he did not regard the relation between a sentence or a thought and its truth-value as a mere *analogue* of that between a proper name or its sense and the object named, but as an *instance* of that relation. This was not part of any general assimilation of all expressions to names: he insisted that the relation between, say, a predicate or its sense and what it stands for is only the analogue of the relation between a proper name or its sense and its bearer. It is due, rather, to a special doctrine of Frege's concerning the grounds on which expressions could be categorized into distinct logical types, one that did not permit the discernment of a distinction of this nature between singular terms and sentences. This peculiar doctrine of Frege's is not important for our purposes: I mention it only to explain an unusual feature of Frege's formal language. This is, namely, that a sentence may meaningfully occur within a more complex sentence in any position in which a singular term might meaningfully have occurred. This makes the formal language very different from natural languages, as it already is in other ways; the divergence is justified by Frege on the ground that sentences stand, on his view, for one or other of two abstract objects, truth and falsity. As I already remarked, to hold that sentences stand for truth-values is not, in itself, to adopt this more radical view that truth-values are objects and sentences therefore complex singular terms of a particular kind: I do not mean to explore this perplexing claim, but needed to mention it in order to render some later remarks about Frege's formal language intelligible.

It is evident that, while Frege took a definite position in the dispute over what "true" primarily applies to, he was vividly aware of the possibility of explaining it as applying to any of the three types of candidate. Truth is not, for him, in the first instance a property of thoughts. There is nevertheless a property that a thought may have which is naturally expressed by saying that it is true. It might seem, from the foregoing exposition, that this property has to be explained in two stages, by invoking a sentence expressing the thought: a thought is true, in this sense of "true", if any sentence expressing it stands for truth. This is not so, however. Just as Frege held that the sense in which a sentence may be said to be true is derivative from that in which the thought it expresses is said to be true, so he also held that the sense in which an expression may be said to stand for something is derivative from a more primitive sense in which it is what the words express—their sense—which stands for that same thing: "the capital of Denmark" stands, in the derivative sense, for Copenhagen because the sense of the phrase stands, in the primary sense, for Copenhagen. What matters, however, is, first, that there *is* a sense in which a thought may be said to be true, and, secondly, that this is a sense to be explained in terms of the more primitive notion of truth as what a sentence or a thought stands for: a thought is true in this derivative sense if it stands for truth, just as a sentence is true in a tertiary sense if it expresses a thought which is true in the secondary sense.

The doctrine is one about the order of explanation, or, at any rate, the order of understanding. We could not grasp what it is for a sentence to be true if we did not regard it as expressing a thought and understand what it is for a thought to be true. In the same way, according to Frege, we cannot grasp what it is for a thought to be true unless we regard it as standing for something, and can distinguish, among the two things for which it can stand, truth from falsity. But we cannot go further than that: we have reached the basic level, beyond which explanations are impossible. Awareness of truth and falsity is implicit in the assertoric use of language: "these two objects", Frege wrote, "are recognized, if only implicitly, by everyone who judges something to be true".

It is not my purpose to resolve the question to what "true" primarily applies: it was introduced here only as bearing on the meaning of Frege's thesis that truth is indefinable. To say that, in a certain language, the number 0, for example, is indefinable is to say that one cannot construct in that language a singular term standing for the number 0, or, more broadly, that one cannot construct a one-place predicate true, under the intended interpretation of the language, of, and only of, the number 0. It was certainly not in this sense that Frege held truth to be indefinable. Nothing is easier than to construct, in his formal language, a singular term standing for truth: any true sentence of the language will serve this purpose. Nor is it difficult to construct a predicate true of, and only of, truth: "$x = (x = x)$" will fulfil that role, as Frege himself in effect pointed out. Indeed, there is no need to *construct* such a predicate: the horizontal stroke, one of the primitive predicates of the language, is interpreted precisely as being true of truth and false of everything else. In this sense, Frege's formal language may be said to have contained its own truth-predicate.

The horizontal stroke is not a truth-predicate in the sense in which that term is ordinarily used by logicians, namely a predicate true of, and only of, true *sentences* of the language. (The term "truth-predicate" is normally extended to cover an arithmetical predicate true of just those natural numbers which correspond, under a certain type of coding of expressions by numbers, to true sentences; for simplicity of formulation, we may here ignore such 'Gödel numbering'.) Frege's horizontal stroke is not true of true sentences, but, rather, of, and only of, what all true sentences stand for. Within a formal language, it is no longer a trivial matter to pass from a predicate representing "true" as applied to what sentences stand for to another one representing "true" as applied to sentences themselves. Even if Frege's formal language were supplemented by a vocabulary for referring to expressions of that language, we could not define from the horizontal stroke a truth-predicate in the standard sense, since we should lack any means of expressing in the language the relation between a sentence and what it stands for. This indeed preserves Frege's system from an additional ground of inconsistency, since it debars us from constructing within it semantic paradoxes such as that of the liar: but our present concern is to understand in what sense Frege held truth to be indefinable. "True" in the sense which Frege considered primary, as a predicate of what sentences stand for, is expressible in his formal language, and, even if not taken as primitive, would be definable in it. "True" in what he considered the derivative sense, as a predicate of sentences, is not expressible in it, principally because the language does not contain a means of expressing the relation between symbols and what they stand for: but it hardly seems that it can be to this that he was referring in calling truth indefinable. The derivative character of the notion consists precisely in its being explicable in terms of the more primitive one, an explanation we can give once we are freed from the constraints of the formal language and can avail ourselves of the notion of an expression's standing for something.

The notion of truth may be encountered, in connection with a formal language, in two different ways. We may be concerned, as in the foregoing discussion, with its expressibility within the language; or we may use the notion in order to lay down how we intend the language to be interpreted. The importance of the latter role is entirely independent of the degree to which, or the sense in which, truth is expressible *within* the language. Even though the language does not itself possess the resources for expressing the notion of truth, we may want to use that notion in order to characterize the intended meanings of its sentences; conversely, if we decide that we do not want to use the notion for that purpose, our decision need not be altered by its expressibility in the language. The distinction does not depend upon its being a *formal* language with which we are concerned. We should not be debarred from applying the predicate "true" to utterances in a natural language by the fact that that language contained no word translatable as "true" and no form of sentence equivalent to an ascription of truth to an utterance. It was plainly that notion of truth which we employ in speaking *about* a language, in order to characterize the meanings of its sentences, rather than that which is expressed *within* the language, that Frege held to be indefinable.

Why should we so much as think of employing the notion of truth in order to state the intended interpretation of a formal language, or the received interpretation of a natural one? In explaining the meanings of the words and expressions of a natural language, our usual method is to give rules for translating them into the language in which the explanation is given, and, in doing so, we have no need of the word "true" save as the translation of a word of the object-language. It was in connection with formal languages that this method was first replaced by a different one: partly because a formal language may have a syntax so different from the natural language used for explaining it that only approximate translations would be possible; and partly because, when we want to prove something *about* a formal language, the notion of one expression's 'meaning the same as' another is a flabby instrument. For these reasons, it is preferable to state the intended interpretation of the formal language *directly*, rather than via the corresponding expressions of English or German. To state its interpretation directly involves eschewing the phrase "means the same as" or even, when speaking of whole sentences, its equivalent, "means that . . .", in the *oratio obliqua* construction: the object is to specify the meanings of expressions of the language without *using* the notion of meaning, but, rather, by laying down those properties of expressions in virtue of which they will have the meanings that they are intended to bear. The result is a semantic theory for the language; and Frege, the first to devise a formal language in the modern sense, was also the first to construct such a semantic theory. A semantic theory for a formal language is not, however, merely a convenient alternative means of specifying an interpretation for a symbolic system which we wish to handle in a more precise mathematical manner than that in which we treat of natural languages: it is a model for what might in principle be done for all languages.

To put a speaker of, say, English in a position to interpret some other natural language, a system of translation is unquestionably the most efficient means. To the extent that the modes of phrase- and sentence-formation in that language differ from those of English, a few grammatical notions, such as that of a transitive verb or of a subordinate clause, will be needed: but they will still be used to frame rules of translation. In knowing English, the student thereby knows what English expressions mean; and, if he does not already understand the phrase "means the same as", he is likely, in the process of learning the other language, to come by a grasp of the concept it expresses. His having grasped that concept would be shown by his asking a question like "How (in the other language) do I say, 'I shouldn't do that if I were you'?"; here "say" means "say something meaning the same as". Just because this process rests upon a tacit grasp of the concept of meaning, however, it can throw no philosophical light on what meaning is: as Davidson has insisted, to explain an expression as having the same meaning as another is not to say what it is to have that common meaning. If we want to attain a clear view of what it is for the words and expressions of a natural language to have the meanings they have, we must know, in principle, how to specify the correct interpretation of such a language without appeal to the notion of meaning; to do so will require us to single out and characterize those features of its expressions their possession of which constitutes their meaning what they do.

Such a theory of meaning for a natural language fulfils a role similar to that of a semantic theory for a formal language. It will, however, be very much more complex. The least important reason for this is that natural languages themselves are vastly more complex than formal ones; other reasons spring from the fact that a theory of meaning must be explicit in a way that a semantic theory need not. A semantic theory for a formal language serves as a practical means for laying down the intended interpretation of that language; it may therefore take for granted whatever the reader may be presumed already to know. A theory of meaning for a natural language is, by contrast, a purely hypothetical entity. No one proposes actually to construct one, or to use one for teaching a foreign language: the only point of considering what form such a theory would in principle take is the philosophical one of throwing light on the concept of meaning and that of a language. A theory of meaning must therefore be conceived of as taking nothing for granted: to the extent that it did, it would be failing to provide the elucidation that constituted its entire purpose.

There is a further evident difference. A semantic theory for a formal language is used to *stipulate* the intended interpretation of the language; but a theory of meaning for a natural language purports to explain how it is actually understood. The semantic theory conveys the intended interpretation of the formal language by laying down what determines as true any given sentence of that language. A reader unfamiliar with the word "true" would not gain from those stipulations a knowledge of how to interpret the language, or even a realization that it served as a *language*: an actual reader will do so precisely because he has a tacit grasp of the connection between the meaning of a sentence of any language and the conditions which determine it as true. That this connection cannot be left tacit by a theory of meaning for a natural language, but must be spelled out, follows from the general necessity that the theory of meaning be fully explicit; but it also follows from the need to explain when such a theory counts as being correct. We could not decide the correctness of a theory of meaning for a natural language simply by asking the speakers. The speakers will certainly not know a theory of meaning for their language in advance; they cannot even be presumed to be able to recognize one as correct when presented with it. It is useless to discuss what form a correct theory of meaning would take if we do not know what would justify us in judging it to be correct: we have therefore to determine the relation between such a theory and the observable practice of the speakers in using the language.

Some philosophers and linguists attribute to a speaker of a language an implicit or tacit knowledge of a theory of meaning which constitutes his knowledge of the language and from which he derives his understanding of its expressions, that is, his knowledge of their meanings. Others reject the concept of tacit knowledge altogether. Three distinct positions are commonly advanced:

(1) Knowledge of a language is a genuine piece of knowledge, albeit tacit or unconscious knowledge, which issues in and explains its possessor's practical competence in using the language.

(2) We may legitimately attribute to a speaker a tacit knowledge of a theory of meaning, but, in doing so, we are not *explaining*, but merely *characterizing*, his practical competence, his possession of which simply constitutes his tacit knowledge of the theory.

(3) Understanding a language does not amount to knowing anything at all, in the sense of knowing something to be the case: it is simply a practical ability, namely to use the language and to respond appropriately to the utterances of others when couched in it.

Between (2) and (3) there appears little more than a difference of terminology; (1), on the other hand, is puzzling. Unconscious knowledge can explain an ability only if its possessor is able to avail himself of it; how, then, can he avail himself of knowledge that he is unaware of possessing? In common discourse, we indeed speak of knowing a language, and treat "knows the meaning of" as synonymous with "understands"; but it is natural at this stage to enquire why we should be disposed to invoke the notion of knowledge in connection with the ability to speak a language. A proponent of position (3) might reply that it is due solely to the empirical fact that no one can speak a language unless he has learned to do so, just as it is likewise an empirical fact that no one can swim unless he has learned to do so (although this is not the case with dogs); we therefore have the same justification for speaking of "knowing how to swim". Now it is common to all three positions that they ascribe to a speaker a certain practical competence lacked by those who do not know the language. Within a practical ability there may, in general, be distinguished a theoretical as well as a practical component. The skill of a ballet dancer, for example, involves not only the ability to perform certain movements of which those not so trained are incapable—the practical component—but also a knowledge of which movements to perform, which is the theoretical component; someone who was a natural ballet dancer in the sense that he could, without any training, execute *fouettés* and the like as soon as he was shown them would, until he was shown the steps, possess only the practical component of the ability and not the ability itself.

One might be tempted to assimilate the practical component to the theoretical one by representing it as a knowledge of what strictly bodily movements—what muscular contractions—would bring about certain desired effects on the motion of the body. The picture here is of an agent as operating the efferent nerves as a signalman operates his levers, the muscles corresponding to the signals on the track and the limbs and torso to the trains controlled by them. The temptation to make this assimilation should be resisted: the dancer is largely unaware of the muscles he is using, but knows, in a straightforward, conscious manner, what steps he has to execute.

Some practical abilities, no doubt, have only a practical component, and others only a theoretical one (for example, the ability to solve Rubik's cube).

Speaking a language has a small practical component, namely the ability to pronounce it correctly; but what interests us is the theoretical component— knowing *what* to say, in the sense of what sounds to utter, rather than knowing how to make those sounds. It is precisely the large theoretical component in linguistic competence that prompts us to describe it as an instance of knowledge. The practical component of a skill could not be acquired by reading a book or otherwise gaining theoretical knowledge; but, by its nature, the theoretical component can be so acquired. It does not follow from this that anyone who has the theoretical component in question actually has the relevant explicit knowledge; someone may be able to "see" what rotations are needed to bring one of the small cubes into its correct position on Rubik's cube without disturbing certain others, and yet be unable to explain the principles he follows. What cannot be supposed is that he does not follow a system capable in principle of being codified and so known explicitly.

This explains why it is so compelling to refer to the ability to speak a language as "knowledge", in a sense more serious than that in which we talk of "knowing how to skate", and to characterize it as implicit knowledge, as on position (2), or to postulate unconscious knowledge to account for it, as on position (1). It may nevertheless seem remarkable that proponents of none of the three positions attempt any direct characterization of linguistic competence, but speak only of the theory of meaning for the language, a theory which is the object of possible knowledge. This failure might seem the least reprehensible on the part of proponents of position (1), since they after all believe that a speaker actually does know the theory of meaning, although only unconsciously; but in fact the failure weakens the credibility of their claim. On their account of the matter, the speaker's tacit knowledge of the theory *explains* his linguistic competence; to evaluate such a claim, we need to be told what are the deliverances of that unconscious knowledge. To exercise a practical ability with an exclusively theoretical component is not, after all, to engage in a species of automatism; the subject, even if unable to state the principles that guide him, is acting quite consciously. We therefore need an account of how unconscious knowledge is supposed to operate; and, to judge whether or not it would explain linguistic competence, we need a description of what precisely linguistic competence consists in.

At first sight, the appeal to knowledge by proponents of position (3) is even less defensible, since they deny that linguistic competence involves knowledge in any sense whatever. If, however, ability to speak a language were just like an inarticulate skill with Rubik's cube, their appeal to knowledge would be entirely justified. Someone who has a skill of this kind acts *just as if* he had a certain body of knowledge: there is therefore nothing problematic in characterizing his skill in terms of the knowledge which would be one means of acquiring it. This is precisely what advocates of position (3) propose as a means of characterizing linguistic competence: namely by stating what body of knowledge someone would have to have if he were to possess such competence by virtue of having that knowledge. If someone explicitly knew a correct theory of meaning for a given language, he would be able to understand any sentence of the language, and hence, if he could apply his knowledge with sufficient rapidity, could use the language himself and comprehend the utterances of others. Speakers do not normally have such knowledge, explicitly or implicitly: but, by stating what someone would have to know if he were thereby to be able to understand the language, we characterize what it is that a speaker is able to do.

This would in most cases be an indisputably reasonable procedure, precisely because there would be no difficulty in converting the enunciation of the given body of knowledge into a description of what someone who has the ability actually does. Thus a description of a sequence of dance steps may serve equally as a means of stating what someone does when performing that dance and as a representation of the body of explicit verbalized knowledge which would enable anyone with the requisite agility to perform it. The same applies to a statement of a strategy, or set of strategies, for solving Rubik's cube. These cases differ from that of language, in that either, as with the dance, there is no purpose requiring explanation, or, as with Rubik's cube, the purpose is independently statable and is known explicitly to the agent.

This may also be said to hold for someone's knowledge of a second language: the object is to produce in that language equivalents of sentences of his mother tongue. So regarded, his knowledge of the second language is explicable as a mastery of a scheme of translation; it is therefore comparable to the other instances of a skill with a largely theoretical component which we have been considering. The same does not hold for his knowledge of his mother tongue. It is constitutive of its being a language that his production of sentences in it is not, like scat singing, devoid of further purpose. The purpose of uttering a sentence, for instance, "I seem to have lost my spectacles", is not, however, one that can be grasped independently of the means used to attain it, namely the use of language. One may first grasp the objective of making every face of Rubik's cube uniform in colour, and subsequently discover or learn a means of doing this; but we do not begin with a conception such as that of informing another of a fact, and then, when we learn language, acquire a method of doing so. Rather, the general purpose and effect of each utterance are part of what we learn when we learn our mother tongue.

For this reason, it is difficult to resolve the dispute about the role of knowledge in an account of linguistic competence: the dispute will be easier to resolve when we have a better understanding of the relation between what is, or might be, known and the practice it explains or characterizes. It is precisely because linguists and philosophers of language do not know how to cast a theory of meaning into such a form as to yield a direct description of linguistic practice that they feel compelled to appeal to the conception of the speaker's knowing such a theory, actually but implicitly or hypothetically and explicitly. The question how such a theory could be converted into a description of the speaker's practice is the same question as that which we asked earlier in a slightly different form: How are we to judge from the observable practice of the speakers of a language whether a proposed theory of meaning is correct?

A semantic theory issues, as we have seen, in a specification of the condition for any sentence of the language to be true; but it leaves the connection between truth and meaning tacit. Theories of meaning for natural languages are usually conceived of in the same way. They may, as in my opinion they should, be more explicit in their accounts of individual words of the language, though not all philosophers of language would agree with that requirement. They may also contain means of differentiating sentences according to the type of force attached to them, which a semantic theory for a formal language does not need. But they are ordinarily thought of as distinguishing the specific contents of sentences—their senses, in Frege's terminology, as opposed to the force attached to them—by what determines them as true. When so conceived, the connection between truth and meaning is usually taken as already understood, just as in a semantic theory of the standard kind. We have to make this connection explicit in explaining how such a theory is to be evaluated by reference to linguistic practice. A natural suggestion is that the theory is confirmed if competent speakers come, by and large, to recognize sentences as true by steps that match those by which they could be determined as true by someone similarly placed but with an explicit knowledge of the theory of meaning. The qualification "by and large" is needed in order to allow, on the one hand, for errors and inattention, and, on the other, for hunches and guesses, wild or inspired; the consequent vagueness is unavoidable. It has, however, to be explained what is meant by a speaker's "recognizing a sentence as true": the language need not itself contain a word for "true", and, if it did, there would be a question about the appositeness of so translating it.

On the face of it, this poses no very great problem. The theory of meaning will presumably indicate a basis on which certain utterances are to be classified as assertoric, either by the form of the sentence uttered or by the tone, manner, or circumstances of its utterance. Independently of his personal motives, a speaker makes an assertion by uttering an assertoric sentence in the appropriate circumstances and manner; his asserting a sentence is to be taken as expressing his recognition of it as true. Hence we may simply equate a speaker's recognition of a sentence as true with his willingness to assert it. Of course, we shall not always know which sentences a given speaker would be willing to assert, other than those he actually does assert and those to which he gives some conventional sign of assent when asserted by others; but such an uncertainty is intrinsic to any inductive enterprise rather than an objection on principle to the matching of theory with practice. The theory of meaning has, indeed, so far been correlated only with assertoric utterances, but it may be presumed that this lacuna can be filled: the utility of the sense/force distinction appears to depend upon its being relatively easy to explain the significance of non-assertoric utterances once the meanings of assertoric ones are known.

To many philosophers of language, an account along these lines offers the definitive solution to the problem of meaning. A theory of meaning takes the form of one laying down what determines any sentence of the language as *true*: and the notion of a sentence's being true is connected with the linguistic behaviour of the speakers in that an assertoric utterance of it is to be construed as expressing that the speaker takes it to be true. Whether or not we view this as a satisfactory solution depends upon what ambitions we conceive on behalf of a theory of meaning; and that in turn depends upon what we regard as being 'the problem of meaning'. It is indeed arguable that a theory of meaning confirmed in this manner by the practice of the speakers determines the meaning of each sentence uniquely and correctly. It is clear, on the other hand, that it falls far short of giving an account of what is involved in speaking a language: it is not an adequate theory of the phenomenon of language.

To see this, imagine first two sheep-dogs, each of which, when guarding the fold on his own, has been trained to emit a distinctive kind of repeated bark if any of the sheep escape; he then tries by himself to round up the sheep, continuing to give the bark until the shepherd arrives with the other dog. To the shepherd, this special bark means "Sheep have escaped from the fold; come and help": but does the sheep-dog mean this by the bark? That would depend upon how he would behave if he were off duty and he heard his colleague giving the same bark. If he was completely unresponsive, he could surely not be said to attach that meaning to the bark: it would be significant only for the shepherd. If, on the other hand, in the absence of the shepherd, he went to give aid to the dog raising the alarm, or, in his presence, prepared to do so, then we could reasonably say that he understood the bark just as the shepherd did.

The same would apply to a small child beginning to acquire language. Suppose him to have acquired the habit of responding to certain observable situations by suitable one-word utterances: others can then use his exclamations as an extension of their own sensory equipment. If, for example, the child says "Pussy", his mother, in the next room, will know that the cat is in there with him. Now can we say that, in saying "Pussy", the child means "There is a cat here"? If the child cannot respond suitably to that utterance when made by others, we cannot say so. Suppose, for instance, that the child is afraid of the cat: before he enters a room, his mother tries to warn him that the cat is there by saying "Pussy", but he takes no notice, comes in, and then becomes alarmed on seeing the cat. In such a case, he does not take "Pussy" as meaning "There is a cat here", but has merely acquired the habit of saying that in response to the sight of a cat.

Now we can imagine a set of adult speakers who are capable of handling assertoric sentences of arbitrary complexity. Let us suppose them capable of going through all the procedures of observation and theorizing, including deductive and inductive inferences, which we employ in ascertaining the truth of sentences; but all they ever do, having established a sentence to be true, is to assert it; in no other way does it affect their behaviour. Here the content of any of their sentences is taken as determined by the manner in which they establish it, in accordance with the proposal already made for justifying a putative theory of meaning. Though these speakers arrive quite correctly at conclusions, they never apply them: they may, for instance, assert a substance to be poisonous, but show no reluctance to eat it. We must suppose that, having established a sentence as true, one of these people will retain it as a truth for use in subsequent inferences; but, while in this respect a *judgement* will have an effect, we may take the principle that an *assertion* has no effect on them in a stricter or a laxer sense. Taken strictly, it will entail that an assertion made by one of them will not add to another's store of truths; taken in a weaker sense, it will allow one speaker's assertions to affect the purely linguistic behaviour of another, in that he accepts it as true and uses it in deriving further truths, provided that each individual's stock of truths in no way affects any of his non-linguistic behaviour: he never acts on what he knows.

Obviously the individuals in this strange community do not speak a language in any ordinary sense: their utterances do not engage with the rest of their activities. Evidently, then, the practice of the speakers of a language, properly so called, must satisfy a further condition if a proposed theory of meaning is to be an adequate representation of the meanings of its sentences. Alternatively expressed, in taking a theory which specifies what determines each sentence as true to constitute a theory of *meaning*, we are presupposing that the speakers satisfy this further condition as well as that concerning how they establish their sentences as true. This further condition is that the speakers act in accordance with the truth of those sentences they take to be true. Our problem is now to explain what 'acting in accordance with the truth of a sentence' may be.

The apparent intractability of this problem is due to a subtle illusion. If we set aside sentences containing so-called evaluative expressions, we can say that what counts as establishing the truth of a sentence is independent of the speaker's particular desires and motivations. It has been repeatedly observed, by contrast, that there is no one course of action consequent upon accepting such a sentence as true: how that affects someone's behaviour will depend crucially upon what his aims are. If we continue to ignore the matter of 'evaluative' expressions, this is perfectly true: but it is a confusion to see it as posing an obstacle in principle to explaining the effect upon action of accepting a given sentence as true. The confusion is due to the error of thinking that any explanation must treat each sentence on its own in isolation from the rest of the language.

It has come to be widely accepted that it is an error to do this when treating of how sentences are recognized as true; the first philosopher to point this out clearly and cogently was Quine in his celebrated article 'Two Dogmas of Empiricism'. The logical positivists had committed precisely this error. Holding that the meaning of a sentence is to be explained in terms of the means by which it can be verified, they applied this principle to each sentence taken by itself, as if it could exist, and have the significance that it has, without the language in which it is embedded. The means of verification must therefore be described independently of the use by the subject of any other sentences; it had accordingly to be taken to consist of one of a set of sequences of sense-experiences. This obviously yielded an account of meaning bearing no recognizable relation to what is actually involved in a speaker's understanding of a sentence. In particular, it allowed no basis for a distinction in meaning between any two analytically equivalent sentences, that is, sentences whose equivalence is demonstrable by deductive reasoning, however complex. It also created a problem about the meanings of logical and mathematical statements: the positivists solved this problem by declaring them to have a meaning of a kind so different that it became little more than a pun to ascribe meaning both to them and to empirical statements.

It was Quine who showed the way out of this impasse. A speaker understands a sentence because he understands the language: we shall therefore arrive at an accurate account of his understanding of the sentence only by appeal to his understanding of other parts of the language. In general, a sentence is recognized as true on the basis of inferential reasoning of some kind, involving the use of other sentences. Hence inference must be treated as an integral part of what in practice counts as the verification of a sentence: logical and mathematical statements are therefore not a special case, but, at most, a limiting one, in which nothing but deductive inference enters into the verification. Furthermore, in explaining the meaning of any given sentence, we do not need to describe the entire route from the infantile *tabula rasa* to the establishment of that sentence, but have only to explain it relatively to the understanding of those sentences from which it can immediately be inferred. If the understanding of a mathematical statement be said to consist in a knowledge of what would count as a proof of it, it becomes obscure how we can understand such a statement without knowing whether, and how, it can be proved: but if our understanding resides in our ability to arrive at it by means of a single inferential step, it ceases to be perplexing that we often do not know whether it is possible to construct a sequence of such steps leading ultimately to it from what we have already established; and the same holds for empirical statements.

An account of this kind looks as though it might be entrapped within language, allowing no place for the impact of sensory perception; but that is a danger Quine has always guarded against. According to him, the language will contain a small class of sentences constituting a limiting case of the opposite kind, namely ones for which the original positivist account is more or less correct: the verification of these observation sentences will consist solely of the occurrence of certain sense-perceptions (including, we may add, observations of the result of some procedure of testing, measurement or counting). Another danger in such an account is that of circularity: the meaning of a sentence is explained in terms of the meanings of other sentences, whose meanings will in turn be explained in terms of those of yet further sentences; there is an evident risk that a path in this tree will lead back to the original sentence. Quine himself does not see this as a serious danger: he inclines to a holistic view of language, according to which the full explanation of the meaning of any sentence will involve an explanation of the entire language. It is far from obvious that such a holistic thesis can avert the danger of vicious circularity; but circularity can be avoided if we adopt a hypothesis that would probably not be to Quine's liking, namely that sentences are to be graded by degree of complexity. On such a hypothesis, an explanation of the meaning of a sentence may presuppose the meanings only of sentences of lower complexity, and will perhaps be given simultaneously with the explanation of certain sentences of equal complexity: it will never involve explaining or presupposing the meaning of any sentence of higher complexity. An understanding of any sentence will involve, on this hypothesis, an understanding of some fragment of the language, a fragment which could, moreover, exist as a language on its own; but an explanation of the language as a whole could be constructed without circularity by starting with sentences of minimal complexity (the observation sentences) and completing the explanation of sentences of any degree of complexity before proceeding to the explanation of those of the next degree.

If this conception is clearly borne in mind, it will be apparent that there would be no greater difficulty in giving a corresponding explanation of meaning in terms, not of how we establish sentences as true, but of what are the consequences for a subject of accepting them as true. To construct such an account, we do not have, for each individual sentence, to survey all the ultimate consequences acceptance of it may have for the actions of an individual, any more than, in explaining meaning in terms of verification, we had to survey all the steps which in any one case might ultimately lead to establishing it. All we need to do is to explain the *immediate* consequences of accepting the sentence as true, again presupposing the meanings of other sentences. Dually to the former case, the immediate consequence of accepting a sentence as true will most usually be the inferential derivation, from it and other sentences already held to be true, of the truth of yet further sentences. Just as, on the verificationist account, the connection with observation was made only at certain particular points, so here the connection with action will be made only at certain points. The judgement by a given individual that a particular sentence is true may not, even in the long term, influence any of his actual actions, possibly including linguistic ones: its only actual consequences might be further judgements which he does not communicate. It always has, however, a potentiality for doing so.

The duality is, indeed, imperfect. Let us call a sentence the acceptance of which has as an immediate consequence an action or sequence of actions by the subject an 'action sentence', by analogy with 'observation sentence'. Many quite ordinary sentences, such as "If you touch the stove, you will burn yourself", would qualify as action sentences under this characterization; but it is easier to think of them as taking a special form, such as expressions of intention like "I will not touch the stove". An observation sentence is determined as such by its meaning, given the character of our perceptual faculties, though there is some variation between individuals, as with the blind, the deaf, those literate in various scripts, and the altogether illiterate. The important difference between the two cases lies in the fact that the point at which a chain of consequences terminates in action depends in large part on the aims and objectives of the individual subject.

It would not be so if all our desires were basic common ones—to avoid pain, preserve our life, and the like; but different people obviously have varying projects and ideals that cannot be accounted for as alternative strategies for reaching common goals. For this reason, the quality of being directed towards action cannot be restricted to the action sentences. The subject's objective may be statable only in a sentence of some complexity, incapable of being directly acted upon: actions result only when recognized as means to the end. We might, therefore, think of the action sentence as expressed, rather, in normative form, say as "The stove is not to be touched": if so, such normative sentences may have figured in several previous steps of the deduction, not themselves action sentences. Thus, in a manner to which there is no analogue in the case of verification, this normative character may be thought of as injected by a sentence expressing an objective of the subject at a stage that may be comparatively remote from the point at which the chain of consequences terminates in action.

This disanalogy with the earlier case is no impediment to the explanation of meaning in terms of consequences. The meaning of a sentence, as understood alike by all the speakers, is, when so explained, a function with arguments of two kinds: the subject's desires, and the other truths he accepts. Its value is a set of consequences, in action and in judgement, both factual and normative. The arguments vary from one speaker to another; the function itself remains the same for all. We are not, in this context, concerned with the celebrated inductive problem of determining beliefs and desires from actions, a problem residing in our having to solve simultaneously for two unknowns. Quine and Davidson have dramatized the philosophical problem of language by imagining how one might arrive, from observation of the speakers, at an interpretation of a hitherto unfamiliar language. The practical difficulties of doing so are, however, only obliquely germane to the philosophical problem how we may elucidate what it is for utterances in a language we in fact understand to have the significance we know them to have. We know what beliefs and what desires our fellow speakers have, in so far as they express them, because we understand the language; our problem as philosophers is to say in what our understanding it consists. Quine's well-known indeterminacy thesis suggests that, if we can find one theory to elucidate this, then we could find a distinct theory which would fit the observable behaviour of the speakers equally well, but would involve attributing to them different beliefs and desires. Now, given any two such theories, the speakers could be asked if either represented their understanding of the language better. If they preferred one, it seems unlikely that they could not give grounds for their preference in terms of what they would say or how they would respond to what others said; if they found them equally acceptable, it seems likely that analysis could reveal a sense in which they were equivalent. If neither of these two resolutions of the dilemma were available, the situation would indeed reveal that both rival theories of meaning had some superfluous content in excess of what is required for characterizing the speakers' understanding of the language; but it seems better to deal with such a crisis only when it actually occurs than to draw morals from a conviction of the possibility of its occurrence.

If we want to avoid circularity in an account of meaning in terms of the consequences of accepting a sentence as true, we must observe the same principle as in the other case: relative to suitable assignments of degrees of complexity, an explanation of the meaning of any sentence can presuppose the meanings only of sentences of lower complexity, and can be given simultaneously only with the meanings of those of the same complexity. Assignment of degrees of complexity is severely constrained by the principle that an understanding of a sentence is derived from its composition: we understand a sentence because we know the meanings of the words and the significance of the ways in which they are combined. This principle is not only intuitively evident, but inescapable in view of the fact that a theory of meaning cannot give the meaning of each sentence outright, since there are potentially infinitely many sentences of the language and the speakers are able to understand sentences they have not previously encountered: the theory therefore has no option but to lay down rules governing the individual words and the various modes of phrase- and sentence-composition from which the meanings of all possible sentences can be derived. For this reason, a compound sentence must always have a higher degree of complexity than any subsentence occurring in it; there is only limited latitude in the assignment of degrees of complexity.

From this it follows that, when the meaning of a sentence is explained in terms of the manner in which we establish it as true, the only inferences that can be taken into consideration are those that lead from premises of lower complexity to conclusions of higher complexity. Conversely, when we explain meaning in terms of consequences, the only inferences considered are those leading from sentences of higher complexity to those of lower. It may be objected that we often come to recognize a sentence as true by means of an argument not all of whose steps are of the first kind, from less complex to more complex; indeed, if it were not so, there would be no such thing as drawing from a given sentence accepted as true the consequence that some simpler sentence is true, as is demanded for an account of meaning in terms of consequences. The converse objection can likewise be made to the restriction upon an account of the second kind. What reply is to be made to these objections?

What we have been considering are two alternative ways of explaining the meanings of the sentences of a language: in terms of how we establish them as true; and in terms of what is involved in accepting them as true. They are alternative in that either is sufficient to determine the meaning of a sentence uniquely; but they are complementary in that both are needed to give an account of the practice of speaking the language. Because either fully determines the meaning of a sentence, these two features of the use of a sentence cannot be assigned independently: given either, the other should follow. There ought, that is, to exist a harmony between these two features of use: it is principally because in the actual practice of speakers such harmony may be imperfect that customary linguistic practice is not sacrosanct or self-justifying, but may be open to criticism.

When the meaning of a sentence is given in terms of the manner in which that sentence may be verified, what is cited is the most *direct* means of verification. A direct verification, in the sense here intended, is one which corresponds step by step with the way in which the sentence is built up out of its constituents, and so with the way in which the truth-value of the sentence is represented by the theory of meaning as being determined in accordance with its composition. For example, if the meaning of the connective "or" is taken as given by the rule of disjunction-introduction, a direct verification of a disjunctive sentence will involve the verification of one of the two disjuncts. Likewise, a direct verification of a sentence like "There are nineteen eggs in the basket" will consist of counting. No one asked to explain how we verify this latter sentence would cite anything else; and yet one can certainly establish it as true in a variety of indirect ways; for instance, from the fact that the shopper who bought them and nothing else started with £9.73 and has £6.12 left, together with the fact that the eggs were of uniform price and cost more than 1p and less than £1 each.

For all sentences other than observation sentences, we have seen that inferential reasoning will play an indispensable part in establishing their truth; but all that are strictly needed for this purpose are inferences leading from simpler to more complex sentences. Once the meanings of sentences are given in terms of the most direct means of verifying them, however, the meanings so given themselves justify the use of indirect means, because of the interrelation between the means of verifying different sentences. If the direct verification of one or more sentences would involve the verification of some simpler one, then if, on whatever basis, say that of testimony, someone has accepted the former sentences as true, he is entitled to accept the simpler one as true also. More generally, if we have a recipe for transforming the verification of one sentence into the verification of another, we are entitled to conclude the truth of the latter from that of the former; such a recipe is precisely what is supplied by a constructive proof.

For this reason, to explain meaning in terms of direct verification is not to deny that indirect verification is possible, but to indicate why it is justified. In particular, it allows us to derive, from the meaning as so given, what is involved in accepting a given sentence as true: for to derive consequences from its truth is just a special case of an indirect verification of those consequences, up to the point when they issue in action. The converse also holds good. An explanation of meaning in terms of consequences takes into consideration only the most *direct* consequences, in an analogous sense. Such an explanation will, however, justify the drawing of indirect consequences: given certain sentences, accepted as true, we shall be entitled to infer any other sentence, any consequence of which would already be a consequence of the given sentences. Among such indirect consequences will be inferences, from less to more complex, of precisely the kind that occur in a direct verification. Hence, if the content of each sentence is given in terms of the consequences of accepting it, that will determine, for each sentence, what should count as verifying it. In this manner, whichever of the two features we take as constitutive of meaning, we can explain the harmony that ought to exist between them and, in virtue of that harmony, derive the other feature.

In the course of the foregoing discussion, a shift of perspective occurred which the attentive reader will have noticed. We began by considering a theory of meaning as laying down the condition for each sentence to be true, and our question was how, by appeal to the observable behaviour of the speakers of the language, such a theory might be judged correct. Identifying someone's taking a sentence to be true with his willingness to assert it, we distinguished two criteria of correctness: how the speakers establish or come to recognize sentences as true; and how so recognizing them affects their subsequent course of action. In discussing these two features of linguistic practice, however, we passed from treating them as providing the standard for evaluating a theory of meaning to regarding them as supplying its substance. From this second viewpoint, we have, not two complementary ways of validating a theory of meaning couched in terms of a sentence's being true, but two alternative types of theories, one couched in terms of a sentence's being established as true and the other in terms of its being treated as true.

The advantage of a theory of either of these last two kinds is that we do not need to ask how to connect it up with linguistic practice: it is framed in terms of linguistic practice. Hence, if a theory of either kind can be devised so as to yield a faithful account of our actual practice, it is preferable to one for which the connection needs still to be made. In such a case, we do not need, for the purposes of a theory of meaning, any such predicate as "is true", but only the predicates "is established (as true)" and "is accepted (as true)", where the parenthesized phrase has no independent meaning. We may very well continue to have a use for the predicate "is true" *within* the language, something easier to explain but of much less philosophical interest. But could a successful theory of either of the two kinds be devised? We cannot say, because we are a long way from solving the many problems of devising a workable theory of meaning of any kind. But, if it should prove impossible to construct a theory of meaning of either of the two kinds, that will almost certainly be because either type of theory would give an inadequate account of our deductive practice: it would license some, but not all, of those forms of inference we customarily treat as valid. If so, and if our deductive practice is to be vindicated, there will be no choice but to fall back on a theory of meaning of the first kind we discussed, one in which essential use is made of the predicate "is true".

To my mind, such an outcome would pose a deep and perplexing problem. We should be falling back on such a theory precisely because we found it impossible to construct one framed directly in terms of a feature of actual linguistic practice. It would seem to follow that the truth-conditional theory on which we had fallen back could not be fully justified by reference to that practice: it would, of its essence, reach beyond it. The theory would, indeed, supply an explanation of our practice, both of what we take as establishing our sentences as true and of what we treat as being the consequences of accepting them. Inasmuch as it explained these features of our linguistic practice, they in turn could be claimed as confirming the theory: but the fact that, by hypothesis, we could not recast that theory in terms of either of these two features would show that its content comprised more than a systematization of our practice.

It might be retorted that, on the hypothesis considered, it would have been yet another feature of our linguistic practice, namely the forms of inference we employ, that had forced us to fall back on the truth-conditional theory of meaning. This, however, is precisely the difficulty. We are not free to employ whatever forms of inference we choose, by convention, to count as valid: our linguistic practice will be incoherent unless we use only those forms of inference for which the assertion of the conclusion is as justified as the assertion of the premisses, according to the meanings of those sentences, however their meanings are thought of as having been given to us. Inferential practice must be faithful to meaning. The hypothesis is that we cannot justify all the forms of inference we use in terms of meaning taken as given in terms of verification. It follows that meaning cannot be taken as so given, unless we are in error in using certain forms of inference: for, by using them, we arrive at conclusions which we could not verify directly even given direct verifications of the premisses. Further, according to the hypothesis, we cannot justify all the forms of inference we use in terms of meaning taken as given in terms of consequences. It again follows that meaning cannot be taken as given in this way, unless our reasoning is, in part, in error: for, by using certain forms of inference, we shall be drawing conclusions the consequences of which would not flow from the premisses. The hypothesis therefore entails that, although deductive reasoning is part of our practice, it cannot without modification be justified by appeal to that practice: it can be justified only by imputing to us a grasp of meaning amounting to more than a grasp of the principles governing our use of the language.

The understanding of the language thus imputed to us will rest upon the notion of a sentence's being true, a notion which, by hypothesis, is not fully explicable in terms of what we actually learn to do when we learn to speak. We, as speakers of the language, will be presumed to have, for each sentence, a conception of what it is for it to be true: it will be in our grasp of that conception that our understanding of the sentence will consist. In applying this assumption to any one particular sentence, say "There are intelligent beings on a planet in the Andromeda galaxy", we do not need to employ the word "true" itself: to grasp what it is for that sentence to be true is just to grasp what it is for there to be intelligent beings on a planet in the Andromeda galaxy. This observation is sometimes made with an air of dissolving any difficulty there might seem to be in imputing such a conception to us; but this is to miss the point in two separate respects. For, first, the word "true" is not eliminable in stating the general assumption, which is what is required in characterizing our understanding of the language as such; and, secondly, the elimination of the word "true" in the particular case does not dissolve the difficulty. The difficulty is one of which some people find it hard to become aware: surely, they think, there can be nothing tendentious or paradoxical in ascribing to someone who understands the sentence quoted above a grasp of what it is for there to be intelligent beings on a planet in the Andromeda galaxy; asked if you knew what it was for that to be so, you would reply "Yes" simply on the strength of your understanding the sentence. To dismiss the matter thus is to ignore the hypothesis under which the whole of the present discussion is proceeding. That hypothesis, applied to the particular case, was that knowing what it is for there to be intelligent beings on a planet in the Andromeda galaxy cannot be exhaustively explained in terms of knowing what would establish that there were such beings, or in terms of knowing what consequences would follow from accepting that there were such beings, or from any other feature of our employment of the sentence: it would be a substantial conception, but no further explicable. It is in the context of that hypothesis that the assumption that we have such a conception of what it is for a sentence to be true becomes opaque; for my part, rather than accept that assumption, I should prefer to believe that some of our accustomed modes of reasoning are unjustifiable and ought to be abandoned.

I do not wish to be misunderstood. I am not asserting that the notion of truth, as employed in the theory of meaning, cannot be wholly explained in terms of those of verification and of consequences. I hope very much that it will prove to be able to be so explained; that would constitute a final resolution of the philosophical problem of truth. If, however, the notion of truth can be explained in terms of those notions, it can also be *replaced* by them, and would be better so replaced. More exactly, in such a case a truth-conditional theory of meaning could, and preferably should, be replaced by one in terms of verification or of consequences. If this cannot be done, we have the alternative of accepting, as essential to an account of our understanding of our language, a notion of truth which in principle resists complete elucidation, or of admitting radical error in accepted modes of reasoning. Perhaps fortunately for our peace of mind, we are not yet in a position to say whether we need face this choice or not.

6

Truth and Meaning

A first consideration of language leads us naturally to ask whether language is prior to thought or thought to language. We have made some progress when we come to see that this question is neither so straightforward nor so fundamental as it seems at the outset. A first move to dispel its deceptively plain appearance is to distinguish between temporal priority and priority in the order of explanation. It is conceivable that thought is prior to language in the order of explanation, but not in the order of acquisition. Its priority in the former regard would involve that, in order to explain what it is for words and sentences to have the meanings that they do, it is necessary to invoke notions relating to the thoughts the speaker uses them to express, or that they call up in the mind of the hearer. For instance, on such a view, it might be that we cannot explain what it is for a proper name or demonstrative phrase to refer to an object save in terms of someone's having a thought about that object: "refer to" is therefore to be explained in terms of "think about". Such a priority of thought over language in the order of explanation requires that we can give an account of what it is to have a thought of a given kind—for instance, what it is to be thinking about a particular object—without reference to the thinker's possessing the means of expressing his thought in words. It therefore implies that it is in principle possible for a being not in possession of a language to have such a thought. But it is quite consistent with that to suppose that an individual's acquisition of the capacity to use a language is always temporally prior to his acquisition of the capacity to frame full-fledged thoughts, or, indeed, that the same is true of the human race as a whole. It might be that it is only the acquisition of the means of expressing thoughts that triggers in us the capability of framing the thoughts so expressible. Something like this must have been the view of Frege, who held that human beings are capable of grasping thoughts only as expressed verbally or symbolically, but that it is no contradiction to suppose that there are beings who grasp the same thoughts as we do, without clothing them in sensible form.

Some gloss is here needed on the expression "full-fledged thoughts". Evidently, some mental activity takes place even in an infant, in the strict sense of a child who has not yet acquired language. Equally evidently, we have to ascribe some desires, beliefs, intentions, and plans to animals. That, in itself, is not enough to justify crediting either infants or animals with such thoughts as

Delivered as a lecture in the Cognitive Science seminar series in Oxford in 1985.

can be expressed in language and attributed to those who command a language. The desires and beliefs of an infant or an animal have, of course, a content; but, in almost every case, there will be non-equivalent formulations of this content, to none of which it will be possible to award a preference, since there is nothing in the behaviour of the infant or animal that could ground the distinction between one way of specifying the belief or desire and another. Furthermore, it will often be the case that *any* formulation will be erroneous, in that it involves the ascription of concepts that the infant or animal cannot possess. An excellent example of Frege's illustrates this vividly. He raises the question whether a dog can "have even an indeterminate idea of what we signify by the word 'one' "; and he says of the dog, in answer:

He will certainly notice a difference between whether he has to defend himself against several other dogs or only against one, but this is only what Mill calls the physical difference. The question depends, rather, on whether he has so much as a dim awareness of that which is in common between the cases in which, for example, he is bitten by one larger dog and in which he chases one cat, that common feature which we express by means of the word "one". This seems to me unlikely. (*Die Grundlagen der Arithmetik*, §31)

It is not, of course, a matter of what is likely or unlikely: the point is, rather, that the dog's behaviour falls far short of requiring, for an adequate description of it, the attribution to him of any recognition of the common element between those two and other situations describable by sentences containing the word "one". His behaviour would have to become immensely more complex to provide a basis for ascribing to him a grasp of the concept "one": indeed, if it were to do so, he would be at least on the verge of an ability to manipulate symbols. And yet, he *can* distinguish, as Frege acknowledges, being attacked by one dog from being attacked by several. We can perfectly well imagine that, on a certain route, he is liable to be attacked by one or more of several dogs that frequent that neighbourhood, and that he adopts a policy of standing his ground if there is only one of them, but retreating if there is more than one: he might cautiously look about to make sure that there really was only one. We should naturally say, "He is looking to see if there is one or more": but, properly speaking, this is not an accurate rendering of the dog's thought, since it would be impossible to have just *that* thought without grasping the concept "one". We have no way of rendering the dog's thought accurately: not merely do we not have such a rendering ready-made in our language, but we cannot even devise one. We cannot do so, because the dog does not have a thought expressible in language: he engages in some mental process that falls short of having the kind of thought a language-user is capable of having.

In addition to all this, the proto-thoughts of which a creature without language is capable—at least a creature of any of the kinds familiar in our experience—can occur only as integrated in his current activity, realized or frustrated: they cannot float free, as adult human thoughts can do. On our ability to entertain thoughts detached from current activity depend not merely science and literature, but casual conversation, as we engage in it for companionship and on social occasions. I do not mean to deny that animals can intelligently and even reflectively devise a means to an end: Köhler's chimpanzee is a clear counter-example. I mean, rather, that the thoughts of which an infant or an animal is capable occur only in the course of, and as contributing to, present activity: he cannot, as a human adult can, suddenly be struck by a thought or get lost in a train of thought. A man may come out of his front door, walk purposively along the street, and then suddenly stop and return to his house: he has remembered something he had forgotten to do, or thought of something it would be a good idea to do. An animal cannot do that; nor can an infant: but quite a small child is capable of it, and it marks a profoundly important stage of development.

I do not mean to suggest that it is either easy or uninteresting to give an account of the mental processes of infants or of animals. Quite the contrary: it is intensely interesting and very difficult, just because of their differences from our own thought-processes. I wish only to stress these differences. When we discuss the relation of thought to language, we are concerned with those thoughts that can be expressed in language. Compared to these, the thoughts of infants and of animals are only proto-thoughts. They can be expressed in words only to a rough approximation: such an expression will almost always be both too precise and too rich to render their content correctly. Moreover, such proto-thoughts, however complex, cannot transcend the context: they can occur only as ingredients in, and as governing, present action; for otherwise, in the absence of language, they would have no vehicle. For these reasons, it is immensely plausible that, for human beings, full-fledged thought—thought that can be faithfully expressed in language—cannot temporally precede the acquisition of a language in which to express it. But, as I have argued, this temporal priority by no means settles the question of conceptual priority. The ability to use language may trigger the capacity to grasp and entertain thoughts, and judge them to be true, without its *constituting* that capacity: for all I have said, it is still open to us to hold that fundamental ingredients of the meanings of words can be explained only by appeal to features of the thoughts we express by means of them.

If what I have said against the temporal priority of thought over language be rejected, the case for its conceptual priority is strengthened: but, even so, the relationship between them is subtle. It is overwhelmingly natural, at first glance, to take it as quite crude: to conceive of a language as a system for encoding thoughts. We cannot, in Oxford, shout loud enough to be heard in London, and, for that reason, we need the telephone: likewise, according to the code conception of language, we need language merely because we happen to lack the faculty to transmit thoughts directly from one mind to another. Since we cannot naturally be heard in London, the sounds we utter, if we are to speak to someone there, must first be encoded by the microphone into electrical impulses, which can be transmitted along the telephone wires to the hearer at the other end; similarly, on this view, since we cannot transmit thoughts directly, we have first, if we are to communicate them, to encode them into something that can be transmitted, sounds or visible marks. Just as the telephone receiver in London decodes the electrical impulses into a simulacrum of the original sounds, so, on this conception, the person we address, our hearer or reader, decodes the sequences of spoken or written words into thoughts which mirror ours.

Despite its superficially compelling character, the code conception of language is irremediably lame. Its deficiency opens up the converse possibility, namely that, even if thought is after all temporally prior to language, language retains the conceptual priority, understood in a weak sense. It can retain it in a weak sense, at most, if thought has the temporal priority: for, in the latter case, since full-fledged thought can occur in the minds of those who have as yet acquired no language, it must in principle be possible to give an account of what it is to have a thought without reference to any linguistic means of expressing it. To deny this possibility would be to maintain the conceptual priority of language over thought in the strong sense: but it remains open to us to hold that, even if some individual has full-fledged thoughts before he acquires any mastery of language, an appeal to his having those thoughts is useless in explaining what makes the language that he learns a means of expressing thoughts. Rather, an account of language—that is, of what constitutes the possession by the words and sentences of the language of the meanings that they have—must begin *ab initio*: that is to say, it must, for an individual who already had, or was capable of having, the thought that he has subsequently learned to express in words, take the same form as it will take for one who has acquired the capacity to think those thoughts simultaneously with the capacity to express them.

What opens up this possibility, and provides a fatal obstacle to the code conception, is the complexity of thought, already illustrated by Frege's example of the dog. Having a thought involves possession of its component concepts: only one who knows what a thief is, and what it is to hide, can have the thought that a thief is hiding in the garden. To be able to have such a thought, he must, therefore, be capable of having other thoughts concerning thieves, and of suspecting or knowing other people or animals to be hiding. That is why it is appropriate to require the dog to have the concept "one", and to be able to have other thoughts involving that concept, if he is to have the thought that he is being attacked by one other dog. If each thought could be grasped as an unarticulated whole, the mastery of a code associating thoughts with sounds or written marks would be relatively unproblematic: the association could resemble that postulated by the empiricists between words and mental images, namely that, when either occurred to us, the other came to mind. But a plausible account of language as a code must establish an association, not merely between sentences and complete thoughts, but between words or phrases and concepts: and, while there is undoubtedly such an event as a thought's occurring to someone, a concept is not the kind of thing of which it makes sense to say that it comes before the mind. A word or an image or the like which expresses or symbolizes that concept may indeed come to mind; but we have then still to explain that association between it and the concept which constitutes its expressing or symbolizing it. The concept cannot come before the consciousness naked and unadorned, not because there is some psychological law inhibiting it from doing so, but because there is no mental process that could reasonably be so described: and so we cannot postulate, between it and some audible or visible expression, a connection that resides in a mechanism of mental association of each to the other.

A language has two functions, as an instrument of communication and as a vehicle of thought. One of the questions facing the philosophy of language is to determine which, if either, is the more fundamental: is it because a language can be used as a vehicle of thoughts that it can also be used to communicate them, or is it, rather, because it is fitted to communicate thoughts that it may serve as the vehicle of an individual's thinking? The code conception of language represents it as needed solely for the purpose of communication: it therefore adopts the strongest form of the view that that purpose is the more fundamental. In adopting this view in so extreme a form, it makes it unintelligible how language *can* be a vehicle of thought; indeed, how there can be such a thing as a vehicle of thought. For it represents thinking precisely as what Wittgenstein so strenuously denied it to be—an inner process which, when speech occurs, *accompanies* the external act of speaking. In such a case, the speech is not the *vehicle* of the thought, which takes place independently of it, but only its outward expression, as inessential to the occurrence of the thought as are the words of the simultaneous translation to the making of the speech which they serve to render intelligible to certain members of the audience. Now, if the spoken words addressed to another are not the vehicle of the thought, then those uttered in soliloquy or rehearsed silently in the mind cannot be its vehicle, either. The thought is then not embodied in the words, whether silent or spoken aloud, in the sense that the act of thinking coincides with that of speaking or mentally framing them. Indeed, if the sentence is an encoding of the thought, and the words composing it code-symbols for its constituent elements, there could be no such thing as thinking in words, any more than it would be possible to make a sound *by* sending electrical impulses along the telephone wire: it would not make sense to conceive of thought as having a vehicle.

Our problem is to explain what it is for a word to *express* a concept. Since the code conception is manifestly untenable, we have to ask whether, in explaining the expression of a concept by a word, it is necessary, or even possible, to make use of the hypothesis that, before he becomes a user of the word, the subject is a master of the concept. We have left unresolved the question whether language is to be explained in terms of thought, or thought explained in terms of language: but we are in a better position to regard the latter possibility as open. In both cases, we require a theory of meaning—a theory explaining in what the meanings of the words of a language consist; but the demands of that theory will be greater or less according as it is presented by what we may call a theorist of language or a theorist of thought. The theorist of thought believes it possible to analyse the structure and character of thoughts independently of the forms of their linguistic expression, and believes it legitimate to appeal to this analysis in explaining linguistic meaning: the theorist of language may deny the possibility of the analysis, and in any case denies the legitimacy of the appeal to it. They can agree to a large extent. They may, for example, agree, concerning a member of the class of singular terms— those words and expressions that serve to pick out particular objects to which we wish to refer—that the linguistic function of even the simplest of them is not exhaustively described as consisting in its referring to a certain object, but that, to understand what is said by the utterance of a sentence containing the term, the hearer must think of that object in a particular way. They differ in how they construe this requirement. The theorist of thought believes that he can explain the notion of thinking about a specific object, and that of thinking of it in a particular way, without reference to language; and he believes, further, that, in learning the language, we are somehow guided to grasp the convention that the use of a certain word requires us to think of an object in some particular way and not another. For the theorist of language, conversely, the notion of thinking of an object in a particular way has to be explained in terms of the employment of one, rather than another, linguistic means of referring to it. He is thus spared the task of attempting to characterize thought independently of its expression; but he has to explain, solely in terms of the use of the language, what it is for a word or expression to refer to or pick out an object, and how there may be different means by which different expressions pick out what is in fact the same object. The disagreement between the two theorists is profound, but it is, so to speak, only profound: when they discuss matters of detail, they may employ the very same formulations; only the foundations of their theories differ.

I said at the outset that we have made a significant step forward when we grasp that the question whether thought is prior to language in the order of explanation, or conversely, has less importance than appears at first sight. The theorist of language faces the formidable task of explaining what, in our employment of language, constitutes the expression of a thought by a sentence, and of doing so without presupposing what it is to have a thought:

his account of what it is for us to take a sentence as meaning what it does will serve as his account of what thoughts are. But the theorist of thought faces an equally formidable task, and, moreover, a very similar one. If we think otherwise, that is only because, by the weight of the philosophical tradition, we suppose that the alternative to analysing thought in terms of its expression is taking it for granted as unproblematic, adopting the attitude that we all know what thoughts are. But the theorist of thought cannot just take the conception of thoughts as given: he has to have, precisely, a *theory* of thoughts, on top of which a theory of meaning—of how sentences express thoughts—is to be built. The theory of thought must explain what it is for someone to have a thought, just as the theory of meaning aims to explain what it is for words and sentences to have the meanings they do. At some point, the account given by the theorist of language must diverge from that given by the theorist of thought in more than the obvious way that the one is talking about sentences and their constituents, and the other about thoughts and their constituents. They will diverge radically if the theorist of thought does not conceive of thoughts as requiring a vehicle, much less so if he thinks they cannot be grasped in their nakedness. But, despite the eventual divergence, the two types of theorist may go much of the way together; and this is why the priority issue is far from being the most urgent.

It took a long time in the history of philosophy for it to be sharply realized that we need to explain what a thought is; partly, I suppose, because, when we do realize that, we feel at a loss how we can begin to explain it. My use of the phrase "a thought" is due to Frege. Before him, it was conventional to speak, not of thoughts, but of judgements—the interior correlates of assertions; but, though much was said about different kinds of judgement, and a certain amount about their structure and the concepts they involved, there was no theory about what a judgement *is*, or what it is to make a judgement. In opposition to the tradition of talking about judgements, to which Bolzano alone had not been a party, Frege insisted that, of what we can judge to be true, we can also consider whether it is true, wonder whether it is true, and the like: different such mental acts, to use a phrase Frege eschewed, may have the same content. This is the analogue of saying that sentences of different forms, for instance assertoric and interrogative sentences, may have the same content: the assertion propounds as true precisely that of which, by means of the question, we ask whether it is true. This content is what Frege called the thought. What makes the distinction between thought and judgement inescapable is that a thought may be a component of a more complex thought, just as a sentence may form a clause within a more complex sentence: even when the complex thought is judged to be true, the component thought is not, in general, thereby also judged either true or false. If we do not draw some such distinction, we shall be in danger of finding a deep mystery in the fact that most words bear exactly the same meanings whether they occur in assertoric, interrogative, or imperative sentences; we shall also find difficulty in explaining why, for example, an imperative cannot be inserted in the antecedent clause of a conditional, but can form one of the two clauses of a disjunctive sentence. We have, indeed, to seek an informative characterization of judgements and of assertions: but this characterization must allow for a precipitation from the judgement or the assertion of its content, as something that can be the content of some other mental or linguistic act. We must say, therefore, that a large ingredient of the meaning of a sentence must be that which Frege called its sense, namely that which determines the content or thought, independently of what he called the force attached to it, determining it as assertoric, interrogative, or the like. The indication of the force may also be an ingredient of linguistic meaning: but it must be regarded as separable from the sense.

What, then, distinguishes thoughts from other constituents of our mental life, from mental images, ideas, feelings, desires, impulses, and the rest? That was the question Frege asked, and was the first to strive to answer: and his first step towards an answer was to say that thoughts, and only they, are apt for being characterized as being true or as being false. An image or a conception of something may be more or less faithful to that of which it is an image or a conception, but it cannot, itself, be meaningfully said to be true or false: what is true or false is the *thought* that it is, in this or that respect, faithful to its object. It always makes sense, of itself, to say of a thought that it is true or that it is false; and whatever it makes sense to describe as true or as false is a thought.

This beginning certainly hits on something essential. It is a touchstone for the success of an account of thought by the theorist of thought that his explanation should display what makes thoughts bearers of truth-values; it is likewise a touchstone for the success of a theory of meaning offered by the theorist of language that it should so explain our use of assertoric sentences as to exhibit utterances of them as bearers of truth-values. Frege did not, however, rest content with singling this out as a feature of thoughts distinguishing them from other objects of mental activity: he converted it into an account of what constitutes a thought. It matters little, from the present standpoint, whether we see this account as a contribution to a theory of meaning or to a theory of thought. Let us take it as the basic principle of a theory of meaning. A theory of meaning has to rest upon a syntax, that is, upon an analysis of the structure of sentences as put together out of their constituent parts. Given a language, there may be alternative syntactic theories relating to it, equally acceptable as yielding the principles by which sentences may be recognized as well formed: but some of these theories may provide a basis for a workable theory of meaning, while others do not. Any theory of meaning must require sentences to be analysed in such a way that their constituents make uniform contributions to the meanings of all sentences in which they occur, with due allowance for ambiguities and for words and expressions with distinct uses. On Frege's theory, these contributions must take the form of something that subserves the determination of the truth-value of each such sentence: what does not subserve this is no part of the sense of the expression in question. Sentences are not, of course, mere strings of words, but consist of different types of expression made to fit one another, and so compose the sentence, in various ways: and the expressions of different types will contribute to fixing how the truth-value of the sentence is determined in different ways, according to their type.

I have here spoken of "the truth-value of the sentence", as Frege frequently did, whereas, of course, it is well known that many sentences—those containing indexical expressions—may be used on one occasion to say something true, and on another something false. Frege was well aware of this, and understood his notion of a thought as involving that, in such a case, different thoughts are expressed: the sentence alone does not suffice to determine the thought expressed. This should be taken into account in a precise statement of the theory; but, for convenience, I shall continue to speak of the sentence as being true or false, or as expressing a true or false thought.

This thumb-nail sketch might make it seem that anyone who understood the components of the sentence and the manner of their composition must thereby know whether the sentence is true or false, a mistake Frege was never tired of repudiating. It is avoided because the theory has two tiers: just as the sentence both expresses a thought and possesses a truth-value, so each constituent expression has both a sense and what I shall call a *value*. The term "value" neither represents a literal translation of Frege's term in German (*Bedeutung*), nor is the standard rendering of it: I choose it as neutral between various controverted alternatives. The value of an expression is that whereby it contributes to the determination of the truth or falsity of the sentence. For instance, a proper name contributes by picking out a particular object: once that object is identified, no further consideration of which proper name was used, or by what means the object was associated with it as its bearer, is relevant to whether the sentence is true or false. Likewise, a (one-place) predicate contributes by being true of certain objects and false of others; given which it is true of, and which it is false of, nothing else matters for the determination of the truth-value of the whole. But these are things of which a speaker who knows the language may be unaware. More exactly, they are not the sort of things of which he may properly be said to be aware. He cannot simply know, of an object, that it is the bearer of a certain proper name, or that a certain predicate is true of it, or anything else about it: here, by "he cannot simply know", I mean that that cannot be the *complete* account of any piece of knowledge that he has. He can know something about an object only as picked out in some particular way, or as thought of in some particular way. How these notions are to be spelled out will be a point of disagreement between the theorist of language and the theorist of thought, but that need not concern us here: both can agree with Kant's dictum, to which Frege was always faithful, that every object must be given to us in some way, and can agree, too, that to be aware that an object, taken as given in a certain way, satisfies a certain condition is not thereby to be aware that it does so when it is taken as given in some other way. The sense of an expression, then, is, for Frege, precisely a particular way in which its value is given. *That* is something that the speaker can grasp. It is in virtue of his grasping the senses of expressions of the language that he knows the language, and is capable of apprehending the thoughts expressed by its sentences; and it is in virtue of the fact that those expressions bear the senses that they do that they have the values, in our technical sense of "value", that they do. Someone who has learned the language knows how the truth-value of each sentence is determined, and thereby knows under what conditions it is true; and, Frege says, the thought it expresses is the thought that those conditions are fulfilled. The sense of each constituent of the sentence is the contribution it makes to the expression of that thought: and this contribution consists in the manner in which the value of that constituent is given to one who has learned the language.

This is a very powerful and attractive theory: in its essentials, it remains that to which more people are attracted than to any other, and also that which has been most satisfactorily worked out in detail. I have stated it as a theory of meaning; but it can readily be adapted by the theorist of thought. So adapted, it says that a thought consists in a particular complex manner of apprehending a certain condition, that, namely, for the truth of the thought. This manner of apprehending the condition can be analysed into components each of which constitutes a particular manner of determining what we earlier called a value, for instance an object or a property, where a property is conceived of as something each object either has or lacks. The condition is then yielded by the structure revealed by that analysis, that is, by how the components fit together to form the whole: for instance, in a simple case the condition may be that the object given in a certain way has the property given in a certain way. All the theorist of thought has had to do in order to adapt the theory was to strip away the reference to the linguistic items: where, for instance, the sense of a name consisted in a particular manner of determining an object as the bearer of that name, the corresponding ingredient of the thought is now taken to be a particular manner of determining an object. The fundamental point at issue between the theorist of thought and the theorist of language is whether it is coherent to strip away the vehicles of sense in this way. For the theorist of language, the relevant condition is the condition for the sentence to be true, but, for the theorist of thought, it is simply a condition, not a condition *for* anything. He may, indeed, say that it is the condition for the thought to be true, as I said in explaining his view; but, if so, he is describing the thinker as apprehending a condition for the truth of the manner in which he apprehends that condition; and it is dubious whether the circularity does not render the description unintelligible. For our purposes, however, this question may be left in abeyance: all that matters is that we have a powerful and attractive theory that can be adopted, in one or other form, by the theorist of thought and by the theorist of language.

The theory has, however, one large defect. This defect is the price paid for the initial distinction between thoughts and judgements, or between the sense of a sentence and the force attached to it: it is that, while the theory explains meaning or thought-content in terms of truth and falsity, it does not say what truth and falsity are. Frege proclaimed truth to be indefinable; he contented himself with the plea that everyone who makes a judgement must know what truth and falsity are. Such an evasion is not tolerable. If philosophical elucidation has any value, a distinction must be drawn between our being able to say something and our knowing what precisely it is that we are saying. The initial distinction between judgement and thought, or between assertion and the mere expression of thought, appeared as a preliminary to an account both of judgements and of mental acts of other kinds, capable of sharing their contents with judgements, or of both assertions and of other linguistic acts likewise related. Frege's account explains thoughts in terms of the notions of truth and falsity, which quite evidently relate primarily to judgements and assertions: unless they are viewed as so related, there is no saying which is truth and which falsity. And then he in effect declares that no account of judgements is possible: for, if truth and falsity are unanalysable, nothing can in general be said about what it is to recognize a thought as true or to assert it to be true.

In order to say anything illuminating about the concept of truth, then, we must link it with that of judgement or of assertion. How can these links be displayed? A judgement or an assertion may be correct or incorrect: it is correct if the thought which is its content is true, incorrect if that thought is false. Plainly, we can in practice directly manifest our grasp of this connection only in circumstances in which we can recognize the thought as true, or in which we may reasonably take the condition for its truth to obtain; and so a first approximation to an account of the notion of truth is to be arrived at by describing in which circumstances a given thought can be recognized as true, and in which we are entitled to treat it as such: for instance, when a speaker is deemed to have had sufficient warrant to assert it. The unique character of judgements lies, however, in their having a further significance than merely being right or wrong: they build up our picture of the world. A philosophical account of the making of judgements which displayed it as no more than a skill, like playing darts, to be acquired and improved, would for that reason be utterly inadequate: a judgement has an enduring importance lacked by the throw of a dart. A judgement is the formation of a belief or the acquisition of a piece of knowledge; and this is manifested by our acting on what we know or believe.

The same is apparent in our mastery of language. A child in the earliest stages of acquiring language is trained to say certain things—"Doggie", for instance, or, somewhat later, "Doggie is asleep"—in certain recognizable circumstances: and the adults are not, at that stage, much interested in whether his remarks have point or relevance, but only in whether he makes them in the *right* circumstances, those that warrant them. But if his ability to do this exhausted his linguistic competence, he could not yet properly be said to *say* that anything was so, such as that a dog was there or that the dog was asleep, any more than a dog that has been trained to bark in a particular way when he sees his master approaching the house can properly be said to be saying that his master is approaching. Both the child and the dog serve as extensions of others' sensory apparatus; but neither can be conceived as making assertions until the relation becomes reciprocal, so that they also become capable of acting on statements made by others. The child normally acquires the two capacities simultaneously, though gradually; the dog usually lacks the second altogether. If there were two dogs who had undergone the same training, and one spontaneously reacted to the other's barking in a special way as to his master's coming home, by getting out his slippers or the like, we should then have a ground for imputing to him the beginning of a language: he is really treating that bark as an assertion.

An account of the link between judgement or assertion and truth therefore requires a characterization, not only of the notion of recognizing a thought or statement as true, but also of that of accepting a thought or statement as true. This means giving an account of what one commits oneself to by making a given judgement. In the linguistic case, we may indifferently look at the matter from the standpoint of the speaker or the hearer: what the speaker commits himself to by his assertion is the same as how the hearer manifests that he takes it as true. Accepting a statement as true involves modifying what one is subsequently disposed to say and do accordingly: it is that which the child has to learn, for the statements in his linguistic repertoire, in addition to learning when he is entitled to make them. The immediate consequence of accepting some statement, or some thought, as true may be to draw some conclusion from it: ultimately, acceptance must issue in action.

Our attitude to testimony forms the most striking refutation of an individualistic epistemology or theory of meaning. Testimony resembles memory in that neither route to knowledge requires a backing. In exceptional cases, when I have particular ground for doubting the reliability of my memory, I may reason that I am unlikely to have remembered *this* event as happening unless it actually did; but it is impossible that, in general, beliefs based on memory should be the result of an inductive inference from the occurrence of the memory-experience, since, without the knowledge memory affords, we should at no stage have anything resembling a basis for such inferences. Likewise, in special cases, one may reason about the probability that what someone says is true, when there is particular ground for suspecting him to be misinformed or lying; but it is impossible that all that we know on the authority of others should be based on such an assessment, since, again, without that knowledge, we should be so ignorant that we should have no basis for estimating the probability that a statement made by another is evidence for its truth. In the general case, remembering something is reason enough for supposing it to have happened; more exactly, there is not sufficient gap between the two for the first to be a reason for the second. In just the same way, understanding someone as asserting that something is so is, in the general case, reason enough for taking it to be so; more exactly, there is not sufficient gap between the two for the first to be a reason for the second. One of the things we have to learn, in learning to use language, is to act appropriately in the light of what we are told; this presupposes that, in normal cases, the question whether to accept it will not arise.

From these sketchy and programmatic remarks, it is unclear whether the programme envisaged can be carried out, or, if so, how. How is the concept of truth related to the composite notions of recognizing-as-true and accepting-as-true? Is it possible, from them, to arrive at the full-fledged notion of a statement's *being* true? Or ought we to say, with Frege, that there is no relation between them, that being true is utterly different from being taken as true and cannot be explained in terms of it?

All goes back to Frege's separation of the act of judgement from its content, or the assertoric force of the sentence from its sense. That appeared as a necessary strategic move; but it threatens to obscure the goal of the strategy. A theory of thought ought not to be concerned only with the *content* of mental acts such as judging, wondering, and supposing, nor a theory of meaning with what is in common between an assertoric sentence and the corresponding interrogative: for there is no way of regarding a thought save as the content of one of those mental acts, nor a meaningful utterance save as effecting one or other linguistic act; one cannot simply *have* a thought, and one cannot simply *express* one, either. A theory of thought must therefore comprise an account of the various mental acts that have thoughts as their contents, and a theory of meaning an account of the different uses to which sentences may be put. Frege, having separated sense from force, provided a theory of sense, and there stopped short: he gave no theory of force, or even indicated whether, or how, one was to be attained. Whether by his example, or through a natural tendency, we are in danger of forgetting what is required of a successful theory, either of thought or of meaning.

A theory of thought must give an account of whatever is involved in the activity of thinking; a theory of meaning must describe the *practice* of speaking a language. This demands, in particular, that the theory of meaning must be able to explain every feature of that practice that depends, intuitively, solely on the meanings of the sentences involved. We invoked the notion of the grounds for making an assertion, or judging a thought to be true, and that of the consequences of accepting a statement or thought as true, as a first indication of how a theory of sense, based on the conception of a thought's being either true or false, could be expanded to a full-fledged theory of thought or of meaning: since they are linked with the assertoric use of language, whereby judgements are expressed, it is surely via them that the notion of truth can be linked to that of judgement. This is surely correct: we need those notions, or something close to them, if we are to give a description of our use of our language, considered as a conventional practice in which we progressively learn to engage as we learn to speak. Nevertheless, we need at this stage to stand back and reconsider our entire strategy of explanation.

The different features of linguistic practice are linked to one another. For instance, one such feature is that of engaging in deductive argument; and the deductive connections that we acknowledge as obtaining between statements are not independent of what we treat as determining those statements as true: we could not simply choose to treat a statement of a certain form as a deductive consequence of others, while demanding, for it to be true, a condition that might remain unfulfilled when those for the truth of the premisses were satisfied. It is for this reason that it is natural, and not erroneous, to regard our sentences as having unitary meanings from which the different ingredients of the use we make of them *flow*. If logical relations between statements are thus regarded, not as being among the things in terms of which their meanings are *given* to us, but as flowing from those meanings, considered as given in some other way, such as the conditions for their truth, room is left for someone to fail to perceive a generally acknowledged deductive relation, without its following that he has failed to understand the sentences. I said that it was 'not erroneous' to conceive of meaning in this way, rather than that it was 'mandatory' or 'correct', because I do not think that we have any sharp everyday notion of what belongs to the meaning of a word or sentence and what is merely a consequence of that meaning: whether we count someone as knowing its meaning depends on whether he knows about it what is generally known and regarded as important, and this varies from instance to instance. It is the task of the theorist to systematize the allocation of meaning, both as between individual words and as between what he deems to constitute the central core of meaning and what he counts as among its consequences. The only constraint is that the theory of meaning that he proposes for a given language must comprise, or directly entail, all that a completely competent speaker of the language is required to know, and nothing that does not follow solely from that.

The theorist of meaning must therefore select some one feature of sentences as that in terms of which he will regard their meanings as being given, and construe the meanings of words as whatever goes to determine this feature of the sentences in which they occur. Equally, the theorist of thought must select some one feature of a thought as determining its content, and construe its constituents as contributions to this, which can similarly serve as contributions to determining the contents of related thoughts. Frege's theory of meaning, or of thought, was one example of such a theory: but there is no reason to suppose that there is any unique choice to be made for the central notion. The first part of a theory of meaning will then display in detail how the meanings of the sentences of the language, in the chosen sense of "meaning", are derivable from their composition: this must then be supplemented by an account of how, in general, the various uses made of sentences in linguistic exchange depend upon their meanings as represented in the first part of the theory.

Thus if, as in Frege's theory, the notion of a sentence's being true is taken as the central notion, the second part of the theory, which is entirely lacking in Frege, must show how what we treat as grounds sufficient to warrant the assertion of a statement depend systematically upon what determines it as true, and, further, how what we take as involved in accepting it as true likewise depends systematically upon how its truth-value is determined. Being true may be different from being taken to be true: but there must be a systematic relation between them. Someone may think, "It takes a philosopher to make a mystery out of this: of course, if I know the truth-conditions of a sentence, I know how to use it". But that is only because he has the concept of truth, and, with it, an implicit grasp of the connection between truth-conditions and use: if, instead of "true" and "false", Frege had employed two otherwise unknown words, the critic would not suppose himself able to derive the use of a sentence from its sense as given by the theory. It is the business of a theory of meaning to spell out explicitly the connection which the critic sees, but is unlikely to be able to state, and, when it has been spelled out, all that we need to know about the concept of truth, as it bears upon meaning, will have been displayed.

It may be possible to supplement Frege's theory in this way; but, even if so, the resultant composite theory no longer has the elegance that the original one did before the need for supplementation was acknowledged. The notions of grounds and consequences admittedly stand at a certain level of abstraction: they are not to be interpreted in any crudely behavioural manner. That is to say, you could not, by observing the speakers of a language you did not know, decide what they treated as justifying the assertion of any given statement, or what they regarded as involved in accepting it: you would have to know quite a lot of the language before you could discover that. Nevertheless, it can hardly be doubted that these notions would have to be employed in any description of the practice of using language: in this sense, they have a direct relation to our actual use of sentences. By contrast, the concept of a statement's *being* true, independently of whether we believe it or can recognize it as such, stands at a far higher level of abstraction. That someone has a certain conception of what has to hold good for a given sentence to be true is not, in general, exhaustively manifested in the use he makes of it, since he will not always be able to recognize the condition for its truth as obtaining, or to take steps that will put him in a position to do so. The concept of truth is obviously not a theorist's notion, but an intuitive one that we all have: but, when it figures in a theory of meaning, it there plays the role of a theoretical notion, connected to linguistic practice only indirectly.

The simplicity of Frege's theory of sense is thus offset by the complexity of the supplementation required to convert it into a complete theory of meaning. It is therefore natural to enquire whether the theory as a whole could be simplified by using as its central notion either that of the canonical grounds for asserting a statement or that of the commitments made by asserting it: by taking the meanings of sentences as given in terms of a particular feature of their use, we simplify the task of connecting meaning with use. We should not, indeed, eliminate it. Whichever feature was chosen as the central notion, the theory must show how the other feature is to be derived from it, just as Frege's theory of sense would have to be supplemented by showing how *both* features could be derived from the sense as given according to that theory. But we should have effected a considerable simplification, since we should have excised a theoretical notion connected only indirectly with use.

Is such an idea practicable? It can only be proved so by actually carrying it out, which no one has done in detail: but certain general doubts may be dispelled at the outset. At first sight, the project calls up the spectre of holism. What counts as grounds for, or as a justification of, an assertion will depend upon what other statements are held to be true. It was an illusion of the positivists that, for each statement, we can conceive of what would justify its assertion in the absence of any other beliefs; obviously, the meaning of at most a very small range of sentences can be given in such a manner. Most statements cannot be justified at all except by appeal to some form of reasoning, deductive or inductive; and this implies that their meanings, if given in terms of what counts as justifying them, must relate to relative justification, by appeal to other statements. This in turn requires, if circularity is to be avoided, that we can, for this purpose, impose a hierarchy upon the sentences of the language, so that the meaning of each sentence can be viewed as given relative only to others of lower rank in the hierarchy. Conversely, in so far as the acceptance of a statement involves a commitment to the truth of other statements, its meaning can be regarded as given only in terms of a commitment to the truth of statements of lower rank.

Much more needs to be said on this matter; but the most important fact is that practice is not sacrosanct. Justification and commitment ought to be in harmony with one another: that is why, if meaning is taken as given in terms of either, the theory must show how the other can be derived from the meaning as so given. The condition for such harmony to obtain is twofold: first, that whatever serves to justify a statement ought also to justify any simpler statement to which acceptance of the first commits us; and, conversely, that all commitments consequent upon acceptance of a statement should already be consequent upon anything offered in complete justification of it. There is, however, a further requirement, which we may call stability. This condition is that we do not demand more, in justification of a statement, than is required for it to carry the commitments we take it to bear; conversely, we should not understand it as carrying fewer commitments than would be warranted by what we require as a justification of it.

These are intuitively reasonable conditions for a language to function as we intend it to do: violation of them will lead to that malfunctioning we call conceptual confusion. There is, however, no a priori reason why a language should perfectly fulfil them. Linguistic practice is enormously complex, and takes a great deal of time to acquire. Justification and commitment are distinguishable features of that practice: there is no more certainty that there will in fact always exist both harmony and stability between them than there is that a machine will always function as intended. For this reason, we cannot demand of a theory of meaning that it will always yield a description of prevailing linguistic practice accurate in all details: on the contrary, the existence of disharmony or instability is more likely to come to light when a systematic account of the working of the language is undertaken, and so the theory of meaning may prompt a change in our employment of it.

Because of the requirements of harmony and stability, a theory of meaning based on justification, which may loosely be termed a verificationist theory, will be equivalent to one based on commitment, which we may term a pragmatist theory: they are therefore not true rivals. That is far from true of either in relation to a theory, like Frege's, based on the notion of a statement's being true, that is, a truth-conditional theory. One reason for preferring a truth-conditional theory is that it will require far less revision in our linguistic practice than a verificationist or pragmatist one; but, given how prone we are to illusion and error, this is a flimsy ground. Far more serious is the suspicion that theories of the other two kinds can give no plausible account of the embedding of sentences in more complex ones, that is, of the logical constants. What, for instance, is the canonical justification of the statement that a given set has an even number of members? Obviously a procedure for partitioning it into two numerically equivalent subsets. But now it is evident that we could not adopt the crudest method of explaining what justifies the assertion of a disjunctive statement, namely whatever justifies one or other subsentence: for the assertion that the number of people in this room is either even or odd is evidently justified in the absence of any justification of either alternative. This may be explained on the ground that we have a procedure for arriving at a justification of one or the other; but in an hour's time it will still be justifiable to assert that the number was either even or odd, although the procedure for deciding will be for ever unavailable. We appear, even in so simple a case, to be pushed back on to saying that we *could have* arrived at a justification of one or other; and we thereby come closer to the conception of one or other alternative's simply being *true*.

The pressure to go the whole distance and admit that we confer upon the sentences of our language meanings determined by our grasp of a conception of what makes them true, quite independently of our means for ascertaining their truth, is immensely strong, and explains the determination so many feel not to allow a truth-conditional account of meaning to be dislodged. The pressure is reinforced by a powerful illusion, which claims many victims: it makes a Fregean theory appear impregnable, and the line of thought I have been pursuing a false track. The victims of this illusion reason that, to grasp the condition for a particular sentence, say "There is life on Mars", to be true one needs to know only one principle governing the notion of truth, namely that for the sentence to be true is simply for there to be life on Mars. Now, they continue: anyone knows this if he has even the most rudimentary understanding of the word "true". But, they argue, if you know this, then you will realize that all that you must, in addition, know in order to know what it is for the sentence "There is life in Mars" to be true is what it is for there to be life on Mars. But, if you understand the sentence "There is life on Mars", you must thereby know what it is for there to be life on Mars; and, conversely, if you know what it is for there to be life on Mars, and also know that the sentence is true just in case there is life on Mars, you must thereby know the meaning of the sentence.

A Fregean theory presupposes *something* about the concept of truth: but the argument I have just rehearsed purports to show that the presupposition is minimal. The fallacy lies in the uncritical acceptance of the notion of knowing what it is for something to be the case (for there to be life on Mars). No progress is in fact made by appeal to this notion: we still need to ask in what having such knowledge is to be taken to consist. If it is taken to amount to a readiness to agree that there is life on Mars when there is compelling evidence that there is, then it is being equated with a grasp of the justification-conditions of the statement; if it is taken to amount to showing that one understands what is involved in accepting the statement, it is being equated with a grasp of the commitment undertaken by an assertion of it. In the one case, we have a verificationist, in the other a pragmatist, account of meaning, and the Gordian knot remains uncut. If, on the other hand, knowing what it is for there to be life on Mars is regarded as the fount of both these abilities, but transcending both of them, we indeed have a truth-conditional account, but one that has failed to evade the difficulties intrinsic to it. It is merely that the obscurity of the notion of a statement's being true has been transferred to that of knowing what it is for something to be the case.

Even apart from the illusion I have just discussed, the pressure to adopt a truth-conditional theory of meaning remains high. But the price is very high, too: too high, I believe, to be paid, at least provided that the issue does not prove to be delusive. In essence, the dilemma is very simple. If the concept of a statement's being true is fully explicable in terms of those concepts employed in a reasonably liberal verificationist or pragmatist theory, then Frege was quite mistaken in supposing the concept to be unanalysable, and the issue between a truth-conditional theory of meaning and other theories is delusive: whatever can be explained using the unqualified notion of truth can be explained without it. I do not believe this to be so, but shall not here argue against it. If it is not so, then a grasp of truth-conditions transcends a mastery of linguistic practice, even if it grounds it. In that case, even if every feature of the use of a sentence is systematically derivable from its truth-conditions, a grasp of those truth-conditions will, in general, involve more than is capable of being manifested in its use. That will mean, in turn, that it is impossible to determine, of another, whether he understands the sentences I utter just as I do: he might attach different truth-conditions to them, or even none at all, and still have learned to use them in a manner not detectably different from my own. And that is absurd. Thought is of its essence communicable. The theorist of thought may not agree; but he should allow that thoughts that *can* be communicated at all can be communicated without residue. For, even if thought is private, the use of language is a social practice; each member of the society can use its language on his own, but the language could not exist save as the possession of the community. That is one reason why I side, in the end, with the theorist of language against the theorist of thought: for I believe that we owe our very natures to our participation in the human life we live together, and, in particular, that we owe our character as rational beings, that is, our capacity for thought, to our ability to use language, which means to use at least one of the languages of men, formed by generations of our forebears.

7

Language and Communication

Language, it is natural to say, has two principal functions: that of an instrument of communication, and that of a vehicle of thought. We are therefore impelled to ask which of the two is primary. Is it because language is an instrument of communication that it can also serve as a vehicle of thought? Or is it, conversely, because it is a vehicle of thought, and can therefore express thoughts, that it can be used by one person to communicate his thoughts to others?

A view that might claim to represent common sense is that the primary function of language is to be used as an instrument of communication, and that, when so used, it operates as a code for thought. On this view, it is only because we happen to lack a faculty for directly transmitting thoughts from mind to that we are compelled to encode them in sounds or marks on paper. If we had the faculty, therefore, we should have no need of language. But the corollary conflicts with common sense: namely that language is not a vehicle of thought at all. Common sense exclaims against this that surely we often think in words: but the advocate of the code theory of language, if he has his wits about him, will reply that we never do any such thing, indeed, that the very notion is unintelligible. Rather, words, spoken aloud or rehearsed in the imagination, often *accompany* our thoughts, but in no way embody them. For, if we should not need language but for the need to communicate our thoughts, we must be capable of having *naked* thoughts (to vary the metaphor once again)—thoughts devoid of linguistic or other representational clothing: thoughts may represent the world, but, to have thoughts, we need nothing that represents *them*. Thus thoughts do not *need* a representation, although, for purposes of communication, they may be verbally represented; and from this it follows that a thought cannot exist—cannot be present to the mind—merely through some verbal or other symbolic representation, which is what it would be for the representation to be the vehicle or embodiment of the thought. The whole substance of the code theory of language is that the speaker encodes his thought as a sentence and the hearer decodes the sentence as that thought: but, if language could be the vehicle of thought, the hearer would not need to decode the utterance nor the speaker to have encoded the thought in the first place. Either no thoughts have vehicles or all thoughts must have them.

What we call 'thinking in words' is, then, according to the code theory of

First published in Alexander George (ed.), *Reflections on Chomsky* (Oxford, 1989).

language, one of two things. It may be thinking *about* how to express our thoughts in words, as with someone rehearsing a speech or lecture or writing a book or article. On this view, we should resist the illusion that the thought is not fully formed until it is articulated in words: it need no more be so than it is for the translator who is considering how to express in a sentence of one language the thought expressed in one of another language.

More usually, the code theorist maintains, the relation of the words to the thought is that of the sound to the written letters. Someone who is fluent in reading a given script, say Roman script, cannot see a written or printed word, for instance a name at a railway station, without mentally attaching a pronunciation to it. If it belongs to a language of whose pronunciation he is uncertain, he may have no confidence that he is mentally pronouncing it correctly; but he is as unable to read it dissociated from any phonetic value as he is unable to see it as one illiterate in that script would do (or as he himself would see a word in a script of which he was ignorant). Likewise, according to the code theorist, we are so overwhelmingly accustomed to speech in our mother tongue, or sometimes in other languages, that, except in moments of emergency, we are unable to entertain thoughts in the forefront of our minds without putting them into words: and so we fall victims to the illusion that the words embody the thought, whereas they merely adorn it. But, he urges, try repeatedly going over, aloud or silently, some familiar words—a well-known quotation or an often-used formula—not abstractedly, but with attention. However hard you try to fasten your attention on the words, you will keep having, in the background or, as it were, skimming between the words, wisps of thought, which you could without difficulty express: and ask yourself whether these background thoughts are also in words. Surely you will agree that they are naked thoughts, he says: the whole conception of thinking 'in' words is spurious. An amusing example occurred in a novel I recently read, in which a character remarked that she was interested to note, while she was thinking through some question, that she did so entirely verbally, thus confirming her long-held opinion that all our thinking is in words: her interlocutor failed to ask her whether her thought "I am thinking in words" was itself in words.

The question was one which exercised Wittgenstein, as illustrated by the following quotation from the *Philosophical Investigations*, in which I thought it best to replace the word "pen" by "pencil": "Speak the line, 'Yes, the pencil is blunt: oh, well, it will do', first thinking it; then without thought; and then just think the thought without the words" (I. 330). Wittgenstein goes on to describe a case in which someone would naturally be described as having had just that thought without words; but remarks that "what constitutes thought here is not some process which has to accompany the words if they are not to be spoken without thought". His idea is surely that, if it were, it would not be difficult to obey the instruction "Just think the thought without the words", whereas it needs a quite special kind of background to make sense of saying of someone that he had such a thought, but not in words. We could say— although Wittgenstein himself does not expressly say this—that thought needs a vehicle of some kind, although this may not consist of words, but of something quite different like actions.

The difficulty of obeying the instruction to think the thought without the words is, however, due, in part, to the ambiguity of the term "thinking". When Wittgenstein speaks of someone's uttering the sentence "The pencil is blunt", thinking it, he does not mean his doing what would ordinarily be described as thinking that the pencil is blunt: there may be no pencil around, or, if there is, it may be quite evidently sharp. Wittgenstein means, rather, that he utters the sentence aware of what the words mean. In Frege's terminology, he grasps the thought expressed by the sentence, without necessarily judging it to be true; or, rather, since no definite thought will be expressed in the absence of any salient pencil, he attends to the meanings of the words, considered independently of any occasion of utterance. Now suppose someone were to say to me, "Think that the pencil is blunt", or, "Think the thought that the pencil is blunt", without raising the question whether I am to think in words or without them: even if it is obvious which pencil is being referred to, what am I to do? If "think" is to be taken in its most usual sense, as in contexts like "I suddenly thought that this would be my last chance of getting a meal that night", then it means "judge" rather than merely "grasp", and I might answer, "I cannot have thoughts to order: the pencil just isn't blunt at all". If, on the other hand, "think" is being used to mean 'entertain the thought', with no implication that it is to be taken as true, then again I am in difficulties, this time because I cannot help but have obeyed the command as soon as it was given: for just understanding the command involved grasping the thought that the pencil was blunt.

It is plain that having a thought is something of a quite different kind from uttering a sentence: it is not merely in a different medium, as it were, but of a different character. A policeman shows me a photograph, and asks, "Have you ever seen this man?": I study the photograph, perhaps trying and failing to evoke a feeling of familiarity, perhaps running through in my mind the facial appearance of a range of slight acquaintances, decide I have never seen the man, and answer, "No". In the context of the question, the word "No" expresses the thought "I have never seen this man". I may have had that thought just before answering, or my answer may have been the first embodiment of my thought. In neither case, however, would it be natural to say that I thought, "No": only that I thought, "I have never seen him". For all that, the thought came to me with no greater articulation than the one-word answer. This is because the content of a thought is much *more* determined by context than that of an utterance. If, for example, I am walking out of my house, the coming to mind of a single personal name, or of an image of the person's face, may constitute my having the thought "I've left behind the book I promised So-and-so". Thoughts, when not framed in sentences, are not framed in some mental language private to the thinker: they are, rather, embodied in (inner or outer) *reactions*, which, in the whole context, are intelligible only as embodying those thoughts. We give verbal reports of such thoughts, at the time or later: asked by my companion, "Why are you turning back?" I will say, "I've left So-and-so's book behind"; recounting my day hours afterwards, I may say, "Just as I was leaving the house, I thought, 'I've left So-and-so's book behind'". Such a report may be called an *interpretation*: it is not read off from an inner tape recorder, but is, as it were, *ascribed* to oneself on the basis of the remembered stimuli and reactions to them. This ponderous terminology, of interpretation and ascription, is not intended to suggest that there is anything dubious about a report of this kind. On the contrary, although my inner reactions, or the inner stimuli that prompted them, may have been hidden from view, anyone who knew what they were, and knew enough about my background, would put the same interpretation on them.

This fact is sufficient to show that, when someone reports his unverbalized or unarticulated thoughts, he is not recalling some inner utterance in a language of the mind: on a few occasions, he may contradict an interpretation suggested by another in favour of a different one, but he cannot intelligibly lay claim to a thought that fails to make sense of his actions and reactions. It is for this reason that the code conception of language is untenable. For language to be a code for thought, thoughts have to be like sentences, and have constituents analogous to words, and the thought-constituents must be matched to the words by some process of association. A word will then evoke the associated thought-constituent in the mind of the hearer, and, for one who wishes to communicate his thought, its constituents will evoke the corresponding words. But this fantasy will not serve as an account of our understanding of language, because there is no such thing as a thought-constituent's coming to mind, independently of any word or symbol that expresses it. To suppose that such a mental event can occur is to have an altogether primitive picture of the character of thinking.

The point is obscured when the term "thought" is used in Frege's way: for Fregean thoughts indeed have constituents, and, for a sentence to *express* such a thought, there must be a certain match between its composition and that of the thought. For instance, no one could have the thought that Venus has an elliptical orbit without possessing the concept of an ellipse; and, in accordance with Gareth Evans's 'generality constraint',[1] this requires that he be able to think of other things as elliptical. Moreover, to grasp a thought involves an apprehension of its complexity: one could not think that the orbit of Venus is an ellipse without being aware that one could judge other shapes to be or not

[1] Gareth Evans, *The Varieties of Reference* (Oxford, 1982), 100–5.

to be ellipses. What does not, in general, have an analogous structure is the *thinking* of the thought—the inner or outer process that, against the necessary background, constitutes having that thought. This is why Frege rightly held that thoughts, in his sense, and their component concepts or senses, are not contents of the mind, as a mental image is: a mental content, as here understood, must be something whose presence does not depend upon there being any particular background.

Were the code theory of language tenable, it would be easy to explain how the words and sentences of a language have the meanings that they do; but it would still be necessary to give a philosophical explanation of what a thought is. For a thought does not resemble a mental image or a sensation: it has the distinctive feature of being, or at least of being capable of being, true or false, and thus relating to reality external to the mind. The same may, of course, be said of a mental image, in so far as it is apprehended as an image *of* a particular thing, and even of a sensation, in so far as it is taken as engendered by some non-mental object or event. A mental image or sensation, considered as such, does not, however, *have* to be so apprehended: it can exist simply as a constituent of inner experience, unintegrated with an awareness of external reality. For this reason, it is highly plausible that what renders an image the image of a certain object is nothing intrinsic to it as an image, but a concomitant *thought* to the effect that it represents that object, and similarly for sensations: hence, if this is right, thought remains unique in its representative character. This representative character requires philosophical explanation. Mental images and sensations are sufficiently explained when a description has been given of what it is like to have them: but a description of what it is like to have a thought, were it possible to give such a thing, would be quite inadequate as a philosophical account of thoughts, since it could not encompass what makes them capable of possessing a truth-value.

The failure of the code theory of language leaves us without an explanation of what it is for an expression of a language to have a meaning. But, if that cannot be explained in terms of a coding of thoughts into sentences by means of an association between words and thought-constituents, it must be explained in such a way as to make manifest how sentences serve to express thoughts, without taking as given a prior understanding of what a thought is. Just such an explanation was in effect essayed by Frege. He insisted that the important thing was the thought, not the sentence; he claimed that the existence of the thought did not depend upon its being grasped or expressed by any rational being; and he also claimed that there might exist beings who could grasp the very same thoughts as we do without needing to conceive them as clothed in language. But his semantic theory made no appeal to an antecedent conception of thoughts: the theory itself sought to explain what it is for a sentence to express a thought without invoking any conception, given in advance, of the thought that it expresses.

That is why Frege is rightly regarded as the grandfather of analytical philosophy, whose distinctive methodology, until quite recently, was to approach the philosophy of thought via the philosophy of language. From such a standpoint, the most important feature of language is that it serves as a vehicle of thought. It is not necessary, in order to adopt this standpoint, to deny that unverbalized thought is in principle possible, nor even to deny, as Frege did, that it is in practice possible for human beings. It is not necessary, either, to deny that thought is possible for creatures who have no language in which to express it. It is necessary only to believe that thought, by its nature, cannot occur without a vehicle, and that language is the vehicle whose operation is the most perspicuous and hence the most amenable to a systematic philosophical account. This is so for two reasons. First, the ascription to a subject of his having a given thought at a particular time can be justified only by the presence of an often extensive background to the occurrence of whatever served as the vehicle of the thought. In the ideal case when the vehicle is a fully explicit verbal expression of the thought, however, the only background to which appeal is needed is the existence of the language and the subject's knowledge of it—an immensely complex but structured phenomenon, relatively isolable from other circumstances. And, secondly, a fully explicit verbal expression is the only vehicle whose structure must reflect the structure of the thought.

From this standpoint, to analyse linguistic meaning along Gricean lines is to pursue an altogether misconceived strategy. When the utterance is an assertoric one, Strawson's version of such an analysis is given in terms of the hearer's recognition of the speaker's intention to communicate that he has a certain belief.[2] McDowell's emendation, that what the speaker wishes to communicate is a piece of information, which may be about anything, rather than only about his own doxastic condition, is undoubtedly an improvement, for language is certainly used primarily as contributing to our transactions with the world, rather than as conveying to one another how it is with us in our thinking parts.[3] It is essential to our most basic acquisition of the practice of using a language that we learn to act on what others tell us; only as a more sophisticated by-product do we learn to use their utterances as revealing their beliefs, and, even then, *their* intention is still typically to inform us that what they say is so rather than to allow us a glimpse of their private convictions. Were it otherwise, it would be, as it were, an afterthought that we could, by making an unintended use of them, gain information from the assertions of others; and we should accept those assertions as true only on occasions on which we had particular reason to trust the speaker's veracity, rather than, as now, whenever we have no particular reason to doubt it.

[2] P. F. Strawson, *Logico-Linguistic Papers* (London, 1971), 172–3, 185.
[3] John McDowell, "Meaning, Communication, and Knowledge", in Zak van Straaten (ed.), *Philosophical Subjects* (Oxford, 1980).

McDowell's formulation, and Strawson's, both suffer, however, from an awkwardness in generalizing them to utterances of all kinds, rather than merely assertoric ones: more importantly, both go astray by in effect helping themselves to the specific content of the utterance instead of explaining what confers that content upon it. Their formulations, in their ungeneralized forms, are candidates for being characterzations of *assertions*, as opposed to questions, requests, and so on: they purport to explain what it is to make an assertion with a certain content, given that we already grasp the notion of something's having that content. That is to say, they aim to characterize asserting that something is the case, on the assumption that we already know what it is to have the information that it is the case (McDowell), or to ascribe to someone a belief that it is the case (Strawson). However, being informed that such-and-such is so and believing that such-and-such is so both obviously involve having the *thought* that such-and-such is so: and thus this strategy of explanation takes as already given the conception of the thought expressed by a sentence, and, at most, explains what it is to assert that that thought is true.

The Gricean line of explanation is hence essentially no more than a sophisticated version of the code conception of language. To understand an assertoric utterance, I must understand two things: that it *is* assertoric, that is, serves to voice an assertion; and what, specifically, it is used to assert. Any explanation of linguistic meaning must, among other things, explain what features of such an utterance enable a hearer to recognize these two aspects of its significance. An explanation of what constitutes a grasp of the concept of being informed that something is so, or of that of believing that something is so, is certainly called for; but let us suppose that such an explanation is to hand. Assume, now, that I, as hearer, do grasp these concepts, and, further, that I am able to recognize the utterance in question as assertoric. What matters, much more than *how* I recognize this—what feature of the utterance indicates to me that this is its character—is what it is for me to take it, rightly or wrongly, as assertoric. Given that I have the general concept of information or of belief, this is at least arguably explicable in the manner of Grice, as amended by McDowell or otherwise. On any account of language, there remains to be explained which features of the utterance convey to me what, specifically, is being asserted: the content of the assertion or, in Frege's terminology, the thought asserted to be true. This formulation, however, makes it appear that we already have a clear conception of what it is for me to grasp the thought, and are concerned only to explain how I identify it as that which the sentence expresses; but, when the philosophy of language is treated as supplying the only route to a philosophical account of thinking, the formulation is misleading. Rather, we need to explain what it is for me to grasp what thought is being asserted in such a manner as thereby to explain what it is for me to grasp that thought at all. By contrast, the Grice–Strawson–McDowell theory assumes that, by some conventional means, I am able to recognize which thought it is that the utterance serves to assert as true; but, in assuming this, it takes my ability to grasp this thought as given antecedently to my recognizing it to be that which is asserted. It thus treats the sentence as *encoding* the thought, rather than as *expressing* it.

The fundamental point made by Frege,[4] and slightly earlier by Wittgenstein,[5] that language enables us to grasp *new* thoughts is often sneered at by those too impatient to stop to reflect upon it. In Chomsky's writings it reappears, heavily emphasized, both in the form that we are able to understand new *sentences*, and more importantly, in the form stated by Frege.[6] If it was merely that we could understand a new way of conveying a familiar thought, a language could be simply a code for thoughts. According to the appropriate version of the code conception of language, we can grasp a large range of thoughts, independently of their formulation in language, and can apprehend relations between them by means of which they may be located in logical space: sentences then serve to pick them out by their coordinates in this space, enabling us to identify the thoughts so conveyed; and a certain redundancy in the coordinate system allows distinct sentences to convey the same thought. This picture of language depends upon taking our grasp of the thoughts that can be conveyed by language as antecedent to our understanding of the language: it is therefore exposed as false by the fact that such an understanding suffices to enable us to grasp quite new thoughts when they are expressed in that language. There is a fundamental difference between expressing a thought and using some conventional means to identify it. Given an invalid argument, the phrase "the weakest additional assumption needed to render the argument valid" picks out a unique thought; but it does not *express* that thought, since it is possible to understand the phrase without knowing which thought it picks out. A sentence expressing the thought, on the other hand, cannot be understood without knowing what thought it expresses. It is an essential feature of anything properly called a 'language' that its phrases and sentences genuinely *express* their meanings. That is the difference between a language and a code; and that is why the mastery of a language enables a speaker to grasp new thoughts expressed in it.

The Grice–Strawson–McDowell theory may, then, conceivably be on the right track to an explanation of a restricted facet of linguistic meaning, namely the assertoric force attached to certain utterances, as contrasted with the interrogative, optative, imperatival, or other type of force attached to others. Here it is unimportant that the overt indicators of the force attached are, in most languages, unreliable and insufficient in number: what matter are the

---

[4] G. Frege, 'Gedankenfüge' (1923), 36; Eng. trans. in G. Frege, *Collected Papers*, ed. B. McGuinness (Oxford, 1984), 390.

[5] Wittgenstein, *Tractatus* (1921), 4.027, 4.03.

[6] See in particular Noam Chomsky, *Language and Problems of Knowledge* (Cambridge, Mass., 1988), 170 and 184.

distinctions that a hearer needs to draw if he is to have understood what has been said. Someone who mistakes a request for a question is not in error merely about the *point* of the utterance, that is, about why the speaker said what he did: he is mistaken about what it was that was said. But a theory of the Gricean type is powerless to explain any other aspect of meaning. For that, an approach along Fregean lines is required: one, namely, that, by explaining what, in general, the specific content of a sentence is, and by displaying the contributions made by particular words to determining the content of sentences that contain them, shows what it is for a sentence to express a thought, and, thereby, what thoughts are.

So far, then, the contest between the view that the primary function of language is that of an instrument of communication and the view that it is that of a vehicle of thought appears to be going decisively in favour of the latter. This was the contest staged by Strawson in his celebrated inaugural lecture 'Meaning and Truth', in which he dubbed proponents of the former view 'communication-intention theorists' and proponents of the latter 'theorists of formal semantics'.[7] If the foregoing argument has been right, communication-intention theories, that is, Gricean theories, at best contribute to that part of a theory of meaning which, in Fregean terms, constitutes the theory of force.

What, then, is needed in order to give an account of that ingredient in meaning called by Frege 'sense'? From the dichotomy drawn by Strawson, it would appear that it can only be what he terms 'formal semantics', that is to say, a theory of sense along Fregean lines, built, like his, on a theory of reference as a basis. If so, does it follow that the primary function of language is to be a vehicle of thought, and that it is the contingent fact that many people happen to know the same language that enables us to put it to a secondary use as an instrument of communication? This is Chomsky's conclusion.[8] Of course, the 'contingent fact' is an essential feature of the way in which we all in practice acquire language: but, from the present standpoint, it is contingent in that it does not follow from the essence of language as language.

On the face of it, a theory of sense of Frege's kind supports such a conclusion. Frege insisted that thoughts and the senses that are constituents of them are equally accessible to all, and hence fully communicable: but, for all that, in an account, of the type he envisaged, of what grasping the senses of expressions of a language comprises, no reference is made to the existence of more than one speaker of the language. On such a theory, for every expression of the language possessing a genuine unity, one who understands the language grasps a particular condition for something to be its referent, that referent consisting of an object or a function according to the logical type of the expression. Attaching a given sense to an expression is thus, on this account,

[7] P. Strawson, *Logico-Linguistic Papers* (London, 1971), 170–89.
[8] Noam Chomsky, *Reflections on Language* (New York, 1975), 71.

personal to the individual speaker. In so far as he wishes to use the language to communicate with others, he will, of course, be concerned to attach the *right* sense to the expression, that is, the sense which it bears in the language; but his attaching a particular sense to it, rightly or wrongly, does not depend upon anything but his own cognitive state, and it does not appear that, for this, he need so much as have any conception of there being other speakers of the language. This fact is vividly illustrated by Frege's remarks in 'Der Gedanke' about the understanding that two speakers may have of a personal name, in Frege's example the name "Dr Gustav Lauben". Leo Peter knows Dr Lauben as a medical doctor who lives in a certain house; Herbert Garner knows, of Dr Lauben, the date and place of his birth, but not where he lives now or anything else about him. Frege comments that "So far as the proper name 'Dr Gustav Lauben' is concerned, Herbert Garner and Leo Peter do not speak the same language; for, although they in fact use this name to signify the same man, they do not know that they do so."[9]

Something very similar holds good of Davidson's account of the matter.[10] In his earlier writings, he emphasized the existence of the whole linguistic community as bearing upon the way in which a theory of meaning for a language might be arrived at, and upon the criterion for its being an acceptable theory: but the theory itself was a body of knowledge that might be possessed by a single individual, his possession of which would enable him to speak the language. In his later work, he has gone a great deal further, taking the primary notion to be that of an idiolect—the language of some individual at a particular time—or refining this notion still further so as to make it relative to a hearer as well as to a speaker: the language that, at a particular time, A uses when he is speaking to B.[11] It is plain from Frege's observations in 'Der Gedanke' that he, too, conceives of a language as an idiolect. He does not take Davidson's step of relativizing the language to both speaker and hearer, since he is less concerned with the language that the subject *uses* as with that which he *understands* (and the manner in which he understands it); the subject is thus considered more in the role of hearer than of speaker. Frege's conception is that a sentence uttered by another will convey to a hearer a thought, and that which thought it conveys will depend upon the senses the hearer attaches to the words, and thus upon the hearer's language. Which thought a speaker intends to convey by a sentence that he utters will doubtless likewise depend largely upon the speaker's language; but this is not the focus of Frege's attention. In any case, the language of speaker or hearer is not conceived of as such a language as German, but as that individual's idiolect: it is to the

---

[9] G. Frege, 'Der Gedanke', 65; *Collected Papers*, 359.

[10] Donald Davidson, 'Radical Interpretation' and 'Belief and the Basis of Meaning', both in *Inquiries into Truth and Interpretation* (Oxford, 1984).

[11] Donald Davidson, 'A Nice Derangement of Epitaphs', in E. Lepore (ed.), *Truth and Interpretation* (Oxford, 1986), 433–46.

expressions of such an idiolect, or at least of a language that might be someone's idiolect, that a theory specifying senses and referents should be taken as applying.

Chomsky embraces with great warmth the conclusion that Strawson, by his endorsement of the communication-intention theory, had sought to defeat, namely that language is primarily a vehicle of thought, and only secondarily an instrument of communication.[12] He cites instances of the many cases in which we employ language with no direct, and sometimes no remote, communicative purpose. These, of course, prove nothing: they serve merely to underline the problem. It is agreed, on both hands, that language serves both purposes: it is easy to cite examples in which it serves the one and other examples in which it serves the other. There is no question, therefore, of its being like the game of bridge. It would be senseless to say that someone, having learned the game of bridge by playing it with others, was now in a position to go off and play it by himself: there is no such thing as playing bridge on one's own. We know in advance, by contrast, that, having learned a language by learning to converse with others, one can then use it in silent, spoken, or, so to speak, written soliloquy: the question at issue is whether it is because it can be used to communicate with others that it can also be used as a vehicle of one's own thought, or whether, conversely, it is because two people are able to use the same language as a vehicle of thought that they are also able to use it to communicate with one another.

The most direct strategy for answering this question is to enquire whether either ability can be explained in terms of the other. It seems, at first sight, that it is straightforward to explain our capacity to communicate by means of language if we assume an ability to use it as a vehicle of thought: given that, for each of two individuals, a sentence of the language expresses the same thought, either of them must be able to communicate that thought to the other by uttering that sentence. At second glance, however, it is not at all so clear, at least in the context of theories of meaning for those individuals' idiolects running roughly along the lines of a Fregean theory of sense and reference.

In order for the speaker successfully to communicate with the hearer, the hearer must understand him as he intended to be understood. The explication that is proposed for the notion of the way in which the speaker intends to be understood is that his idiolect can be correctly characterized by a certain theory of meaning: the hearer will then understand him as he intended if the hearer's idiolect—or at least the idiolect attributed by the hearer to the speaker—is characterized by the same theory of meaning. The status of such a theory of meaning is open to dispute. At one extreme, it may be taken as merely a theory propounded from the outside, playing no actual role in the mechanism that governs either speaker's or hearer's linguistic behaviour. At

[12] Chomsky, *Reflections on Language*, 61–2 and 69.

the other extreme, that represented by Chomsky, the speaker's knowledge of his language is identified with his knowledge of such a theory. Since the speaker obviously has no explicit knowledge of more than a few fragments of such a theory, this must be classed as unconscious knowledge; and, if anyone objects to the notion of unconscious knowledge, he is to be pacified by the replacement of the word "knowledge" by "cognition". This is not offered as the outcome of conceptual analysis, but as an empirical scientific hypothesis, specifically a psychological hypothesis. It is guarded from attack as embodying a mythological conception of an immaterial psychic mechanism by the identification of psychology as neurophysiology on an abstract level: the theory of meaning is an abstract description of a structure within the brain. Since a subject cannot be expected to have even an abstract awareness of much that goes on within his brain, it is unsurprising that his knowledge of the theory should be unconscious.

On the face of it, this account is open to the criticisms that Frege and Husserl brought against psychologism: meaning becomes private and hence no longer in principle communicable. This is to say that faith is required if we are to believe that we communicate with one another. The hearer must presuppose that he is interpreting the speaker as the speaker intends: but the speaker's intention and the hearer's interpretation are, at best, constituted by inner states of each respectively, not accessible to themselves, let alone to the other. Frege insisted on the communicability of thoughts, as contrasted with the contents of consciousness: thoughts are not contents of consciousness, but, being common to all, are objective extra-mental entities existing independently of our grasping or expressing them. Notoriously, this doctrine fails to explain how thoughts can be communicated by language. It is not enough that the senses should themselves be objective: their attachment to the words whose senses they are must likewise be objective, or at least objectively ascertainable, and that is something that cannot be independent of us.

If communication is not to rest on faith, it is necessary to maintain that any misunderstanding can come to light. The hearer may indeed be construing the speaker's words in accordance with the wrong theory of meaning; if so, there must be something that the speaker is liable to say or do, in virtue of the way he intends what he says to be understood, that would demonstrate to the hearer that his understanding of the speaker has up to now been incorrect. But it is not enough to make such a claim: it must be made out. We are here taking it that a theory of meaning for an idiolect of the 'formal semantic' type will conform to the Fregean prototype in issuing in an assignment, to every possible utterance of any (assertoric) sentence of the language, of the condition for that utterance to be true. What has, therefore, first to be done, in making out the claim, is to explain in detail the consequences such a theory has for what a speaker may say and do. It naturally cannot be demanded of such an explanation that it should enable us to predict what any given speaker will say, let alone what he will do, in response to the utterances of others; but, since it is by a speaker's linguistic and non-linguistic behaviour that we must judge whether or not some given theory of meaning, of the Fregean type, can be taken as governing that speaker's idiolect, it must be possible to state the basis of such a judgement. Consequently, the explanation will lay down the principles that determine what behaviour on the part of a speaker is consistent with a given theory of meaning for his idiolect: in other words, it will exhibit the connection between the theory of meaning for a language and the actual use of that language.

It is precisely the lack of any such connecting explanation that makes theories of meaning constructed after the Fregean prototype so unsatisfying and so hard to evaluate. Davidson, for instance, has emphasized that, in proposing a truth-theory of the kind he has advocated as the proper form for a theory of meaning, he is turning a Tarskian truth-definition on its head.[13] He is not, like Tarski, defining the property of being true, taking the meanings of the sentences as antecedently explained without appeal to the notion of truth: rather, he is taking as given an understanding of what it is for a statement to be true, and explaining the meanings of words and sentences of the language by laying down when utterances made by means of them are true. It follows that someone can derive the meanings of those words and sentences from the truth-theory only if he grasps, at least implicitly, whatever Davidson is presupposing him to grasp concerning the notion of truth. What he must grasp is, precisely, the manner in which the truth-conditions of utterances of a sentence go to determine its use: that is, when it is appropriate to utter it, and what are the consequences, for speaker and hearers, of such an utterance. We are disposed to overlook the need for such a connecting explanation because we do, of course, have an implicit grasp of the notion of truth: but a philosophical elucidation demands that it be made explicit.

That there is something to be made explicit is evident from the fact that the result of replacing the word "true" as it occurs in the truth-theory by some arbitrarily invented word would yield nothing with any pretensions to being a theory of meaning: but it is far easier to see that there is something that needs to be made explicit than to make it so. Davidson, we may say, commits the opposite error to that made by the classical theories of truth such as the correspondence theory. To know what proposition a sentence expresses is to know what it means: hence, by asking after the condition for any given *proposition* to be true, rather than for the truth of an utterance of a given sentence, those theories in effect assumed that meanings could be assigned to the sentences of a language in advance of determining the conditions for them to be true. Once such an assumption is made, all hope of arriving at a genuinely explanatory account is lost, because the notions of meaning and

---

[13] Donald Davidson, 'Reply to Foster', in *Inquiries into Truth and Interpretation*, 173.

truth can only be elucidated together, as part of a single theory. Davidson, on the other hand, assumes that he can take the notion of truth as already understood, and explain that of meaning in terms of it: and this condemns his explanation of meaning to be as sterile as was that of the notion of truth in the classical theories.

Supplying an explanation connecting the theory of meaning for an idiolect with the linguistic behaviour of the subject would only be the first step in making out the claim that, on an account of language given in such terms, communication does not need to rest on faith. Whatever the exact status of such a theory of meaning, two such theories will need to be invoked in explaining the process of communication: that governing the speaker's idiolect and that attributed to the speaker by the hearer. The claim is that any divergence between the two theories in the truth-conditions they assign to any sentence must be capable of being revealed by something said or done by speaker or hearer. The second step in establishing this claim would therefore have to be a demonstration, by appeal to the connecting explanation, that a divergence in the assignment of truth-conditions would always result in a divergence in linguistic or associated behaviour, potential if not actual.

It is a long way from being evident that such a demonstration would be possible. It would clearly be possible if the condition for the truth of every utterance were such that we could be credited with an ability, in particular favourable circumstances, to recognize whether the condition obtained or not: but it is obvious that that is far from being so. To this it may be said that those (including Davidson) who accept the thesis of the indeterminacy of translation would not maintain the possibility of any such demonstration: use, for them, does not uniquely determine meaning. Then why not simply conclude that, for them, communication does rest on faith, or else is only to a limited degree possible? Precisely because they further contend that, to the extent that use leaves meaning undetermined, there is no fact of the matter concerning what someone means: there would therefore be no substance to a faith conceived as underlying communication, nothing, in other words, that would be left uncommunicated. If so, the original notion of meaning, regarded as captured by a theory of meaning, was unnecessarily refined, and may be coarsened. Theories of meaning will stand to others in an equivalence relation, holding between any two theories just in case they cannot be distinguished by anything a speaker says or does: and the expressions of two idiolects may be held to have the same coarse meaning just in case those idiolects are governed by two equivalent theories. A characterization of coarse meaning will be given, not by a single theory of meaning, but by an equivalence class of such theories. Coarse meaning will both determine and be determined by use: fine meaning, on the other hand, may, for present purposes (or for all), be disregarded, since there is no fact of the matter whether it attaches to an utterance or not.

The word "meaning" is used in a sense relevant to the present enquiry if, under it, there is a genuine difference between someone's attaching one meaning to an expression and his attaching another, so that successful communication depends upon the correct apprehension of meaning in this sense. But, on reflection, it becomes unclear that it is of any importance to us whether or not it would be possible to demonstrate that use determines meaning, in such a sense of "meaning". If it would not, then communication certainly depends upon an irreducible residue of faith. But, even if we had such a demonstration, it would remain that truth-conditional theories of meaning for idiolects are not autonomous. That is to say, the criterion for whether a given theory of meaning governed a speaker's idiolect would be whether, in the course of linguistic interchange, he always spoke and responded in a manner consistent with it; and this would apply whether or not his mastery of his idiolect were supposed to consist in his having 'internalized' the appropriate theory of meaning. But, if that is so, it seems that the possibility of using language to communicate with others cannot, even in principle, be a contingent feature of having a language: for ascribing an idiolect to a subject would appear to have no substance save in virtue of his use of it to communicate with others.

A possible reply to this would be that the behaviour, linguistic and non-linguistic, by means of which we might judge how a speaker intended his utterances to be understood, that is, on the account under consideration, what his idiolect was, is merely *evidence* for the hypothesis that he has internalized a certain theory of meaning and that the representation of that theory in configurations of his brain issues in such behaviour. Does such a reply rebut the argument?

Our question was whether an account according to which the primary function of language was as a vehicle of thought could explain how it can also be used as an instrument of communication. Any such explanation must consider what constitutes successful communication, in order then to show how an understanding of language as a vehicle of thought is a sufficient basis for it. Successful communication takes place when the hearer understands the speaker as the speaker intended. What, then, constitutes a subject's understanding the sentences of a language in a particular way? Is it what he says and does, or would say and do, when engaged in linguistic interchange? Or is it, rather, his having internalized a certain theory of meaning for that language? If it is the internalization, then indeed his behaviour when he takes part in linguistic interchange can at best be strong but fallible evidence for the internalized theory. In that case, however, the hearer's presumption that he has understood the speaker can never be definitively refuted or confirmed: he can only have evidence that he has done so, which falls short of being conclusive. So regarded, communication does rest ultimately on faith—faith that one has hit on the very theory of meaning that one's interlocutor has internalized.

The only escape from the absurdity of this conclusion is to treat the supposedly internalized theory of meaning, not as constitutive of the speaker's attaching the meanings that he does to his words, but, indeed, as an empirical hypothesis to explain what enables him to use the language to express those meanings. It then becomes irrelevant to the philosophical task of explaining what it is so to use them, that is, what it is to attach a certain range of meanings to the words and sentences of the language. There is now no obstacle to taking a speaker's understanding the language in a particular way as consisting in his being disposed to say certain things in certain circumstances and to respond in certain ways to the utterances of others; and, in this case, whether two participants in a linguistic exchange understand one another will either already be manifest from what they say and do or, at worst, could be made manifest if the exchange were continued in one or another way. But now the internalized theory of meaning has fallen out of the picture (the philosophical picture, though not the scientific one): no attempt is now being made to explain the possibility of using language for communication on the basis of an existing understanding of it as a vehicle of thought.

When the theory of meaning for a speaker's idiolect is not conceived as internalized by him or as the content of a piece of knowledge of any kind that he possesses, the matter stands differently. In this case, the theory of meaning is intended merely as a systematization of the understanding which he manifests in his use of the language. As was argued above, it can in fact be at best a truncation of such a systematic description, needing to be supplemented by an explanation which links the truth-conditions which the theory ascribes to (certain types of) utterances with the linguistic and related behaviour by means of which he manifests his understanding. The question now naturally arises whether the detour through truth-conditions was not superfluous. If a complete account of what it is for the words and sentences of a language to have (in the mouth of a given speaker) the meanings that they do requires a specification of how truth-conditions determine use, and if the only criterion for whether such an account is correct lies in its agreement with the use actually made of them, should we not obtain a simpler account by describing that use directly, without invoking the notion of a statement's being true or being false (independently of whether it is or can be recognized as such)?

That was certainly Wittgenstein's idea. In his later work, he treated the notion of truth as essentially a shallow concept, wholly explicable in Ramsey's way by appeal to the schematic principle that, for each statement "A", "It is true that A" is equivalent to "A".[14] The meaning of a statement or form of statement is therefore not to be explained by stating the condition for it to *be* true, but by describing its use. He understood a description of the use of a statement to consist in saying: under what conditions we should be disposed to

[14] The most explicit statement occurs in the unhappy appendix on Gödel (Wittgenstein, *Remarks on the Foundations of Mathematics*, 3rd edn. (1978), I, app. 1).

make it; to what criteria we should appeal to decide whether it was true and hence to be accepted; what might subsequently compel us to withdraw it; what anyone commits himself to by making it or by accepting it as true when another makes it; what consequences, if any, follow from someone's making it; what we take to be the point of making it on a given occasion; what we take to be the point of having such a form of words in the language—just those things (except the last) by means of which one speaker may judge whether he is understanding another as he intends. The occurrences of the word "true" in the phrases "decide that it is true" and "accept it as true" are not here supposed to be understood in terms of any more substantial notion of a statement's being true than that yielded by Ramsey's equivalence. Accepting or rejecting a statement made by another, checking whether it was warranted, and evaluating circumstances as warranting or as not warranting an assertion made at once or subsequently—all these are activities which demand to be described in any full account of the practice of using language: they are all components of that practice. A statement's satisfying the condition for it to *be* true, on the other hand, is certainly not in itself a feature of its use. The question at issue is whether there is nevertheless a need to appeal to it in a characterization of linguistic practice. Wittgenstein's view was clearly that there is not, but, as things stand, neither that view nor its contrary can be more than an *opinion*: without a detailed account of how linguistic practice may be exhibited as depending on or derivable from the truth-conditions of sentences of the language, it is impossible to decide the question with assurance.

There are two components of Wittgenstein's view: his hostility to systematic theories and preference for piecemeal descriptions; and his rejection of the centrality to an account of meaning of the notion of truth—that is, of a statement's being true, independently of its being accepted or being recognizable as true—in favour of a direct description of use. The second does not depend on the first. Providing piecemeal descriptions admittedly makes it far easier to give the appearance of dispensing with the notion of truth; but, by the same token, it cannot be established that the notion is genuinely dispensable until it has been shown how a comprehensive and hence necessarily systematic account can be constructed without it. Systematization is not motivated solely by a passion for order: like the axiomatic presentation of a mathematical theory it serves to make a clear separation of the concepts and principles assumed from those explained or derived. A piecemeal description of the use of a particular expression or form of sentence will inevitably presuppose an understanding of much of the rest of the language: only a systematic theory can reveal on what basis it is possible to explain in general what linguistic meaning is and how our understanding of sentences depends upon our understanding of the words composing them and of the constructions they employ. By his refusal to contemplate even an outline of a systematic theory, Wittgenstein left it uncertain whether his strategy of describing linguistic practice without appeal to the notion of truth could or could not be successfully executed.

The same holds good of his strategy for philosophical enquiry. He wished to replace the philosophical study of phenomena by a study of the kind of statement we make about phenomena. But such a study, if it is to yield illumination, cannot accept whatever is normally or frequently said as immune to criticism: statements do not in general acquire authority from the frequency with which they are made. We need, rather, to distinguish what is merely customarily said from what the principles governing our use of language and determinative of the meanings of our utterances require or entitle us to say. To draw such a distinction, it is not enough merely to confine oneself to describing what may be observed to happen, or of assembling reminders of what everyone knows, as Wittgenstein claimed that a philosopher should do: the distinction does not draw itself, but requires some theoretical apparatus. The very methodology that Wittgenstein employed rested on general ideas concerning meaning that could be vindicated only by an outline of the very thing that he repudiated, namely a systematic account of how a whole language functions; and so, to borrow a phrase of his, his entire philosophy hangs in the air.

Thus his rejection of a general theory is not only not a consequence of his dismissal of the notion of truth as a deep one essential to a grasp of the notion of meaning, but is an obstacle to evaluating that dismissal. But his negative attitude to the notion of truth should also be distinguished from his positive insistence on use as the determinant of meaning. Even if the negative view is wrong, a theory yielding specifications of the truth-conditions of sentences of a language can be at most a part of an explanation of their having the meanings that they have; whether it is even such a part depends upon whether it is possible to supplement it with a description of the uses of sentences as determined by their truth-conditions.

Does it follow that language has to be considered as essentially an instrument of communication—not indeed because it is a code for thought, nor because meaning can be explained in terms of the intention to induce belief, but because, without reference to the communicative use of language, an assignment of truth-conditions is without substance? Such a conclusion would be natural; but, as thus stated, it would be unwarranted. My argument has been that a truth-theory is without substance if it is not linked to an account of the way in which language is used: the link between truth-conditions and use must be such as to display the manner in which the use of any particular sentence is determined by the condition for the truth of any utterance of it. But that does not show that the use of the language must be a use in communication. It could in principle be a use by a speaker who employs his language (perhaps always aloud) only for the expression of his own thoughts, resolves, judgements, and uncertainties; and a passage from the

Philosophical Investigations suggests that Wittgenstein himself accepted this as a possibility:

A human being can encourage himself, give himself orders, obey, blame and punish himself; he can ask himself a question and answer it. So we could imagine human beings who spoke only in monologue; who accompanied their activities by talking to themselves.—An explorer who watched them and listened to their talk might succeed in translating their language into ours. (This would enable him to predict these people's actions correctly, for he also hears them making resolutions and decisions.) (I. 243)

This passage immediately precedes Wittgenstein's attack on the conception of a private language, in the sense of one that another person cannot understand. It intimates that Wittgenstein has no objection to the conception of a language which, as a matter of contingent fact, only one person actually does understand—or, at least, that he has, in this context, no concern with that conception. It does so by means of the fantasy of a language in fact understood by many people, but not used by them for communicating with each other. The explorer would find it much harder to hit on the scheme for translating the language of any one of these people if his language did not coincide with that used by the others; but the coincidence of their languages makes no difference in principle. None of them holds himself responsible to the way the others speak; if his way of using certain words diverges from that of others, he will not know it and would be unaffected by the knowledge if he had it: the language of each is therefore in principle private to himself. One might ask how the people in this fantasy acquired their knowledge of the language, but one is plainly not intended to do so: Chomsky, who attributes so much of our linguistic ability to innate dispositions, would surely not cavil at the thought of people born with a complete knowledge of a specific language, considered only as a theoretical possibility. A language that is used for communication can also be used by each for speaking to himself: why, then, should there not be a language that is only used in the latter way?

Such people could, of course, form a society of only the most primitive type. They could have no money, and only the most casual form of barter; they could make no concerted plans, hold no councils, elect no leaders; they could give no undertakings and engage in no contracts; they could ask no questions, impart no information, issue no warnings and no threats, utter no endearments, and make no declarations of love or friendship: and all the while, each would be capable of the most sophisticated solitary thoughts, reasoning, and plans.

Reflection on the details of this fantasy quickly shows its utter absurdity: but absurdity does not imply logical impossibility. The idea of some human beings using language only in soliloquy indeed conflicts with fundamental features of human life and human nature, and with our mode of acquiring language; but it should not be treated as a self-contradictory supposition, since the difference between the use of language in soliloquy and in dialogue is not great enough to deprive a language so used of the character of meaningful language. But if the supposition is at least logically possible, Chomsky's claim, as against Strawson, that the primary function of language is as a vehicle of thought, and not as an instrument of communication, would appear after all to be vindicated. Is that, in the end, to be our conclusion? No. Our conclusion should be, rather, that our original question, which of these two is the primary function of language, was misconceived; and that both of the contestants in Strawson's heroic struggle are in error.

Could we not save the thesis that language is primarily an instrument of communication by regarding the people in Wittgenstein's fantasy as communicating with *themselves*? Is not someone writing in his private diary communicating with his future self? If so, is not someone soliloquing communicating with his present self? Chomsky very reasonably objects to such a description on the score that it stretches the notion of communication so far as to obliterate the distinction between the use of language in converse with another and its employment by someone talking to himself: the whole question which of the two reveals the essence of language is then rendered nugatory.[15]

Chomsky's objection is wholly just if the description is meant as a defence of the thesis that the primary function of language is as an instrument of communication. Nevertheless, taken in itself, and not as a plea in defence of that thesis, the description has considerable point. The use of language for self-addressed utterances, whether silent or aloud, is an imitation of its use in linguistic interchange, and involves nothing essentially different. We are inclined to exaggerate the contrast between them because we tend to conceive of soliloquy solely as the audible aspect of a thought-process, whereas, when we think about dialogue, we attend to the very various things that can be done by means of verbal utterances. But the things that someone does when he is addressing only himself are just as various as those done by someone addressing another. He does not merely frame propositions and acknowledge some of them as correct: he asks himself questions, draws conclusions, forms resolves, makes plans, reproaches himself, exhorts himself, ridicules himself; treats himself, in other words, much as he would an interlocutor.

It is indeed true that to describe someone as communicating with himself is to obliterate the whole distinction between using language as an instrument of communication and as a vehicle of thought: but the fact that such a description is not merely possible, but has a point, shows that the opposition between the two functions of language is a shallow one. The true opposition is between language as representation and language as activity: and it is operating as an activity in soliloquy as much as it is in dialogue.

[15] Chomsky, *Reflections on Language*, 71.

Philosophy of language takes its origin from a wonder at the power of language to possess a significance so greatly transcending the surface reality. Two people are talking together: that is to say, each in turn utters sounds of a certain kind. But we know that what is happening reaches far beyond the sounds that are all that is evident to gross observation: they are narrating events, asking questions, propounding hypotheses, advancing grounds and objections, and so forth. How is it that, by merely making certain sounds, they can do these complicated things? More exactly, what is it to do those things? These are the questions philosophy of language seeks ultimately to answer: and, when the stage is set in this way, a particular strategy for answering them presents itself with overwhelming naturalness. Namely, the preliminary answer must be that the participants in the conversation are speaking a language that they both understand: so the understanding of a language is the notion that has to be explained; it is the explanation of this notion that will resolve our perplexity. When the matter is viewed in this way, the understanding of a language is seen as something that each of the two speakers has in his head: it is what he has in his head that makes the sounds he utters the bearers of meanings, and enables him to construe those uttered by the other as bearers of meanings. Communication is possible between two individuals, according to this picture, when they have the same thing in their heads: the business of the philosophy of language is to say what it is that they have in their heads that makes their utterances meaningful. The standard answer is that what they have in their heads is a theory of meaning, usually construed as a theory determining the truth-conditions of sentences of the language. From all this it is apparent why the primary notion must be that of an idiolect, and why the key to an account of meaning is what Strawson called 'formal semantics'.

It is this picture that prompts us to conceive of the significance of language—what makes a language a language—as residing in its capacity to represent reality: a sentence says how things are if it is true, and to understand the sentence is to grasp how things are if it is true. This natural disposition was what was attacked by Wittgenstein, who saw much deeper into the nature of language than either of Strawson's two embattled armies, when he wrote that we have to

make a radical break with the idea that language always functions in one way, always serves the same purpose: to convey thoughts—whether these thoughts are about houses, pains, good and evil, or whatever (I. 304)

and that

we are so accustomed to communication through language, in conversation, that it seems to us as if the whole point of communication lay in someone else's grasping the sense of my words, which is something mental, and, so to speak, absorbing it into his own mind. If he then does something further with it as well, that no longer belongs to the immediate purpose of language (I. 363)

Our position to think in the manner Wittgenstein is satirizing is reinforced by the Fregean heritage. It was observed above that if one asks, as Frege did, what distinguishes thoughts from mental contents such as images, the answer must be that they present themselves as assessable as true or false. It is then overwhelmingly natural to regard language, by means of which thoughts are expressed, in the same light. Of course, this cannot be a simple misconception: the representative power of language is both genuine and central. The illusion is threefold: in thinking, first, that this representative power can be isolated from all the other features of language; secondly, that those other features can be explained in terms of it, or left to take care of themselves without explanation; and, thirdly, that the representative power consists in the speaker's being in the correct interior states. If this were the true account, communication would indeed rest on faith. Since it obviously cannot rest on faith, there must be an adequate outward manifestation of understanding, consisting in a complex interplay between linguistic exchange and related actions. It is this interplay which a genuine account of linguistic meaning has to make explicit, a task which 'formal semantics', in the sense of truth-conditional theories of meaning, unjustifiably shirks.

It is also this interplay towards which I intended to gesture by speaking of language as activity. What was meant was not the banal point that to utter a sentence is to do something, just as to comb one's hair is to do something. It was, rather, this: that the significance of an utterance lies in the difference that it potentially makes to what subsequently happens.

Even for an account of the role played by language in the transmission of information—in enabling us to build up our picture of the world—a specification of the conditions for the truth of our sentences is wholly inadequate, even if it is genuinely needed and even if it can avoid triviality, both of which there are strong grounds to doubt: for since the condition for the truth of any but a very limited range of statements is not one which, in the most favourable situation, we can simply observe to obtain, such a specification will leave largely unexplained what is to be treated as a sufficient ground for accepting a statement of each given type. Until the task shirked by theories of meaning, as these are conceived by the 'formal semanticists', is carried out, we are simply not equipped to form any opinion about whether the appeal to the notion of truth provides an essential first step towards a description of the activity of using language, whether it is a harmless but unnecessary detour, or whether it is a useless and confusing blind alley.

8

The Source of the Concept of Truth

Hilary Putnam began his 1976 John Locke Lectures on 'Meaning and Knowledge' by observing that "the nature of truth is a very ancient problem in philosophy". It is certainly a problem that has greatly preoccupied Putnam himself; in my opinion, he is an outstanding member of that minority of philosophers who have grappled with what makes the problem so intractable. It is not this problem that I intend to address in this essay, however, but, rather, an antecedent question, namely: How do we ever come by the concept of truth?

If the concept of truth is as central to the content of a thought as Frege maintained, and as Wittgenstein, after him, maintained in the *Tractatus*, how is it that there is uncertainty about its application? The most striking example of such uncertainty is the still unresolved question concerning the truth-conditions of indicative conditionals of natural language. For Frege, for the *Tractatus*, and, indeed, for Davidson, any difference about the conditions under which a statement should be accounted true must reflect a difference in the interpretation placed upon it, or in the thought it is taken to express. Yet, surely, the philosophers who engage in disputes about indicative conditionals all understand such conditionals in exactly the same way; what they disagree on is how the concept of truth ought to be applied to them. How, if Frege and the rest are right, could any uncertainty arise about this, given agreement in practice about what the conditionals mean?

Only the boldest of philosophers—Ryle, for instance—have attempted to resolve the problem of indicative conditionals by denying that they admit assessment as true or false at all; but this has been a thesis frequently advanced concerning other large classes of utterances that we should normally classify as statements. There is, however, an important distinction to be made between such claims, according to whether the utterances of the given class are admitted to be informative or not. A straightforward emotivist account of ethical statements, for example, does not allow any informative content to such an utterance as "Rape is wicked": according to it, such an utterance merely registers an attitude that the speaker has to rape. By contrast, Hilbert's way of construing arithmetical propositions involving quantification over all natural numbers concedes to them a great deal of informative content: it

First published in George Boolos (ed.), *Meaning and Method: Essays in Honor of Hilary Putnam* (Cambridge, 1990).

merely denies that they are statements assessable as true or false. Suppose that "$A(\ )$" is a decidable predicate of natural numbers. For any particular natural number, say 103, the proposition "$A(103)$" is then uncontroversially an informative statement. The existential proposition "For some n, $A(n)$" is taken by Hilbert to be an incomplete communication of any particular such instance: one is entitled to enunciate it if one knows of any specific number of which one can show that it satisfies the predicate "$A(\ )$". So understood, the utterance of an existential proposition obviously conveys information: there is no specific statement that one who accepts the utterance as justified is in a position to assert, but the justification requires the speaker to be in a position to assert some one of an infinite range of informative statements. The same holds good, on Hilbert's account, of the utterance of the free-variable form "$A(x)$", or, what is the same, of the form "For every n, $A(n)$" with an initial universal quantifier. Such an utterance is justified if the speaker has an effective means of arriving, for any given natural number n, at a proof that it satisfies the predicate. We can view this as another kind of incomplete communication. Someone who cited a specific effective means of finding a proof of each instance of the proposition would be making a particular kind of informative statement, even if it should be classified as a metamathematical statement rather than an arithmetical statement proper. One who merely enunciates the universally quantified proposition is making an incomplete communication of such a metamathematical statement. Here the informative character of the utterance is even less in doubt, since one who accepts the utterance as justified is now in a position to assert each of infinitely many arithmetical statements, namely the instances of the quantified proposition.

Why, then, on Hilbert's view, are such propositions not to be classed as genuine statements, true or false? Plainly because the condition for someone to be entitled to make any such utterance is inseparably connected with his own cognitive position: lacking such an entitlement does not provide an entitlement to enunciate any alternative proposition. The mere fact of not being in a position to cite a true instance of "$A(n)$", for instance, does not entitle anyone to assert the negation "Not $A(x)$" of the free-variable statement, which would be tantamount to asserting "For every n, not $A(n)$"; and likewise, the mere fact of lacking any means of showing, for each n, that "$A(\ )$" applied to it does not entitle one to assert "For some n, not $A(n)$". Hilbert assumed that the sentential operators are to be explained by the two-valued truth-tables: for this reason, an arithmetical proposition involving unrestricted quantification over the natural numbers cannot be subjected to such operators, if the outcome is to be a meaningful statement. Such a proposition is to be explained in terms of what justifies an utterance of it, not in terms of the conditions for its truth and falsity; although informative, it is therefore not a statement proper, and the operations of negation, disjunction, and conditionalization cannot be applied to it.

The intuitionists in effect accepted the Hilbertian characterization of the meanings of the existential and universal quantifiers, but denied that statements formed by means of them were incapable of being subjected to negation or the other sentential operators. For them, it was necessary only to explain the sentential operators in the same manner, rather than by truth-tables: that is, to give the meanings of the sentential operators by specifying, for each operator, what would justify the assertion of a statement of which it was the principal operator. With all the logical constants explained in this same manner, rather than by a stipulation of the conditions for the truth or falsity of statements involving them, there would be no obstacle to forming by their means statements of indefinitely high complexity.

There are two components of the intuitionists' claim: (1) that an intelligible use of all the logical constants could be attained by an explanation along these lines; and (2) that our existing use of the logical constants ought to be explained in this way, or, at least, (2a) that *one* of our existing uses of them should be so explained. (1) is incontestably plausible within mathematical discourse; whether it is plausible when extended to empirical discourse is less clear. The case to be made for (2a), when applied to negation, is far from negligible. For a linguistic practice involving the making of claims, to be assessed as justifiable or unjustifiable, rather than as true or false, must still involve a recognition of the incompatibility of claims. The claim to be able to cite a number to which the predicate "$A(\ )$" applies is, for example, incompatible with the claim to have a means of showing, for any given number n, that the predicate does not apply to it; and any workable linguistic practice involving the making of such claims must incorporate a recognition of this incompatibility. For this reason, such a practice has, as it were, a place already prepared for the introduction of a non-classical negation, according to which the negative utterance "Not B" expresses a second-order claim to be entitled to make a claim incompatible with the claim that would be made by the utterance of "B". Such a negation would easily be recognized as having the characteristics of intuitionistic negation. For instance, it would easily be seen that "Not: for some n, $A(n)$" was equivalent to "For every n, not $A(n)$"; but that from "Not: for every n, $A(n)$", "For some n, not $A(n)$" would not follow.

For the present, however, this is a side-issue: our immediate concern is with the picture of the genesis of the concept of truth supplied by Hilbert's discussion of the quantifiers. The concept of truth is born from a more basic concept, for which we have no single clear term, but for which we may here use the term "justifiability". We have seen that, even if we operate with the classical conception of a large class of utterances that constitute assertions of statements with determinate truth-conditions, we shall still need to acknowledge that not all informative utterances belong to that class. Other informative utterances may be classified, not as assertions of statements, but as expressions of claims: statements are to be assessed as true or false, but claims as justified or unjustified. Such claims are clearly illustrated by Hilbert's account of arithmetical propositions involving unrestricted quantification. The claim may be justified by the speaker's ability to cite a true statement from some large range, or by his possessing an effective means of establishing the truth of any given statement from such a range, or, as on the intuitionistic interpretation of the conditional, of establishing the truth of some one statement, given any way of establishing that of a certain other statement. In these cases, the condition for the justification of a claim has been formulated in terms of the truth of certain statements; but it does not follow that the notion of the truth of a statement is prior to that of the justifiability of a claim, since the conditions could just as easily have been formulated in terms of the justifiability of certain other claims (as the intuitionists would insist that they should be).

From this it is clear how it is possible that a certain form of statement, such as the indicative conditional, should be well understood, and yet disagreements arise about its truth-conditions. What is well understood, and what is sufficient for grasping the use of that form of statement in practice, is the condition for an assertion of it to be justifiable. More exactly, such an understanding of it does not yet require it to be construed as a statement, nor an utterance of it as an assertion, in the strict sense in which the terms "statement" and "assertion" were used above. Such an understanding amounts to a mastery of the use of that form of sentence to express a claim. That does not rule out its being taken as amounting to a statement with determinate truth-conditions, since an assertion is a particular species of claim; but it leaves it open whether it can be so construed, and, if so, what its truth-conditions should be taken to be.

Why, then, if this is how things are, do we need the notion of truth, or that of a statement, in addition to those of justifiability and the expression of a claim? Hilbert's treatment of arithmetical propositions once more supplies the answer. We are here setting aside non-informative uses of language, such as questions, requests, commands, and so forth, and concerning ourselves only with informative utterances, whether assertions or expressions of claims. To understand the use of a given sentence, considered as used on its own to make a complete informative utterance, we need only consider it as the expression of a claim: we need to know what counts as justifying such an utterance, and we need to know no more than this. If, however, we interpret any of the sentential operators of our language as truth-functional, we shall need to attribute more to the meaning of the sentence than the condition for the justifiability of an utterance of that sentence on its own, if we are to understand the result of applying any such operator to the sentence. For Hilbert, it was just because we can associate with a quantified arithmetical proposition only justification-conditions, and not truth-conditions, that we cannot intelligibly apply negation or any other sentential operation to it. If, then, we have in the language sentential operators which we construe as truth-functional, or as partly truth-functional, we must interpret sentences to which they are applicable as having determinate truth-conditions.

A sentential operator may be called partly truth-functional if the justifiability of an utterance involving that operator requires, for its formulation, mention of the truth or falsity of at least one of its subsentences. An operator's being taken as even partly truth-functional, in this sense, is sufficient to force us to regard any sentence capable of occupying that position as endowed with conditions for its being true or false.

To speak more exactly, all this has been expressed the wrong way round. The concept of truth is far from being wholly a construct of theoreticians. Philosophers who discuss how the concept should be applied to the indicative conditionals of natural language are engaging in a theoretical discussion: it is just because we do not have any intuitive conception of how it should be applied to them that disputes arise over the matter. The philosophers who engage in such disputes are therefore asking how best the concepts of truth and falsity should be applied to such utterances in order to construct a semantic theory faithful to actual linguistic practice, one that derives the use we make of sentences of our language from a specification of their truth-conditions. But the concept of truth is not an invention of theoreticians: it is an intuitive notion with which we operate in natural language; and our linguistic practice is in part guided by our apprehension of conditions for the truth or falsity of what we say. We cannot be said intuitively to regard any sentential operators as truth-functional, since that is a theoretical notion: ordinary speakers do not need, and can rarely pause, to ask which connectives yield sentences whose truth-value depends only on those of their subsentences. Still less can we be seen as intuitively regarding particular sentential operators of natural language as partly truth-functional: for this is not even a familiar theoretical notion (and, as such, awaits further explanation). Rather, it is the existing use of certain operators, which we learn as we acquire our language, that prompts us to form an intuitive conception of the *truth* of sentences to which they can be applied, as opposed to the justifiability of an utterance of such a sentence on its own. This occurs when an operator is used in such a way that the condition for the justifiability of an utterance involving it could not be framed in terms only of the justifiability of certain of its subsentences; we are then compelled to form a pre-theoretical notion of what it is for such a subsentence to be objectively true or false, independently of whether an utterance of it on its own would be justifiable or not.

At least if we subsume tenses to sentential operators, the point is easily illustrated by the future tense. We have two distinct uses of the future tense— what may be called the future tense proper, and the future tense expressing present tendencies. The latter is exemplified by the sentence "There was going to be a meeting, but it will not now take place"; the former by "They are thinking of cancelling the meeting, but I feel sure it will take place"; to this one might add, "I have said all along that there was going to [or: would] be one". What establishes the difference between these two uses of the future tense? More precisely, what allows room for a differentiation between them? The use of a simple sentence in the future tense, considered as uttered on its own, could not allow us to discriminate between the two uses: for such an utterance will be justifiable if and only if the tendencies prevailing at the time of utterance are for events to occur as stated. One way of distinguishing, however, is by the behaviour of the associated compound past-future tense "was going to . . .", which we may view as the result of applying the past-tense operator to the original future-tensed statement. Another way is by the behaviour of a conditional whose antecedent is (tacitly) in the future tense. Usually, the antecedent is taken as being in the future tense proper: in a sentence like "If you go into that room, you will die before nightfall" (which, when translated into Italian, say, would have a future-tensed antecedent), the event stated in the consequent is predicted on condition of the truth of the antecedent (construed as in the future tense proper), not of its justifiability; otherwise stated, on its truth when understood as being in the future tense proper rather than as in the future tense that expresses present tendencies. But the distinction between the two ways of construing a future-tensed sentence, and hence between the truth and the justifiability of an utterance of it on its own, arises only because of the behaviour of more complex sentences formed from it: conditionals of which it is the antecedent, and sentences with compound tenses.

This thesis must be distinguished from a related one for which I argued in my article of 1959 on 'Truth'.[1] There I claimed that the rationale for recognizing certain forms of sentence as violating the principle of *tertium non datur* rested solely on the behaviour of such sentences as subsentences of complex ones, never on the use of them when uttered on their own. This is to say that, given concepts of truth and falsity, the incentive for regarding certain sentences as being, in certain circumstances, neither true nor false is always to achieve a means of systematizing their behaviour as constituents of more complex sentences, usually by a tacit or explicit appeal to a three- or other many-valued semantics. Here I am making a stronger claim, namely that the very concept of the truth of a statement, as distinct from the cruder concept of its justifiability, is required only in virtue of the occurrence, as a constituent of more complex sentences, of the sentence by means of which the statement is made.

Which operators compel us in this way to replace the conception of justifiability by the more refined concept of truth? "And" plainly does not: the linguistic effect of uttering a conjunction of two sentences is barely distinguishable from that of uttering the two sentences in succession, each as a

---

[1] Reprinted in *Truth and Other Enigmas* (London, 1978).

complete sentence. "Or" is a more promising candidate, but by no means a compelling one. Certainly, its ordinary use in natural language could not be captured by a straightforward intuitionistic explanation, to the effect that a disjunctive utterance "*A* or *B*" is justified just in case either the utterance of "*A*" or that of "*B*" would be justified; but a more complicated explanation might be given without appealing to the concept of truth. We must first recall that a non-classical negation can readily be introduced in terms of justifiability alone. The utterance of "*A* or *B*" may now be thought of as expressing a conditional claim to be able to justify the claim "*A*", given a justification of "Not *B*", or, conversely, to justify the claim "*B*", given a justification of "Not *A*": this is, in effect, to take the logical law *modus tollendo ponens* as giving the basic meaning of disjunction.

Given such an argument for dismissing the claims of the connective "or" to prompt us to recognize the concept of truth in addition to that of justifiability, it would seem natural to dismiss the claims of the connective "if" on similar grounds. It lies to hand, after all, to explain "if" in intuitionistic style: the utterance "If *A*, then *B*", so understood, would express a conditional claim to be able to justify the claim "*B*", given a justification of "*A*"; this would be to take the law *modus ponendo ponens* as giving the basic meaning of the conditional. The fact is, however, that such an explanation would signally fail to fit the use of "if" in natural language.

Some may feel sceptical that there is any such difference between "or" and "if", as used in natural language; and it is not a major part of my thesis that there is. If someone accepted the general lines of my argument, but held that our use of "or" as effectively prompts us to form the concept of truth as does our use of "if", he would do little damage to the argument as a whole. The interpretation of "or" proposed above in effect equates "*A* or *B*" with "If not *A*, then *B*, and, if not *B*, then *A*", understood intuitionistically, a rendering of course weaker than the ordinary intuitionistic interpretation of "*A* or *B*". On this interpretation, various statements would fail to be logically true that are classically so: for instance, "Either for some *n*, *B*(*n*), or, for every *n*, not *B*(*n*)". It is, however, arguable that the use of the standard logical constants in natural language embodies a great part, though not the whole, of classical logic. Perhaps everyday linguistic practice is not coherent in this regard, that is to say, not systematizable: perhaps classical laws that would be intuitively rejected as invalid are nevertheless derivable from laws that would be intuitively accepted. However this may be, it remains plausible that the classically valid schema cited above would be recognized by the speakers of natural language as logically compelling, and this calls in question the proposed interpretation of the "or" of natural language.

Such an argument exposes an ambiguity concerning the basis on which the connective "if" was rated a better candidate than "or" for being one whose use prompts us to form the concept of truth. We are seeking to discern the genesis of this concept. The thesis that I have been maintaining is that, for a mastery of the simplest part of linguistic practice, a grasp of the concept of truth, however implicit, is not required, but only of the coarser concept of justifiability; but that the more refined concept is needed in order to master the use of certain means of forming complex sentences from simpler ones. The problem is, then, to seek an understanding of how the use of certain linguistic constructions forces us to refine the concept of justifiability so as to arrive at that of truth. It is no part of this thesis that the concept of truth is spurious or redundant: we really do have such a concept, and Frege was not far off target in saying that truth and falsity are known, "even if only implicitly, to everyone who ever makes a judgement". A little more accurately, we may say that an implicit grasp of the concept of truth is required for construing certain utterances as assertions of statements rather than mere expressions of claims.

Now, once we have the concepts of truth and falsity, it is open to us to interpret such a connective as "or" truth-functionally; and it is unsurprising that we should at that stage be disposed to accept logical laws relating to it that are classically, but not intuitionistically, valid. Our doing so will then properly be called part of the practice governing the use of that connective in natural language; but it does not follow from this that it was the use of that connective which originally prompted us to form the concept of truth. Our mastery of common linguistic practice is, of course, acquired in stages. At a stage when we are implicitly operating only with the notion of justifiability, and not yet that of truth, we can, still without needing to form the latter notion, learn enough of the use of "or" to be able to utter disjunctive sentences appropriately, and to respond appropriately to disjunctive utterances of others. At that stage, we shall have only an imperfect grasp of the use of "or" in natural language, but one whose imperfection is unlikely yet to be apparent to us. Only after we have acquired the concepts of truth and falsity shall we be able to perfect our knowledge of the conventional use of the connective "or"; but, despite the imperfection of our knowledge at the earlier stage, it was not our introduction to the use of disjunctive sentences that *forced* us to form the concept of truth. What forces us to do so is the use of conditionals. Although there is indeed a way of understanding conditionals that can be explained in terms of justifiability, rather than of truth, it does not yield even a plausible approximation to the actual use of conditionals in natural language; and that is why it is their use that forces us to form an implicit notion of truth.

As already remarked, it is of minor importance whether or not I am right to think that the use of disjunctive sentences does not, of itself, have this effect: it is very clear that the use of conditionals does so. A conditional assertion is justified provided the speaker can offer a conditional justification of the consequent, but the condition under which the consequent needs to be justified is the *truth* of the antecedent, not the existence of a justification for it. We have already seen that this holds good when the antecedent is in the future tense; but it holds equally in all other cases, for example, when the antecedent is an existential sentence. In themselves, existential statements are like disjunctions. The fundamental justification for an existential claim is the ability to cite a specific instance. It is only after we have come to regard existential sentences as carrying truth-conditions and hence as expressing assertable statements that we acknowledge indirect demonstrations of existential statements; as with disjunctions, this exemplifies the extension of a primitive use by appeal to a truth-conditional conception of content. But a conditional whose antecedent is an existential sentence "For some x, $A(x)$" cannot be interpreted in terms of the primitive notion of the justifiability of an utterance of the antecedent on its own: to justify the conditional assertion, we must be able to justify the consequent, not on the assumption that we can *cite* an object of which the predicate "$A(\ )$" holds good, but on the weaker assumption that there *is* such an object, known to us or not.

It is precisely because occupancy of the position of antecedent of a conditional constitutes that context which most clearly demands that a sentence be regarded as having truth-conditions rather than merely justifiability-conditions that it is the context invariably chosen by those, notably Peter Geach, who wish to appeal to the occurrences of sentences of a given class as subsentences of complex ones in order to refute a philosophical thesis that sentences of that class are not even informative. Geach holds that the admissibility of ethical sentences as antecedents of conditionals suffices to disprove the emotivist interpretation of them: according to him, such a sentence as "If lying is wrong, then it is wrong to get your little brother to lie" (his example) would be unintelligible unless the antecedent "Lying is wrong" were a full-fledged assertoric sentence with determinate truth-conditions. The cogency of this argument is uncertain, since it is open to the emotivist to claim that a non-truth-functional explanation of conditionals of this particular type would be in place: in the present setting, we need note only that the selection of this particular context—as antecedents of conditionals—to be that in terms of which the argument is stated reflects the peculiar power of the context to demand interpretation in terms of truth-conditions.

It is now clear why it is that philosophers, who perfectly well understand indicative conditionals, as used in natural language, nevertheless find themselves involved in disputes about when they are properly to be called 'true'. The reason is that we possess no intuitive conception of truth for indicative conditionals. And the reason for that is that nothing in our actual use of such sentences forces us to form such a conception; and, more particularly, that we hardly have a use for conditionals whose antecedents are themselves conditionals, that is, for conditionals of the form "If, if A, then B, then C". They are not, indeed, completely ruled out. In particular, if "C" is a logical consequence of "If A, then B", for instance if "C" is "If not B, then not A", such a conditional would be accepted as making an intelligible and correct claim. In general, however, we should attach no clear content to an indicative conditional whose antecedent was itself an indicative conditional; and this is the same as to say that, while we understand what claim a speaker makes by enunciating an indicative conditional, we have no definite conception of what condition must hold for such a conditional to be true, independently of anyone's reasons for believing it true.

Many claims and counter-claims have been made on behalf of Tarskian truth-definitions that have little to do with Tarski's original intentions. Indeed, it is unclear whether his own later estimation of the significance of such a truth-definition did not diverge considerably from his original intentions; in any case, so much has been said on the subject without deference to Tarski's own views that we may here leave aside the question what those views were. It is frequently conceded that a Tarskian truth-definition does not tell us much about the concept of truth; but it is even more frequently claimed, on behalf of such a definition, that, by yielding what Davidson calls T-sentences for sentences of the object-language, it at least determines the application of the predicate "true" to them. It is, however, clear that it is powerless to do even that in any intuitively doubtful case. If this were not so, the problem of the condition for the truth of an indicative conditional could be very rapidly cleared up: we should need to note only that such a sentence as "If Anna is coming from Cambridge, she will pass through Bedford" is true if and only if, if Anna is coming from Cambridge, she will pass through Bedford. But this helps us not at all. We shall readily grant one half of the biconditional, namely that, if the sentence "If Anna is coming from Cambridge, she will pass through Bedford" is true, then, if Anna is coming from Cambridge, she will pass through Bedford. But that half will not tell us when the sentence *is* true. To learn that, we shall need the other half of the biconditional, to the effect that if, if Anna is coming from Cambridge, she will pass through Bedford, then the sentence "If Anna is coming from Cambridge, she will pass through Bedford" is true. But such a stipulation does not help us, precisely because we do not know how to interpret conditionals of the form "If, if A, then B, then C".

We may, quite accurately, express this as follows. The conditional "If, if Anna is coming from Cambridge, she will pass through Bedford, then the sentence 'If Anna is coming from Cambridge, she will pass through Bedford' is true" constitutes one-half of the relevant T-sentence; let us call such a conditional a T'-sentence. The T'-sentence purports to lay down a condition under which the sentence "If Anna is coming from Cambridge, she will pass through Bedford" is true. We can grasp what this condition is, however, only if we know the condition for the truth of the antecedent of our T'-sentence. But this antecedent is precisely the conditional "If Anna is coming from Cambridge, she will pass through Bedford", whose truth-condition we are trying to establish: hence we are no further on. Of course, the same might be said of the specification of the condition for the truth of any sentence whatever, if expressed in a metalanguage that includes the object-language. Normally, however, the fatuity of the procedure, considered as a means of *specifying* the condition for the truth of the sentence of the object-language, is partly disguised from us by the fact that we already have an intuitive conception of the condition for its truth, a conception closely connected with our use of conditionals of which that sentence forms the antecedent.

It would be a mistake to suppose that there is some effective means of passing from the justifiability-condition of an assertion to the truth-condition of the statement asserted. Still less would it be right to think the transition is of a nature that someone with a tacit grasp of the notion of a justifiable assertion is already equipped to understand. On the contrary, the transition is a major conceptual leap. Nevertheless, the general principle that governs it is clear to anyone who has made that leap, as we all did at an early stage in our acquisition of our mother tongues. We suppose given a sentence an utterance of which is understood as expressing a claim, which claim is taken as justified provided the speaker is able to demonstrate that he possesses a certain cognitive ability. This sentence is now to be used in contexts which demand that a truth-condition be attached to it. What will this condition be? Save, of course, in the special case in which the sentence relates overtly to the cognitive state of the speaker, it must be a condition independent of the speaker's cognitive state (or of anything else peculiar to him), and relating solely to some state of affairs obtaining independently of our knowledge. In general, it will consist in the maximal such state of affairs the obtaining of which would be guaranteed by a justifiable claim expressed by the utterance of the sentence. Thus the utterance of an existential sentence expresses a claim to be able to cite a specific instance: if the claim is justified, the maximum that it guarantees, independently of the speaker's cognitive state, is that there should be such an instance, whether known or not. Since an ability to demonstrate any one instance would establish that the claim was justified, the condition for the sentence to be *true* will then be the truth of at least one of them. The condition for the truth of a universally quantified sentence is similarly arrived at from the condition for the justifiability of a claim expressed by uttering it. Again, the condition for the truth of a sentence in the future tense proper is the bare residue that remains when we prescind from the speaker's possession of inductive grounds or grounds in his own intention for the claim expressed by enunciating it, namely the occurrence of the event predicted, independently of the existence of any means of foreseeing it.

The adoption of the concept of truth does not, of course, render that of justifiability otiose; but, in an obvious manner, it makes the latter dependent on the former: an assertion will now be regarded as justifiable provided the speaker was in a position to know, or had good grounds for believing, that the statement asserted was true. The effect is sometimes conservative, sometimes not; that is to say, it sometimes preserves the original notion of justifiability, and sometimes extends it. It is conservative over sentences in the future tense: it remains the case that intention and inductively based causal principles form the only basis for prediction, and so the justification for asserting a future-tensed statement must be the same as that for a predictive claim. It is also essentially conservative over universal quantification. On the other hand, the availability of the notion of truth leads to an extension of the conditions for justifying an existential assertion. The acquisition of the concept of truth automatically generates the concept of falsity. The essence of the concept of truth is that a statement is conceived of as being true or otherwise independently of the speaker's cognitive state and of human cognition generally, in virtue of an objectively existing reality; and this conception provides of itself for the recognition of just one condition that must obtain if the statement fails to be true, namely its being false. Given the notions of truth and falsity, and the interpretation of universal quantification as logical product and existential quantification as logical sum, a justification for denying a universally quantified statement must count as a justification for asserting the existential quantification of the negation of the predicate; and so an indirect justification of an existential statement must be admitted alongside the primitive direct justification.

If the foregoing account of the genesis of the concept of truth is correct, what follows? The account is not concerned with the *explicit* introduction of the concept: it has nothing to say about the use of the word "true" in the language. It is concerned, rather, with a prior implicit grasp of the concept, that is to say, with the creation of a *place* for it to occupy. According to this account, our mastery of the most primitive aspects of the use of language to transmit information does not require even an implicit grasp of the concept of truth, but can be fully described in terms of the antecedent notion of justifiability. But comparatively more sophisticated linguistic operations, and, above all, the use of compound tenses and of conditional sentences, demand, for a mastery of their use, a tacit appeal to the conception of objective truth; and so we have, in our conceptual furniture, a place exactly fitted for that concept as soon as it is explicitly introduced.

This is why any critique of the concept is so fiercely resisted. If it were merely a tool of theorists attempting to devise a semantic theory adequate to account for our existing linguistic practice, it would not appear so indispensable. The same would hold good if our possession of the concept of truth consisted solely in our ability to employ the word "true" within the language, for a large part of the use of that word can indeed be explained simply by appeal to the equivalence principle, that, for any statement "A", "It is true that A" is equivalent to "A". But the concept is neither of these things. Rather, it is deeply embedded in our implicit grasp of the use of our language: not, admittedly, of its most primitive part, but of forms of expression learned at a comparatively early stage, long before we explicitly apply any theoretical notions to our language or the practice of using it. It is for this reason that a criticism of a truth-conditional account of meaning, and, with it, of a realistic interpretation of our language, appears so threatening to the entire conceptual framework of our thinking.

For all that, the account here proposed is no *defence* of the concept of truth, realistically conceived. It does not attempt to explain in what a speaker's grasp of the condition for the truth of a statement consists, nor provide any answer to the charge that any formulation of such a condition begs the question whether it is coherent to attribute to anyone a grasp of such a condition. It simply contends that our linguistic practice cannot be fully described in terms of the notion of justifiability, and that, in achieving a mastery of it, we appear to be compelled to adopt the conception that with most of the informative sentences of our language (though not, for instance, with indicative conditionals) are associated determinate conditions for their truth that obtain independently of our knowledge or abilities.

That has no suasive power against anyone convinced that the concept of truth which, in this way, we tacitly acquire is nevertheless spurious. A tacit acquisition of the concept consists in gaining a mastery of a use of sentences a systematic account of which requires explicit use of the concept. As observed above, its tacit acquisition involves a conceptual leap; but, just because this is so, it is open to challenge. In general, a concept whose acquisition demands a conceptual leap is vulnerable to sceptical attack. Our acquisition of the concept of infinity involves just such a leap; and, for that very reason, no compelling refutation can ever be offered of a radical finitism whose proponents purport not to understand what it means to say that there are infinitely many things of a certain kind, whether natural numbers or stars. Likewise, the view may be consistently maintained that the leap required for a tacit attainment of the concept of truth takes us, not on to firm ground, but into a chasm. That is what, for mathematical statements, the intuitionist holds, and what, for statements of all kinds, the verificationist holds: we are under an illusion that we have acquired a genuine concept or have mastered a coherent linguistic practice.

Thus an intuitionist will not be dissuaded by its being pointed out that the practice of classical mathematicians is not wholly explicable in terms of constructive proof, but rests, instead, upon a conception, tacit or explicit, of the objective truth or falsity of mathematical statements, independently of our capacity to prove or refute them. He knew that already: that is why, rejecting such a conception as untenable, he believes that a just understanding of the meanings of mathematical statements demands a revision of classical practice. Now, although intuitionistic mathematics contains several profoundly subtle ideas, the connection between meaning and justification that it proposes for mathematical statements is peculiarly simple. So simple a connection could not plausibly be suggested for empirical statements: there has to be some definite conceptual advance, some genuine increase in the sophistication of our linguistic practice, that corresponds to the conceptual leap. But what may be called generalized verificationism, or possibly generalized constructivism, must argue that this advance need not be a leap. The concept which corresponds to the full-fledged realist notion of truth, but which, on this view, is the most we are entitled to, is indeed more refined than the straightforward concept of justifiability; but it will still be one that can be explained, even if in a complex and subtle way, in terms of justifiability, and so requires no leap to attain.

In this essay, I have taken no sides in this dispute, either as restricted to mathematics or as extended to other areas of discourse. In several writings, I have addressed the issue because it is my firm conviction that the concept of truth requires more explication by defenders of a truth-conditional account of meaning, and of a realistic conception of the relation between thought and the world, than it has yet received from them; until such an explication is supplied, their views are still unacquitted of the incoherence with which their critics charge them. Here I have sought only to diagnose the deep entrenchment in all of us of a realistic conception of truth, which explains the fanatical commitment of its philosophical defenders and the sense which its critics have of flying in the face of common sense.

9

Mood, Force, and Convention *(1976)*

In his 'Moods and Performances',[1] Donald Davidson very properly distinguished between the mood of a sentence (indicative, imperative, optative, interrogative) and the use to which it is put on a given occasion of utterance (to make an assertion, to give an order, to express a wish, to ask a question), or, in Frege's terminology, the force with which it is uttered. Mood is a feature of the form of the sentence, force relates to the significance of the utterance. Several questions arise concerning mood and force; though these questions are interrelated, it is important to keep hold of the distinctions between them, and I shall therefore give them numerical labels. There are two main questions concerning force. Question (1) is: What is it to attach each of the distinguishable kinds of force to an utterance? To ask this is to ask for a statement of the significance that is conferred on an utterance by attaching to it, for example, an assertoric or an interrogative force; in other words, to ask what it is to make an assertion, or to take someone else as having made one, and what it is to give a command, or to take someone else as having given one, and so forth. Question (2) is: Under what conditions is it correct to say that someone has made an utterance with a specific type of force, has, for example, made an assertion or asked a question? This is virtually indistinguishable from the question: How do we recognize an utterance as carrying a specific force, as being, for example, an assertion or a command? For mood, too, there arise two questions at the outset. We may label as Question (3) the question: What is the linguistic function of mood (i.e. its semantic function in a broad sense of "semantic")? Finally, Question (4) differs from Question (3) in calling only for a syntactic analysis; it is: What is the logically correct representation of mood?

Since, for brevity, I shall refer to these questions solely by their numerical appellations, I here recapitulate. Question (1) asks what each kind of force is; Question (2) asks under what conditions each kind of force attaches to an utterance, or how we recognize it as being so attached; Question (3) asks for the semantic function of mood; and Question (4) asks for its syntactic analysis.

Question (1) is, without doubt, the deepest and most difficult of these

Forthcoming in Bruce Vermazen and Merill B. Hintikka (eds.), *Essays on Davidson: Truth and Interpretation* (Oxford).

[1] In A. Margalit (ed.), *Meaning and Use* (Dordrecht, 1979); repr. in D. Davidson, *Inquiries into Truth and Interpretation* (Oxford, 1984). Originally presented at the conference in memory of Yehoshua Bar-Hillel held in Jerusalem in April 1976, of which the volume edited by Margalit forms the proceedings.

questions; but, while 'Moods and Performances' treats of Questions (2), (3), and (4), it does not explicitly raise Question (1). At first sight indeed, Question (1) is the only one of the four that raises any difficulty at all. For it lies to hand to say that mood is simply a force-indicator; the mood of the sentence conventionally indicates the force with which it is uttered. In so far as this is correct, it simultaneously answers Questions (3) and (2). The linguistic function of mood is to indicate the force attached; and, given that the speaker knows the language, he asks a question just in case he deliberately utters a sentence in the interrogative mood, makes an assertion just in case he deliberately utters one in the indicative mood, and so on. As for Question (4), the answer to Question (3) also determines the answer to it, once we have grasped Frege's point that force attaches only to the sentence as a whole, not to any of its constituent subsentences or to any other particular component of it. If, then, mood is a force-indicator, its representation in natural language by means of the inflexion of the main verb or the word-order in the main clause is misleading, and it must be represented as an operator applied to the sentence as a whole, one that does not affect the sense, i.e. the truth-conditions, of the sentence, but determines an altogether different feature of the significance of an utterance of it.

It is important to note that, even if all this is correct, it takes us not one inch towards an answer to Question (1). To say that someone makes an assertion just in case he deliberately utters a sentence in the indicative mood, or, since the indicative mood is a somewhat imperfect indicator of assertoric force, just in case he deliberately utters an assertoric sentence, is a possible answer to Question (2); considered as an answer to Question (1), it is circular. Assume that we have succeeded in characterizing assertoric sentences in terms of their form; our answer to Question (3) involves that the utterance of a sentence of that form indicates the significance of the utterance, what the speaker is doing by uttering it, namely making an assertion. Question (1) asks what it is for an utterance to have that significance, what it is that a speaker does when he makes an assertion: to reiterate that he utters an assertoric sentence is merely to repeat what we already knew, the means by which he does it.

Davidson calls in question the straightforward answers to Questions (2), (3), and (4) which we have been considering. He agrees, indeed, that mood is a force-indicator; but, according to him, it gives only a prima-facie indication of the force with which the sentence is uttered, an indication that may be misleading. The relation between mood and force is not so simple as at first appears: "there are many utterances of indicative sentences that are not assertions . . . while assertions can be made by uttering sentences in other moods . . . And similarly for the other moods; we can ask a question with an imperative or indicative . . . or issue a command with an indicative." So, while the mood of the sentence provides a partial answer to the question how we recognize the force of an utterance, the answer is incomplete, and more needs to be said to attain a satisfactory answer to Question (2). As for Question (4), we can see that this, too, is more complex than appeared at first sight if we ask a subordinate question, which I shall label Question (4a): Should mood be represented by an operator applied to indicative sentences, or one applied to 'neutral' sentences? 'Neutral' sentences do not exist in natural language: they correspond to what Wittgenstein called 'sentence-radicals'. A neutral sentence is one that has determinate truth-conditions, but carries no force and is, therefore, devoid of mood. The utterance of such a sentence effects no linguistic act; the speaker would not, by this means, succeed in *saying* anything, in 'making a move in the language-game'. Frege's answer was, of course, that the force-indicator must be attached to just such a neutral sentence; since it is only to whole sentences that the force is attached, neutral sentences are precisely what are needed to serve as constituents in a complex sentence, and, likewise, to be that to which the force-indicator is to be attached. That neutral sentences do not exist in natural language is due, on his view, in part to our representing mood as we do, not, as in a logically correct symbolism, by an operator attaching to the sentence as a whole, but by the inflexion of the main verb or the word-order in the main clause, and in part by the irregular behaviour of the indicative mood. The indicative mood is not a fully-fledged force-indicator, since it is used in constituent clauses of complex sentences, including subordinate clauses of non-assertoric ones, such as the antecedents of conditional imperatives, whereas the interrogative and imperative moods cannot figure in subordinate clauses. But a constituent clause cannot carry any force and therefore, in a correct representation, would have no mood. Since the constituent subsentences would then be neutral, the complex, to which the force-indicator was to be attached, would also be neutral.

To this view of Frege's is opposed the conception that no operator is required for a representation of the indicative mood. On this view, there is no need to invent any special neutral sentences or sentence-radicals; as Davidson says, the operators representing the non-indicative moods will then be attached to *indicative* sentences. Davidson himself makes no explicit pronouncement on Question (4a): but, as we shall see, it is of great importance for his own theory.

In his approach to the general Question (4), Davidson is actuated by a concern special to himself. He remarks at the outset that Frege held that an adequate account of language requires us to attend to three features of sentences: reference, sense, and force. Davidson holds, on the other hand, that a theory of truth patterned after a Tarskian truth-definition tells us all we need to know about sense, and that therefore the study of sense comes down to the study of reference. He would like to be able to say the same about force. But what would it be to assert the same about force? Davidson glosses this question as follows: "I want to consider force in the only form in which I am certain that it is a feature of sentences, that is, as it serves to distinguish the moods. And the question I am concerned with is: can a theory of truth explain the differences between the moods?" To give an affirmative answer, it is necessary for him to be able to represent the mood-operators by indicative or neutral sentences, which themselves have truth-conditions and can therefore be handled by a theory of truth. He does this by extending to them his well-known paratactic analysis of sentences involving indirect speech or ascribing propositional attitudes. The utterance of a sentence in a given mood is to be decomposed into "the utterance of a core sentence that is moodless, and the utterance of another sentence that specifies the mood"; this second sentence is called by Davidson a 'mood-setter'. Here Davidson appears to be violating the distinction he himself drew between mood and force. Mood, properly speaking, is a grammatical notion, relating to the form of the sentence; what Davidson intends, presumably, is that the so-called mood-setter should specify the *force* attaching to an utterance of the sentence. Since he wants no allusion to grammatical form, he invents words, "sertive", "impish", and "rogative", to express the content of these 'mood-setters'. "The utterance of a normal imperative, say 'Put on your hat', is then to be thought of as an utterance of a neutral sentence, 'You will put on your hat', accompanied by an utterance of 'This utterance is impish'." In accordance with Davidson's view on Question (2), he remarks that the second of the two components, the mood-setter, is not guaranteed to be true; if, for example, someone uses an interrogative form to make an assertion, the mood-setter ("This utterance is rogative") will be false. There is, moreover, no *convention* that determines when the mood-setter is true.

At first sight, Davidson is siding with Frege's answer to Question (4a). He disclaims the intention of reducing all the moods to the indicative; and he expressly says that the core sentence is neutral and moodless. In emphasizing the absence of any guarantee that the mood-setter is true, he says that "there is no suggestion that an utterance of an indicative, say, must be an assertion, or that it is if certain conventions are observed". In this last remark, an indicative sentence is taken as a representative example; it therefore strongly suggests that an assertoric utterance is, like an imperative one, to be decomposed into a neutral core sentence and an accompanying mood-setter. But, if so, there is a difficulty for the theory, and for any other that refuses to treat force-indicators as, in Frege's term, *sui generis*. The core sentence is neutral; but the mood-setter must surely be regarded as assertoric. If *A* says to *B*, "Put on your hat", he is, on Davidson's account, to be viewed as having uttered the core sentence "You will put on your hat". He did not, however, *say that B* would put on his hat, the sense of making that assertion; that is why the core sentence must be taken to be neutral. *A* is also to be viewed as having uttered the sentence "This utterance is impish"; but, this time, he cannot be taken merely to have uttered a further neutral sentence, but as having, truly or falsely, *said that* his other utterance was impish. So, if the mood-setter is to be taken as genuinely indicative, and not merely as neutral like the core sentence, it, too, must in turn be decomposed into a mood-setter, "This utterance is sertive", and a neutral core. Obviously, infinite regress is thus generated: mood refuses to be fully analysed out.

Davidson was surely conscious of this: it was presumably in order to avoid this trouble that he specified his theory as applying only to the *non*-indicative moods. But then we must ask why the indicative mood should be treated in a special way. The only satisfactory answer can be to adopt the view opposed to Frege's concerning Question (4a). On this view, the indicative mood is not, semantically considered, one mood among others: rather, it represents the absence of any particular mood. An indicative sentence, so regarded, is, always and only, simply a sentence that has certain truth-conditions; it is what, on Frege's theory, a neutral sentence or sentence-radical is conceived to be, something that, in Frege's terminology, expresses a thought but carries no particular force. For this reason, we do not need to *invent* neutral sentences: we already have them. There is then no infinite regress; but, after all, Davidson's theory does involve a reduction of all the moods to the indicative.

How can this be? Is there no stronger sense in which *A* said that his own utterance was impish than that in which he said that *B* would put on his hat, namely that, in both cases, he expressed the relevant thought? Yes, indeed, there is: *A* asserted the one thing, and did not assert the other, and, moreover, will have been recognized as asserting the one but not the other. It is just that there was no linguistic indicator of his making an assertion in the one case which was absent from the other. The whole point of Davidson's answer to Question (2) is that, while mood is an indicator of force, it is neither a certain nor an indispensable indicator; so why not just say that we neither have nor need any indication of assertoric force?

On the question whether there actually is in natural language a feature of sentences indicating assertoric force, Frege was inclined to waver. If we say that the indicative mood is the sign of assertoric force, we run against the fact that the verb in a subordinate clause may be in the indicative mood. But, once we have grasped that the force attaches to the sentence as a whole, and not to its constituent subsentences, why should we not say, as Frege sometimes did say, that the indicative mood of the main verb functions in natural language as an assertion sign?

It seems that we might well say this; but, since the viability of Davidson's answer to Question (4) turns on our *not* saying it, let us ask instead whether we have to say it. In asking this, we have to address ourselves to Question (3), what it is that the mood of a sentence does. For Davidson, it gives a prima-facie indication of the force attaching to the utterance, though, in a particular case, this indication may be misleading; in some such cases, we can see at once that it is misleading, in others we may be perplexed or actually misled. In order to decide whether the indicative mood, considered as that of the main verb, is semantically, a genuine mood, or registers the absence of mood, we have to ask whether its use gives a prima-facie indication that an assertion is being made, or, more generally, of the force with which the utterance is endowed, or whether it gives no such indication at all.

The fact that the utterance of an indicative may sometimes serve to ask a question or to give a command is not decisive, any more than the fact that the utterance of an interrogative may sometimes serve to convey an assertion has any tendency to show that the use of the interrogative mood is not a prima-facie indication that a question is being asked; it follows from Davidson's answer to Question (3) that we have no right to require more than a *prima-facie* indication. Some would argue that there is no *one* such type of linguistic act as that of assertion, that the general notion of 'assertion' is made to cover a wide variety of different uses of sentences, so that, by specifying that someone made an assertion and that what he said had such-and-such truth-conditions, one has by no means completely determined the significance of his utterance. Such a contention is of great interest and importance; but it, too, even if correct, is not conclusive for the present question. Giving commands is not the only typical use of the imperative, which also serves to make requests, to give advice or instructions ("Cook for half an hour in a moderate oven"), or even to express a wish ("Have a good time"). It is an over-simplification to say that the use of the imperative mood is a prima-facie indication that the utterance is endowed with one specific kind of force, that of command; rather, it gives a prima-facie indication that the utterance carries some one of several distinguishable types of force.

To make out that the indicative mood was really a non-mood, one would have to show that its use gave no indication whatever of the force attached to the utterance. This it is impossible to do: at the very least, the use of the indicative mood is a prima-facie indication that the speaker is attaching to what he says a force distinct from any of those which the use of the interrogative, imperative, and optative moods are typically used to convey. The absurdity of treating sentences in the indicative mood as neutral is borne in on us most strongly when we contemplate a use of interrogative sentences, not as calling for an answer, that is seldom commented on. The use I am alluding to is distinct from the asking of rhetorical questions; a rhetorical question may be taken as the use of an interrogative sentence to make an assertion. But in the course of a speech or lecture, or a piece of writing, a speaker may pose a question, not rhetorically in this sense, nor as calling for an answer from his audience, but merely as a preliminary to giving an answer or to saying something towards an answer: the question serves to point the direction of his ensuing remarks. One fact that makes it difficult, at first, to accept Frege's notion of the neutral sentence is that we cannot isolate such a thing: there is no such thing as a complete utterance to which no force whatever is attached, the bare expression of a thought. This, of course, is how it ought to be on Frege's theory; but it is nevertheless a fact which creates an initial resistance to accepting that theory. But, if there is anything which comes close to being the mere expression of 'an assumption proposed for judgement', it is a question of the sort to which I am referring, when it takes the form of a sentential question (Yes/No question). Hence, if the indicative mood, taken as distinguished from the interrogative one, really were the means of framing a neutral sentence, it would be perfectly adapted, far better than the interrogative mood, for the propounding of such assumptions. It needs no remarking that, if a speaker were to attempt so to use it, he would utterly fail to convey to his audience what he intended: the indicative mood is, ordinarily, a sign of assertoric force.

It follows, I think, that Davidson's answer to Question (4), the paratactic analysis which allows him to claim that nothing need be added to a theory of truth in order to account for mood, cannot be sustained. His answer to Question (3), that mood is a prima-facie indicator of force, certainly seems acceptable, at least prima facie. We are not disposed to resist the qualificatory phrase, since it is evident that mood is a very imperfect indicator of force; in particular, we do not have moods to distinguish all the types of force that would have to be recognized in a serious analysis, as has already been pointed out for the case of imperatives. Someone who mistakes a request or a piece of advice for a command is certainly misidentifying the force which the speaker intended to attach to his utterance; but, save by the use of explicit performatives ("I advise you . . .", "I should like to ask you to . . ."), we have no linguistic forms which serve to distinguish these types of utterance. But an adequate evaluation of Davidson's answer to Question (3) depends on consideration of his answer to the closely linked Question (1).

We may begin by scrutinizing his examples of utterances whose force belies their mood. As an interrogative sentence used to make an assertion he gives "Did you notice that Joan is wearing her purple hat again?"; as an imperative used to ask a question he cites "Tell me who won the third race", and as an indicative similarly used, "I'd like to know your telephone number"; and as an indicative used to issue a command, "In this house we remove our shoes before entering". When combined with Davidson's paratactic analysis, these examples produce a very curious effect. If we follow the mode of decomposition blindly, we should, for the first sentence, obtain the core sentence "You noticed that Joan is wearing her purple hat again", and the mood-setter "This utterance is rogative". But, for this genuinely to be a case in which the mood belies the force, we should have to say that the mood-setter was false; presumably, therefore, that the speaker's utterance was not rogative but sertive. This would involve attributing to the speaker an assertion that his hearer had noticed that Joan was wearing her purple hat again; and this seems quite implausible. What Davidson presumably wants to have is that the speaker's utterance was tantamount to an assertion that Joan was wearing her purple hat again. This would compel us to take the core sentence as being "Joan is wearing her purple hat again", something that grammar would not easily lead us to. But, now, the mood-setter must remain "This utterance is rogative", since, for one thing, the sentence *was* in the interrogative mood, and, for another, we should not otherwise have a case of an interrogative sentence used to make an assertion. This way of taking it, however, makes the utterance indistinguishable from "Is (not) Joan wearing her purple hat again?", used to frame a rhetorical question. No doubt we could say that the original utterance had the same point as the rhetorical question, but it is scarcely indistinguishable from it; for one thing, a rhetorical question, strictly so understood, calls for no answer, while Davidson's example invites not only such a response as "Is she really?", but also one like "No, I didn't".

Similar remarks apply to the other examples; to obtain the effect Davidson intends, we have always to transform the core sentence from its apparent indicative or neutral form; for instance, in the last example, the subject must be changed. This is an indication that something has gone wrong with his account; and what has gone wrong is that he is conflating two things which ought to be kept distinct, what the speaker actually says and the point of his saying what he did. Someone who says, "Tell me who won the third race", could have achieved the same effect by saying, "Who won the third race?"; but that does not mean that he was using the imperative sentence in some deviant way, that he was *not* requesting his hearer to tell him who won the third race. No doubt, the speaker in the first example could have made his point just as well by saying, "You may or may not have noticed, but Joan is wearing her purple hat again"; but this should not lead us to say that, by saying what he did, he was not, as he appeared to be, asking his hearer whether he had noticed that Joan was wearing the hat in question. To talk of the *use* of sentences naturally tends to blur this distinction; but it is a distinction that we must maintain if we are to hope to be able to give a systematic account of how language functions, that is, a theory of meaning. It is, indeed, of great importance that, when we engage in converse with others, we are always occupied, not merely in trying to understand what it is that they are saying, but also in grasping the point that they have in saying what they do, their intentions in saying it. In doing this, we estimate their intentions and motives in the same kind of way as that in which we estimate their intentions in their non-linguistic behaviour. What it is that someone says, on the other hand, is determined, not by his particular intentions, but by what is involved, as such, in knowing the language, together with the words he used and the circumstances in which he used them. It is determined, that is, by what is particular to that language, and is or might be different in other languages, in other words by the conventions whose acquisition constitutes learning the language. To give a theory of meaning, a description of how a language functions, is to give a systematic account of these conventions; such an account will determine the meaning of each utterance just so far as fixing what it is that he actually says. It will not yield an explanation of the point that he may have in saying it; but it does not need to, since that is something that we divine in the same sort of way as we grasp other intentions, without making any further appeal to what belongs to the use of that language, and hence may be left, from the standpoint of a theory of meaning, to take care of itself.

If we do not make this distinction, but count everything that belongs to the point of a speaker's utterances as part of their meaning, we are liable to conclude that no systematic theory of meaning is possible, just because the point of an utterance can often not be derived from its structure. It is tempting to ascribe such a conclusion to the later Wittgenstein, who certainly rejected an account of sense in terms of truth-conditions and who seems also to have rejected the Fregean distinction between sense and force. There hovers at the back of much of his later writing the idea that no systematic account of language is possible, but it is not a thesis that he ever states explicitly. On the other hand, he does give an example of the underivability of the point of an utterance from its structure in the *Philosophical Investigations*, where he says that, if I say, "Milk me sugar", it is no part of the meaning of what I say that you should stand and gape at me, even though it has that effect and that was my purpose in saying it. Unfortunately, the example is too crude for it to be easy to know how far Wittgenstein would have pressed the distinction. If, in a suitable context, I say, "Either he is your brother or he isn't", you are likely to understand me as meaning to convey that there are no borderline cases; on the other hand, if, in the course of a proof, a mathematician says, "N is either prime or composite", you are unlikely to take him as making a similar point, but, rather, as preparing you for an argument by cases. There is, however, no way to derive the point of either utterance from the structure of an instance of the law of excluded middle; so, if we adhere to a conception of the meaning of each individual sentence as its use, regarding use as comprising all that is conveyed by any utterance of it, we shall conclude, from these and countless other like examples, that a systematic theory of meaning is unattainable. We can view such a theory as attainable only if we relegate part of what takes place when we communicate with one another to an area that lies outside the proper province of language.

Unlike Wittgenstein, Davidson does not reject Frege's idea of the senses of sentences as specifiable by a statement of their truth-conditions, despite his disagreement with Frege over the relations between a theory of sense and a theory of reference; so he does not conclude to the impossibility of a theory of meaning. But, because he does not make a distinction between the force attached to an utterance, which goes to determine what the speaker is saying, and the point he has in saying it, but subsumes both under a general notion of the use to which he puts his utterance, he would like, similarly, to extrude any

account of force from a theory of meaning, and associate it with the general
procedure of divining someone else's intentions. This he cannot quite do,
because mood is an undeniable feature of sentences, and has therefore to be
accounted for somehow by a theory of meaning; but, without a distinction
between the force of an utterance and its point, it is impossible to account for it
correctly.

   It would be wrong to suggest that the line between the force of an utterance
and its point was always a sharp one. The intention underlying a certain form
of utterance may be so common that we are uncertain whether to say that a
recognized convention is involved or not; and we may have a choice over
whether to say so, although, in general, conventions are not to be multiplied
without necessity. Thus, I think that none of Davidson's examples is an
example of what he claims it to be; but in the case of the third one, "I'd like to
know your telephone number", I find myself inclined, at first sight, to say that
the form "I should like to . . ." is often conventionally used to make a request,
and that therefore the sentence is not properly described as in the indicative
mood. (The term "mood" must, of course, be used somewhat differently in a
semantic and in a grammatical context; but in this case we do not need the
qualification "save in a grammatical sense", since, grammatically, the sentence
is in the conditional mood.) But, if we were to yield to this inclination, what
should we say of someone, seated in someone else's sitting-room and
addressing his host, saying, "I am feeling a bit cold"? Is that a conventional
form of request to be placed nearer the fire or have the heating turned up? If we
said that, we should surely have trespassed over the line which marks off force
from point. Rather, what is being appealed to is not any special linguistic
convention, but the ordinary rules of courtesy; but, if we say that, why should
we not say the same about sentences beginning "I should like to . . .", rather
than ascribing a distinct force to "I should like to use your lavatory" and to "I
should like to see Istanbul once in my life"? Probably the only special
convention we should regard as governing the form "I should like . . ." is that
which allows it to be used in explicit (or virtually explicit) performatives; if
someone says, "I should like to thank you for the trouble you took", he *is*
thanking his hearer, who would be quite wrong to reply, "I shall look forward
to your doing so".

   Even if Davidson's examples fail of their purpose, the point that they were
intended to sustain, that mood is not an infallible indicator of force, is not
thereby refuted. He argues that, even if we had a Fregean assertion-sign in our
language, the mere utterance of a sentence prefaced by this assertion-sign
could not of itself guarantee that an assertion had been made: it would remain
possible to use such a sentence for another purpose. This remark, as it stands,
is certainly correct. The archetypal case is Frege's example, about which Frege
himself was confused, of the utterance of an actor when, in the play, the
character he is playing makes an assertion. Here, we may say, the assertoric

utterance is governed by a special convention, applying to all that happens on the stage from the first to the final curtain. The assertoric force is not exactly *cancelled* by this convention, since the audience, if they are to follow the play, must be able to tell the difference between the *character's* making an assertion and his asking a question, but it is, as it were, *transposed* by the convention, so that the audience understands that the *actor* is not making an assertion, but acting the making of one. But there are also cases of a different sort, involving, not a special use of language, but a special use of the form of a sentence, as when an assertoric sentence in the future tense is used to give a command ("You will go to your room immediately"), or when an assertoric sentence is used to ask a question (e.g. "There are more Japanese than Indians in the country?", uttered in an incredulous tone). In English, the asking of questions by means of a non-interrogative form is rather rare, in some other languages much more common; even here, the spoken sentence would have to carry an interrogative intonation, and the written one a question mark, so that one cannot say that there is no indication of the force. In any case, it seems quite proper to regard it as a feature of the language whether assertoric sentences can normally be used in this way; when my *Teach Yourself Italian* book remarks that it is quite common to do so in Italian, it is surely not concerning itself with something non-linguistic. We may say that, in learning our language, which involves learning to handle the moods correctly, we learn whether, and how far, the indicative mood permits of such subsidiary uses; in these cases, therefore, we are still concerned with something governed by a linguistic convention.

This is not the sort of case that Davidson wishes chiefly to draw attention to. Rather, his interest lies in cases in which there is no prior convention: ones in which a speaker utters a sentence in such a way as, on the face of it, to make an assertion, knowing that his hearer will realize that he cannot actually have meant to make that assertion, and that they will therefore cast round for, and probably hit on, the real intention behind his utterance. For instance, *A* says to *B*, "Do you know who you are talking to? I am the Duke of Marlborough", to which *B* replies, "And I am the Prince of Wales". We could hardly speak of a convention whereby one evinced disbelief in another's assertion by making an obviously false reply; it is a very natural thing to do, and is readily understood even by one who has never heard it done before. Of course, in such cases, the line between force and point, which Davidson does not want to draw at all, becomes blurred; we are hard put to it to say whether *B* has asserted nothing at all, or has shown his disbelief in what *A* said by making an obviously false assertion in reply. Davidson proposes it as a necessary condition for making an assertion that the speaker represent himself as believing what he says. By this criterion, *B* has not asserted anything; let us accept that such cases can and do occur.

How does Davidson think that Question (2) is to be answered? He scouts the idea that we can make any progress in arriving at an answer by appeal to Austin's distinction between the 'normal' or 'serious' uses of language and the 'etiolated' or 'parasitical' uses. He does not mean to deny that such a distinction can be drawn, and, indeed, it follows from the paratactic analysis he later gives, and which I have already discussed, that it can; the 'serious' uses will be just those in which the 'mood-setter' is *true*. Quite generally, if mood is an indicator of force, but only a prima-facie indicator, then we can distinguish a 'serious' utterance as one for which the prima-facie indication is unmisleading. His point is, rather, that this does not tell us when the mood-setter is to be said to be true, and when false; it does not tell us how we are to discriminate a 'serious' utterance from a 'parasitic' one. And one suggestion which he rejects, and which he attributes to me, is that there exist conventions which enable us to determine, from the circumstances in which an utterance is made, whether or not the utterance is to be accounted 'serious'. There certainly *are* some such conventions, as I observed in connection with plays; but let us grant that those conventions do not cover every case. Indeed, Davidson insists, with some reason, that, even if they did, they would be liable at any moment to be flouted. He refers, in this connection, to what he calls 'the autonomy of linguistic meaning'. That is to say, language is never proof against the introduction of new deviant uses, either of words in new senses or of sentences to serve new purposes; and very often we grasp what a speaker intends by such a deviant use, although we have no previously existing convention to guide us. Hence, however elaborate we made our specifications, we could never draw up a set of conditions, in terms purely of linguistic forms, such that any speaker who knew the language would be making an assertion just in case he deliberately uttered a sentence satisfying those conditions; our stipulations would always be liable to be falsified tomorrow.

What, then, is Davidson's answer to Question (2)? He does not offer a precise one, but only indicates the direction in which we are to look, by saying that "there is an element of intention in assertion". This seems, indeed, very reasonable. Davidson hardly needed to invoke the occurrence of 'parasitic' uses, uses when the prima-facie indication is misleading, whether or not there is any convention governing them, to make it seem so; he had only to remark on the fact that mood is a very imperfect indicator of force. The imperative may, quite normally, be used to give a command, make a request, or give advice; the interrogative may be used, quite normally, to ask a question or, again, to make a request or an offer ("Would you like a drink?"). We no more have sufficiently many moods to distinguish the types of force with which we invest our sentences than we have letters to distinguish the vowel-sounds of English; and context does not always suffice to determine the force of an utterance, even assuming that utterance to be 'serious' or 'normal'. Suppose, for instance, that *C* is telling a story about a holiday in France, and *D* interrupts to ask, "Can you speak French?", to which *C* responds, "Avec plaisir", and continues his story in French; at the end of the story, *D*, having evinced the appropriate amusement, amazement, or other emotion, may remark, "I wasn't asking you to speak French, but enquiring whether you could do so". *C* had misunderstood the force of *D*'s utterance; but there was nothing but probability to guide him, the probability, namely, of *D*'s having the one or the other intention.

But, now, what is the relevant intention? In the case of assertion, our natural inclination is to follow the clue given by Davidson's connection of assertion with belief, embodied in his remark that, to make an assertion, one must represent oneself as believing what one says. Assertion thus appears as the external expression of an interior act (a judgement) or the external manifestation of an interior state (a belief). Of course, it may be a sham manifestation, that is, a lie, just as a manifestation of pain may be a sham; but what, on this view, characterizes an assertion is that it purports to be, or is intended to be taken as, a manifestation of belief. And we may hope to extend this to the other types of utterance: a question purports to be an expression of curiosity, a command an expression of desire, and so on.

In so far as Davidson is right in saying that there is an element of intention in assertion, he could, with equal right, have said the same about asking questions or giving commands. Both because the utterance may not be a 'normal' one and because interrogative sentences may also be used to make requests or offers, the utterance of an interrogative sentence does not of itself guarantee that a question has been asked; both because the utterance may not be a 'normal' one and because there are other uses of imperatives, the utterance of an imperative sentence does not guarantee that a command has been given. If the context was insufficient to decide the matter, then all that determines that the speaker was not asking a question or giving a command is the intention with which he uttered the sentence. And so we have, in all these cases, to ask the same question: What is the relevant intention?

It is certainly true that assertion has some intrinsic connection with belief. This is shown by Moore's paradox: a speaker nullifies his assertion if he reveals that he does not have the corresponding belief. But, in this, assertion stands in contrast with commanding and asking questions. A speaker may give a command and yet not represent himself as desiring obedience, or anything resulting from obedience: he might, for example, add, after giving the order, "And I just hope you disobey, because this time I'm really going to throw the book at you"; or he might wash his hands, like Pilate. In neither case does he nullify the command: the command stands. Likewise, someone may ask a question, but not represent himself as ignorant of, but wanting to know, the answer; he may, for example, be an examiner. We cannot even say that he wants, or represents himself as wanting, the person addressed to give the answer: he may be hoping that he will stand tongue-tied before him, or, if he is Joseph McCarthy, that he will refuse to answer on the ground that the answer may incriminate him; or he may be wholly indifferent what the outcome is.

When someone utters an interrogative sentence, which could be taken as used to make a request or an offer, with what intention must he have uttered it for him truly to be said in fact to have been asking a question? When someone utters an imperative sentence that could have been taken as embodying a request or a piece of advice, or an indicative one that could have been taken as conveying a prediction or as an expression of the speaker's intention, with what intention must he have uttered it for it to be true to say that he actually gave a command? We have no answer to hand save, in the one case, "the intention to ask a question", and, in the other, "the intention to give a command". That, usually, is how we clarify our intentions when a misunderstanding arises; we deploy, in our discourse, the notions of the various kinds of force, by saying, for example, "I was not advising you, I was *telling* you". It is, indeed, unthinkable that such a characterization of the requisite intention should be irreducible. It must be possible to make it explicit what it is to give a command, or to be taken as having given a command, without invoking the notion of giving commands as already understood; it is because the speaker relies on his hearer's implicitly understanding what it is to give a command that he can clarify his utterance in this way, and this understanding evidently depends upon a prior understanding of those utterances, unambiguous in themselves or by reason of circumstances, by means of which commands are given. But, as speakers of the language, we do not have an explicit account to hand; it is as philosophers of language that we may seek thus to make explicit what, in ordinary discourse, is left implicit and, thereby, to answer Question (1) as it relates to commands. The two points to note here are these. First, the notion of intention may rightly be appealed to in answering Question (2): it has no place in an answer to Question (1), precisely because an answer to Question (1) must give the content of the intention that is invoked, in cases of ambiguity, in answering Question (2), the intention, namely, to invest the utterance with a certain force. It is the same with ambiguity of sense. If someone says, "I did not notice the slip", the context may be insufficient to determine whether he meant by "slip" an error or a garment, and, in that case, it is only his intention that constitutes his having meant one or the other. His intention was to use the word in a certain sense, or to be taken as so using it; but we should fall into circularity if we then attempted to explain what it was for the word to bear one or other sense, or to be taken as doing so, by once again invoking this intention of the speaker's. Secondly, although Davidson does not himself discuss Question (1), he has no secret means of evading it: as soon as we enquire what is the intention which, in cases of ambiguity, makes an utterance to have been invested with one kind of force rather than another, we see that we can give an informative answer only by answering Question (1).

Mood, Force, and Convention

So: not to determine which a (for a) but to have to utter a concept of what is sentence is some force:

pragmatic

My appeal to the notion of convention was intended to relate, not as Davidson supposed, to Question (2), but to Question (1). The claim was not that linguistic conventions suffice, in every case, to determine the force attached to an utterance; it was that to know what it is to ask a question, or to give a command, or to make an assertion or request, etc., is to be master of a certain *use* of sentences, which use is constituted by conventions, linguistic and non-linguistic, which are part of a common practice that has to be acquired. What makes an utterance a command (Question (2)) is a combination of the mood of the sentence and the surrounding circumstances, supplemented, in cases when these do not suffice, by the speaker's intention. But what it is for it to be a command (Question (1)) is given by the whole complex social practice in accordance with which one individual is recognized as having authority over another in a certain respect, and may impose sanctions of varying kinds for disobedience to commands issued on that authority. (A good example of socially recognized authority is that which I believe Professor Anscombe once mentioned, the authority each person has over who may enter his room.) It is not part of this thesis that every difference of force must be marked by a feature of the linguistic expression: it is integral to the thesis that to grasp what it is for a sentence to carry a particular kind of force is to be master of a practice—of what Wittgenstein called a language-game, which has to be learned and whose existence depends upon a common participation in it by the speakers of the language. Let us label this Thesis A.

If I have understood him aright, Thesis A already conflicts with Davidson's view of the matter. It does not, however, exhaust what I intended when I characterized force as depending upon convention. It would be quite consistent with Thesis A to hold that, in explaining certain kinds of force, in answering Question (1) as relating to them, we should have to appeal to interior states of the speaker, to his beliefs, desires, and perhaps intentions. I wished, however, also to maintain what we may call Thesis B, that no such appeal is needed, indeed that any such appeal will involve a circularity.

Giving commands, asking questions, and making bets are all purely external activities in the sense already stated, namely that they are in no way frustrated by any disavowal by the speaker of their most common internal accompaniment: if a man, having laid a bet, says that he does not expect to win it, that does not cancel the bet. But, as we noted, assertion *is* tied in this manner to belief, as making a request is to desire: if, having asked for a drink, I add that I do not want a drink, I either produce puzzlement or am understood as having withdrawn my request. This makes it natural to suppose that, in explaining the language-game of assertion, we must allude to the speaker's beliefs, and that, in explaining that of making requests, we must allude to his desires. Thesis B does not, of course, deny that any adequate account of assertion and belief, or of request and desire, must exhibit the connection between them: what it denies is that, in explaining assertion, we can take it as already understood what it is to have the belief evinced by a given assertion, and likewise with request and desire. It is a thesis concerning the proper order of explanation.

Let us first ask what the relation is between someone's having a certain belief and his holding to be true a sentence of his language expressing that belief. Is his having that belief to be explained in terms of his holding that, or some similar, sentence to be true? Or is his holding the sentence to be true to be explained in terms of his having the belief it expresses? It is plain that, in general, we must opt for the former alternative. The latter is possible only when the belief is one that can intelligibly be ascribed to someone independently of his mastery of language; without taking time to argue the point in this essay, I shall take it as common ground that this is true only of a small proportion of our beliefs. Now to say that a belief cannot intelligibly be ascribed to someone who lacks the language in which it can be expressed is to say that any account of his holding that belief must invoke his mastery of such a language. That means, in turn, that, to a first approximation at least, we have to explain having the belief as holding to be true a sentence, in a language understood by the subject, which expresses that belief: we cannot, therefore, appeal to the belief as explaining what it is to hold that sentence to be true.

We have now to decide a second question of priority in the order of explanation, namely between making an assertion and holding a sentence to be true. Is assertion an external manifestation of belief, or is belief the interiorization of assertion? Since we have already decided that, in general, belief is to be explained in terms of understanding a language and holding a sentence of that language to be true, the question comes to this: Is assertion an external manifestation of holding to be true the sentence by uttering which the assertion is made, or is holding the sentence to be true an interiorization of assertion?

This question brings us face to face with the concept of truth. For, on the face of it, if someone is to be said to hold a sentence to be true, he must grasp the concept of truth, though, admittedly, his grasp of the concept need only be an implicit one—he need not have a word for 'true', still less be able to explain it. Furthermore, if a grasp of the sense of a sentence is to be explained as consisting in a knowledge of its truth-conditions, then even to ascribe to someone an understanding of a sentence involves attributing to him an implicit grasp of the concept of truth. Now this may be objected to. We may say of someone that he trusts someone else without ascribing to him a grasp of the concept of trust or of trustworthiness, or that he finds something interesting without ascribing to him a grasp of the concept of interest or of being interesting. But, at any rate, we, in describing someone as trusting another or as taking an interest in something, are making explicit use of the concepts of trust and of taking an interest, and may therefore be fairly challenged to explain these concepts. Similarly, if we make use of the notion of someone's holding to be true a sentence that he understands, we must be prepared to explain what it *is* to hold a sentence to be true; and if we explain understanding a sentence as taking it to be true if and only if such-and-such a condition obtains, we must be prepared to explain what it *is* so to take it. We can say what it is to take an acquaintance as trustworthy, or to take something as interesting: but what is it to take a sentence as *true*?

We can take a short way with this question by saying that to take a sentence as true is to be prepared to assent to it, and then selecting some simple behavioural token of assent, such as nodding when another utters the sentence (in an interrogative tone or otherwise). But this is to bypass the real issue. A behavioural account of trusting displays what trust is, and a behavioural account of showing an interest in something displays what interest is: but to talk of nodding is not to explain what assent is, since nodding is only a gesture of assent, not an exemplification of it. To register assent is to make a certain move in the language-game; if assertion is to be explained as an external manifestation of belief, then giving a sign of assent must be explained likewise. If we are going to explain assertion as a manifestation of belief, and belief as taking to be true a sentence understood by the subject, we cannot explain taking a sentence to be true in terms of assertion or of assent.

If meaning is to be explained in terms of truth-conditions, and understanding is correlative to meaning, then an even more blatant circularity threatens us from the other side of the biconditional. Taking something to be interesting just in case a certain condition is fulfilled is, at least roughly, being prepared to treat it as interesting as soon as one is persuaded that that condition is fulfilled. But, if we explain understanding a sentence as taking it to be true just in case a certain condition obtains, then we cannot, in this context, explain taking it to be true just in case that condition obtains as being prepared to treat it as true as soon as one takes that condition to obtain. We cannot do so because taking the condition to obtain is tantamount to believing it to obtain; and our strategy was to explain belief in terms of taking to be true a sentence which one understands.

It cannot here be pleaded that the theory of meaning merely states that the sentence is true if and only if a certain condition holds, not that the speakers in any sense *know* this. Whether an account of what it is for the sentences of a language to have the meanings that they do needs to appeal to the notion of an individual speaker's understanding the language is a difficult question. If this question is decided affirmatively, a further, equally difficult, question arises: Is an individual speaker's understanding of the language to be explained as his having an implicit knowledge of the theory of meaning that governs the language, or in some more subtle way that does not invoke the concept of knowledge? But, however these questions are to be answered, the fact remains that it is the notion of *understanding* with which we are here concerned, since we proposed to appeal to it in explaining both what it is for someone to have a given belief and what it is for him to make an assertion.

An understanding of a language is the mastery of a *practice*. Hence whatever place the notion of truth may have in a correct account of that in which the understanding of a language consists, it must be connected up with the practice of speaking the language. Indeed, that which a theory of meaning for the language is concerned to explain is the existence of this practice; and hence, in the same way, that theory will explain what it is intended to explain only if the theoretical notions it employs are connected up with the practice, including the notion of truth, in so far as it is taken to play an essential role in the theory. The question whether the theory of meaning needs to invoke the notion of an individual speaker's understanding of the language is thus the question whether the description of a conventional practice needs to appeal to the notion of an individual's mastery of that practice; and the question whether a speaker's understanding of the language is to be explained as his implicit knowledge of the theory of meaning is the question whether the mastery of a practice is to be explained as the implicit knowledge of a theoretical description of the practice. But, to repeat, the notion with which we are concerned in the present context is not that of a sentence's having the meaning that it has, but that of a speaker's understanding that sentence, together with that of his taking it to be true. In explaining the latter notion, we are surely unable to evade the notion of truth; in explaining that of understanding a sentence, it is at least obscure how Davidson could avoid invoking it.

It is only in relation to the practice of speaking a language that we can give any content to the notion of a sentence's being true. We have seen that it is necessary to distinguish between the question when a sentence has a certain force (Question (2)) and the question what it is for it to have that force (Question (1)). To say, for a certain variety of force, that there was no answer to Question (1) would be, in effect, to say that the conception of that kind of force was spurious; and then Question (2) could not seriously and significantly be asked. No one can sensibly be said to know, for example, that an utterance is an assertion if such-and-such conditions are fulfilled if that is *all* he knows about assertion; unless he knows, in some implicit manner, what assertion is, all he can be said to know is that an utterance made under those conditions is *called* an 'assertion'. In a precisely analogous way, we must also distinguish between the question under what conditions a sentence is true and the question what it is for a sentence to be true. For a theory of meaning that admits a distinction between sense and force, it is that part of the theory which constitutes the theory of sense that provides an answer to the question under what conditions any sentence of the language is true; for Davidson, the theory of sense simply is a theory of truth, that is, a theory which permits the derivation, for any sentence, of its truth-conditions. But no one can sensibly be said to know the theory of truth, in this sense, if that is all he knows about truth. Unless he knows, in some implicit manner, what truth is, he cannot be said to know a sentence to be true, or to know that it is true under such-and-such conditions; all that he can be said to know is that it is to be *called* 'true', absolutely or under such-and-such conditions.

I have here slipped back into appealing to the notion of implicit knowledge, which can be quite difficult to avoid; the sort of knowledge involved is that spoken of when it is said that someone does, or does not, know the difference between right and wrong, where he may be allowed to know the difference even if he has no words for "right" and "wrong". It might be objected that we are concerned with someone's *holding* a sentence to be true, which need not amount to his *knowing* it to be so, and with his *understanding* it, which need not be explained as his knowing its truth-conditions; and, earlier, I allowed a similar objection. But the question whether, in the phrase "knowing what truth is", the verb "to know" is appropriate and to be taken at face-value, though an important and interesting one, is not here to the point. An implicit knowledge of what it is for a sentence to be true consists in having a mastery of the practice of speaking the language, whether or not the word "knowledge" is justifiably used in this connection; more exactly, it is that part of a mastery of the practice of speaking the language which is not represented by the theory of sense. If *we* are to explain in what that practice consists, and what it is for someone to have mastered it, we must make the connection, in our theory of meaning, between that practice and our theory of sense. This means that we must make explicit, in our theory of meaning and our theory of understanding, what it is that someone would not know if all he knew, in any sense, about the language and about truth was the theory of sense, the specification of the truth-conditions of the sentences. The part of the theory of meaning that establishes this connection will be the theory of force; and it is this that will explain what it is for a sentence to be true. The theory of force will contain a direct description of, for example, the language-game of assertion, that is, of the practice of speaking the language in so far as it involves the making of assertions; and it will do so without invoking any more about the notion of truth than is given by the theory of sense, i.e. by that part of the theory of meaning which specifies the *content* of each sentence, irrespective of the force attached to it. This much about the notion of truth we may legitimately invoke, since otherwise we shall have no uniform notion of assertion at all, and shall not have justified segmenting our theory of meaning into a theory of sense and a theory of force. But more we cannot invoke, on pain of leaving tacit what it was our object to make explicit: for what else there is to the concept of truth is precisely that which establishes the connection between the truth-conditions of the sentence and the use to which it is put, the significance conventionally attached to an utterance of it.

I am not arguing that the notion of assent has no place in the explanation of what it is to take a sentence as true. I am arguing, rather, that to explain what it is for a sentence to be true involves describing the practice of speaking the language, and that to explain what it is to take a sentence as true involves giving an account of what it is to have a mastery of that practice. We therefore cannot describe that practice, or any ingredient of it such as assertion, or explain in what a mastery of it or of that ingredient consists, by appeal to the notion of holding a sentence to be true. To explain what it is to hold to be true a sentence that one understands, we have to explain what it is for it to be true; and we have to do this by describing what it is to *treat* the sentence as true, namely by asserting it, assenting to it, etc. The connection between assertion and belief is not to be denied: but we cannot explain what it is to make an assertion by appeal to the notion of belief, because the notion of belief is, in general, subsequent to that of holding a sentence to be true, and the notion of holding it to be true is subsequent to that of treating it as true, one exemplification of which is asserting it.

Theses A and B are quite independent of there being moods or other conventional force-indicators. It would be in principle consistent with those two theses that the language should be wholly devoid of mood, so that the hearer had always to guess what force was attached to the utterance. It is surely improbable that such a language would be workable or could be easily learned; but Theses A and B do not rule it out. They maintain, rather, that what it is to make an assertion, to give a command, or the like, is to engage in a certain conventional practice, without the existence of which there would be no such thing as using sentences as carrying the relevant kind of force; and, further, that this practice is, and must be, describable without appeal to interior states such as intention, belief, and desire, since those states are propositional attitudes not, in general, ascribable to one who has not already mastered the language-game in question. The conventions to which I intended to allude are not those which determine whether, for example, an utterance is to be taken as an assertion, but those without which there would be no such thing as the assertoric use of sentences, those by reference to which an account is to be given of what it is to make an assertion.

Although Davidson, by ignoring the distinction between force and point, greatly exaggerates the extent to which mood may belie force without this being explicable by appeal to any special linguistic convention, there is no ground to doubt that such cases occur. But Davidson drives towards a picture entirely different from that which I have just tried to sketch. That he never quite presents this alternative picture is due to his having to reckon with the undeniable phenomenon of mood; but I think that he would like to consider mood as, in principle, quite inessential. Suppose, then, a language wholly devoid of mood, which, whether a genuine possibility or not, I have already acknowledged as not incompatible with my own Theses A and B concerning how Question (1) is to be answered. According to Thesis A the distinction between the different kinds of force with which a sentence could be uttered would depend upon the existence of a variety of language-games a move in which could be made by the utterance of that sentence. Without mood to indicate force, a hearer must guess the speaker's intention: but the intention in question would be to engage in one rather than another language-game, each such language-game being constitued by conventions which determine the significance of an utterance. Suppose, as an analogy, that there were two distinct games played with chess-men on a chessboard, having the moves and the initial position in common, but not the principles governing win and loss; and suppose also that we, very inconveniently, possessed no means of indicating in advance which of these games we proposed to play. Then the player with the black pieces would have to guess, from his opponent's opening move, which game he was meaning to play. The move would have one significance or another according to which game was being played: but this significance would be conventionally determined, namely by the rules of the game in question. (*not by the intention alone*)

Davidson's picture is entirely different. On his view, force is not a matter of a conventional practice at all: all that is conventional about the language is the *sense* of the words, that is, what goes to determine the truth-conditions of each sentence, the content that may be in common between one uttered assertorically and one uttered interrogatively or imperatively. More exactly, since our language does have mood, whose significance is undoubtedly conventional, all that would be conventional about a language that lacked mood would be the senses of the words (in the Fregean sense of "sense"). In apprehending the force attached to an utterance, a hearer would be doing just what I earlier said he is doing in grasping the *point* of an utterance, namely divining the intention of the speaker, where this intention is one that does not relate to any convention that has already to be established or to have been acquired. According to me, a hearer has to ask himself, "What could the speaker's purpose be in asserting that so-and-so (or in asking whether so-and-so, etc.) in this context?", and so to estimate the speaker's intention in uttering a sentence with such-and-such truth-conditions and with such-and-such a force. If the language is devoid of mood, he must also ask himself, "What force is it likely that the speaker intended to attach to his utterance?", just as, if the speaker uses an ambiguous word or construction, he must ask himself, "In what sense is it likely that he intended his utterance to be understood?" But, just as the possible senses of a word depend on distinct alternative conventions governing its use, so, according to me, do the different possible forces that may be attached to an utterance, where the *point* of an utterance expressing a given sense and carrying a given force is not a matter of any established linguistic convention. For Davidson, however, the same is true of force. For him, the question the hearer has to ask himself is "What could the speaker's purpose be

in uttering, in this context, a sentence with such-and-such truth-conditions?"
Or, at least, this would be his question if the language were devoid of mood.
And, in answering this question, he will seek to characterize the speaker's
intention without reference to any further linguistic convention. He will, by
giving such an answer, determine *both* the force and the point of the utterance;
or, rather, there is no distinction to be drawn between these two features of it.
Force is not, for Davidson, something governed by convention at all, and so
no viable distinction between it and the point of an utterance needs to be made.

This explains why Davidson fails to make the distinction between force and
point even for a language, like the one we have, that does have moods. It is
plain that a failure to draw the distinction leads in this case to definite error, in
that it obstructs any adequate account of mood. Davidson's account makes
inevitable a misdescription of his own examples. The point of asking, "Did you
notice that Joan is wearing her purple hat again?", may be to draw attention to
Joan's hat, or, more subtly, to prompt the question "Has she worn it before?",
and to be able to reply, "Dozens of times", while dishonestly adding, "I should
not have mentioned it if I had not thought you knew"; but what nevertheless
makes it a genuine question is that, like other questions, it calls for an answer.
Force is, as it were, a tactical, not a strategic notion: it does not relate to the
long-term aim, but to the form of linguistic or non-linguistic response, if any,
which is called for, and the commitment, if any, undertaken by the speaker (it
being the latter which differentiates an offer from a mere enquiry). Mood is an
indicator only of the immediate tactical role of the utterance, not of its
strategic intent. But I do not wish to be taken as arguing that this mistake of
Davidson's reveals, by itself, any fault in his general conception. It would be
consistent to allow that a distinction between force and point was required for
an account of mood, while holding that, for a language devoid of mood, such a
distinction, though it might be drawn, would not be needed. Whether that
distinction would be needed, in that case, depends upon whether the
significance of an utterance could be satisfactorily explained without invoking
any recognized linguistic conventions other than those that determine sense.
This, in turn, depends, in part, on whether we have any means of explaining
what it is to ascribe to someone any of the beliefs which he is capable of
expressing without presupposing that he has a mastery of the assertoric use of
language. I have argued that we have no such means. This is a deep issue, and I
do not pretend to have done more than give hints in favour of my conjecture,
and against Davidson's, concerning how it is to be resolved. As Davidson in
effect remarks, to construct an account of assertion satisfying the conditions
demanded by Theses A and B is far from easy; only when it has been done will
there be anything describable as a demonstration of those theses.

10

Frege and Husserl on Reference

In his excellent book *Husserl*[1] Professor David Bell challenges the customary assimilation of Husserl's "theory of *gegenständliche Beziehung* [objectual reference]", as expounded in his *Logische Untersuchungen* (1900–1), "to Frege's theory of *Bedeutung*" (p. 140), with Husserl's meaning (*Bedeutung*) assimilated to Frege's sense (*Sinn*). He argues that Frege's notion of *Bedeutung* is one of "genuine, full-blooded, relational reference" (p. 130), whereas Husserl's notion of reference is "adverbial". Citing a host of Husserl experts and other commentators (including myself) as having misconstrued the text, he sees this as a critical point of Husserl exegesis:

This is a crucially important issue; for, in it, there come to a head a number of problems—to do with intentionality, meaning, objects, reference, the nature of phenomenology, the degree of Husserl's commitment to methodological solipsism, and the nature of his commitment (if any) to realism—problems the solutions we provide to which will in large part determine what, in general, we make of Husserl's early philosophy as a whole. (p. 133)

It certainly seems that whoever is wrong on this point must be misinterpreting Husserl's *Logische Untersuchungen* from start to finish.

The problem arises out of the contrast between two modes of assigning the object of what Brentano called a 'mental act', or of a linguistic one. In one mode, it may rightly be said that no one can make a request, for example, unless he makes it of somebody; a child writing a letter can, in this mode, truly be said to be asking Father Christmas for a toy train. This is the intensional mode: the verb "to ask" is taken as creating an intensional context. There is also an extensional mode: in this mode, we may truly say that there is no one to whom the child is addressing his request. Any adequate account of the activity of requesting must make room for both these modes. The problem concerns all propositional attitudes—all states relating to what Frege called 'thoughts'—as well as to all actions that express or convey them. It is thus not restricted to linguistic acts like making a request or an assertion, as the reference to Frege's theory of *Sinn* and *Bedeutung* might suggest. Frege's view was that we human beings can grasp thoughts only as expressed in language, which implies that language is involved in our assumption of any propositional attitude; but this

Excerpted from a review of D. Bell, *Husserl* (London, 1990), *Philosophical Quarterly*, 41 (1991), 484–8.

[1] (London, 1990.) All page numbers in this essay refer to the same work.

is a subsidiary thesis which, for present purposes, may be set on one side. The theory of *Sinn* and *Bedeutung* was not, for Frege, exclusively about linguistic expressions, in that thoughts do not owe their existence to being expressed, but have as intrinsic constituents the senses of the words composing the sentences that would express them, while *Bedeutung* attaches primarily to the sense and only mediately to the expression.

We are thus faced with the problem of reconciling the two modes of speaking of the object that someone's thought is about or to which his propositional attitude relates. These are the extensional and the intensional modes, and they reflect two ways of thinking about the object; that way of thinking about it that corresponds to the extensional mode of expression we may term 'the extensional conception', and that which corresponds to the intensional mode of expression 'the intensional conception'. Bell presents the problem on his pages 133–5. He terms the extensional conception a 'relational theory' of intentionality, and sees it as embodied in Frege's theory of *Bedeutung*. The intensional conception contrasted with it he terms an 'adverbial theory' of intentionality. His contention is that those interpreters of Husserl whose views he is controverting have mistaken him as holding a relational theory, whereas in truth he held an adverbial theory. He goes on to identify a relational theory as a realistic one (p. 135); that is why he takes it that the topic bears crucially upon the nature of Husserl's commitment (if any) to realism.

As Bell himself says, however, the problem is not one of choosing whether to adopt one or the other type of theory: it is that of finding a way to *reconcile* them. We cannot do without the intensional mode of expression; without it, we should be unable to recognize that intentionality characterizes all propositional attitudes, or to state certain facts that indisputably *are* facts. But we can hardly dispense with the extensional mode, either: without it, we could not indicate wherein there is a greater difference between asking Father Christmas for a toy train and asking one's aunt for one than between asking one's aunt and asking one's mother. The fact that both Husserl and Frege had a means of reconciling the two conceptions, or at least the two modes of expression, suggests that, even if Bell is right, the opposition between the two philosophers in this regard is not one of essential doctrine, but only a disagreement over which part of the composite theory, the relational part or the adverbial part, the notion of reference each employs is to belong to.

Bell indeed believes that Husserl had a strategy for reconciling the two conceptions. He describes this (p. 134) as the proposal that we construe "the relation between my intentional object and the 'corresponding' real object, if there is one" as "a weaker and more distant one" than that of identity, "say, one of 'correspondence' "; on such a view, "when I am minded in a certain intentional way, there will be *some* (as yet unspecified) relation" between the two. As we shall see, this is not a completely accurate way of characterizing

Husserl's thought; but, to the extent that it serves this purpose, it equally well serves that of characterizing Frege's, though Bell does not remark on the fact. What, on Frege's view, the thinker *grasps* is the sense. This sense has, or, sometimes, unhappily lacks, a *Bedeutung*, which is the object about which he is thinking. If there is such an object, the sense is not identical with it, but constitutes, rather, a particular way in which that object is given to the thinking subject. No difference between the views of Frege and of Husserl has therefore yet been demonstrated.

Why is the foregoing characterization of Husserl's view inaccurate? It is so because it suggests a conception that Husserl emphatically repudiates. That it amounts, not merely to an infelicitous choice of words, but to a definite misinterpretation, is witnessed by Bell's arguing (p. 138) that "the intentional object to which an expression has *gegenständliche Richtung* [objectual directedness] can never be the same as the object (if any) that would be assigned to that expression as its Fregean *reference* [*Bedeutung*]". Husserl expressly contradicts this in a passage from the *Logische Untersuchungen* (Investigation V, appendix to §§11 and 20). This passage is quoted by Bell himself a few lines further on; the passage also repudiates the conception suggested by Bell's initial characterization of Husserl's view.

It is a serious error to draw a real distinction between "merely immanent" or "intentional" objects, on the one hand, and "transcendent", "actual" objects which may correspond to them, on the other. . . .. It need only be said to be acknowledged *that the intentional object of a presentation is the same as its actual object, and on occasion as its external object*, and *that it is nonsensical to distinguish between the two*.

Intentional objects do not form an ontological category: to speak of them is merely to adopt the material mode of saying what, in the formal mode, relates to a singular term standing in an intensional context. To say that Father Christmas is the intentional object of a child's expectation is just to say that he expects Father Christmas, where, obviously, the intensional mode of expression is being used; it is not to say that there is a special kind of object forming a constituent of the child's consciousness, or immanent in his act of expectation, still less that he is not expecting a cheery old gentleman with a white beard, but something altogether more ethereal. In such a case, we may say that the object is 'merely intentional', meaning that a falsehood would result from interpreting the statement that the child expects Father Christmas in accordance with the extensional mode of expression; but, as Husserl remarks, to call the object 'merely intentional' "does not mean that it *exists*, but only in the *intentio* (as a real component part of it), or that there exists therein some kind of shadow of it". What it means, rather, is, as he says, that "the intention, the act of meaning [*das 'Meinen'*] an object of such a kind, exists, but the object does not" (ibid.). All this Bell, very honestly, quotes; but he does not draw the conclusion from the plain sense of the passage, namely that, when the object is 'merely intentional', there is no existent object, outside the mind or within it.

It further follows from what Husserl says here that, in happier cases, when the object is not *merely* intentional, there is no question of correspondence, or of any other relation short of identity, between the intentional object and the actual one: when the child is expecting his mother, it is *his mother*, that actual lady, whom he is expecting. It might be objected that Husserl ought not to have attributed even identity between the intentional and the actual object, if the intentional object is not a genuine object at all: he ought not to have muddled up the intensional and the extensional modes of expression. But that is just how we do speak: we say, for example, "He's been expecting his mother for an hour or more, but she's only just come in now", and also, "He is expecting *someone*, but not a real person". If we use the vocabulary of 'intentional objects' at all, we can only say what Husserl said.

A map represents the terrain, a portrait its sitter, in virtue of a certain correspondence between them; but, for that very reason, it is not intrinsic to the map or the portrait which terrain or sitter, if any, it represents—as Husserl observes, "the pictorial character is obviously not an intrinsic feature of the object that functions as a picture" (ibid.). That is why the notion of a mental representation—a 'shadow'—is, for Frege and for Husserl, quite misguided. A singular thought has, on Frege's theory, a constituent which would be the sense of the singular term in a sentence expressing that thought. This thought-constituent or sense has a *Bedeutung*, which is the object that the thought is about; the sense *is* no more and no less than a particular way of singling out that object. It is in virtue of this sense that the subject is thinking of that object. Husserl says the same: "an expression attains objectual reference only through having a meaning, and . . . it can be justly said that the expression designates (names) the object *in virtue of* its meaning" (*Logische Untersuchungen*, Investigation I, §13).

Being directed towards a particular object is thus intrinsic to the Fregean sense, just as it is, for Husserl, intrinsic to any intentional act: "the reference to an object is a peculiarity belonging to the act-experience in accordance with its essential constitution" (*Logische Untersuchungen*, Investigation V, §20). We must not, however, think of a Fregean sense as an intermediate station *en route* to the referent, as if the thinker aimed at the sense, which then readdressed the thought to the referent. The sense is itself the route; the entire route, and nothing but the route. The sense may be regarded as an object, but to grasp it is not an instance of that object's being given to us; it is a way in which the *referent* is given to us. Grasping a sense and thinking *of* that sense are two quite different things. Husserl says similarly that "we intend [*meinen*] the object and not its meaning" (*Logische Untersuchungen*, Investigation I, §34). If, in grasping it, the sense were given to us as an object, then, in accordance with the principle common to Kant and Frege, it would have to be given in some particular way. There would then be a particular means by which we apprehended the sense, and, in the linguistic case, identified the sense as that borne by the expression; whereas, on the contrary, everything that goes to determine the referent is part of the sense. We apprehend the referent *through* the sense; the sense simply is a way of conceiving of the referent.

Husserl's conception of how the desired reconciliation should be effected between the intensional and extensional conceptions of an object of thought thus appears very closely to resemble Frege's. It has seemed to some that a reconciliation along these lines must rule out the possibility of sense without reference, or, what is the same thing, of an intentional object that does not exist: for, if the thought is intrinsically directed towards an object, how can there fail to be an object towards which it is directed? To argue thus is, on the face of it, to condemn the reconciliation as imperfect; for it can hardly be denied that there is a sense in which the child was asking Father Christmas for a toy train, and the problem was, in part, to accommodate this presumptively legitimate way of speaking. It would not be to the present purpose to discuss whether Frege's theory or that maintained by Husserl in the *Logische Untersuchungen* can really make room for singular thoughts or intentional acts that lack an existent object. Still less would it be to the purpose to discuss whether they *ought* to make room for them, or whether, contrary to first impressions, it would, rather, be a merit of their theories if they did not. All that matters here is that neither Frege nor Husserl perceived any difficulty in accommodating failed reference. For them, the sense or meaning is, as it were, directed at a particular point in the space of objects; whether or not there is actually an object at that point is a further question. Bell insists (p. 135) that, within the constraints imposed by Husserl upon a phenomenological investigation, that further question cannot be addressed; but that, if so, does not differentiate the two thinkers, since Frege equally declined to address it in 'Über Sinn und Bedeutung'.

Bell does indeed succeed in pointing to a signal difference between Frege and Husserl, namely in the latter's talk of intentional objects. Frege would certainly never have allowed himself to speak of objects that did not exist; but the difference, nevertheless, is no more than terminological, since, as we have seen, intentional objects no more form a *kind* of object than places in novels form a kind of place (although, if the place actually exists, the place in the novel *is* that place). There is a strong suggestion in Bell's chapter on the *Logische Untersuchungen* that Husserl is unconcerned with reference to objects external to the mind (see, for example, p. 104). Since he himself quotes from Husserl examples concerning Napoleon and the Schloss in Berlin (pp. 121, 139), the suggestion cannot be sustained. It may be said with justification that Frege and Husserl owe us an account of how we can know, or at least reasonably presume, that, in a particular case, we are thinking about an actual object (or have succeeded in referring to one, addressing a request to one, etc.). Frege could plead that the general question did not fall within his subject, and that, as regards logical objects at least, he had shown how, in a purified language, a reference could be assured for all singular terms constructible in it. Husserl's philosophical concerns were wider; Bell may well be right in conjecturing (p. 135) that it was his failure to provide a satisfactory answer to the question that drove him towards his later transcendental idealism. It remains that Bell has failed to prove that, when he wrote the *Logische Untersuchungen*, Husserl was not a realist, in the intended sense, or that his theory of our reference to objects, in thought or language, was in this respect different from Frege's.

11

Realism

The term "realism" is constantly used by philosophers, in various connections, to characterize certain philosophical views; but it is rare for them to attempt to explain what they mean by calling a view realistic or non-realistic. I here attempt to analyse the concept of realism.

It is clear that one can be a realist about one subject-matter, and not about another: though someone may have a general inclination towards realistic views, it is plain that there is no coherent philosophical position which consists in being a realist *tout court*. This may be expressed by saying that one may be a realist about certain entities—mental states, possible worlds, mathematical objects—and not about others. But it seems preferable to say that realism is a view about a certain class of *statements*—for instance, statements in the future tense, or ethical statements—since certain kinds of realism, for instance realism about the future or about ethics, do not seem readily classifiable as doctrines about a realm of entities. So, in every case, we may regard a realistic view as consisting in a certain interpretation of statements in some class, which I shall call 'the given class'.

So construed, realism is a *semantic* thesis, a thesis about what, in general, renders a statement in the given class true when it is true. The very minimum that realism can be held to involve is that statements in the given class relate to some reality that exists independently of our knowledge of it, in such a way that that reality renders each statement in the class determinately true or false, again independently of whether we know, or are even able to discover, its truth-value. Thus realism involves acceptance, for statements of the given class, of the principle of bivalence, the principle that every statement is determinately either true or false. Acceptance of bivalence is not, as we shall see, sufficient for realism, but it is necessary to it. It follows that, on a realistic interpretation of some class of statements, the classical logical constants can always be intelligibly applied to those statements; for instance, classical negation or existential quantification, classically construed. Realism does not, of itself, exclude the possibility of intelligibly applying to statements of the given class some non-classical logical operators. For instance, realism concerning mathematical statements is usually called Platonism: and a Platonist, although he admits non-constructive mathematical reasoning as valid, may quite legitimately take an interest in whether or not a proof is

First published in *Synthese*, 52 (1982), 55–112.

constructive—legitimately so, because a constructive proof gives more information than a non-constructive one. Having this interest, he could, if he liked, introduce symbols for constructive disjunction and constructive existential quantification into his mathematical language. Where "OR" is constructive, and "or" classical, a proof of "*A* OR *B*" must not merely prove "*A* or *B*", but must also provide an effective method of finding a proof either of "*A*" or of "*B*"; a proof of "For each natural number *n*, *A(n)* OR *B(n)*" must supply an effective method for finding, for each value *k* of "*n*", a proof of "*A(k)*" or a proof of "*B(k)*"; where "SOME" is constructive and "some" classical, a proof of "For SOME natural number *n*, *A(n)*" must supply an effective method for finding a number *k* and a proof of "*A(k)*". These constructive logical constants plainly do not obey the classical laws: for instance, "*A* OR not *A*", the law of excluded middle, cannot in all cases be asserted. The admission of these non-classical logical constants does not, in itself, in the least impair the realistic interpretation of mathematical statements—at least, of those that do not contain such logical constants. What *would* rule out a realistic interpretation would be the view that the constructive logical constants were the only ones that could intelligibly be used in a mathematical context, that classical disjunction and classical existential quantification could not intelligibly be applied to mathematical statements. It is not the admissibility of non-classical logical operations, but the inadmissibility of classical ones, that entails a rejection of realism.

Rejection of the principle of bivalence for statements of some given class always involves a repudiation of a realistic interpretation of them; and adoption of an anti-realistic view often turns critically upon such a rejection of bivalence. But sometimes it is not the principle of bivalence that is the crucial question. To have a realistic view, it is not enough to suppose that statements of the given class are determined, by the reality to which they relate, either as true or as false; one has also to have a certain conception of the manner in which they are so determined. This conception consists essentially in the classical two-valued semantics: and this, in turn, embodies an appeal to the notion of reference as an indispensable notion of the semantic theory. Statements of the given class will ordinarily include ones containing expressions of generality: and, within the two-valued semantics, there will be associated with such expressions a definite domain of objects. Reference is a relation between a singular term, of a kind that can occur within statements of the given class, and some one object within the domain. We might, in a particular case, be concerned with a class of statements that contained no (closed) singular terms, but only expressions of generality; but that will not affect the crucial role within the semantic theory of the notion of reference. It will not do so because of the characteristic way in which, within the two-valued semantics, the truth-value of a statement involving generality—universal or existential quantification—is conceived of as being determined. The truth-value of a quantified statement is, on this conception, determined by the truth-values of its instances, so that the instances stand to the quantified statement just as the constituent subsentences of a complex sentence whose principal operator is a sentential connective stand to the complex sentence: the truth-value of the quantified statement is a truth-function of the truth-values of its instances, albeit an infinitary one if the domain is infinite. The truth-value of a universally quantified statement is the logical product of the truth-values of its instances, that of an existentially quantified statement the logical sum of the truth-values of its instances. These operations, these possibly infinitary truth-functions, are conceived of as being everywhere defined, that is, as having a value in every case: in other words, the application of the operation of universal or of existential quantification to any predicate that is determinately true or false of each object in the domain will always yield a sentence that is itself determinately either true or false, independently of whether we are able to come to know its truth-value or not. (Thus, on this semantic theory, it is correct, on the *semantic* level, to say that universal quantification amounts to infinite conjunction, existential quantification to infinite disjunction; such a remark ceases to be true only at the level of *meaning* (sense), since to know the meaning of a quantified statement it is not necessary to know the meanings of all its instances.) Here, of course, by an *instance* of a quantified statement is simply meant the result of filling the argument-place of the predicate with a singular term, that is, of removing the quantifier and replacing each occurrence of the variable that was bound by that quantifier by that singular term.

Now, in an actual language, there may not be, for every object in the domain, a singular term referring to that object. We can handle such a language in either of two ways. On what is essentially Frege's approach, instead of constructing a semantic theory for that language, we construct one for an expansion of it: this expanded language is obtained by enriching the original language by adding sufficiently many singular terms for there to be, for each object in the domain, a term referring to it. A semantic account of how the sentences of this expanded language are determined as true or as false will, of course, cover all the sentences of the original language; and, in this account, the notion of reference plays a crucial role. It does so precisely because the semantics is such that, once the truth-values of all the atomic statements are given, the truth-value of every complex statement, built up from the atomic ones by means of the sentential operators and the quantifiers, is thereby also determined; and the determination of the truth-value of an atomic statement, formed by inserting singular terms in the argument-place or argument-places of a one-place or many-place predicate, goes via the referents of the singular terms.

The other approach is that of Tarski. On this approach, we regard complex sentences as, in general, built up, not necessarily from atomic sentences properly so called, but from atomic *open sentences*, that is, from expressions that resemble sentences save that *free* variables may occur where, in an actual (closed) sentence, a singular term might stand. Just as the Fregean approach required consideration of a language expanded from the original one, so the Tarskian approach may require modification of the original language. It is being presupposed that, in that language, generality is expressed by means of the notation of quantifiers and variables (or, at any rate, that the language has first been modified to that extent in order to apply classical semantics to it). This presupposition entails that *bound* variables occur in some sentences of the language; but there is no necessity that the original language should admit any such device as *free* variables, nor, therefore, even allow the formation of open sentences. However this may be, the manner in which a quantified sentence is determined as true or false is explained, on the Tarskian approach, not in terms of the truth-values of its various instances, but in terms of the open sentence that results from removing the quantifier and replacing each occurrence of the variable that it bound by a free variable. In order to do this, we have to invoke the notion of the truth or falsity of an open sentence under an assignment of some object in the domain to the free variable, or of objects to the various distinct free variables, when there is more than one; this is often expressed as the notion of the *satisfaction* of the open sentence by an object or sequence of objects from the domain. Instead of considering the replacement of the bound variable by different singular terms, each with a fixed reference to one particular object, we consider its replacement by a single free variable, regarded as capable of receiving different assignments to it of an object from the domain. It is plain, however, that this is a mere variation on the idea embodied in the Fregean approach. Under any one particular assignment, the free variable behaves exactly as if it were a singular term having the assigned object as its referent. Save in a very special case, we shall still need to introduce the notion of reference in addition to that of an assignment of values to the free variables. Suppose that the language contains some individual constants (proper names) and some function-symbols (like "$+$") or functional expressions (like "the wife of . . ."). The individual constants or proper names must be taken as having references in the usual way; to the functional expressions will correspond functions, of appropriate degree, over the domain. We shall then have to explain, inductively, the notion of the reference of a simple or complex singular term, which may be either open or closed, that is, may or may not contain free variables, under any given assignment to the free variables, as follows: what a free variable refers to, under the assignment, is the object assigned to it; what an individual constant refers to, under the assignment, is simply the object it refers to; what a complex term, say $f(t_1, t_2)$, formed by means of a function-symbol, refers to under the assignment is the value of the corresponding function for those objects as arguments to which the constituent terms (here t_1 and t_2) refer under the assignment. The only case in which we can dispense altogether with the notion of reference in favour of that of an assignment is that in which the language contains neither any individual constants or proper names nor any function-symbols or other device for forming complex terms; and, even in this case, the notion of reference is being surreptitiously appealed to, since the possible assignments to a free variable are, in effect, different interpretations of it as an individual constant. Thus, even if our original language does not actually contain any (closed) singular terms, and even if we formulate the semantic theory in Tarski's manner, in terms of satisfaction, the notion of reference still plays a crucial role in the theory.

A semantic theory is not itself a theory of meaning, since it does not concern itself with what is known by a speaker and constitutes his grasp of the use of an expression: a knowledge of the meaning of a predicate does not consist in knowing of which objects it is true and of which it is false, and a knowledge of the meaning of a sentence does not consist in knowing its truth-value. But a semantic theory is plausible only in so far as it provides a base on which a theory of meaning can be constructed. The semantic theory seeks to exhibit the manner in which a sentence is determined as true, when it is true, in accordance with its composition, its internal structure. It does so by specifying, for each type of expression, what has to be associated with an expression of that type in order that, for every true sentence in which the expression occurs, we can exhibit the manner in which that sentence is determined as true in accordance with its composition. Let us say that, for any particular expression of any given type, that which must, according to the semantic theory, be so associated with it is its *semantic value*.

Now some semantic theories do not admit that every well-formed sentence with a definite sense is, independently of our knowledge, determined either as true or as not true. A characteristic way in which this comes about is illustrated by the intuitionistic semantic theory for mathematical statements sketched by Heyting. In this semantics, the semantic values of the component expressions of a sentence jointly determine a decidable relation between that sentence and an arbitrary mathematical construction which obtains just in case that construction constitutes a proof of that sentence. A sentence may then be said to be true if and only if there exists a construction that constitutes a proof of it: but, since the phrase "there exists", in this definition, is itself interpreted constructively, we may not assert, for an arbitrary mathematical statement with a well-defined meaning, that there either does or does not exist a construction which is a proof of it, nor, therefore, that it either is true or is not true. Within such a semantic theory, we cannot say that the semantic values of the components of a sentence determine that sentence either as true or as not true, but only that they determine what, if there be such a thing, will render it true.

A semantic theory of this kind is, evidently, a highly non-realistic one, since it involves rejecting the principle of bivalence. A realistic theory, on the other hand, incorporates the principle of bivalence, the principle that every meaningful sentence is determined as true or as false, and so entails the weaker principle, namely that every meaningful sentence is determined as true or as not true. Without at present enquiring more closely into the rationale that may be offered for admitting a distinction between a statement's failing to be true and its actually being false, let us say that a semantic theory which involves the weaker principle is an *objectivist* semantics: a realistic semantics is necessarily objectivist, but an objectivist semantics need not be realistic. An objectivist semantics incorporates a notion of truth which is not closely linked to the possibility of our recognizing a statement as true: on such a semantic theory, a statement may be true even though we have not recognized it as such, and, possibly, even though we have no means of doing so. By contrast, in such a semantic theory as that of Heyting for mathematical statements, intuitionistically interpreted, the only admissible notion of truth is one directly connected with our capacity for recognizing a statement as true: the supposition that a statement is true is the supposition that there is a mathematical construction constituting a proof of that statement.

In any objectivist semantic theory, it will be possible to regard the semantic values of the components of any sentence as jointly determining it either as true or as not true; and so we may describe such a semantic theory as specifying, for each type of expression, what has to be associated with an expression of that type in order that every sentence in which the expression occurs should be determined as true or otherwise. Thus, in particular, according to the classical two-valued semantics, there must be associated with each proper name or other singular term an object from the domain, with each one-place predicate a mapping from the domain into the set of the two truth-values, *true* and *false*, with a sentential connective a truth-function, with a sentence, considered as capable of serving as a constituent in a more complex sentence, a truth-value, and so forth.

An understanding of a sentence must involve a grasp of how it is determined as true, if it is true, in accordance with its composition: hence a theory of meaning must ascribe to a speaker of the language an implicit grasp of the underlying semantic theory. A grasp of the meaning of a specific expression will thus involve a knowledge of the kind of semantic value it may have, in virtue of the linguistic type or category to which it belongs. It will not, in general, amount, in any straightforward way, to a knowledge of the semantic value of the expression, since, on any objectivist semantic theory, once we know the semantic values of all the component expressions in some sentence, we are in a position to say whether that sentence is or is not true, whereas we can understand the sentence without being in any such position. It is natural to

say that whether or not a sentence is true depends both on its meaning and on
the way the world is, on the constitution of external reality; and, since the
semantic values of the component expressions together determine whether or
not the sentence is true, it is plain that, in associating particular semantic
values with these expressions, we have already taken the contribution of
external reality into account. But, given the way the world is, whether a
sentence is or is not true depends upon its meaning; so, given the way the world
is, the semantic value of an expression depends only on its meaning. It follows
that a grasp of the meaning of a specific expression must be something which,
taken together with the way the world is, determines the particular semantic
value that is has. Thus meaning must be something that determines semantic
value: in Frege's terminology, sense determines reference. (For Frege, the
notion of reference applies not only to singular terms, as I am here taking it,
but to expressions of all categories; it thus coincides with what I am here
calling semantic value, at least within the two-valued semantic theory, which
Frege of course advocated.) To say that meaning determines semantic value
does not just mean that, if the meanings of two expressions coincide, so do
their semantic values. Rather, its having any particular semantic value is to be
explained in terms of its having a certain sort of meaning. A grasp of its
meaning just is the conception of its having a semantic value that depends in a
certain way on how the world is: on an objectivist semantic theory, to know
the meaning of an expression consists in knowing the condition for it to have
any given semantic value. In Frege's terminology, the sense of the expression is
the mode under which its reference is presented to us; to keep the metaphor,
but employ the terminology being used here, its meaning is the manner in
which its semantic value is given to us. It is in this way that a semantic theory,
while not itself being a theory of meaning, forms a base for such a theory, and is
plausible only if a viable theory of meaning can be constructed on it as base. To
vary the metaphor, it provides a framework for a theory of meaning; it lays
down the terms in which such a theory must provide a model for that in which
the understanding of an expression of any given category must consist.

If, in particular, our semantic theory is an objectivist one, then any theory of
meaning that can be erected on it as base will be one under which a knowledge
of the meaning of a sentence will consist in a grasp of what has to be the case for
it to be true, where, in general, truth is regarded as determinately attaching to
certain statements and failing to attach to others independently of our
knowledge. It is important to notice, however, that this observation holds
good only as regards that understanding of a sentence which is sufficient to
yield a comprehension of its significance when it forms a complete utterance—
of what, for example, is the content of an assertion made by means of it. A
knowledge of the condition that must hold for a sentence to be true need not
suffice for an understanding of the sentence as it might occur as a constituent in
a more complex sentence, that is, of the contribution it makes to determining

the condition under which that more complex sentence is true: for that, we may need to know more than simply under what conditions the constituent sentence is true. For instance, if the language contains modal operators, explained in terms of a semantics of possible worlds, the semantic theory may allow that a grasp of the content of some sentence, considered as a complete utterance, amounts to a knowledge of what has to be the case for it to be true: but constituent subsentences will not contribute to determining this solely in virtue of whether or not they are true, that is, true in the actual world, but also in virtue of their being true or false in various possible worlds. It is characteristic of the two-valued semantics, however, that, according to it, that understanding of a sentence which is enough to supply a grasp of its content when it serves as a complete utterance suffices also for an understanding of its significance when it occurs as a constituent in a more complex sentence. From this it follows that no distinction can be made between a sentence's failing to be true and its being false; hence the relatively weak principle common to all objectivist semantic theories, that every statement is determinately either true or not true, can be strengthened to the principle of bivalence, that every statement is determinately either true or false. In any case, a theory of meaning for which the two-valued semantics serves as a base is a *truth-conditional* meaning-theory; one according to which to grasp the meaning of a sentence consists in a knowledge of the condition that has to obtain for it to be true.

Now some interpretations of the statements in some given class fail to be realistic, not because they involve a repudiation of the principle of bivalence, but because they diverge from a theory of meaning of this kind. This may be because they are not truth-conditional in form, that is, not constructed on the basis of an objectivist semantics: they deny that an understanding of the statements in question is to be explained in terms of a grasp of the condition for such a statement to be true. Alternatively, they may accept this general characterization of that in which an understanding of a statement consists, but reject the account embodied in the two-valued semantics of the mechanism whereby a statement is determined as true or false; they may, for instance, repudiate the conception whereby a determination of the truth-value of a statement containing a singular term proceeds via an identification of an object as the referent of that term. An example of a rejection of realism on both counts would be Wittgenstein's view of statements ascribing inner sensations to people. In one passage of the *Philosophical Investigations* (I. 352), Wittgenstein does, it is true, inveigh against the principle of bivalence for such statements (or, rather, against the law of excluded middle, which, for him, accepting as he did the redundancy theory of truth, amounted to the same thing). He writes:

Here it happens that our thinking plays us a queer trick. We want, that is, to quote the law of excluded middle and to say: "Either such an image is in his mind, or it is not: there is no third possibility!" . . . When it is said, "Either he has this experience, or he does not"—what primarily occurs to us is a picture which by itself seems to make the sense of the expressions *unmistakable*. "Now you know what is in question."—we should like to say. And that is precisely what it does not tell him.

But, in fact, Wittgenstein is not particularly interested in denying the principle of bivalence for ascriptions of inner sensations or images, save in queer cases, such as if someone says that the stove is in pain. The thrust of the argument is not that bivalence fails: it is, rather, first, that we cannot employ the notion of reference to explain how expressions for inner sensations function ("if we construe the grammar of the expression of sensation on the model of 'object and name', the object drops out of consideration as irrelevant" (I. 293)), and, secondly, that an understanding of ascriptions of inner sensation cannot be explained as consisting in a knowledge of the condition for them to be true. The condition for an ascription of pain to someone to be true is plainly not that he manifests pain-behaviour. Hence, if we attempt to give a truth-conditional account of the meaning of such ascriptions, we are forced to resort to the conception whereby I understand the word "pain" in the first instance from my own case, namely by giving myself a private ostensive definition of the word, and then transfer it to the experiences of others by analogy: the condition which I apprehend as being that under which "Henry is in pain" is true is then, on this conception, that it should be with Henry as it is with me when I am in pain. Having, as I think successfully, but at least to his own satisfaction, exposed the chimerical nature both of the private ostensive definition and of the supposed analogical transference, Wittgenstein concludes that the understanding of pain-ascriptions is not to be represented on the model of a grasp of truth-conditions. Our philosophical perplexities arise, according to him, precisely from the use of this model: for, if we use it, we are forced to choose between two alternatives. One is to seek for conclusive and publicly accessible grounds for ascribing pain to someone, and to declare the existence of such grounds to be that which renders such an ascription true; this is behaviourism. The other is to deny the possibility of any publicly accessible and absolutely conclusive grounds, and, on that score, to hold that what renders a pain-ascription true is something inaccessible to any but the one to whom the pain is ascribed, and hence that our understanding of pain-ascriptions rests on our grasp of what it is for such an in principle inaccessible state of affairs to obtain. The solution is to abandon the attempt to give a truth-conditional account of the meanings of statements of this form. We have, rather, to accept that an understanding of pain-ascriptions consists in a mastery of their actual use. This involves knowing that the presence of a pain-stimulus and the manifestation of pain-behaviour together supply an entitlement for an ascription of pain; knowing when one of these does, and when it does not, supply such an entitlement in the apparent or demonstrable absence of the other; and knowing what justifies withdrawing an ascription of pain for which there had been such an entitlement. (To display pity for the sufferer and to gloat over his sufferings are two possible manifestations of a belief that he is in pain: but, in view of the callousness which is also a prevalent human attitude, it seems difficult to maintain that such a belief is incompatible with behaviour no different from that towards a broken chair.) It is, on this account, part of our understanding of the word "pain" that we recognize that a report by a speaker that he is himself in pain does not require grounds or justification, but also that it is to be assessed like any other pain-behaviour. It is not that the speaker attaches a private meaning to the word "pain" under which he knows that he is in pain, as he understands "pain". Rather, the significance of his utterance depends upon his use of the word as part of the public language, and so on his grasp of the connections between pain, pain-stimuli, and pain-behaviour; for instance, an apparently sincere declaration on his part that he did not in the least mind being in pain would call in question the meaning, and thereby the truth, of his report.

The rejection of a realistic view of statements of some given class has often been associated with the maintenance of a reductionist thesis concerning them. Reductionism, properly so called, is the thesis that there exists a translation of statements of the given class into those of some other class, which I shall call the reductive class. This translation is proposed, not merely as preserving truth-values, but as part of an account of the meanings of statements of the given class: it is integral to the reductionist thesis that it is by an implicit grasp of the scheme of translation that we understand those statements. The most celebrated example of a reductionist thesis is that embodied in classical phenomenalism: the given class here consists of statements about material objects, and the reductive class of statements about sense-data. Reductionism in this sense may indeed afford a ground for rejecting realism concerning statements of the given class, even when it does not provide any reason for repudiating the principle of bivalence as applied to them. To take an example of Frege's, suppose that we have a method for translating statements containing terms for and quantification over directions into ones containing only terms for and quantification over straight lines, and that a grasp of this scheme of translation is accepted as being integral to our understanding of statements about directions. In the *Grundlagen der Arithmetik*, Frege claimed that the necessity to invoke such a translation in order to explain the meanings of statements about directions would not render it improper to ascribe a reference to terms for directions, since it is only in the context of a sentence that a word has a meaning. Provided that an expression really does function logically as a singular term, that is, that certain patterns of inference govern sentences containing it, and provided that we have laid down determinate truth-conditions for sentences containing that expression, then, according to Frege, it is entirely proper to ascribe a reference to that expression (a reference to an object); any question that may remain as to whether it actually has such a reference will not be a semantic question, but a factual one, namely a question as to the truth of an existential sentence of the kind for which we have laid down the truth-conditions. In the example, we have laid down the truth-conditions of statements about directions precisely by means of the translation, provided, of course, that it is assumed that statements about lines already have determinate truth-conditions. Hence, according to Frege, the setting up of such a translation actually supplies a justification for ascribing reference to terms for directions, or, in another terminology, for admitting directions into our ontology: no better justification can be required for acknowledging the existence of abstract objects than that we know what must hold good if sentences concerning them are to be true.

Even in the *Grundlagen*, this was, for Frege, a merely hypothetical case: for rather special reasons, he did not in fact think that it was possible to translate statements about directions into statements about lines. Furthermore, his stance on this matter in his later writings is somewhat unclear. But, in *Grundlagen* at any rate, his espousal of the hypothetical thesis is unequivocal: *if* we had such a translation, then we should, by that very fact, be justified in ascribing a reference to terms for directions.

I do not wish to controvert this thesis: given an acceptance of the scheme of translation as providing a correct account of the meanings of statements about directions, nothing is gained by a philosophical protest to the effect that "there are not really any such things as directions". Such a protest springs, however, from the perception of a genuine and important fact: the fact, namely, that adoption of this form of explanation for statements about directions represents the abandonment of a realistic view of such statements. Realism is abandoned, not because a truth-conditional account of the meanings of the statements is impossible, nor, necessarily, because there is any reason to repudiate the principle of bivalence as applied to them, but because the notion of reference no longer plays any role in the account of their meanings. Even if, relying on Frege's principle that a term has reference only in the context of a sentence, we continue to ascribe reference to terms for directions, we do not need to invoke the notion of reference, as applied to such terms, in order to explain how a sentence containing such a term is determined as true or false: the determination of the truth-value of the sentence does not proceed via the identification of an object as the referent of the term. Indeed, just because it is only in the context of a sentence that such a term is conceived of as having a reference, the notion of reference, as applied to that term, has not been explained by the use of anything characterized as identifying an object as its referent; and, for all that has been said, there may be no process that can legitimately be so characterized. Suppose that we have the simplest kind of statement about a direction, a sentence formed by inserting in the argument-place of a suitable one-place predicate a term for a direction. Then, under the given account of the meanings of statements about directions, the canonical means by which we establish the atomic sentence as true or as false is not by identifying some direction as being that to which the term refers, and then determining that the predicate is true of it; it is by first translating the sentence into a statement about lines, and then determining, by whatever are the appropriate means, the truth-value of the resulting statement. In this process, the notion of reference as applied to terms for lines may need to be invoked, if we have a realistic theory of meaning for statements about lines which here form our reductive class: but the notion of reference as applied to terms for directions, however defensible, plays no role in the account of the meaning of the original sentence. And, because this is so for atomic sentences about directions, it is so also for sentences involving quantification over directions: we shall determine such sentences as true or as false not by considering their truth-values as the values of infinitary truth-functions whose arguments are the truth-values of their instances, but by first applying our translation scheme to obtain some statement about lines, and then determining the resulting statement as true or as false.

It may be for reasons of this kind that phenomenalism was always reckoned to stand in opposition to realism concerning statements about material objects; but I think that another, imperfectly apprehended, reason underlay this classification. I have emphasized that realism concerning a given class of statements requires adherence in all respects to a certain pattern of explanation for statements of the given class, a certain style of meaning-theory for those statements: any divergence from that pattern constitutes an abandonment of realism in its full-fledged form. A very radical type of divergence is involved when, as with Wittgenstein's view of statements ascribing inner sensations, it is denied that it is possible to give a truth-conditional account of the meanings of the given statements; if this is denied, it becomes relatively unimportant whether the principle of bivalence is abandoned or not. On the other hand, when the divergence takes the form of dispensing with the notion of reference, as playing a crucial role in the semantic account of statements of the given class, perhaps because of the acceptance of a reductionist thesis concerning those statements, and does not involve either a rejection of a truth-conditional account of their meanings or a repudiation of bivalence, we have only a comparatively mild species of anti-realism. Probably the great majority of anti-realistic views are ones whose most characteristic expression consists in a rejection of the principle of bivalence: very plain examples are a constructivist view of mathematical statements, under which a mathematical statement is true only if we are in possession of a proof of it, and false only if we are in possession of a refutation; and neutralism concerning the future, under which future-tense statements are not in general determinately true or false.

Now although there is just one logic, the familiar classical logic, which accords with an acceptance of the principle of bivalence, there is no one logic with accords with its rejection: to reject the principle of bivalence is, in itself, merely to adopt a negative position, and is compatible with the acceptance of a variety of semantic theories and a variety of resulting logics. In some cases, the semantic theory advocated by the anti-realist will involve, not merely the rejection of bivalence, but the abandonment of a truth-conditional theory of meaning, because the semantic theory underlying his theory of meaning is not of the objectivist type: he does not admit, for statements of the given class, any notion of truth under which each statement is determinately either true or not true, independently of our knowledge. In other cases, the semantic theory he advocates, although not embodying the principle of bivalence, will remain objectivist in character, and therefore compatible with a theory of meaning under which a grasp of the meaning of a sentence consists in a knowledge of the condition that has to obtain for it to be true. In the former case, we are concerned with an anti-realist view of a very thoroughgoing kind; in the latter, with a less radical type of anti-realism, although one more radical than a view which leaves the principle of bivalence intact, but merely calls in question the role of the notion of reference in the meaning-theory.

There are other cases, however, in which the opponent of realism does not actually take the step of rejecting the principle of bivalence, but in which it appears that his position would be strengthened were he to do so: and these cases are rather hard to classify. It has already been remarked that opposition to realism is frequently associated with acceptance of a reductionist thesis, and not incorrectly so. But it has often been associated also with acceptance of a weaker form of thesis, which I shall call a *reductive* thesis. A reductive thesis, like a full-fledged reductionist thesis, is concerned with the relation between two classes of statements, the given class and the reductive class. A reductionist thesis claims the existence of a translation from statements in the given class into statements in the reductive class; a reductive thesis more modestly claims only that no statement of the given class can be true unless some suitable statement or statements of the reductive class are true, and, conversely, that the truth of those statements of the reductive class guarantees the truth of the corresponding statement of the given class. It is, once again, essential that the reductive thesis be advanced, not as a mere observation concerning a connection between the truth-conditions of statements of the two classes, but as part of an account of the meanings of statements of the given class: the proponent of the thesis holds that an understanding of those statements involves an implicit grasp of their relation to statements of the reductive class, that is, an implicit acceptance of the reductive thesis.

In order to bring out the difference between a reductionist thesis and the weaker philosophical proposition I have labelled a reductive thesis, it is worth while to consider the different possible reasons an adherent of the weaker thesis might have for not advancing the stronger one.

1. He might hold that, for any particular statement A of the given class, there will in general be infinitely many statements of the reductive class the truth of

any one of which will guarantee the truth of A, and such that the truth of A requires the truth of one of those statements. If the language does not contain a mechanism whereby we can form a statement, belonging to the reductive class, tantamount to the disjunction of those infinitely many statements, then it will be impossible actually to translate A into a statement of the reductive class. Alternatively, he might hold that the truth of A entailed the simultaneous truth of the statements in some infinite subset of the reductive class, and was guaranteed only by the truth of all of them: and, again, if the language contained no device for forming a sentence tantamount to the infinite conjunction of the statements in that set, it would be impossible actually to give a translation of A. Or, again, he might combine these views: the truth of A might guarantee, and might require, the truth of all the statements in some one out of infinitely many infinite subsets of the reductive class, so that a translation of A could be given only as an infinite disjunction of infinite conjunctions of statements of the reductive class. Just such a reason as this has been advanced by some philosophers as a ground for denying the possibility of translating statements about material objects into statements about sense-data, while admitting the correctness of a weaker reductive thesis concerning these two classes of statements.

2. Quite a different ground has been given for denying the possibility of an actual scheme of translation. This is, namely, that it is impossible to introduce a vocabulary adequate for expressing statements of the reductive class without thereby introducing one adequate for the expression of statements of the given class. This need not mean that the given class becomes a subclass of the reductive class, thereby rendering the reductive thesis entirely nugatory: the reductive class may be characterized in such a way that, although the entire vocabulary by means of which statements of the given class are expressed may occur in statements of the reductive class, it does so only in a restricted type of context. Nevertheless, when the two classes are related in this way, there can be no question of a translation of statements of the given class in a manner that eliminates its characteristic vocabulary. An example might be a reductive thesis concerning mathematical statements, the thesis, namely, that a mathematical statement A can be true only if the statement ⌜We possess a proof that A⌝ is true: the given class consists of mathematical statements, the reductive class of statements to the effect that we have proofs of such statements. Such a reductive thesis is quite compatible with the view that, for any given mathematical statement, there is no way in which to express the general notion of something's being a proof of that statement that does not require the use of that statement itself as a subordinate clause, or, more generally, that there is no way of characterizing all possible proofs of a given statement without employing a vocabulary adequate for the expression of the statement in question. Accordingly, a reductionist thesis could not be maintained: there could be no scheme for translating mathematical statements

into statements about our possession of proofs of them. Another example would be a reductive thesis, such as has been advanced by some philosophers (Łukasiewicz, C. I. Lewis, and, at one time, A. J. Ayer) concerning statements in the past tense, to the effect that such a statement cannot be true unless some statement about the existence of present (or perhaps also future) evidence and memories is also true; if every trace of the occurrence of the alleged past event has disappeared, the statement that it occurred is devoid of truth. This reductive thesis could be maintained even though it was denied that there could be any translation of past-tense statements into ones in the present and future tense, on the ground that any such translation would require allusion to memories, and that there is no way to characterize a memory of an event without the use of the past tense. A similar ground has also been given for denying the possibility of translating material-object statements into ones about perceptual experience: our perceptual experience is, on this view, so coloured by our interpretation of our sense-impressions as revealing to us the constitution of material objects and their disposition in three-dimensional space that there can be no way of characterizing that experience without the use of a vocabulary already adequate for the expression of material-object statements.

This second type of ground for rejecting reductionism while accepting a reductive thesis deserves a closer scrutiny. It might be objected that the overlap of vocabulary is no impediment to a translation. We might still be supposed to be capable in principle of understanding statements of the reductive class in advance of understanding those of the given class: at such a stage, our understanding of the vocabulary needed for expressing statements of the given class would be only partial, for we should understand it only in those restricted contexts in which it occurs in statements of the reductive class. For instance, we might understand a mathematical vocabulary only within contexts governed by "a proof that . . ."; or we might understand the past tense only in contexts governed by ". . . remembers that . . .". If this assumption were made, there would be no obstacle to an informative translation of statements of the given class: we should be translating statements in which certain expressions occurred in a context of one kind into statements in which they occurred only in contexts of another kind. And, it might be urged, the possibility of such a translation is implicit in the claim that the reductive thesis forms part of an account of the *meanings* of the statements of the given class: if we could not understand statements of the reductive class antecedently to a knowledge of the meanings of those of the given class, how could the reductive thesis operate as an explanation of those meanings?

This objection is perfectly reasonable, so far as our present characterization of this second ground for resisting reductionism while accepting a reductive thesis goes. It shows, however, that we have not yet fully characterized that ground. In a case of this kind, the reductive thesis is not intended to be understood as a partial explanation of the meanings of statements of the given class after the manner of a reductionist thesis and, perhaps, of other reductive theses. That is to say, the reductive thesis is not intended to explain the meanings of statements of the given class by formulating their truth-conditions in terms that can be understood antecedently to an understanding of those statements, as a reductionist thesis is certainly intended to do. It is precisely because, in a case of this sort, it is *not* supposed that statements of the reductive class are even in principle intelligible in advance of an understanding of those of the given class that the reductionist thesis is rejected. The reductive thesis makes an important contribution to circumscribing the form which a theory of meaning for statements of the given class must take, namely by saying something about the appropriate notion of truth for statements of that class; but it is not intended to offer an explanation of those statements in terms of other statements regarded as capable of being antecedently understood.

3. A third ground for rejecting reductionism while accepting a reductive thesis is very seldom appealed to: it is that, while, for any statement *A* of the given class there must be a statement *B* of the reductive class in the truth of which the truth of *A* consists, we have no effective means of identifying, for each statement *A*, the corresponding statement *B*. This appears to be Donald Davidson's reason for denying the possibility of translating psychological into neurophysiological statements: I know of no other actual example of an appeal to such a ground for denying a reductionist thesis.

Very often maintenance of any reductive thesis is taken as constituting in itself a rejection of realism for statements of the given class. This is, however, a mistake. A reductive thesis does not, of itself, imply that we cannot give a truth-conditional account of the meanings of statements of the given class; it does not imply that bivalence fails for those statements; it does not even imply that the notion of reference does not play its standard role in the explanation of how those statements are determined as true or as false. An example might be the reductive thesis, for psychological statements, embodied in so-called central-state materialism: the reductive class, in this case, consists of statements about the states of the central nervous system. Such a thesis has no tendency to cast doubt upon whether any specific statement ascribing a psychological state to an individual is determinately either true or false: rather, it tends to reinforce the presumption that it will be one or the other, since it is assumed that his central nervous system either is or is not in the corresponding state at any given time. It does not even call in question the ascription of reference to terms for particular psychological states, since these can be construed as referring, in a certain manner, to the corresponding neurophysio-logical states. In fact, we can see that, in this example, we do not arrive at an anti-realist position even if the reductive thesis is strengthened to a full-fledged reductionism: if there is a one–one correspondence between describable psychological states and describable neurophysiological states, then terms for the former can be construed as referring, in a particular manner, to the latter. What, in the example concerning directions and lines, deprived the notion of reference of any significant role in the account of the meanings of statements about directions was that we tacitly assumed that, in the process of translating such statements into statements about lines, we did not simply replace a term for a direction by a term for a line, or by a term of any other kind, but effected a transformation under which that term disappeared altogether. If we had been concerned with a translation under which a term for a direction was replaced by a term for, say, a maximal class of parallel lines, then we should not have said that the notion of reference, as applied to terms for directions, no longer had any part to play in the meaning-theory: we should have said, rather, that terms for directions were being construed as referring to classes of parallel lines. In this latter case, therefore, we should have a reductionist thesis that in no way impugned a realistic interpretation of statements about directions. Reductionism is, therefore, not intrinsically anti-realist: it depends on the character of the translation proposed. *A fortiori*, a reductive thesis does not in itself involve any rejection of realism.

The principal reason why philosophers have often confused an advocacy of a reductive thesis with the repudiation of realism is that the reductive thesis frequently represents a first step in an argument leading to the rejection of bivalence. For instance, it is first claimed that a mathematical statement can be true only if there exists a proof of it; and then the second step is taken, namely to observe that there is no ground for assuming that, for any intelligible mathematical statement, we must be able to construct either a proof or a disproof of it of the kind that we are able to grasp. It then follows that we have no entitlement to assert that every mathematical statement is either true or false. In general, a reductive thesis may lead to a rejection of bivalence if the correspondence between the given class and the reductive class is of a particular kind; given the reductive thesis, the second step in the argument may be cogent even though a realistic interpretation is allowed for statements of the reductive class. The general form of the second step consists in pointing out that, for any particular statement A of the given class, there is no guarantee that there should be any true statement, or set of true statements, of the reductive class whose truth would entail the truth of A or would entail the truth of $\ulcorner$Not A$\urcorner$, the given class being taken to be one closed under negation; where the falsity of A is identified with the truth of its negation, as it is usually natural to do, it follows, given the reductive thesis, that a statement of the given class cannot be assumed to be either true or false.

This second step, leading to a rejection of bivalence, and, therefore, of realism concerning the given class of statements, often very naturally follows upon the reductive thesis. For instance, if statements about the past are considered as needing to be rendered true, when they are true, by what lies in the present or the future, it will inevitably be inferred that a past-tense statement need not be either true or false. Or, again, to take an example not so far used, if a psychological statement is regarded as requiring to be rendered true by corresponding behaviour on the part of the individual concerned, if it is to be true at all, it is almost equally natural to conclude that a psychological statement will not in all cases be either true or false: the individual may not behave in such a way as to render either that statement or its negation true. It is, however, a mistake to suppose that a reductive thesis leads inevitably to a rejection of bivalence, or that it always represents a repudiation of realism. We have to look at the particular case to see whether, given the reductive thesis, the second step can be taken: the relation between the given class and the reductive class may be such that—given a realistic interpretation of the reductive class—for any statement A of the given class, we are assured that either there will be some true statement B of the reductive class such that A is true in virtue of the truth of B, or there will be some true statement C of the reductive class such that the negation of A is true in virtue of the truth of C. We have already considered a case in which it is natural to say this, namely when the given class consists of psychological statements, and the reductive class consists, not of statements about behaviour, but of neurophysiological ones.

Realism about a certain class of statements is thus compatible with acceptance of a reductive thesis concerning that class: and we may label a realistic view that is combined with, and, perhaps, even rests on, a reductive thesis *sophisticated realism*. In this sense, central-state materialism represents a form of sophisticated realism concerning psychological statements. Opposed to all reductive theses applied to a given class of statements is what we may call an *irreducibility thesis*: the thesis, namely, that no reductive thesis holds good for that class. In characterizing the general notion of a reductive thesis, I did not need to place any restrictions on the two classes of statements considered: if the two classes can be chosen in such a way that the reductive thesis becomes trivially true and hence philosophically unilluminating, that is no objection to the concept of a reductive thesis. Probably, however, in order to give a clear explanation of what I intend by speaking of an irreducibility thesis, I ought to circumscribe the type of class for which such a thesis can be propounded, and the type of class about which the irreducibility thesis asserts that it cannot serve as a reductive class for the given class. To state such restrictions accurately is, however, not easy to do, and I shall therefore leave the notion of an irreducibility thesis to this extent incompletely specified: I do not think that any serious misunderstanding will result. A reductive thesis offers an informative general answer to the question "What makes a statement of the given class true, when it is true?" or "In virtue of what is such a statement true, if it is true?" An irreducibility thesis is, conversely, to the effect that, for a statement of the given class, no non-trivial answer can be given to this question; or, at least, that no non-trivial general answer is possible. A trivial answer to the question what makes a statement A true, if it is true, is one that consists, actually or in effect, of simply repeating the statement; and a trivial general answer to the question what makes any statement of a certain class true, when it is true, is one that amounts to no more than saying, "That statement's being true". For instance, a constructivist has an informative general answer to the question, "What, in general, makes a true mathematical statement true?", namely "The existence of a proof of that statement". A platonist, on the other hand, that is, one who adopts a realistic interpretation of mathematical statements, can give no answer to the question "What makes Goldbach's conjecture true, if it is true?", save "Every even number's being the sum of two primes", that is, by formulating Goldbach's conjecture; and, to the general question "What makes a mathematical statement true, when it is true?" he can do no better than to reply, "The constitution of mathematical reality". Since mathematical reality is composed of mathematical facts, that reply is quite uninformative: it amounts to saying that each true mathematical statement is rendered true by the fact which it states. An informative answer to the question what makes a statement of some class true, when it is true, sheds light on the notion of truth appropriate for statements of that class, and gives an indication of the type of semantic theory, and therefore the type of meaning-theory, required for them: it is therefore desirable when it can be attained. But we cannot expect in each case to be able to find an informative answer; in some cases, only a trivial answer may be possible.

As already explained, a realistic interpretation of a certain class of statements does not require the maintenance of an irreducibility thesis concerning them. It is, however, characteristic of a number of disputes over the tenability of a realistic interpretation that the critic of realism maintains a reductive thesis, while its defender rejects not only that, but any conceivable, reductive thesis, and so propounds an irreducibility thesis. The term "naïve realism" is well known from philosophical literature, although it is sometimes difficult to grasp what is intended by it. For the present, let us say that *naïve realism* concerning statements of a given class consists in the combination of a realistic interpretation of them with an irreducibility thesis; how far this agrees with the accepted use of the term we shall enquire later.

Now an interesting distinction between reductive theses can be drawn by asking whether subjunctive conditionals are admitted as belonging to the reductive class. In some cases, the plausibility of the reductive thesis depends heavily upon their admission. Notoriously, for instance, the first step in the phenomenalist translation of material-object statements into sense-data statements was supposed, in most cases, to consist in the formation of a subjunctive conditional the antecedent of which would state the condition for a suitable observation to be made and the consequent of which would state the making of a positive observation: the celebrated prototype was the rendering of "There is a table in the next room" by "If anyone were to go into the next room (and switch on the light), he would see a table". Of course, this was only a first step, since at this stage both antecedent and consequent are expressed in material-object vocabulary: they would then be subjected to further transformations, in order to obtain equivalents couched solely in sense-datum vocabulary; but, in the process, the subjunctive conditional form would persist. The need for the admission of the subjunctive conditional form in statements of the reductive class arose from the fact that the phenomenalists were not prepared to be sufficiently tough-minded as to declare only those material-object statements true which have actually been observed to be true. A similar inclusion of subjunctive conditionals among the statements of the reductive class is very characteristic of a number of reductive theses. A behaviourist wants to assert an intrinsic connection between the concept of knowledge or of expectation and that of its manifestation, between the concept of belief and that of its avowal, between that of intention or of emotion and its expression. But he hardly wants to deny that a man may have knowledge which he does not display, an expectation that he never manifests, and so forth: so he is disposed to say that "X expects E to happen" is true provided that X would show surprise if he were to discover that E had not occurred, that to ascribe an intention to someone is to say that he would act in accordance with it were the occasion to arise, and the like. Other reductive theses, on the other hand, make no appeal to subjunctive conditionals. One who takes a constructivist view of mathematical statements does not hold that such a statement is true provided that there *would be* a proof of it under favourable conditions; he is content to say that it is true only if there actually *is* such a proof. Even in the mathematical case, however, there are contexts in which it is natural to appeal to subjunctive conditionals. A constructivist may be more or less radical: he may be content, like the intuitionists, to appeal to procedures that could in principle be effectively carried out, or he may, like the strict finitists, rely only on procedures that can in practice be carried out. A constructivist of the less radical variety would accept a computation procedure that would in principle effectively decide the application of some predicate to any natural number as imposing a determinate meaning on that predicate, of such a kind as to make it true or false of every natural number: for instance, by factorization we can decide whether or not a number is prime, or is square-free. A radical constructivist will object that, for sufficiently large numbers, we could not in fact decide the application of the predicate by that means: the less radical one may then be tempted to reply that, nevertheless, the predicate is true of such a number provided that, if we *were* to apply the decision procedure, we *should* obtain an affirmative result. A case in which an appeal to subjunctive conditionals is completely out of the question is that of a reductive thesis concerning statements about the past. For an anti-realist about the past, a past-tense statement can be true only if there is present evidence for its truth. He may well allow that it may be true, given such evidence, even if we are unaware of that evidence: but there is no plausible but non-trivial thesis to the effect that it is true just in case, under such-and-such conditions, there *would be* present evidence for its truth.

If subjunctive conditionals are excluded from the reductive class, it will usually be fairly obvious whether or not the reductive thesis entails a rejection of bivalence for statements of the given class. When subjunctive conditionals are admitted to the reductive class, however, it is a great deal more delicate to decide whether, given the reductive thesis, bivalence will fail: it depends on how many subjunctive conditionals are considered as holding good. This problem was particularly acute for the phenomenalist. For the naïve realist, or for any realist who rejected the phenomenalist reduction, any significant statement about the physical universe, for example, "There are living organisms on some planet in the Andromeda galaxy", must be determinately true or false, at least within the limits imposed by the vagueness of some of the terms occurring in it. From the truth of such a statement, the truth of a subjunctive conditional concerning the results of observation under suitable conditions, in our case, "If we were to travel to the Andromeda galaxy and inspect all the planets in it, we should observe at least one on which there were living organisms", would follow; from its falsity, the truth of the opposite subjunctive conditional would follow, where the opposite of any conditional is that conditional having the same antecedent and the contradictory consequent. The realist therefore had good ground for holding that, of any pair of such opposite subjunctive conditionals, one must be true and the other false. The phenomenalist, however, was in a different position. For him, the affirmative subjunctive conditional was not a *consequence* of the material-object statement, but equivalent to it in meaning: it represented the first step in the translation of that statement. The phenomenalist could not, therefore, argue, as the realist could, that, *because* the material-object statement was either true or false, so one or other of the pair of opposite subjunctive conditionals must be true. For him, a decision on whether the material-object statement had to be either true or false must depend upon a prior decision as to whether it was necessary that one or other of the two subjunctive conditionals must be true.

Now one who adopted a realistic interpretation of material-object statements could well afford to hold a reductive thesis concerning subjunctive conditionals. On such a view, for any subjunctive conditional, we can always give an informative answer, even if a rather complicated one, to the question in virtue of what it is true, if it is true: such an answer would allude to general laws and, perhaps, to tendencies, intentions, and the like. If the phenomenalist likewise accepted a reductive thesis concerning subjunctive conditionals, he would be more or less forced to grant that material-object statements, understood in his way, did not satisfy the principle of bivalence. For the realist, an essential ingredient in an informative answer to the question what renders the subjunctive condition, "If we were to inspect the planets in the Andromeda galaxy, we should observe one on which there were living organisms", true, if it is true, would be "There being living organisms on some planet in the Andromeda galaxy". But, for the phenomenalist, this could not be part of an *informative* answer to that question, since, for him, it is simply to reiterate the subjunctive conditional in a disguised form: the phenomenalist had, as it were, a much more slender basis of categorical truths on which to support those subjunctive conditionals which he could consider true. For the phenomenalist who accepted a reductive thesis concerning subjunctive conditionals, a subjunctive conditional could not be true in virtue of the truth of some material-object statement whose truth we might never know: it could be true only in virtue of some actual reports of observation, expressible as sense-datum statements, together with laws stating observed or at least observable regularities connecting our observations. On such a basis, it would be quite implausible that, for any material-object statement, either the subjunctive conditional which represented the first step in its translation, or the opposite one, would have to be true: and so the consequence would be a denial of the principle of bivalence for material-object statements, and, therefore, a thoroughgoing repudiation of realism.

What is surprising is that, in the actual historical development, very few phenomenalists appear to have taken that position. Rather, they appear to have rejected any reductive thesis concerning subjunctive conditionals, while continuing to maintain a reductionist view of material-object statements. To reject a reductive thesis concerning a certain class of statements does not, of itself, afford any ground for accepting the principle of bivalence as applied to them: it merely disposes of one argument to show that bivalence fails. Independently of any reductive thesis concerning subjunctive conditionals, for example, it would be hard to maintain that they satisfy the principle of bivalence, if the falsity of a subjunctive conditional be equated with the truth of the opposite conditional. Few could be found to hold that such a subjunctive conditional as "If the next Pope to be elected were an Englishman, he would take the name Adrian" must, in this sense, be determinately be true or false, that is, that either it or its opposite must be true. It could, indeed, be argued that this is not the natural way to understand the word "false" as applied to subjunctive conditionals, that it should, instead, be so taken that the falsity of the foregoing subjunctive conditional would involve the truth only of "If the next Pope to be elected were an Englishman, he would not necessarily take the name Adrian", rather than that of the opposite conditional "If the next Pope to be elected were an Englishman, he would not take the name Adrian". On this latter way of understanding the notion of the falsity of a subjunctive conditional, the opinion that subjunctive conditionals are determinately either true or false would be much more widespread. Let us speak of *strong* bivalence for subjunctive conditionals when the falsity of a conditional is equated with the truth of its opposite, and of *weak* bivalence when its falsity is equated with the truth of the statement resulting from inserting "not necessarily" in the consequent. The appropriate application of "false" to subjunctive conditionals is not, however, to the present point. If we call subjunctive conditionals with "might", "would perhaps", or "would not necessarily" in their consequents *permissive* conditionals, and those with plain "would" or "would not" in their consequents *straightforward* conditionals, it is plain that the first step in the phenomenalist translation of a material-object statement will always yield a straightforward, not a permissive, subjunctive conditional; this will normally be the case under any reductionist thesis admitting subjunctive conditionals in the reductive class. In particular, the phenomenalist translation of the negation of a material-object statement *A* will be the opposite subjunctive conditional to that which is the translation of *A*. Hence, for the phenomenalist, the question whether the principle of bivalence holds for material-object statements is the question whether strong bivalence holds for subjunctive conditionals of the kind which serve as their translations into the sense-datum language: it makes no difference whether strong bivalence is or is not what "bivalence" should be taken to mean when applied to subjunctive conditionals.

Now it is impossible to hold that subjunctive conditionals satisfy the principle of strong bivalence quite generally. The reason is that there are obvious cases in which it is neither true to say that, if it had been the case that *A*, then it would have been the case that *B*, nor true to say that, if it had been the case that *A*, then it would not have been the case that *B*. A very wide class of such cases is provided by those in which an additional condition is required to determine the consequent: that is, where, for some additional statement *C*, we can truly say (1) that, if it had been the case that *A*, it might or might not also have been the case that *C*, (2) that, if it had been the case that *A* and that *C*, then it would have been the case that *B*, and (3) that, if it had been the case that *A* but not *C*, then it would not have been the case that *B*. Now, since subjunctive conditionals cannot be held to be generally subject to strong bivalence, the most that can be claimed is that strong bivalence holds for some restricted range of subjunctive conditionals. The most characteristic reason for supposing this is the belief that there is some underlying class of categorical statements such that, for any subjunctive conditional in the given range, there is some categorical statement in the underlying class that would support it, and that these categorical statements are subject to bivalence. For instance, we may have a test *T* for the possession of some property *P* by a body. The statement "The body *x* possesses the property *P*" then gives support to the subjunctive conditional "If *x* were to be subjected to the test *T*, it would pass that test". If statements ascribing the property *P* to a body are realistically interpreted, they will be regarded as subject to bivalence: at any given time, any particular body either has the property *P* or does not have it. It will then follow that, for any subjunctive conditional of the form "If *x* were to be (have been) subjected to the test *T*, it would pass (have passed) it", either it or the opposite conditional must be true. This assurance reflects the fact that a realistic interpretation has been adopted for statements of the form "*x* has property *P*": we could say that the belief that subjunctive conditionals of this form satisfy strong bivalence simply expresses acceptance of a realistic view of statements ascribing the property *P* to a body.

The phenomenalists appear, however, not merely to have rejected a reductive thesis for subjunctive conditionals, but, further, to have retained the belief, natural for anyone taking a realistic view of material-object statements, that strong bivalence holds good for the subjunctive conditionals resulting from the phenomenalist translation. This belief on the part of the phenomenalist could not have the same basis as the corresponding belief held by a realist. For the phenomenalist, such a subjunctive conditional would not *rest on* the corresponding material-object statement, that is, it would not be true in virtue of the truth of that statement, together with the laws of nature, since it would be a translation of it. In so far as the phenomenalist rejected a reductive thesis for subjunctive conditionals, they need not rest on anything at all: there need be no non-trivial answer to the question in virtue of what such a statement was true.

This extraordinary situation reveals how close the classical phenomenalist actually was to his opponent, the realist. In terms of the analysis of the concept of realism I am here putting forward, a phenomenalist of this kind diverged from a realistic view of material-object statements neither in repudiating the principle of bivalence as applied to them nor in rejecting a truth-conditional account of their meanings. Indeed, in only one respect could he be said to diverge from realism, as I have analysed it, namely if he denied that the notion of reference, as applied to names of material objects, played any role in the account of how a statement containing such names was to be determined as true or as false. Whether he could be said to deny this would depend upon the details of his translation into the sense-datum language, details which were, notoriously, never forthcoming: specifically, on whether, in the process of translation, a name for a material object would be replaced by a term for some complex of sense-data, or whether it would be dissolved altogether so that no corresponding term remained in the sense-datum sentence. It thus becomes highly dubious whether a classical phenomenalist can properly be described as having held an anti-realist view at all. His principal disagreement with those who called themselves realists lay in his acceptance of a reductionist thesis concerning material-object statements; and, as we have seen, neither a reductive nor even a reductionist thesis is sufficient for a rejection of realism. It would be better to say that the distinction between those who called themselves realists and those who called themselves phenomenalists was that the former were naïve realists, at least as I earlier explained the term "naïve realism" while the latter were sophisticated realists, concerning material objects.

An outcome which involves that a philosophical view like phenomenalism that would ordinarily be taken as a prototype of anti-realism is better regarded as a sophisticated version of realism may seem to be a *reductio ad absurdum* of my proposed analysis of the concept of realism; but I do not think so. The disposition to classify phenomenalism as an outstanding example of anti-realism is partly to be explained as due to a failure to distinguish clearly between anti-realism, properly so called, and advocacy of a reductive thesis. But it is not wholly due to that confusion. It springs also from a perception of the irrationality of the classical phenomenalist's position: he had neither ground nor motive for accepting strong bivalence for the subjunctive conditionals resulting from his translation of material-object statements. We can reasonably regard his having done so as due to a lingering attachment to a realistic view of material-object statements; and, so regarded, he was not genuinely an anti-realist. But we can equally view him as having failed to pursue his ideas to their natural conclusion. Given his reductionist thesis about material-object statements, the natural line for him to have taken was to accept a reductive thesis for subjunctive conditionals generally, and, on that very ground, to have rejected strong bivalence for the subjunctive conditionals resulting from his translation; he would then have had to reject the principle of bivalence for material-object statements. Had he taken such a position, he would, on the present analysis of the concept of realism, have been an anti-realist of a fairly thoroughgoing kind; and it was surely an imperfect perception that this was the natural consequence of his principal contention that made it seem so obviously correct to classify the phenomenalist as an opponent of realism.

For all that, philosophers have frequently failed to distingush between a reductive thesis and the repudiation of a truth-conditional meaning-theory of the standard kind; it is the latter which is constitutive of anti-realism. Not only is a reductive thesis by itself insufficient for a rejection of realism: it is also unnecessary. Realism requires us to hold both that, for statements of the given class, we have a notion of truth under which each statement is determinately either true or false, and also that an understanding of those statements consists in a knowledge of the conditions under which they are true. Either proposition may be denied without appeal to a reductive thesis. To speak more exactly, almost any anti-realist doctrine seems to lend itself to expression by means of a reductive thesis: but, in some cases, this thesis proves to be only a loose and inessential formulation of the doctrine, while in others it plays an essential role.

To illustrate this, let us examine in more detail the case of neutralism with regard to the future. The neutralist does not believe that there is any definite future course of events which renders every statement in the future tense determinately either true or false. There is a wide variety of different forms of neutralism; but it is common to a great many of them that, if a future-tense statement is (now) true, then it can be so only in virtue of something that lies in the present. This is, as it stands, a reductive thesis; but it is only a very rare type of neutralist who will combine this thesis with the view that it is solely by grasping how a future-tense statement is determined as having present truth that we attain an understanding of such statements. A neutralist of this type (an example of which is provided by Peter Geach) in effect holds that the only intelligible use we have for the future tense is that in which it expresses present tendencies; there is therefore no difficulty whatever for him in allowing that something was going to happen, but is now no longer going to happen. There can be no disputing that we do have such a use of the future tense, exemplified by a newspaper announcement reading, "The marriage arranged between X and Y will not now take place"; a Geachian neutralist differs from everyone else in maintaining that it is the *only* coherent use of the future tense that we have. He is thus in some difficulty how to explain the use of the future tense to make bets; it is not apparent why, on his view, a bet about what will happen in two years' time should not be settled immediately.

If the present truth or falsity of a future-tense statement depends only on what lies in the present, the possibility is open that such a statement may be true at one time but not at another; or, to speak more precisely, it is possible that some future-tense statement, made at some time, is rightly assessed at that time as not being true then, although, when made at another time, is then rightly assessed as being true at *that* time. If a sentence contains only an indexical temporal indicator, such as "a week from today" and the identity of the statement made by means of it is taken as fixed by the identity of the sentence used, then, of course, this possibility will be admitted by everyone, whatever his metaphysical view of the future; but a neutralist admits the possibility even for a statement made by means of a sentence containing a non-indexical temporal indicator like "in the year 2001". Most neutralists will, however, wish to place some restriction upon such possibilities; and, if any restriction is imposed, and if an awareness of that restriction is essential to an understanding of the future tense, it ceases to hold good that an understanding of future-tense statements consists solely in a knowledge of what will confer on them present truth. Typically, a neutralist will hold that, once a future-tense statement is true, it cannot at any later time cease to be true. Such a neutralist will regard a future-tense statement as acquiring truth only at a time at which there is something more than a mere *tendency* for things to go that way, something that confers a certain kind of physical necessity upon the statement. (Necessity of this kind is thought of as possessed by all true present-tense and past-tense statements, but only by some future-tense ones, those, namely, which follow from some true present-tense statements together with some general laws of nature.) On his conception, a future-tense statement that is not at present either true or false may later become true, either at the time to which it refers or at some intervening time; but, unlike a Geachian neutralist, he does not allow that a future-tense statement may be true now, but later cease to be true or even become false. For such a neutralist, then, in order to understand statements in the future tense, one must indeed know the sort of thing that can confer on them present truth, namely physical necessity; but one must know more besides. One must also know that, if a future-tense statement is now true, it is *necessarily* true, in the relevant sense of "necessarily"; that is, one must know the connection between what may render such a statement true now and what may render it true at a later time, and, in particular, at the time to which it refers; and one must know that, by the time to which it refers, it will have become determinately either true or false. (We are here considering only statements whose reference is to a definite future time.) An admission by a speaker of the possibility that a future-tense statement, although now true, might later cease to be true would serve, on this view, to show that he did not fully understand the central use of the future tense, even if he rightly judged of the present truth or otherwise of any such statement. From this it follows that, for such a neutralist, an understanding of future-tense statements does not consist solely in knowing what is required to confer on them present truth; one must also know the connection between their truth at one time and their truth at a later time.

A neutralist of this kind diverges from a realistic view of statements about the future not only, and not principally, because he rejects the principle of bivalence for them, but because he holds that, for an understanding of them, we need to appeal, not to the notion of a statement's simply being true, but to that of its being true at one or another time. He is a believer in variable truth-value in a sense stronger than that in which this can be said of one who accepts that there is a definite future course of events, but employs a tense logic. A tense logic differs from a representation of temporal indicators as arguments for predicates in that the temporal indicators, figuring as sentential operators in the tense logic, can be indefinitely iterated. This requires that a sentence— that to which such an operator can be applied—be regarded, not as being simply true or false, but as being true at certain times and false at others, the atomic sentences thus being taken as present-tensed. The metaphysical implications of this device for handling temporal reference, considered in itself, are, however, minimal. It appears as no more than a recognition of the indexical character of some temporal indicators, which makes iteration significant in the way that compound tenses like the future perfect and pluperfect are significant; when the temporal reference is non-indexical, the tense logic may admit the sentence to be either true at all times or false at all times, or, in other words, simply true or simply false. A neutralist of the kind we are considering may also be said to believe in variable truth-value in a sense more serious than that in which a Geachian neutralist does so. A Geachian neutralist allows that a sentence in the future tense, with a non-indexical temporal indicator, may be used at one time to say something true and at another time to say something false; but, just because, on his view, there is no constraint on the different truth-values the sentence may have at different times, there is no serious sense in which he is taking it to make the same statement on the different occasions of utterance.

A neutralist of our kind can be said to hold a reductive thesis; but it is quite wrong to compare him with an anti-realist who derives from a reductive thesis the failure of bivalence, since the neutralist does not regard the meanings of future-tense statements as given by the conditions under which they are (now) true. A better representation of the theory of meaning he favours for future-tense statements is a variant on a semantic theory in terms of possible worlds. A 'world' here consists of the actual present state and past history of the world, together with some complete possible future history of it, where the notion of possibility is correlative to that of necessity as employed by the neutralist: a future event is possible if it does not follow from the present state of the world, taken together with the laws of nature, that it will not occur. The central notion for such a semantic theory is not that of a statement's being true absolutely, but of its being true in a 'world'. The set of possible 'worlds' continually diminishes with the passage of time; that is to say, the various 'worlds' may be regarded as forming paths in a (mathematical) tree, the nodes of the tree—the points at which the paths diverge—corresponding to a state of a 'world' at a particular time, each state being common to many 'worlds'. A statement may therefore be said to be true in a 'world' W at a particular time t just in case it is true in every 'world' V such that the state of V at t is the same as the state of W at t. It is the basic contention of the neutralist that no one 'world' is the actual world; there is no *actual* future course of events. But, at any time, we may pick out an actual state as being the state-of-the-world at that time: hence, at any time, we may characterize as assertable those statements which are true at that time in any 'world' of which the actual state is a state. When the meaning-theory of our neutralist is represented in such a manner, no reductive thesis can be attributed to him at all: he cannot even formulate a reductive thesis, since he admits no notion of absolute truth, but only the notions of being true in a 'world', being true in a 'world' at a time, and being actually true at present. He cannot, therefore, strictly speaking, be said to reject the principle of bivalence, which requires the notions of absolute truth and falsity for its formulation; we can, indeed, loosely describe him as rejecting it, on the ground that, while he holds each statement to be either true or false in each 'world', he denies that, for each particular time, each statement is either true in a given 'world' at that time or false in that 'world' at that time, and hence, in particular, that each statement is actually either true or false at present. His rejection of realism is more accurately described as consisting in a repudiation of two-valued semantics that results from his having discarded altogether the notion of a statement's being absolutely true.

One form which an anti-realistic view may take is, thus, the replacement of the notion of absolute truth-value by a notion of relativized truth-values. The resultant semantic theory may still be objectivist, in that the (relativized) truth-value of a statement need not depend on our knowledge of it or our capacity to know it: in the foregoing example, there may be many statements that are actually now true even though we do not know that they are and perhaps can never know. Another type of anti-realism, perhaps the most interesting, consists in rejecting an objectivist semantics, even though it may still be allowed that to understand a statement is to know the condition for it to be true. The notion of truth admitted in such a meaning-theory will be one closely linked to our recognition of truth. Now this tendency is already evident in many reductive theses that afford a ground for rejecting bivalence. The reductive thesis is often arrived at by considering on what basis we are accustomed to assert a statement of the given class, and then declaring that such a statement can be true only if there is such a basis for an assertion of it. Thus, we assert subjunctive conditionals on the basis of general laws; we make assertions about the past on the basis of memories, records, and other present traces; we make psychological statements on the basis of behaviour; and we make statements about the physical world on the basis of observation. The thought underlying the reductive thesis is that, since our use of statements of the given class is governed by a knowledge of the kind of basis on which they may be asserted, a grasp of their meaning could not involve a notion of truth as attaching to them independently of such a basis. But, in most of these cases, the reductive thesis, while leading to a rejection of bivalence, does not call in question an objectivist theory of meaning; a statement of the given class may still be considered as determinately either true or not true. The mere existence of a basis for asserting a particular statement, the existence of something such that, if we knew it, we should take ourselves as entitled to assert that statement, is sufficient for its truth; it is not required that we should know that there is such a basis, or even be in a position to discover the fact. If, then, statements of the reductive class—statements to the effect that there is a basis for assertion— are themselves realistically interpreted, it will follow that each statement of the given class will be determinately either true or not true.

Sometimes, however, it does not work in this way. Consider, once again, the case of mathematical statements. A platonist will admit that, for a given statement, there may be neither a proof nor a disproof of it to be found; but there is no intelligible anti-realist notion of truth for mathematical statements under which a statement is true only if there is a proof of it, but may be true because such a proof exists, even though we do not know it, shall never know it, and have no effective means of discovering it. The reason is evident: we can introduce such a notion only by appeal to some platonistic conception of proofs as existing independently of our knowledge, that is, as abstract objects not brought into being by our thought. But, if we admit such a conception of proofs, we can have no objection to a parallel conception of mathematical objects such as natural numbers, real numbers, metric spaces, etc.; and then we shall have no motivation for abandoning a realistic, that is, platonist, interpretation of mathematical statements in the first place.

If we wish to say that a mathematical statement can be true only if there exists a proof of it, we have, therefore, only two choices. We can interpret "exists" as meaning concrete existence, our actual possession of a proof; in this case "is true" becomes a tensed predicate of mathematical statements, a statement being able to change from not being true to being true, although not conversely. Each statement is then either true or not true at any given time, although it may be neither true nor false, where its falsity involves the existence of a disproof; but there will be no question of its being objectively true, although we (collectively) are unaware of its truth. Alternatively, we may construe "exists", and therefore "is true", as tenseless. We shall, in this case, have to interpret "exists" constructively; we can then rule out the possibility of a statement's being neither true nor false, since its not being true would be tantamount to its being false, but we cannot assert, in advance of a proof or disproof of a statement, or an effective method of finding one, that it is either true or false. Because, on this second interpretation, "exists" is understood constructively, we shall still be unable to conceive of a statement as being true although we shall never know it to be true, although we can suppose true a statement as yet unproved.

Instead of allowing ourselves to be entangled in these difficulties, it seems better to represent a constructivist theory of meaning for mathematical statements as dispensing with the notion of truth altogether. This notion is replaced, as the central concept of the meaning-theory, by that of something's being a proof of a statement, as explained earlier in connection with Heyting's semantics for intuitionistic mathematics in terms of constructions. In the present context, what is important about such a shift is that it no longer appears that a first step towards this anti-realistic interpretation of mathematical statements consisted in the adoption of a reductive thesis: just as with the neutralist, no reductive thesis can even be formulated, since the notion of truth is unavailable. The difference is that the neutralist meaning-theory remained objectivist in the modified sense that there may be something, of which we are not aware, which would justify the assertion of some future-tense statement if we were aware of it; whereas the only thing which will justify the assertion of a mathematical statement is the existence of a proof, and, when "existence" is not interpreted platonistically, this is something of which we cannot be unaware.

The possibility of stating the anti-realist view of mathematics without formulating a reductive thesis at all is closely connected with there being an objection, of the second of the types we listed, to a proposal to translate mathematical statements into statements about proofs. We listed three generic types of objection to reductionism: one of the second type rested on the claim that statements of the reductive class are not intelligible antecedently to those of the given class; for example, that statements about mathematical proofs cannot be understood independently of the statements proved. A case in which this objection does not appear to arise is that of a reductive thesis about psychological statements, the reductive class consisting of statements about behaviour. Here it seems natural to say that statements reporting someone's behaviour can be understood independently of statements ascribing to him a mental state or psychological character: we can even state the quality of an action, as brave, generous, prudent, or the like, without presuming an understanding of an ascription of the corresponding character-trait to an individual. An actual theory of meaning for psychological statements, based on the reductive thesis, will require a detailed scheme for assigning, to each psychological statement, a range of statements about behaviour, or of sets of such statements, the truth of any one of which would establish the truth of the psychological statement; this would hold good even if the thesis did not amount to a full-fledged reductionism, so that an actual translation was not in question. Such a scheme might be very complicated and very hard to construct; it would remain that, in so far as our interest lay in explaining psychological statements, we could, in constructing it, take a theory of meaning for statements about behaviour as already given, just because they were assumed to be intelligible in advance of the psychological statements.

When, as in the mathematical case, the meanings of statements of the reductive class cannot be taken as given in advance of those of the given class, the problem of giving a meaning-theory for the latter is quite different. We have, in such a case, simultaneously to devise theories of meaning for statements of the reductive class and for those of the given class. For instance, we have, for each mathematical statement A, to characterize what, in general, is to count as a proof of A: this will obviously depend, in some systematic manner, on the composition of the statement A, on its internal structure. What we have to do, therefore, is first to lay down, for each atomic statement, what is to count as a proof of it, and then to give, by means of a stipulation relating to each mode of sentence-composition—the use of the various sentential operators and of each type of quantifier—an inductive characterization of what is to count as a proof of a complex statement. For each mode of sentence-composition, we shall assume it known what is to count as a proof of the immediate constituents of a sentence so formed (in the case of a quantified sentence, of its instances); and we shall, in terms of that, state what is to count as a proof of such a sentence. A simple example would be the stipulation that a proof of an existential statement $\exists x A\ (x)$ is to be a proof of some statement of the form $A\ (t)$, where t is a term, together with a proof that t stands for some element of the domain of the variable x.

We shall, by this procedure, have gone a long way towards explaining the meanings, not only of statements of the reductive class, but of those of the given class itself. In the general case, we shall have explained what it means to say that something is a ground for asserting an arbitrary statement of the given class. If the reductive thesis is to the effect that a statement of the given class is true if and only if there exists a ground for asserting it, and if a statement that there exists such a ground is regarded as determinately true or false, or at any rate as capable of being true independently of our knowledge, what remains will be to explain the meaning, that is, the truth-conditions, of such an existential statement: when this has been done, we shall have explained simultaneously the meanings of statements of the reductive class and of the given class. In the mathematical case, however, this final step is redundant, because we are not considering a proof as something that may exist independently of our having constructed it or having an effective method of constructing it. Hence, once we have laid down, for an arbitrary mathematical statement, what is to count as a proof of it, we have, from the constructivist standpoint, thereby determined the meanings of all mathematical statements. Constructively regarded, the meaning of such a statement is given as soon as we know when we are entitled to assert it. We shall be entitled to assert it just in case we possess a proof of it; and, for each statement, it has been inductively stipulated what is to count as such a proof. It is for this reason that, in a case of this kind, the reductive thesis falls away as irrelevant. There are not, in a case like this, two separate tasks, to explain the meanings of statements of the reductive class and to explain, in terms of them, the meanings of statements of the given class. There is only one task, to explain simultaneously the meanings of statements of both kinds; and, in executing this task, we do not need to appeal to or to introduce any notion of truth for statements of the given class—in the example, for mathematical statements—considered as attaching to them independently of our being aware of grounds for asserting them.

The constructivist's view of mathematical statements can be formulated by enunciating, as a first step in his argument, a reductive thesis concerning them, and it is quite natural to express it in this way. But what makes it natural is the analogy with anti-realist views of other classes of statements; and this analogy we have seen to be in part misleading. What makes it misleading is that we do not end up with any objectivist notion of truth for mathematical statements; for that very reason, the reductive thesis is not an essential ingredient of the constructivist view. It follows that, just as a reductive thesis need not lead to an anti-realistic interpretation of statements of the given class, so an anti-realist view need not incorporate any reductive thesis. An anti-realist view can be arrived at by means of an argument intended to show directly, without the mediation of a reductive thesis, that, for statements of the given class, we possess no legitimate objectivist notion of truth, no notion of truth transcending our capacity to recognize such statements as true, and, *a fortiori*, no notion of truth subject to the principle of bivalence. It must be admitted that, save in relation to mathematics, an anti-realist view resting on a non-objectivist semantics has seldom been formulated; but that may be largely because the distinction between the different possible forms that a rejection of realism may take was unclear to those who were disposed to reject it.

We can at least conceive of a version of anti-realism of this kind for statements about physical reality, one that does not rest upon any reductive thesis in the sense in which a constructivist interpretation of mathematical statements does not really rest upon a reductive thesis. Even if such a view has never been adopted, even if no one ever does adopt it, it will remain of philosophical interest to consider how it might be rebutted, just as philosophers concern themselves with the refutation of solipsism or other extreme sceptical opinions. Phenomenalism embodied a reductionist thesis, and it was therefore integral to it to maintain that sense-datum statements could be understood antecedently to the material-object statements that were to be translated into them. It was, indeed, this ingredient of phenomenalism that was subject to the heaviest criticisms, criticisms that eventually brought about its downfall. But an anti-realism about the physical world which did not rest upon a reductive thesis would adopt just the opposite view: there would be no reductive class of statements intelligible independently of material-object statements. Instead, the claim would be that a theory of meaning for statements about physical reality would have to take, as its central notion, not that of the truth of such a statement, but that of conclusive ground for asserting it. The meaning of such a statement would have to be given by specifying, in accordance with its composition, what was to count as such a ground. Such a specification would have to relate to our faculties of observation; but, since not every statement about physical reality is capable of serving as a report of observation, it would have to relate also to those means of establishing such statements as true which involve inference, either deductive or inductive. Very likely, since we do not often expect to attain certainty about the truth of statements concerning the physical world, it would be necessary to consider the meanings of such statements as given, not in terms only of what counted as a *conclusive* ground for asserting them, but in terms of a ground of the strongest attainable kind: given such a ground for asserting a given statement, we can rule out the possibility that we shall subsequently be presented with stronger contrary grounds, but cannot rule out the possibility that we shall meet with contrary grounds of equal strength. Or perhaps we might have to invoke some weaker notion yet. It is not to my purpose here to go into the difficulties which would attend the construction of a theory of meaning of this kind. My intention is only to indicate the possibility of such a position, which represents a form of anti-realism not vulnerable to many of the objections successfully brought against phenomenalism. In the present context, an important feature of it is that, since, unlike mathematical statements, statements about physical reality have grounds of so various a kind that we have no single word for them corresponding to "mathematical proof", it would be highly unnatural to express an anti-realist view of this kind by means of a reductive thesis. The most important point is that, natural or unnatural, such a way of expressing it would be to a high degree misleading.

We saw that there are two genera of realists, those that accept an irreducibility thesis for statements of the given class, whom we termed *naïve realists*, and those that propound some reductive thesis for them, whom we termed *sophisticated realists*. In just the same way, there are two principal genera of anti-realists, though many species within each genus. One genus consists of those who arrive at their anti-realist position via some reductive thesis, which constitutes an indispensable ingredient of their theory of meaning for statements of the given class. Such anti-realists we may term *reductive anti-realists*; examples are phenomenalists and behaviourists. The other genus consists of those whose anti-realist view does not rest upon any reductive thesis; these we might term *outright anti-realists*. Various as they are, there belong to this genus most neutralists about the future, mathematical intuitionists, and adherents of Wittgenstein's account of ascriptions of inner sensations. By and large, their views tend to be more interesting than those of reductive anti-realists.

I have taken realism as requiring acceptance, in all its details, of a classical two-valued semantics and of a truth-conditional theory of meaning based on that semantics. This might be objected to, on two counts. It might be said, first, that what is essential to realism is that the meaning of a sentence be regarded as given in terms of what has to hold for it to be true, absolutely and timelessly, where the notion of truth is understood in an objectivist way: but that the mechanism whereby the condition for the truth of a sentence is determined in accordance with its composition is, in some respects at least, metaphysically irrelevant. Granted that, if we are to have a realistic interpretation, this mechanism must involve the notion of reference, there is no necessity that the sentential operators be truth-functional in the sense of being definable by two-valued truth-tables. There is a weaker and a stronger sense in which someone may be said to know the meaning of a sentence. In the weaker sense, all that is required is that he know its content when used as a complete utterance, for instance that he grasp the significance of an assertion made by uttering just that sentence. If the meaning of the sentence is to be explained in truth-conditional terms, then, in order to know its meaning in this weaker sense, it is sufficient that someone should know no more than under what conditions it is true and under what conditions it is not true. In the stronger sense, however, a speaker may be said to know the meaning of a sentence only when he also knows the contribution which that sentence makes to the meaning of a more complex sentence of which it is a constituent, that is, the contribution that it makes to determining the condition for the more complex sentence to be true. It does not, however, violate the general principle of a truth-conditional meaning-theory that the knowledge, in the weaker sense, of the meaning of a sentence should not suffice for the knowledge of its meaning in the stronger sense. There is no reason why a subsentence of a complex sentence should contribute to determining the condition for the truth of the complex sentence only via the condition for the subsentence to be true or not to be true: it may well contribute in some more complicated way. The truth or otherwise of the complex sentence may depend, not just on whether or not the subsentence is true, but on whether it fails to be true for a reason of one kind or for a reason of another kind. When this is so, we shall need a many-valued semantics to explain the sentential operators or other devices for forming complex sentences: the different undesignated values will represent different ways in which a sentence may fail to be true; if there are also distinct designated values, they will represent different ways in which a sentence may succeed in being true. Whether or not a complex sentence is true will then depend, not just on whether its constituents are true or not, that is, on whether they have designated or undesignated values, but on the different ways in which they succeed in being or fail to be true, in other words, on the specific values that they have. It will remain that, to know the meaning of any sentence in the weaker sense, that is, to grasp its content when it stands on its own, it is necessary to know only the condition for it to have some designated value, the condition, namely, for it to be true; if we want to know the meaning of the sentence only in this weaker sense, we shall not need to know the conditions for it to have specific undesignated values or specific designated ones. Now our objector's claim is that, in order to have a realistic interpretation of a class of sentences, all that need be assumed is that to know the meaning of a sentence in the weaker sense, to know its content, is to know the condition for it to be true: the details of the mechanism by which this condition is determined in accordance with the way the sentence is put together out of atomic sentences are of no metaphysical importance.

The second prong of this objection is a protest against the assumption that I have hitherto made, that realism demands an unqualified assent to the principle of bivalence. A formulation of the principle invokes not only the concept of truth but also that of falsity; and, it is objected, while the concept of truth usually has a fairly natural application to the statements of any given class, that of falsity depends for its application on much more *ad hoc* conventions. In most cases that I have here discussed, in fact in all save that of subjunctive conditionals, I equated the falsity of a statement with the truth of its negation, that is, of what looks at first sight like its negation. The reductive thesis then led to the conclusion that not every statement need be either true or false. But, the objector says, this same conclusion could have been expressed less dramatically by saying that what looked like the negation was not the real negation; and, if we so expressed it, we should have no reason for claiming any departure from realism. Since whether or not someone is a realist cannot depend on the partly arbitrary question how he chooses to apply the word "false", it follows that not every repudiation of the principle of bivalence is incompatible with realism: we have to distinguish those grounds for rejecting bivalence which are compatible with realism from those which are genuinely incompatible with it. One type of violation of bivalence that would be perfectly compatible with realism would occur if we adopted a many-valued semantics, of the kind which the first part of the objection maintained to be consistent with realism, but gave the name "falsity" to just one out of several undesignated values. A motive for doing so might be to enable us to identify some unary sentential operator as a negation operator, one that converted every true sentence into a false one and every false sentence into a true one. In any case, the objector may add, it is foolish to attach much importance, when treating of sentences of natural language, to the principle that a sentence is false just in case its negation is true, or, at least, to treat it as a guide to when a sentence should be called 'false'. The reason is that we do not, in natural language, have a sentential negation operator; we cannot, therefore, be guided mechanically by syntactic form in deciding what is the negation of any sentence, but have to reflect. The principle connecting falsity and negation can serve only to guide us what to take the negation of some sentence to be, once we have already decided when to call it 'false': it cannot serve the converse purpose.

This two-pronged objection expresses opinions that I once held. I used to think that one could classify semantic theories involving departures from the principle of bivalence into those which did and those which did not entail a rejection of realism. I no longer think that this can be done by appeal just to the form of the semantic theory: *any* modification of the principle of bivalence, or, more generally, of the standard two-valued semantics, involves potentially a rejection of some realistic view. Anti-realism, which, as we have seen, can assume a wide variety of forms, is, as such, a negative doctrine: it is correlative to a corresponding species of realism. Where we are disposed to interpret sentences of a certain range in accordance with a two-valued semantics, any divergent way of understanding them will appear to us an anti-realist doctrine; where we have no such inclination, the observation that some departure from the two-valued semantics is called for will not seem anti-realist in character, but will appear merely to be a comment on the underlying semantic mechanism of those sentences. There need be no difference, however, in the form of the semantic theory proposed in each case: the difference may lie solely in our having had, in the one case but not in the other, a disposition to treat those sentences at their face-value, as it were, that is, to apply to them the simplest form of semantic theory, the two-valued one. Whenever some non-classical semantics or some non-truth-conditional meaning-theory is proposed, there is a possible form of realism to which the proposal stands in opposition, which would be embodied in a truth-conditional meaning-theory based on a two-valued semantics. In some cases, this possible realistic view would lack all plausibility; in others, it may be merely out of fashion; and in others again, it may be a live alternative. It will depend on which of these states of affairs obtains whether the proposal strikes us as anti-realist in character: but the question is external to the form of meaning-theory that has been proposed.

Admittedly, we need to reflect in order to decide what is the negation of a sentence of a given form: for this reason, to equate the falsity of a sentence with the truth of its negation is not to appeal to a mere syntactic criterion, but, rather, to what we intuitively regard as the condition for the sentence to be false, since the principle that the negation of a statement is true if and only if the statement is false is what guides us in deciding what to recognize as being the negation of a given statement. But, for that very reason, an appeal to the concept of negation, as applied to sentences of natural language, is an appeal to our intuitive conception of the conditions under which they are rightly said to be false. Hence, if some reductive thesis has the consequence that some sentence need not be either true or false, when its falsity is equated with the truth of what is ordinarily taken to be its negation, that result does not merely reflect an arbitrary decision to apply the word "false" to that sentence in a particular way; rather, it undermines a realistic interpretation which we are unreflectively disposed to adopt for that and similar sentences. In any case, the fact that natural language does not possess a sentential negation operator ought not to be overstressed. Natural language does possess a regular means for negating a predicate, a means which breaks down principally in the presence of modal auxiliaries like "must" and "may". Reflection is needed to decide what is the negation of a quantified sentence: but, when we have what is apparently a singular term as the grammatical subject, there is normally no difficulty in saying what would ordinarily be taken as the negation of that sentence, namely the result of negating the predicate. If we accept some reductive thesis for a class of statements that yields an objectivist semantics for those statements, we could indeed propose to use the word "false" so that a statement was false just in case it was not true, thus saving the principle of bivalence at the cost of divorcing the concept of falsity from that of the truth of what would ordinarily be taken as the negation of the statement. Contrary to what the objector maintains, however, such a proposal would not enable us to preserve a realistic interpretation of statements of that class. If what appears to be the negation of a singular statement is declared not to be its real negation, this can be explained in either of two ways: either what was apparently a singular term is not genuinely one, and then we must abandon a semantic account which involves assigning a reference to that expression; or the operator which apparently negated the predicate does not function in an ordinary two-valued manner. In either case, although we have formally preserved the principle of bivalence, we shall have had in some way to diverge from the two-valued semantics; and we shall thus have abandoned a purely realistic interpretation of statements of the given class. We shall, in particular, have opened the way for the introduction of a 'genuine' negation operator which carries a sentence in the given class into one not in that class, i.e. one under which the given class is not closed; and it was integral to the realistic account of statements of that class to suppose it closed under negation.

The distinction between any form of objectivist semantics and a non-objectivist semantics is, indeed, the most important one: an adherent of a non-objectivist semantics could not count as a realist from any perspective, whereas an adherent of an objectivist semantics is an anti-realist only to the extent that a straightforward two-valued semantics holds any attraction. Consider someone who believes that there is no *one* intended model for set theory, so that the central notion for a semantics for set-theoretical statements is not that of simply being true, but that of being true in a model belonging to some class K; a set-theoretical statement will be absolutely true only if it is true in all models belonging to K, so that there will be some set-theoretical statements that are neither absolutely true nor absolutely false. The sentential operators and quantifiers are to be interpreted in the two-valued manner relatively to each model. Compared with the intuitionists' account of mathematical statements, a proponent of such a view is very little removed from an out-and-out platonist; for him, each set-theoretical statement is determinately either true or false in each particular model, independently of our knowledge. There is, however, nothing to distinguish this conception formally from that of a neutralist about the future, who thinks that there is no *one* actual future course of events, but is prepared to treat the sentential operators and quantifiers occurring in a future-tense statement as to be interpreted in a two-valued manner relatively to each possible future course of events. In both cases, we shall have a classical logic for set-theoretical statements and for future-tense statements respectively, since, in each case, the semantic values which a sentence may assume form a Boolean algebra, although not the two-element one: in both cases, therefore, the law of excluded middle will hold, although not the principle of bivalence as stated in terms of absolute truth and absolute falsity. We shall certainly regard the neutralist as an anti-realist, since the conception under which every statement about the future already has a determinate truth-value exerts a strong attraction. The idea that there is some one intended model of set theory has less power; but the view proposed is, nevertheless, an anti-realist one when contrasted with a wholly realistic view of set theory, one according to which every set-theoretical statement is absolutely true or absolutely false, because, in making such statements, we have in mind some one particular abstract structure, even though we have not fully succeeded in characterizing it, and, perhaps, cannot ever do so.

Whenever we allow that the truth-condition of a complex sentence depends on more than the conditions for its constituent sentences to be true or not to be true, we create the possibility for a disagreement between a realistic and a non-realistic interpretation. We shall have a realistic interpretation whenever it is held that the mechanism whereby the truth-condition of a sentence is determined could be explained by means of the two-valued semantics, with, perhaps, some slight adjustment of the syntactic analysis of the sentence. It was already remarked that a tense logic, when not founded upon any neutralist view of the future or any anti-realist view of the past, does not involve any divergence from realism, even though it requires a non-two-valued semantics, namely a semantics in terms of relativized truth-values, of a sentence's being true or false at each particular time. This, we saw, was because the tense logic could be viewed as a variation upon a two-valued semantics for a language in which temporal indicators appeared as arguments of predicates. What makes this possible is that we should treat the temporal indicators in such a language as genuinely having reference: so the tense logic does not appear to involve any genuine departure from realism. Now, formally speaking, a semantics for a language containing modal operators appears very similar: we again employ a notion of relativized truth-values, relativized in this case to possible worlds rather than to times. When this kind of semantics was first introduced, therefore, it might have seemed natural to say that it did not involve any departure from realism either. In line with the objection we are considering, it might have been claimed that this semantics embodied a divergence from two-valued semantics with no metaphysical implications: obviously, the truth-condition of a modal statement could not depend solely on the conditions for its constituent subsentences simply to be true; but that would not affect the fact that we were regarding their meanings as determined by their truth-conditions, with respect to a notion of truth under which each was determinately either true or false. But, in saying this, we should have been wrong. A semantics of possible worlds brings with it the possibility of a new form of realism, realism concerning possible worlds, as advocated, for example, by David Lewis. To be a realist about possible worlds, to believe that there really are such things as possible worlds, is, as Lewis says, to treat the adverb "actually" as indexical, as indicating position in modal space in the way that "here" indicates position in physical space. And to do this is to regard modal logic as strictly comparable with tense logic. To treat modal statements in terms of a semantics of possible worlds is, on this view, no more than a variation on a treatment of them by means of a two-valued semantics for a language in which each predicate has an additional argument-place for a possible world; in such a language, a variable ranging over possible worlds would need to be explained in the same way as any other sort of individual variable, namely by ultimate appeal to the notion of reference to a possible world. To reject realism about possible worlds is, in effect, to deny that a straightforward two-valued semantic theory could be given for such a language: to speak of possible worlds is only a *façon de parler*, and there is no such thing as reference to a possible world. To know whether or not we have a realistic interpretation of some class of statements, it is necessary to look, not merely at the formal structure of the semantic theory, but at the entire meaning-theory constructed on it as foundation. Even then, we shall not classify a given interpretation as anti-realistic unless there is some form of realism with which to contrast it. The mere possibility of a view compared to which a given interpretation would be anti-realistic supplies no guarantee that such a view will ever actually be proposed: probably, when the semantics of possible worlds was first introduced, it appeared unthinkable that anyone would adopt a realistic view of possible worlds. But we can be secure that our interpretation of some class of statements will never appear an anti-realistic one, when compared with some other view, only if that interpretation embodies a completely unmodified two-valued semantic theory.

What is sound about the objection is that it is not the mere adherence to or rejection of the principle of bivalence that marks the difference between a realistic and an anti-realistic interpretation. Impressed by the fact that many philosophical views which involved rejecting some form of realism turned on, or at least naturally led to, a repudiation of bivalence, I have been guilty in the past of speaking as though what characterizes anti-realism is the rejection of bivalence, so that, provided one accepts bivalence, one is a realist. The price of adopting this excessively simple criterion was to be forced to distinguish between metaphysically significant and metaphysically insignificant grounds for rejecting bivalence: for instance, it did not appear that one who, like Frege and Strawson, held that a singular statement containing an empty proper name was neither true nor false need be any less of a realist than one who, like Russell, declared that it was false, on the ground that the proper name was a disguised definite description, to be interpreted according to Russell's theory of descriptions. Another price of adopting bivalence as the shibboleth for discriminating realists from anti-realists was the necessity to admit different senses of "realism", since some philosophical debates over certain forms of realism (for example, the realism concerning universals which is opposed by nominalism) patently did not involve any disagreement about bivalence. The mistake lay in concentrating on only one feature of the two-valued semantics. There really is nothing to choose between the Russell view and the Frege–Strawson view of sentences containing empty proper names in respect of realism. This is not, however, because the topic is metaphysically neutral. Both views stand in opposition to a realism of a Meinongian kind, which would take all proper names as referring to objects, whether existent or non-existent, and would construe statements of the form "*a* is *F*" as meaning "*a* exists and is *F*". Russell's theory departs from Meinong's idea that reference can be ascribed to every proper name by declaring that ordinary proper names are not, as they appear, genuine singular terms, and, being definite descriptions, are not to be explained in terms of the notion of reference at all.

The Frege–Strawson account departs from it by invoking the distinction between sense and reference to explain how a genuine singular term may lack a reference, and by repudiating bivalence. We do not see either theory as anti-realist, because we no longer take Meinongian realism seriously, and our attention is concentrated upon the disagreement between Russell on the one hand and Frege and Strawson on the other. But it is a mistake to say that the dispute has nothing to do with any question concerning realism; and still more of a mistake to say that we can recognize this to be so from some formal characteristics of the competing views.

We have, up to now, been considering realism solely as a *semantic* doctrine, a doctrine about the sort of thing that makes our statements true when they are true: the fundamental thesis of realism, so regarded, is that we really do succeed in referring to external objects, existing independently of our knowledge of them, and that the statements we make about them carry a meaning of such a kind that they are rendered true or false by an objective reality the constitution of which is, again, independent of our knowledge. Very often, however, realism, or, to speak more exactly, naïve realism, is taken as also having an epistemological component: it is considered to be part of a naïve realist view that we have a direct acquaintance with the external objects about which we speak. It is readily understandable how this epistemological thesis comes to be associated with naïve realism. Naïve realism, as I characterized it above, embodies an irreducibility thesis, to the effect that there can be no informative answer to the question what, in general, makes a statement of the given class true, when it is true. We certainly cannot expect that, for any statement or class of statements we choose to consider, there will be an informative answer to this question. But, when it is possible only to give a trivial answer to the question, there must be a non-trivial answer to the further question in what our knowledge of the condition for such a statement to be true consists. If this question, too, admitted only a trivial answer, then we should have no account of the meanings of such statements, that is, no account of what a speaker knows when he understands statements of this class; and this would be absurd, because a knowledge that we are able to acquire must be a knowledge of which we can give an account. Now realism is primarily a semantic doctrine; but, as we have seen, this should not be interpreted as meaning that a realistic interpretation of some class of statements consists simply in the adoption of a certain semantic theory, in the sense in which logicians speak of a semantic theory. A semantic theory in this sense gives an outline sketch of the manner in which a sentence is determined as true, when it is true, in accordance with its composition; it is plausible only in so far as it is possible to construct, on the semantic theory as base, a complete theory of meaning. A theory of meaning must do much more than simply analyse the way in which a sentence is determined as true, when it is true, in accordance with its composition: it has, among other things, to say what a speaker knows when he understands an expression of the language, and to explain how the speaker's understanding of an expression determines it as having whatever semantic value it has, its semantic value being that whereby it contributes to determining the truth or otherwise of any sentence in which it occurs. Hence, in so far as the meaning-theory takes a truth-conditional form, in so far as it equates the understanding of a sentence with a knowledge of the condition that must obtain for the sentence to be true, it has to explain in what a speaker's knowledge of that condition consists. When it is possible to give a non-trivial answer to the question in virtue of what a sentence of a certain form is true, if it is true, we have already an explanation of what a speaker must know in knowing the condition for a sentence of that form to be true. But, when no non-trivial answer can be given, a further explanation must be supplied by the meaning-theory. The simplest way in which the meaning-theory can do this will consist in attributing to the speaker a capacity, in favourable circumstances, to recognize the condition as obtaining or not obtaining. Just because we cannot state informatively what will render the sentence true, when it is true, the faculty of recognition thus attributed to the speaker will be a faculty of *unmediated* recognition; neither the speaker nor the meaning-theorist can say *whereby* he recognizes the condition as obtaining. That which renders the sentence true is the very thing of which we are directly aware when we recognize it as being true.

Now the claim that we possess such a faculty for direct recognition of a condition of a certain kind is an epistemological one; and we see, from this, why epistemology enters into the matter. Realism and anti-realism are metaphysical doctrines; and it has been an implicit contention of the present analysis of the concept of realism that metaphysical questions, at least ones of this type, are at root questions belonging to the theory of meaning. It is impossible, however, to keep the theory of meaning sterilized from all epistemological considerations, because meaning is, ultimately, a matter of *knowledge*. The meaning of an expression is what a speaker must know if he is to be said to understand that expression; the meaning-theory for a language displays what anyone must know if he is to be said to know, or to be able to speak, that language. For this reason, the purely semantic explanation previously given of what naïve realism consists in does not completely tally with the way in which the term "naïve realism" has traditionally been used: it stated only part of what has usually been taken as involved in being a naïve realist. For example, a realistic interpretation of statements about the past involves accepting the principle of bivalence as applied to them: they are determinately true or false, independently of whether we know their truth-values or, in a particular case, have any means of knowing. Anyone who takes this view—and very few philosophers have dared to contradict it—is unlikely to admit any reductive thesis for statements about the past, considered as a class; there will be no non-trivial answer to the question what, in general, renders a past-tense statement true if it is true. By our original criterion, therefore, the standard view of statements about the past should count as a naïvely realistic one. It would usually be thought, however, that more was required for naïve realism about the past: namely, a view to the effect that we are directly acquainted with past states of affairs, that memory affords us direct contact with them.

It is not altogether easy to see what this additional epistemological component of naïve realism, as ordinarily understood, amounts to. It might be said that our knowledge of the past in memory is indeed direct, in the sense that a report of memory is not ordinarily the conclusion of an inference: I do not conclude to the truth of the past-tense statement because that is the most plausible explanation of the memory-experience that I have. On occasion, indeed, something like this may happen. I may have the impression that I remember a certain event, then feel uncertain that I have not made a mistake of memory, and finally conclude that I must have remembered correctly, on the ground, say, that I have hardly ever made mistakes of that particular kind, or that I should be unlikely to have thought of such a curious event had I not actually witnessed it. But a case of this kind must necessarily be exceptional: we could not suppose ourselves to know enough about the past to make any such inferences if we did not take most of our memories to be correct; in fact, if all memory is called in question, we are left without any knowledge of the past at all. The claim that, in memory, we are in direct contact with the past event must, however, mean more than just that reports of memory are not, in general, based on inference, since the same may be said of knowledge based on the testimony of others. On many occasions, I may doubt whether someone else is to be trusted in what he asserts; he does not know enough about the subject, he has proved unreliable in the past, he is not always veracious. On other occasions, I may at first entertain such doubts, and then set them at rest by some particular consideration: the individual in question is unlikely to lie to *me*, and, although he has made mistakes, he has always been right on questions of this specific kind. In such a case, I may be said to conclude to the truth of what he says on the basis of an inductive inference. But the normal case is not of that kind: for, if I call in doubt the truth of everything for which I have only the authority of others, I should simply know far too little about the world to be able to judge, on an inductive basis, of the reliability of any but a very few of the things that are said to me. It is our normal practice to accept other people's assertions, just as it is our normal practice to take what we remember to have happened as having happened. Just as it is only when we have a special reason for mistrusting our own memories that we look for further grounds for supposing things to have been as we remember them, so it is only when we have a special reason for doubting the truth of what someone else says that we look for further grounds for accepting it. This is not due to laziness, or because "life is too short": without its being ordinary practice to take what another asserts as true, we could not have a language; part of what a child has to learn in learning language is to accept and act on what other people say. Lying subverts the institution of language: if most members of a society started to lie most of the time, they would cease to be able to communicate. For the same reason, it is a priori impossible that most assertions should be mistaken.

For present purposes, the point is that 'direct knowledge', as the naïve realist speaks of it, must mean more than "knowledge not arrived at as the conclusion of an inference". When I accept a statement on the testimony of another, I am not normally concluding to its truth on the strength of an inference: nevertheless, that is the prime case of knowing something indirectly, of knowing it "not of my own knowledge", as the lawyers say. What the naïve realist appears to mean in speaking of direct knowledge is that a Cartesian doubt is excluded. If my knowledge of the past, in memory, is the outcome of a direct contact that I now make with the past event, then it must be *senseless* to suppose that I should have this memory even though the past event did not occur. Thus, for the naïve realist, the connection between that which renders a statement true and our knowledge of its truth is an intimate one, just as it is for the anti-realist: from what it is like to know it to be true, we see just what it is for it to be true. Only, they draw opposite conclusions. The anti-realist draws the conclusion that the statement cannot be true unless we know it to be true, at least indirectly, or unless we have the means to arrive at such knowledge, or at least unless there exists that which, if we were aware of it, would yield such knowledge. The naïve realist believes that the statement must be determinately true or false, regardless of whether we are able, in the particular case, to perceive that which renders it true or false; but it is our capacity, in favourable circumstances, to perceive directly that which renders true or false other statements of the same type that constitutes our understanding of what it is for the given statement to be true or to be false.

The naïve realist faces a twofold difficulty. He has, first, a problem to explain how we ever come to make a mistake in making a judgement on the favoured basis: if memory is a direct contact with past events, how can a mistake of memory occur? Secondly, he has a problem about the connection between our mode of coming to know the truth of a statement and the consequences we take it to have: if memory is a direct contact with a past event, which must, therefore, still exist in some manner if I am to be able now to apprehend it, how can I know that that event has not changed somewhat since it originally occurred? The question is, of course, senseless: but it is difficult to argue it to be senseless without, at the same time, rendering senseless the notion of a direct contact with past events.

A realist who is not, in my sense, a sophisticated realist, that is, who does not accept any reductive thesis for statements of the given class, but who also does not accept the epistemological component of naïve realism, is in an intermediate position: we might call him a *semi-naïve realist*. The semi-naïve realist has difficulties of his own. He has to explain in what our knowledge of the condition for a statement of the given class to be true consists; he cannot, for this purpose, invoke even our most straightforward means of knowing such statements to be true in the way that the anti-realist and the naïve realist do; at least, he cannot assign it such a leading role. He usually has recourse to some type of analogy; we are supposed to transfer to statements of the given class some feature of our understanding of some more primitive class of statements, where our understanding of these more primitive statements can be explained in a naïve realist fashion. But I do not wish to go further into the debate between the protagonists of the different metaphysical (or metaphysico-epistemological) positions. My sole aim has been to characterize them; that is, to explain the concept of realism as applying to philosophical views which may be adopted on a wide variety of different questions.

Cartesian doubt has two features. It is doubt entertained in the teeth of the best possible evidence, unimpaired by any contrary evidence; and it is all-encompassing. Descartes wished to entertain every doubt that is not by its nature *senseless*; and he wished to doubt simultaneously every proposition which, taken by itself, it would be possible to doubt. The naïve realist's response is to declare the doubt senseless; even Cartesian doubt is then excluded. It is this which gives its special character to his conception of *immediate* knowledge, knowledge by direct apprehension of that which renders the proposition true. Without a grasp of this curious idea, we cannot understand much that is to be found in empiricist epistemology. Consider, for instance, Locke's doctrine of secondary qualities. Locke says, of colours, that they "are nothing in the objects themselves but powers to produce various sensations in us". Ayer, in his *The Central Questions of Philosophy*, attributes to Locke the view that "colour is nothing in the object itself", without adding the phase "but powers . . .". At first sight, this is as unwarranted as if someone, accused of being nothing but a social climber, should say, "He said that I was nothing": we should naturally construe Locke as saying that colours, in the objects, are only powers to produce sensations, and, in a later passage, he does precisely so express himself. Ayer is not misrepresenting Locke, however; for Locke also says, in yet another passage, that colours "are not really in" the bodies. Now how does it come about that Locke makes this seemingly unjustifiable transition from his own doctrine? If, in the objects, colours are powers, then the colours are presumably in the objects, though, indeed, only as powers: why, then, does Locke contradict himself by saying that the colours are not in the objects? It seems that Locke is offering an analysis of the concept of a colour, considered, at least, as a property of an opaque surface, as being a disposition of a particular type, namely a power: what more is added to this analysis by remarking that the colours are not in the objects? Are the powers, then, not in the objects? It is, after all, the body that has the power: the power is not floating independently in space, at a location where the body happens to be; when the body moves, the power moves with it, for the power, on Locke's formulation, is a power *of the body* to produce sensations in us. If, then, the colour is a power, and the power is in the body, what can possibly be meant by saying that the colour is not in the body?

Not surprisingly, it is easy to feel totally baffled by this notion of Locke's that colours, and other secondary qualities, are not *in* the physical objects. It cannot be understood unless we bear in mind the epistemological component of naïve realism, the notion of direct contact with, or immediate awareness of, the object and its properties. Locke wishes to depart from naïve realism, so far as secondary qualities are concerned: but he is attracted to it. A naïve realist about the physical world supposes that, in perception, we are in direct contact with physical objects: we know them as they really are. When, under normal conditions, I perceive an object, a Cartesian doubt is impossible, according to the naïve realist: it would be senseless, given my perceptual state, to suppose that the object was not present or was otherwise than I perceive it to be; mistakes occur only because perception does not always take place under normal conditions. My ability to judge the truth of material-object statements on the basis of observation constitutes, for the naïve realist, my knowledge of what has to be the case for those statements to be true: so the very meaning of an ascription of perceptible qualities to an object is given by reference to the process of perceptual recognition of those qualities, and can only be so given. Now a disposition of any kind is not a quality of which we can be directly aware in such a way; a disposition is something that is manifested on some occasions and not on others, and may be variously manifested in differing circumstances. For instance, our concept of colour, as a property of an opaque surface, is not to be explained, as the naïve realist is forced to suppose, solely in terms of the appearance of a surface 'under normal conditions'; it is not irrelevant to that concept that there is a connection between the colour of a surface and its appearance under various abnormal conditions, under a coloured light, under excessive or inadequate illumination, or from too far away to allow resolution into its differently coloured regions. Now, as Locke understands the word "colour", a colour is a disposition, and is really in the object. But, as a naïve realist understands the word "colour", a colour cannot be a disposition, for then perception, under normal conditions, would not be an immediate awareness of the object as it really is: so, as the naïve realist understands "colour", Locke's view entails that objects do not have colours. It is the conflation of these two conceptions of what the word "colour" means that produces Locke's contradictory remarks.

The naïve realist's notion of immediate awareness, consisting in a direct contact between the knowing subject and the object of his knowledge, is probably in all cases incoherent: it is certainly extremely difficult to formulate it intelligibly. The proper response to Cartesian doubt is to deny, not the meaningfulness of each individual expression of doubt, but the possibility of professing simultaneously every doubt which, taken by itself, is meaningful if neurotic: it is the generality of Cartesian doubt, not its contempt for evidence, which is the point at which it should be attacked. Bertrand Russell maintained that we could not know for certain that the world was not created two minutes ago, complete with all our apparent memories and with all the apparent traces of past events. Most philosophers do not trouble themselves with a Cartesian doubt of this kind; it is too absurd to entertain seriously, but they tacitly agree with Russell that, if someone succumbed to it, philosophy could do nothing to dispel it. Many years ago, I heard Professor Anscombe argue that what makes such thoroughgoing Cartesian doubt absurd is that, if we came across a society of people in whose language there was an inflexion of the verb such that we could establish no correlation between the sentences containing verbs in this inflexion to which they assented and what had previously happened, we could not intelligibly suppose that this inflexion represented their past tense, but that their memories were hopelessly astray. This argument was being advanced from a Wittgensteinian standpoint, but it agrees equally with that of Quine and many others; and it is surely fundamentally correct. Naïve realism, as traditionally understood, was a doctrine advanced by philosophers to whom epistemological considerations were of paramount importance, and one of whose primary objectives was to defeat scepticism; being an incoherent doctrine, it failed as a weapon in this particular battle, and this led to too easy a victory for idealism. In more recent philosophy, it has been realism, in a semi-naïve or sophisticated form, which has, for the most part, attained too easy a victory. Many of the problems expressible as disputes for and against one or another species of realism are still live issues, or ought to be. In tackling them, we need a clear formulation of what realism consists in, and a clear view also of the various forms which it can take, and the various forms which a denial of realism can take. In most of these disputes, naïve realism, as traditionally conceived with its epistemological component, is no longer a serious contender. This very fact may, but ought not to be allowed to, obscure the importance of the distinction between the sophisticated realist and what, in the later part of this essay, I have been calling the semi-naïve realist; above all, it should not lead us to mistake the sophisticated realist for the anti-realist.

12

Existence

Some philosophers regard the problem of existence as the central question of all philosophy; others, distinguishing between existence and being, would rather bestow that title upon the investigation of the concept of being. To yet others, however, such an attitude savours of mystagogy. For them, the concept of existence, which they would unanimously refuse to distinguish from that of being, is a very thin concept, essentially captured by the theory of the existential quantifier as employed in the notation of mathematical logic. If it has caused perplexity in the past, that is only because formal logic had not yet supplied philosophers with an adequate analysis of the structure of sentences involving generality, nor, therefore, if one wishes to speak in such a manner, of the thoughts or propositions expressed by such sentences. Now that we have such an analysis, the apparent mystery is dissolved, and it can be recognized that there is little to say about what existence is, however much there may be to say about what exists and why, and about what does not exist and why not. In particular, further investigation of the concept of existence cannot be made to yield any substantial metaphysical conclusions; anyone who purports to extract them from it thereby betrays that he has committed some elementary logical blunder.

For philosophers of this latter turn of mind, it was Kant who, though he lacked the benefit of even an approach to modern logical theory, had the insight to take the first step to a correct solution by his doctrine that "exists" is not a real, but only a logical, predicate;[1] and it was Frege who, thanks to his invention of modern logic, was able to give the definitive solution, which he expressed by saying that existence is a concept of second level, something, that is, which can be ascribed, not to individual objects, but to first-level concepts such as *satellite of Mars*. According to this account, when we say that satellites of Mars exist, we are not ascribing a property, the property of existing, to those objects which fall under the concept *satellite of Mars*. If we were, and meant to be understood as saying that *all* satellites of Mars had this property, then, if such a statement is construed as meaning that, if anything is a satellite of Mars, it has the property of existing, it would be compatible with there being no satellites of Mars. Even if we were assured that Mars has some satellites, the

First published in D. P. Chattopadhyaya (ed.), *Humans, Meanings and Existences*, Jadavpur Studies in Philosophy, v (Delhi, 1983).

[1] Mr Arindam Chakrabarti first brought me to realize that Kant did not hold the doctrine usually attributed to him, that "exists" is not a predicate at all.

question would arise, if existence were a property of objects, whether all of Mars's satellites had the property, or only some of them, whereas such a question is patently senseless; in fact the proposition that there are satellites of Mars plainly embodies all that we wished to assert in asserting such satellites to exist. That assertion ascribes no property to the objects Phobos and Deimos: it says something about the concept *satellite of Mars*, namely that there are objects falling under it; otherwise expressed, it says, about a certain *kind* of object, namely satellites of Mars, that there are objects of that kind. Kant drew from his thesis that "exists" is not a real predicate the conclusion that there can be no analytically true existential statements. For Frege, the conclusion was too strong, and, indeed, untrue, since, for him, there are logical objects, which include the numbers, and a statement asserting the existence of logical objects expresses an analytic truth: Kant's mistake, according to Frege, lay not only in a defective analysis of the structure of sentences, but in an excessively narrow characterization of analyticity. Frege agreed with Kant, however, in condemning the ontological argument for the existence of God as fallacious. This argument has the general form:

> Whatever is God has the property X.
> Anything that has the property X has also the property of existing.
> Therefore, God exists.

The fallacy of such an argument, according to Frege, lies in the second premiss: such a form of sentence is misbegotten, and, in a properly constructed language, could not even be expressed.

The appeal of this solution depends upon the plausibility of equating such a statement as "Egg-laying mammals exist" with "There are egg-laying mammals". Evidently, for ordinary conversational purposes, these two statements are equivalent. If, however, it is once admitted, quite generally, that "Xs exist" means the same as "There are Xs", the ontological argument is blocked at the outset. The question is not whether "exists" is a predicate, it is, rather, whether, if "exists" is treated as a predicate, it is to be taken as one that is true of everything, or as one that is true of some things and false of others. To equate "Xs exist" with "There are Xs" is to choose the former option, since, if there are objects that do not exist, these may include Xs, and this would render "There are Xs" true without thereby making "Xs exist" true, this being understood as meaning "Some Xs exist". In holding "exists" not to be a real predicate, Kant meant that, in stating an object to exist, we in no way determine its character. Since this could not be so if there were some objects that existed and others which did not, Kant's authority can be claimed for the view that "exists", considered as a predicate, is true of everything; that is why his discussion was a step towards the correct solution.

A proponent of the ontological argument must therefore maintain that there are objects that do not exist, that is, that we do not quantify only over what exists. He can cheerfully admit that the range of quantification is often tacitly restricted to what exists; such a tacit restriction occurs when, in the normal way, someone asserts that there are egg-laying mammals, which is why his assertion could as well be expressed by saying that egg-laying mammals exist. He must maintain, however, that there are some contexts in which there is no such restriction, for instance such a statement as "Jews and Arabs trace their descent to the same person". What makes this statement true is that both Jews and Arabs trace their descent to Abraham; but it would ordinarily be understood in such a sense that its truth would remain undisturbed by the historical discovery that there was never any such person. On the face of it, therefore, the statement means that there is some person, who may or may not have existed, to whom both Jews and Arabs trace their descent; this interpretation requires us to allow that there are individuals who have never existed.

The proponent of the ontological argument has, however, to do more than make out that there are objects which do not exist. If the first premiss of the argument is construed as of the same form as the second, namely as meaning:

For any object *a*, if *a* is God, then *a* has the property *X*,

then the conclusion must be of the same form, namely:

For any object *a*, if *a* is God, then *a* exists.

This conclusion amounts to saying "Everything that is God exists", understood as without existential import, whereas since "*X*s exist" is being construed as meaning "Some *X*s exist", the desired conclusion was "Something is God and exists". A defender of the argument must therefore understand the first premiss to mean:

That object which is God has the property *X*.

If the argument, so understood, is not to beg the question, it must be possible to use such a phrase as "that object which is God" to pick out a specific object in advance of knowing whether or not it exists. That is, it must be a semantic possibility to refer to a specific non-existent object, and an epistemic possibility to know a statement about a specific object to be true without knowing that object to exist. In which cases can we have such knowledge?

If there are singular statements which we can know to be true without knowing whether the object referred to exists, these must include ones in which the predicate is, implicitly or explicitly, part of the means by which the object is specified, as in "Socrates' eldest uncle was male". Existential statements, however, cannot be included in this class, on pain of admitting an ontological argument for the existence of an object of any possible kind; for otherwise we could obtain such an argument merely by adding the requirement of existence to the specification of the object. Hence, even if "exists" is regarded as a predicate, and as one true of some objects and false of others, it must be one of a very peculiar sort; and if we so regard it, we shall be hard put to it to explain this peculiarity.

The proponent of the Fregean view thus faces the difficulty of explaining such statements as "The Jews and Arabs trace their descent to a common ancestor" without allowing that there are non-existent individuals; and the proponent of the ontological argument faces that of explaining why existence cannot be one of the properties by which a possible object is specified. Of these, the latter difficulty is the greater: no plausible solution to it has ever been offered by the friends of non-existent objects. Frege offered a solution to the former difficulty, namely that, in a statement such as that about Jews and Arabs, we should take the quantification as being, not over human beings at all, but over the *senses* of personal proper names and other singular terms intended to refer to human beings. Of the advantages and awkwardnesses of this solution I do not propose to speak. The Fregean has at least this great advantage over his opponent, that the difficulty faced by the opponent is a quite general one, whereas that faced by the Fregean relates only to two special categories of statement, though admittedly broad and important ones. The temptation to interpret a statement as involving quantification over non-existent objects arises only when, as with the statement about Jews and Arabs, it involves the ascription of beliefs or other propositional attitudes, or when it explicitly involves modal expressions such as "possibly" and "might have been". Statements of these two categories are notoriously troublesome for semantic theory; we are therefore justified in setting them on one side at the outset of any enquiry into the concept of existence. Having done so, we may then agree to equate "*X*s exist" with "There are *X*s", that is, to repudiate the conception that there are objects that do not exist, trusting that some means of handling statements of these two categories—Frege's or some other—will be able to be found that does not require us to revive that conception.

That may be thought a cavalier attitude to non-existent but possible objects at a time when such objects not only flourish more vigorously than they ever did in Meinong's day, but now have complete possible worlds to inhabit (alongside the actual objects also found in many of those worlds). It is undoubtedly true that any adequate investigation of the concept of existence or of actuality would involve a very thorough enquiry into the notion of possible worlds. Nevertheless, the first steps may be taken in concert by those who believe in possible worlds and those who do not, without raising the large point of disagreement between them. What makes this possible is that both believers and disbelievers are agreed that a statement is true *simpliciter* just in case it is true with respect to the actual world. According to possible-worlds semantics, each statement is to be considered as true or false with respect to each possible world, including the actual one; most will be true with respect to some and false with respect to others. A statement will be true absolutely, however, just in case it is true with respect to the actual world. If it contains modal expressions, then, in evaluating its truth with respect to the actual world, we may have to consider, of subsentences contained in it, whether they are true with respect to other possible worlds. If it contains no modal expressions, on the other hand, we need consider nothing but the actual world in order to determine whether or not it is true with respect to that world, and hence absolutely. In particular, when we are concerned with the truth or falsity of an unmodalized statement, we may take the domain of quantification to comprise only objects that actually exist.

Admittedly, advocates of possible-worlds semantics insist that we cannot explain the meaning of such a statement without allusion to the conditions for its truth or falsity with respect to other possible worlds. I believe this claim to be either empty rhetoric or the product of confusion; by sticking to questions about the condition for the (absolute) truth of a statement, however, and avoiding discussion of its meaning, we can avoid even this controversy.

It seems, then, that, at least until we tackle modal statements and those ascribing propositional attitudes, the Fregean analysis of existence is unassailable. To those who believe that there is no deep riddle of existence, this conclusion is thoroughly satisfactory; and yet, to their irritation, the concept of existence will not lie down and be still. Articles continue to be written about it, expounding new theses and drawing metaphysical conclusions from them. Is this a revival of obscurantism, or does a genuine ground for perplexity about the concept persist?

The question is not whether Frege's analysis adequately explains one use of the verb "to exist", but whether there are others to which it cannot be applied. This question may be asked of two types of context: first, those in which the verb is subject to a significant temporal qualification, or to a modal auxiliary such as "might" or "could"; and, secondly, singular existential statements in which the subject is a proper name or other singular term. Philosophers differ about which of these two types they see as presenting the greatest difficulty for a Fregean analysis. Geach, for instance, plainly sees significantly tensed existential statements as presenting the greatest challenge, whereas the late Gareth Evans, in his posthumous book *The Varieties of Reference*,[2] treats tensed and modalized existential statements as unproblematic, and devotes all his attention to singular indicative ones without a significant tense. It is this latter type with which this essay will be concerned.

If existence is to be considered a second-level concept, that is, a property of first-level ones, it must be senseless to ascribe existence to objects, or to deny it of them. Frege put the matter as follows:

Let us consider the sentence "There is a square root of 4". It is clear that we are not here talking about a specific square root of 4, but about a concept. . .. A great difference

[2] Ed. John McDowell (Oxford, 1982).

obtains between the logical position of the number 2, when we say of it that it is a prime number, and that of the concept *prime number*, when we say that there is something which is a prime number. In the former position only objects can stand, in the latter only concepts. It is not only linguistically inadmissible to say "There is Africa" or "There is Charlemagne", but it is nonsensical.[3]

It is thus apparently a consequence of the Fregean analysis of existence that there can be no singular existential statements.

The matter cannot be dismissed so lightly, however. Inadmissible as it may be to say "There was Charlemagne", it is perfectly proper to say "There was such a person as Charlemagne" or "Charlemagne really existed". In the passage just cited, Frege allows only one way of explaining this, when he goes on to remark that:

We can indeed say "There is something that is called 'Africa' ", and the words "is called 'Africa' " designate a concept.

If we take this observation in the simplest way, it is not to the point. Someone might come to the conclusion that there was never any such person as Socrates, and express this by saying, "Socrates did not exist"; but he would not be meaning to exclude the possibility that anyone was ever called "Socrates"; his assertion would be consistent with there having been millions bearing that name.

In order to explain the content of such a statement as "Socrates did not exist", we have, therefore, to recognize that the speaker is concerned with a particular *use* of the name "Socrates", in the sense in which I make a different use of the name "Mars" according as I am employing it to refer to the planet, to the Roman god, or to a chocolate manufacturer. Occurrences of a proper name in different uses are thus, on this conception, a special case of occurrences of homonyms; what occur are really different words that happen to be pronounced and spelled alike. To amend Frege's suggestion along these lines, we should have to regard someone who says that Socrates did not exist as asserting the non-existence of a referent of the name "Socrates" as used in a particular way: he is not actually using the name, on this view, nor talking about it, considered as something identified phonetically and orthograph-ically, but talking about a particular use of it. The suggestion, so amended, has lost most of its attraction. On any view, the truth of the statement involves that, under a particular use of the name, it has no referent. On any view, the speaker is, after all, undoubtedly using the name. On Frege's suggestion, whether amended or unamended, he is not making that use of it under which, if his statement is true, it has no referent. On the amended version of the suggestion, however, he is alluding to that use. Plainly, if it is possible to

---

[3] 'Über die Grundlagen der Geometrie', *Jahresberichte der deutschen Mathematiker'-Vereinigung*, 12 (1903), 372–3: Eng. trans. in G. Frege, *Collected Papers*, ed. B. McGuinness (Oxford, 1984), 282.

explain the statement in such a manner that the speaker is not using the name in a special way to talk about another use of it, but simply making that use of it under which, if he is right, it has no referent, we shall have a simpler account.

Other observations of Frege's suggest a solution which, if it can be made to work, would have this effect, and which has found many adherents. Speaking of the word "is" as it occurs in 'The Morning Star is Venus', he says that it

is obviously not the mere copula, but, as regards its content, is an essential part of the predicate, so that the whole predicate is not contained in the word "Venus". One could say instead, "The Morning Star is none other than Venus" . . . and "is" in "is none other than" is now genuinely simply the copula. What is here predicated is therefore not *Venus* but *none other than Venus*. These words stand for a concept, under which, indeed, only a single object falls; but such a concept must still always be distinguished from the object.[4]

This concept seems far more apt for our purpose than that of *being called* '*Venus*', since it assumes the use of the name, in this case to stand for a planet, as fixed, while not involving reference to that use. If, then, we treat "Venus exists" as meaning "There is something which is identical with Venus", we shall have hit on an interpretation which allows the statement to be meaningful without invoking any supposed special use of the name "Venus". It does this by assimilating the singular existential statement to a general one via its analysis into "There is something which . . ." and ". . . is identical with Venus". At the same time, it remains a singular statement, since it also admits an analysis into "There is something which is identical with . . ." and "Venus": so viewed, "exists" in "Venus exists" is being treated precisely as a predicate true of every object, since everything is identical with something, namely itself.

Our fundamental assumption, that "exists", in so far as it functions as a predicate, is one that is true of everything, implies, independently of any debatable logical doctrine, that the statement "Venus exists", though it may tell us something, cannot tell us anything about the planet Venus; for if we know that, by using the name "Venus", we succeed in referring to an object, then we know that the statement is true. The case is similar to that of identity-statements; I may well learn something by being told that Byzantium is the same city as Istanbul, but what I learn is not that a certain city stands in a particular relation to itself. It is a mistake to infer from this that a statement of identity is about the names occurring in it; and it is likewise a mistake to infer that "Venus exists" is about the name "Venus", if by that we mean that the name is not being used in the ordinary way, but in a special way, as referring to itself. The notion of what a word or expression refers to, when used within a serious semantic theory, belongs to a systematic account of what determines sentences in which it occurs as true or false, and does not relate directly to the

---

[4] 'Über Begriff und Gegenstand', *Vierteljahrsschrift für wissenschaftliche Philosophie*, 16 (1892), 194; *Collected Papers*, 184.

knowledge that is conveyed by means of those sentences. If we use the word "about" in such a way that a statement is held to be about what the words occurring in it refer to, then what a statement is about need not in all cases coincide with what we learn something about when we come to know the statement to be true. Just this, of course, was one of the fundamental motives for Frege's distinction between reference and sense.

Unfortunately, though the solution being considered explains why "Venus exists" is true and "Venus does not exist" is false, it does not explain why "Vulcan exists" is false and "Vulcan does not exist" true, where "Vulcan", as the reader will recall, was the name once given to the hypothesized planet whose orbit lay within that of Mercury. There is undoubtedly such a concept as *being identical with Venus*, under which alone Venus falls; but, since there is no such planet as Vulcan, it seems questionable that there is any such concept as *being identical with Vulcan*. Furthermore, the solution fails to explain why "Venus exists" gives any information at all. Without considering statements of identity connecting two names to be *about* those names, we can still recognize that such a statement could not be informative, for anyone who grasped the use of both names, if a grasp of their use involved knowing whether or not they referred to the same object. In the same way, such a statement as "King Arthur existed", or, equally, its negation, cannot be informative, for anyone who grasps the use of the name "King Arthur", if a grasp of its use involves knowing whether or not it refers to anyone.

Empty proper names have long been a thorn in the flesh of philosophers of logic. They raise particular problems for those who hold the thesis enunciated by Kripke in the words "the linguistic function of a proper name is completely exhausted by the fact that it names its bearer".[5] If this thesis is correct, it would seem that, if a name is empty, it fails of its sole function, and that therefore its presence in a sentence must destroy the linguistic effect of that sentence as surely as would a piece of gibberish.

Kripke stated his thesis with the intention of tying together two views which he held concerning proper names which, in themselves, are independent of one another. One was a view about the reference of a proper name in a possible world other than the actual one: namely that, being a rigid designator, it must refer to the same object in that world as that to which it refers in the actual world. The other was a view about what determines the reference of a proper name in the actual world. The two views could both be exhibited as following from the single thesis about the linguistic function of a proper name, which I shall label thesis L. Unfortunately, thesis L is itself ambiguous, since it is not clear what should count as belonging to the 'linguistic function' of a word. There are two possible interpretations of the thesis, a weak and a strong one. On the weak interpretation, what is meant by the 'linguistic function' of an

---

[5] 'A Puzzle about Belief', in A. Margalit (ed.), *Meaning and Use* (Dordrecht, 1979), 240.

expression is its semantic role, where the semantic role of an expression is that fact about it in virtue of which it contributes to determining the truth or falsity of any sentence in which it occurs. For brevity, when I wish to make clear that I am considering thesis L under this weak interpretation, I shall refer to it as thesis L_w. Now some confusion is caused by Kripke's habit of repeatedly contrasting his views with those of Frege: the similarities are as noteworthy as the differences. In the present instance, thesis L_w was a thesis of Frege's, to which he attached very great importance; many of his other views would become untenable if thesis L_w were rejected. For Frege, the truth or falsity of a sentence is determined by the references of the expressions contained in it; once we know the reference of any such expression, no further feature of it is relevant to whether the sentence is true or false. For present purposes, it does not matter what he took the references of expressions other than proper names to be: in all cases, what I called the semantic role of an expression consisted for him in its having the reference that it has. In the case of a proper name, the reference is simply the object for which it stands or which we use it to talk about, in other words, its bearer: this is precisely the thesis L_w.

From this it followed, for Frege, that the presence in a sentence of an empty name, one without a reference, did destroy the most obvious linguistic effect of uttering that sentence. The most obvious effect of uttering a sentence is that you say something true or false; and Frege held that, if the sentence contained an empty name, you would fail to achieve either effect—you would say nothing true *or* false. It is this that gives rise to the difficulty, on his theory: if someone seriously asserted that Vulcan existed, he would not even be saying something false, according to Frege, since the name "Vulcan" does not refer to anything; equally, one who retorted that Vulcan does not exist would not be saying anything true.

It is true that, even if Kripke intended his thesis L to be understood only in the weak sense, there are two important differences between Frege's doctrine and his. In one respect, Frege's doctrine is weaker, since he held thesis L_w with a reservation which Kripke would not admit. Frege held that, in a sentence used to ascribe to someone a belief or other propositional attitude, a name occurring in the substantival clause that states the content of the belief does not refer to the object of which it ordinarily serves as the name, but to its own ordinary sense. He could continue to hold in full generality that a word contributes to determining the truth-value of a sentence containing it in virtue of its reference alone: but he could do so only by holding that its reference, and thus its linguistic function, differs according to whether it occurs in an ordinary context or in one of this special kind. Hence, in particular, an empty name, whose presence in an ordinary context will deprive the sentence of truth-value, will not in general do so when used in an ascription of belief: "Vulcan has an almost circular orbit" is neither true nor false, but "Professor Higgins believes that Vulcan has an almost circular orbit" may conceivably be true. Kripke, on the other hand, means thesis L to apply to an occurrence of the name in every context: if a name refers to anything at all, it refers to the same thing wherever it occurs (at least so long as it is being used in the same way), and its doing so is its sole linguistic function.

In another respect, however, Frege's doctrine is stronger than Kripke's. Kripke's thesis L is intended to apply only to proper names, not to all singular terms; but Frege's thesis that a name contributes to determining the truth-value of a sentence containing it solely in virtue of its reference, and thus, in ordinary contexts, of the object for which it stands, is meant to cover, under the term "name", all singular terms whatever, including those composed of several words like "the planet nearest the Sun".

If we understand thesis L in the weak sense, the possibility stands open of distinguishing between the linguistic function of a word and that which confers that linguistic function upon it. That this may have been the interpretation intended by Kripke is suggested by the distinction he draws between the reference of a name and the way in which its reference is fixed. So understood, his thesis differs from Frege's view only in the two respects just mentioned: important differences, indeed, but occurring against the background of a fundamental agreement.

A stronger interpretation of thesis L, which we may label L_S, is that a proper name lacks a sense. One way of expressing this is to say that the fact that it has the bearer that it has is a *bare* fact, incapable of elaboration or explanation. This formulation requires a gloss, however. In one sense, the fact that the letter A is the first letter of the Roman alphabet is a bare fact: if you did not know the order of the letters of the alphabet, there is nothing about those letters from which you could deduce it. In another sense, it is not a bare fact: the order of the letters is constituted by our learning to recite them in that order, and using that order to arrange or locate words in an index, directory, or dictionary; it would be nonsense to conceive of them as having an order independently of our treating them as having one. Now to say that a proper name, say "Oslo", lacks a sense is to maintain that the fact that it denotes a particular city is a bare fact in that sense in which it *is* a bare fact that A is the first letter of the alphabet. It thus does not involve holding that the name's denoting that city is independent of our treating it as doing so; nor does it exclude our being able to spell out in detail what is comprised in our so treating it.

It is plainly not enough, for the thesis L_S to hold, that we should be able, for each particular name, to spell out what constitutes our treating it as a name of the object for which it stands. At the very least, it must be demanded that the account be such as to leave no room for a distinguishable use of another name with the same bearer, a use which would equally merit the description "treating the word as a name of that object". Even this would not be enough, however: for it would merely embody the thesis that two names could not have distinct senses and the same reference, not that they lacked senses altogether. If there was nothing uniform in the accounts of what is involved in our treating one word as the name of one object, and of what is involved in our treating another word as the name of another object, then those two accounts would manifest the distinct senses borne by those two names. We could not even say, in such a case, that reference determined sense: for we should have no way of grasping the use of the name in the language simply from knowing to which object it referred. It would not even do to suppose that, for each sort of object, cities, rivers, people, etc., there was a uniform account of what it is to treat a word as the name of a particular object of that sort; for this would embody only a modified version of the thesis L_S, one which allowed each name to possess a sense that determined to which sort of object it referred, though not to which particular such object. The thesis, as it stands, demands a wholly uniform account, not relativized to sorts, of that in which our treating a word as the name of an arbitrary object consists, an account which thereby completely specifies, for any given object, the use of such a word.

It might be conceded that, if any account were to be given, the thesis L_S would require that it be uniform, but objected that the thesis does not demand, but merely allows, the possibility of such an account. The phrase "treating a word as the name of a certain object" is self-explanatory, it might be pleaded; it needs no spelling out. Such a plea should be rejected. Explaining what it is for a word to be a name, and explaining what it is for a word to be the name of a particular object, are one, in the same way as it is the same thing to explain what it is for a man to be a father and to explain what it is for him to be the father of a particular individual. We learn to recognize which words in the language are names and which are not, and this requires us to grasp what it is for a word to be a name; it is unthinkable that it should be impossible to explain what it is that we grasp, save by using the word "name" itself (whose meaning we also had to learn). The denial that proper names have senses puts a greater burden on any explanation of what a name is than the view that they have them. To the extent that the use of a word is not fully determined by the fact that it is the name of a given object, an explanation of what it is for a word to be a name need not characterize the whole use of such a word. If proper names lack senses, however, the whole use of a name consists in its being the name of a certain object; so, conversely, an explanation of what it is for a word to be a name must completely specify the use of any name, given its bearer. Furthermore, we cannot clearly comprehend the claim, embodied in thesis L_S, that the use of a proper name can be fully described as consisting in treating it as the name of a specific object until it *has* been spelled out what constitutes so treating it: for, until that is spelled out, the implausible consequence would appear to follow that *any* perplexity over the identification of an object as the bearer of the name—for instance, over the identification of the place where one is as Oslo—must reflect a failure to grasp the use of that name.

It does not need to be spelled out, however, for us to recognize that, if the use of a name simply consists in our treating it as referring to a particular object, then, if it had no bearer, it would have no use. The converse, indeed, does not follow. It does not follow from the fact that a grasp of the use of a name entails an awareness of the existence of its bearer that the name lacks a sense; for it may still be that that use could not be fully described merely by saying that it was treated as a name of that object, even when it was spelled out in what, in general, treating a word as the name of an object consists. It is certainly plausible that there are proper names for which the weaker condition holds; for instance, someone could hardly be said to have mastered the use of the name "the Sun" for whom there was a question whether or not such a heavenly body existed.

Frege is celebrated for having maintained, in his mature period, that every proper name that has a definite use has a sense. There can be no such thing, according to him, as simply treating an object as the referent of a name; it must always be a matter of our treating that object which is given to us in such-and-such a way or identifiable by us by such-and-such a means as the referent. Thus, while he accepted thesis L_W for all singular terms, though with a reservation for special contexts, he denied thesis L_S as forcefully as possible. It is a mistake to think of Frege as having attributed senses to names solely in order to explain their semantic role in the special contexts: such an explanation would be unintelligible unless they had senses governing their employment in ordinary contexts.

It is unnecessary for us to adjudicate the question whether all proper names have senses or whether there are some that lack them: our concern is only with such names as can significantly occur in singular existential statements. If a grasp of the use of a name "a" requires knowing that it has a bearer, then the statement "a exists" is not even in principle informative; if it does not, but may plausibly be thought to do so, the statement will not in practice be informative. If it is a well-known fact that a name, say "Robin Goodfellow", has no bearer, then it will be impossible, at least in practice, to use the name seriously with the intention of referring to an object; since the negative existential statement "There is no Robin Goodfellow" will be uninformative to those who know the use of the name, it can plausibly be construed as being about that use. We are therefore concerned only with names like "King Arthur" for which it is disputable whether or not they have a bearer. Such a name must have a sense. If the question whether or not there was such a person as King Arthur is to be understood so as to have a determinate answer, and as having the same answer for all—at least for all participants in a particular discussion of it—then they must be using the name "King Arthur" in the same way. Their use of it cannot simply consist in their all treating a certain man as the bearer of the name, since otherwise the question whether there was such a man could not arise between them.

The sense of a proper name, when it has one, consists in an agreed means of determining, for any object, whether or not it is the bearer of the name: whether it yields an *effective* method of doing this will necessarily depend on how the object is given, and we need not assume that it always or even ever does so. More exactly, this is what constitutes a *complete* sense borne by a proper name, that is, one which uniquely determines the bearer of the name, if any; a partial sense will consist in an agreed means of ruling out certain objects as candidates for being the bearer of the name. The occurrence in a sentence of an empty name will not rob that sentence of the ability to express a definite thought if the name has a complete sense; for in that case the thought will involve the subsidiary thought that the condition for the name to have a bearer is fulfilled. Precisely this was Frege's conclusion: such a sentence will still express a thought, even though the fact that the name has no referent prevents the thought from being either true or false. Suppose, Frege argued, using a different example, that I come to believe that there was such a man as King Arthur, having formerly doubted it: the thoughts that I find expressed by Geoffrey of Monmouth by the use of the name "King Arthur" will not thereby have changed from those I previously took him as expressing.[6] What determines the thought expressed by a sentence containing a proper name is the *sense* of that name, not its reference; the capacity of the sentence to express a thought depends upon the name's having a sense, not upon its having a referent, which, even if it has one, will normally not be the sort of thing that can be an ingredient of a thought.

Those who assert the existence of names having reference but no sense could not endorse this principle; but its essence would be retained if it were said that the expression of a thought by a sentence containing a name requires that the name have a use, where, if a name has a sense, its use is determined by that sense, but, if it lacks a sense, its use is determined by its reference. As we have already seen, the notion of a particular use of a name is inescapable: if we do not distinguish different uses of what is phonetically and orthographically the same name, we lose all right to speak of *the* bearer of any name. Frege would not have allowed that a name could have a reference but not a sense; but he subscribed to the weaker thesis that it may have a sense the possession of which requires the existence of a referent. Apart from his problematic observations about the pronoun "I", his doing so is apparent from his having held the presence of empty names to be an avoidable defect in a language, and aspiring to construct a symbolic language free of this defect: in such a language, the sense of every name would be such as to guarantee it a reference.

That a name lacking reference may still have a sense resolves our uncertainty whether, if King Arthur did not exist, there is any such concept as *being identical with King Arthur*. If the question whether King Arthur existed has a definite sense, either according to the common understanding of the

---

[6] See G. Frege, 'Einleitung in der Logik' (1906), *Posthumous Writings*, trans. P. Long and R. White (Oxford, 1979), 191.

words or according to a particular interpretation being put upon it, there must
be a definite condition which someone must have fulfilled for him to have been
King Arthur: to fulfil that condition is precisely to fall under the concept
identical with King Arthur. If there was no such person, then there is nothing
falling under that concept, and so the statement "King Arthur did not exist" is
straightforwardly true. If there was such a person, our grasp of the concept
does not involve our knowing that there was, and so the statement "King
Arthur existed" is informative.

Such a solution involves conflict with Frege's other doctrines. The price of
admitting names with sense but no reference, as Frege did, is to create a
tension between his principle that a sentence's being true or false depends upon
its parts' having a reference, and the sister principle which he also held, that its
expressing a thought depends on their having a sense; more generally, between
the principle that a well-formed expression has reference only if all its parts do,
and the principle that it has sense if all its parts do. The principle about
reference of course follows from the generalization to expressions of all types of
the thesis L_W. From the principle about reference, it follows that, if King
Arthur did not exist, the phrase "identical with King Arthur" lacks a reference,
and thus does not stand for any concept after all, and that no sentence
containing the name "King Arthur" can be either true or false, including the
sentence "No one was identical with King Arthur". So long as we accept these
Fregean principles, we can explain why "King Arthur did not exist" expresses
a thought, but we cannot explain how it can express a true one.

There are two possible responses. One is to modify Frege's principle
concerning reference. We can still maintain the principle as applied to the
semantic role of an expression, saying that whether a sentence has a truth-
value, and, if so, which, depends only on the semantic roles of the expressions
occurring in it: we need only refuse to make Frege's identification between a
name's having a bearer and its having a semantic role. Two names both of
which lack a bearer may be allowed to have the same semantic role, at least in
ordinary contexts: but they need not be denied to have any semantic role
whatever, and hence their presence need not deprive a complex expression of
semantic role or a sentence of truth-value.

A more radical response is to deny that empty names are really names.
Barry Miller, for example, defining non-fictional names as "names of
individuals that do or have existed", writes that "there is the same absolute
distinction between fictional proper names and non-fictional ones . . . as . . .
between predicates and non-fictional proper names".[7] He does not mean that
the distinction is as great: he really means that it is the same distinction. He
explains it thus: "A non-fictional proper name refers to a particular
individual. . . . A fictional proper name is only a disguised definite description,

<hr/>

[7] Barry Miller, 'In Defence of the Predicate "Exists" ', *Mind*, 84 (1975), 345.

and as such is applicable to exactly one individual but to no one in particular."[8] Since a name of an existent individual is *ipso facto* a non-fictional name, by the definition, it is somewhat surprising to learn that a fictional one applies to just one individual, even if to none in particular; possibly Miller means that, if used seriously to speak about an actual individual, it is intended to apply to exactly one. It is, of course, also intended to apply to a particular one; but we may grant that there is no particular individual—in fact, no individual at all—to whom or which it is intended to apply. At any rate, it is clear that a fictional name is, for Miller, not a genuine name, but a disguised predicate of a particular kind (the kind that can apply to at most one thing): as he later remarks, "if 'Phlogiston does not exist' is true, then 'phlogiston' can be only a predicate, but never a name."[9]

To say that a name without a bearer is really a predicate is a means of escape from maintaining the obvious falsehood that it can have no genuine, serious use. Miller offers, as a ground for this thesis, the distinction between a particular individual and exactly one individual. The proposition "Socrates is thinking dark thoughts" is, he says, about a particular individual, Socrates, since only he can make the proposition true. If we replace "Socrates" by a definite description, however—let us say "the MP who assaulted Mrs Thatcher"—we obtain a proposition that is not *about* any individual, since "there is no particular individual required to make" it true: "it would be true if there were any ... one ... individual" satisfying the description (and, I presume, thinking dark thoughts).[10] To the objection that only the MP who actually assaulted Mrs Thatcher (if any did) could make the proposition that that MP is thinking dark thoughts true, Miller would obviously reply that, if things had been different, someone else might have answered that description, whereas, however different things were, no one other than Socrates could possibly have been Socrates.

This is a point that has become familiar; whatever its merits, though, it cannot be used to show "King Arthur"; or even "Ossian", to be a predicate, since it is no more possible for anyone other than King Arthur to have been King Arthur than for someone other than Socrates to have been Socrates. We can imagine a state of affairs in which the child who actually grew up to be a philosopher and to be judicially poisoned died in infancy, but in which some other child with the same name grew up to look like Socrates and to do and suffer all that he did: but, at least according to the present thesis, this state of affairs would not be one in which that other man would have *been* Socrates, even though he would have been the man we should then refer to as "Socrates". The same must obviously apply to King Arthur if he existed; it also applies if he did not. Even if there was never any historical person to whom

---

[8] Ibid.
[9] Ibid. 351.
[10] Ibid. 340–1.

"King Arthur" refers, we can imagine a state of affairs in which there was; but it is as true to say that the person to whom, in that state of affairs, we should use the name "King Arthur" to refer would not *be* King Arthur as to say that, in the other hypothetical case, the person we should refer to as "Socrates" would not *be* Socrates. "King Arthur" is used as a proper name, not as a predicate; even if it fails of its objective of referring to someone, it does not thereby cease to behave linguistically as a proper name. If "King Arthur" were truly a proper name, though empty, it might be argued, then it would be the name of someone existing in merely possible worlds, whereas merely possible objects cannot be named. On the contrary, if we agree to talk in terms of possible worlds at all, it is just because we cannot name possible objects that, if King Arthur did not in fact exist, it is impossible that anyone should have been King Arthur: just this is what shows that "King Arthur" is not a predicate.[11]

Even if empty proper names cannot be equated with predicates, may there not be a difference in logical category between them and what Miller calls 'non-fictional' names? The use of the term "fictional name" as equivalent to "empty name" serves falsely to suggest that it is only by ignorance of the way a name is being used that one can be in doubt whether it is fictional or not: on the contrary, even if the name "King Arthur" occurred only in what purported to be factual narrative, there would still be a question whether or not there was such a man. With non-fictional and fictional names distinguished according to whether they have or lack a bearer, the proposal to regard the two classes as forming distinct logical categories runs foul of the principle that a speaker who knows the use of an expression thereby knows what goes to determine its logical category. The classification of expressions by logical category relates to the way in which they are used, to what combinations of them are intelligible and what implications are recognized as holding between sentences containing them. Hence the significant distinction cannot be between empty names and those that have a reference; it must lie, rather, between any name for which it can come into question whether or not it has a bearer, without its thereby coming into question whether it has a use, and those names whose use guarantees that they have bearers. So considered, "Socrates", though for Miller a non-fictional name, belongs in the former class, since it can intelligibly be questioned whether Socrates ever existed.

The point of maintaining that, if King Arthur did not exist, the phrase "King Arthur" is a predicate, is principally to allow that "is King Arthur" or "is identical with King Arthur" stands for a concept, since, as Frege observes, it is no bar to a predicate's standing for a concept that it is not true of anything. At this stage, however, the proposal to regard empty names as predicates has

---

[11] "Phlogiston", as a mass term, is a special case. To the extent that it behaves as a predicate, that is not because there is no such substance; a mass term like "water" sometimes behaves as a proper name, as in "Water is a compound", and sometimes as something resembling a predicate, as in "The stuff in the bottle is water". "Phlogiston" is no more of a predicate than "water" is.

dwindled to something indistinguishable from its rival, the modification of Frege's principle concerning reference. If we modify it as suggested, "is identical with King Arthur" will not only retain its sense if King Arthur did not exist, but will stand for a concept under which nothing falls. This will satisfactorily explain why, in that case, "King Arthur did not exist" should be a true statement; unfortunately, it will not explain why "King Arthur was not married" should not be. If there is such a concept as *being identical with King Arthur*, under which no one has ever fallen, must there not also be such a concept as *being married to King Arthur* under which no one has ever fallen? If the emptiness of the first concept renders "King Arthur did not exist" true, why should not the emptiness of the second render "King Arthur was not married" true?

This is sometimes explained as a difference in the scope of the operator "not" in the two sentences. A distinction is drawn between external and internal negation: it is held that in "King Arthur did not exist", the negation is external, being applied to the sentenc "King Arthur existed", taken as a whole; but that in "King Arthur was not married", the negation is internal, being applied only to the predicate, and not to the whole sentence "King Arthur was married". This formulation is unhappy, and violates another principle of Frege's, which may be called that of the completeness of the values of a function. A predicate or functional expression is classified by Frege as incomplete, because it has one or more argument-places; a singular term or a sentence, by contrast, is complete. In an analogous sense, concepts, relations, and functions are incomplete, objects and truth-values complete. There can be functions of higher level, e.g. ones taking concepts as arguments. The principle of the completeness of values says, however, that a function, of whatever level, can have only objects or truth-values as values; there cannot, for example, be a function mapping concepts on to concepts. If there were an internal negation operator, transforming a predicate into another predicate, it would stand for just such a function; hence there can be no such operator.

The ground for the principle of the completeness of values lies in a deeper principle, which may be called Frege's principle of concept-formation. Stated in terms of expressions, rather than of what they stand for, this says that a complex predicate is not to be thought of as put together out of simpler expressions which are its parts, but as formed from a sentence by removing from it a name, perhaps in more than one occurrence; and analogously for other incomplete expressions. This has the direct consequence that there can be no internal negation operator, or any other operator whose application results in the formation of a predicate.

Frege's principle of concept-formation was a great discovery, on which he based his explanation of the capacity of deductive reasoning to yield new knowledge. We can, however, obtain the same effect as that aimed at by the distinction between external and internal negation without violating the principle, which no more requires us to construe "King Arthur was not married" as the negation of "King Arthur was married" than it requires us to construe "Someone is not amused" as the negation of "Someone is amused". The desired effect can be obtained, then, by taking "King Arthur was not married" to be of the form "For some X, X was (identical with) King Arthur and X was not married". On such a view, the name "King Arthur" genuinely fills the argument-place of ". . . did not exist" in the sentence "King Arthur did not exist", that is to say, it genuinely fills the argument-place of "It is not the case that for some X, X is identical with . . .". In the sentence "King Arthur was not married", on the other hand, the name does not genuinely fill the argument-place of ". . . was not married"; rather it acts as an expression, "For some X, X was King Arthur and . . . X . . .", of the same type as a quantifier.

At first sight, this conclusion is intolerable, since we shall need to apply it, not only to proper names which we believe to be or suspect of being empty, but to all whose use could be grasped by some one for whom the existence of its bearer was not a closed question; but to apply it to "Socrates" in "Socrates was not married" seems to stretch credulity to breaking-point. On reflection, however, some such conclusion is inescapable. Once we have accepted that a predicate containing an empty name may nevertheless be false of an object (or even true of one), we can only regard the predicate ". . . was married to Arthur" as being false of everyone if there was no such man as Arthur; it must then be true to say "No one was married to Arthur". If, now, "Arthur was not married" is to be reckoned as false, we can hardly deny the equivalence between it and "Arthur was married to no one"; we must therefore deny that between this latter sentence and "No one was married to Arthur". This involves abandoning a thesis of Frege's that goes far less deep than those previously cited, to the effect that occupying the position of grammatical subject has no logical significance; the only plausible explanation for its having such significance is that the subject-term functions as an operator with wide scope.

It is natural to object that, on this account, every proper name, in every occurrence, functions as an operator rather than as a term, at least if it is not guaranteed a reference. For instance, we want "Guinevere was not married to Arthur" to come out false if Guinevere did not exist but true if she existed but Arthur did not; we have therefore to read it as meaning "For some X, X was Guinevere and it is not the case that, for some Y, Y was Arthur and X was married to Y". There is no harm in admitting this comment to be legitimate. We are striving to allow sentences containing certain empty names not only to express thoughts, but to express true or false thoughts; and that involves allowing that such an empty name has a semantic role, and hence denying that the semantic role of a proper name must always consist in its having some particular object as bearer. If one's conception of a genuine proper name is that of a term whose semantic role is guaranteed to be just this, then the outcome of any such enterprise will necessarily be to deny to names whose use does not guarantee them a bearer the status of genuine proper names in this sense; but this is no objection to the enterprise until a demonstration is provided that everything in natural language that looks like a proper name is one in this restricted sense. More precisely, the admission of empty names as not robbing of truth-value every sentence in which they occur has the inevitable effect of allowing a substantive distinction according as a name not guaranteed not to be empty is viewed as occurring within or outside the scope of some operator like the negation operator or a quantifier. Since Frege's principle of concept-formation ought not to be violated without dire necessity, and since it prohibits us from admitting internal operators, the only way in which we can invoke the notion of scope for names is by regarding them as themselves being, at least in certain contexts, operators of a kind: this upshot is intrinsic to the enterprise, and cannot by itself prove the enterprise to have been mistaken.

Much of what I have said amounts to a defence of what is known as free logic as being an apter representation of natural language than the standard logic in which every term is assumed to have a denotation; at least of that feature of free logic which allows the occurrence of terms not denoting an element of the (proper) domain, though not of that which allows the (proper) domain to be empty, since I have said nothing about whether it is a truth of logic that at least one object exists. Free logic, as usually presented, is, however, clumsy in its characterization of the semantic role of an empty name, which it treats as denoting a null object lying outside the proper domain. This has the effect of making assignments of truth-values to sentence containing empty names somewhat arbitrary; we need to take the semantic role of an empty name to consist in its having no bearer, not in its having a non-existent or otherwise peculiar one. For this reason, my remarks are perhaps better seen as a defence of the undervalued and misleadingly entitled proposal of Quine for the elimination of proper names. This involves transforming every sentence containing the name "Mrs Thatcher" for example, into one containing quantifiers and a predicate ". . . thatcherizes", understood as meaning what we mean by ". . . is Mrs Thatcher". The proposal has been resisted for two different reasons. First, it is rightly thought that an understanding of a quantified sentence demands an understanding of what it is for the predicate to which the quantifier is attached to be true of any given object, and wrongly thought that this requires that, for every object, the language should afford a means of picking it out that was guaranteed not to fail. Even if there were such a requirement, this would yield no objection to Quinean treatment of those names for which we lacked a guarantee that they were not empty; but the requirement is spurious. The supposition that the identification of the bearer of a name may be a complex process whose success is not certain in advance in no way impedes our conceiving of an understanding of a simple or primitive predicate as consisting in a grasp of what it is to be true of an object so identified; nor does the explanation of a complex predicate's being true of a given object as consisting in the truth of a sentence obtained by putting a name of that object in the argument-place of the predicate presuppose that we can be certain of having formed such a sentence.

The other objection lodged against Quine's proposal is that proper names behave quite differently from predicates, or from terms like definite descriptions formed from predicates. If it is meant that all names are guaranteed a bearer, it is simply false: we should have no problem if it were not. In other respects, the claim is undoubtedly true: but these are aspects in which the difference carries over to what may be called 'proper predicates' like ". . . thatcherizes". Thus, it may quite truly be observed that, while Neil Armstrong always was Neil Armstrong, even before he was named, he became the first man to step on the Moon only at a certain time; or that, while he could never have been anyone other than Neil Armstrong, he might easily not have been the first man to step on the Moon. These observations have, however, only to do with the behaviour of the predicate ". . . is Neil Armstrong", as contrasted with that of ". . . is the first man to step on the Moon", in contexts involving modal and temporal operators. There is nothing to lead us to think that a Quinean proper predicate like ". . . armstrongizes" would not behave in exactly the same way; there can therefore be no valid objection to Quine's proposal from this quarter.

The misconceived distinction between internal and external negation is sometimes used as a ground for maintaining that non-existence is not a property, even though existence is one. This would follow only if some reason could be cited why internal negation cannot be applied to the predicate ". . . exists": as it is, all that an advocate of the distinction between external and internal negation is entitled to claim is that in "King Arthur did not exist" the negation is external, so that, by asserting it, we do not ascribe non-existence to King Arthur, but only deny that existence may be ascribed to him. The notion of internal negation gives us no ground to doubt that, for every property, or for every concept in Frege's terminology, there is a complementary property or concept: if we adhere to Frege's principle of concept-formation, so that there can be no internal operators, this follows at once from the fact that every sentence can be negated. Thus the predicate which stands for the concept of non-existence is simply "It is not the case that . . . exists": it is a predicate false of every object, since ". . . exists" is one true of all. It is, of course, quite true that, in asserting that King Arthur did not exist, I am not aiming at predicating non-existence of an object, although, if I speak falsely, that is what I do. Even if I speak falsely, I can also be correctly described as ascribing to the concept *identical with King Arthur* the property of having no object falling under it; and that I also do if I speak truly. That is not to say that, even if I speak truly, the sentence I uttered cannot be analysed as composed of the name "King Arthur" and the predicate ". . . did not exist": only that the legitimacy of such an analysis does not of itself warrant describing one who asserts the sentence as applying that predicate to an object, since obviously I can make a statement about an object only by using a term that refers to it. The terminology of making a statement about something, predicating something of something else, etc., simply fails to fit this case: when it is not used to indicate the information conveyed or the focus of interest, it can be explained only in terms of reference; I speak about whatever I refer to. It must, then, break down if we allow that there are terms in the language which lack a reference, but are not devoid of a semantic role. So far as I can see nothing disastrous has happened when it does break down. We can still satisfactorily explain how the language works, how its sentences are determined as true or false, and what is involved in understanding them; I know no argument to show that the terminology of making a statement about something must be applicable to every case, or that something precious is lost if it is not.

For a singular existential statement, as made on a given occasion, to be problematic, three requirements must hold. The first is that it must be possible to raise the question whether the statement is true without betraying linguistic misunderstanding; equivalently that

1. it must be possible on the relevant occasion to use the singular term forming the subject of the sentence competently but without knowing whether or not it has a referent.

The second is that it must be in principle possible that the question of existence should be settled, affirmatively or negatively, to the satisfaction of all; that is that

2. it must be in principle possible to settle the truth or falsity of the existential statement.

The third is that a 'metalinguistic' solution should be inappropriate; that is that

3. it must be implausible, or at least in no way compelling, to explain the existential statement by representing it as a statement about the relevant use of the singular term.

It was argued in the foregoing that, if requirements (1) and (2) are met, there must be a condition which must hold if the singular term is to have a referent, and which is not necessarily known to hold by anyone who grasps the relevant use of the term: the content of the affirmative existential statement will then be that this condition obtains. There will be such a condition only if the term, as so used, has a sense. The sense of the term will consist in the condition that any given object has to satisfy to be the referent of the term: the condition for it to have a reference is then that there is some such object.

In *The Varieties of Reference*, Gareth Evans holds, in effect, that this is an over-simplification. For him, there are no utterances of singular terms that do not carry a sense, understood in a Fregean manner as the way in which the object is presented by that use of the term. The relevant distinction is not, therefore, between terms that have a sense and those that lack one: it is between descriptive terms and those which he calls 'information-linked'. A use of a term is information-linked if "in order to understand an utterance containing a referring expression used in this way, the hearer must link up the utterance with some information in his possession".[12] Evans holds that demonstrative expressions are information-linked in this sense. In support of this, he quotes G. E. Moore:

Can we say that "that thing" = "the thing at which I am pointing" or "the thing to which this finger points" or "the nearest thing to which this finger points"? No, because the proposition is not understood unless the thing in question is *seen*.[13]

It seems that there are more expressions than those like "red" and "pretty" that the blind are unable to understand.

Descriptive terms include definite descriptions and a minority of proper names, those, namely, introduced by such a stipulation as

Let us call whoever invented the zip fastener "Julius".[14]

It is very important for an understanding of Evans's position that, so far as descriptive terms are concerned, he is willing to accept an account of singular existential statements involving them that is essentially like that so far argued for in this essay. Since they are descriptive, there is indeed a condition that an object has to satisfy to be the referent of such a term: the significance of the term consists in the association of this condition with it, and it therefore retains that significance even if it lacks a referent. This comes out very strongly in connection with Evans's criticism of Kripke's account of negative singular existential statements.

Kripke has proposed that one who truly says, "*a* does not exist", should be understood as meaning, "There is no true proposition that says of *a* that it exists". Evans's answer is that, if there is no proposition expressed by "*Fa*", there can be no proposition expressed by "There is a proposition which says of *a* that it is *F*", either: if the significance of "*a*" is contaminated by its having no referent, that of "proposition which says of *a* that . . ." must be equally contaminated.[15] He then considers a retort to this objection, namely that, if the reference of "*a*" is fixed by means of a definite description, the sentence "*a* is *F*" will still not express a proposition if nothing satisfies the description, but it

---

[12] Evans, *The Varieties of Reference*, 305.
[13] G. E. Moore, *Commonplace Book 1919–1953*, ed. Casimir Lewy (London, 1962), 158.
[14] *The Varieties of Reference*, 31.
[15] Ibid. 350.

will nevertheless be clear in what circumstances it would express a true proposition, and this is enough to render the description "proposition that says of *a* that it is *F*" intelligible, even though it applies to nothing. To this Evans replies that the retort relies on a distinction which, quoting me, he rejects as unjustified. The distinction is that between an ascertainable condition for an utterance to be true and one for it to express a proposition at all. If we are concerned solely with the content of that utterance, rather than with the behaviour of the sentence uttered when subjected to linguistic operations such as negation, there is no warrant for such a distinction: what is being represented as the condition for a proposition to have been expressed should be taken as part of the content of the proposition.[16]

Thus, for Evans, the occurrence in a sentence of a *descriptive* term lacking a reference does not deprive that sentence of significance or block it from expressing a proposition. He takes issue with me, however, in that he believes that the occurrence of an information-linked term without a reference always has this effect. The utterance of an information-linked term cannot be understood by anyone not in possession of the relevant information, and making appropriate use of it; and one can make such a use only if one believes, and rightly believes, the information to be veridical.[17]

Evans's clear distinction between information-linked terms and descriptive ones, and his careful and elaborate discussion of the former, mark a great step forward: in particular, he shows more plainly than anyone has done before why it is so grave a mistake to equate, as Kripke does, the ascription to a term of a Fregean sense with a characterization of it as descriptive. For our purposes, however, only two questions are of importance: (i) *Must* the understanding of an information-linked term require the existence of a referent? (ii) If so, must not such a term violate requirement (1) above for a term that can be the subject of an informative existential statement? We may set aside the question whether or not Evans is right to the extent of thinking that there are *some* information-linked terms an understanding of which is possible only in virtue of their having referents; we have noted that it is plausible that "the Sun" is one such term. Our concern remains only with such terms as can occur in informative singular existential statements.

The question is of importance to us because, according to Evans, most proper names are information-linked:[18] "Julius", as explained above, is not, but "Socrates" and "King Arthur" are. How, then, if "*a*" is an information-linked term, can we ever ask, "Does *a* exist?"? Plainly, it can happen only because we are not always sure whether what we have is information. Evans uses the word 'information' as signifying something independent of the subject's beliefs: his having the information does not require him to believe

16 Ibid. 350–1 and n. 13.
17 Ibid. 330–2.
18 Ibid. 310.

that it is veridical;[19] indeed, he goes further, and uses the word to include misinformation. I may not be sure whether what I seem to see may not be an illusion; or whether a purported informant is sincere or is bluffing me; or whether what I am reading is fiction or factual narrative. When, in such a case, I make an affirmative existential claim, the truth of my claim amounts to the veridicality of the information. The task Evans sets himself is to explain how this comes about.

He explains it as an exploitation of the make-believe use of language. Such a use occurs in fiction; it may also occur when two or more people are the victims of a perceptual illusion, which they recognize as such. A case of this kind is discussed in detail by Evans: two people who both appear to perceive a little green man in front of them can, without error, feign to make reference by using a demonstrative expression like "that little green man". Given that they really are suffering from an illusion, they do not thereby refer to anything. They are, however, engaging in a form of discourse the aim of which is not to make statements that are literally true, but to utter sentences that count in the make-believe game as expressing true statements; Evans spells out the conventions that determine what counts as true and as false in the game. The analogue is a conversation about the characters in a novel, conducted in the style of reference to real individuals. Evans thinks it better to characterize such a conversation, not as literal discourse about fictional characters, regarded as abstract objects in no way resembling real people, but as feigned discourse about human beings; there are standards of correctness and incorrectness, but these do not involve literal truth and falsity, but only what count in the game as making true statements and as making false ones.

It is because Evans is surely right to hold that the use of language in what is intended to be understood as fiction is a special use that we cannot speak of the condition that would have to be satisfied for a real person to be the referent of a fictional name such as "Becky Sharp" in Thackeray's *Vanity Fair*. Thackeray was using the name *as* a fictional name; there may well be real individuals known as "Becky Sharp", but that particular use of the name is determined by the novelist's manifest intention: there can therefore be no question of its referring to a real person.

This conclusion, not overtly stated by Evans, is in line with a general principle which Evans, observing that it agrees with a remark he quotes from me, states thus: "a *necessary* condition for a speaker to have referred to an object by the use of an expression is that it be the intended referent of that use of the expression".[20] An important thesis of Evans's appears, however, not to conform to this principle. This is that if, in the case in which two speakers engage in make-believe discourse involving the use of the phrase "that little green man", they are in fact mistaken in thinking themselves to be suffering

---

[19] Ibid. 123.
[20] Ibid. 318; see M. Dummett, *Frege: Philosophy of Language* (London, 1973), 149.

from an illusion, then they are, unknown to themselves, referring to the little green man actually present.[21] Here Evans's necessary condition appears not to be fulfilled: not only do the speakers not think they are referring to anything, but they are not even meaning to refer to anything.

Evans has, however, an argument for his claim that, in such a case, the speakers are referring to something without knowing it. The argument rests upon the rules of the make-believe game. Those rules, as expounded by Evans,[22] require the outright acceptance, as true in the game, of certain principles: in the present instance, of the principle that the speakers' visual impressions are veridical. The rules further require that, if the counterfactual conditional "If it had been the case that A, it would have been the case that B" is (literally) true, and "A" is true in the game, then "B" is true in the game. If, in the present instance, either of the speakers takes "A" as "My visual impressions are veridical" and "B" as "I am referring to a little green man", he will be able to derive, by this rule, that the statement that he is referring to a little green man is true in the game. Now it was required that the counterfactual be *literally* true; and, in the version of the example we are presently considering, its antecedent is true also—contrary to what they suppose, the speakers' visual impressions *are* veridical. Hence the consequent must be true: they must in fact be referring to the little green man who is actually there.

This argument appears to me fallacious. There is no reason to suppose the counterfactual "If their visual impressions were veridical, they would be referring to a little green man" to be true: it might well be that, if they were aware that their visual impressions were veridical, they would keep very quiet about the whole matter. The relevant counterfactual is not this, but a more complex one, namely, as expressed by one of the speakers, "If my visual impressions were veridical, and I were saying what I am now saying, but intending it to be understood literally rather than as an utterance in a make-believe game, I should now be referring to a little green man". This counterfactual *is* literally true; and, in the game, the multiple antecedent is true, since *in the game* they are indeed speaking literally. But we cannot infer, from the fact that they are not under an illusion, that they are actually referring to a little green man, since the other condition, that they intend to be understood literally, does not itself literally hold.

The analogue would be that of someone mistaking a factual narrative for a piece of fiction. If such a reader uses the names of the characters, after the manner of someone discussing the characters in a novel, it would be a mistake to say that he was thereby in fact referring to the real individuals of whom the narrative treated; for he would lack the requisite intention. What makes this compelling is the consideration that make-believe discourse based on a

---

[21] *The Varieties of Reference*, 362.
[22] Ibid. 354.

narrative does not require the speakers to take that narrative to be fiction. What differentiates someone speaking in a make-believe way of the characters of the narrative from someone speaking literally about the individuals whose deeds the narrative relates is the criterion for speaking correctly. It is part of the make-believe game that everything in the narrative is taken as unquestionably true in the game, no information about the characters being admitted from any other source, and it is on this basis that a statement is judged as true or false in that game; but someone speaking literally about the actual individuals aims to make statements about them that are true in fact. It is no bar to playing the make-believe game that one takes the narrative to be intended as factual and to be largely reliable: but, in engaging in that game, a speaker is not referring to the actual individuals. One may even contrast the King David of the Book of Samuel and the King David of the Book of Chronicles, who, as occurring in two different works, are two different characters, although the writers meant to refer, and did refer, to the same actual man.

Evans thus appears to be mistaken in claiming that the speakers engaging in make-believe discourse on the basis of what they take to be an illusion are referring to something actual if they are not in fact victims of any illusion; this claim is incompatible with his own principle making intention a necessary condition for reference. Now the simplest way to approach Evans's account of problematic singular existential statements is to consider a version of the example in which the speakers are unsure whether they are suffering from an illusion or not. Even before they have resolved this question, they may engage in make-believe discourse in which they use the phrase "that little green man". They may, however, come to opposite conclusions about whether their visual impressions are illusory: one may express his by saying, "That little green man exists", and the other may contradict him, saying, "He does not exist". How are we to understand them?

The existential statements, affirmative and negative, are no longer part of the make-believe game. The difficulty is that they involve the use of an information-linked term, which, when literally used, is, on Evans's view, devoid of significance if it has no reference; so, if they *are* suffering from an illusion, the existential statements would appear not to express any propositions. Evans's ingenious solution is that they should be understood as tacitly containing the adverb "really": the one is saying, "That little green man really exists", and the other, "That little green man does not really exist". He is certainly right to say that these statements tolerate the addition of "really" without change of content; and he points out that other existential statements do not. If, for example, we say of someone that, if his parents had never met, he would not have existed, we cannot express this by saying, "He would not really have existed".

On Evans's account, the adverb "really" functions as a kind of sentential operator, which could be read as "it is really the case that . . .". The negative existential statement should therefore be construed as of the form "Not (really (that little green man exists))". The operator "really" is in place in a context in which a make-believe use of language has been employed, or is at least possible; and it serves, in part, to indicate that the statement which it governs is to be taken literally. We cannot simply say, however, Evans argues, that "really" serves to cancel the make-believe convention; for, if we do, we have no explanation of the existential statements. Rather, he suggests, the correct account of it is:

(I) A sentence "Really (*A*)" is true absolutely just in case "*A*", when used in the make-believe game, expresses a proposition in that game, and this proposition is literally true, not just true in the game.[23]

Evans's idea that the existential statement, whether affirmative or negative, somehow exploits the make-believe use of language, and that this fact is shown by the possibility of bringing out its force more clearly by inserting the adverb "really", evidently contains an important insight: for how could anyone say, "That little green man does not exist", as opposed to "There is no little green man there", save by adverting to the perceptual impressions that could serve as a basis for a make-believe use? As it stands, however, his proposal involves multiple difficulties.

Let us, for convenience, abbreviate "that little green man" as "*g*". Evans admits the existence of a first-level predicate ". . . exists", understood as true of everything: there is therefore a simple existential statement "*g* exists", which he writes as "$E(g)$", and which expresses a true proposition if "*g*" refers to something, and fails to express a proposition when "*g*" does not refer to anything. As uttered by a speaker in our example, however, "That little green man exists" should not be construed as "$E(g)$" but, rather, as "Really ($E(g)$)". Now Evans is clear that the sentence "That little green man does not exist", as uttered by the other speaker, is to be represented as the direct negation of the first speaker's statement, and hence as "Not (really ($E(g)$))". But, then, it appears from (I) that the condition for the truth of "Not (really ($E(g)$))" ought to be the failure of the condition for the truth of "Really ($E(g)$)": namely that either "$E(g)$" does not express any proposition when used in the make-believe game, or it does express such a proposition, but that proposition is not literally true. So understood, however, the negative statement would not genuinely be exploiting the make-believe game; and that was not Evans's intention.

There is, of course, a reply to this. Evans is operating with a theory according to which an utterance of a meaningful sentence may fail in two distinct ways, either by expressing a false proposition, or by expressing none at all. It therefore cannot be assumed that the negation of a sentence will express

[23] Ibid. 370.

a false proposition whenever the sentence fails to express a true one: when the sentence expresses no proposition, its negation will express none, either. Perhaps, then, a more exact formulation of Evans's (I) would be:

(II) "Really (*A*)" expresses a proposition just in case "*A*", when used in the make-believe game, expresses a proposition in that game; "and, further, "Really (*A*)" expresses a true proposition just in case the proposition expressed in the game by "*A*" is literally true.

This formulation still does not resolve the difficulty. The phrase "The sentence '*A*' expresses a proposition in the game" is to be construed as "'*A*' counts in the game as expressing a proposition", not as "There is a proposition which '*A*' counts in the game as expressing", so the fact that "*A*" expresses a proposition in the game gives us no licence to speak about the proposition that it expresses in the game. If, in a play, one of the characters dies, a death occurs in the play; but we cannot speak of "that death" save when we engage in the make-believe use of language. Even if the actor playing that character were actually to die at that moment, his death would not be *that* death—the death of that character; nor, if the character represented a historical individual, would the actual death of that individual be the death of the character in the play.

We have two cases, according as the speakers are or are not suffering from an illusion. Suppose, first, that they are not. Then, according to Evans, when they use the phrase "that little green man", even only in make-believe discourse, they really are referring to something. Hence, if one of them were, in the game, to say, "That little green man exists", understood simply as "$E(g)$", he would be not only expressing a true proposition in the game, but actually expressing a proposition which was literally true. We have seen, however, that this is an error: no one intending only to say something in the make-believe game can thereby, unknown to himself, also say something literally; all that we can say is that, had he used the same sentence literally, he would have said something true. If, on the other hand, the speakers are suffering from an illusion, the case is worse, since, even on Evans's account, they do not actually refer to anything when they use the phrase "that little green man", and hence do not express any genuine proposition by saying, "That little green man exists".

We might attempt yet a further reformulation, as follows:

(III) "Really (*A*)" expresses a proposition just in case "*A*", when used in the make-believe game, expresses a game-proposition; and, further, "Really (*A*)" expresses a true proposition just in case that game-proposition is literally true.

This is no improvement, however. There *are* no game-propositions: expressing a proposition in the game is no more to be described as actually expressing a game-proposition than eating a mango in a dream is actually eating a dream-mango. The whole point of the account of fictional discourse as a special make-believe use of language is to relieve us of the need to say what the story-teller is talking *about*: he is not talking about fictional characters, but feigning to talk about real people. By the same token, he is not expressing story-propositions: he is feigning to express genuine ones. Moreover, even if there were game-propositions, formulation (III) would not resolve the difficulty that, contrary to Evans's opinion, one cannot, by expressing a game-proposition, express a literally true proposition, real or fictitious.

Evans's intention is plain enough; but it would be wrong on that ground to dismiss these difficulties as mere awkwardnesses of formulation. The question is not what he intended, but whether what he intended solves the problem as he conceived it. The problem, so conceived, is that "that little green man" is an information-linked term, so that, if it has no reference, no sentence containing it can express a proposition. Evans's intention is that "Really $(E(g)$)" shall express a proposition just in case "$E(g)$" expresses a proposition in the game, and shall express a true proposition just in case "$E(g)$" does, when understood literally. As we have seen, however, Evans did not believe that we are at liberty simply to stipulate that such-and-such a form of sentence shall, in certain circumstances, be deemed not to express a proposition: that is why his own formulation (I), unlike the reformulations (II) and (III), contained no such express stipulation. He thought such a stipulation unwarranted and pointless; that is why, unlike Kripke, he did not see the problem as arising for descriptive names. On Evans's view, we ought to regard an utterance of a meaningful sentence as failing to express a proposition only when we are compelled to; and we are compelled to only when the sentence contains an information-linked term lacking a reference.

How, then, does this square with his account of "Really $(E(g))$? This sentence is to express a proposition, not on condition that "g" has a reference, but on condition that "$E(g)$" expresses a proposition in some make-believe game; the proposition expressed by "Really $(E(g)$)" is, in turn, to be true or false according as "$E(g)$", used literally, does or does not express a proposition. It is, however, impossible to see why the condition for "Really $(E(g)$)" to express a proposition should be what Evans takes it to be unless that sentence is being used to say something about a particular use of the sentence "$E(g)$" or, rather, since there is nothing special about the use of the predicate "E", of the term "g". It is the occurrence of the visual impressions which make it possible to play a make-believe game in which the term "g" is used; and it is the possibility of this use of "g" which guarantees that "Really $(E(g)$)" expresses a proposition. That proposition cannot, in general, be about the referent of "g", used literally, since, if the proposition is false, there is no such referent: it must therefore be about a certain use of the term "g".

I am not here endorsing an account of "That little green man (really) exists" as being about the relevant use of the term, "that little green man": I am arguing only that it is the sole account consistent with Evans's statement of the problem. It is not consistent with his full statement of it, however: for he imposes, as a condition for a correct solution, the same requirement that was stated above as requirement (3), namely that the existential statement should be construed as involving the relevant *use* of the singular term, rather than metalinguistically, as a statement *about* that or any other use of it.[24] In the nature of the case, however, by holding that the term, when used literally, *cannot* be significant if it lacks a reference, he has precluded himself from arriving at any solution that meets requirement (3): the solution he offers can only be interpreted as flouting that requirement so long as it is held that the simple "$E(g)$", understood literally, can never express a false proposition.

A proper name or a demonstrative term cannot be understood save as being used in a particular way. We earlier forswore any attempt to argue that every specific use of a term involved using it to express a Fregean sense; but it has become plain that this must be so for any term capable of occurring as subject of an informative existential statement. There are, however, distinct aspects of the use that is made of a term. It may be used literally or in a make-believe manner: but, for any term capable of being used in both manners, both kinds of use require a basis; for either kind of use, a different basis determines a different use. An information-linked term is one the basis for whose use consists in something that may be taken as giving information about the world. Evans's discussion emphasizes that the basis for a literal use and for a make-believe use may be the same: in his example, the basis is a set of visual impressions. His mistake is to assume that the falsity of the informational basis deprives the term, literally used, of significance, so that no sentence containing it can express a proposition: once we cease to regard such a term as, at best, possessing a bare reference, not mediated by a sense, such an assumption loses any sufficient ground.

Suppose that there is an ancient manuscript concerning which there are two plausible theories, each with powerful but far from conclusive grounds: that it is of the seventh century, and describes contemporary events; and that it is of the ninth, and was intended as a pure romance. The narrative concerns a king, Abbanes. Some, believing the document to contain reliable history, confidently make statements about Abbanes; others, believing it to be fiction, employ the name only in a make-believe use; others again, taking an agnostic view, are willing to use the name literally, conscious that it may have no reference. The use of the name to refer to a seventh-century king relates essentially to that single document; if the narrative does not supply sound information, the name, in that use, has no reference. But we have no ground to go further and declare that, if the information is unsound, the name has no significance and that sentences containing it express no thought.

It might be argued that the name has significance only if it is *possible* that it

<hr>

[24] Ibid. 344.

has a reference. If the document does not give genuine information, there is a sense in which that is not possible, the sense, namely, in which there could not have been such a man as Abbanes: there are no possible worlds containing Abbanes. In that sense, however, as we have seen, the same applies to any empty proper name, including descriptive names: it is a mark of distinction between proper names and definite descriptions, not between descriptive and non-descriptive names. If, to take Evans's example, there was no one person who invented the zip fastener, the name "Julius", as specified by him, has no referent: but, by the same token, there could not have been such a man as Julius. If someone who in fact died in infancy had grown up to invent the zip fastener, he would not have *been* Julius, though he would be the person we should then refer to as "Julius": this applies whether or not there is in fact a referent of the name "Julius". This is simply a feature of proper names in general, and, in particular, of the behaviour of predicates of the form ". . . is *a*", where "*a*" is a proper name. It cannot show that there is no condition for a proper name to have reference; it shows only that, in specifying such a condition, we are not concerned to distinguish certain metaphysically possible worlds from others.

Metaphysical possibility, in the sense in which Kripke employs the phrase, is not the relevant type of possibility. What gives the name "Abbanes" a literal use is that it is consistent with what we know that the name should have a referent. The condition for its having one goes through the document: it involves its giving reliable information. That this condition is of a different kind from that attaching to descriptive names is, however, no ground for declaring it a condition for the *significance* of the name.

What makes it possible for someone to use an information-linked term in the make-believe fashion is that his possessing the relevant information requires neither that it be veridical nor that he believes it to be so. Evans argues that he nevertheless could not *use* the information to attain an understanding of a literal use of the term unless he believed it to be veridical[25]; moreover, his *falsely* believing the term to have reference can surely not confer significance on it. Now indeed he could not take the term to have a reference unless he believed the information to be veridical; but the possibility of employing the term to ask an existential question shows that its significance does not depend upon its having a reference. There may perhaps be information-linked terms that cannot be understood unless they have a reference, when the existence of a referent is a necessary condition for the possession of even putative information, of the relevant kind; if so, such terms cannot possibly be the subjects of informative existential statements. In arguing that all information-linked terms are of this kind, Evans commits himself to solving a problem that does not arise and cannot be solved, and so blemishes an otherwise impressive and original theory.

[25] Ibid. 331–2.

13

Does Quantification Involve Identity?

How are "every", "some", and their like related to "the same as"? Is there any ground for saying that an understanding of the former—of expressions of generality—presupposes an understanding of the latter—of expressions of identity? Let us begin with formalized languages, those framed by use of the apparatus of predicate logic. In a second-order language, identity is definable, so no problem arises. If, in a first-order language, identity is taken as primitive, it is at least unproblematic that an interpretation of the language must involve *a* relation of identity over the domain. But suppose that a language is framed within first-order logic *without* identity: is there then any need to assume that an interpretation of the language will involve or invoke a relation of identity over the domain?

The idea that there is such a need is forcefully expressed in the following quotation from Quine's review of *Reference and Generality*:[1]

This doctrine [Geach's denial of the existence of an absolute relation of identity] is antithetical to the very notion of quantification, the mainspring of modern logic. Quantification depends upon there being values of variables, same or different absolutely; grant quantification and there remains no choice about identity, not for variables. For a language with quantification in it there is but one legitimate version of '$x = y$'.

Now why should this be so? Why, if the language contains no identity-predicate, should the mere assignment of a domain to the variables involve assuming a relation of identity between its elements? The response that suggests itself it that, given a domain, the *possibility* of defining a relation of identity over it—the minimum reflexive relation—is always open. A more detailed form of argument to this effect might run as follows. If we are engaged in giving a verbal *statement* of the interpretation of the object-language, we have first to specify the domain of the variables. To give the interpretation of the non-logical constants, we have to be able to refer in the metalanguage to elements of that domain, or to pick out subsets of it. In order to know whether a given interpretation is admissible, that is, intelligible, we must know when two terms of the metalanguage pick out the *same* element of the domain, since

First published in Harry A. Lewis (ed.), *Peter Geach: Philosophical Encounters* (Deventer, 1991).

[1] W. V. Quine, review of P. T. Geach, *Reference and Generality*, *Philosophical Review*, 73 (1964), 100–4.

the requirement that one and the same element, considered as picked out by each of two distinct singular terms of the metalanguage, should behave differently in respect of the satisfaction of some predicate of the object-language will render the interpretation contradictory and so inadmissible. Hence, to give an interpretation relative to a domain presupposes a relation of identity defined over it. And, according to the present argument, the same applies to the case in which we have only a mental apprehension, rather than a verbal statement, of the interpretation. In such a case, we must grasp the domain, and have some means of picking out—mentally alluding to—its elements; and, in apprehending the interpretation of any predicate relative to this domain, we must in the same way know under what conditions two such allusions are to the same or to distinct elements.

In any case, as Quine has pointed out, for any first-order language L we can *define* a relation $=_L$ which will satisfy the axioms for identity. This relation is to be defined as follows:

$$x =_L y \leftrightarrow \left[\bigwedge_{j=1}^{k} \bigwedge_{i=1}^{n_j} \forall z_1 \ldots \forall z_{i-1} \forall z_{i+1} \ldots \forall z_{n_j} \right.$$

$$\left. (P^{(j)} z_1 \ldots z_{i-1} x z_{i+1} \ldots z_{n_j} \leftrightarrow P^{(j)} z_1 \ldots z_{i-1} y z_{i+1} \ldots z_{n_j}) \right].$$

Here $P^{(1)}, \ldots, P^{(k)}$ is an enumeration of the finitely many primitive predicates of L, where each predicate $P^{(j)}$ ($1 \leq j \leq k$) is of degree n_j; given the actual values of $k, n_1, \ldots, n_k$, we can of course write out the definition in full.[2] The definition captures the notion of being indiscernible relative to the language L. Given that $=_L$ is an identity relation in the sense of one satisfying the standard axioms for identity, what problem remains? We may try enunciating two possible theses:

(1) The defined symbol $=_L$ *must* always be interpreted as genuine identity.
(2) The defined symbol $=_L$ *can* always be interpreted as genuine identity.

Of these, (1) is obviously false. Given any model M of a theory T in L, if M has an infinite domain, we can always find another model M' of T by adding a new element b to the domain which behaves with respect to the interpretations of the predicates of L just like some fixed element a of the original domain; $=_L$ will then come out as holding between a and b. On the other hand, (2) is equally obviously true. Given any model M of a theory T in L, $=_L$ will be interpreted as an equivalence relation over its domain, indeed a congruence relation with respect to the predicates of L. We can therefore find a new model M^* of T whose domain consists of the equivalence classes into which the

---

[2] The definition as stated is adapted for the case when the only non-logical constants of L are predicates. It will be obvious how it is to be modified for the general case in which L contains also function symbols.

domain of M was partitioned by the relation which interprets $=_L$; in M^*, $=_L$ will come out as genuine identity. So far, then, we have found no problem.

The quotation from Quine occurred as part of an attack on Geach's doctrine of relative identity, and I turn to Geach's article 'Ontological Relativity and Relative Identity' for a formulation of that view.[3] Geach claims that for no language L can $=_L$ denote absolute identity. Since he does not believe that there is any such thing as absolute identity, he has a little difficulty in explaining what it is that he is saying that $=_L$ cannot be interpreted to mean. One attempt he makes is to say that, while $=_L$ expresses indiscernibility within L, absolute identity would consist of indiscernibility within any possible language; he goes on to criticize quantification over all possible languages as suspect in view of the semantic paradoxes. I will not spend time discussing how grave this suspicion is: we do not need to invoke the totality of all possible languages. In giving the familiar proofs of the falsity of thesis (1) and the truth of thesis (2), I did not appeal to any such totality: the 'genuine identity' referred to in those theses was simply the identity of the metalanguage. A relativist may seize on this, and remark, "You cannot escape relativization to a language: you must speak always of identity as expressed in some language, not as independent of any particular language". This remark, taken in one way, is patently true, indeed platitudinous; taken in another way, it is patently false. It is platitudinous in the sense that, if I am speaking English, and use the word "identical", I mean it to be understood in the sense that "identical" bears in English, just as with any other word that I use; or, again, if we, speaking English, contemplate a speaker of a language L' asking, in L', whether the relation denoted by $=_L$ for some third language L is really identity, we shall perceive that he is asking whether the interpretation of $=_L$, as stated in L', coincides with the relation expressed by the identity-predicate of L'. The remark is patently false in the following sense: that if we ask in English whether $=_L$ does or does not denote the relation of identity, there is nothing wrong with our question; it is not ambiguous or incomplete. We do not need to qualify the word "identity" as "identity in English", any more than we need to do when we say that the rules of baseball are identical with those of rounders.

Geach says, "We can never so specify what we are quantifying over that we are secure against an expansion of our vocabulary enabling us to discriminate what formerly we could not." What, then, is his thesis? We might state it as follows:

(3) For any theory T in a language L, there exists an extension T' of T in an expansion L' of L such that the truth of T' demands that the interpretation of $=_{L'}$ does not coincide with that of $=_L$.

Geach uses "theory" to mean 'interpreted theory' and "language" to mean

---

[3] P. T. Geach, 'Ontological Relativity and Relative Identity', in M. K. Munitz (ed.), *Logic and Ontology* (New York, 1973).

'interpreted language'. We begin, therefore, with a model M of T, and advance to a model M' of T' of which M is a submodel. Now, clearly, if the domain of M is infinite, we shall be able to find a model M' of T itself whose domain properly contains that of M, such that $=_L$ does not denote identity over the new elements. But that is not what Geach had in mind: he meant that $=_{L'}$ will not be interpreted as coinciding with $=_L$ over their common domain. Whether this can happen or not depends not only upon how the domain has been specified, but also on the interpretation of the predicates of L. If, in M, they were so interpreted that $=_L$ does not come out as the identity relation over the domain D_M, then the situation envisaged by Geach is possible. If, however, the predicates of L were so interpreted that $=_L$ came out as the identity relation over D_M, then no such possibility exists. The general thesis (3) is therefore plainly false.

Nevertheless, Geach has a formal argument to support his view. He attributes to a believer in absolute identity the thesis:

(4) For any language L, we can so construe L that, if $=_L$ holds between x and y, then x and y are absolutely identical.

If "absolutely identical" is understood to mean 'genuinely identical', i.e. 'identical' (as the word "identical" is used in the metalanguage), then this is just another formulation of that thesis (2) which we have seen to be evidently true. Geach has, however, a refutation of it. Suppose that the theory T, expressed in the language L, is ontologically committed to the existence of men. Let L_0 be a proper sublanguage of L, and suppose that $=_{L_0}$ holds between men if and only if they have the same surname. Let T_0 be the restriction of T to L_0. Then, Geach says, on thesis (4) T_0 is ontologically committed to the existence of creatures for whom possession of the same surname is a criterion of absolute identity. But, in that case, T is also committed to the existence of such creatures, "since a theory picks up the ontological commitments of each subtheory". But this, he triumphantly concludes, is absurd; hence thesis (4) must be false.

This argument depends upon an oscillation between taking a language, or a theory, to be interpreted and taking it to be uninterpreted. Given a model M of T (formulated in L), by restriction we obtain a model M_0 of T_0 (formulated in L_0) having the same domain as M. In the case imagined, $=_{L_0}$ will not, in M_0, denote identity. But that does not disprove thesis (4), which merely stated that there would be *some* model of T_0 in which $=_{L_0}$ denoted identity. If we consider such a model, say M_1, it need not be a submodel of M: but it is only for *interpreted* theories that a subtheory can be claimed to carry over its ontological commitments to the main theory. Indeed, this claim needs very careful statement if it is to have any cogency at all: M_1 might in fact happen to be a submodel of M, namely by containing, within its domain, just one man for each surname; and then there would be no reason at all why the theory T, with the model M, should 'pick up' the requirement that $=_{L_0}$ should express identity over the domain of M.

The fact is that, even though Geach himself engages in it, discussion of the matter along the lines we have so far pursued misses the point of Geach's real concern. Theses (1) and (2) are formulated on the assumption that, in the metalanguage, we can intelligibly speak of *the* identity-relation over the domain of an interpretation. Given this assumption, it requires no elaborate argument to refute thesis (1), and it is vain to attempt to refute thesis (2); so Geach has no need of any arguments which appear to be aimed at refuting either thesis on its own terms. What he really wishes to do is to challenge the terms in which they are formulated, that is, to challenge the assumption that we may reasonably speak of *the* identity-relation over a given domain.

One of Geach's principal contentions is that it can *always* happen that, for some expansion L' of a language L, $=_{L'}$ comes out as a finer equivalence relation than $=_L$; as we continue to expand the language, we might get finer and finer equivalence relations *ad infinitum*. How can this be, we may ask, if we happened to start with a language L for which $=_L$ comes out as the identity-relation over the domain, or if we happened at some stage to arrive at a language for which this was so? The answer is that we are begging the question in supposing this to be an intelligible possibility: we are presuming that, given a domain, there must be some one determinate relation over it which constitutes genuine identity, *the* identity-relation associated with that domain. In specifying the domain, we do not, according to Geach, provide for any such relation; if we did, then there would be a limit to the process by which, for L taken as ranging over a sequence of more and more inclusive languages, $=_L$ may come to express a finer and finer equivalence relation: but, since we do not, there is no such limit.

Geach's central concern is thus with the way in which we specify the domain of an interpretation. Logicians usually say merely that, in giving an interpretation, we need to specify a non-empty domain, without bothering themselves with the means by which this is to be done. (Sometimes they add that the domain must be taken to be a *set*, and, in this, a severe restriction may be implicit: but, to make it explicit, we should have to go very deeply into the notion of a set.) How, then, do we specify a domain? Suppose that our metalanguage is English, or some other natural language. Then one natural way to specify a domain would be by the use of a count noun, either unrestricted or restricted by some predicate embedded in a relative clause: thus we might say that the domain was to consist of dogs, or of all dogs now alive in California. For present purposes, however, this seems an unpromising approach. It is a cardinal doctrine of Geach, and one that we should hardly want to deny, that, for any count noun "A", the expression "the same A as" has a determinate sense: so, for a domain specified by means of the count noun "A", the relation expressed by "is the same A as" will surely constitute an identity-relation which is the limit of all possible interpretations of $=_L$, for variable L, over that domain. If, for example "A" is "dog", we can hardly introduce an interpretation under which a is the same dog as b, but a satisfies some predicate which b fails to satisfy.

It is for this reason that, instead of considering a specification of a domain by means of a count noun, Geach treats instead of a specification by means of a list, finite or infinite; I shall make no cavil about the idea of an infinite list. He insists that a list, used for this purpose, may contain repetitions. In order that we may use it to specify a domain, we do not need to know whether it contains repetitions or not. Indeed, it does not make sense to ask whether any element is listed twice—we can only ask, for this or that count noun "A", whether two entries mention the same A; the answer may be different, according to the count noun we select; and there is no *one* count noun which is the right one to use for this purpose.

These remarks hang oddly together with the thesis to which Geach subscribes, as do I, that to every proper name is associated some determinate criterion of identity, given that he acknowledges that a list is a string of proper names; indeed, without affecting the issue, we could allow the list to contain singular terms other than proper names. It is not that Geach has gone back on this thesis concerning proper names, since he reiterates it in the very article, 'Ontological Relativity and Relative Identity', under discussion. If to two proper names occurring in the list there are associated conflicting criteria of identity, it would not appear to make sense to say that they denoted the same object; and, when the same criterion is associated with two names, that criterion determines the sense of asking whether a repetition is involved, without the need for any arbitrary choice. Given an assignment, to each entry on the list, of an appropriate criterion of identity, it seems that an identity-relation over the elements of the domain specified by the list had thereby been determined, one that will, as before, set bounds to the fineness of the interpretation of any $=_L$.

In any case, we must enquire whether, in specifying the domain by means of a list, we thereby impose any constraints upon the interpretations that may be given relative to this domain, or whether we are allowed to make any entry behave differently, with respect to the interpretation of some predicate, from any one other entry. If the proper names making up the list are thought of as having senses associating with each of them a criterion of identity, we should surely want to impose the constraint that any two names which, according to the relevant criterion of identity, denoted the same object must behave alike in respect of the interpretation. Even if the names are not said to have such senses, there must be some means employed for fixing their reference, since otherwise there would be no content to calling them 'names'; and, at least in the case in which, for some two entries, the *means* of fixing their reference completely coincided, we should expect a ban on allowing them to behave differently with respect to any interpretation. In any case, whether or not any such constraints are imposed, it would seem that the *list* itself, taken together with those constraints, if any, sets a bound to the fineness of any equivalence relation expressed by some $=_L$. For, even if there are no constraints, we surely cannot get any finer equivalence relation than that which holds between the object corresponding to each entry and itself, but not between any such object and the object corresponding to any other entry. After all, even if we do not mind a list's being repetitive, we shall want it to be exhaustive; we want to be sure that, for each item we wish to include, there is at least one entry to which it uniquely corresponds. It seems, therefore, that we must employ some criterion for what merits separate inclusion in the list; this criterion must be such that, for any count noun "A", if we want to admit interpretations such that, if x is not the same A as y, then x may satisfy some predicate which y fails to satisfy, then there is no entry on the list to which x and y both correspond. For, of course, the picture aroused by the conception of specifying a domain by means of a list is that the interpretations of the predicates over this domain are given by citing the entries, or n-tuples of entries, on the list which satisfy those predicates.

It is, however, exactly this which Geach denies. The insistence on the possibility that the list may contain repetitions was really beside the point: the real point is that it may contain compressions. "If", he says, "we list the things we are quantifying over by their names, one of these names may turn out to be not a proper name but a shared name, of objects that we now can discriminate but previously could not." How does it come about that we make this new, finer, discrimination? Not, surely, by an expansion of the formal object-language. If we discover that some name, "a", occurring on the list is really a shared name, we shall, presumably, replace it as quickly as possible by two or more new names, say "b" and "c". Until we have made this distinction between b and c, we have no means of introducing into the expanded language a predicate which is true of b but not of c, since we have no means of formulating the intended interpretation of such a predicate; the discrimination cannot, therefore, be a consequence of the fact that $=_L$ does not hold between b and c, although $=_L$ did, since we cannot even make the stipulations that have this effect until we have first distinguished between b and c. How, then, does this discovery that "a" was really a shared name differ from a *change* in the domain of quantification? In what sense does the domain remain the same?

What, indeed, does such a discovery consist in? We may, admittedly, have made a mistake in listing "a" in the first place: we may have been using the name "a" indifferently for each of two twins, whom we wrongly took to be the same person, and now we discover our mistake. It must be acknowledged to be obvious that no specification of a domain is immune to a mistake of this sort: but, while the domain we specify when we replace "a" by "b" and "c" is that which we were all along aiming to specify, the original specification was simply wrong, and did not fully succeed in its aim. Evidently, Geach did not have cases of this sort in mind; so let us change the example. Suppose, now, that we live in a society familiar with the phenomenon of identical twins, but in which the word "person" is so used that a pair of twins is construed as a case of the bilocation of a single person: "*a*" names such a bilocated individual. Later, under foreign influence, this society adapts its use of the word "person" so that twins are counted as distinct people, and this particular pair are now named "*b*" and "*c*". This time, no mistake is involved, at least not a *mere* mistake: there is conceptual change. Again, we must concede that no specification of a domain is proof against revision under the pressure of such conceptual change. But, this time, it is unclear in what sense the revised list specifies the *same* domain as the original one; in attempting to view it as doing so, we only assimilate this case to that in which a mistake is involved. In any case, our new capacity—better, propensity—to discriminate between the twins as distinct individuals is not due to any enrichment of the object-language. On any reasonable choice of the language L, as originally interpreted over the domain given by the list containing "*a*", $=_L$ will now be regarded as failing to hold between the twins; for example, if "*Fx*" means "*x* is in England" and "*Gx*" means "*x* is in Spain", it may be that "*Fx*" is true of one twin and false of the other, and "*Gx*" true of the other and false of the one, although, originally, we rated "*Fx* & *Gx*" true of the object denoted by "*a*".

So far, then, it appears that Quine was right: the interpretation of a first-order language L demands that a domain be specified for the variables; in specifying such a domain, we cannot avoid determining an identity-relation over it which constitutes the finest possible interpretation of $=_L$, and determines the admissibility of proposed interpretations of the predicates of L relative to that domain. However, Geach's principal concern seems to be with natural, not with formalized, languages: and so we have to ask, for natural languages, the analogue of the question we have been considering for formalized languages. It could even be thought that Geach could quite consistently have conceded the point about formalized languages, say by allowing that the specification of a domain for the variables of such a language always involves the use of some count noun "*A*", and hence that "is the same *A* as" will express the identity-relation associated with that domain, and yet have maintained his contention for natural languages. For reasons that I shall explain, I do not think that this is quite true: but that is far from obvious at first sight.

Natural languages differ from formalized languages in the manner by which they express generality. Their means of doing so differs in two respects from that of a quantificational language. (1) They lack the machinery of quantifiers and variables: the noun-phrase, containing the indefinite article or some word like "some" or "every", stands in the argument-place of the predicate; sometimes a pronoun serves as a variable bound by this noun-phrase, sometimes the effect of further occurrences of the bound variable is obtained by a range of devices including the use of connectives between words or phrases that fall short of being clauses. (2) Usually the operative noun-phrase contains a common noun, namely one admitting a plural, expressing more than a formal concept, specifically a count noun. (By a noun expressing a formal concept is meant one with no informative content, that is, one the applicability of which, when it is correctly used, cannot be meaningfully questioned. The word "thing" is the prototype of such a word: if someone says, "That was a terrible thing to happen", his hearer cannot appropriately reply, "It was terrible, all right, but I shouldn't call it a thing".) I shall consider only restricted generality, of the kind expressed by a phrase containing a count noun, and not that expressed by one containing a mass term, nor yet unrestricted generality, both of which raise different problems. For our purposes, feature (1) is unimportant: our problems would be unaffected by the introduction of bound variables, namely if, instead of saying, "A dog rushed out and bit Henry", we said, "For some dog x, x rushed out and x bit Henry". The important point is not whether or not variables are used, but that there is not a fixed number of sorts of variable, given in advance, each with its associated domain; instead, the range of generality is indicated by the count noun occurring in the noun-phrase.

A count noun is naturally taken to be a noun "A" that can occur in contexts of the form "There are just n As" or "There are just n As which are F", when the latter means "There are just n As each of which is F". A count noun must therefore admit both a singular and a plural, and be capable of occurring as a predicate "is an A"; and, necessarily, the phrase "is the same A as" must have a determinate sense.

What *is* the analogue, for natural languages, of the question we asked about formalized languages? It emphatically is *not* the question: Is there an absolute relation of identity? One version of a negative answer to *that* question would be to say that the phrase "is the same as" has a clear sense only when the context determines a count noun "A" such that we can replace the phrase by "is the same A as". Far from wishing to controvert *this* thesis, I accept it as true. A stronger version is to say that it sometimes holds, for particular count nouns "A" and "B", that we can truly say that something is the same A, but not the same B, as something else. I do not wish to controvert even this stronger thesis: under some possible uses of certain count nouns, it is indisputably true.

For any count noun "A", let us say that "is the same A as" denotes an identity-relation. The analogue of our original question is, now: Is there, for any expression of restricted generality of the kind with which we are concerned, a definite identity-relation associated with the range (or domain) of generality? It may seem quite trivial to answer this question. An expression of restricted generality of the kind with which we are concerned is effected by means of such a phrase as "Every A", "Some A", "Every A which is F", "Some

A which is *F*", etc., where "*A*" is a count noun. It may, then, seem obvious that, for any such phrase, the identity-relation associated with the range of generality will be that expressed by "is the same *A* as". However, we shall see that this cannot be so certainly concluded in every case: although I shall return an affirmative answer to the question, it will not be quite so easily arrived at.

Geach characterizes a word "*A*" as a count noun if it is subject to the following pattern of explanation. First we introduce the expression "is the same *A* as" as standing for some equivalence relation. Secondly, we use the predicate "is an *A*", which is definable as meaning "is the same *A* as something": this, he says, is a case of derelativization comparable to the definition of "is a father" as meaning "is the father of someone". In neither case could we proceed the other way round: we could not first introduce the predicate "is a father", and then explain what it was to be someone's father; likewise, "is the same *A* as" is not paraphrasable as "is an *A* and is (absolutely) the same as". Next, we explain sentences of the form "There are just *n A*s" as holding good just in case we can assign the natural numbers from 1 to *n* "to such objects in a domain as are *A*s"—that is, to those objects of which "is an *A*" is true—according to the principle that the same number is to be assigned to an object *x* and to an object *y* if and only if *x* is the same *A* as *y*.

The expression "is the same *A* as" may or may not be explicable by some verbal definition: Geach considers an artificial example in which it is. We introduce the word "surman" by laying down that "is the same surman as" is to hold between two men if and only if they have the same surname. The expressions "is a surman" and "There are *n* surmen" are then explained in accordance with the general stipulations.

I wish to single out two particular classes of what are ordinarily reckoned as count nouns that are not subject to Geach's pattern of explanation. Consider, first, the word "father". This certainly functions as a count noun in the ordinary sense: it admits a plural, and we can sensibly ask, "How many fathers are present tonight?" Geach is precluded from saying that it accords with his pattern of explanation, since he cannot claim that "is a father" is to be explained as meaning "is the same father as someone"; on the contrary, he is committed to the more plausible view that it should be explained as meaning "is the father of someone". Indeed he expressly acknowledges this in his paper 'Names and Identity',[4] saying, " 'is a brother' is a derelativization not of 'is the same brother as' but of 'is brother of' ". There is no reason to hold that "is the same father as" is logically prior to "is a father"; on the contrary, "is the same father as" is most naturally explained as meaning "is a father and is the same man as". Geach actually concludes that "is the same brother as" is "an ill-formed expression generated by false analogy".[5] He says that "It could be

---

[4] P. T. Geach, 'Names and Identity', in Samuel Guttenplan (ed.), *Mind and Language*, Wolfson Lectures, 1974 (Oxford, 1975), 157.
[5] Ibid. 156–7.

legitimate only if 'is a brother' were its derelativization". The suggestion appears, therefore, to be that a noun that does not fit the preferred pattern of explanation by reference to which Geach characterizes count nouns cannot meaningfully appear in the gap within "is the same . . . as". The suggestion is implausible in itself; if it were correct, it would follow that there is not the connection which Geach claims in 'Ontological Relativity and Relative Identity'[6] between what Frege called statements of number and what Geach admits as count nouns; more specifically, it would follow that not every noun which can immediately follow such an expression as "There are three . . ." can appear in the gap of "is the same . . . as". The point does not apply only to count nouns "*A*" such that "is an *A*" is to be explained as "is an *A* of something", but, equally, to such a noun as "baker". There is an intuitive absurdity to saying that "is a baker" is to be explained as meaning "is the same baker as someone", which is borne in on us when we ask how we might explain "is the same baker as": the obvious way to explain the latter phrase is as meaning "is a baker and is the same person as", while "is a baker" has a straightforward explanation as meaning "is a person who earns his living by baking bread". The latter explanation, if taken as primary, yields just the right meaning for "is the same baker as", showing that there is no reason to take the latter as logically prior to the former. I shall call count nouns "*A*" such that "is the same *A* as" is to be explained as meaning "is an *A* and is the same *B* as", for some other count noun "*B*", *derivative count nouns*: they form one important class not subject to Geach's pattern of explanation.

Consider, now, the noun "nationality". There is some uncertainty whether we should allow "is the same nationality as" to occur only in contexts such as "Persian is the same nationality as Iranian", or also in contexts like "Henri is the same nationality as Pierre". Some would say that sentences of the latter form exhibit an ungrammaticality of the same sort as that which they would detect in such a sentence as "She was wearing a kind of kimono" (instead of "She was wearing a kimono of a kind"), and which is seen, grossly, in "He kind of slumped in his chair", and that we ought only to say, "Henri is of the same nationality as Pierre", or "Henri has the same nationality as Pierre"; certainly the suggestion is in line with French and German, although both admit the "a kind of . . ." formation. I do not wish to legislate on the grammatical point: we can consider both alternatives.

"Nationality" is certainly a count noun: it admits a plural, and we can sensibly ask, "How many nationalities are represented at this conference?" If we rule out sentences like "Henri is the same nationality as Pierre", then "is the same nationality as" can express only an equivalence relation defined over nationalities. In this case, "is a nationality" is indeed equivalent to "is the same nationality as something"; nevertheless, the noun "nationality" is not subject

6 'Ontological Relativity and Relative Identity', 290.

to Geach's pattern of explanation, for two reasons. First, "is the same nationality as" does seem to be paraphrasable as "is a nationality and is the same as"; indeed, just because it is over *nationalities* that the equivalence relation is defined, we can hardly think of "is the same nationality as" as being introduced before "is a nationality" is understood. Secondly, "is a nationality" is not *only* explicable as "is the same nationality as something"; it is better explained as meaning "is the nationality of someone". Frege long ago described a pattern according to which a count noun like "nationality" may be thought of as being introduced. We first introduce "has the same nationality as" or "is of the same nationality as" as expressing an equivalence relation between human beings, in this particular case one definable as "is a citizen of the same country as". Next, we form the operator "the nationality of . . .", so used that "the nationality of x is the same as that of y" is equivalent to "x has the same nationality as y". Finally, we explain "is a nationality" as meaning "is the nationality of someone". (The only feature of Frege's account which I have omitted, and the only controversial one, is the detailed means of taking the second step, of introducing the operator "the nationality of . . .".) I shall call count nouns subject to Frege's pattern of explanation *abstract count nouns*: other examples are "weight", "status", and "species" (in the last case, the operator takes the form "the species to which . . . belongs").

If we adopt the second alternative, and admit "Henri is the same nationality as Pierre" as grammatical, thus regarding "is the same nationality as" as expressing an equivalence relation between human beings, then indeed the phrase, so understood, must be viewed as having priority in the order of explanation over other phrases involving the word "nationality"; it will not be equivalent to "is a nationality and is the same as". But the noun will still not exhibit Geach's pattern of explanation, because "is a nationality" will not be equivalent to, let alone be definable as, "is the same nationality as someone": Henri is the same nationality as Pierre, but neither is a nationality. In fact, the word "nationality", so used, is subject to precisely the same Fregean pattern of explanation as before, save that the equivalence relation is expressed by "is the same nationality as" in place of "has the same nationality as".

For any count noun "*A*", whether of the type of "surman", of "baker", of "nationality", or of none of these, I shall call the relation expressed by "is the same *A* as" a *relative identity-relation*. It will be noted that, for different replacements of "*A*", a phrase of the form "is the same *A* as" may function in different ways, according as (1) it does or does not stand for a relation between things of which "is an *A*" is true, and (2) it permits suppression of the count noun "*A*" without ambiguity, wherever it is properly used.

We have looked at two important classes of count nouns not subject to Geach's pattern of explanation; their existence shows that not all words that would ordinarily be classed as count nouns are subject to that pattern. It is, however, comparatively unimportant that some words naturally thought of as count nouns do not conform to that pattern of explanation; the important claim made by Geach is that some do so. But we need to ask whether, if a count noun "*A*" has been introduced in accordance with Geach's pattern of explanation, that manner of introduction completely determines its use in the language. For instance, have Geach's stipulations concerning his artificial word "surman" completely specified the use of this noun? Geach thinks so: he insists that, in sentences involving this word, "we need not use" other "words in some artificial sense that I have negligently failed to specify". At first sight, however, there are many possible contexts that Geach has not provided for. We expect that any count noun "*A*" will figure, not only in the three contexts Geach explicitly considers, namely "is the same *A* as", "is an *A*", and "There are just *n* *A*s", but also in contexts of the following kinds: "is an *A* which is *F*"; "There are *n* *A*s which are *F*"; "some *A*"; "every *A*"; "an *A*" in subject position (including grammatical direct and indirect object position, after a preposition, etc.); "some *A* which is *F*"; "every *A* which is *F*"; and "an *A* which is *F*" in subject position. It does not appear that these contexts have been automatically provided for as soon as the three contexts which Geach deals with have been stipulated for. And, on reflection, it seems that all these other contexts will have been wholly or largely provided for if we lay down which predicates may be significantly applied to *A*s, and under what conditions each such predicate is true of some one given *A*. With derivative count nouns, this presents no problem: we shall apply to bakers just the same predicates that we apply to men, subject to the same satisfaction-conditions. It is different with "nationality" or "species". The things that can be said of nationalities are not at all the same as those that can be said of people, and an understanding of the word "nationality" depends upon knowing what things can be said of a nationality and under which conditions it is true, for instance that someone can be said to acquire or to be deprived of a nationality, and the like. Similarly with "species": things can be said of a species that cannot meaningfully be said of any of its members, for instance that it is extinct, and things that can be said of a species and can also be said of its members, e.g. that it is degenerate or that it is 10,000,000 years old, are said of the species in a different sense. I do not mean to place a strong construction on "in a different sense" here; I mean only that the condition for a species to be degenerate is not to be explained in terms of the condition for any of its members to be degenerate.

Once we have laid down which predicates can be applied to *A*s, and under what conditions they are true of a given *A*, we are in a position, not merely to understand the use of "*A*" in any of the contexts I listed, but also to introduce proper names of *A*s. In this connection, the expression "proper name of an *A*" must be treated with caution. By Geach's stipulations, Jimmy Carter is a surman, and hence, in one sense, "Jimmy Carter" is the proper name of a surman; but this is not the sense in which "Jimmy Carter" is the name of a man. This can be seen from the fact that "Jimmy Carter is now the President of the

United States" does *not* follow from "Jimmy Carter used to grow peanuts and the same surman is now the President of the United States". In a special sense, "Jimmy Carter" is the name of a man but is not the name of a surman; and I shall express this sense by saying that "Jimmy Carter" *designates* a man and does not *designate* a surman. The sense, namely, is this: that "*y* is *F* and Jimmy Carter is the same man as *y*" entails "Jimmy Carter is *F*", whereas the same entailment fails when we replace "man" by "surman". This supplies the sense in which Geach holds, and I entirely agree, that with every proper name is associated some criterion of identity, usually, perhaps always, expressible by "is the same *A* as" for some count noun "*A*"; and, in this sense, the language does not as yet contain any proper names that designate surmen. If we wished to introduce them, we should have to lay down the conditions under which a given surman satisfied a predicate significantly applicable to it; and it is that stipulation which Geach appears to have omitted to make.

It is apparent from Geach's practice that he wishes to apply to surmen the same predicates as those we apply to men; so we may enquire after their satisfaction-conditions. Two possibilities occur immediately: (1) a predicate is true of a surman just in case it is true of every man who has the corresponding surname; or (2) a predicate is true of a surman just in case it is true of some man who has the corresponding surname. Since Geach speaks of surmen living in Leeds, (1) is unlikely to accord with his intentions, since, under (1), it is improbable that any surman lives in Leeds. But, now, if we adopt (2), are we to say that "Some surman is both alive and dead" is true or false? If we apply the condition directly to the complex predicate "is both alive and dead", it comes out false; yet there plainly exist *x* and *y* such that *x* is alive and *y* is dead and *x* is the same surman as *y*. What we have run into here is scope trouble: is condition (2) to be applied to the predicates "is alive" and "is dead" taken separately, and the sentence then construed in the usual way as arrived at by conjunction and existential generalization, or is it to be applied directly to the complex predicate? One possible choice would be to lay down that the scope is always to be taken as narrowly as possible, that is, in the example, in the first of the two ways just canvassed; in this case, the sentence "Some surman is both alive and dead" will come out true.

Now this would be a perfectly coherent way of speaking, even if it would have some rather paradoxical-sounding consequences; but, on reflection, it seems unlikely to be a correct interpretation of Geach's intentions. For one thing, he says that "if *x* is a surman in Leeds, then *x* has a heart in his breast, guts in his belly, and so on". When scope difficulties are involved, the interpretation of a sentence is very sensitive to how we construe its internal structure; but if we take "*x* has guts in his belly" to mean something like "For some *y* and for just one *z*, *y* is a gut and *z* is a belly, and *y* is in *z* and *z* is part of *x*", this predicate will not, under the proposed convention, be true of any surman; no surman will have just one belly, but will have as many of them as there are men bearing the corresponding surname. Much more important, however, is the fact that Geach is convinced that he has no need to *specify* the conditions under which such a predicate is to be true of a given surman: he continues, "These predicables will be true of x in their ordinary everyday sense; to make these predications true, we need not use words in some artificial sense that I have negligently failed to specify". How has it come about that I have (I hope) at least made it appear that some such specification is required, whereas it appears obvious to Geach that none is needed?

The reason is that I have been assuming that, when a predicate is applied to a surman, the identity-relation associated with such a predication will be that given by "is the same surman as". What is meant here by speaking of "the associated identity-relation"? The fact is that, just as the phrase "proper name of an A" has to be treated with caution, so has the phrase "predicating something of an A". In *one* sense, when I say, "Jimmy Carter comes from Georgia", I am predicating something of a surman; but, in *another* sense, I am not, because I have attached the predicate to a name which does not, in our special sense, designate a surman, but, rather, designates a man. If x is a surman, and x lives in Leeds, and x is the same surman as y, does it follow that y lives in Leeds? Evidently not, when "x" and "y" are taken as ranging over men; but how is it when they are taken to range over surmen, that is, when we construe "x is a surman", not as a predicate applying to certain elements of the domain, but as indicating that "x" is to range over surmen?

The answer is that it depends how we construe the expression "ranging over surmen". The critical question is what is the identity-relation associated with the given expressions of generality. The phrase "x is the same A as y" expresses such an identity-relation just in case "For some x and y, x is F and x is the same A as y and y is G" is taken to entail "For some x, x is both F and G"; for example, "is the same surman as" expresses the identity-relation associated with the expression "some surman" just in case it is a sufficient condition for the truth of "Some surman is both alive and dead" that, for some x, x is alive, and, for some y, x is the same surman as y, and y is dead. Geach's conviction that there is no stipulation that he has failed to make arises from the fact that he does *not* want to make the relation expressed by "is the same surman as" play this role in connection with expressions like "some surman"; and we may express this by saying that he does not wish to introduce into the language any expressions of generality for which the relevant range consists of surmen—he does not want to quantify *over* surmen at all. That is why he can say that all predicates applied to surmen are to be taken "in their ordinary everyday sense": when an expression like "some surman" is used, the associated identity-relation will be given, not by "is the same surman as", but by "is the same man as", and so "Some surman is both alive and dead" will come out as false, since we cannot find a case in which x is a surman, and x is alive, and, for some y, y is dead and y is the same *man* as x.

Geach does not wish to quantify over surmen in any other sense than that of restricting the domain to those men who satisfy the predicate "is a surman". Just as there is a broader and a narrower sense of "proper name of an *A*", and a broader and a narrower sense of "predicating something of an *A*", so there is a broader and a narrower sense of "quantifying over *A*s". In the broader sense, to quantify over *A*s is to quantify over a domain each element of which satisfies the predicate "is an *A*"; but, in the narrower sense, it involves using an expression of generality with which is associated the identity-relation expressed by "is the same *A* as". Because Geach wishes to quantify over surmen only in the broader, not the narrower, sense, the word "surman", as he intends it to be used, will function precisely like a derivative count noun such as "baker" save in the two special contexts "is the same surman as" and "There are *n* surmen". These two perturbations of the familiar pattern will produce some paradoxical-sounding results; for instance, "There is just one surman in Llanellyn" and "Some surman in Llanellyn is over 30" may both be true, while "Every surman in Llanellyn is over 30" is false. This is not to suggest that there is any incoherence in the use of "surman" as proposed by Geach; reflection should, however, make it evident that "surman" will not behave in the same way as any existing word in the language.

It is thus apparent that, for every expression of restricted generality of the kind with which we are concerned, there must be *some* identity-relation associated with it. It will not, however, hold in all cases that with an expression like "some *A*" is associated the relation expressed by "is the same *A* as", which is why the short way with our question about expressions of generality in natural language is not in fact a correct response. To understand an expression of the form "some *A*", it is not enough that one should have mastered the expression "is the same *A* as": knowing how to use "is the same surman as" does not tell us whether "Some surman is both alive and dead" is to be reckoned true or false. What we have to know is which is the right identity-relation to appeal to in judging statements involving "some *A*": whether that expressed by "is the same *A* as", or some other. Geach is anxious to insist that, when *x* is the same *A* as *y*, there may always be some count noun "*B*" such that *x* is not the same *B* as *y*. The correct answer is, I think, that it depends whether "is the same *A* as" expresses the identity-relation associated with the domain of the variables "*x*" and "*y*": if it does, then there can be no such count noun "*B*". But suppose that, for the sake of argument, we concede this claim of Geach's. It remains that, when the phrase "some *A*" is used, we must know whether or not "is the same *A* as" expresses the associated identity-relation: otherwise we cannot determine the truth of sentences of the form "Some *A* is both *F* and *G*". On the way of construing sentences involving the word "surman" that I have attributed to Geach, it counted as a relevant objection to the truth of "Some surman is both alive and dead" that, although *x* is alive, and *y* is dead, and *x* is the same surman as *y*, still *x* is not the same *man* as *y*. But, now, suppose that I observe, of some man now taking tea with me, that he is the same man as the one who presided over last night's meeting: can I infer that some man both presided over that meeting and is now having tea with me? I cannot make this inference unless I know that the fact that it is the same *man* is conclusive here. Suppose it said that, although it is the same man, it is not the same whatnot, where "whatnot" is some suitable count noun: how am I to know that this is not a valid objection to the inference? I cannot know this, unless I know that, for the relevant domain—that invoked in using the expression "some man" and for these predicates, the relation expressed by "is the same man as" plays a quite special role, a role which other identity-relations which may be defined over that domain do not play; that it is *the* identity-relation associated with that domain.

Geach gives an actual example of a range of words which he claims are count nouns subject to his pattern of explanation. These are specifications of the ambiguous word "word": e.g. "token word", "dictionary-entry word", "orthographic word", "phonetic word", etc. Now I think it is plain that such expressions do *not* behave like "surman" on the way of construing it sketched above—nor, indeed, given Geach's explicit stipulations, on any other—since the predicates we apply differ in different cases. A dictionary-entry word may be said to be invariable, but not an orthographic word; an orthographic or phonetic word may be ambiguous, but not a dictionary-entry word; a token word, but not a phonetic word, may be almost illegible. The most important fact to note about this example, however, is that there are two distinct ways of understanding the account which Geach gives of these expressions. One is to take "orthographic word", "dictionary-entry word", and "phonetic word" as related to "token word" as "surman" is related to "man": "x is the same orthographic word as y" would then be defined to mean "x is a token word and y is a token word and x has the same spelling as y", while "is an orthographic word" would be defined to mean "is the same orthographic word as something". It would then follow, as Geach says, that every element of a domain specified as consisting of words was, simultaneously, a token word *and* an orthographic word *and* a dictionary-entry word, etc. On this interpretation, we start with a domain of token words, and define, over it, a number of equivalence relations, expressed as relative identity-relations, such as that expressed by "is the same orthographic word as". Here "token word" plays in relation to "orthographic word" exactly the role that "man" is supposed to play in relation to "surman". But, then, what about the nouns "token word" and "man" themselves? Are they to be taken as subject to Geach's pattern of explanation for count nouns? If so, over what domain is the relation expressed by "is the same token word as" or that expressed by "is the same man as" defined? If Geach were to deny that "token word" and "man" exemplify his pattern of explanation, we should have another, and most important, class of count nouns not subject to that pattern.

It does not seem, however, that he would take that view; for he speaks of "token word" as a count noun alongside "dictionary-entry word" and the rest, and, for him, it is a criterion for "*A*" to be a count noun that "is an *A*" should have to be explained in terms of "is the same *A* as" by derelativization. This conflicts with the suggested interpretation of Geach's account of nouns like "orthographic word", for, under that interpretation, "token word" was taken as already understood and as being used to fix the domain over which the various relative identity-relations were to be defined; we should then have no need to *introduce* "token word" by specifying the sense of "is the same token word as" as standing for an equivalence relation over that domain. This suggests a different interpretation of Geach's account: one under which "token word" plays no distinguished role in fixing the domain over which the various relative identity-relations are to be defined, and under which no other count noun plays such a role; the domain is given *first*, antecedently to our defining over it *any* identity-relation. This is in harmony with the thesis I have already rejected, the thesis which it is the main burden of this essay to confute: that a domain may be specified without associating any particular identity-relation with it.

Much of what Geach says supports this second interpretation. He writes,

The word "word" . . . is ambiguous. It may mean "token word", or "dictionary-entry word" or various other things. Despite this, I may specify as the universe of discourse the words in a given volume in my room at Leeds; for I could give each word in the volume a proper name and get a finite list of them. The ambiguity I have just mentioned is an ambiguity over what shall count as *the same* word; but since a list specifying a domain . . . need not be nonrepetitive, this need not worry us. The count of token words, of orthographic words . . . and of dictionary-entry words, may be different in each case; all the same, each thing in the universe is the same token word as itself *and* the same orthographic word as itself *and* the same dictionary-entry word as itself, and thus *both* is a token word *and* is an orthographic word *and* is a dictionary-entry word. I dismiss the protest that this result is incoherent because the entity in question must be of only one of these three kinds; there is no "must" about it. We have in view an entity that belongs to the field of these different equivalence relations, and therefore comes under three different counts using different count nouns; *each* of the count nouns applies—that is how count nouns are used. It is on the contrary the question "But which is it *really*?" that is incoherent and unintelligible.[7]

Now it is true enough, on Geach's account, that of each element in the domain we can truly predicate "is a token word", "is an orthographic word" and "is a dictionary-entry word"; but, if we adopt the first interpretation of that account, under which the domain is originally fixed as consisting of token words (say because the proper names occurring in Geach's list have associated with them the criterion of identity expressed by "is the same token word as"), it

---

[7] Ibid. 294.

does not in the least follow that the question, "Which is it *really*?" is devoid of sense. On the contrary, to the question "What is it?" asked of an element of the domain, the answer "It is a token word" will have a distinguished place, because it alone will indicate the identity-relation associated with the domain. This suggests, therefore, that, of the two interpretations, it is the second that corresponds with Geach's intentions: it suggests that we are supposed to select a domain for our variables in advance of fixing *any* identity-relation for it, and that "is the same token word as" denotes one of the equivalence relations which we only subsequently define over this domain.

It is just here, therefore, that Geach's views concerning natural language link up with those concerning formalized languages with which I began: for the domain of definition of the relations expressed by phrases of the form "is the same *A* as", Geach requires the same amorphous sort of domain, given by a list whose entries may later be discerned to be shared, rather than proper, names, as that which he wanted to invoke in speaking of an interpretation of a formalized language. Of the equivalence relations mentioned by Geach in the example, that expressed by "is the same token word as" happens to be the finest; but we may later see fit to introduce another, defined over the same domain, say one expressed by "is the same runcible word as", which is yet finer. If, originally, we listed the elements of the domain by giving a separate entry to each distinct token word in the volume, it will now prove that some of our entries each correspond to distinct runcible words, and hence are not, after all, proper names, but only shared names. This is why the plausible suggestion made earlier, that Geach could have conceded the point for formalized languages, but still have maintained his position for natural language, is not in fact correct: if his thesis about formalized languages crumbles, so does his thesis about natural language.

As I see it, the truth of the matter is this. The different criteria of identity associated with count nouns and with proper names are not criteria for the obtaining of different equivalence relations between determinate objects. Reference to an object requires that we have some criterion of identity for the object referred to; hence the criterion of identity associated with a count noun must be understood before reference is possible to any object for whose identity it is the appropriate criterion. These criteria of identity may be thought of, at least in the first place, as criteria for the truth of statements of identity between things referred to ostensively. The question "Is this the same as that?" where the demonstratives are supplemented by pointing gestures, is indeed indeterminate: we have to insert a count noun after "the same" to make it a determinate question. This is enough to show that demonstrative pronouns do not have to be understood as tacitly associated with any particular criterion of identity on each occasion of their use, and that, for this very reason, they are not, in general, to be taken as picking out determinate *objects*. Below the level at which we employ genuine predicates of objects, predicates such as "is loyal to his friends" or "has visited Nigeria", which can be understood only as defined over a domain of objects, there is a level at which we employ quasi-predicates which need not be so understood, but can be attached to demonstratives unqualified by any count noun: and it is in respect of this more basic level of discourse that we can truly say that no particular relation of identity is presupposed. But the question "Is *a* the same as *b*?", where "*a*" and "*b*" are proper names, *requires* no supplementation by a count noun, though it will always *admit* one, since a criterion of identity is already associated with the proper names. What is more, as was asserted by Quine in the quotation with which we began, though it is by no means so obvious, the same holds good of the determination, for particular values of the variables, of a formula "$x = y$" of a formalized language; for the specification of the domain of the variables likewise requires the invocation of an associated identity-relation.

POSTSCRIPT (1978)

This essay was written in November 1976, and given in that month as a lecture at the University of California, Berkeley, at Stanford University, and at the University of Mexico. It overlaps extensively with an earlier, unpublished essay, 'Geach and Quine on Identity', and is printed here in almost exactly the form in which it was originally written. Since writing it, I have had the opportunity of reading H. W. Noonan's 'Objects and Identity'[8] and Nicholas Griffin's *Relative Identity*[9]. I have not, however, thought it advisable to complicate and lengthen this essay by relating the views expressed in it to those of either writer. With Griffin's book, the views advanced here do not, I think, have a great deal in common. It is otherwise with Noonan's thesis. His approach to the topic and mine are radically different; but, in reading his thesis, I found many of the points I had made here made also by Noonan, of course quite independently and sometimes in a very different manner. To give just two instances, he gives great prominence to the distinction between the narrower and the broader sense in which a name may be said to be the name of an *A* (the former being expressed by him by saying that it is the name OF an *A*); he also uses the very same example, of the count noun "nationality", that I used. Naturally, there is also a great deal in Noonan's thesis on matters not discussed here. I hope it is clear that in this essay I have attempted no comprehensive treatment of the topic of relative identity; my aim has been solely to answer the question embodied in the title, and the corresponding question for natural language.

---

[8] Ph. D. thesis, Cambridge University, 1977. Pub. in book form with the same title (The Hague, 1980).
[9] (Oxford, 1977).

14

Could there be Unicorns?

The earliest investigations into sentential logic, including non-classical logics, used the notion of what was originally called a 'matrix', and we may call a 'valuation system', particularly for proving independence of axioms in an axiomatic formalization. This generalized the two-valued system by admitting more than two truth-values, and distinguishing them as 'designated' or 'undesignated'; when operations on these truth-values corresponding to the logical constants had been specified, a valid formula was one obtaining a designated value for every assignment of truth-values to its sentence-letters. This was a very clumsy tool of investigation, and was capable of improvement in two ways. On the one hand, the distinction between designated and undesignated values could be replaced by a binary relation between values, in terms of which the relation of entailment could be defined between a set of formulas and a formula, or, more generally, between one set of formulas and another; a valid formula then became one entailed by the null set. This does not concern us here: an improvement that preceded it was to treat the 'values' as sets of points in an underlying space. This worked extremely well for intuitionistic logic, but was even more natural for the usual modal logics. For these were standardly assumed to be classical with respect to the ordinary logical constants "not", "and", "or", and "if"; only the modal operators "possibly" and "necessarily" functioned non-classically. A valuation system for such a modal logic was therefore virtually forced to be a Boolean algebra, with the Boolean operations of complementation, intersection, and union corresponding to "not", "and", and "or"; only the algebraic operations corresponding to the modal operators were non-Boolean. Since a Boolean algebra is always isomorphic to a field of subsets of some underlying set, the transformation of such a valuation system into one in which the value of a sentence-letter or formula was a subset of points in an underlying space was very straightforward.

Such a representation made it possible to view the fundamental notion, not as that of a value possessed by a formula (relatively to an assignment to the sentence-letters), but as that of its being true or not being true *at* any given point of the space. Its value was the set of all points at which it was true; but

Revised version of 'Könnte es Einhörner geben?', *Conceptus*, 17, (1983), 5–10. Not previously published in English.

this fell away as a subsidiary notion. The generalization of the two classical truth-values to many was thus replaced by a *relativization* of them to the points of the space. Since, for the modal logics, the ordinary operators were interpreted as Boolean, the truth or falsity at a point of a formula whose principal operator was not a modal one depended only on the truth or falsity at *that* point of its immediate subformulas. The same could not hold for one whose principal operator was a modal one: its truth or falsity at that point had to depend on the truth or falsity of its immediate subformula at *other* points.

The replacement of systems of many truth-values by a relativization of the usual two truth-values to the points of a space had great advantages for the logician. The underlying space was, in general, and, in the finite case, always, much smaller than the system of values representable as subsets of it, and its structure (when it had one) much more perspicuous: it was, to take intuitionistic logic as an example, much simpler to handle a partially ordered set with a topology on it than a lattice of points corresponding to its open subsets. Moreover, these systems of relativized truth-values lent themselves much more readily to interpretation as supplying a semantics for the logic in question—as opposed to a mere algebraic characterization—than had the valuation systems with many truth-values. Thus, in the case of the modal logics, the points of the space could be understood as possible worlds, in accordance with the old idea of Leibniz: to speak of a formula as being true (under a given interpretation) at a point was to speak of it as being true in the corresponding possible world. Subsequently, this idea, which had proved so fruitful in logic, was revived by philosophers, largely through Saul Kripke's influence, for use in discussing modality as it figures in natural language.

This development seems at first sight unsurprising; there was something paradoxical about it, all the same. For the idea of adapting the Leibnizian notion of possible worlds had already been used for a proof of the completeness of the strongest modal system, S5, before it occurred to anyone to adapt it for weaker modal systems, or, indeed, to use relativized truth-values for other non-classical logics. On a Leibnizian understanding, "Possibly *A*" is true just in case "*A*" is true in *some* possible world, and "Necessarily *A*" just in case "*A*" is true in *every* possible world. This could be used to explain the modal operators in S5: "Possibly *A*" could be understood as being true in any given world just in case "*A*" was true in some possible world, and "Necessarily *A*" as being true in any given world just in case "*A*" was true in every possible world. No structure need be put on the underlying space of possible worlds: each world was to be considered as possible absolutely.

For weaker modal logics, the space of possible worlds needed a structure: indeed, as far as modal logic is concerned, the discovery could be expressed as being that, with a suitable structure imposed on that space, the Leibnizian idea would work for all modal logics. Suppose we are given a valuation system ('matrix') of the old-fashioned kind, with eight values, for demonstrating the unprovability in S4 of some formula valid in S5. We interpret the system in the usual way as a Boolean algebra, consisting of all subsets of a set of three elements, that is, of a space of three possible worlds. If we treat each of these worlds as possible relatively to both the other two (and to itself), we shall not obtain the original 'truth-tables' for the modal operators; but we shall do so if we lay down that a world y is to be considered possible relatively to a world x just in case, whenever "p" is true at y, "Possibly p" is true at x. (Alternatively, that "Necessarily p" is true at x only when "p" is true at y.) This allows us to specify that "Possibly A" is true in any given world just in case "A" is true in some world possible relatively to it, and that "Necessarily A" is true in a given world just in case "A" is true in every world that is possible relatively to it. The truth or falsity in a particular world x, under a given assignment, of a formula whose principal operator is modal will then depend only on the truth or falsity of its immediate subformula in worlds accessible to x (that is, possible relatively to it). In this way, every modal logic can be characterized in terms of the restrictions placed on the relation of accessibility (of relative possibility).

The *logical* discovery, as regards modal logics, was thus that the Leibnizian conception can be extended to logics weaker than S5 by means of a structure imposed on the space of possible worlds by an accessibility relation defined on it; the use of the Leibnizian conception to characterize S5 was already known. By contrast, the philosophical applications, to analyse modality as involved in sentences of natural language, have treated as fruitful only the type of possible-worlds structure that characterizes S5. In these, the accessibility relation is essentially superfluous: since accessibility is required to be an equivalence relation, we need never consider more than one equivalence class, within which every world is possible relatively to every other. Thus the idea that represented an advance in studying the formal properties of modal logics was not that which was eagerly taken up by philosophers; that was, rather, one that had been known to logicians for a little time.

How can the relation of relative possibility fail to be an equivalence relation? This may hold because what constitutes a possible state of affairs depends on how things in fact are; by extension, what, in some possible world, constitutes a possible state of affairs will depend on how things are in that world. If so, it may be hypothesized that a certain state of affairs T is possible only if another state of affairs S obtains. Suppose first that S does not in fact obtain, but is possible. Then there is a possible world u (possible relatively to the actual world) in which S obtains. In u, T will be possible, which it is not in the actual world: it will follow that the relation of relative possibility is not transitive. Or suppose that both S and T in fact obtain, but that S does not obtain in a certain world v, possible relatively to the actual world. Then the actual world is *not* possible relatively to the world v, since T holds in the actual world. It follows that the relation of relative possibility will not in these circumstances be symmetrical. So far as I know, however, no intuitively plausible example of a failure of the accessibility relation to be both transitive and symmetrical has ever been proposed. I aim in this essay to suggest one.

2

At the beginning of 'Naming and Necessity', Kripke remarks that he does not believe that there might have been unicorns; the matter is further referred to in a discussion printed in *Synthese*,[1] at the end of which Quine remarked, "We'll never know whether Michael agrees"; I shall, in what follows, falsify this prediction. "Unicorn" is, of course, exceptional among terms for mythical beasts in applying to a biologically possible animal; centaurs, by contrast, are six-limbed vertebrates. What grounds can be given for Kripke's contention that it is not metaphysically possible?

To say that there could not have been any unicorns obviously presupposes that there are in fact none. How do we know that there are no unicorns? Admittedly, the surface of the globe has been pretty well explored; but new species certainly turn up. For all we know, there may be, in some inaccessible place, animals resembling the unicorns depicted in paintings, on tapestries, and in heraldry. If we found them, we should almost certainly say, "There are unicorns, after all". Should we be right to call such creatures 'unicorns'? This question is crucial: for, plainly, if we *should* be right to call them 'unicorns', it will follow that there might be unicorns; indeed, that there may actually be some. What grounds, then, can be given for saying that there could not have been any unicorns, or, more precisely, that, if there are in fact no unicorns, then it is not the case that there might have been?

If the term "unicorn" had a purely descriptive content, so that it simply *meant* 'animal resembling the unicorns of the pictures', there would be no room for argument about the matter; such beasts might very well exist or have existed. But the word is, or, rather, purports to be what philosophers call a 'species term', which means that if it applies to anything at all, it applies exclusively to animals of some one species, genus or family (or, possibly, order). Given that there are no unicorns, "unicorn" is a mock or spurious species term, as "Sherlock Holmes" is a mock personal proper name, and "Hermes Trismegistus" a spurious one. If there were unicorns, it would be a genuine species term; anyone who thinks that there might have been unicorns must rank it as a putative species term. Kripke has promoted a vogue for speaking of 'natural kinds', a term taken as covering both chemical substances and animal and plant species. The term is, in my view, unfortunate, since these are rather different types of thing, and the words used for them behave differently. Perhaps prompted by the classification of both under the

---

[1] *Synthese*, 27 (1974), 509–12.

same head of 'natural kinds', what Kripke stresses about animal species is that membership of a single species (or genus, etc.) requires identity or similarity of internal structure. In my view, what matters is genetic affinity—a common descent: internal structure is merely a reliable clue to this, rather than a separate criterion. If there were creatures on Mars resembling terrestrial tigers in external appearance *and* internal structure, they would still not be tigers unless they were descended from terrestrial ones, or conversely.

It remains that what primarily makes it a matter for debate whether there could be unicorns is that "unicorn" purports to be a species term and yet gives no clue to anything but the external appearance of the animals; neither their biological affinities nor their internal structure are specified by it. It would be possible to invent a term for a hypothetical species having a precise taxonomic and evolutionary location, and so with a determinate internal anatomy. On some views, if there were in fact no such species, it would *still* be proper to deny that there could have been animals of that species. On other views, it would not, although it would be right to deny the possibility of unicorns. In any case, the two questions would have a very different character.

We can distinguish three possible theories about species terms that yield arguments to show that, given that there are no unicorns, and never have been, it is not true that there might have been any. All three are based on the fact that, if there were unicorns, "unicorn" would be a species term like "tiger". The second and third are variants of one another; but the first is quite distinct. It appeals to an alleged analogy between species terms and proper names of individuals and places; in doing so, it relies upon a doctrine which makes the original introduction of a proper name decisive for its reference. By contrast, the second and third arguments pay no attention to the manner in which the term "unicorn" was introduced, but turn solely upon conditions for the application of a species term, independently of how it was introduced into the language.

The first argument may indeed be combined with the second or third, but they are intrinsically independent. To recognize that species terms differ from those with a purely descriptive content like "marine animal" in no way entails any doctrine about the reference of proper names or any assimilation of species terms into the category of proper names. The only connection is that the assimilation is made on the strength of a species term's being one for a 'natural kind', since plainly a term with a purely descriptive content could not be compared to a proper name without emptying the expression "proper name" of meaning. Now in such a use as "The mountain gorilla is rapidly becoming extinct", a case may evidently be made for taking "the mountain gorilla" to be functioning as the proper name of a species. In a sentence like "I have never seen a mountain gorilla", on the other hand, the phrase "mountain gorilla" is equally evidently not a proper name, but a common noun-phrase. The thesis underlying the first argument is that, even in such uses, a species term inherits some of the special features of proper names. That is the *only* bearing that the fact that "unicorn" purports to be a species term has on the first argument; conversely, its resemblance, if any, to a proper name is quite irrelevant to the second and third arguments.

3

Argument (1). The first argument appeals to the *origin* of the term "unicorn". Species terms, the argument runs, form a subclass of the more general class of terms for natural kinds, which also include mass terms like "water" and "gold" for chemical substances. Terms for natural kinds essentially resemble proper names of persons and of places, it continues, in that their reference depends upon the reference they were intended to have when they, or their ancestors, were first introduced.

According to this theory, a proper name, in a given use, is tied to the manner of its introduction. How its reference is determined when it is first introduced is left somewhat hazy; but once introduced, to use it in the same way is to use it with the intention that it have the same reference, and it *will* then have the same reference, despite any false beliefs the speaker may have concerning its bearer, or his lack of any beliefs.

The theory must be modified to allow an exception for an inadvertent shift of reference, as in Gareth Evans's compelling example of "Madagascar", unintentionally transferred to the island from a part of the mainland. Such a shift can occur only if the object to which the name is transferred is accessible—can be observed or visited, or at least is one to which we already have some means of referring. In such a case, the use of the name may perhaps be said to have remained constant, since the speakers intended to use it with the same reference as before; but it should be allowed that the *sense* has altered.

It is not to the present purpose to discuss this theory, in its original or modified form: what concern us are cases in which the name will have had no bearer when it was first introduced. There are two kinds of such case. The first is that of a proper name, say "Guy Pringle" in Olivia Manning's novels, introduced as that of a fictional character. Having been introduced in this way, it remains the name of a fictional character. No one you could meet, however similar his characteristics and life history to that of the character in the novels, could *be* Guy Pringle; and therefore it is not true that there *might have been* such a person as Guy Pringle. This continues to apply, according to the argument, even if a mistake is later made, and the name "Guy Pringle" comes to be taken as that of a genuine individual, and has, for some time, been used exclusively as such. We are then under the illusion that there was such a person as Guy Pringle, or, more exactly, that there was a person to whom the name "Guy Pringle" referred. But, given that the name was introduced (in this use) as in fact it was, and that it continues to be used in the same sense, there are no conceivable circumstances which would render any actual person its bearer, since there could be nothing that constituted the name's referring to that person. It is therefore not true that Guy Pringle *could have been* a real person.

This conclusion is surely correct. In the usual case, anyone who knows the name will be well aware that it is the name of a fictional character, and can therefore use it in the same sense only as the name of a fictional character: it would be as meaningless to suppose that it could, *in that sense*, have named a real person as to suppose of a real person that he could have been a purely fictional character. Once it has been generally forgotten that the name was introduced as that of a character in fiction, the question arises how speakers take its reference as being determined. If they think of it as referring to a real person answering to a certain description, and would in no way be deterred from that understanding of it by learning that it had originally been used for a character in a story, they have certainly altered its original sense; and that is the only condition under which it will be admissible to say that there was, or at least could have been, such a person.

The other case in which the name lacked a bearer when first introduced is that of a mistake made at the outset. The reference of the name may have been fixed by a definite description, wrongly thought to have application; or it may have been introduced ostensively on the basis of a mistaken observation. The same will then hold good as before, on this theory. The original mistake will continue to deprive the name of reference, provided that its sense remains unaltered; and it therefore *could* not have had a reference.

This argument is less strong. Consider a name which everyone in fact believes to have a reference, say "Charlotte Corday"; and suppose, for present purposes, that there actually was no such person, and that the story of Marat's assassination is spurious. Then our use of the name is founded upon a mistaken belief; but, still, that belief might have been correct, and then the name *would* have had a reference. It is the same with most empty definite descriptions or mistaken observations: there might have been something answering to the description; the observation might not have been erroneous. If a proper name had been introduced on the basis of such a mistake, we cannot say that it *could not have had* a bearer. Admittedly, in our hypothetical case, it would make no sense to say that *that person*, Charlotte Corday, might or could have existed; but we could properly say that there might have been *such a woman as* Charlotte Corday.

4

According to this first argument, the same goes for the term "unicorn". If it, or, rather, the ancestor of the term, was introduced with serious intent by someone who had glimpsed some real creatures (say a species of rhinoceros), then, however unlike the unicorns of the pictures may be to the animals he saw, it is *they* that would rightly be called 'unicorns'. In this case, it is not merely that there might have been unicorns; there actually are, or, at least, once were, unicorns. If, on the other hand, the term, or its ancestor, was originally introduced as a piece of deliberate romancing, then, even though the mistake was later made of misinterpreting romance for factual narrative, and later yet the original romance was forgotten, it can never be correctly applied to any actual creature, no matter how much it resembles the unicorns of the pictures. It follows that, in that case, there could not be, and could never have been, any unicorns. The third possibility is that the term was introduced with the serious intention of applying it to real animals, but on the basis of some garbled travellers' tales. In this case, too, the existence of unicorns would not be a possibility, on this theory: an analogy would hold with a proper name allotted to an individual or place falsely believed to exist.

Any thesis about the meaning or reference of a word must draw its substance from how we use it or should use it in hypothetical circumstances. There is no possibility of a statement's failing to be true, in virtue of some fact, if all speakers of the language would agree that that fact did not invalidate its claim to be true. The present argument does not rest on what we should actually say. If, in some inaccessible part of the world, we found animals resembling the unicorns of the pictures, we should surely call them 'unicorns'; perhaps we should say, "So there are unicorns, after all". If we did, this would not of itself invalidate the argument from the origin of the term; for it might be that, in saying this, we should be using the word "unicorn" in a sense different from that it had originally had. What the proponent of the argument needs to make out is that such a change *has not yet taken place*. He is not in a very strong position in maintaining this, precisely because it is *now* clear to us that we should apply the term "unicorn" to such creatures, if they were discovered; but he can plead that a foreseen change may nevertheless be a change.

The criterion by which such a theory is to be judged is its accord with our actual linguistic practice. Does the theory that lays central emphasis upon the origin of a putative term for a natural kind give an accurate account of our linguistic practice in using such a term? In one direction, it plainly does not. However compelling the evidence might be that the term "unicorn" was originally introduced on the basis of a momentary glimpse of a rhinoceros, we should not be led by it to apply the term, save jocularly, to a rhinoceros, or to reclassify the word "unicorn" as one for a real, rather than a legendary, animal: the contribution of the traditional depictions and descriptions of unicorns to the way we use the word is greater than that. This case should therefore be classified with that in which the term "unicorn" was introduced on the basis of a mistake of observation.

Concerning the other direction, it is more difficult to decide, since the discovery of animals closely resembling those illustrated in the pictures would incline us to suppose that the word had, after all, been introduced by someone who had seen one. We have to suppose that evidence was produced to the contrary, to the effect either that the originator of the term was overtly engaged in romancing, or that he was serious but deceived by false reports. We should be reluctant to accept so amazing a coincidence; but what if the evidence was irrefutable? There still remains no question how we should in fact speak in this situation. We should certainly still call the newly discovered creatures 'unicorns'; the only question is whether, by so doing, we should be conferring a new sense on the word.

Without doubt, what is phonetically and orthographically the same word may be used in different senses, sometimes related, sometimes unrelated. When the word is capable of being applied in both senses to the same thing in the same circumstances, so that it can be asked in which of the two senses it is being so applied, the distinction between those senses is mandatory and will be acknowledged by any competent speaker. But when the senses are related, although the word cannot be applied to the same thing in both senses, or cannot be so applied in the same circumstances, no ambiguity can arise, and it is therefore unnecessary for speakers of the language to be conscious of the distinction. In any such case, an element of theorizing is always involved in distinguishing them as *two* senses. There is often, indeed, a point in making such a distinction: for instance, when it is plausible that one of the two senses could be grasped without grasping the other, but not conversely. (It cannot be explained what it is for a person to be generous without first explaining what it is for an action to be generous.)

When it is not necessary for a speaker to be aware of the distinction between the two senses, a theory which does not require that distinction to be made is normally to be preferred, on grounds of simplicity, to one which does; especially is this so when it would be difficult to persuade an ordinary speaker that such a distinction existed. For this reason, the theory that, by calling the newly discovered creatures 'unicorns', we should, if the word had originally been introduced as a fictional term or as the result of a mistake, have changed its sense, has a poorer claim on our acceptance than the theory that, by being guided by the traditional descriptions of unicorns, we should be being faithful to the sense it presently possesses. This does not settle the matter, indeed; it does not refute, but only weakens, the first of the three arguments against the possibility of unicorns.

Roland is a character of romance, but not a *mere* character of romance: the name "Roland" at least purports to name a historical figure. It also purports to be the name he bore in his lifetime; but let us suppose it known, instead, that it was subsequently introduced to refer to someone whose acts were believed to be remembered, but whose name forgotten. As we saw, if historical research then established that there was no one to whom such acts could be credited, we could not say that, though Roland did not exist, he might have done, since "Roland" would not refer to anyone; but we could properly say that there could have been such a man as Roland. In the same way, if the word "unicorn" were proved to have been introduced mistakenly but seriously, we could not say that the species unicorn could have existed. But we *could* say (at least as far as the present argument goes) that unicorns could have existed: as "the species unicorn" is a singular term that behaves in many ways like the personal name "Roland", so "unicorn" is a general term more comparable to the phrase "such a man as Roland".

This leaves us only with the case in which "unicorn" was originally used as a piece of conscious romancing, without any intention of taking it to apply to any actual creatures. To allow, in this case, that there could be unicorns is to treat the word "unicorn" as behaving very differently from the name "Guy Pringle". Why should it do so? The analogy between proper names and everyday (rather than scientific) names of species is very far from perfect. A person, other than an infant, already has a name: we should not call him by the name of a fictional character unless that *was* his name; if it was, and he tallied in other respects with what was told of that character, we should doubt whether the character was, after all, fictional. A fictional place—an island, say—would offer a better analogy to a fictional species; but even places have to be *given* a name. It might be natural to give an island the name of a fictional one, if the correspondence was very close; but, since it had to be *decided* what the island was to be called, no one would suppose that the use of that name for the newly discovered island was a mere continuation of its use for the fictional one.

More importantly, it is rare for us not to know whether a personal name or place-name is fictional or not. By contrast, while it is fairly well known that many in the Middle Ages believed that there really were such animals as unicorns, few people know whether the term was first introduced as a fictional one, as a result of a glimpse of some real creatures, or in consequence of some misunderstanding of travellers' tales or of invention by the travellers; I certainly do not. The word "unicorn" is therefore quite unlike "Sherlock Holmes", which everyone knows to have been invented as the name of a character in stories. The fictional origin either of a proper name or of a general term undoubtedly affects the use that we make of it, and thus its sense; but only when it is *known* that its origin was fictional. Even for a personal name, we do not hold ourselves responsible to the intentions of whoever introduced it if its origin is no more than conjectural. Whatever those intentions may have been, the name may, in the course of time, have been *attached* to a particular individual, regardless of the name by which he was known during his life. This would be a shift of reference from a fictional to a real person, and would involve a change of sense even if we were unaware that such a shift had occurred. In other cases, we may take what was originally a fictional name to be, or purport to be, that of a real person; if there is or was in fact no actual person identifiable as its bearer, we have once more a use of a name founded upon a mistake. The question whether there was such a man as Hermes Trismegistus, for example, is not the question whether the name has come down to us from a man called "Hermes" (or "Thoth") in his lifetime, nor yet whether the first person to speak of Hermes Trismegistus was consciously romancing or was referring to some real individual, but whether there was an ancient sage to whom that name at some stage became attached.

The disanalogy between species terms and proper names is thus not so great after all, once we compare cases of both in which the origin is unknown. Even if the word "unicorn" originated as deliberately fictional, the fact is not generally known, and perhaps will forever be unknown to anyone. There is therefore no reason why it may not have been subject to an unwitting change of sense, from being regarded as intrinsically fictional in view of its known fictional origin to being treated as having an application determined by its descriptive content. It is surely more plausible to explain the fact that, if we encountered animals resembling the unicorns of the pictures, we should call them 'unicorns', by supposing that a shift in its sense *had already taken place* before the encounter than by the hypothesis that that encounter would foreseeably prompt us to change the sense the term now has for us. We are not yet in a position to say for sure that this may hold for the term "unicorn", since we have so far examined only the first of the three arguments against this supposition; but that argument has proved to do nothing to rule it out.

5

What we have, in fact, been discussing is the proposition that there may be unicorns. I have argued, not yet that there may be, but that the theory that the origin of a species term is integral to its meaning fails to show that there cannot be. Our question was, however, whether, granted that there are no unicorns, and never have been any, there *might* nevertheless have been some. We accepted a swift transition from the proposition that there *can be none* to the proposition that there *could not have been any*; we ought now to scrutinize this more closely. The transition was effected, for the case of proper names, as follows:

No one you could meet . . . could *be* Guy Pringle; and therefore it is not true that there *might have been* such a person as Guy Pringle.

Is the transition justified?

The difference between "There may have been such a person as Sherlock Holmes" and "There might have been such a person as Sherlock Holmes", or, at least, the only difference we need consider, is that "might" is counterfactual in character, whereas "may" always carries the proviso "given all that we know". "There may be unicorns" means that it is possible that all we know should hold good, and there be creatures that would rightly be said to be unicorns. "There might have been unicorns", on the other hand, means that it is possible that things should have been otherwise than we know them to be, and that there should then have been creatures that would rightly have been said to be unicorns. No difference in the *kind* of possibility involved is relevant in this context. Kripke distinguishes between epistemic and metaphysical possibility, and is disposed to see "may" as relating to the former and "might" to the latter. The distinction arises, according to him, because a thing's essential properties may not be those by means of which we identify it. It is essential to the Evening Star to be identical with the Morning Star, but it is not in that way that we pick out the referent of "the Evening Star"; we used to determine a metre as the length of the standard metre rod, but being the length of that rod was not essential to *that length*, as the fact that we now identify the same length by a different means makes apparent; if it is now 12 noon GMT, it is essential to the present moment that it is 12 noon GMT, but it is not by looking at our watches that we decide that something is happening *now*. In none of these cases does the question of error in our identifications arise. It is not, for example, that something, although the same length as the standard metre rod, could be shown nevertheless not to be a metre long, as an animal having the same outward appearance as a tiger could be shown nevertheless not to be a tiger; it is just that the property by reference to which we are identifying the length as one metre is not essential to it.

No such divergence is relevant to the present issue. We are concerned with the conditions, if any, under which it would be correct, by the canons of our existing linguistic practice, to call an animal a 'unicorn'. Our initial identification of the species to which an animal belongs—a tiger, for example—is indeed ordinarily based on outward appearance and behaviour: the sense of a species term always comprises a descriptive content relating to externals. Its being a species term involves that we understand this content as neither necessary nor sufficient for assigning a species to an individual animal. It is not necessary, since there may always be freaks and atypical varieties; it is not sufficient, because, to belong to the species, an animal must be genetically akin to other members, and must therefore resemble them internally as well as externally: an identification of the species by superficial appearance may therefore be overturned on closer inspection.

At first sight, this may seem analogous to the cases of the metre and the Evening Star. We fix the reference of "tiger" by external appearance; but the essential properties of tigers are their genetic affinities and their internal anatomy. But the analogy is lame. The essential properties of a thing, in the relevant sense of the expression, are those which, when we are entertaining hypothetical circumstances, it must be thought of as still having if we are to speak of *it* as figuring in those circumstances. When we describe imaginary conditions as obtaining, we do not lose our grasp on what we are referring to if we imagine the Evening Star as not visible in the evening sky, since we know it to be a planet with a particular position in the solar system, whereas various factors might interfere with its visibility. But, although the typical external appearance of tigers is neither necessary nor sufficient for the assignment of any individual animal to that species, it by no means follows that we should retain our grip on what was being referred to if it were imagined that the species existed, but that that appearance were no longer typical of it. We could do so only to a very limited extent, because, although external appearance does not determine internal anatomy, anatomy goes a long way to determine external appearance. There could doubtless be tigers without stripes, but while in the kingdom of heaven the lion may lie down with the lamb, in the world we live in there could be no herbivorous tigers. Nor could there be tigers lacking a feline carriage or gait, nor yet, though size is a poor indicator of taxonomic relationship, could there be tigers as large as elephants or as small as mice. If we attempt to imagine otherwise, we simply lose the sense of calling the beasts so imagined 'tigers': we might *stipulate* that we were speaking of animals resembling actual tigers in their internal organization, but we could not leave this to be understood merely by employing the word "tiger".

To say that the property by means of which we ordinarily identify some object is not among those essential to it is to say that, in describing hypothetical circumstances, we can retain our grasp of what is being referred to even when we imagine it to lack that identifying property. For us to be able to do so, its having the essential properties it has must be part of our *existing* understanding of the term by which we refer to it. This does not contradict the dictum that essence is to be discovered, perhaps empirically. We must know the *sort* of thing to which the term refers, and thereby the criterion of identity for things of that kind, even if we do not at present know how to apply that criterion: we must know, for instance, that "the Evening Star" refers to a celestial body, even if we do not know whether it is a planet, a star or something else, and have the conception of identifying such a body by its position in the universe. (Those who do not, but conceive of "the Evening Star" merely as denoting a visual object, like, say, "the Aurora", do not as yet understand the term as we do.) Likewise we may know how to identify giant pandas, for example, by their appearance, without knowing their internal structure or place in the evolutionary tree: but we must know that "giant panda" is a species term, and the criterion for belonging to the same species. In hypothetical circumstances, the Evening Star will be the same celestial body as that actually identified by its appearance in the evening sky; giant pandas will be animals of the same species as that we in fact identify by its well-known appearance. There is no place here for mystification about trans-world identity: the same criterion applies here as in other contexts. This shows in our practice, or potential practice, in face of actual change. We are already agreed that, in altered future circumstances, the Evening Star will be the same celestial body as that *now* identified by its appearance in the evening sky; giant pandas will be animals of the same species as that we at present identify by its well-known appearance. Questions about what is called 'metaphysical' possibility are questions about our *existing* criteria for determining reference or application.

There are two questions before us. The first is: Given the way we know the world to be, could there be animals which, if we knew of them, we should rightly call 'unicorns' in accordance with the principles governing the present use of the word? Briefly expressed, may there be unicorns? The second is: In imagining the world to be different from how we know it to be, could we consistently describe it as containing unicorns, conforming thereby to the actual present sense of the word, and relying upon that for the intelligibility of the description? Briefly expressed, could there be unicorns? The first question turns on the requirement made by our existing linguistic practice for identifying any animal as a unicorn, and whether, the world being as we know it to be, that requirement could be met. The second question turns on the very same requirement. In everyday speech, the transition from denying that there may actually have been such a person as Sherlock Holmes to denying that there might have been such a person as Sherlock Holmes would be dubious, since, by using "might have", we indicate that we are prescinding from some of the facts we know to hold; it would normally be allowable to include among these the fictional origin of the name. Clearly, however, such a use of "might have" was not what Kripke had in mind. We may therefore agree that the condition for something to be rightly called a 'unicorn' in hypothetical circumstances must be the same as that for anything we actually encountered to be rightly called a 'unicorn'. The distinction between epistemic and metaphysical possibility thus plays no role in resolving the present problem.

6

Argument (2). The second argument to show that, if there are no unicorns, it is not true that there might have been some, is quite different, and appeals in a more substantial fashion to the fact that "unicorn" is a (putative) species term. The crucial consideration, according to this argument, is whether there are or are not in fact any animals resembling the unicorns of the pictures: if there are such animals, they *are* unicorns, provided that all or most of them are of the same species; but, if there are none, there could be no unicorns. In brief, the argument for this latter conclusion is that, in the absence of any animals we should identify as unicorns if we knew of them, there is no determinate species, actual or hypothetical, to whose members the term "unicorn" could correctly be applied. The underlying assumptions of this argument are these: first, that it is a necessary condition for an animal to belong to a species (genus, etc.) that it share a common descent with other members of that species or genus, and hence have the same anatomical structure as they; and secondly that in the first instance we identify an animal as belonging to a given species by its external appearance and observable behaviour, knowing that there must be a type of anatomical structure distinctive of that species, determining a place for it in the evolutionary tree, but without having to know what, specifically, what place or what structure that is. Thus an animal is identified as, say, a tiger in virtue of its having the characteristic external appearance and behaviour of a tiger; but we shall allow that, for it to have been *correctly* so identified, it must have the same anatomical structure as other creatures so identified, and share a common descent with them.

This second argument allows that, if we do come to discover animals resembling the unicorns of the pictures, we shall be right to call them 'unicorns'. According to it, if there are in fact animals resembling the unicorns of the pictures, and all or most of them in fact belong to a single species, they *are* unicorns; there will then be unicorns in some merely possible worlds, too, although all such possible unicorns will necessarily have the same anatomical structure and position in the evolutionary tree as actual unicorns. If, on the other hand, there are no animals in the actual world resembling the unicorns of the pictures, then not only are there no unicorns, but there *could* not be, since there will be no determinate condition that an animal must satisfy for it to be a unicorn: there will thus be no unicorns in any possible world. Creatures in another possible world will be tigers, on this account, only if *they* have the same ancestry and anatomical structure as the animals we identify by their appearance and behaviour as tigers. On the presumption that there are no creatures we identify as unicorns, or should so identify if we encountered them, there is no condition the satisfaction of which would make an animal in any possible world a unicorn; therefore, since there are no unicorns in the actual world, there are none in any possible world, either. If there are no creatures in the actual world resembling the unicorns of the pictures, there are no unicorns, and it is not true that there might have been; but, if (unknown to us at present) there *are* some such creatures, they are unicorns, and, since there may be such creatures, there may be unicorns.

Argument (2) may be dramatized as follows. Suppose that in some possible world *v* there are animals resembling the unicorns of the pictures. Now the legend of the unicorn in no way determines the anatomical structure of the animals. We may therefore suppose that there are also animals in another possible world *u* resembling the unicorns of the pictures equally closely, but greatly differing from the creatures of world *v* in their skeletal structure and the arrangement and type of their organs. The creatures of the two worlds, *u* and *v*, have quite different biological affinities with other species, and, therefore, different evolutionary origins. Since "unicorn" is intended to be a species term, they cannot both be unicorns, being evidently of unrelated species: since there is nothing to choose between them on the basis of our understanding of the word "unicorn", we must say that neither qualify as unicorns.

The argument is incoherent. Its proponent would like to assert that, if there were animals in the actual world resembling the unicorns of the pictures, and all or most of the same species, they would *be* unicorns; but he cannot do so consistently with his maintaining that, if there are no unicorns in the actual world, there are none in any merely possible world, either. He cannot do so, because to talk about how things would be in the actual world in hypothetical circumstances just is to talk about how they are in certain possible worlds: the terminology of possible worlds was supposed to explicate or regiment our everyday use of subjunctive conditionals and modal auxiliaries like "might" and "could". There nevertheless is something the theorist wishes to assert about the actual world: he can consistently express it only by using an indicative conditional, and saying, "If there are animals, most of them of the same species, that resemble the unicorns of the pictures, they are unicorns". The indicative conditional does not succeed, however, in expressing all that he wishes to say. However sure he feels that there are in fact no animals resembling the unicorns of the pictures, he still wishes to declare that, if there *were*, we should be right to call them 'unicorns' provided that they were of a single species; but he cannot say this without contradicting his stated view that there are no unicorns in possible worlds if there are none in the actual world.

It might be protested that the fact that an indicative conditional is correct does not always guarantee the correctness of the corresponding subjunctive one, even though the indicative conditional can be asserted without knowing whether the antecedent is satisfied. But why does it not? In asserting an indicative conditional, we may properly take into account anything we know or reasonably suppose to be so. In considering grounds for a subjunctive conditional, on the other hand, we have to exclude some such facts: those, namely, that the truth of the antecedent would render impossible or improbable. That is what can justify us in asserting an indicative conditional in a case in which its subjunctive counterpart should be rejected. Nothing of the kind applies in the present example. The theorist's ground for saying that, if we encounter animals of a single species that resemble the unicorns of the pictures, we shall do right to call them 'unicorns', is that he thinks that a species is to be picked out, in the first instance, by its external appearance; and the hypothesis of our encountering such animals in no way affects either the truth or the plausibility of this principle. Argument (2) is thus intrinsically unstable.

Argument (3). The third argument is a variant of the second, intended to escape the inconsistency just noted. According to argument (1), if "There might have been unicorns" is false, so is "There may be unicorns". According to argument (2), by contrast, "There may be unicorns" is unconditionally true, whereas "There might have been unicorns" is false unless unicorns in fact exist. Argument (3) restores the symmetry: it holds that we neither shall nor should ever be right to call any animals 'unicorns'; more modestly, that, if we ever do, we shall not be using the word in its present sense, no matter how closely those animals resemble the unicorns of the pictures.

Argument (3) attempts to escape the inconsistency by making the decisive factor, not the presence or absence of animals resembling the unicorns of the pictures, whether known to us or not, but the existence of animals which we *now* identify as unicorns: since there are none, there is no condition to satisfy which would make an animal a unicorn, and therefore there neither can nor could be any. Does this avoid the inconsistency? It is plainly possible that there should be animals resembling the unicorns of the pictures; there may in fact be. It is also possible both that they should all be of the same species and that we should encounter them. Unless some reason can be given to show that, even in such a case, we should be wrong to call them 'unicorns', the same conclusion will follow as before, namely that in a possible world in which such conditions obtain, there are unicorns. We cannot say, indeed, that such conditions *may* obtain, because we know very well that they do not; but, failing some further ground of objection, we must say that they might obtain. Simply by altering the factor taken to be decisive, therefore, the inconsistency cannot be evaded: such a strategy would work only if the decisive factor were one that *could* not hold.

Argument (3) has thus to be strengthened; how this can be done is best shown by dramatizing it. The result is closely similar to the dramatization of argument (2): it differs in postulating distinct species of unicorn-like animals, not in different possible worlds, but in the *same* one. Suppose that in two inaccessible parts of the globe we were to find animals exactly resembling the unicorns of the pictures in external appearance, but that examination revealed that their anatomical structure was distinctly different, and that they were not merely of different genera, but of different orders. They could not both be unicorns: since there would be no reason to call one species 'unicorns' in preference to the other, it follows that we should be wrong to call either 'unicorns'; more exactly, that, if we did, we should be further determining the sense of the word "unicorn". In practice, if the discovery of one species preceded that of the other by a significant interval, we should be likely to apply the term "unicorn" to whichever we had discovered first.

Arguments (2) and (3) both take it as an necessary condition for an animal to belong to a species that it have the anatomical structure common to members of that species. Both agree that, to identify an animal as belonging to a particular species, we do not have to know the anatomical structure distinctive of that species. For both, there can be unicorns in other possible worlds only if there are unicorns in this one. Their conclusions differ, however: argument (2) merely yields the conclusion that it is not true that there might have been unicorns, while allowing that there may be some, while argument (3) involves denying that there may be. The reason for the difference lies in a disagreement about the condition to be satisfied for there to be unicorns in the actual world. For the theory underlying argument (2), it is enough that there be animals which, if we discovered them, it would be natural for us to call 'unicorns'; for that underlying argument (3), it is required that there be actual animals to which we *already* give the name "unicorns".

According to argument (3), what matters about the word "unicorn", as we now have it, is the fact that there is nothing to which we actually apply it. For a term to denote an actual or possible species, it is not required that we should know the anatomical structure characteristic of the species; but it is required that that anatomical structure be determinate. It can be determinate only if there are some actual animals to which we apply the term (all or almost all of them of the same species). It is the fact that there are no actual animals we call 'unicorns' that rules it out, not merely that, although there are no unicorns, there might have been, but that there may in fact be some.

What argument (3) shows, in the form in which it was stated above, is that, if there are two unrelated species, both resembling the unicorns of the pictures in external appearance, the members of neither can rightly be called 'unicorns' without changing the existing sense of that word. It does not follow that, if there were in fact only one such species, its members could not rightly be called 'unicorns' without changing the sense of the word: to reach this conclusion, a further premiss is needed. This would have to be that if, in accordance with the sense that it now bears, a term like "unicorn" applies to a given object, it must do so independently of the existence or non-existence of anything that played no part in that object's coming into being. This additional premiss enables us to infer that it would never be in accordance with the present sense of the word "unicorn" to apply it to the members of any species if there was so much as a possibility of there being some unrelated species whose members could with equal right have come to be called 'unicorns'. Since the possibility cannot be excluded, it follows that there are not, could never have been and could never be any such creatures as unicorns in the present sense of the word.

The additional premiss is unjustified. There may be two equally good claimants to be the referent of a definite description: if so, neither has a valid claim. But if either claimant had existed without the other, its claim would have been valid: for the definite description to have a referent, it is not required that it be impossible, but only that it be false, that more than one claimant should exist. Matters are no different for proper names or for species terms. There may be two individuals with equally good claims to be the bearer of a personal proper name. For instance, a detective agency has a collection of photographs which they take to be of someone involved in a case, and, not knowing the man's real name, use for convenience a nickname of their own invention. But, unknown to the agency, the photographs may in fact depict two separate people (say identical twins). The same may happen with a historical individual: two saints with the same name may become confused, and their life stories intertwined. When there are two equally good claimants to be the bearer, there is no bearer; but if either of the two had existed, and the other not, that one would have unambiguously been the bearer of the name. Likewise, we may agree that, if there were two unrelated species equally resembling the unicorns of the pictures in outward appearance, neither would *be* unicorns, but deny that, simply because that is a *possibility*, if there were only one species looking like that, its members would still fail to have a just claim to be what we call 'unicorns'.

8

The upshot of our discussion is, then, that there *might* be unicorns, and, indeed, just possibly may be. There would be unicorns if there were a single species or genus of animals resembling the unicorns of the pictures. Let us assume, however, that there is not in fact any such species or genus: there are no unicorns. The pictures and verbal descriptions of unicorns do not suffice to determine what their biological affinities would be, if there were any. They might, for instance, be of the order Artiodactyla, like deer, or of the order Perissodactyla, like horses. In the language of possible worlds, there are no unicorns in the actual world w, but there is a possible world u in which there are unicorns, which belong to the order Artiodactyla, and another possible world v in which there are also unicorns, which in that world belong to the order Perissodactyla. How can this be reconciled with argument (2)? In world u, any animal, to be a unicorn, must have the same anatomical structure as the unicorns in u, and hence, in particular, must belong to the order Artiodactyla. It follows that the world v is not possible relatively to u, and, conversely, that u is not possible relatively to v. How about the actual world w—is that possible relatively to either u or v? It would at first seem so, since the principal difference we have stipulated is that there are no unicorns at all in w. But u is a world in which it holds good that unicorns are necessarily of the order Artiodactyla, whereas in w it is possible for unicorns to be of the order Perissodactyla. Since a proposition necessarily true in u is possibly false in w, w cannot be possible relatively to u, although u is possible relatively to w. The relation of relative possibility (accessibility) is therefore not symmetrical. That is not to say that it is not possible in *u* that there should be no unicorns. There will be a world *s*, possible relatively to *u*, in which there are no unicorns, and likewise a world *t*, possible relatively to *v*, in which there are again no unicorns.

What we need to accommodate the relations between these various modal statements is the modal logic S4: in a possible-worlds structure for S4, the relation of accessibility is transitive but not symmetrical. The accessibility relations between the five worlds we have mentioned are as shown in the following diagram:

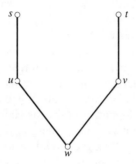

We may suppose that the differences between the worlds are just those mentioned: that *u* and *v* are exactly like *w* save for containing unicorns of their respective types, while in *s* and *t* all non-modal propositions hold good that hold good in the actual world. They differ from *w*, however, in respect of the modal propositions true in them. In *s* it is true to say that, if there were unicorns, they would be of the order Artiodactyla, and in *t* that, if there were unicorns, they would be of the order Perissodactyla, whereas, in *w*, it holds that unicorns, if there were any, might be of either order. In an S4 semantics, worlds can differ in respect of the truth relatively to them of modal propositions alone.

How, then, can the inhabitants of *s* *know* that unicorns, if there had been any, would have belonged to the order Artiodactyla? If all non-modal facts that hold in *w* hold in *s*, they cannot know without direct insight into modal truths; if all knowledge of modal truths is based on knowledge of non-modal ones, they cannot know at all. So if there are no unknowable truths, or if modal truth is always supervenient upon non-modal truth, S4 cannot be the correct logic for modality. This may partly explain why relativization of the accessibility relation has failed to attract philosophers.

To this there is an answer: namely that it is only in the *actual* world that modal truths are supervenient on non-modal ones. The equation of a possible world with a way that the (actual) world might be is wrong: the world *s* in the foregoing diagram is not a way the world might be, but a way we should allow that the world might be if the world were as it is in *u*. This answer gives a distinguished place, *sub specie aeternitatis*, to the actual world. According to

David Lewis's modal realism, by contrast, "actually" is just an indexical adverb like "here". For God, there is no distinction between the actual world and other possible worlds: all are equally actual for him, just as every place is present for him. But an S4 logic cannot sustain this conception: the actual world is, in itself, special, not just from our point of view. A possible world like *s* is no more than a construction. It is a construction we make in considering which statements, modal and non-modal, would hold good in such a world as *u*, and hence which modal statements will in fact hold good. That *s* is not really 'a way the world might be', but, rather, 'a way the world might be considered to be if things were different in a certain respect', might arguably be taken as showing that the accessibility relation should not, after all, be taken to be transitive; we should then have to adopt the modal logic T, rather than S4. This is not the place to argue this delicate point, however. What is clear is that, if our space of possible worlds has *no* structure, as in a semantics for S5, then, from the standpoint of the semantics, all possible worlds are on the same footing; it then becomes difficult to resist the claim that all are equally real. But, when that space is given some structure, the actual world occupies a distinguished position; and then the modal realism which most people find intuitively absurd becomes untenable.

15

Causal Loops

1

I was originally asked by the organizer of this series to give a talk about the direction of causality. After I had accepted, he later rang me up and asked me to put something in about time travel, as it figures in science-fiction stories; so I gained the impression that my talk was intended to offer a little light entertainment to round off the series.

Let us begin, then, with what I presume is the first of the time-travel stories, H. G. Wells's *Time Machine*. Most of the book is taken up with the time traveller's experiences in the very remote future; but it opens with a meeting between him and a friend to whom he tries to explain his invention of a device for travelling in time. Time, he says, is just another dimension, like the spatial ones; after all, what lacked all duration simply would not exist. He then demonstrates time travel with a miniature time machine that he has constructed, in all but size just like that in which he proposes to travel. He sets it on the table, adjusts the controls for it to travel into the future, and switches it on: its appearance becomes blurred for a second, and then it vanishes. Where has it gone? Into the future. Since it has no occupant to bring it to a halt or reverse it, it will never be seen again.

Suppose you are the time traveller's friend, and that this has just happened. The time machine has incontestably disappeared: but has it really gone into the future? It is 6 p.m. on Friday. If the time machine has gone to tomorrow, Saturday, even though only passing through, it should be there tomorrow. But it is not, and the time traveller does not expect it to be. What, then, does it *mean* to say that it travelled into the future, if it is not there when the future comes? Of course, the reason why we are supposed to be unsurprised at not finding it there tomorrow is that we think that, by then, it is far ahead of us. We are playing the tortoise to the time machine's Achilles (in a race in which they start from the same point). When the tortoise reaches the 100-yard post, he should not expect to see Achilles there: he passed it long ago, and is at the 1,000-yard post by then. The picture to which Wells is surreptitiously appealing is that of a fourth dimension along which we are already travelling at a certain rate, namely an hour per hour: the time machine simply goes much faster, say at a day per hour. On this picture, any given location along this fourth dimension

First published in Raymond Flood and Michael Lockwood (eds.), *The Nature of Time* (Oxford, 1986).

will be in a certain state at any given time, say *now*: so it will make sense to say, at 7 p.m. on Friday, that the model time machine has *now* reached 6 p.m. on Saturday, and, at 6 p.m. on Saturday, that it is *now* more than three weeks ahead. Thus at 7 p.m. on Friday—that is to say, when *we* are at 7 p.m. on Friday—it is true of 6 p.m. on Saturday that there is then a model time machine on the table; but, of course, by the time we have reached 6 p.m. on Saturday, it will no longer be true of that time—that location in the fourth dimension—that any such time machine is at that, or any other, place. I need not waste your time exposing the incoherence of this picture. A writer of popular books on time, J. W. Dunne, gained a reputation in the thirties by taking quite seriously the very picture to which Wells was appealing. Observing that time travel involves two kinds of time, that along which the journey is made and that which the journey takes, he thought that the argument must be able to be reiterated, arriving at the conclusion that there must be infinitely many temporal dimensions. It seems at first sight, therefore, that the whole idea of time travel rests on a primitive misrepresentation.

Yet it seems to make sense when we introduce a traveller: is it, then, consciousness that makes the difference? Wells assumes that travel in time is like travel in space, in that, in order to reach a given time, you have to pass through the intervening times. If, then, we agree that, for something which remains in a particular place to pass through any given time, it must be in that place at that time, we must revise our picture of the time traveller's journey into the future. There will be no flickering and disappearing on the part of the time machine: it must remain where it is throughout the interval between his getting into it and his getting out of it in the remote future. The only special feature is that time will pass with immense rapidity for him: at the remote future date at which he switches off the machine, he will have aged only a week or so. It is not just an effect on his consciousness, therefore: all his bodily processes will have been tremendously slowed down. This, from the standpoint of everything else, is the effect of the time machine. Nothing appears unusual about it (save possibly its resistance over long periods to decay): it merely slows down any process taking place within it.

We can now revise the story of the model time machine. Let us suppose there was placed in it a small watch—one of those that show the day of the week as well as the time. When the machine is set going, nothing spectacular happens: it remains where it is. It is only that the watch appears to have stopped: by 6 p.m. on Saturday, it is reading only "7 p.m. Friday".

This may perhaps deserve to be called a 'time machine', but it hardly appears to be a vehicle for *travelling* in time in any but a highly subjective sense. A quite different interpretation is obtained if we allow a jump to occur: if it is set to advance twenty-four hours, the machine, when started at 6 p.m. on Friday, immediately vanishes; it as suddenly reappears in the same place at 6 p.m. on Saturday, the watch it carries being exactly one day slow. Here it is not only what the machine carries that behaves unusually, but the machine itself in relation to its environment, involving a gross discontinuity; possibly the most surprising thing is the displacement of the air molecules in anticipation of its reappearance.

An analogous interpretation of a backward move in time carries greater difficulties. Suppose that the time traveller sets the model machine to jump to twenty-four hours earlier. Then at 6 p.m. on Thursday it must suddenly have appeared on the table: the time traveller and his friend might be able to verify this if a movie camera had been trained on the room since before that time. What, then, happens at 6 p.m. on Friday? There are two cases. In the first, the time traveller starts the machine off, whereupon it promptly disappears. His friend exclaims, "Where's it gone?", looks around, and spots it on the mantelpiece: on examining it, they find that the watch reads five past six, Saturday. The explanation is that, on Friday morning, the cleaning lady came in and removed the machine to the mantelpiece in order to polish the table. As a variation on this, we may suppose that, when the time traveller and his friend entered the room, they found such a machine already on the table. The time traveller puts his machine close beside it, sends it back to Thursday, at which point it vanishes: when his friend asks, "Where's it gone?", he points to the one that has been there all the time, and says, "That is it". In this case, the cleaning lady put it back on the table after polishing, but not exactly in the same place. Whatever the details, the time machine was bilocated during the period from 6 p.m. on Thursday to 6 p.m. on Friday.

The other possibility is that in which no one came into the room during that period. In this case the machine will already be on the table, when the two friends enter the room, and in the exact position from which the time traveller is to set it in action. He must produce his exemplar of the machine from his attaché case, and, having set the controls, hold it over the other exemplar and, at precisely the right moment, press the "On" button and let it fall. To the friend's eye, it will merge with the machine already there. This is puzzling enough; more puzzling is the apparent ability of the time traveller, by choosing to set his machine beside that already present rather than to engage in the delicate operation I have just described, to bring it about that someone or something moved the machine during the preceding twenty-four hours.

Both with the forward and with the backward jump, we are concerned with a causal sequence: the machine carries a watch in order to make the sequence clear. Without such a device, a gap in the existence of an object is, on the face of it, a phenomenon symmetrical with respect to past and future; but we should always prefer to interpret such a gap as a forward than as a backward jump in time, especially if the object reappeared in the place at which it had vanished. This is because we take the career of the object to run in the direction earlier-to-later: its position at the moment of disappearance is explained by its career up to that point, not by anything that happens subsequently, whereas its position at the moment of reappearance requires explanation. Likewise, we shall prefer to interpret a period of bilocation, introduced by the sudden appearance of the object at a new place, and ended by a coalescence of the two exemplars at that place, as a backward jump in time.

Backward movement that traverses the intervening time is even more difficult to envisage. In this case, not only must the physiological processes of the time traveller be slowed down, from the standpoint of the ordinary observer, but they must be reversed: his blood, for instance, must collect oxygen from all over his body and deliver it to his lungs, from where he expels it through his nose or mouth. A visitor from the future—say from 2085—will make an abrupt appearance in his time machine; more exactly, two exemplars of the machine must appear side by side simultaneously. From one of them the visitor steps out leaving within the other a similacrum of himself whose bodily processes are slowed down and reversed in the way described: provided that no one tampers with its controls, the machine from which he stepped henceforward behaves in an unsurprising way, and, if carefully preserved, may survive intact (say in a museum) until 2085. If we suppose that the visitor does not return to the time from which he came, he (the exemplar not in the machine) will die in, say, 2020, having been born in, say, 2045. From the latter date onwards, therefore, there will again be two exemplars of him; the younger of them constructs the time machine and positions it. Note that he cannot leave it standing for any length of time and then climb in and switch it on, since it would then have been in the way of itself. He has, rather, to set its controls, have it hoisted above the correct position—which is occupied by that one of its other two exemplars which is not in the museum, but contains himself living backwards—climb in, give the signal for it to be dropped, and simultaneously press the "On" button: he and it will then coalesce with their other exemplars and vanish, leaving only the surviving machine in the museum.

2

I now turn to a philosophical argument which you are unlikely to hear propounded by any philosopher. It is, rather, a piece of popular philosophy. This is the fatalist argument to show it to be pointless to attempt to bring about, or to prevent, any future event. One version of this argument relies on the assumption of determinism—the assumption, in conflict with modern physics, that every detail of what will occur at any future time is causally determined by the present state of the universe. I wish, however, to consider, not this, but the crudest version of the fatalist argument, which relies, not on causal predetermination, but simply on truth and falsity. This was frequently applied, during the bombing of London in the Second World War, to being killed by a bomb. So applied, it ran like this. Either your name is written on any given bomb, or it is not. If it is, then you will be killed by that bomb whatever precautions you take. If it is not, you will survive the explosion, whatever precautions you neglect. In the first case, any precautions you take will be fruitless: in the second, they will be redundant: hence it is pointless to take precautions.

Proponents of this argument were not superstitious enough to believe that anyone's name was literally written on a bomb: they employed this figure of speech to mean, "The bomb is going to kill you". The general form of the argument is therefore this. Concerning any future event, either it will take place or it will not. If it is going to take place, any action taken to bring it about will be redundant and any taken to prevent it will be fruitless. If it is not going to take place, any action taken to bring it about will be fruitless and any taken to prevent it redundant. Hence it is always pointless to attempt either to bring about or to prevent any future event.

This fatalist argument is not to be dignified by the name of "paradox". A paradox, in the strict sense, is an apparently cogent argument, based on apparently true premisses, leading to a palpably false conclusion, such as that Achilles cannot overtake the tortoise. In a wider use, the term is applied also to valid arguments, based on true premisses, leading to apparently false, or highly surprising, conclusions: it is in this use that people speak of the paradox of voting. But the fatalist argument is a blatant piece of sophistry: no one would accept this reasoning unless he had a strong motive to believe the conclusion. There is, nevertheless, a good reason not just to dismiss it without further attention, but to try to locate the fallacy exactly.

One attempt would be to deny that statements about the future—statements to the effect that a given event will or will not occur within a given interval—are either true or false. Someone who takes this line may, after a moment's reflection, be willing to grant that they are either-true-or-false, but still deny that they are either: true, or: false. For example, you will either be killed or not be killed by the bomb, but you won't *either* be killed by it *or* survive it. This sounds incoherent. It is an attempt to express an understanding of the connective "or" according to which a disjunction may be true even though neither of the two subsentences is true. W. V. Quine once wrote of this as a "fantasy": but in fact there is no difficulty, for various applications, in constructing a plausible logic which allows it to occur. (The logic of vague statements provides a possible example, quantum logic another.) On the other hand, the idea does not, in my view, yield an effective rebuttal of the fatalist, who will probably win the dispute if his opponent adopts this line. But the principal objection to this strategy is that it is far too heavy for the task in view. It does not expose a fallacy recognizable by all, but invokes a questionable revision of the logical principles we ordinarily accept; and it does so on the basis of the metaphysical idea that the future is, as it were, unavailable to render statements about it true or false. Surely the fatalist's argument was a sophistry uncoverable without wading into the deep waters of metaphysics or the foundations of logic.

A natural alternative attempt consists in saying that it may be precisely the precautions that I take that are responsible for my escaping the bomb: the fatalist cannot therefore be justified in inferring, from the hypothesis that I shall not be killed, that I shall not be killed even if I take no precautions, since otherwise he would be entitled to draw the same conclusion from the assumption that I shall escape death thanks to the precautions I am going to take, and to them alone. Suppose, for instance, that, when I emerge with the rest from the shelter, we find that everyone within a half-mile radius of my house has been killed. I shall then very naturally say, "If I hadn't taken shelter, I should have been killed"; and I mean this to imply that, if anyone had said of me beforehand, "If he does not take shelter, he will be killed", he would have spoken truly. It cannot therefore have been true to say, as the fatalist would have us suppose, that if I had not taken shelter, I should *not* have been killed.

This is much more along the right lines, but it has two defects. First, if accepted, it shows that the fatalist argument must be wrong, which we probably already believed it to be; but it fails to show exactly where it went wrong. Secondly, it leads us into another morass: quite a shallow one, compared to metaphysics and the validity of the law of excluded middle, but a morass all the same. This is the interpretation of "if . . . then . . ." statements: the objector will soon get bogged down in arguments about what they mean and in what circumstances they are true. We shall do better not to call in question the fatalist's principle, according to which the truth of a conditional follows from the assumed truth of its consequent. "If . . . then . . ." certainly can be used in that way, however else it can be used; the fatalist has therefore not yet made a mistake by so using it.

Where, then, do we stand? Let us call the event I want to bring about, surviving the raid in our example, "E", and the action I propose to take, in our case taking refuge in the shelter, "A". The fatalist begins by saying:

> Either E will occur or it will not.

Whatever we think about it, we have agreed not to call this in question. He goes on to say:

> If E does not occur, it will not occur even if you do A.
> If E does occur, it will occur even if you omit to do A.

We have agreed not to object to these statements, either, that is, to interpret "if", as it occurs in them, so that they are true. The fatalist proceeds:

> If E does not occur, A, if you did it, will have been fruitless.
> If E does occur, A, if you did it, will have been redundant.

The first of these two statements can hardly be challenged: if I took shelter, but was nevertheless killed, my taking shelter was fruitless. In general, an action done for a certain purpose, and for that alone, must be fruitless when the purpose is unfulfilled: that is what it *is* for an action to be fruitless. It is otherwise with the fatalist's second claim: an action performed for a purpose that is in fact realized is not thereby redundant. A is redundant, when E occurs, only if E would have occurred even if A had not been performed: this is what the second objector was aiming at. The fatalist has not shown this to be so: he has claimed only that, if E is going to occur, it will occur even if you do not do A. This indicative conditional, being of a kind whose truth is guaranteed by the truth of its consequent, will not support the corresponding subjunctive conditional. The fatalist has in fact made no claim that can be embodied in a subjunctive conditional; and so he has no right to assert that, when E occurs, A, if performed, will be redundant.

This, now, seems a satisfactory refutation of the fatalist argument; and you may therefore be breathing a sigh of relief that we must be going to move on from this tedious sophistry. I am, however, going to try your patience a little longer: I should rather a cleaner refutation. The one just given is messy because it appeals to a subjunctive conditional. Subjunctive conditionals crop up all over the place: all sorts of notions, when we attempt to analyse them, appear to depend upon them. And yet the meaning of a subjunctive conditional is enormously obscure; they have been a thorn in the side of analytic philosophers for many decades. Even more obscure than their meaning is their point: when we have devised some theory to explain their truth-conditions, we are at a loss to explain for what purpose we want to have sentences with those truth-conditions in the language at all. Very important things may hang on them: whether the accused is guilty of murder may depend on whether the deceased would still have died if the accused had not acted as he did. But that is no answer to the question about their point: for, in such a case, we have *given* the subjunctive conditional such a point, and the question is why we should do so.

I should therefore like to be able to state the refutation of the fatalist argument without invoking so opaque though everyday a form of expression. To dwell on this a little, let me recall to you a paradox with which some readers may be familiar. In problem cases, when we are faced with conflicting considerations, it is hard to make up our minds which counterfactual conditionals we should count as true. Moreover, even when we have made up our minds, it is difficult to be sure that the basis on which we decide their truth and falsity is the very same as the basis on which actions are to be judged rational or irrational. Rationality is what the fatalist is talking about: whether it is rational to take precautions or to try to bring something about or prevent it. Now that is very well brought out, it seems to me, by Newcomb's paradox, which I shall here present in a slightly modified version.

Imagine that a rich and eccentric psychologist offers an opportunity for acquiring money to selected individuals. In each case he first interviews the candidate, and then informs him that he has placed equal sums of money in each of two boxes. The candidate is free to choose whether to open only one box or both of them; in either case, he keeps the contents of any box that he has opened. He must, however, make his choice in advance; he cannot first open one box and then decide whether or not to open the other. If the psychologist estimates, on the basis of the interview, that the candidate will choose to open both boxes, he puts £10 in each box; if he estimates that he will choose to open only one, he puts £1,000 in each. Over many trials, the psychologist has never lost more than £1,000 to any one candidate, nor less than £20: he has got it right every time, even with candidates who said in the interview that they would choose to open one, or both, boxes and then, in the event, made the opposite choice. All this is explained to the candidate.

Smith, when his turn comes, argues, "The money is already in the boxes. Whether each contains £10 or £1,000, I shall get twice as much if I choose to open both boxes"; he accordingly does so, and receives £20 in all. Jones says to him, "You were a fool: you should have chosen to open only one box", but Smith replies, "If I had opened only one, I should have got no more than £10". Jones may well retort, "Not at all: if you had opened only one, the psychologist would previously have put £1,000 in each". Now which is right? If the question is, which of their judgements about the truth of the counterfactual conditionals best accords with our established ways of judging such matters, it is arguable that Smith has the better case. If so, all that follows is that he has a more accurate grasp of the existing use of such sentences: it does not show that Jones will be acting foolishly when his turn comes, and he chooses to open only one box, obtaining £1,000. He thinks to himself, "I am free to open both or only one. If I choose to open only one, I shall reduce to zero the probability that I shall receive £2,000, but shall vastly increase the probability that I shall receive at least £1,000, and vastly reduce the probability that I shall receive no more than £20. Since it is in my power to affect the probabilities in this way, it would be irrational of me not to do so". His reasoning does not turn on the truth or otherwise of subjunctive conditionals, but on factors that it is proper to invoke in determining what he has a rational motive to do; and he ends up with £1,000 to prove it. (See the Appendix for a defence of this line of reasoning against an attempted rebuttal by John Mackie.)

Let us, then, return to the fatalist and try to avoid using these subjunctive conditionals in refuting him. One thing is evident concerning subjunctive conditionals, namely that, though distinct in meaning, they are often closely related to the corresponding indicative ones. A subjunctive conditional is often to be counted as true just in case, in different circumstances, an assertion of the corresponding indicative conditional would have been warranted. Thus we have already remarked that, if I later truly say, "If I hadn't taken shelter, I should have been killed", this implies that, if I had earlier said, "If I do not take shelter, I shall be killed", I should have been right. Some kind of converse holds also, but to enquire exactly what would land us back in the morass of trying to explain subjunctive conditionals, which we are anxious to avoid. The fatalist is not, after all, interested in subjunctive conditionals, but is trying to persuade us that it is never reasonable to do anything in order to bring about, or prevent, a subsequent event. He is therefore not really concerned with whether or not we say later that the action was redundant, which indeed turns on the truth of a subjunctive conditional: he is arguing that we can never have a reasonable motive for doing it at the time.

So when do we consider that we have a reasonable motive for doing A in order that E should later occur? Given that we want E to occur, and that it is reasonable to want that, one condition will be satisfied if we have good ground to take doing A as a sufficient and non-superfluous condition of E's occurring. We shall have good ground to take it as a sufficient condition if we have good reason to assert that, if we do A, E will occur; and we may take it as a non-superfluous condition if we have no ground for asserting that, if we do not do A, E will occur—still more, if we have a ground for asserting that, if we do not do A, E will not occur. If we have such grounds, all the fatalist can pit against them is the observation that, if E is going to occur, then it will be true to say that, even if we do not do A, E will occur. Now the supposition that the indicative conditional "If we do not do A, E will occur" is true is no obstacle to the truth of the conditional "If we do A, E will occur", for, since these are conditionals whose truth is guaranteed by the truth of their consequents, both can be true together. The fatalist is therefore not, at least on this horn of his dilemma, attempting to undermine our treating A as a sufficient condition of E. He wishes only to undermine our treating it as a non-superfluous condition. He intends us to reason thus: If we knew that the conditional "If we do not do A, E will occur" was true, we should regard A as superfluous. But whether A is superfluous or not cannot depend on whether we *know* the conditional to be true: that only determines whether we *think* it to be superfluous. Hence the supposition that the conditional is true implies that A *is* superfluous. Of course, we cannot conclude outright that it is, since we do not know whether the conditional is true or not. We do, however, know that either that conditional or one whose truth implies that it will be fruitless to do A must be true: and hence we know that doing A must either be fruitless or superfluous.

That is how he wants us to argue: but we should, of course, resist such a train of thought. Unlike the similar notion of being redundant we considered earlier, no explanation of what it is for an action to *be* superfluous is available. It is not available since it could not be provided without the use of subjunctive conditionals, which we are eschewing: whether, when we explain such a notion by appeal to them, we have really supplied a firm foundation for it is yet another question I shall not attempt to answer. In the present setting, we have no use for the notion of an action's *being* superfluous, but only for that of our reasonably regarding it as superfluous. The difference is that whether we can reasonably so regard it or not is a matter of what we know or have grounds for believing: no argument can therefore be put forward to the effect that it must in fact be superfluous if a certain conditional, which we have no grounds for taking to be true, in fact holds good.

To have a reasonable motive for doing A in order that E should later occur, we do not, of course, need a ground for regarding doing A as a sufficient condition for the occurrence of E: it is quite enough that we have grounds for regarding it as more probable that E will occur if we do A than if we do not. That, however, is not the only condition: we must also regard ourselves as free to do A or not as we choose. Again, that is overstated: we need only reasonably suppose that we are likely to succeed if we try. More exactly, we must have no ground for thinking that we shall fail save for some reason independent of whether E occurs or not. Normally, I regard starting my car as something I am free to do if I choose; but if, one morning, I find the battery flat, I might ask my son to have it charged. When I return in the evening, I may try to start it. Succeeding in doing so is very nearly a sufficient condition of the battery's having been charged; but I do not regard myself as starting the car in order that the battery should have been charged, but as seeing whether I can start it in order to find out whether the battery was charged. That is because, in this case, I do not suppose that I am free to start the car if I choose, or that, if I fail to do so, this will be explicable independently of the event in which I am interested.

It is natural to think that the topic I am aiming to discuss raises the issue of free will. That issue I believe to be a very difficult and important one, about which most that has been written, from any standpoint, is gravely inadequate; and I do not wish either to deny or to assert that, in any fully adequate discussion of the present topic, it would have to be considered. I believe, however, that it is possible to get a very long way with the surrogate notion of someone's reasonably regarding himself as free to do something if he chooses. Whether he reasonably so regards himself is not a question of whether he has free will: it is a purely empirical question, turning principally on whether or not he has experienced difficulties in performing the action in the past, and on the character of those difficulties, and, secondarily, on the experience of others in this regard.

3

I shall say nothing further about the fallacies of fatalism; but I hope that, despite its being quite obvious that it is fallacious, you have managed to attend to what I have said to show it so, since, as I said at the outset, there is a good reason for exploring this matter. This reason I have so far left unstated. It is this. When people—including philosophers—consider the question whether it would ever be possible, or even reasonable to try, to affect the past, they frequently come out with an argument that is the exact analogue of the fatalist argument. That is to say, their doing this is the best you can usually hope for. If you are not so lucky, they will say things like, "You can't change the past: if something has happened, it has happened". But, if you are lucky, they will see straight away that the question is not one of changing the past in the sense of making something that yesterday had happened last week become, today, something that did not happen in that week, any more than affecting the future consists in making something which yesterday was not going to happen next week become, today, something that will happen next week. It is those who avoid this confusion who put forward the analogue of the fatalist argument.

How do they argue? Suppose it is proposed to perform an action *B* in order that a previous event *F* should have occurred. Those I have in mind open their argument by observing that either *F* has occurred or it has not. If it has occurred, they say, it has occurred whether we do *B* or not: in this case, then, doing *B* is redundant. If *F* has not occurred, then doing *B*, for this purpose, will be fruitless. In either case, therefore, it is pointless: we can do nothing, and cannot ever reasonably suppose that we can do anything, to bring it about that something has happened.

I said that the fatalist argument is not a paradox: it is too obviously fallacious for that. But its analogue, used to show that we cannot affect the past, might be called an anti-paradox. The conclusion seems as obviously true as that of a paradox seems obviously false; but the argument appears valid only for this reason. The argument, being the exact analogue of the fatalist's, is as grossly fallacious as his. It nevertheless impresses a large number of people, including professional philosophers, who, ostensibly on the strength of it, thereupon dismiss the entire issue as unworthy of further consideration.

It thus seems to follow that, in certain circumstances, if we were lucky enough to discover them, it would be reasonable for us to perform an action *B* in order that a previous event *F* should have occurred. These circumstances are as follows:

(1) The performance of *B* approximates, in our experience, to being a sufficient condition for the previous occurrence of *F*: more exactly, there is a sufficiently high positive correlation between them for the performance of *B*, in a case in which we do not otherwise know whether *F* has occurred, significantly to increase the probability that it has.

(2) We can find no ordinary causal explanation for the occurrence of *F*, on those occasions when it is followed by the performance of *B*; or, at least, we can discover no ordinary causal connection between *F* and *B* which would explain why *B* should be correlated with *F*.

(3) So far as our experience goes, *B* is an action which it is in our power to perform if we choose. That is to say, we do not have, or only very rarely have, the experience of trying to perform *B* and failing; and, when we do have it, an explanation for our failure is readily forthcoming that makes no appeal to the previous non-occurrence of *F*.

Now it seems that these conditions would at most provide a motive for the action *B* in circumstances in which it was not known whether *F* had occurred or not: for, if it were known, the analogue of the fatalist argument would apply. If *F* were known to have occurred, it would appear superfluous to perform *B*; if it were known not to have occurred, it would appear fruitless. But this suggests that it could easily be arranged that one of the conditions (1)–(3) was violated, provided that it was possible to perform the action *B* in cases in which it was known that *F* had not occurred. If it were not possible, this might be regarded as a violation of condition (3); but suppose it possible. The challenge may now be issued to perform *B* when *F* is known not to have occurred. Nothing analogous can happen in the case of an action *A* designed to bring about a subsequent event *E*, since our knowledge of the future is in part based on our intentions. If we take ourselves to know, independently of our intentions, including the intention to perform *A* or not to perform it, that *E* will not happen, that can only be because we do not suppose that the performance of *A* can, in the circumstances, bring about the occurrence of *E*; if, on the other hand, our conviction that *E* will not take place is based on our intention not to do *A*, we cannot accept a challenge to do *A* without losing our ground for supposing that *E* will not occur.

If we accept the challenge to perform *B* when *F* is known not to have occurred, it seems that one of two things must happen: either we shall do *B*, in which case the correlation of *B* with *F* will be weakened; or we shall find that we cannot do *B*, in which case our belief that it is an action which it is in our power to do is undermined. Now, of course, a single trial may not have a significant effect. A single instance in which a performance of *B* was not preceded by *F* will not greatly lower the increase in the probability of *F* which we attribute to a performance of *B* when it is not known whether *F* took place or not; and a failure to perform *B* owing to causes apparently quite unconnected with the non-occurrence of *F* may be dismissed as coincidence. The failure may not even have the appearance of an unsuccessful attempt: an urgent summons to a forgotten appointment may account for our not even making the attempt.

The situation changes significantly only if there are repeated trials. We may assume that the outcomes are mixed: sometimes *B* is performed; on other occasions something of an explicable and apparently unconnected kind occurs to prevent the attempt or frustrate its success. Conditions (1) and (3) will not be sufficiently preserved, however, to justify maintenance of the belief that doing *B* is a way of bringing it about that *F* occurred if all the outcomes are of one or other of these kinds: we must suppose that a third type of outcome occurs with significant frequency. This is that *B* is performed, but it subsequently proves that the information that *F* had not happened was erroneous, owing to an error of observation or in the transmission of the report. If this happens often enough to enable conditions (1)–(3) to be preserved to a degree sufficiently great to warrant maintenance of the belief in the efficacy of *B*, it will tend to change our attitude to evidence that *F* did or did not occur. Originally we made the natural assumption that we could, on occasion, know whether or not *F* had occurred independently of our intentions—precisely the assumption that cannot be made in relation to any future event which we believe ourselves to have the means of bringing about or of preventing. It was because we made that assumption that we were able to establish the correlation between the performance of *B* and the previous occurrence of *F*. It was also because we made this assumption that we took it for granted that there was no point in trying to bring it about that *F* occurred when we have clear evidence that it did not. Although we placed sufficient reliance on the correlation between *B* and *F* for the performance of *B* to count as increasing the probability that *F* occurred in cases in which we had no evidence of an ordinary kind about whether it did or not, we trusted such evidence so much more than we trusted the correlation that the performance of *B* did not significantly affect our estimate of the probability of *F*'s having occurred in cases in which we possessed that evidence, even though we knew that evidence for a past event can sometimes prove mistaken. Now, however, we shall be impelled to abandon this assumption. The performance of *B* is now felt to increase the probability that any report we have that *F* did not occur will be found to be in error: we therefore no longer believe that the performance of *B* is irrelevant to our judgement of the probability of *F*'s having occurred when we have other grounds to go on. Since we still regard performing *B* as being, by and large, within our power to do when we choose, it follows that the formation of an intention to do *B* is likewise relevant to such a judgement. In the intermediate stage, the performance of *B* merely increased the likelihood that a report that *F* had not occurred would be found to have been in error: but the final result will be that we shall take that action, or even the formation of an intention to perform it, as itself grounds for doubting any such report, even in the absence of any contrary evidence of the usual kind.

Thus what stands in the way of our supposing it rational to do anything in order that something else should previously have occurred is not the logical fact that the event in question has already either occurred or not occurred, or the metaphysical status of the past as fixed, in contrast to the fluid condition of the future, but our assumption that, of any past event, we may have evidence for its occurrence or non-occurrence whose strength can be estimated independently of our intentions. This assumption is, of course, based, not only on causal connections from earlier to later, but on the absence of any comparable connections in the reverse direction—that is, connections that we might use to attempt to bring it about that certain events had previously occurred. Just because the assumption is so deeply engrained in us, we should feel the strongest psychological resistance to recognizing any such connection; but, were we to recognize one, we should have, to that extent, to modify that assumption. This would profoundly alter our conception of evidence about the past, but it would not produce conceptual chaos.

4

What is our conception of the temporal priority of cause over effect? Not, plainly, that there must be a temporal gap between an immediate cause and its effect, but, rather, that a causal chain runs always in the earlier-to-later direction. Each link in the chain is a process, whose initiation is the immediate, and thus simultaneous, effect of the arrival at a particular stage of the process that constitutes the preceding link. The subsequent continuation of the process is not treated as requiring causal explanation, but only its deviation, if any, from some norm, which is to be explained by the continuous (and simultaneous) operation of some causal influence. It is the fact that it is the *subsequent* continuation of the process, once initiated, that calls for no explanation which gives a temporal direction to the causal chain.

Can we imagine a world in which the temporal direction of *all* causal processes is reversed? If memory is treated as a natural process, we should lack the faculty of memory in such a world, and have, instead, the analogous faculty of precognition; and it now becomes difficult to say whether, in imagining this, we have not simply switched the words "past" and "future", that is, whether we have genuinely imagined a different state of affairs. If, on the other hand, we exempt memory from the time-reversal, then, again, there seems little difficulty if we suppose that we are mere *observers*—a kind of intelligent tree, able to communicate with one another, but to engage in no other action or form of interference with the course of events that we witness. If, on the other hand, we imagine ourselves as interacting with such a world, we shall have to exempt intention, as well as memory, from the reversal of causal direction, if we are to preserve any ordinary conception of action at all, since it is integral to the concept of intention that there be a high correlation between forming intentions and carrying them out. For us to be able to form future intentions at all, we should have to have a cognitive attitude to the future not wholly analogous to our present attitude to the past; it would nevertheless be somewhat analogous to that, in that our knowledge of what was to happen would rest in part on our intentions and in part on inferences from present traces of future events parallel to the inferences we now make concerning past events of which we find present traces. In consequence, we should regard far fewer actions as in our power to perform than we now do. This would mitigate the weakening of our confidence in our memories that would result from the phenomenon on which I have commented, that we should no longer believe, in general, that we could have knowledge of what had happened independent of our intentions. All this makes the thought experiment difficult: but, as far as I can see, it is not impossible.

In such a world, remote causes would be connected to their preceding remote effects by causal chains running in the later-to-earlier direction. In discussing the coherence of the conception of bringing about the past—doing something in order that some subsequent event should have occurred—I ignored the question whether such a chain could be discovered between the action and the earlier event. In doing so, I failed to provide a true analogue to earlier-to-later causal connections. A correlation between temporally separated events can of course be observed, and, so far, provides evidence only for the hypothesis that there is some causal connection between them. That the earlier lies on a direct causal chain linking them can only be fully confirmed, or disconfirmed, by the identification of such a chain, and hence the integration of the connection into our system of causal explanations; but the hypothesis that it does can be supported by observational evidence that the later event is not equally well correlated with an immediately antecedent condition, in cases when the earlier event is inhibited. The same applies when we reverse the temporal order of the two events. It could occur that every attempt to correlate the earlier event with some earlier link in a recognized causal chain leading to the later one breaks down. Indeed, this must happen if the conditions I stated for it to be rational to attempt to bring about the past are to be satisfied. In that case, the later event was a voluntary action: discovering that the earlier event was equally well correlated with some event that was earlier still and led to the performance of the action would destroy the belief that the action was in our power to perform, and turn trying to perform it into a way of finding out whether the earlier event had occurred. But, even so, we have, at best, an analogue of the case in which there is some supporting evidence for the hypothesis that a certain event is a remote cause of some subsequent one, not of that in which that is as secure a belief as any concerning causality can be. For that, we should need a chain linking the later event to the earlier one, composed of processes whose *previous* stages were taken to require no explanation, given what ended them. Is it a coherent idea that we might recognize the existence of such a chain, even though our general system of causal explanations ran, as now, in the earlier-to-later direction?

It is certainly the complete absence of anything to fulfil the role of such a causal chain that makes parapsychology—at least, that part of it that treats of alleged instances of precognition—appear utterly unscientific: but is this in the nature of any purported case of backwards causation, or due only to the feebleness of parapsychology? The difficulty of the idea plainly decreases the further we move from the sphere of processes which we are capable of interrupting. Any attempt to consider anything as simultaneously subject to influences in both temporal directions is liable to collapse in complete incoherence. Let us consider the model time machine once more, and suppose that it travels backwards continuously in time. Let us first suppose the room to be empty from 5 p.m. on Thursday until 5.55 p.m. on Friday, when the time traveller and his friend enter. The camera records the following scene. At 5 p.m. on Thursday the table is bare. Precisely at six, two model time machines appear abruptly on the table side by side; inside one is a watch which reads 7 p.m. Friday and is running normally, and inside the other one that gives the same reading and is running backwards at the rate of two and a half minutes per hour. Both machines continue in the positions at which they appeared until 6 p.m. on Friday, at which moment the time traveller, having taken a simulacrum out of a box, sets its controls and holds it over the machine containing the watch now telling the right time (the other reads 7 p.m. Saturday), drops it, pressing the "On" button: both it and the machine on to which he drops it vanish, leaving only the machine with the fast watch.

Now suppose that, at 10 o'clock on Friday morning, the cleaning lady comes in. Is it possible that she should take both exemplars of the time machine from the table and put them on the mantelpiece? There is no difficulty about her doing this to the exemplar in which the watch is running normally: but it is impossible that she should do it to the one that is travelling backwards in time, or, otherwise expressed, within which all processes are slowed down and reversed. She cannot do it, because we have assumed

(1) that the time traveller started the machine on its backwards journey on the table; and
(2) that that journey, which occupies it from 6 p.m. on Friday to 6 p.m. on Thursday, is a process which has the temporal analogue of the property of requiring no explanation for its continuance, once initiated.

What is this analogous property? Described in our ordinary earlier-to-later terms, it is that of being a process which, from a certain moment t on, will continue until the terminating event. The terminating event in our case is the time traveller's pressing the "On" button. The moment t will be either the initial event—in our case the sudden appearance of the time machine at 6 p.m. on Thursday—or the very first moment of any intervening action on the machine. It follows that no such intervening action, with *subsequent* causal consequences, such as the cleaning lady's removal of the machine to the mantelpiece, can occur: for those consequences cannot ensue, given the stated assumption about the character of the process the machine is undergoing during those twenty-four hours.

We must not conclude that, while it is undergoing this process, the machine has become an immovable object: the impossibility is a logical, not a physical, one. What made the supposition that the cleaning lady moved the machine impossible was our assumption that, when the time traveller and his friend entered the room, the machine was on the table, and that he pressed the "On" button as he let it fall to the table. The following sequence is consistent. At 6 p.m. on Thursday, the machine (or, rather, the two exemplars of it) appears suddenly on the table. The cleaning lady comes in the next morning, and removes the machine undergoing backwards travel to the mantelpiece, and the other one to a shelf. That evening, the two friends find the two exemplars in those positions, and, as he sets the "On" button, the time traveller drops his exemplar on to the one on the mantelpiece.

This last is, I think, a coherent description; but it has puzzling consequences. Why was the machine on the mantlepiece when the time traveller and his friend entered the room? Its position at that time is doubly determined: by the fact that the cleaning lady put it there; and by the fact that the time traveller subsequently set it going there. On the other hand, there is no reason at all for its being on the table at the moment when the cleaning lady picked it up. Its presence on the table is not accounted for by the cleaning lady's picking it up, which serves only to explain its *subsequent* position; and it is not accounted for by its having previously been on the table, since it was at that time undergoing its backward journey, any phase of which serves only to explain *previous* phases. The price of admitting things to be subject to causal influence in both temporal directions may be that for some phenomena we have a multiple explanation, while for others we have none.

5

If there are causal chains running in the reverse as well as in the usual direction, there is a possibility of causal loops. They often occur in science fiction: one such story that amused me concerned a fifth-rate but conceited artist. One day he is visited by an art critic from a century ahead, who explains that he has been selected for time travel so that he could interview the artist, who is regarded, in the critic's time, as by far the greatest artist of the twentieth century. When the artist proudly produces his paintings for inspection, the critic's face falls, and he says, in an embarrassed manner, that the artist cannot yet have struck the inspired vein in which he painted his (subsequently) celebrated masterpieces, and produces a portfolio of reproductions that he has brought with him. The critic has to leave, being permitted, for some unstated reason, only to remain for a limited length of time in the past, and the artist manages to conceal the portfolio, so that the critic has to leave without it. The artist then spends the rest of his life producing the originals of the reproductions by carefully copying them in paint.

The natural reaction to such a cycle is that there is no explanation for *its* occurrence. The existence of the reproductions is to be explained, in the usual way, by reference to the existence of the originals; and the existence of the originals can likewise be explained by reference to that of the reproductions from which they were copied: but there is no reason whatever for their joint existence—no reason why there should be any paintings and reproductions like that.

Reflection on such examples throws a little light upon a puzzling feature of the philosophy of St Thomas Aquinas. In his proof for the existence of God as First Cause, Thomas says that you cannot go back to infinity in a sequence of causes, that is, that you cannot have an infinite descending causal chain, where by a descending causal chain I mean a sequence each term of which other than the first is a cause of the preceding term. The thought is evidently modelled on the principle that you cannot have an infinite descending chain of (cogent) grounds. A proof, if it is to carry conviction, must have premisses. It might be possible to give a precise characterization of an infinite deductive structure, in the form of a tree: each statement stands below one or more other statements from which it follows by a valid principle of inference. Since it is infinite, however, there must be at least one branch of the tree that does not terminate, that is, has no tip; and, if so, the proof establishes nothing. The point of a deductive proof is that truth is transmitted downwards: given the truth of the premisses, the truth of the conclusion is guaranteed. In the infinite proof, we have no reason for accepting any of the statements occurring along the infinite branch as true, and hence no reason whatever for accepting the conclusion. It is natural to think that Thomas regarded causes in the same light: an infinite descending causal chain would offer *no* explanation for the existence or occurrence of the first term in the chain.

What is puzzling is that Thomas elsewhere argues that we have no ground in reason for believing the universe to be of finite age (he thought that revelation supplied such a ground). Why, then, can we not prove that the universe must be of finite age by appealing to the impossibility of an infinite descending causal chain? And, if we cannot, why can we not refuse the conclusion to the existence of God as First Cause by proposing that the universe has always existed? The standard response of the commentators to the latter question is to say that we require an explanation of the existence of the sequence as a whole. I used to think this response absurd in itself, and lacking any warrant in the texts. Whether warranted or not, it cannot be dismissed offhand as absurd in itself. A causal cycle of length *n* is a special case of an infinite descending causal chain, one in which every block of *n* terms repeats; and the intuitive reaction to the supposition that there could be such a cycle is precisely that it would leave the existence of the cycle as a whole unexplained.

There is a passage in Thomas's writings in which he attempts to resolve the problem caused by his denial of the absurdity of a universe without temporal beginning by distinguishing two types of descending causal chain, one of which may be infinite and the other of which cannot. In making the distinction, he employs the terms *per se* and *per accidens*, which seem capable of a wide variety of applications in mediaeval philosophy. The idea is that it is intrinsic to the existence of certain things that they should have been produced in a certain way, whereas in other cases it is merely a contingent fact that they are always produced in a particular manner: when the chain is of the former type, it must be finite, but when of the latter, it may be infinite. As a specific example of the latter type, Thomas cites a chain composed of human beings, each term of which other than the first is a parent of the preceding term. It is not intrinsic to the existence of human beings that they have parents, Thomas thinks: after all, Adam and Eve had none. The difficulty is to cite examples of the former type. Here is one that is attributed to Wittgenstein. You come upon a man, and hear him say, "Four, three, two, one, nought. Whew!!" You question him, and he replies, "From eternity I have been running through the sequence of natural numbers backwards, and I have just got to the end". It is plain that this strikes us as conceptually absurd in a way that its opposite does not, or at least as measurably *more* absurd than its opposite. If there were a Greek legend of a sinful mathematician condemned in Hades to count through the natural numbers for eternity in ascending order, this would appear far more intelligible than Wittgenstein's fantasy. A causal sequence of the order-type of the positive integers appears less baffling than one of the order-type of the negative integers: why? I suppose the thought behind the intuitive reaction is this. When the sinful mathematician says, "31", for example, at a particular moment, his reason is that he had just said, "30": and his reason for saying that can be traced back to his reason for saying "Nought" at the outset, which in turn lay in the sentence of the infernal judge. In the same way, the reason for Wittgenstein's friend having said, "31", at a particular moment lay in his having just previously said, "32". *This* reason, however, cannot be traced back to anything, and so he can have no reason to be engaged in the countdown at all: he has no reason to utter the name of any particular number because there is no reason why he should be engaged in the entire process. Once more, it seems that there can be no adequate ground for the occurrence of any term in the sequence, because there is no ground for the occurrence of the sequence as a whole.

6

I am not going to attempt to resolve this perplexing matter. I shall not end, as Wittgenstein once ended a lecture, by saying, "For the moment, I shall leave you puzzled": there is no "for the moment" about it, because I am deeply puzzled myself, and, if I tried to take the matter further, should probably talk utter nonsense. I shall end only by remarking that there is a possible means of affecting the past that I have not considered, namely if time is itself cyclic, so that the recent past is also the remote future and conversely. In this case, of course, the terms "past" and "future" do not, relative to any moment and frame of reference, distinguish disjoint temporal regions; hence, even if all causal chains run in the same temporal direction, anything that affects what subsequently happens thereby also affects what has happened. It does not follow from that that there are causal loops, since all effects might dissipate within a small fraction of the length of the entire cycle; but the possibility of loops is open, leaving us with the puzzles I have confessed that I do not know how to resolve.

DISCUSSION

Q. There's a stock objection to backwards causation which has to do with people killing their grandfathers and so forth. You seem to be trying to avoid this problem by saying that, in some sense, the probability of a past event always falls short of certainty, that you can't actually *know that* a past event happened. And that seems a very counter-intuitive thing to say.

A. Well actually, I didn't even say that there were not events of which you *could* know for certain that they had happened. But in general it *is* a matter of probabilities and assessing reports that we get. The situation I envisaged was this. There's a type of event *F* and a type of action *B*. You believe on the basis of past experience that you're free to perform *B* or not as you choose. Moreover, you regard *B* as a sufficient condition of the previous occurrence of *F*. That's also based on empirical evidence. Finally, you've got no other explanation for the occurrence of *F*, no ordinary causal explanation that accounts for the correlation that links them. Those were the assumptions. The question then is whether these assumptions are cotenable. Someone who thought they were not might issue the following challenge: you can show that you can't hold all of these together if you keep trying to perform *B* in conditions in which you take yourself to know that *F* has not occurred. Now perhaps in some cases responding to that challenge *would* violate one or other of those beliefs. You might find yourself just unable to do *B* in many of those cases. Then you would give up your belief that you were free to do *B* or not. Or you might find that you frequently did it. And there it was: you've got *B* being performed on many occasions when *F* has not occurred. That weakens the belief in the correlation, perhaps to vanishing point. I'm not denying that those are possibilities.

What I was considering, however, was whether things could so turn out that, even though you respond to this challenge, these conditions—conditions in which I maintained that it would be rational to do *B* in order that *F* should have occurred—still sufficiently persist. And what I said was that this can only happen if it frequently then turns out that the report that *F* did not occur was erroneous. Now you can't deny that very often we do find that we've made mistakes about what has happened in the past. One just can't legislate that out of existence. So I'm entitled to suppose that, in a hypothetical case, that happens sufficiently often so as not to destroy, though it may weaken, the other assumptions. What it then does is a very peculiar thing. And that, I think, helps to explain why we have such a resistance to the idea of backwards causation, or doing something in order that something else should have happened. We find that what gets weakened is our normal assumption that you can tell whether or not an event has occurred independently of your intentions. And now the intention to do *B* becomes itself a ground, in some cases, for supposing that *F* has occurred, even when there are no other reasons. Of course not from the beginning. It's just that finding so often, when we do *B*, that it turns out that *F* has, after all, occurred puts you in that frame of mind.

Now that's a very big conceptual change. But I don't think it produces conceptual chaos. A lot of people think that the idea of backwards causation—at any rate backwards causation that we could get a handle on in order to bring about what has happened—is complete nonsense. But I don't think so. It's certainly not nonsense because of the analogue of the fatalist argument. If the fatalist argument is no good in the hands of fatalists, then it's no good here.

Q. Logicians seem concerned to rescue ordinary people from the pathological consequences of logic choppers who are distorting language. And they do this by sophisticated arguments which are, ultimately, appeals to common sense. Now we've been hearing in other lectures about causality from the point of view of quantum theory, where we get paradoxes like Schrödinger's cat. I wondered how a logician would regard that. Is that kind of causality outside the preserve of logicians?

A. Not at all. Nothing is outside the preserve of logicians. That's by definition. If logic doesn't cover every realm of discourse, then it isn't logic. But continue with your question. (I'm not going to talk about Schrödinger's cat, if that's what you were hoping.)

Q. I wondered if you felt that these paradoxes of quantum theory could also eventually be reduced to common-sense terms, if we had sufficient insight into the common usage of such expressions as 'causality'.

A. I think that's a misconception of what I said. I do not think that it's a matter of common usage. Quite the contrary. Of course you have to respect common usage to some extent. Those words you use and don't specially explain are best used in accordance with their accepted meanings. Otherwise you'll be misunderstood or will make claims that are quite unjustified. But solutions to philosophical problems that turn simply on appeals to common usage are, for the most part, spurious in my opinion. And that is precisely why, for example, I tried to get away from these subjunctive conditionals. You can spend a lot of time discussing in what circumstances the statement "If I had done so-and-so, such-and-such would have happened" is true. And when you've finished doing that, if you're not careful—unless you tie it up in some way—all you've got is an account of the way we normally use conditionals of that form. And it hasn't answered the question you seriously wanted to answer. Particularly is this so if you concentrate on how the word "cause" is used, and how it's connected with a temporal direction. Now, if someone wants to know whether it's reasonable for him to do something when his motive is that something should have happened—which some people regard as absolutely ridiculous—it's a cheat to fob him off with explanations in terms of how we use the word "cause". That's not the question. Whether it would be

370   *Causal Loops*

called a cause, or is rightly called a cause, may be an interesting question, but it is not the question he was asking. If it's not called a cause, then all right, perhaps we'll call it something else. But the question is: Is there any sense in doing this thing? So you've misunderstood me if you thought I was making appeals to common usage. And I wasn't making appeals to common sense either. In fact I thought I was flying in the face of common sense to some extent.

Q. Can I put something to you that arose in a previous lecture? Paul Davies mentioned a fascinating thought experiment that John Wheeler has been writing about, in which it looks as though there's backwards causation. What you have is a light source, a screen with two apertures, a lens with an image screen in front of it, and two photon detectors. Now the image screen is made up of slats which can be opened like a venetian blind. If the slats are open, the photons will pass through them, and the lens will deflect each photon into the upper or lower detector, depending on whether it has gone through the lower or the upper aperture. If they are closed, on the other hand, one will get interference fringes on the screen, just as in the classic Young's two-slit experiment. And the way this would normally be explained is that, when the slats are closed, each photon exhibits wavelike behaviour and goes, so to speak, through both apertures. If the slats are open, however, then, because the detectors enable one to tell which aperture the photon goes through, the accepted wisdom is that it behaves like a particle, and just goes through one aperture or the other. But Wheeler pointed out that you can delay the decision as to whether to have the slats open or shut until after the photon has passed through the screen containing the apertures. Then it looks as though it's a matter of retroactively causing the photon, as the case may be, to behave like a wave or like a particle. But it struck me, listening to your talk, that actually this kind of backwards causation is totally benign in terms of your account. For suppose that you are the experimenter and you want to know, after the photon has negotiated the apertures but before it reaches the image screen, whether it has gone through just one aperture or, as it were, spread out between the two. It is quite clear that there is, in principle, no way of knowing that independently of knowing your own intentions: specifically whether you intend to open (close) the slats, assuming them to be closed (open), or to leave them as they are. I wonder if you have any comments on this.

A. Well I think you've already made the comment which I was intending to make! As for benign, I don't mean that it's easy to swallow. What is particularly difficult is to put such phenomena into any coherent system of causal explanations. Still, I do think that what you said is absolutely right. As I understand it, there is, in the kind of case you describe, no possibility of generating causal loops. And this is surely a crucial consideration in its favour.

APPENDIX. MACKIE ON NEWCOMB'S PARADOX

Newcomb's paradox involves a case in which I can choose between two courses of action, knowing that one or other of two situations obtains, but not knowing which: the outcome will depend both on my choice and on the situation that in fact obtains. The principle of dominance lays down that if one of the two courses of action will, in *each* of the two situations, produce the more favourable outcome for me, I must rationally choose that course of action. In the version of Newcomb's paradox discussed by the late J. L. Mackie in 'Newcomb's Paradox and the Direction of Causation',[1] one box is open to view, and contains $1,000, and the other is closed, and contains either nothing or $10,000: I have the option of either taking only the closed box or both of them, in both cases keeping the contents. The pay-off matrix is therefore as follows:

	The closed box is not empty	The closed box is empty
I take the closed box only	$10,000	$0
I take both boxes	$11,000	$1,000

The strategy of taking both boxes dominates that of taking only the closed box, since in either situation I get $1,000 more.

Bar-Hillel and Margalit, in 'Newcomb's Paradox Revisited',[2] had argued that the principle of dominance fails to apply when the choice of strategy affects the probability that one or other situation obtains. Mackie denies this, and maintains that the principle fails only when the choice of strategy causally determines, or at least influences, the situation. The immediate argument he gives against Bar-Hillel and Margalit is, however, irrelevant. It is given in terms of an example of theirs concerning the relations between Israel and Egypt: but I shall here transpose his argument to the Newcomb context. So transposed, it is as follows. Suppose that, before I make my choice, I get a glimpse of the inside of the closed box, without being sure that I have seen aright. And suppose that, if the closed box appeared to me to be empty, I am strongly moved to take both boxes, whereas, if it appeared to me to contain $10,000, I am moved to take only it. Then my taking only the closed box makes it more probable that it is not empty: but this provides no rational ground for me to depart from the principle of dominance.

Mackie's argument looks plausible, partly because it is very swift, and partly because it is *not* transposed to the Newcomb context: but it is doubly wrong. First, it violates the conditions of the paradox, which involve that I have no basis for judging whether the closed box is empty or not save by reference to my own choice of strategy. Secondly, and crucially, it affects the probabilities as judged by a third party, but not by me. If *you* know that I have had a glimpse of the closed box, but do not know what I (thought I) saw, and if you know how this glimpse is likely to affect my choice of strategy, then my taking only the closed box makes it more likely, for you, that I saw money in it, and hence that it has money in it. Having had the glimpse, however, my choosing only the closed box does not, for *that* reason, make it more likely *for me* that there is money in it, because it makes it not in the least more likely, for me, that I thought I saw money in it: I already know what I thought I saw. Mackie's argument therefore provides no counter-example to the thesis of Bar-Hillel and Margalit, which was that the principle of dominance fails, as a criterion of rational choice, whenever my choice of strategy affects the probability that *I* (rationally) assign to the obtaining of the two possible alternative situations. I shall here defend that thesis, which I shall label the BHM thesis.

The assumption of the paradox is that, in every instance in which someone chose to take both boxes, the closed box proved to be empty, and, in every other instance, it contained $10,000: all those choosing both boxes got $1,000, and all those choosing only the closed box got $10,000. Mackie is of course quite right that I have to ask myself

[1] *Canadian Journal of Philosophy*, 7 (1977), 213–25.
[2] *British Journal for the Philosophy of Science*, 23 (1972), 295–303.

whether I can extrapolate. If I decide that this regularity was pure coincidence, I may rationally follow the principle of dominance: on this hypothesis, my choice of strategy will not weigh with me in estimating the probability that the closed box contains $10,000. This case, too, is irrelevant to the BHM thesis.

Mackie goes further, however, and insists that, if I do not dismiss the regularity as coincidental, I must ask myself *how* it occurs. If I decide that someone's choosing to take only the closed box *brings it about* that it contains $10,000, when otherwise it would have been empty, then, Mackie agrees, it will be rational for me to ignore the principle of dominance and choose to take only the closed box. This will happen, Mackie says, if I conjecture that, by some trickery, the $10,000 are inserted into the box after the subject has announced or otherwise demonstrated that he will adopt the strategy of taking only the closed box. He adds that it will also happen if I suppose that backwards causation is operating. Once more, these cases are not at issue between Mackie and Bar-Hillel and Margalit: they are agreed that the principle of dominance fails in cases such as these.

What if I decide that the regularity is not coincidental, but that my choice of strategy does not bring about the condition of the closed box? How can I suppose this? The agent whose money goes into one or both boxes claims to be a psychologist with a deep understanding of character, who puts $10,000 into the closed box if, and only if, he predicts that the subject will choose to take only that box. Now, Mackie says, I can hold that the regularity is not coincidental, without supposing that my choice of strategy brings about the condition of the closed box, by believing the psychologist's claim. In that case, he claims, I have decided that each person is determined by his character to adopt one strategy or the other, and that it is the psychologist's perfect assessment of this character that determines the situation, namely whether the closed box is or is not empty. But, if I think this, Mackie maintains, I must recognize that my choice of strategy is not free: I therefore do not need to make up my mind what to do. More exactly, he does not actually say that I do not need to make up my mind: what he says is that the question "What is it reasonable for me to do?" is idle.

Obviously, this is wrong: for me the question is not idle at all. Here I am, wavering between taking both boxes and taking only the closed one, and trying to decide which it is reasonable for me to do. The thought "My choice is not really open: the psychologist already knows which I shall do" may fill me with despair: but it will not help me to decide, and it equally will not dispense me from deciding.

A compatibilist, in philosophical jargon, is one who believes that our possession of free will is compatible with complete causal determinism. Mackie remarks that, in a case like that under consideration, I may be free "in a sense which compatibilists might find sufficient". He claims, however, that the compatibilist must interpret the question "What is it reasonable for me to do on this occasion?" as meaning "What sort of action is in general most advantageous in circumstances of the type to which those now obtaining belong?" On Mackie's own view, these are two quite different questions, although, in most circumstances, they have the same answer. To the second question, he has no doubt of the answer in the present case: it is in general more advantageous to take only the closed box. But the peculiarity of Newcomb's paradox, he argues, is that it splits the two distinct questions apart. In the particular case under consideration, in which I am supposing that each person's choice is determined in advance by his antecedent character, the first question *has* no answer, according to Mackie: there is nothing it is reasonable for me to do, since I believe that my choice is not free.

Mackie's conclusion thus appears to be that, if Bar-Hillel and Margalit are compatibilists, their thesis is after all correct, but only because it does not mean what it appears to mean: being compatibilists, they are forced to put a deviant construction on the notion of rational choice. If the notion is understood in the standard way, however, namely as a non-compatibilist interprets it, then the BHM thesis is incorrect.

The conclusion seems implausible: it makes the solution to Newcomb's paradox turn on the perplexing issue of free will and determinism, whereas it hardly seems that one has to resolve this issue before deciding what is the rational choice for one of Newcomb's subjects to make. Certainly it is unnecessary to have any opinion about the issue to acknowledge that, in the case in question, I have to make up my mind what to do, and shall want to do so rationally. Mackie acknowledges that a determinist could allow that I was capable of being influenced by rational argument: but he takes this only as a breach in the determination of my choice by my character. Perhaps others can advise me before I make my choice of strategy, and perhaps they may persuade me to do what I should not otherwise have done; but, then, there is, after all, a little room between my character and my choice, even though I am not really free.

The question is not, however, whether some third party, who holds determinist opinions, will allow that I might be influenced by rational argument. It is not even whether Mackie can admit that such a determinist could consistently allow this: it is whether *I*, the subject, holding determinist opinions at least about the choice with which I am faced, can, on Mackie's view, consistently seek or entertain such advice. It is obscure how I can. According to Mackie, I ought to regard the question "What am I to do?" as idle. What does it mean to regard that question as idle? Perhaps that I should not view myself as having any choice to make. If so, there will, nevertheless, be such a future event as my selection of a strategy: but, perhaps, on Mackie's view, that should not be described as my making a *real* choice, whatever *that* means. Well, whatever it means precisely to say that I should regard the question what I am to do as idle, Mackie certainly intends it to imply that the question what is the rational thing to do does not arise for me: if it did, he would be guilty of failing to pronounce on which strategy would be rational in such a case.

Now, it might be said, even though I believe my selection of a strategy to be determined by my character, I may still consistently suppose that it may be affected by extraneous factors, such as listening to somebody's advice. I may indeed suppose that: but what motive have I, on Mackie's account, for subjecting it to such factors? The only motive I might have is that they would tend to make my choice more rational: but Mackie's position is that, having once adopted a determinist view of my forthcoming selection of a strategy, I can no longer regard it as rational or irrational. Even if someone comes unasked to offer me advice, how can I listen to it and be swayed by it? The effect of advice on my subsequent actions is not an adventitious one, like that of alcohol or a good night's sleep: it is supposed to operate through my understanding of the words and my estimation of their truth. But any advice I receive will be to the effect that one strategy or another is the more rational: and I am expected by Mackie, if I am rational, to suppose that the categories of rationality and irrationality do not apply to my selection of a strategy.

In any case, we can simply set up the paradox to make the intrusion of advisers impossible: after I commit myself to being a subject of the experiment, I have no opportunity to take anyone else's advice until after I have chosen. All the same, I can still revolve the considerations in favour of each strategy in my own mind: perhaps no adviser would be able to put before me any consideration that had not already occurred to me. I still must ask myself, "What shall I do?": however convinced I may be that my choice is fore-ordained, I still must make it.

Suppose that I explain the fact that the closed box has, in the past, proved empty in just those instances in which the subject chose to take both boxes by appeal to the psychologist's discernment of character, without supposing him infallible: there have been 2,000 previous subjects, and I estimate that he is liable to make a mistake once in every 5,000. I might still believe in a strict determination of choice by antecedent character; but I might not believe that, thinking that some actions, though only a very few, are out of character. On this view, my choice is then free, though largely constrained; but it will make no sense to say that the question what I am to do is *largely* idle. The question is either idle or it is not: either my choice can be described as rational or irrational, or it cannot. Mackie's view is that, in this case, I must, if I am rational, follow the principle of dominance: the small margin of error on the psychologist's part makes all the difference, because, since I have a degree of freedom, even though so small a degree, the question what it is reasonable for me to do now genuinely arises, and, when it does, it is always rational to follow the principle of dominance when the choice of strategy does not causally determine the situation. It would therefore be irrational for me to take into account the fact, as I consider it to be, that the probability that I am the one subject in 5,000 about whom the psychologist is mistaken is only 1/5,000. Mackie attempts to soften the unconvincing ring of this answer by giving a tendentious description of the case: he says that the subject may be able to "break free from his own established character by a heroic effort of will", and that if that character tends very strongly to make him take the closed box only, "he should make a supreme effort to break free from it and take both". Plainly, however, this need not be a correct account of how the matter appears to the subject at all. The description would fit if he were conscious that, in those circumstances, his judgement was liable to be warped, and was trying to bring to bear a previous resolution, made when it was more reliable. If, on the other hand, he has no particular reason to distrust his present judgement, talk of a supreme effort is inapplicable: if, upon reflection, he is disposed to take only the closed box, he has no motive to act contrary to his judgement.

Still, in considering this last case, Mackie has found himself no longer able to evade the question he has for so long refused to face: and his answer is quite implausible. It is plain that, if the psychologist really is a good predictor of each subject's choice of strategy, those who make the choice Mackie considers to be irrational will do much better than those who make the other choice: and this needs some explaining. He explains it by saying that "rationality as a character trait, defined as a strong tendency always to do what, if one were free to choose, would then be the more advantageous thing to do, is not necessarily the most advantageous character trait to have". The definition is faulty: the rational agent will not always do, and may not even tend to do, what is in fact most advantageous, since he may be badly misinformed. Roughly speaking, a wholly rational agent is one who always does what, on the basis of what he knows, is most likely to be the most advantageous thing; more exactly, one who maximizes expected utility. This cannot but be the most advantageous character trait to have, or, more exactly, the most likely to be advantageous. There can be cases in which an imperfectly rational action proves more disastrous than an unintelligent one, as when a chess player's opponent prepares a trap he will fall into only if he is a fairly good player; and there can be cases in which misinformation, or an incorrect assessment of probabilities, will lead a rational agent into worse trouble than an irrational one, because the latter happens to hit on a policy that would have been rational for someone correctly informed: but there cannot be a case in which, on the basis of given information, an irrational policy has a greater chance of being advantageous than a rational one. Any policy compliance with which has a strong probability of not yielding the greatest advantage simply cannot be that which a rational agent will adopt.

The only kind of freedom relevant to the paradox is that I am free to take one box or both in the sense that I can rule out the possibility that I should attempt to take both and find myself unable to, or attempt to take only one and be unable to avoid taking both. Suppose that I believe that I am, in *that* sense, wholly constrained. I think, that is, that, if there is nothing in the closed box, I shall simply be unable, if I try, to take only it, and that, if it contains $10,000, I shall similarly be unable to take both boxes. Then, indeed, the question "Which shall I do?" has become idle for me: it will, I believe, turn out the same whichever I decide. But, if I do *not* think that, the question is not idle, independently of any opinions I may hold about determinism. In this case, I regard myself as free, in this, the only relevant, sense, to take only the closed box or to take both. My decision reasonably affects for me the probability that the closed box contains $10,000 rather than nothing. How could it reasonably fail to do so? For any onlooker, my decision *obviously* affects that probability: it has not failed in a single one of the preceding 2,000 cases. And I am, in this matter, in exactly the same position as the onlooker. The onlooker may not know how to explain it; I may not know how to explain it: but, if I do not dismiss the psychologist's past predictions as coincidental, my own choice must affect my estimate of the probability that one situation obtains or that the other does. Moreover, my choice of strategy is the *only* circumstance of which I know that bears on that probability. I thus have a choice between doing something that will, with a very high probability, result in my getting $1,000 and doing something that will, with a very high probability, result in my getting $10,000. Plainly, BarHillel and Margalit were right to conclude that the rational thing for me to do is the second. *After* I have done it, the rules governing the assertion of counterfactual conditionals may entitle me to assert, "If I had taken both boxes, I should have got $11,000"; but that is only a remark about our use of counterfactual conditionals. *Before* I make my choice, I should be a fool to disregard the high probability of the statement "If I take both boxes, I shall get only $1,000". That is not merely a remark about our use of the word "probability", nor even about our use of the word "rational", but about what it is rational to do.

16

Common Sense and Physics

1. THE PROBLEM

In *The Central Questions of Philosophy*,[1] Professor Ayer enquires into the compatibility of "the scientific view of the nature of physical objects and that which can be attributed to common sense". We are presented with a threefold choice. One possible answer is that physical theory constitutes, in Ramsey's terminology, a secondary system, the primary system being the world as conceived by common sense, or, rather, as we learn later (pp. 142–5), an attenuated version of it, stripped of dispositional and causal properties. The primary system embodies "the sum total of . . . purely factual propositions" (p. 33); the function of the secondary system is "purely explanatory", and the entities to which it refers, in so far as they cannot be identified with those figuring in the primary system, are simply conceptual tools serving to arrange the primary facts (pp. 109–10). This, then, is simply a version of instrumentalism: the actual facts, the hard facts, those that we really believe to obtain, are those of the primary system; the statements of scientific theory represent fictions, in which we do not really believe (as Ramsey confessed that he did not really believe in astronomy), but which we devise as a vivid means of encapsulating patterns and regularities detectable amongst the primary facts. Ayer thinks that such a distinction between primary and secondary systems is inescapable; but, in the present instance, he doubts whether it is necessary to relegate so much to the secondary system.

The second possible answer is to transfer "all the perceptible qualities of things to the observer's account, leaving things, as they are in themselves, to be represented by the necessarily imperceptible objects of physical theory" (p. 110). This is objectionable because it involves locating imperceptible objects in perceptible space; and it is dubious whether the notion of a spatial system of which none of the elements can be observed is even intelligible (p. 86).

The third possible answer, and that which Ayer himself favours, is to conceive of physical particles as being the minute parts of perceptible objects, so that their being imperceptible is not a necessary part of their nature, but

First published in G. F. Macdonald (ed.), *Perception and Identity: Essays Presented to A. J. Ayer* (London, 1979).

[1] A. J. Ayer, *The Central Questions of Philosophy* (London, 1973), 108–11. All subsequent page references in this chapter refer to the same work.

simply an empirical consequence of their being so minute. On this view, it is simply an empirical fact that particles which are individually colourless compose coloured objects when enough of them come together; it is a further consequence that we are actually in error when we believe that the surfaces of physical objects are continuous.

What is the question to which these are rival answers? We could, entirely properly, formulate it as "What are the hard facts concerning the physical world?"; but this is not Ayer's way of framing it, and would lead us into a discussion of the very important, but very general, distinction between hard and soft facts. A formulation more in accordance with Ayer's discussion, and having the right degree of generality, would be "How are we to conceive of physical objects as they are in themselves?" And so our first task is to scrutinize the notion of an object "as it is in itself".

We might say that the enquiry how things, in general, are in themselves—not just material objects—is *the* metaphysical enquiry. Here, of course, "as they are in themselves" stands opposed to "as they appear to us". This contrast is stated by Ayer in discussing the view (p. 82) that physics falsifies naïve realism. This view he links with the thesis that tables, for example, are not really coloured; and in elucidating this thesis he says (p. 84), of those who hold it, that "they want to distinguish between things as they are in themselves and things as they can appear to us, and to count as the real properties of physical objects only those properties that they possess independently of our perceiving them". There is no doubt that this is a correct characterization of a very strong and very broad current in philosophical thought. We commonly deploy a distinction between how things appear and how they really are; and it is therefore natural to try to push this distinction to the limit. This seems to me the best way in which to view the so-called 'argument from illusion'. If this is regarded as an argument, properly so called, with premises and a conclusion, it is difficult to make out what are the premises and what the conclusion. Rather, it is a *starting-point*. We start with the existence of a distinction, or distinctions, between how things appear and how they really are; and we want to take it as far as we can, or, at any rate, to see how far it can be taken. It is, of course, possible to point out that the contrast between how a thing appears and how it really is is not made at one level: the notion of appearance is not applied uniformly, and so the correlative notion of reality is not applied uniformly either. But we might compare this situation with what Wittgenstein said about possibility. Wittgenstein observed that, at least in most contexts, "can do such-and-such" may be glossed "can do such-and-such so far as . . . is concerned", where the dots are filled in in some specific way. But, even if we grant this, we may legitimately enquire whether there is any *absolute* sense of "can" that falls short of "does", one that is the conjunction of all the relativized senses. In the same way, we may enquire whether there is a way of characterizing a thing that will fall on the side of how it really is, or how it is in itself, as opposed to how it appears, *however* that distinction is applied; and it is this concern which powers a great deal of metaphysical enquiry.

2. REALISM

The thesis that tables and the like are not really coloured was, as we saw, attributed by Ayer to the proponents of the view that physics falsifies naïve realism; and, in the passage (pp. 108–11) with which we are chiefly concerned, the second and third of the three possible answers to our question are stated to be alternative means of upholding realism, while the first answer relegates physical theory to the status of a secondary system. The realism in question is "a realistic view of the status of physical particles" (p. 110). Now it appears to me that the traditional manner of using the philosophical term "realism", which Ayer follows, blurs an important distinction. Of course, there is no question of anyone's simply being a realist *tout court*: one may be a realist about a certain subject-matter, or, as it seems to me better to say, one may adopt a realistic interpretation of a certain class of statements, and not about some other subject matter, or of some other class of statements. Objections to a realistic interpretation of a given class of statements frequently take their rise from a form of reductionism: one says that a statement of the given class cannot be true unless some statement, or perhaps set of statements, of some other class, which I shall call the *reductive* class, is true. For instance, it is said that a statement ascribing a mental state to somebody cannot be true unless some one of a range of statements about his behaviour is true, statements which may be required to be categorical or may be allowed to include subjunctive conditionals. Here the reductive class consists of statements about the person's behaviour; on another view, it might consist of statements about his neurophysiological condition. Such a thesis is obviously of philosophical interest in itself: I shall call it a *reductive* thesis. A reductive thesis concerning statements ascribing mental states to individuals may be said to be a thesis about that in virtue of which such statements are true, when they are true; or to offer an answer to the question of in what mental states consist. The thesis that, for a given class of statements, there is no other class of statements with respect to which a reductive thesis holds—that is, that there is no reductive class—I shall call an *irreducibility* thesis.

   Now, although reductive theses are intrinsically interesting (at least when the given class has been characterized in such a way as not to make them trivial), it seems to me a mistake to make rejection or acceptance of such a thesis a touchstone of whether one adopts or repudiates a realistic interpretation of the given class. The reason why it can seem so is that the step of propounding a reductive thesis is very often a preliminary to a further step.

One observes that, for any particular statement of the given class, there is no guarantee that there will either be true statements of the reductive class which render that statement true, or be true statements of the reductive class which render its negation true (the given class is assumed closed under negation). From this it is inferred that there is no guarantee that an arbitrary statement of the given class will be either true or false: such statements do not satisfy the principle of bivalence, so long as the falsity of such a statement is equated with the truth of its negation. And it is in taking this step that a realistic interpretation of the statements of the given class has been abandoned. That is, the touchstone of realism ought to be whether it is held that we possess a notion of truth for statements of the given class relative to which they satisfy the principle of bivalence—the principle, namely, that every statement is determinately either true or false.

The advantage of characterizing realism in this way lies in two facts. First, the acceptance of a reductive thesis does not inevitably lead to the repudiation of realism: one need not take the second step in the argument. From a reductive thesis it does not in itself follow that bivalence fails for statements of the given class: one has to look at the particular reductive thesis proposed to see whether that consequence is plausible or not. For instance, those who hold that a statement ascribing a mental state to someone, if true at all, will be true in virtue of some neurophysiological condition of that person are likely to place a realistic interpretation on statements ascribing mental states, by the criterion of realism formulated above. And, secondly, the repudiation of realism does not require the prior acceptance of a reductive thesis: that is simply a familiar route to it. One might hold an irreducibility thesis concerning statements of some given class, and yet believe that the idea that we had, for such statements, a conception of truth relative to which bivalence was satisfied was an illusion. I do not pretend that, in using the term "realism" in the way proposed, we shall be precisely conforming to traditional philosophical practice. On the contrary, the point of the proposal is to enable us to keep clearly in mind a distinction which, under the traditional use of the term, has frequently been blurred. Whether my terminology is happy is a matter of minor importance; what is important is to maintain the distinction.

All four combinations are possible. If one takes a realistic view of a given class of statements, one may nevertheless admit that some reductive thesis holds for that class; or one may regard the class as irreducible. I shall say that a realist of the first kind is a *sophisticated realist*, one of the second kind a *naïve realist*. Equally, if one repudiates realism concerning a class of statements, one may do so on the strength of some reductive thesis to which one adheres; but one may also do so while admitting that class to be irreducible. I shall call the former a *reductive anti-realist*, the latter an *outright anti-realist* (it would be stretching the term too far to call him 'naïve').

I have so far avoided the label 'reductionist'. A reductionist is usually thought of as one who not merely accepts a reductive thesis, but also holds that it is in principle possible to translate statements of the given class into statements of the reductive class; and this is just the way in which Ayer characterizes that position (p. 66). Obviously, one may accept a reductive thesis, but deny the truth of reductionism, for any of several reasons. First, one may, without abandoning the reductive thesis, concede that statements of the reductive class are not intelligible independently of statements of the given class. For instance, one may claim that a mathematical statement, if true at all, can be true only in virtue of the truth of a statement to the effect that we are in possession of a proof of it, but admit that it is impossible to frame a vocabulary in which statements of the latter kind can be expressed without thereby introducing a vocabulary adequate for the expression of the mathematical statements themselves. This is emphatically *not* Ayer's ground for denying the possibility of translating statements about physical objects into statements about sense data (see pp. 91–3). Secondly, one may hold that we have no way of effectively identifying, for any statement of the given class, that statement of the reductive class that must be true if it is to be true. This seems to be Donald Davidson's reason for not holding that psychological statements are translatable into neurophysiological ones; but, again, no such suggestion appears in Ayer. Thirdly, one may think that, to ensure the truth of a statement of the given class, the truth of the statements in some infinite subset of the reductive class is needed; or that the truth of a statement of the given class guarantees the truth of only one out of infinitely many statements in the reductive class; or one may combine these views. If our language does not contain the apparatus for forming the necessary infinite conjunctions and disjunctions, actual translation will be impossible. This is one of Ayer's two reasons for not being a reductionist (p. 107). The other is that a translation would necessitate admitting subjunctive conditionals into the reductive class, and Ayer feels uncomfortable about such conditionals. I do not classify this as a distinct ground for rejecting reductionism while accepting a reductive thesis, since it would seem that, where the premiss was cogent, conditionals would have to be admitted to the reductive class if even the reductive thesis was to hold. What is important is that even reductive anti-realism does not require reductionism in this full-fledged sense.

On the strength of his rejection of reductionism, Ayer claims to be a sophisticated realist (p. 108). Now, Ayer's second argument against reductionism tells equally against a reductive thesis. It is this. To find, for an arbitrary statement about material objects, a statement about percepts the truth of which would render the material-object statement true, it would be necessary to allow the statement about percepts to take the form of a subjunctive conditional. But any class of subjunctive conditionals is itself pre-eminently a reducible class: some reductive thesis must hold good for it (Ayer expresses this by saying that conditionals do not belong to the primary system—see pp. 142–5). The argument, as thus stated, is not cogent: it shows only that the class of statements, including conditional ones, about percepts is not an *ultimate* reductive class for material-object statements, that we can carry out a further reduction. It would become cogent only if it were claimed, in addition, that the truth of a conditional concerning percepts could be explained only in terms of the truth of suitable (categorical) material-object statements, so that the latter formed a reductive class for conditionals about percepts: then, indeed, the class of material-object statements would be effectively irreducible. There is, however, no suggestion of this kind in Ayer's discussion of subjunctive conditionals (pp. 150–5): he says that we accept a conditional on the basis of a generalization of law, which differs from a generalization of fact in that we treat it as projectible. Of course, this calls for a detailed discussion of what induces us to treat a generalization as projectible; but there is no explicit claim that we should never so treat generalizations concerning percepts without adverting to material-object statements we consider true.

However this may be, it seems clear that Ayer does not accept even a reductive thesis concerning material-object statements. He is therefore not a sophisticated realist in the sense I gave to that term above; if he is a realist at all, he is a naïve realist in my sense. Now, Ayer does say explicitly (p. 152) that the principle of bivalence does not hold for subjunctive conditionals in general; but, since he does not accept a reductive thesis, we cannot infer that he is not a realist, in my sense, about material-object statements. It is very hard to say whether he is or not: he does not appear to be concerned with this issue in respect of material-object statements couched in everyday language. He *is* concerned with it in regard to the statements of physical theory; for instrumentalism—the view that scientific theories form mere 'secondary systems'—does constitute a rejection of realism, in my sense, for scientific statements. The question he raises concerning material-object statements of everyday language, on the other hand, is not whether they may all be considered as determinately true or false independently of our knowledge, but, roughly speaking, whether they may ever be considered true at all: more exactly, the curious question whether material objects really have perceptible qualities.

In calling himself a sophisticated realist, Ayer is certainly using the term "sophisticated" in a technical sense. Sophisticated realism stands opposed to naïve realism; and naïve realism, as Ayer characterizes it (pp. 65–6), appears to incorporate what I have here called naïve realism, and an epistemological thesis besides. The epistemological thesis Ayer expresses as being that "we perceive physical objects not through a screen of sense-impressions but directly". It is clear that this obscure form of words is meant to exclude the possibility of Cartesian doubt concerning reports of observation, but I shall not, in this essay, discuss Cartesian doubt. We shall have a great deal of trouble with the epistemological thesis here attributed to the naïve realist—a thesis which may, again obscurely, be expressed as that, in observing an object under favourable conditions, we know it as it really is.

3. PERCEPTIBLE QUALITIES

Ayer employs the notion of a perceptible quality, but does not define the term; and there are several different possible ways of using it.

(1) The weakest sense is that under which a quality or relation is perceptible provided only that we can frequently judge, with high probability, that an object possesses it, or that it holds between two objects, just by looking at, listening to, feeling, tasting, or smelling that object or those objects. Let us call qualities and relations that satisfy this condition *observable* ones. There are obviously a great many observable qualities: being cylindrical, for example.

As soon as we frame stronger requirements, we step into a morass. I shall first list the conditions I wish to consider, and attach labels to the classes of qualities and relations satisfying them, and then make a number of comments.

(2) A very strong requirement is that, whenever it is possible to override a judgement to the effect that an object possesses the quality, or that the relation holds between two objects—that is, based on looking at or otherwise observing the object or objects—then it is possible to override it by appeal to judgements also so based but to the opposite effect, possibly made under different conditions or by a different observer. I shall call qualities and relations satisfying this condition *simple observational* ones.

(3) A requirement stronger than (1) but weaker than (2) is that any judgement that can be made about whether an object has the quality, or whether the relation holds between two objects, can be made on the basis solely of perceptual comparisons, in the relevant respect, of one object with another, not necessarily the given object or objects, under varying conditions. Qualities and relations satisfying this condition will be called *complex observational* ones.

Simple and complex observational qualities and relations will be taken as together comprising *observational* qualities and relations.

(4) We may require that a characterization of what it is for an object to possess the quality, or for two objects to stand in the relation, must involve essential reference to human perceptual faculties. I shall call a quality or relation that satisfies this condition *intrinsically perceptual*.

(5) Finally, following Locke, we may say that a quality is a *primary* observable quality if no explanation of our ability to perceive an object as having that quality can be given that does not expressly appeal to the object's possession of the quality, and similarly for relations. For instance, we do not expect any account to be forthcoming of how we are able to discern by feeling it that a moderately small object is spherical that does not appeal to the object's being spherical. I shall here be very little concerned with this interesting property of certain observable qualities.

The definitions of simple and complex observational qualities and relations were so framed as not to exclude their being vague: it was not required that the possession of the quality or subsistence of the relation be completely determined in every case by any set, finite or infinite, of actual or possible observations, or by anything else. It may be said that there can be no vague qualities or relations, but only vague *expressions*, which, as Frege would say, therefore do not stand for any qualities or relations at all. We might, of course, just define a vague quality to be what a vague predicate stands for; but, it will be said, there can be no vagueness in nature, in the world, only in language. This presumably means that the world cannot be such as to require vague predicates to describe it, although *we* may be, for various reasons, forced to employ them; but I am inclined to suspect that this attitude represents a deep but unwarranted philosophical prejudice.

For all that, there are grounds for thinking that there can be no simple observational *qualities*. The defining condition for such qualities implies a further condition, which I shall call the *indiscernibility condition*: namely that, if one object possesses the quality, and no relevant difference between it and another object can be perceived, then the second object possesses it. It seems indisputable that we do habitually use a number of adjectives—for example, "red" and "sweet"—as if standing for a quality subject to this condition. At the same time, in view of the non-transitivity of perceptual indiscernibility, to which Ayer alludes (p. 90), it is incoherent to suppose that there is any quality that always satisfies the condition.

It does not follow, however, that there are no simple observational *relations*. For the indiscernibility condition to apply to a given quality, we must have a suitable notion of perceiving a relevant difference. In the case of colours, tastes, and the like, we do: we make judgements, based on observation, that two objects are or are not perceptibly distinct in colour, as well as judging that a single object is, or is not, red. But consider the relation of being perceptibly distinct in colour itself, which may, of course, be viewed as a quality of pairs of objects rather than as a relation between objects. Then we lack any notion of a perception of a relevant difference between two pairs of objects; we cannot say, "If you judge those two objects to be perceptibly distinct in colour, then you must judge those two other objects to be so also, because there is no perceptible difference, between the two pairs, in the colour distance of the members of the pairs". Since, therefore, we lack a notion of a perception of a relevant difference, we cannot even state the indiscernibility condition for this relation. Hence, while there is an incoherence in supposing that there is a simple observational quality of redness, there is not the same reason for thinking that there is any incoherence in supposing that there is a simple observational relation of perceptible difference in colour.

An objection might be made as follows. If having a specific shade of colour were a simple observational quality, then, given an object with that quality, it would be a necessary and sufficient condition for another object to have the quality that it be perceptibly indiscriminable in colour from the given object. The indiscernibility condition required only that perceptual indiscernibility from an object having the quality be a *sufficient* condition for possession of the quality. We expect it to be a *necessary* condition also when the quality is not only observational but also specific or cospecific (a cospecific quality is the negation or complement of a specific one). Now let us say that a pair of objects has quality Q just in case those objects are perceptibly distinct in colour. Then our argument that the indiscernibility condition is inapplicable to quality Q amounts to saying that there is no perceptible relation between pairs of objects such that, for any pair having quality Q, another pair will have quality Q if and only if it stands in that relation to the first pair. This is indeed surprising, inasmuch as we should expect quality Q to be a cospecific quality. However (the objection goes), it does not show that the indiscernibility condition is inapplicable: for this, we need only a perceptible relation which yields a *sufficient* condition for the second pair to have quality Q. But the relation that holds between the pair $\{x,y\}$ and the pair $\{u,v\}$ when x is perceptibly indiscriminable in colour from u, and y from v, is such a relation: since we cannot see any relevant difference between x and u, or between y and v, we are forced to say that, if $\{x,y\}$ has quality Q, then so must $\{u,v\}$ have it. But if x,u,v,y is a sequence such that no two adjacent terms are perceptibly distinct in colour, but x and y are, the conclusion will be false: there is therefore no such simple observational relation as being perceptibly distinct in colour.

The argument is fallacious, however. The condition that x be perceptibly indiscriminable in colour from u, and y from v, is *not* sufficient to make us say that the pair $\{x,y\}$ cannot be perceived as differing in a relevant respect from the pair $\{u,v\}$: the mere fact that we perceive x and y as distinct in colour, and do not so perceive u and v, makes the two *pairs* perceptibly different in the relevant respect, even though we can see no relevant difference between the individual *objects* x and u, or between y and v.

A similar fallacious objection would be one based on the possibility of converting a relation into a quality by fixing one of its terms. If, the objection runs, being perceptibly indiscriminable in colour is a simple observational relation, then being perceptibly indiscriminable in colour from the surface *s* is a simple observational quality. Hence, if *t* is not perceptibly distinct in colour from *u*, and *t* is not perceptibly distinct in colour from *s*, then *u* cannot be perceptibly distinct in colour from *s*, by the indiscernibility condition; and we appear to have proved the transitivity of indiscernibility of colour, which we know to fail. The mistake in this argument lies in the premiss of fixing one term of a simple observational relation need not yield a simple observational quality. A simple observational quality was defined as one to determine the possession of which by an object we did not need to observe more than that object; but, in deciding whether *t* is perceptibly distinct in colour from *s*, we shall need to look at *s* as well as *t*, and there was nothing in the definition of a simple observational *relation* to make us think otherwise.

Still, it may be said, it is a matter of common experience that there are no simple observational relations, even if we lack an irrefutable argument to show that there can be none. Consider, for instance, perceived equality of length for juxtaposed objects. If I have a metre rule, and am asked to sort lengths of string into those that are more than 29 centimetres long and those that are no more than 29 centimetres long, I shall in some cases be uncertain; but, if perceived equality of length were a simple observational relation, no such uncertainty could arise. Moreover, if I am instructed to sort the lengths of string into those that are *definitely* over 29 centimetres long and those that are not *definitely* so, I shall still sometimes be uncertain. However, all that this argument shows is that, if perceived equality of length is taken to be a simple observational relation, it is irremediably vague; and, as was already noted, this was not ruled out by the definition of a simple observational relation. We did not reject simple observational qualities on the score merely of their exhibiting the very general feature of vagueness of application, but because they had a very special type of vagueness that engendered actual inconsistency. In any case, we have no argument to demonstrate that there are no exact simple observational relations.

If there are, after all, no simple observational relations, there can be no complex observational qualities or relations. Suppose, following Nelson Goodman, that we define *x* to be *indirectly discriminable* in colour from *y* just in case, for some *z*, *x* is perceptibly distinct in colour from *z*, but *y* is not; or conversely. Then, if (direct) perceptible discriminability in colour is a simple observational relation, indirect discriminability is a complex observational one, vague or exact according as the former is vague or exact. Goodman's idea, by allowing us to introduce complex observational colour qualities related to indirect indiscriminability as the simple observational ones were supposed to be related to direct indiscriminability, gets us over the difficulty that there can be no colour qualities satisfying the indiscernibility condition; but such a device works only if direct indiscriminability is a simple observational relation.

In the definitions of simple and complex observational qualities and relations, I have left an uncertainty about whether it is allowable, in making a comparison, to juxtapose the objects, or whether a comparison between non-adjacent objects must be made with them *in situ*. If we allow juxtaposition, we shall of course get a wider class of qualities and relations. For instance, if, in that case, we had a notion of equality of length considered as determined solely by very direct and straightforward methods of measurement, involving only comparison of juxtaposed objects, and not measurement of angles, calculation, and so on, then equality in length would be a simple or a complex observational relation according as we made only direct comparisons or used a yardstick. However, the important fact is that there are many observable qualities which are not observational at all: for instance, shape qualities, the application of which even to objects of the right size and distance for us to be able to judge of their shape by looking may always be checked by measurement (of distances and angles), the result of which overrides the purely perceptual judgement when it disagrees with it. Measurement may reveal that the base of the tin is not circular, and hence that the tin is not cylindrical, even though no observer can detect the deviation from circularity just by looking. Ayer refers to this fact (p. 77); but he rather brushes it aside. Colour qualities have a better claim to be observational. For instance, when presented with one of the familiar kind of optical illusions, we determine that a figure really is a rectangle, and not, as appears, a trapezium, by some crude measurement; but we determine that an area of the figure is really white, and not yellow or grey, by covering up the rest of the figure and seeing how it looks then, and thus by means of a test of the sort allowed for observational qualities. In the former case, we no longer appeal to any perceptual judgement about shape; but, in the latter case, we still rely on a perceptual judgement about colour, but we change the conditions under which it is made.

There remains some doubt, especially for those who believe that there is no vagueness in nature, whether there are any simple observational relations, and hence whether there are any observational qualities or relations, simple or complex, at all: certainly we use many familiar terms as standing for simple observational qualities the existence of which involves a contradiction. We must suppose that there exist non-observational qualities the extension of which approximately coincides with our application of such terms; and when, in the sequel, I speak of observational qualities, I must, whenever necessary, be taken as referring to such approximately observational ones.

The notion of an intrinsically perceptual quality also calls for some explanation. It is a plausible hypothesis that some or all of the affective qualities—being funny, boring, macabre, eerie, interesting, and so forth—are, in an analogous sense, intrinsically affective. Various people, such as Bergson and Freud, have attempted to say in what being funny, considered objectively, consists: "considered objectively" means "formulated without reference to the capacity to evoke amusement in us". The problem is this. Suppose that we had got as far as being able to feed narrative stories into a computer: it could then answer examination questions about them, of the type "What reason did Jane give for returning to Paris?"; or perhaps it could produce on its console a cartoon depicting the sequence of events. We want now to programme the computer to give sensible answers to the question "Was that story (*a*) hilarious, (*b*) mildly amusing, or (*c*) not funny in the least?": what instructions are we to give it? Only if we had a theory of humour of the kind Bergson and Freud so unsuccessfully attempted to construct could we begin to set about this task. And perhaps there is no such theory. Perhaps being funny is incapable of analysis save in terms of reactions evoked in us: perhaps we are the only creatures in the universe who can perceive this quality, so that it is impossible in principle to design an instrument to detect its presence, unless that instrument incorporates one or more human beings. That is the hypothesis that the quality of being funny is intrinsically affective.

What would it be for a quality to be, in a similar way, intrinsically perceptual? If, in the definition, we replace "human perceptual faculties" by "the perceptual faculties of terrestrial animals", we can imagine that taste qualities had so turned out. Intense research had wholly failed to uncover the physiological mechanism of taste; and repeated efforts had established no correlation between the taste of a substance and its molecular structure or any other feature of its physical or chemical constitution. Perhaps it was found that sodium chloride could be separated out, by getting people to taste minute quantities of it, into two chemically indistinguishable substances—one twice as salt in taste as ordinary table salt, and the other quite tasteless: we might find ourselves forced to admit that our impression that chemically identical substances taste alike was an illusion owing to most samples' having the same mixture of substances distinguishable only by taste. This would not *prove* that taste qualities were intrinsically perceptual: that would be only a hypothesis—the hypothesis, namely, that terrestrial animals were the only things in the universe that responded differentially to, and could therefore be used to detect, qualities of taste. It would then hold good that the *only* characterization of what it is for something to be sweet, for example—the only characterization we could ever attain—would be that it tastes sweet to human beings, bears, and similar creatures.

4. THINGS AS THEY ARE IN THEMSELVES

The formulation of Ayer's original question with which we came up was "How are we to conceive of physical objects as they are in themselves?" We saw that Ayer connected this with the question whether the scientific view of the nature of physical objects is compatible with that attributable to common sense, and, further, with the question whether tables are really coloured. Now, as already remarked, the main question takes its rise from the fact that we admit a distinction, or distinctions, between how things really are and how they appear. For there to be a world—that is, an external environment—that we all inhabit, there must be a distinction between how things appear to one person and how they actually are. From this it does not follow that we need admit any distinction between how things appear to us generally and how they really are: I may take as correct etiquette what is not actually correct etiquette, but it is impossible that we should all take as correct etiquette what is not actually so. Nevertheless, we do in fact extend the distinction we make between how material objects appear to one observer and how they really are to a distinction between how they appear to any (human) observer and how they really are. This is in part a consequence of the fact that the majority of the predicates that we use as standing for observable qualities do not stand for observational qualities: the results of physical operations, or of mental ones such as counting, provide criteria for their application that override judgements based on unaided observation. But even for predicates standing for observational qualities we admit the distinction. To any normally sighted person who looks up when he is out of doors on a clear day, it undoubtedly looks as though there is something blue overhead; but the only candidate for being something that really is blue is a purely visual object. Equally, if he looks up on a clear night, he will see the stars twinkling; but the stars do not really twinkle: they only appear to twinkle—though, of course, they really do so appear.

But these, after all, are cases of mistakes—very natural mistakes, but still mistakes: unless otherwise instructed, anyone will naturally suppose that there is a blue dome above the clouds, and that the light emitted by the stars fluctuates rapidly in intensity. Is there any reason to admit a distinction between how things appear to all of us and how they really are, when no mistake is in question? If such a distinction is admissible at all in cases when no mistake is involved, it cannot be one that requires us to say that the object in question is not as it appears to be; for this would entail that, in taking it to be as it appears, we had made a mistake, when, by hypothesis, no mistake was in question. It does not follow that there is not a legitimate distinction between different ways of characterizing the qualities of objects. The contrast is now not between the qualities that things appear to have and those different qualities that they really have: it is between a method of characterizing those qualities that they are agreed to have in terms of our own perceptual capacities and one that is independent of our modes of perception; it is therefore not a matter of discovering that they lack certain qualities that we wrongly supposed them to have. The attempt to say what things are like in themselves is an attempt to find a means of characterizing them that is independent, not only of the particular position and circumstances of an individual observer, but also, more generally, of the situation of human beings, located on the surface of a certain planet at a particular stage in its history, being of a certain size, and having a particular range of sensory faculties. The making of such an attempt in no way involves us in thinking that a description that is not independent of these things, but is given in terms relative to or explained by reference to our own position and observational capacities, is *incorrect* in any way: only that it does not accomplish what is achieved by a description that is independent of these contingent facts.

Thus the distinction between "how things are in themselves" and "how they appear to us" bifurcates into two quite different, though related, distinctions: that between what is true of the world and what only appears to be, but is not actually, true of it; and that between what may be called an absolute and what may be called a relative form of description. A description in relative terms may, in itself, be perfectly correct; but, in reflective moods, and, to a considerable extent, for practical purposes, we prefer a description in absolute terms. One of the things that a scientific theory aims to do is to attain an accurate description of things as they are in themselves, or as they really are, in this sense—that is, a description in absolute terms; and such a description need not invalidate, in the sense of showing to be incorrect, the form of description in relative terms that we employ in everyday life.

But, if this is so, why is an impression to the contrary so widespread amongst philosophers? Why is it regarded as a problem, as Ayer regards it, whether a scientific description is compatible with a common-sense one, and, if so, how the reconciliation can be effected? Why should Ayer concern himself with those who think that his table is not really brown? Ayer himself does not think that there is good reason to deny that his table is brown; but he treats the matter as a serious problem, one requiring a subtle philosophical theory to meet the challenge. He wants a theory according to which subatomic particles are colourless only as "an empirical consequence of their being so minute", i.e. smaller than the wavelength of light; and he thinks that he has to work hard to get such a theory, and so escape the rival theory according to which all physical objects, however large, are in principle colourless. But why cannot we dismiss this rival theory as involving an elementary confusion between the two types of distinction between how things are in themselves and how they appear? Any normally sighted person, we might say, can see at a glance that there are plenty of coloured material objects: the question is not whether the surfaces of objects have colour, but in what their having any given colour consists. Perhaps those who think that all (material) objects are colourless, and those who are frightened that, if we do not relegate science to the status of a 'secondary system', in the Ramsey–Ayer terminology, we may have to allow that material objects are colourless are making the mistake of confusing the adoption of a reductive thesis concerning statements ascribing colours to objects with the repudiation of a realistic view of such statements—when in fact, as we have seen, the two are independent of one another. Indeed, even the rejection of realism concerning a given class of statements does not involve us in saying that no statement in that class is ever *really* true. Someone who takes a constructivist view of mathematical statements has in no way to deny that there are true mathematical statements: he merely rejects the idea that each statement of classical mathematics is determinately true or false, independently of our knowing, or having the means of knowing, its truth-value. In any case, the question here at issue is not that of realism concerning statements about material objects, in the sense in which I am using 'realism': it is, rather, the question of whether a reductive thesis holds good for such statements, where the reductive class consists of statements couched in the terms of physical theory. Modern physics does undoubtedly offer many affronts to common sense: but it does not appear that the denial that objects are coloured is one of them.

5. COMMON SENSE

Against this it may be objected that to say that most people can see at a glance that the world contains many coloured objects is an application of the paradigm-case argument. If so, it may be possible to rebut it by the standard means for rebutting paradigm-case arguments: namely, by agreeing that we normally assume that we can tell whether something is brown by looking at it, but contending that, in calling it "brown", we ordinarily understand ourselves as attributing to it a property which, if physical theory is not a mere secondary system, it does not actually have. To argue thus is, in effect, to reject the claim made earlier that there is a way of construing the distinction between how things are in themselves and how they appear to us that does not involve that the appearance is delusive. On this account, a physicist who agrees that Ayer's table is brown will not be using the word "brown" in the same sense as that in which it is used by most people in everyday speech; at least, he will not be so using it if he believes that a description of the table in terms of physical theory is a description of it as it really is, rather than just giving a convenient summary of certain regularities we should observe if we subjected the table to a variety of experiments.

Now, without doubt we may properly speak of certain views as forming, at a particular period and within a particular culture, a part of common sense. A common-sense view is a conception on which most of those who belong to that culture at that time habitually rely in their everyday thinking. It is not required that they should actually hold it to be correct—they, or some of them, may know, or think, otherwise: what matters is that their ordinary thinking proceeds *as if* it were correct. It was remarked above that modern physical theory offers many affronts to common sense. It has often been remarked that common sense always lags behind scientific theory, and one thing that common sense has still not absorbed is relativity theory; it seems reasonable to say that common sense continues to take temporal intervals and spatial distances and therefore shapes as absolute.

To speak about common sense in this way, however, as something that lags behind the advances in scientific theory, is to reject the picture of it that some philosophers appear to use: the picture of a single, unified, permanent 'theory of the world', an acceptance of which, at least as a basis for one's ordinary, everyday thinking, is simply part of what is involved in being a sane adult human being. There is no such single unchanging theory. It is, for instance, a mistake to think of anyone, however little educated, in our own society as entirely ignorant of science or as uninfluenced by it in his common modes of thought. On the contrary, all are profoundly affected, in their view of the world and of ordinary things in it, by the smatterings of scientific knowledge that they possess. Perhaps the most striking example of this is the way in which our thought is permeated by the knowledge of the molecular structure of matter, which informs the way we think about mixtures of liquids. We have learned to think about these on the model of mixtures of granular solids such as sugar and salt: so much does this image dominate us that it is virtually impossible to think oneself back into those conceptions which seemed natural when a liquid was thought of as homogeneously filling the whole space it occupied. St Thomas says that, if a small quantity of water is added to wine, it becomes wine. Even if we prescind from our knowledge that wine is already a mixture, this seems to us insane; but that is because we surreptitiously appeal to the granular model to explain to ourselves what a mixture is. We cannot recapture the mode of thought natural if a liquid is taken to be completely homogeneous; we have no idea how, under such a conception, we are to describe what takes place when one liquid is added to another and thoroughly stirred.

Again, in assessing the conception that a 'plain man' has of phenomena of light, it is wrong to think of him as innocent of the idea of radiation. He has a wireless and a television set; he has, perhaps, an electric heater, of which one part works by convection and the other by radiation; he has a camera, and knows about the exposure of a film to light; he has X-ray pictures taken at the hospital; he has heard of radio astronomy and perhaps of X-ray astronomy; he has possibly read newspaper articles about the ozone layer and ultra-violet radiation. For a philosopher who believes that there is such a thing as *the* common-sense view of the world, a natural response to remarks such as these is to say that all they show is that there are no plain men in our society. If, he thinks, we could find a society whose members remained uncorrupted by scientific knowledge, those people would retain the pure, unadulterated common-sense view. But this is an error. Even if we find people who have nothing that we should classify as scientific knowledge, they will have some general account of phenomena of their experience, even if a wholly erroneous one, and, even if most of them have only smatterings of this theory, it will colour the way they find it natural to think about the world. The idea of *the* common-sense view of the world is as much a myth as that of the noble savage (or, indeed, that of the savage). Even if a philosopher who believed the myth were to scour the earth and succeed in finding, in some remote corner, a group of people who accepted just what he had described as constituting *the* common-sense view of the world, it would prove nothing to his advantage: it would show only that he had made a lucky guess about one possible conception of reality; but that conception would have no special standing, among all the different conceptions that have prevailed amongst men of different times and places. The belief in a unique common-sense view is contradictory: it postulates a theory that is, somehow, not a *theory*. It has to be a theory, since, in this context, "view" and "conception" are mere stylistic variants on "theory": it has, that is, to be something in which people may be said to believe, or, at least, to think in accordance with, even if they do not suppose it to be true. Creatures who did not have a theory in this, perhaps fairly low-grade, sense of "theory." would hardly be *men* at all, but only a kind of talking animals; they would lack the curiosity and the capacity for reflection that are essential marks of being human. But, at the same time, the common-sense view has *not* to be a theory, in that, whenever we find people whose view of the world does not coincide with it, we shall be able to say that their view has been distorted by whatever theory is prevalent in their society. There is, however, no view or set of views that has such a privileged status; no view that men would take if only they were left alone by society to form what view was natural to them; for they owe their language, the vehicle of their thought, and their very humanity to being members of a society.

Philosophers of the kind who raise the problem of reconciliation that Ayer is striving to resolve claim to descry a tension not merely between common sense and particular ingredients of current scientific thought, but between common sense and science as such. Such a tension is not discerned by the 'plain man' in our society. There are not, for him, two distinct realms—one of science, which describes things in peculiar ways for arcane purposes of its own, and the other the world of common sense; rather, the fragments of scientific knowledge that a man possesses enter into his picture of the world without any feeling of their being an alien ingredient that has no business to be there. As technology advances, new things become part of everyday experience. They will not, indeed, be fully understood by most people, just as the purely natural phenomena encountered are not fully understood; but, in so far as they are understood, they are understood in the only way they can be, by incorporating scientific ideas into our picture of the world as a whole.

If common sense is culturally conditioned and subject to historical evolution, if it can itself digest scientific ideas and diverges from scientific theory only because the process of digestion is slow and imperfect, then there cannot be an opposition in principle between it and science; nor can we owe to common sense any duty of accepting it, reconciling it with science, or enshrining it as a primary system, with science demoted to secondary status. We can owe it nothing at all: philosophers need make no presumption that the views which, in their particular age, make up the common sense of the day are in some fundamental sense the true ones, subordinate to which any other conception, whether of scientific or of philosophical origin, must find a place if it can.

That is not to say that a philosopher need not pay any special attention to common sense, that he may dismiss it with the brusque remark that, if common sense conflicts with the truth, then so much the worse for common sense. Common-sense views enter into our understanding of the words we use in everyday speech, and it is this that makes them particularly tenacious and makes us at first resist as unintelligible any theory that conflicts with them. I am not among those who hold that it is impossible in principle to draw any distinction between the meanings we attach to our words and our acceptance as true of statements involving them; but it would be absurd to deny that what we take to be true often bears strongly on the way we take the meanings of our words as being given, or that, given the meaning attached to some predicate, the truth of some substantial proposition needs to be assumed if it is to be believed to have an application. An abandonment of a common-sense view may therefore require a certain shift in the understanding of words, a shift rendered more palatable by a philosopher's effort to bring the common-sense view to light and to analyse the change of meaning demanded.

6. 'THE COLOURS ARE IN THE OBJECTS'

We have still to discover just what view is imputed to common sense by those philosophers who think that a scientific account, if accepted as part of a primary system, would require us to believe that Ayer's table is not brown, as common sense understands "brown". On the face of it, if the alleged common-sense view is to be one that conflicts not merely with the particular scientific account of colour that we have, but with any conceivable such account, so that common sense is in opposition, not merely to particular scientific theories, but to science as such, it must be to the effect that colours are intrinsically perceptual qualities, in the sense in which, in the imaginary situation described above, taste qualities would be. On reflection, however, it seems doubtful that this can capture what is alleged to be the common-sense view. Does anyone credit common sense with the view that no scientific account of what enables us to perceive any observable, or, perhaps, any observational, quality will ever be forthcoming? Surely everyone would agree that common sense is simply indifferent to the feasibility of such accounts; or, if anything, in our culture, has a prejudice in favour of it. An expression of the view imputed to common sense which some philosophers favour is to say that colours (and other observational qualities) are *in* the objects. Ayer (p. 85) quotes Locke as asserting that "colours are nothing in the objects themselves"; and certainly Berkeley made use of a similar form of expression (disagreeing with Locke about his primary qualities—not, like the self-appointed champion of common sense, about his secondary ones). But this is a very strange form of words, which does not, at first sight, convey any clear sense whatever. What can it mean?

If the alleged common-sense view is not that colours are intrinsically perceptual, can it be that they are *primary*, in the sense explained above— namely that any explanation of our capacity to perceive an object as brown must make essential appeal to its being brown? That hardly seems right as it stands. If we are told that our ability to distinguish things that taste sweet from those that do not is due to some feature of the shapes of the molecules of sweet substances, it could hardly be maintained that here was an affront to common sense. But what, then, *is* meant when it is contended that, for common sense, the colour (or the taste) is *in* the object? Perhaps we are going astray because we have not given due weight to the requirement that the scientific account be regarded as part of a *primary* system, i.e. that it be claimed that it describes the object as it really is in itself. Perhaps it is not the scientific account itself that is regarded as conflicting with common sense, but this claim on its behalf. Let us see if we can make any progress by viewing the matter in this light.

Could it not be said that the meanings we ordinarily attach to words for observational qualities render those qualities intrinsically perceptual in a weaker sense—one that does not, just because those meanings relate to the observational character of the qualities, rule out a scientific account of the relevant perceptual faculty? We learn the meanings of expressions for observational qualities by learning to recognize those qualities by observation, and learning also the cases in which a judgement about the possession of such a quality is to be withdrawn as mistaken. Now, an intrinsically perceptual quality was defined to be one that could be characterized only by reference to human perceptual faculties. If we add the requirement that the characterization be such as to involve no shift in our everyday understanding of an expression for the quality, we obtain a weaker notion, that of being what we may term an *inherently perceptual* quality. Thus, colours of opaque surfaces, as expressed in our everyday vocabulary, are not intrinsically perceptual qualities, because they can be characterized, in a rather complicated way, in terms of propensities to reflect light of certain frequencies. But such characterizations, if taken as ways of giving the meanings of words such as "brown" and "red" as applied to opaque surfaces, involve a shift in the way those meanings are given, since they are ordinarily understood as given by reference to our observational capacities. Hence, the qualities for which they stand, though not *intrinsically* perceptual, are *inherently* perceptual. Perhaps the thesis being imputed to common sense is that all observational qualities are inherently perceptual.

Here we seem to have come closer to our goal; but we have not attained it. For the thesis, as now formulated, can hardly be denied: it follows from the simple fact that we normally acquire, and should normally explain, all expressions for observational qualities by reference to our capacity to recognize such qualities by unaided observation. But we can now make the following suggestion. The thesis that is being imputed to common sense, the thesis expressed by saying that colours, tastes, and so on are *in* the objects, is that, in describing an object as it is in itself, each quality that we ascribe to it for which there is an expression in everyday speech must be characterized by the use of that expression in a manner that preserves its meaning as ordinarily understood. The fact that this thesis requires so elaborate a statement is, in itself, no objection to its being regarded as implicit in common-sense conceptions: such conceptions may well be confused or inchoate. On the assumption that this, or something very like it, is the thesis which, in the opinion of some philosophers, is embedded in the common-sense view of the world, we have now to ask whether it really is so embedded.

7. CORRELATION AND NORMAL CONDITIONS

Let me say at the outset that I do not for a moment believe that any such thesis can be attributed to common sense. The question then arises why, if it cannot, it has appeared to many philosophers that it can. I shall try to answer this question before arguing that the thesis is not attributable to common sense. The mistake made by the philosophers who think otherwise rests on two inaccurate modes of thought. The first consists in conceiving of physical theory as though it had originally come into existence quite independently of our everyday experience of, and reflection upon, observable qualities. According to this picture, a physical and chemical theory had been developed for some reason or other—say, for explaining mechanical and chemical interactions and phenomena of electricity and magnetism; then, subsequently, people had the bright idea of connecting this theory with ordinary observable qualities of objects, so as to yield, in conjunction with the findings of physiologists, an explanation of our capacity to observe such qualities. The model here is an explanation of taste qualities in terms of chemical structure (or molecular shape), or, perhaps, the theory of sound in terms of longitudinal waves in the air. The scientific account is, on this picture, viewed as the discovery of a *correlation*: some observable quality is found to be correlated with some property describable in terms of physical or chemical theory, and then the physiologists are called in aid to explain how this property affects our sense organs. Philosophers who see the matter in this way attribute to common sense the idea that, even if an observable, or, at any rate, an observational, quality can in this way be correlated with a physical property, and the latter used to give a causal explanation for our capacity to perceive the former, still there can be no question of *identifying* the one with the other: the object's possessing the observational quality cannot be taken to *consist* in its having that physical property by means of which our capacity to perceive the observational quality can be explained.

This is a picture that fits certain cases, such as taste qualities—and it may seem natural in view of the esoteric character of contemporary physics, with its quarks, collapses of wave packets, and black holes; but it is, in general, a false picture. Physical theory was not first constructed to explain phenomena of which we have little direct perceptual experience, and then subsequently applied to give a causal account of our sensory faculties. It has, on the contrary, grown from the effort to formulate laws governing everyday phenomena, describable in terms of observable qualities: there is a continuous development from the steps we are forced to take even in everyday life to frame an adequate description of the world we observe and live in to the abstruse physics of today. In the course of its growth, physical theory has, naturally, come to embrace ever more recondite phenomena, integrating them, sometimes as a first step, sometimes only at a late stage, with the more familiar ones. Thus, for example, the adjective "heavy" certainly denotes an observable quality; and, from its birth, physics employed the notion of weight. Later, it split off the notion of mass from that of weight, needing the former notion to formulate laws governing mechanical phenomena having nothing to do with falling or pressing downwards. Only when a heliocentric account of the planetary system had liberated us from the idea that "up" and "down" denote directions from any point in the universe could the problem of weight be converted into the problem of gravitation—a big generalization, indeed, but a natural and inevitable one given the altered view of the macrocosm. And, as for weight, so also for light and heat. Physics reached the point it is now at by continuing to explore the world, and to seek an adequate description of it, in a manner wholly continuous with what everyday observation forces upon us.

The second mistaken idea underlying the false conception of what common sense entails is that the use of expressions for observational qualities is properly described by saying that their application depends upon the judgements we make when the observation is conducted 'under normal conditions'. The idea is that we learn to discount judgements made under special conditions known to give rise to error: it has become a cliché, in philosophical discussions of perception, to say that an object has those observational qualities it is judged to have by normal observers under normal conditions. Thus, someone who has been handling ice will overestimate the temperature of things he touches; while anyone is liable to misjudge the colour of a surface if he sees it under, say, a sodium vapour lamp. This gives rise to the conception that we may, quite literally, distinguish between delusive appearances, on the one hand, and, on the other, seeing (hearing, feeling) an object as it really is—for instance, seeing it in its true colours. Of course, we can, and do, make a distinction between circumstances in which we are prone to make incorrect judgements, or unable to make any at all, and ones in which we shall probably judge correctly; and we sometimes draw this distinction by speaking of seeing an object as it really is. But for a philosopher to place great weight on this form of words is for him to allow no place for a distinction between what I earlier called a description in absolute and one in relative terms, or, at least, for contrasting the two forms of description as a description of the object as it is in itself and as one in terms of how it appears to us: it allows no conception of the object 'as it appears to us' save when a *mistake* is involved. If our perception of an object 'under normal conditions' is a perception of it as it really is, then a description of it as it really is must be a description of it as we then perceive it—that is, by the use of observational predicates, understood as being explicable only by reference to observation.

Only brief reflection is required in order to reveal that the whole terminology of 'normal conditions' involves a crude over-simplification. It is a well-known fact that a piece of metal, being a much better conductor, feels much colder to the touch than a piece of wood when both are at room temperature. Are we, then, to say that a thermometer records real—i.e. observational—temperature inaccurately? If not, what are the 'normal conditions' under which we perceive the true temperature of a piece of metal? Common experience familiarizes us with the phenomenon of resolution, as when, in driving, a distant blur resolves itself into separate street lights. But what are the 'normal conditions' for viewing an object the surface of which appears to the naked eye, however close, to be uniformly coloured, but resolves into dots under magnification? What are 'normal conditions' for viewing the Milky Way? Or for viewing the sun, an oxyacetylene torch, or a nuclear explosion? Is the 'normal' mode of observing a reflecting surface with the eyes focused on that surface or, behind it, on the image? The only general sense that can be given to "perceiving the object as it really is" is 'perceiving it under conditions in which one is not liable to make an error of judgement'; and the conditions required will vary according to the particular predicate we are judging to apply or not to apply, and, sometimes, cannot be stated at all, if the judgement is to be based on unaided observation. Given a particular predicate—say, a colour predicate such as "brown", or other predicate, such as "shiny", characterizing the visual appearance of an opaque surface—there will often be a range of conditions under which an observer will probably give a correct judgement: in the case of "brown" or "shiny", when the object is illuminated by a white light giving a degree of illumination between a certain minimum and a certain maximum. But that does not mean that, provided that the necessary 'normal' condition holds, a surface to which such a predicate is correctly applied will present a unique visual appearance: appearances which will evoke the description "brown" or "shiny" will vary enormously in detail, according to the position and brightness of the light source or sources, the position of the observer and the focus of his eyes, the placing of objects which cast shadows or the variously coloured surfaces of which reflect on to the observed surface, and so on. The notion of 'normal conditions' is a myth, except in the restricted sense stated above: anyone accustomed to the use of observational predicates knows at least implicitly, and will recognize on reflection, that they stand for essentially dispositional properties, for a propensity to present a range of appearances under a variety of conditions. This is obvious enough in the case of predicates such as "shiny" and "moiré": a shiny surface must glint, from some angles at least, but where the gleams are seen depends on the position of the eye and of the light source. But it is fairly obvious for "yellow", and the like, also, even as applied to matt surfaces—as only a moment's contemplation of, say, the walls of a room will normally suffice to convince anyone not already conscious of the fact.

To see how much the habit of talking in terms of 'normal conditions' distorts the character of our actual perceptual experience, let us consider a world in which it would be entirely appropriate: one in which, under certain conditions of observation, a complete characterization of the visual appearance of a surface would be given in terms invariant under any change in the circumstances of the observer, provided only that those conditions continued to obtain. Suppose that there were only colourless, transparent objects and matt, opaque ones; and, within quite a wide range in intensity of illumination, including daylight on the darkest and on the brightest day, the appearance of an object did not change (so that there would be no shadows when the light was sufficiently bright). We may suppose also that we never saw any source of light—the sky was always clouded, we never rose above the clouds, and there was no fire or incandescence. In such a world, we could say that in daylight we saw the real colours of objects, in a sense much stronger than we can, in our world, give to that phrase: for, in the daylight, the visual appearance of a surface would be independent of the position of the observer, provided that he could see it at all. The description of something as of a particular shade of green would tell me all about the colour impression that anyone would get who saw it in daylight: there would be nothing further to say that would depend on his position or the quality or direction of the light. In such a world, at least in respect of visual surface qualities, the notion of 'normal conditions' could be employed with full appropriateness; but we have only to compare that world with ours to see how very crude and inadequate a notion it is for characterizing our use of observational predicates. In the world imagined, it might be natural for people to adopt, as part of their common-sense view of the world, a thesis like that we have taken to be expressed by the odd phrase "the colours are in the objects"; but our world is very unlike that one.

8. A PLAIN MAN'S VIEW OF COLOURS

I have argued that there can be no such thing as a common sense uninfluenced by theory. Nevertheless, it may be worth attempting to describe how a moderately thoughtful person, not given to philosophical speculation, might conceive of the visual qualities of objects if he were quite innocent of scientific knowledge, but relied only on facts of everyday experience. The most obvious fact is that, to be seen, a surface needs to be in a light; and the second most obvious is that light is something positive, darkness a privation—there are sources of light but no sources of darkness. Light can, however, be blocked; and the most elementary observation of shadows suffices to prompt the conception of light as emanating from light sources in straight lines. It would, on the other hand, be wrong in this context to speak of light as travelling, since, to gross observation, the illumination of a surface when a light source is activated is instantaneous. Gross observation does serve to inform us that the eye is the organ of sight: this is a fact known to everybody, and embodied in the everyday use of the verb "to look".

Now, how would a scientifically uninstructed person conceive of the mechanism of sight? That there is such a thing as reflected light is apparent from the common experience of shiny and reflecting surfaces; but need he think of matt surfaces as reflecting light? He would know that light has to fall on a surface for it to be visible; but must he think that it is by light entering the eye that we see? Plato indeed suggested a different idea, that rays from the eye strike the illuminated surface; but, actually, the most banal facts speak against such a conception. For one thing, there could, on such a view, be no expectation that the same objects would be opaque both to light and to the eye rays; but it is a fact that everybody takes for granted that an object which, if placed between the light source and the surface, will throw the surface into shadow, will also block our vision if interposed between the surface and the eye. For another thing, we can certainly see light, as we know if we look directly at a light source. It is difficult to think of the light from a source as not being continuously between the source and the surface it illuminates, but as jumping the gap between them, because, if an object is placed between them, it is illuminated. On the other hand, we cannot normally see the light between the source and the surface. There could be other explanations of this fact; but the overwhelmingly most natural thing to think is that the light, transmitted from the source, is not itself a source, but that we see the surface that it strikes only because it is reflected into our eyes. This is reinforced by the fact that a matt surface will affect the apparent colour of an adjacent surface (for example, a cream-coloured wall takes on a blue tinge near a bright blue box); and it is well known that, with the same strength of light, a room panelled in dark though shiny mahogany is darker than one with matt white walls, and that we are dazzled by sunlight on snow. On the strength of all these facts of common experience, even a quite uninstructed person would quite naturally form the idea that we see by light entering the eye, and that even a matt surface reflects.

I have not specifically discussed the colour predicates, our ordinary understanding of which is quite complicated: we grasp the distinguished roles of black and white, so that we should be baffled by the expression "black light", and know that what is needed, in any case of doubt, to determine the colour of a clear transparent substance is to put a white surface behind it. It was remarked above that, on a quite ordinary understanding of colour predicates, as applied to opaque and transparent objects, they stand for dispositional properties: no one who has ever noticed—and who has not?—the varied appearance of a uniformly coloured surface, from one area to another, as light from different sources strikes it, as parts lie in shadow and other parts are tinged by reflections from nearby objects, could conceive of them otherwise. This does not hold good, indeed, for colour words as applied to light sources; but, then, we do not ascribe colour to light itself in the same sense as we ascribe it to objects considered as retaining their colours in the dark: we can ask, of an opaque surface, what degree of illumination allows us to judge most reliably of its true colour, but the brightness of a light source is an intrinsic feature of its visual appearance. But the foregoing discussion was intended to bring out that the most familiar facts, with which we need to be acquainted for practical purposes, lead us beyond a merely programmatic conception of visual qualities of surfaces as consisting in propensities to display systematic ranges of different appearances under different conditions of observation. They lead us, that is, to an embryonic theory of that in which such propensities consist— namely in the ability to emit, reflect, absorb, or transmit light of different kinds: in view of our capacity to perceive light, if not too intense, as of different colours, by looking at the sources, it is surely not improper here to speak of "kinds" of light. This illustrates the contention advanced above that physical theory grows out of our everyday understanding of the world and is continuous with it. At the same time, it displays how enormously more sophisticated is the sort of view that is really to be ascribed to common sense than the crude conception of a quality directly recognizable 'under normal conditions'. Were it not that this style of talk has become a fairly venerable philosophical tradition, one would think that philosophers who indulge in it had never seen mirrors, varnished furniture, shot silk, velvet, expanses of water, or cups of coffee, and had never really looked at the variety of other surfaces, of diverse textures, which they encounter every day.

9. KNOWING AN OBJECT AS IT REALLY IS

Now, the thesis expressed by saying such things as that "the colours are in the objects", the thesis imputed to common sense by many philosophers, we formulated as the thesis that, to characterize an object as it is in itself, we have to attribute to it what observational qualities it has by means of expressions understood as essentially involving reference to our perceptual faculties. It remains unclear to me, however, whether this formulation yet succeeds in capturing all that is intended. For it appears intuitively that the recognition that an observational quality is dispositional in character itself involves a rejection of the imputed thesis. Someone who thinks that being yellow, like being shiny, is a matter of presenting a variety of visual appearances under a variety of conditions surely does not believe that the colour yellow is in the object, or in the surface, in the intended sense. If this is not so, then Ayer's discussion of Locke rests on a phrase wrenched out of context. Ayer quotes (p. 85) Locke's famous remark that the secondary qualities "are nothing in the objects themselves but powers to produce various sensations in us" (Ayer adds a comma after "themselves" which is not in my edition of Locke's *Essay*). One would naturally take the "nothing" as going with the "but"—that is, construe the sentence as meaning that they are not anything other than such powers; but Ayer, in the very next paragraph, speaks of Locke as "holding that colour is nothing in the object itself", without including the phrase introduced by "but", as if the sentence were to be construed to mean, "They are nothing in the objects themselves; they are, on the other hand, powers to produce sensations in us". On the face of it, this is as unwarranted as if someone, told that he was nothing but a social climber, were to complain, "He said that I was nothing". However, if the idea that colours and the rest are dispositional qualities— 'powers', in Locke's terminology—excludes the view that "colours are in the objects" is intended to convey, the transition is warranted; and Locke himself slides easily from one manner of expression to the other, saying (*Essay*, II. viii. 15), "they are, in the bodies . . ., only a power to produce those sensations in us", and, a little later (II. viii. 17), that they "are no more really in" the bodies than "sickness or pain is in manna".

But, if Ayer is right and Locke is right on this point, then our formulation was inadequate. Suppose that some predicate is explained as applying to a surface if it presents a certain kind of appearance when viewed in certain lights, from certain angles and certain distances, and other kinds when viewed in other lights, from other angles and distances, and we regard this form of explanation as essential to its meaning. Then the predicate qualifies as one that can serve to characterize an object as it is in itself, under our formulation of the thesis. On the other hand, it has been explained in a dispositional manner, as a power of producing certain sensations in us under certain conditions; and it ought not so to qualify, if Locke and Ayer are right, and as I too feel, if we are to interpret the thesis correctly. I find it immensely hard to express that interpretation of it. It is as if it were thought that, in perception, whenever it is not delusive, we enter into communion with the object; we know it as it is known by God. Hence the importance of the conception of 'normal conditions': it does not matter if there are many conditions under which we do not perceive the object truly, so long as there is a type of condition under which we know it as it is; but to explain a predicate as meaning that it has this appearance under these conditions, that appearance under those, is to leave no place for a notion of knowing it as it really is. The appearances have, in such a case, become as extrinsic to the quality ascribed to the object as is the smarting sensation to the astringent quality of the lotion. (Why do we actually use two different words here? Perhaps because the smarting can continue when all the lotion has been wiped off. But, then, a taste can linger, too, as can the burning sensation produced by an excessively hot curry.)

Ayer cannot explain the notion of knowing an object as it really is in terms of knowing it as God knows it, since he does not believe in God (pp. 211–35); and, although I do, I should hesitate to say that we can know the natural world as God knows it, or even approximate to doing so. (It may well be, however, that part of the allure of science and philosophy, considered as attempts to say what the world is really like, lies in just such an idea.) But, if one sets that explanation aside, it is difficult to express the notion except metaphorically.

10. MEANING

However that may be, once the step of regarding a quality as dispositional is taken, it becomes very easy to take the further step of identifying the quality with that feature of the constitution of the object that confers on it the relevant propensity; and that transition, too, Locke of course makes without hesitation. This is because we are naturally prone to regard dispositional properties as resting on non-dispositional ones; whether or not there are irreducibly dispositional properties, whenever we can find a convincing causal explanation of a disposition, we tend to identify having that disposition with the constitution that explains it. Now, in the case of colours and other visual surface qualities, even before we have any actual scientific knowledge, the complex character of our visual experience forces on us an interpretation of such qualities in terms of propensities to affect (different kinds of) light in various ways; and this already carries us beyond an account of those qualities in terms of how a surface appears to us, although the colours of light itself are still explained only in terms of our capacity to recognize them. The stage is thus already set for an identification of colour qualities with physical properties not in any way characterized in terms of our own colour vision; when a workable theory of light is available, we are at once ready to make this identification.

It may be objected that, in making the identification, we shall be being unfaithful to the meanings of our colour words as these were originally given to us. After all, the contention was never that a physicist, speaking as a physicist, had no right to use the form of words "Ayer's table is brown"; only that, in so far as he interpreted the adjective "brown" in terms of the spectral reflection curve of the surface of the table, he was not using it in accordance with its ordinary meaning. This is quite true. But the original contention went further than this: it embodied the claim that, on the physicist's account, the table is *not* brown, as "brown" is ordinarily understood. It is this claim which is false. The idea that we may identify the colour of a surface with a feature of its spectral reflection curve, that that is what its having that colour consists in, is precisely the idea that, as a matter of physical necessity, just those things that are brown in the new sense may correctly be said to be brown in the original sense. Let us consider once more the analogy with affective qualities such as being funny. Someone who wants to devise a 'theory of humour' asks, "What does being funny consist in?" If someone else answers, "It consists in the propensity to evoke amusement in us: that is what the word 'funny' *means*", he will reply, "Of course; but I want to know what feature of an event, remark or story, describable in principle by someone devoid of a sense of humour, *makes* it funny in that sense". If, now, he succeeds in finding such a feature, then, if he henceforward uses the word "funny" as meaning 'possessing that feature', he will have modified the meaning of "funny"; but his theory will be acceptable just in case all and only those things that possess the feature are funny in the original sense, i.e. amuse us: hence no one will have any warrant to say to him, "You are maintaining that nothing really is funny, in the original sense of the word 'funny' ". Modifications in the meaning of a general term that, as a matter of theoretical necessity, leave the extension of the term unaffected are the easiest for us to accept; indeed, we usually feel no resistance, but a positive attraction, to them. This is particularly true of terms expressing physical concepts, precisely because the process whereby an individual acquires such concepts is itself a complicated and gradual one: as we advanced from the childhood stage of learning to apply colour words to brightly coloured pictures in a book to mastery of the phenomena of light and colour with which we are familiar as adults, we had repeatedly to modify our understanding of those words. Some philosophers have been so impressed by our willingness to accept modifications of meaning that they have rejected the notion of meaning as altogether useless. This is, in my opinion, a mistake: it suggests that everyone is, at any time, free from all constraints on what sentences he may intelligibly propose for acceptance, when in fact the modifications of meaning that we readily accept are those which do not require us to reject as false sentences that we had previously accepted as true; and, when a modification does call for such revision, we shall accept it only when we can obtain a clear view of the principles governing the new meaning of the term and of the theory that makes the modification mandatory or desirable. The process by which meanings undergo modification is a subtle and complicated one, that requires detailed study; there is no easy way to dispense with such study by jettisoning the whole notion of meaning. But that does not mean, either, that our conception of the world can be faithfully described by ignoring the considerations that induce us to modify the meanings of our words; still less does it entitle a philosopher to say that, whenever we are prompted to accept such a modification, the statements that we previously made are, by that very fact, rendered false.

11. ABSOLUTE AND RELATIVE FORMS OF DESCRIPTION

The notion of a direct apprehension, in perception or by other means, of an object as it *really* is seems to me a spurious one, and certainly not an ingredient of a common-sense view of the world, as the common sense of ordinary people goes: it is a philosophers' notion, going back at least as far as Locke, and falsely imputed to the plain man by philosophers. On the other hand, the notion that we have been considering—that of a *description* of things as they are in themselves—is an entirely different one; and this really plays an important role in our thinking. Whenever one can be attained, we give preference to a form of description that is independent of the particular circumstances and position of the observer. That is why, to common sense, our vocabulary for assigning three-dimensional shapes to objects and giving their location, relative to one another, in three-dimensional space is pre-eminently one by which things are described as they are in themselves; for, as already remarked, it is a common-sense view that shape predicates are independent of viewpoint and stand in no need of relativization to the circumstances of the observer. The interpretation of our essentially two-dimensional visual impressions as three-dimensional, the conception of objects as disposed in a three-dimensional space in which we also are, is so fundamental to our ability to form a conception of the world at all and to engage in any kind of action, and so integrated with our perceptual experience, that it may be denied that it can serve as a pattern to be followed in other cases. It does, however, form just such a pattern: the practice of taking the physical world to admit of a description independent of viewpoint, and of regarding such a description as representing it as it actually is, is rooted in our most primitive experience of it. Imagine, for example, that the heavenly bodies, while having negligible proper motion, were vastly nearer to us than in fact they are, so that we could detect appreciable parallax in moving a few hundred miles over the earth's surface. Such parallax would not, of course, enter into our immediate visual experience, like a landscape seen from a train. Nevertheless, we should regard the resulting representation of the heavenly bodies as disposed in three-dimensional space not merely as a convenient means of summarizing the changes in the appearance of the night sky as we moved about the earth, but as depicting the actual state of affairs.

There is no a priori reason why the world should admit a description in absolute terms. One can, for instance, imagine a world in which the apparent colours of objects varied, in a totally unsystematic manner, according to the distance from them of the observer. In such a world, we could not describe an object simply as yellow, but only as yellow from within a certain interval of distance from it. But, if, now, we suppose that, although there was no general correlation between the apparent colour of an object from 2 feet and that from 20 feet, still objects were found to split up into a manageable number of different types, any two objects of the same type behaving in the same way in respect of its apparent colour from varying distances, then a vocabulary for assigning objects to these types would serve the function that, in our language, is served by the vocabulary of colour words as applied to objects. There is no guarantee that we shall be able to devise an observer-independent vocabulary; but we always seek for one, and, the world being as it is, we always find one. As far as colours are concerned, for example, it is far from irrelevant that, although we are liable to make mistakes if we try to estimate the 'true' colours of objects seen under coloured light, we know that the changes induced by such light in their apparent colours are not random, just as the apparent uniform colour of a multicoloured object seen from too great a distance for us to resolve the surface into its components is not random. Knowledge of this kind plays an important part in our conception of colour qualities; and this is a further reason why the conception of 'normal conditions' is so misleading.

Just as, in considering the extraterrestrial cosmos, we extend the procedure of giving spatial descriptions independent of the position of the individual observer to obtain ones independent of our location, as a species, on the surface of this planet, so, as we learn more about physical properties and about the physiology of perception, we attain forms of description that are independent of our particular range of sensory faculties. Even before we have any scientific account of sound, it is natural to think of a sound as something that is given off, its finite velocity being evident to ordinary observation, as in thunderstorms and when we see and hear a distant gun being fired. As with the more complex case of visual surface qualities, this conception prepares us to accept the identification of sounds with waves in the air when the scientific explanation of them becomes available: to resist that identification would be to insist on a pointless duplication. But, even before we know this explanation, we shall be willing to sever the tie between the notion of sound and our own perceptual capacities: the possibility of sounds too high for us to hear cannot be ruled out as contradictory even before we identify sounds with sound waves. Perhaps, until that identification is made, the possibility requires that there be organisms (for instance, dogs) sensitive to such humanly inaudible sounds; but, when it is made, not even that requirement is necessary for the conception to be intelligible. In the same way, the programmatic notion of kinds of light by means of which we may conceive of colour phenomena before we have any actual theory of light gives way to an understanding of those phenomena that reveals the highly contingent character of our colour perception. Not only does it become intelligible to say that insects are sensitive to ultra-violet 'light', which is invisible to us; but, even restricted to the visible spectrum, the colour of an opaque surface, as we discriminate it, is not to be equated to its spectral reflection curve, but stands, rather, in a complicated one–many relation to it. Having arrived at this stage of understanding, we subsume the concept of light under the more general one of electromagnetic radiation, and regard propensity to reflect, absorb, or transmit radiation of different wavelengths as a more accurate replacement of the experientially based notion of colour. In doing so, we are not rejecting the lessons taught by our everyday experience: we are simply remaining faithful to that quest for a description of reality in absolute terms that we have from the outset taken as a quest for a description of it as it is in itself.

12. THE CAUSAL THEORY OF PERCEPTION

I have argued that there is no conflict in principle between science and common sense, and that therefore, contrary to Ayer, no subtle theory is called for to allow each its proper place: though common sense lags behind science, science grows out of common sense and is continuous with it. If I am correct, then Ayer is wrong in what he says (pp. 82–8) about the causal theory of perception. I do not believe that the notion of cause, as such, is integral to the concept of perception: all that is integral to the latter concept is that my perceptions should always afford some ground, even if one that can in some cases be overridden, for supposing things to be as I perceive them. If someone believes, with Malebranche, that the presence of the object and my perception of it are joint effects of some further cause, his belief does not violate the concept of perception, so long as he allows that my perception supplies a reason for taking the object to be there. (I owe this point to Mr John Foster.) But it does not follow from this that there must be more to our perceiving objects than their causing us to have certain perceptual experiences. Ayer argues that, if perception is to be from the outset linked to the causal action of the object on the percipient, there can be no barrier against a total scepticism (p. 87); he is here following Hume, whom he quotes with approval (p. 86) as saying that "the philosophical system" contains all the difficulties of "the vulgar system" with others peculiar to itself. The reason is that, if we link perception with cause at the outset, then, Ayer thinks, we shall convert the objects perceived into "unobservable occupants of an unobservable space". Hence we have to assume a primitive notion of perception explicable without reference to the notion of causality: a link with causality can be made only at a later, secondary stage in the development of the concept of perception. This supposed primitive notion of perception is presumably that which we earlier found it so difficult to express, one under which perception (when it takes place under normal conditions) is a kind of immediate awareness of the object as it really is, a communion with it in its essential being.

We here see more clearly the genesis of this curious idea; but it is conceived in the womb of philosophy, not of common sense. To conceive of perception, even at the outset, as the causal action of the object—more exactly, for any of the senses that operates at a distance, of something emitted by the object—on the percipient does not reduce the object to an unobservable occupant of an unobservable space: how could it do so, when, by hypothesis, it is the object being observed? We need not postulate the existence, let alone the validity, of any more primitive notion of perception to save the objects of observation from this unfortunate fate. Not only is the observed object by hypothesis observable: it can also perfectly well be described. The only descriptions we can initially frame are expressed by words the meaning of which is given in terms of our own observational capacities; but, as I have argued, that does not make those descriptions incorrect, even though, for greater understanding of the world, we seek descriptions of a different form. The trouble seems to be that, although Ayer starts with a more or less correct delineation of the distinction between a description of things as they are in themselves and one in terms of how they appear to us—that is, between a description in absolute and one in relative terms—he soon forgets the nature of this distinction. He begins (p. 84) by elucidating the statement that physical objects are not really coloured as meaning that being coloured "is not an intrinsic property of the object", i.e. is not a property that it possesses "independently of our perceiving" it: this can certainly be understood as meaning that to describe an object as coloured is to use a relative rather than an absolute form of description, in the terminology I have been using; and the statement that physical objects are not really coloured, when understood in this way, will be correct if the term "coloured" is regarded as explicable only in terms of our faculty of colour vision. But, in what he writes subsequently, it appears that he has forgotten that he has elucidated "is not really coloured" in this very special sense: he takes it, thenceforward, in the other, more straightforward, sense under which the appearances are delusive—that is, in the sense in which to say that something is coloured, when really it is not, is to say something untrue. If we take perception as being, from the outset, linked with causality, then, he thinks, we must regard the object as being, in itself, as it would be described in the causal account of the sensory process. But, then, forgetting that the qualification "as it is in itself" relates to the form, not to the correctness, of the description, he infers that, on this view of perception, the object will lack colour or any other observable quality, and hence will itself be unobservable. But the dilemma is a spurious one: no such consequence follows.

13. INSTRUMENTALISM

So far this essay has read as a whole-hearted repudiation of instrumentalism, the view according to which scientific theories have only the status of "secondary systems"; and I wish to back-pedal somewhat. Science begins by borrowing concepts, such as those of weight, heat, light, and force, from everyday discourse, and subjects them to progressive refinement. It has been argued here that this process is continuous with that of forming a coherent picture of the physical world in which we engage in ordinary life, and that, for that reason, we have no option but to take science as revealing what the physical world is like in itself. But, somewhere in the course of scientific development, the character of the theories changes. Properties, such as those of 'colour' and 'strangeness', now attributed to fundamental particles, have no connection with ordinary experience: they are mere labels for ingredients of a purely mathematical model. Now instrumentalism is usually thought of as a doctrine about the ontological status of theoretical entities, or the semantic status of theoretical statements (semantic status, not epistemological status, as is sometimes inaccurately said: the question is what their truth consists in, not how we know them to be true). It is, in effect, the rejection of realism for theoretical statements: there is no objectively existing reality that renders such statements determinately true or false; rather, they are not to be interpreted literally at all, but are to be viewed as pictures that help us to master complicated regularities governing real, i.e. straightforwardly observable, phenomena.

In order to evaluate such a doctrine, it is necessary to gain a clear view of what is to be counted as a theoretical statement, in the relevant sense. For this purpose, a theoretical statement may be considered one on which we have not conferred a definite semantics—that is, the conditions for the truth and falsity of which we have not determined: it functions only as part of a theory which behaves in a Duhemian fashion, forming a sort of coagulated lump within the language; we have means of judging the correctness or incorrectness of the theory as a whole, but not of individual statements belonging to it. To characterize theoretical statements in this way is, indeed, to prejudge the issue between instrumentalism and realism in favour of the former: if theoretical statements are ones on which we have not conferred determinate truth-conditions, it must be superstition to believe in an objective reality that determines them as true or as false. But a plausible formulation of instrumentalism must find a convincing way of circumscribing the range of statements to which it applies—those to be regarded, for this purpose, as theoretical. The usual formulations of it either leave this range quite unspecified, or, more often, treat as theoretical any scientific law that rises above the level of a straightforward generalization (for example, the law of the rectilinear propagation of light). A law may be said to rise above the level of a mere generalization if it effects some modification of our concepts. Precisely because it does so, it cannot be considered, as can a simple empirical generalization, as having associated with it in advance determinate conditions under which it holds good. We do not, for example, start with a conception of light as travelling along certain paths, and subsequently notice that, in most cases, the paths in question are straight lines: adoption of the principle of the rectilinear propagation of light is likely to be simultaneous with the introduction of the notion of the path along which light travels. But it is a mistake to infer from that that the statement, once adopted, remains without definite truth-conditions: the modification of our concepts once effected, we know what observations will suffice to show that the law does not hold in full generality.

When instrumentalism is in this way applied to every scientific statement that rises above the level of simple generalization, it becomes utterly implausible, and it is no wonder that it is resisted; we have here another example of the frequent phenomenon that realism scores too easy a victory, because the alternative to it has been incorrectly formulated. As I have tried to argue, a statement such as that light travels in straight lines is virtually forced on us in the attempt to make sense of our everyday experience; and many other scientific laws are arrived at by a process essentially the same in character as that by which, in ordinary life, we form a picture of the world we live in. Hence, if instrumentalism is to have any claim on our consideration, it must be maintained that the critical line, beyond which we begin to deal in theoretical statements properly so called, is crossed not as soon as anything recognizable as a scientific theory is framed, but at some much later stage in the development of science. Just when this occurs will be very hard to say. It is a problem in the theory of meaning; and the theory of meaning is not yet in a sufficiently well-developed state for us to be able to give a ready answer to the question when we may be considered to have conferred determinate truth-conditions upon any given range of statements: that is, indeed, the central question over which the participants in a dispute about whether statements of a given class admit a realistic interpretation disagree with one another. It will be the task of scientific realism to maintain that there are no theoretical statements in the required sense—that, in other words, no line can be drawn: the progress of science is, on a realist view, everywhere continuous with the kind of attempt we make, even before science begins, to understand our world and arrive at a description of it as it is in itself. Earlier in this essay, I did indeed express such a view, but I do not really want to commit myself to it: I wish to remain agnostic about whether it is possible to delineate a range of theoretical statements for which the instrumentalist thesis is plausible. The theses for which I wish to contend are the following: that instrumentalism, if correct at all, is so only for the most rarefied statements of scientific theory; that there is no conflict in principle between scientific truth and a common-sense view of the world, and, therefore, no problem of reconciling them or necessity to opt for one or the other; that there is no legitimate notion of knowing an object, by immediate awareness, as it really is, when this is taken as involving more than that we have not made a mistake; but that there is a legitimate notion of a description of an object as it is in itself, and that we cannot but view science, at least before it transcends some critical level of abstraction, as attempting to arrive at such descriptions.

Instrumentalism constitutes a very special form of reductive thesis, applied to theoretical statements of physical science, the reductive class consisting of non-theoretical statements about the physical world. A thoroughgoing scientific realist needs to refute instrumentalism, presumably by an argument along the lines sketched above. But, when he has done so, he has not thereby established as correct a realistic interpretation of the statements of physical theory: he has merely rebutted one line of criticism. There may be—indeed, there is—a form of argument to show that we should not adopt a realistic interpretation of statements about the physical world in general, whether scientific or everyday statements, theoretical or non-theoretical ones; and the scientific realist has also to meet this more general challenge. There are also quite specific considerations concerning the character of quantum theory which yield a strong case for saying that, so long as physics incorporates that theory, a realistic interpretation is ruled out—this is another very particular attack which the scientific realist has to face. These issues are remote from the topic of the present essay; but, because we tend to have an endemic prejudice in favour of realism, we are always allowing it to score too easy a victory; and I did not want to be guilty of abetting this process.

17

Testimony and Memory

The law distinguishes, among the things that a witness knows, those that he knows 'of his own knowledge', and allows him to testify only to them. This is in part because his confirmation of another witness's testimony adds no weight to it if he derived his knowledge only from that other witness's having told him. That is not the only reason, however. Only in special cases, such as a deathbed declaration, is second-hand evidence admitted at all. That is due both to the impossibility of testing it under cross-examination, that is, of probing its foundations, and to the well-known phenomenon of the corruption of information as it passes from its source along a chain of second-hand and third-hand transmitters. Historians, on the other hand, must perforce admit information given at second or later hand, since, very often, no other is available. The prejudice of the law against it has nevertheless often exerted a strong influence upon epistemologists; those subject to this influence consider that what a lawyer would deem me to know 'of my own knowledge' marks an upper bound to what I may genuinely be said to know at all.

The tide of philosophical opinion is now flowing in the opposite direction: philosophers have become chary of denying the title of knowledge to anything which, in common unreflective discourse, anyone would ordinarily be said to know. Epistemologists of quite a recent period, on the other hand, were wont to follow an ancient tradition in sundering a genuine, strong sense of the verb "to know" from its everyday application. In doing so, they were guided by certain principles governing the concept of knowledge which they found intuitively compelling. Which such principle, then, could be invoked to justify the ruling that, in the genuine sense of "to know", I cannot be said to know more than what the law courts would recognize me as knowing of my own knowledge? A principle to which this role may naturally be assigned is that no one may be said to know that for which it is possible for someone else to have better evidence, or firmer grounds, than his. If I know something by having been told, then my informant must have had better evidence than I do; or, if he did not, *someone* must have had. When one who attended a lecture informs me of what the lecturer said, his evidence is better than mine, for there is an additional opportunity for my information to be erroneous. My informant may have misheard, or misunderstood, or misremembered, in which case both of us will be astray; but, even if he made none of these mistakes, *I* may mishear, or misunderstand, what he tells me, or, later, may misremember it. Hence,

Forthcoming in Arindam Chakrabarti (ed.), *Knowing from Words* (Dordrecht).

according to this principle, I know, at best, only in what its proponent considers to be the weak sense of having been truly told and not forgotten; but, having evidence less strong than could be had for the proposition in question—indeed, less strong than that which my informant *does* have—I do not know at all, in the genuine, strong sense of "know".

How, then, is the principle to be applied? I knew yesterday, say, that I was sitting in a garden, for I saw the garden all around me. Am I now able to know, in the philosopher's strong sense of "know", that I was sitting in a garden yesterday? Certainly, for the lawyer, I can know this of my own knowledge, for there is no one who can offer better evidence to this effect, though others can corroborate it if they saw me there: but can the philosopher allow that I genuinely know it? I know it because I remember sitting in the garden: but should this count as having the strongest conceivable evidence? It is certainly not the strongest evidence anyone could have for that proposition: for, while I was sitting in the garden, my evidence was stronger. It is very like the case of knowing through having been told: it is only because I had stronger evidence yesterday that I can claim to know now. It was stronger, because there was less opportunity for a mistake. I might have been deceived, and have been sitting in some place cunningly got up to look like a garden; but today there are further possibilities of error that did not exist yesterday, such as that I am confusing what I was doing two days ago with what I was doing on that immediately preceding today, or mistaking a dream for an actual occurrence, or misremembering in yet some other manner. Memory may be said to be the testimony of one's past self. Does the epistemologist's principle allow one to claim genuine knowledge of anything which one knows only by remembering having witnessed it?

Perhaps to apply the principle so strictly as always to reject such a claim would be to abuse it. Perhaps we ought not to interpret it as denying knowledge to anyone on the ground that he has not the best possible evidence for the truth of the *proposition* he claims to know: for this would rule out, not merely all knowledge of the occurrence of a future event, but, equally, all knowledge of any observable past event; it would render our 'genuine' knowledge in the highest degree evanescent. How, then, should we interpret it—if we are to subscribe to it at all? Perhaps only as demanding that, if I am at any time to sustain my claim to know something, it must be impossible for anyone to have, *at that time*, better evidence than I do for what I claim to know. The principle, thus interpreted, is certainly more liberal than under its strict interpretation. But has it not become too liberal? Under its lax interpretation, it could not rule out knowledge of the future, which many philosophers have declared impossible in principle, in the strong, and allegedly genuine, sense of "knowledge". I fully intend to give a lecture tomorrow morning, and know of nothing that is likely to prevent me from doing so. It is of course possible that someone else presently knows of something that might prevent me, and also knows how I may circumvent this obstacle. But if, in fact, no one knows of the likely occurrence of any such obstacle, and if, in fact, I shall lecture tomorrow, without having to overcome any particular obstacle, it holds good that no one is, or could be, in a better position than I to judge that I shall be lecturing tomorrow; and then, under the lax interpretation of the principle, a knowledge of this fact may now be attributed to me. Those who deny the possibility of a knowledge of the future are usually motivated by some stricter version of the principle. However strong may be the evidence that someone now has for some event's occurring tomorrow, the evidence available tomorrow for its then occurring—or not occurring—must be stronger; and hence no one can *know* today that it will occur.

This argument has a certain speciousness. The lax interpretation of the principle has the discouraging effect of robbing it of cogency; the strict interpretation the yet more unwelcome effect of excluding the possibility of knowing the past. Of course, we can patch up the principle to make it yield precisely the result we hanker after. To do this, it is enough to substitute "at that time or subsequently" for "at that time" in the foregoing formulation of the lax interpretation. The principle, thus emended, reads as follows: If I am at any time to sustain my claim to know something, it must be impossible for anyone to have, at that time or subsequently, better evidence than I now do for what I claim to know. Under this third interpretation, the principle allows knowledge of the past, but rules out knowledge of the future, just as intuition—some people's intuition, at any rate—would have it do. Of course it does; for it has been expressly framed to have just those consequences. But, for that very reason, it lends no support to, and provides no justification for, intuition. We are inclined to think that, while we may have well-founded *beliefs* about the future, we could not, in principle, *know* what was to happen; at the same time, we should be horrified to think that the same held good concerning the past. To vindicate these views which we find ourselves disposed to hold, we ought to appeal to some principle not overtly asymmetrical with respect to past and future; one, such as that enunciated above, which makes knowledge, by fiat, asymmetrically related to past and future has no probative force, but merely reiterates what our unreflective inclinations predispose us to think.

Knowledge *is* asymmetrically related to past and future, it may be objected; that is to say, we stand in different cognitive relations to them. All the more reason why we should have no need to *make* knowledge asymmetrical with respect to past and future by fiat. If it is already asymmetrical about this axis, we are not required to adopt a temporally asymmetrical criterion for what is to count as knowledge: the asymmetry ought to show itself when we apply a criterion formulated symmetrically, if that asymmetry resides in the nature of things, and not just in our language.

There is no doubt that we are cognitively related to the past in a different way from that in which we are cognitively related to the future. Memory delivers to us information, not mediated by inference and independent of our wishes, concerning what we have previously witnessed, and is largely outside our control: we cannot decide *what* to remember, and only to a limited extent whether or not to remember. Our non-inferential information about the future is constituted by our intentions, and is of a quite different character. Its scope is much more restricted, namely to our own actions and what is under our control; and it is itself under our control. We form intentions, modify, revise, and abandon them; and we do so in the light of our wishes. Do these differences justify an asymmetrical criterion for what is to be reckoned as knowledge? Can they justify denying the title of knowledge to a conviction, founded on inductive evidence, on our own intentions, or on a mixture of the two, that some event will occur next week, on the ground that, even if the conviction is sound, we shall next week have better evidence than now for the occurrence of that event? If so, can they at the same time justify according the title of knowledge to a conviction, founded on inductive evidence and on memory, that some other event took place last week, despite the fact that, last week, we had better evidence for its occurrence than we have now? Of course, we have the right to use the word "knowledge" as we wish, and hence, if we so choose, to apply it in a temporally asymmetrical manner; but, if we do, is this because such a use happens to accord best with our conduct of our lives, or are we responding to some intrinsic difference between a well-founded conviction concerning the future and a well-founded conviction concerning the past?

Suppose that I know of myself that I frequently misremember events that I have witnessed, but seldom fail to carry out an intention I have formed. Despite my faulty memory, I have, on some occasion, a strong recollection of a scene at which I was recently present, and no specific reason to doubt it. I have also formed a resolution about a course of action to be undertaken tomorrow, and no reason to expect any impediment to executing it. Some philosophers, whose number is probably greater nowadays than it used to be, find no difficulty in the notion of knowledge of the future, in any admissible sense of "knowledge", no matter how strict. Others, however, among whom I should include myself, feel disposed to allow that, in the case imagined, my recollection consitutes knowledge of the past scene, but to deny that I could claim to *know* what my actions will be tomorrow. What can motivate such an inclination? The answer "The fact that my conviction about what will happen tomorrow may prove to be wrong" is surely inapposite. My conviction may indeed prove to be wrong; but so may my recollection, and, given my assumed character, is much more likely to do so.

The reason lies, rather, in this. My recollection may well be wrong; but, so long as I trust it, I cannot separate the knowledge I suppose myself to have now from the knowledge I surely had at the past time. For the former is derived from the latter; more exactly, it simply *is* the knowledge I had as an eyewitness, maintained in being. By contrast, my intention to act in a certain way tomorrow, though intrinsically more trustworthy, is not derived from the knowledge I shall have tomorrow of how I am then acting. The two pieces of information concerning my actions on that day have different sources, and neither derives from the other; my actions derive from my previously formed intention, but my knowledge of those actions as I perform them does not so derive. This does not necessarily involve a contrast between knowledge by observation and knowledge in intention. The knowledge I shall have tomorrow of what I am then doing may be partly based on observation, but may be largely constituted by the non-observational knowledge we have of our voluntary actions as we are performing them—a type of knowledge stressed long ago by Professor Elizabeth Anscombe in her well-known book *Intention*. But, even if the knowledge I shall have tomorrow of my actions is wholly of this non-observational character, it will not *derive* from the intention I have today to act in that way: my *actions* may derive from that intention, but my knowledge that I am performing them does not.

This serves to explain why, whatever we may think about the possibility of knowing the future through our own intentions, or through observed regularities, or through a mixture of the two, we cannot refuse to accept foreknowledge as genuine knowledge. Christ knew that St Peter was going to deny him, not because he read Peter's character, still less because he intended that he should so act, but because he had foreknowledge of the betrayal. In this case, therefore, Christ's knowledge of the coming event was derived from the event itself; and, for that reason, it truly ranks as knowledge of the future. The concept of foreknowledge is, of course, perplexing on its own account: not, however, as violating the principle that we cannot know the future, but as an instance of backwards causation. Christ's capacity for foreknowledge is explained theologically, by reference to his divinity. Someone who rejects the theological belief will reject the story; but that in no way impedes his ability to *understand* the story, or his willingness to allow that, according to the story, Christ *knew* that Peter would deny him.

All this leads, not to yet a fourth interpretation of our principle, but to a modification of it. The new version will run thus: no one may be said to know something if there is or could be someone possessing evidence for it both stronger than his and derived from a different source. No temporal asymmetry enters into the formulation of this revised principle. It allows us to have knowledge of the past. It rules out the possibility that, constituted as we are, we should know the future; and yet it admits that, if there is such a thing as foreknowledge, it is genuine knowledge. It thus accords with intuition; at least, with the intuitions of those disposed to believe that our ordinary convictions about the future, however strong, do not amount to knowledge. For those so disposed, it therefore satisfies all the criteria we have so far elicited from our discussion for being the principle we seek, that is to say, the right principle.

Those who think that our everyday assurance about the future, based on our own intentions and on inferences from the present by appeal to principles of causality, sometimes constitutes knowledge could not have accepted our original principle, under its strict interpretation, and would have had no motive for emending the lax interpretation by making it temporally asymmetrical and thus ruling out knowledge of the future, though not of the past. Equally, they will be unable to accept the revised principle, since it, too, excludes knowledge of the future on an ordinary basis. They would presumably therefore have had little inclination to espouse a principle of this kind at all, a principle, namely, at which we here first arrived by considering the motivation for denying that testimony can transmit knowledge. In assessing the strength of this motivation, it remains of interest to enquire how the concept of knowing something by being told it by another fares in the light of the revision of the principle which our discussion has led us to adopt.

Before we do so, however, we must revise it still further. As was pointed out to me by Dr Timothy Williamson, the revised principle, as stated, admits a Gettier-type objection. Suppose that I know some proposition "A" to be true, and consciously infer from this to the truth of the disjunctive proposition "A or B". Given that it is possible for someone to know the truth of the proposition "B", he might likewise infer the truth of "A or B". Now, if someone arrives at a deductive consequence of things that he knows by means of a long and intricate argument, it is reasonable to count that argument as part of his evidence for accepting that consequence, rather than confining the evidence he has for doing so to the evidence he has for the various premisses of the argument. It nevertheless appears contrary to reason to dispute that, if someone knows a given proposition, and directly and explicitly infers from it a weaker proposition which is, glaringly, a logical consequence of it, then he knows that weaker proposition also. If so, the one who, knowing "A" to be true, inferred that "A or B" was true, must be said to know the truth of "A or B"; and likewise the one who, knowing "B" to be true, drew the same conclusion. But the source of the latter's knowledge of the disjunctive proposition is plainly quite different from the source of the former's; and it may be that his evidence for the truth of "B", and hence for the truth of "A or B", was stronger than the other's evidence for the truth of "A". We then have here a counter-example to the revised principle.

We can escape this refutation in one of only two ways. Either we must deny that someone who knows a proposition also knows an obvious consequence of it that he expressly draws; and this seems counter-intuitive. Or we must hold, since "B" might have been any proposition, that no one knows anything for which he has evidence possessing less than the maximal strength which the evidence for any proposition whatever might have; and this is flagrantly contrary to our intentions in formulating our revised principle, and, indeed, to the deliverances of intuition. "Intuition" here means merely the sum of our untutored inclinations to apply the term "knowledge" to certain cases and withhold it from others. Such intuitions may be an uncertain guide, but only in so far as they either lead us into irresoluble antinomies, or present us with a concept palpably of little interest or use. Until they have been shown to do one or the other, we are bound to respect them, since after all the concept of knowledge is our concept. We are therefore debarred from either of these two escape routes, and must amend our principle or abandon it.

An adequate emendation must necessarily be somewhat complex; the following appears to meet the case. Let E be a piece of evidence for a proposition "A". We may then define the proposition $P(E, "A")$ to be the strongest proposition for which E is evidence as strong as it is for "A". Our emendation of the revised principle will then be as follows: no one may be said to know a propositon "A" on evidence E if it is possible for someone to have evidence stronger than E, and derived from a different source, for the proposition $P(E, "A")$. Having stated this emendation, we may in what follows ignore it: for, in all the examples considered, $P(E, "A")$ will coincide with "A".

Our revised principle did not involve the asymmetry between past and future embodied in the formulation of the third interpretation of the original principle. It also corrected another asymmetry. The second or lax interpretation of the original principle exhibited no asymmetry between past and future; but we set it aside as allowing extensive knowledge of the future. That second interpretation did, however, involve another asymmetry: it treated the times at which the purported knowledge is possessed differently from the subjects to whom it is ascribed. It denied a subject's claim to knowledge at a given time if, at that time, it was possible, either for that subject or for any other, to possess stronger evidence for the content of the purported knowledge. Under this interpretation of the original principle, the time at which someone possesses evidence for the proposition in question is crucial; but the identity of its possessor is quite irrelevant. Why this difference? If it matters *when* the evidence is available, why should it not equally matter *to whom* it is available? If, in this second formulation of the unrevised principle, we were to interchange subjects and times, we should arrive at the following: no one can be said to know the truth of a proposition if it is possible that *he* should have, come to have, or have had, better evidence for it than in fact he has. We may call this the second lax interpretation of the original principle. The first lax interpretation allowed knowledge of previous or subsequent events, both of which the strict interpretation appeared to rule out; but it might well be construed as excluding knowledge of other people's sensations or inner states. I see you scratching, and conclude that you have an itch; but can I, according to the first lax interpretation, claim to *know* that you have an itch? According to that interpretation, I cannot do so if it is possible for anyone else at this time to have stronger evidence that you have an itch than I do; but surely you are in just that position. You *feel* the itch, whereas I just see you scratching: surely you have better evidence. I may, of course, ask you, "Do you have an itch?", and you may reply, "Yes". Yet you may have misheard or misunderstood my question, or I may have misheard your answer, or you may have been lying: and so you still have the stronger evidence, or perhaps we should say, you are in a better position to judge. The second lax interpretation concurs with the strict one in denying any possibility of knowing the past or the future; but it does allow me to claim that I know you have an itch, because *I* could never have better evidence for this proposition than I now have. Of course, we could combine the first and second lax interpretations to produce a third, maximally lax, one. On this maximally lax interpretation, the hypothetical cases which defeat a claim to knowledge by merely being possible must be restricted to those in which the stronger evidence is possessed at the given time by the claimant himself. But we are no longer in the business of seeking a satisfactory interpretation of our original principle: we have rejected that principle altogether in favour of our revised principle. The present excursus has been solely for the sake of pointing out another advantage of that revised principle. The third interpretation of the original principle involved an asymmetry between past and future, and that seemed unjustifiable. The second interpretation—that is, the first of our lax interpretations—involved an asymmetry between times and subjects; and that seems equally unjustifiable. Our revised principle involves neither asymmetry; and this should strengthen our confidence that it—or, more properly, its emended version—is correct.

How does the revised principle handle the case of my claim to know that you have an itch? Well, if I merely see you scratching, you have a better ground on which to judge that you have an itch than I have; moreover, my ground is not derived from yours. The principle will therefore in this case adjudicate my claim unfavourably. But, if I ask you, and you tell me, the matter stands differently. You will remain on firmer ground, indeed; but my ground for judging you to have an itch is derived from yours, and therefore has the same source; and so, according to the revised principle, the fact that you are in a better position to say, and that there is more scope for error in my case than in yours, does not defeat my claim to know.

It may be said that this is no complete solution to the problem of our knowledge of others' sensations. If I see you drop a heavy weight on your foot and then hop about, clutching that foot and uttering agonized cries, do I have to ask you before I can claim to know that you have hurt your foot? Surely not: but this does not call our revised principle in question. Doubtless there are cases in which the subject is in no better position to know what sensation he is experiencing than the onlookers: that only means that neither of our principles, however interpreted, will impugn the onlookers' claim to know.

Often, however, as it seems to me, I cannot know unless you tell me, even though, in some cases, I may have good grounds for an opinion. The revised principle is the only one which rules in such a case that, before you tell me, I cannot know, but allows that, if you do tell me, then I do know.

The analogy between memory and testimony is very strong. In forming a belief, or adding an item to one's stock of knowledge, on the strength of a memory, one does not, in the normal case, arrive at it by any process of inference. There are exceptions. If I know that my memory is particularly unreliable, and I have the impression of remembering having witnessed some event, I may reflect on the probability that, in this instance, my memory has misled me; estimating that, in the particular circumstances, this is highly unlikely, I may conclude that the event indeed occurred. An inference is here required to rebut a doubt prompted by experience. But, in the normal case, no particular doubt arises. I remember something as having happened in my presence; and my remembering it *is* my adopting the belief, or my coming once more to know, that it took place. I perform no rapid surreptitious piece of reasoning to the effect that I am under the impression that I remember the event, that in my case such impressions usually prove to be veridical, and that therefore it is likely that the event occurred: I simply judge the event to have occurred, in the consciousness that my warrant for the judgement is that I remember it.

Exactly the same holds good for coming to believe or to know something by being told it. In the normal case, this is not effected by any process of inference. There are, again, special cases. I may know, from experience, that a particular informant is generally unreliable, through dishonesty or proneness to error, or that he is especially unreliable about a certain subject-matter. I may therefore consider, concerning something he has told me, the probabilities that he is mistaken or deceiving me, and decide that, in that specific case, the probability of either supposition is low, and so conclude to the probable truth of what he said. But such reflections are exceptional. If someone tells me the way to the railway station, or asks me whether I had heard that the Foreign Secretary has just resigned, or informs me that the Museum is closed today, I go through no process of reasoning, however swift, to arrive at the conclusion that he has spoken aright: my understanding of his utterance and my acceptance of his assertion are one; I simply add what he has told me to my stock of information.

It might be questioned whether these features of memory and of the receipt of testimony are epistemological principles or mere psychological phenomena. Maybe it is simply in our nature to accept the deliverances of memory or the assertions of others without, usually, any scrutiny or reflection; but may it not also be that, if we are to possess knowledge acquired by either means, we must be able to supply as backing an argument corresponding to the inference we omitted to draw? According to this suggestion, if I am to be said to know what someone else has told me, and do not know by any other means, I must be able to supply a specific ground for supposing my informant himself to have been well informed on the matter and to have been speaking truthfully, even though, in originally accepting what he said, I did not advert to those grounds. Likewise, if I am to be credited with knowing something that I once witnessed and have subsequently remembered, I must be able to supply a specific ground for supposing that, in this case, my memory was veridical, even though, when the recollection first came to me, I trusted it without adverting to the ground I had for doing so. If either of these suggestions—let alone both—were adopted, we should have to confess to knowing pitifully little. Try the experiment of building up a stock of knowledge from a base consisting only of what you know from present observation and present ratiocination, prescinding, at the outset, from all that you remember. At the first stage, admit only those memories which, on the basis only of what you presently know, you have a particular reason for supposing reliable. At later stages, if you ever reach a later stage, admit only such memories as you have, at that stage, reason to rely on. It is plain that the outcome of this exercise will be to leave you reckoning yourself to know practically nothing at all. You cannot, at the initial stage, appeal to past experience or past regularities, or any general knowledge of what usually happens, to supply a warrant for trusting any of your memories; and therefore you will not contrive to add any of them to your meagre initial stock. In fact, you will not advance beyond your initial position: you will be trapped in a cognitive solipsism of the present moment.

The same applies to the experiment of building up a stock of knowledge from what you know of your own knowledge, that is, independently of anything you have been told. In this experiment, you will be allowed at any stage to add information you have received from others only if, at that stage, you have specific grounds for taking it to be trustworthy; and, at the outset, you may add such information only if such grounds are to be found within your unaided observation and reasoning. This time you may get a little way beyond your initial position. Able to appeal to memory, you may be in a position to assure yourself that certain informants are reliable reporters of what they themselves observed. You will, however, seldom be able to add to your stock of knowledge anything you were told by someone who himself had it from someone else: for, to do that, you would have to know who your informant's informant was, and have independent evidence that *he* was reliable. It is again plain that the body of knowledge which you will end up with as a result of this second exercise will be miserably thin; you are trapped in something not far extended beyond cognitive solipsism.

These considerations show that, if the concept of knowledge is to be of any use at all, and if we are to be held to know anything resembling the body of truths we normally take ourselves to know, the non-inferential character of memory must be accepted as an epistemological principle, and not as a mere psychological phenomenon. Memory is not a *source*, still less a *ground*, of knowledge: it is the maintenance of knowledge formerly acquired by whatever means. Certainly knowledge, like everything else, is subject to decay. Certainly knowledge first acquired long ago is less secure than knowledge at its first acquisition. But it is the same piece of knowledge as that originally acquired, and, if it has neither corrupted nor come under particular suspicion of having corrupted, it is still *knowledge*. If error has crept in, it is no longer knowledge; if our assurance has failed, it is no longer knowledge: but, if it has suffered damage of neither of these kinds, we need no further warrant for it than that which made it knowledge when we first acquired it. We need no particular reason to take things to be as we remember them, save when we have some weaker contrary ground for not so taking them; but we always need a particular ground for declining to take them as we appear to remember them.

To view the matter otherwise is to destroy, not only the concept of the past, that is, of the world as having a temporal extension, but also the concept of a person. We are what we are, good or bad, because of our history; and we know what we know because of our cognitive history. What we are are people, who develop and interact, acquiring a picture of the world constantly added to and modified, and in part crumbling; and this picture includes ourselves, as persisting agents and subjects of a stream of variegated experience. To deny that knowledge persists is to convert us into momentary agents and momentary subjects. It is also to dissolve the conception of the world itself as a changing reality or shifting habitat; for it is only through our memories that we form any conception of the past and hence of time. To preserve that conception, we must acknowledge the propriety of the practice we originally adopted when we first learned to use the past tense. Our adoption of it was due in part to a universal natural disposition, in part to our acquisition of the linguistic device of tenses. For us, the first and only possible route to a mastery of the use of the past tense lay through our learning to employ it for the expression of our memories. At that stage, there was no possibility of failing to take things as having been as we remembered them; the only way in which we could have avoided doing so was by failing altogether to acquire any conception of how things had previously been, that is, to acquire the concept of the past. We had not the conceptual equipment required for doubting our memories; and to have done so, if we had been capable of it, would have been to violate a linguistic rule, thereby manifesting our failure to grasp the meaning of the past tense. As adults, our grasp of its meaning is enormously richer, allowing us in every case to attach a significance to the question whether we have remembered correctly. Our understanding of the past tense, our concept of the past, is nevertheless still founded upon the base which constituted our initial imperfect grasp of it: the assumption, namely, that memory is the retention of knowledge previously acquired. To reject that assumption by supposing that acceptance of our memories always requires specific justification therefore continues to embody a fundamental misunderstanding of our own language, and hence of our own being: it subverts the very concept of the past.

It may well be thought to have been unnecessary to have argued all this at such length: to very few nowadays would it appears contentious. The point of doing so lies in the almost exact analogy between memory and testimony; for the principal object of our enquiry is to establish on what grounds it is proper to allow that we can acquire genuine knowledge by means of testimony, and, in particular, to arrive at grounds that retain their validity in the face of an admissible form of restrictive principle of the kind with which we began. In the case of testimony also, if the concept of knowledge is to be of any use at all, and if we are to be held to know anything resembling the body of truths we normally take ourselves to know, the non-inferential character of our acceptance of what others tell us must be acknowledged as an epistemological principle, rather than a mere psychological phenomenon. Testimony should not be regarded as a *source*, and still less as a *ground*, of knowledge: it is the transmission from one individual to another of knowledge acquired by whatever means.

If remembering something is to count as retaining a knowledge of it, it must have been known when originally witnessed or experienced; if it was derived from a misperception or misapprehension, the memory cannot of course rank as knowledge. The same naturally applies to taking something to be so, having been told it: the original purveyor of the information—the first link in the chain of transmission—must himself have known it, and therefore have been in a position to know it, or it cannot be knowledge for any of those who derived it ultimately from him. There is in practice far more danger that what is transmitted by testimony is not knowledge, either because it has deteriorated in transmission or because it was not knowledge in the first place, than that what is retained in memory is not knowledge. We cannot always be sure of the status of what we unhesitatingly take to be true: and so we often think we know what we do not know, even when it is in fact so, and often know what we do not feel certain, and therefore do not know, that we know.

Just as the mode of my present knowledge of some fact may consist in my remembering it, so an individual's personal acquisition of a piece of knowledge may consist in his having been told it. One of the many things language does for us, however, is to render knowledge a communal possession, or at least a communicable, and so transmissible, property. There is a fluctuating body of knowledge possessed in common by a community, not of course in the sense that all its members are cognizant of everything it comprises, but in the weaker sense that it is in principle accessible to all. It is in reference to this knowledge possessed by the society as a whole that lecturers and writers—historians and scientists in particular—say, "We know this, we do not yet know that". There is, indeed, also a larger body of personal knowledge, for the most part of less importance, which is still communicable, but the means of access to which is far less clearly marked. Certainly knowedge, like everything else, is liable to be corrupted in transmission. Certainly knowledge acquired by transmission through many mouths or hands is less secure than knowledge as apprehended by its discoverer. But it is the same piece of knowledge as that originally discovered, and, if it has neither been corrupted nor come under particular suspicion of having been corrupted, it is still *knowledge*. If error has crept in in the course of transmission, it is no longer knowledge; if one to whom it has been passed on does not feel assured of it, he does not *know* it: but if, in being passed from individual to individual, it has undergone neither distortion nor a weakening of confidence, we need no special warrant for accepting it or for giving it the title of knowledge. The only warrant that can be demanded for it is that which relates to its primary source, which can be supplied only by its discoverer and those who know the relevant details of its discovery, or who have rediscovered it for themselves. We need no particular reason to take things to be as others inform us that they are, save when we have some weaker contrary ground for not so taking them; but we always need a particular ground for declining to take them to be as we are told that they are.

To view the matter otherwise is to subvert the whole institution of language: to subvert it in something of the way that the liar does, but more far-reachingly. If we subvert the institution of language, we dissolve our own being. Just as we are constituted by our pasts, so we are constituted by our membership of human society. We function only as distinct individuals. If we were transformed into mere components of a collective, as an army to some degree attempts to transform the soliders, and as the Colonels' regime in Greece succeeded in a more thoroughgoing way in transforming those it employed to administer torture to its prisoners, we should, at least as long as we remained in that condition, have ceased to function as human beings. But, equally, we function only as members of a human society. A wolf-child cannot operate as a member of a human society, indeed can hardly function at all in a human environment. He has been formed by wolf society, and can function only as a member of it; and so he too no longer functions as a human being. It would, of course, be wrong to say that either one of the Greek torturers or the wolf-child had ceased to *be* a human being, for to kill either one or the other would still be murder: but neither functions as a human being.

We are in large part constituted by our membership of a human society, and, above all, by having language and making almost unceasing use of it during our waking hours. We acquired our language from others, and could only have done so; for a language is a social institution, and cannot exist save as a social institution. It is not a rule of etiquette, or a device for saving time, that we should accept what others tell us: it is fundamental to the entire institution of language. There are two principal aspects to a mastery of what Wittgenstein calls the 'use' of linguistic expressions, most easily distinguished if we restrict ourselves to assertoric utterances. One is to know when we are entitled to say something; the other is to know how to act on what others say. Suppose that a child has, for some suitably restricted vocabulary, mastered only the first aspect of its use. That is, he utters assertoric sentences on appropriate occasions, namely when he is in a position to recognize the situations that warrant those assertions: he says, "Doggie is sleeping", when he observes the dog asleep, and so on. Then adults can use him as an extension of their observational capacities; they can, for instance, tell from his utterance that the dog is asleep, even though they cannot see it. Is this enough for us to attribute to the child an understanding of his own utterances? Not if he remains incapable of using the assertoric utterances of others in the same way, even when they are couched in the restricted vocabulary that he knows. That is, not if he is unable to react appropriately to what others attempt to tell him. In such a case, he is unable to use others as an extension of his own powers of observation. He has not begun to master the second aspect of use: he does not know what it is to act on what others say, and he therefore does not know what it is to take what they say as true.

This is a fantasy, of course: we do not learn first the one aspect of use and then the other, but acquire them both simultaneously. We can, however, imagine a dog that has been trained to emit certain special signals by barking in a particular way in certain observable situations, say when a wolf is approaching the fold. Can we say that the dog is telling us that a wolf is near? Certainly not if he evinces no particular response to another dog's giving the same special signal: he has merely been trained to give the signal in the relevant situation, and has no idea that he is telling anyone anything. If, on the other hand, he does react appropriately to hearing the signal from the throat of another dog, and especially if he does so spontaneously, without having been trained to, the whole aspect is altered. The point of the fantasy concerning the child was to draw attention to two distinguishable, though closely related, components of a linguistic practice. If a child does not respond appropriately to an assertion addressed to him, or if, when it calls for no immediate response, he fails subsequently to modify his actions accordingly, then he does not understand the sentence used, even if we know him able to come out with a similar sentence for himself in a suitable situation. To respond appropriately is to act on the truth of the assertion; and such a response of course involves accepting it as true. Acquiring the practice of acting on what others tell one therefore comprises learning what is involved in accepting what they say, and learning to do whatever is so involved. In this way, a disposition to accept what others tell one is central and fundamental to acquiring language at all: unless one does so, one cannot be said to understand language. As one's mastery of language deepens, one learns to curb this fundamental disposition in certain cases. One learns the various possibilities of error on the part of others; one learns also how language may be employed dishonestly. One recognizes then that one may sometimes be justified in not accepting what one is told; one recognizes also that, in some cases, a special reason is required for accepting it. But the foundation-stone cannot actually be removed without causing the entire edifice to collapse. The institution of language, and, with it, the existence of human society our membership in which goes to constitute us as human beings and thus as what each of us is, rest upon certain fundamental assumptions: and one of these is that knowledge is transmitted by means of language. To make this assumption is to treat accepting what we are told, without the need for any further special reason for accepting it, as the normal case. About this, there is a strong impulse to say: we cannot but do so.

What would be the point of saying, "We cannot but do so"? What is the point of Wittgenstein's saying, "Just try—in a real case—to doubt someone else's fear or pain" (*Philosophical Investigations*, I. 303)? Surely, even if it is true that the sceptic, who believes it to be unjustified to accept what is said to one unless one has a specific reason for believing it, cannot help doing so all the same, this fact will cut no ice with him: he will continue to regard what he cannot help doing as unjustified. The point, however, is not that he cannot help doing it, but that, in so far as he can succeed in refusing to do it, he is repudiating something on which the whole institution of language rests and thereby converting the language that is his, and in which his thinking is conducted, into a private language from which the meaning will leach out.

A radical sceptic denies that we have any reason to believe what we believe. A mild sceptic merely says that, although it is reasonable to *believe* it, we do not *know* it. Suppose a mild sceptic concedes that we are often right to take what we remember as having been so or what we are told is so to be true, but maintains that we do not know either one or the other: what memory retains and testimony transmits, he argues, is *information*, but not *knowledge*. Is it important to combat his contention?

The verb "to know", as a tool of converse, plays different roles in different contexts: one cannot elicit from its manifold use a precise criterion for its application to all cases. Notoriously, it frequently signifies no more than the possession of a piece of information. Sometimes, as in "I know what he'll say", it means even less than that—something like "I can tell you" or "I have an opinion". It is also often used to rule out doubt, as in "I *know* I left it in here" or "I *know* she would have telephoned if there'd been anything wrong". It is sometimes used to claim greater authority, as in "I *know* where the Warden was yesterday, because I happened to see him". It is, I think, for this latter reason that the Creeds begin "I believe . . ." rather than "I know that . . .". The believer is not wishing to represent his faith as doubtful; but, even if he claims the authority of divine revelation for his belief, he cannot properly say "I know . . ." if the unbeliever has the same access to that revelation as he has, the difference between them being only that the believer *trusts* it.

For all that, philosophers constantly seek a precise criterion for something to be knowledge. If no such criterion can be vindicated by appeal to the common concept of knowledge, what is the point of their quest? The point of the search is not evident in advance. It becomes apparent only from what is found: any notion of knowledge framed by means of a precise criterion derives whatever interest it has from the criterion adopted. There is no antecedent truth about what is known and what is merely reasonably believed that would make one proposed criterion wrong and another right: we can seek no more than a way of drawing the line that marks a significant difference between what lies on one side and what lies on the other. In this essay I have operated, not with a criterion, but with a principle of distinction that, in my view, marks such a difference; I have no wish to claim that those to whom it does not appeal are objectively mistaken. There is no determinate right or wrong in this matter.

The principle distinguishes between knowledge and belief according to whether it ultimately derives from the securest possible source for information of the kind in question, but allows that knowledge can be retained and that it can be transmitted from one subject to another. It demands that the channel by which it is transmitted be a normal one; but it does not require that channel to be itself secure. A sceptic can, if he wishes, deny this, thereby confining knowledge to awareness of that with whose source the subject is presently in contact; presumably, on this basis, a mathematician could not be said to know the truth of any theorems other than those of which he could currently cite a proof. Yet, in so characterizing knowledge, the sceptic cannot claim to be more in the right than one who accepts the proposed principle; he can claim only to have drawn the line in what strikes him as a more interesting place. What he cannot reasonably do is to admit memory, but not testimony, as a channel for the transmission of knowledge; the analogy between them is too close for the line to run between them.

The mild sceptic is no menace; merely an eccentric who chooses to use the term "knowledge" in a fashion that renders it largely useless. The radical sceptic proposes to do more than adjust the use of a term: he believes that we ought not to accept the deliveries either of memory or of testimony unless we have particular reason to do so. It would plainly be impossible for anyone to strip himself of every belief that would never have been formed if he had obeyed this maxim from childhood: but might it not be possible for him to follow it henceforward, though retaining those beliefs he already had, saying to himself that, while he could not rid himself of most of them, he would no longer *form* any beliefs unreasonably?

The idea that it is unreasonable to believe something to be so on the sole basis of having been told that it is so is as myopic as the idea that it is unreasonable to believe something to have been so on the sole basis of remembering it as having been so. In believing what I am told, I may go wrong for either of two reasons: because my informant was lying, or because he made a mistake. For reasons of the kind that have become associated with the name of Davidson, we can know a priori that, among human beings generally, lying is rare. If it were not that most assertions seriously made are made in the belief that they are true, our words could not mean what they do mean. They mean what they mean because they are *used* to mean that; and it is only because lies are exceptional utterances on the part of any speaker that he may be said to be using words in accordance with their meanings, even when he is lying. In the normal case, therefore, the *presumption* must be that, in making an assertion, a speaker is saying what he takes to be true; it is not reasonable, or even a piece of prudential caution, to flout that presumption, because it is a presupposition of our understanding the assertion, or of the existence of the language in which it is couched. Reason does not demand that the presumption be maintained in *all* circumstances. It obviously does not need to be maintained when the speaker is known to be one addicted to lying; it also does not need to be maintained when there is strong incentive for the speaker to lie, save when he is known to be exceptionally honest. But to repudiate the presumption in normal circumstances is to undermine our assurance that we so much as understand the content of anything that is said to us; it therefore cannot be reasonable to do so.

Even a sincere speaker may transmit misinformation as the result of a mistake. Epistemologists are greatly occupied with mistakes, but philosophers of language frequently write as though they were impossible. How is it possible to think the thing that is not? The problem seems still to be with us. Experience makes its impacts at the periphery of our linguistically formulated theory of the world, and we adjust the theory accordingly. Our mastery of the language in which it is formulated consists in our knowledge of which adjustments are appropriate to different possible new, or recalcitrant, experiences: how, then, can we go wrong? Otherwise expressed, to understand a statement is to know what counts as entitling us to assert it; so how, if we understand it, can we ever assert it unjustifiably? In accordance with these conceptions, it ought to be that everyone who has the same evidence about something should have the same beliefs about it; but, notoriously, opinions are infinitely various. The most important reason is the salience of hypothesis and judgement in the formation of our beliefs. We adopt what seems to us to be the only, or the most likely, explanation of the facts; but we fail to think of the best explanation, or, by ill luck, to hit upon the true one. In deciding what to think, we are forced to estimate probabilities when objective measures or objective tests of significance are lacking, and our estimates differ without the common content of our thoughts coming into question. Since error is so pervasive, is not the sceptic right to refuse to accept the judgements of others, and rely solely on his own?

It is not enough to point out to the *radical* sceptic that this applies primarily to the original informant, rather than to its transmitters, and that we have already allowed that knowledge cannot be gained by testimony unless the original informant genuinely knew what he told to others, whereas if what he said expressed only his *opinion*, no one can obtain knowledge by hearing it reported. The radical sceptic is not concerned merely with denying that knowledge can be gained from testimony; he denies that it ever supplies any reason for belief. His scepticism thus does not really relate to the process of transmission, but to the *authority* of the original informant: he is, in effect, denying that anyone can ever have the authority to tell anyone else anything.

Despite this disanalogy, to a large degree the same applies to fallibility as to insincerity: assigning to our words and those of others the meanings we take them to have excludes the possibility that more than a minority of our beliefs should be mistaken. It is here a matter of degree, however. The greater the role played by the postulation of hypotheses and the subjective estimation of probability in the formation of our beliefs, the more space there is for agreement upon meanings in the face of divergence of opinions; the less weight, therefore, attaches to any one individual's opinion. Clearly, I can accept something on the authority of another only if he has or had access to evidence I do not possess, or has reflected more upon it, or is more skilled at thinking about or judging of such matters; failing these conditions, he can merely tell me what he thinks, not what I should think. The degree and basis of another's authority will depend on the type of proposition involved. It remains that, for a great range of propositions, though mistakes can never be ruled out, there is the same presumption against them as that in favour of a speaker's truthfulness; the example of mathematical theorems asserted by competent mathematicians suffices to show that this range does not comprise only reports of observation. Radical scepticism on this ground is as unreasonable as on the ground that I can trust only myself to tell me the truth.

18

What is Mathematics About?

The two most abstract of the intellectual disciplines, philosophy and mathematics, give rise to the same perplexity: what are they *about*? The perplexity does not arise solely out of ignorance: even the practitioners of these subjects may find it difficult to answer the question. Mathematics presents itself as a science in the general sense in which history is a science, namely as a sector in the quest for truth. Even those least instructed in other sciences, however, have some general idea what it is that those sciences strive to establish the truth about. Historians aim at establishing the truth about what was done by and what happened to human beings in the past; more exactly, to human beings after they had invented writing. Physicists try to discover the general properties of matter under the widest variety of conditions; more generally, of matter and of what it propagates, such as light and heat. But what is it that mathematicians investigate?

An uninformative answer could be given by listing various types of mathematical object and mathematical structure: mathematicians study the properties of natural numbers, real numbers, ordinal numbers, groups, topological spaces, differential manifolds, lattices, *and the like*. Apart from the difficulty of explaining "and the like", such an answer is uninformative because it is given from within: one has to know some mathematics—even if, in some of the cases, only a little—if one is to understand the answer, whereas the sample answers to the questions concerning history and physics could be understood without knowing any history or physics.

Some maintain, nevertheless, that mathematics is a science like any other. The claim is unconvincing prima facie: what is immediately striking about mathematics is how *unlike* any other science it is. It is true that, in the more mathematicized sciences such as physics, there may be elaborate deductions from initial premises, just as there are in mathematics; but they play a different role. In mathematics, their purpose is to establish theorems, that is, mathematical truths; in physics, they serve to elicit consequences of a theory, which can then be used to make predictions but also to test the theory. The word "theory" is used quite differently in mathematics and in the other sciences. In physics, biology, and so forth, it carries the connotation of a hypothesis; however well established a physical or biological theory, it always

Delivered as a talk to a conference on 'Mathematics and Mind' held at Amherst, Mass., in April 1991. Forthcoming in Alexander George (ed.), *Mathematics and Mind* (New York).

remains open to refutation or revision. In mathematics, there is no such connotation. We are all familiar with the idea of observations designed to test—to confirm or refute—the general theory of relativity; but we should be unable to conceive of observations designed to test number theory or group theory.

The most determined effort to represent mathematics as empirical in character was made by John Stuart Mill; but he achieved little more than to point out, what is in any case evident, that mathematics can be *applied* to empirical reality. That, indeed, is a salient feature of mathematics that any philosophical account of it must explain; but it is not to be explained by characterizing mathematics as itself an empirical science. Our very vocabulary indicates the difference. We do not speak of 'applying' a physical theory when we draw physical consequences from it, but only when we base some technological innovation upon it. Even someone who accepted all Mill's arguments would have no ground for regarding mathematics as a science like any other; it would still differ markedly from all others. For Mill, the axioms and definitions of mathematics are derived from very general facts apparent to untutored observation; but the theorems are still consequences drawn by deductive reasoning from those axioms and definitions, without further appeal to observation, let alone to refined observations made in artificially created conditions or with the help of sophisticated instruments. Moreover, as Frege pointed out, the mathematical notions whose application Mill was anxious to locate solely in physical reality have in fact far wider application. It is misleading to say that we encounter the natural numbers, for example, in the physical world; for, while physical situations may indeed need to be described by citing a natural number as the number of physical objects of some given kind, non-physical situations may equally need to be described by citing a natural number as the number of non-physical objects of some given kind, for instance as the number of different proofs of the fundamental theorem of algebra, or, indeed, of roots of an equation. The same holds good of sets. These notions are too general for us to locate them in any particular realm of reality; as Frege maintained, they apply within every sector of reality, and the laws governing them hold good, not only of what we find to exist, but of all of which we can frame intelligible thoughts.

If mathematics is not about some particular realm of empirical reality, what, then, *is* it about? Some have wished to maintain that it is indeed a science like any other, or, rather, differing from others only in that its subject-matter is a super-empirical realm of abstract entities, to which we have access by means of an intellectual faculty of intuition analogous to those sensory faculties by means of which we are aware of the physical realm. While the empiricist view tied mathematics too closely to certain of its applications, this view, generally labelled 'platonist', separates it too widely from them: it leaves it unintelligible how the denizens of this atemporal, supra-sensible realm could have any connection with or bearing upon conditions in the temporal, sensible realm that we inhabit.

Like the empiricist view, the platonist one fails to do justice to the role of proof in mathematics. For, presumably, the supra-sensible realm is as much God's creation as is the sensible one, and conditions in it therefore as contingent as in the latter. The continuum hypothesis, for example, might *happen* to hold, even though we can apprehend neither its truth nor anything in which its truth is implicit. That there may be mathematical facts that we shall be forever incapable of establishing is a possibility admitted by some mathematicians and philosophers of mathematics, though denied by others. When admitted, however, it is normally admitted on the ground that our inferential powers are limited: there may be consequences of our initial assumptions that we are unable to draw. If these are first-order consequences, we could 'in principle' draw them, since they could be elicited by reasoning each step of which was simple; but the proofs might be too long and complex for us ever to be able to hit on them, or even follow them, in practice. If they are second-order consequences, we may be unable even in principle to see that they follow. But, if we take seriously the analogy between our supposed faculty of intuition and our perceptual faculties, there is no reason why there may not be mathematical facts that are in no sense consequences of anything of which we are aware. We may observe a physical object without either perceiving all its features or being able to deduce all of them from what we do perceive; if mathematical structures are merely the inhabitants of another realm of reality, apprehended by us in a manner analogous to our perception of physical objects, there is no reason why the same should not be true of them. There are indeed hypotheses and conjectures in mathematics, as there are in astronomy; but, while both kinds may be refuted by deducing consequences and proving them to be false, the mathematical ones cannot be established simply by showing their consequences to be true. In particular, we cannot argue that the truth of a hypothesis is the only thing that would explain that of one of its verified consequences; there is nothing in mathematics that could be described as inference to the best explanation. Above all, we do not seek, in order to refute or to confirm a hypothesis, a means of refining our intuitive faculties, as astronomers seek to improve their instruments. Rather, if we suppose the hypothesis true, we seek for a *proof* of it, and it remains a mere hypothesis, whose assertion would therefore be unwarranted, until we find one. True, we seek to make our methods of proof ever more explicit and precise. This is not analogous to the improvement of the instruments, however. Methods of proof serve to elicit consequences, not to yield a more extensive evidential base; if the hypothesis is to be established, this must be done, not by testing its consequences, but by exhibiting *it* as a consequence of what we already know. Platonism can no more explain these differences between mathematics and the natural sciences than empiricism can, for both go astray by claiming to discern too close an analogy between them.

A brilliant answer to our question, but one now generally discredited, was given by Gottlob Frege and sustained by Russell and Whitehead. It was, essentially, that mathematics is not about *anything in particular*: it consists, rather, in the systematic construction of complex deductive arguments. Deductive reasoning is capable of eliciting, from comparatively meagre premises and by routes far from immediately obvious, a wealth of often surprising consequences; in mathematics, such routes are explored and the means of deriving those consequences are stored up for future use in the form of propositions. Mathematical theorems, on this account, embody deductive subroutines which, once discovered, can be repeatedly used in a variety of contexts.

This answer, generally called the 'logicist' thesis, was brilliant because it simultaneously explains various puzzling features of mathematics. It explains its methodology, which involves no observation, but relies on deductive proof. It explains the exalted qualification it demands for an assertion: in other sciences, a high degree of probability ranks as sufficient ground for putting forward a statement as true, but, in mathematics, it must be incontrovertibly *proved*. It explains its generality; it explains our impression of the necessity of its truths; it explains why we are so perplexed to say what it is about. Above all, it explains why mathematics has such manifold applications, and what it is for it to be applied. It allows that mathematical statements are genuinely propositions, true or false, and hence accounts for what is manifestly so, that mathematicians may be interested in determining their truth-values regardless of the uses to which they may be put; at the same time, it explains the content of those propositions as depending on the possibility of applying them, and thus justifies Frege's dictum that it is applicability alone that raises arithmetic from the rank of a game to that of a science. By contrast, Wittgenstein's account of mathematics, which lays even greater stress on application, makes the existence of pure mathematicians a phenomenon for pathology. It will be my purpose in this paper to maintain that the logicist answer, if not the exact truth of the matter, is closer to the truth than any other that has been put forward.

The classic versions of logicism both ran aground on the problem of the existence of mathematical objects, those abstract entities of which mathematical theories, taken at face-value, treat, and above all the elements of the fundamental mathematical domains, that of the natural numbers and that of the real numbers. The aim of representing a mathematical theory as a branch of logic is in tension with recognizing it as a theory concerning objects of any kind, as its normal formulation presents it as being: for we ordinarily think of logic as comprising a set of principles independent of what objects the universe may happen to contain. Frege nevertheless believed that the truth of number theory and analysis demanded the existence of those objects with which, on the face of it, they are concerned; and so he had to justify the belief in their existence, while reconciling it with the purely logical character of arithmetical statements. In trying to achieve this, he ran into actual contradiction. Russell and Whitehead, greatly concerned with the need to avoid contradiction, tried to construct foundations for mathematics in accordance with the more natural conception of logic as independent of the existence of any particular objects: their classes are not genuine objects at all, but mere surrogates, statements about them being explained as a disguised means of talking about properties of objects, properties of such properties, properties of properties of *those* properties, and so on upwards. Frege had never given any good reason for insisting on the genuine existence of mathematical objects; perhaps the only plausible reason lies in the difficulties encountered by Russell and Whitehead in trying to dispense with them. The price they paid for doing so was that, in order to ensure the existence of sufficiently many of their object-surrogates, they had to make assumptions that could not be rated as logical, or even likely to be true. The axiom of infinity, saying that there are infinitely many concrete objects, was needed to secure that the natural numbers did not terminate; the axiom of reducibility, saying that there are sufficiently many properties of things of a given type definable without speaking of all properties of those things, was needed to guarantee the completeness of the real-number system.

More recently, Hartry Field has advanced what may be seen as a modification of the logicist thesis. Frege argued that the application of a mathematical theory, outside mathematics or within it, requires, to warrant it, a stronger claim than the consistency of the theory being applied. Suppose that a theorem in one mathematical theory T is proved by appeal to another, auxiliary, theory S. It is then not enough, Frege reasoned, to know that, if the theory T is free from contradiction, then so is the combination of T and S: for that would warrant us in claiming no more than that we shall not involve ourselves in contradiction if we accept the theorem, whereas we wanted to be in a position to *assert* that theorem; and for that, Frege held, we must know the auxiliary theory S to be *true*. Field argues that we need claim nothing so strong as truth on behalf of a theory in order to warrant its applications. If we want to show that a mathematical theory S can be legitimately invoked as an auxiliary to some other theory T (which may be a scientific theory or another mathematical one), we need only claim something intermediate between the logical truth of S and its consistency relative to T, namely that the conjunction of T and S is a conservative extension of T. This means that anything expressible in the language of T that could be proved from T together with S could already be proved—perhaps at greater length and with greater difficulty—in the theory T on its own.

Field, too, is concerned with the existence of mathematical objects. He agrees with Frege, as against Russell and Whitehead, that the truth of a mathematical theory demands the existence of the mathematical objects of which it purports to treat: that is his reason for denying the truth of the theory, since he disbelieves in the existence of any such objects.

To give substance to the claim that, when the theory *S* is added to the theory *T*, it yields a conservative extension of *T*, we must be able to formulate *T* without reference to whatever objects of the theory *S* are regarded as objectionable; achieving such reformulations is the major part of Field's programme. His motivation for seeking to explain the applications of mathematics without recognizing the existence of mathematical objects lies in his general disbelief in abstract objects of any kind. It is on this that criticism has centred: can he really formulate scientific theories without appeal to abstract objects?

For Frege, on the other hand, the error which blocked any reasonable philosophy of mathematics was the failure to recognize that abstract objects may be quite as objective as concrete ones (in his terminology, non-actual objects as actual ones). He characterized abstract objects much in the way that philosophers are disposed to do today, namely as objects lacking causal powers; by 'objective' he meant something that is neither a content of consciousness nor created by any mental process. It is a common complaint about abstract objects that, since they have no causal powers, they cannot explain anything, and that the world would appear just the same to us if they did not exist: we can therefore have no ground to believe in their existence. For Frege, such a complaint would reveal a crude misunderstanding. He gave as an example of an object that is abstract but perfectly objective the Equator. If you tried to explain to someone who had never heard of it what the Equator was, you would certainly have to convey to him that it cannot be seen, that you cannot trip over it, and that you feel nothing when you cross it. If he then objected that everything would be exactly the same if there were no such thing as the Equator, and that therefore we can have no reason for supposing it to exist, it would be clear that he had still not understood what sort of object we take the Equator to be. What has to be done is to explain to him how the term "the Equator" is used in whole sentences: how it is to be determined whether or not someone has crossed the Equator, or whether some natural feature lies on it or to the north or south of it, and so on. That is all that can be done, and all that needs to be done: if he still persists in his objections, there is nothing we can do but pity him for being in the grip of a misleading picture.

Thus reference to an abstract object is to be understood only by coming to grasp the content of sentences involving such reference, and it is only by specifying the truth-conditions of such sentences that it can be explained what such an object is: it is only in the course of saying something intelligible about an object that we make genuine reference to it. This, indeed, holds good for all objects, concrete or abstract; but the failure of philosophers to appreciate the dependence of reference upon the context of a proposition tempts them to dismiss the object referred to as mythological only when it is abstract, since sentences involving reference to concrete objects include those in which they are indicated by means of demonstrative terms, which is to say that concrete objects can be encountered. For Frege, however, to treat mathematical objects such as numbers as fictitious because abstract is to commit as crude a blunder as to do the same for the Equator, one which springs from the same misunderstanding about what referring to an object involves.

In this, Frege was surely right. He did not, however, take his *general* defence of the existence of abstract objects as dispensing us from any work in particular cases, but only as pointing to the kind of work that needed to be done. In each case, we have to specify the truth-conditions of sentences containing terms for objects of the kind in question; in those with which he was concerned, for natural numbers, or cardinal numbers in general, and for real numbers. And this was, for him, a highly problematic task, but one that he believed he could solve. The first lesson of the contradiction was that he was woefully mistaken in that belief.

If we reject Field's all-encompassing nominalism, his programme takes on a different aspect. Much of the criticism directed at it falls away, once the task is no longer that of avoiding reference to all abstract objects; it continues to be of interest because it focuses on the problem which defeated both Frege and Russell, of either justifying or explaining away reference to specifically mathematical objects, and remains a problem even after the general objective of eliminating all reference to abstract objects has been discarded. Field's programme then becomes a new strategy for resolving the problem of mathematical objects. Nevertheless, Field envisages the justification of his conservative extension thesis as being accomplished only piecemeal. For each mathematical theory, and each theory to which it is applied, the demonstration is to be carried out specifically for those two theories; no presumption is created by the successful execution of the programme for one case that it will work in others. If, for example, it is shown that real analysis yields a conservative extension when adjoined to Newtonian mechanics, real analysis will not have received a general justification as a mathematical theory, but only in application to Newtonian mechanics. Now suppose that some millionaire is converted to Field's philosophy of mathematics and endows an institute to carry out Field's programme for all scientific theories and all mathematical theories which find application to them; and suppose that the institute is uniformly successful: it has so far examined every existing scientific theory, and every application of mathematics made within it, and has succeeded in each case in establishing Field's claim. Then it has still not established that claim for future applications of other parts of mathematics to existing theories, nor for applications of mathematics to scientific theories yet to be devised. Long before this stage, however, we should have become dissatisfied with the institute's work. For each mathematical theory, we should surely demand a guarantee that it would always yield a conservative extension when adjoined to any scientific theory, so that it would be justified once and for all; and we should also require an explanation why it demonstrably did yield a conservative extension when adjoined to every known scientific theory. Such an explanation would have to turn on the character of the mathematical theory itself, independently of the particular scientific theories to which it was applied; and it would presumably provide the sought-for guarantee. Without such an explanation, we could hardly suppose that we had reached the fundamental truth of the matter; for it could not very well be a mere fortunate coincidence that the theories devised by the mathematicians just happened to yield conservative extensions when adjoined to the theories developed by physicists and other scientists. It is difficult to think what such a general explanation could be, unless it were that mathematical theories, if not logically true in the strict sense, have some closely related property. Field's thesis is not a single one, but a bundle of numerous particular theses; and, as such, it lacks the generality that is required of an adequate account of the applicability of mathematical theories.

Once we have achieved the required reformulation of the theory T to which some mathematical theory S is to be applied, Field's strategy is to prove a representation theorem for T. To avoid unnecessary detail, I will illustrate this by Field's own preliminary example. Here T is (an adaptation of) Hilbert's axiomatization of Euclidean geometry, while S is the theory of real numbers. T is formulated without reference to numbers of any kind, but with variables ranging only over geometrical objects; it is based on axioms governing primitive predicates expressing properties of and relations between them. In Hilbert's original formulation, there were three sorts of variable, for points, lines (determined by any two distinct points), and planes (determined by any three non-collinear points); Field prefers to conceive it as using variables only over points. In this case, there will be a four-place predicate holding between points x, y, z, and w just in case the line segment xy is congruent to the line segment zw, and a three-place predicate saying that y lies between x and z on some line. Then a partial rendering of Hilbert's representation theorem states that there will be a binary function d from the points in any model of T into the non-negative real numbers such that

$$d(x,y) = d(z,w)$$

just in case xy is congruent to zw and

$$d(x,z) = d(x,y) + d(y,z)$$

just in case y is between x and z. By laying down suitable conditions on the distance function d, we could prove a converse, namely that any structure on which was defined a function d satisfying those conditions could be converted into a model of *T* by explaining segment-congruence and betweenness in the manner just stated.

This helps to explain how real numbers can be used as an auxiliary device for proving results within this particular theory, namely the theory *T* of Euclidean geometry; it does not, of course, illuminate the uses of real numbers in other applications. Field remarks that the function d is unique only up to multiplication by a positive constant. This of course reflects the obvious fact that a quantity—here a distance—does not by itself determine a real number alone, but only in conjunction with a unit. What uniquely determines a real number is a ratio between distances: if we replaced d by a function e of four arguments, giving the ratio of the distance between *x* and *y* to that between *z* and *w* (where *z* and *w* are distinct), we could reformulate the representation theorem so that e would be unique. (We should then require that *xy* be congruent to *zw* just in case $x = y$ and $z = w$ or $e(x,y,z,w) = 1$, and that *y* be between *x* and *z* just in case $y = z$ or $e(x,z,y,z) = e(x,y,y,z) + 1$.) We need not do this, of course: it is enough to observe that if real numbers are uniquely determined by ratios between distances, it at once follows that there will be distance functions d obtained from one another by multiplication by positive real numbers. (Any such d will be obtainable from e by setting $d(x,y) = e(x,y,a,b)$ for suitable fixed distinct *a* and *b*.) Furthermore, real numbers correspond uniquely to ratios, not merely between distances, but between quantities of any one type. Hence, given an adequate analysis, such as that aimed at in measurement theory, of what, in general, constitutes a range of quantities, we have a hope of a general explanation of why there will be a unique mapping of pairs of objects that have these quantities on to the real numbers or on to some subset of them. From these sketchy remarks, it is possible to glimpse how such a general explanation might be made to yield a theorem of which a whole range of corollaries ensuring a representation by means of real numbers were special cases. We should then have secured the desired generality for explaining the applications of real numbers on Fieldian lines. Such a theorem would encapsulate the general principle for applying the theory of real numbers.

This, however, would do nothing to convince Field of the existence of real numbers. Frege held that real numbers *are* ratios between quantities. Once we have abandoned the superstitious nominalist horror of abstract objects in general, there would be nothing problematic about the existence of real numbers in the context of some empirical theory involving quantities of one or another kind, if they were identified with ratios between those quantities. What real numbers there were would depend upon what quantities there were: there would be no danger of our not having sufficiently many real numbers for our purposes.

The difficulty about mathematical objects thus arises because we want our mathematical theories to be pure in the sense of not depending for the existence of their objects on empirical reality, but yet to satisfy axioms guaranteeing sufficiently many objects for any applications that we may have occasion to make. The significant distinction is not between abstract objects and concrete objects, but between mathematical objects and all others, concrete or abstract. Plenty of abstract objects exist only contingently, the Equator, for example: their existence is contingent upon the existence of concrete objects, and upon their behaviour or the relations obtaining between them. Ratios between empirically given quantities would be dependent abstract objects of this kind. By contrast, the existence of mathematical objects is assumed to be independent of what concrete objects the world contains.

In order to confer upon a general term applying to concrete objects—the term "star", for example—a sense adequate for its use in existential statements and universal generalizations, we consider it enough that we have a sharp criterion for whether it applies to a given object, and a sharp criterion for what is to count as one such object—one star, say—and what as two distinct ones: a criterion of application and a criterion of identity. The same indeed holds true for a term, like "prime number", applying to mathematical objects, but regarded as defined over an already given domain. It is otherwise, however, for such a mathematical term as "natural number" or "real number" which determines a domain of quantification. For a term of this sort, we make a further demand: namely, that we should 'grasp' the domain, that is, the totality of objects to which the term applies, in the sense of being able to circumscribe it by saying what objects, in general, it comprises—what natural numbers, or what real numbers, there are.

The reason for this difference is evident. For any kind of concrete object, or of abstract object whose existence depends upon concrete objects, external reality will determine what objects of that kind there are; but what mathematical objects there are within a fundamental domain of quantification is supposed to be independent of how things happen to be in the world, and so, if it is to be determinate, *we* must determine it. On the face of it, indeed, a criterion of application and a criterion of identity do not suffice to confer determinate truth-conditions on generalizations involving some general term, even when it is a term covering concrete objects: they can only give them a content to be construed as embodying a *claim*. So understood, an existential statement amounts to a claim to be able to give an instance; a universal statement is of the form "Any object to which the term is recognized as being applicable will be found to satisfy such-and-such a further condition". An utterance that embodies a claim is accepted as justified if the one who makes it can vindicate his claim, and rejected as unjustified if he fails to do so; a universally quantified statement is shown to be unjustified if a counter-example comes to light, but is justified only if the speaker can give adequate grounds for the conditional expectation he arouses. The difference between such an utterance and one that carries some definite truth-condition is that the claim relates to what the speaker can do or what reasons he can give, whereas the truth-condition must be capable of being stated independently of his abilities or his knowledge.

This is not, however, how we usually think of quantified statements about empirical objects. We normally suppose that, given that we are clear what has to be true of a celestial object for it to be a star, and when a star observed on one occasion is the same as one observed on another, we need do nothing more to assure definite truth-conditions to statements of the form "There is a star with such-and-such a property" or "All stars have such-and-such a property". This assumption reflects our natural realism concerning the physical universe. Whether this realism about the physical universe is sound, or (as I myself strongly suspect) ought itself to be challenged, is a question not here at issue: what matters in the present context is the contrast between what we standardly take to be needed to secure determinate truth-conditions for statements involving generality in the empirical case and in the mathematical one.

We are, indeed, usually disposed to be quite as firmly resolved that our mathematical statements should have truth-conditions which they determinately either satisfy or fail to satisfy as we are that this should hold good of our empirical statements. This is something that it never occurred to Frege to doubt. He acknowledged the necessity for specifying the truth-conditions of the statements of a mathematical theory; unfortunately, he persuaded himself that the domain of the individual variables could be determined simply by laying down the formation rules of the fundamental terms and fixing the criterion of identity for them, which he did by means of an impredicative specification, and produced an ingenious but fallacious argument to this effect.

Despite his realism about mathematics, even Frege did not think that mathematical reality determined the truth or falsity of statements quantifying over a domain of mathematical objects, without our needing to specify their truth-conditions; and his successors, mindful of the disaster that overtook him, have accepted the need to specify the domain outright, or to form some conception of it, before interpreting the primitive predicates of a theory as applying to elements of that domain. Notoriously, however, we have found little better means of accomplishing this task than Frege had. The characterizations of the domains of fundamental mathematical theories such as the theory of real numbers that we are accustomed to employ usually convince no one that any sharp conception underlies them save those who are already convinced; this leads to an impasse in the philosophy of mathematics where faith opposes incredulity without either possessing the resources to overcome the other. Moreover, this outcome seems intrinsic to the situation. A fundamental mathematical theory, for present purposes, is one from which we originally derive our conception of a totality of the relevant cardinality: it appears evident that we cannot characterize the domain of such a theory without circularity.

What is the way out of this impasse? We may approach this by asking after the error that underlay the assumptions which led Frege into contradiction—not that involved in his fallacious justification of those assumptions, but in the assumptions themselves. We have grown so accustomed to the paradoxes of set theory that we no longer marvel at them; and yet their discovery was one of the most profound conceptual discoveries of all time, fully worthy to rank with the discovery of irrational numbers. Cantor saw far more deeply into the matter than Frege did: he was aware, long before, that one cannot simply assume every concept to have an extension with a determinate cardinality. Yet even he did not see all the way: for he made the distinction between concepts that do, and those that do not, have such an extension an absolute one, whereas the depth of the discovery lies in the fact that it is not. Taken as an absolute distinction, it generates irresoluble perplexity. We are thoroughly at home with the conception of transfinite cardinal numbers; but consider what happens when someone is first introduced to that conception. A certain resistance has first to be overcome: to someone who has long been used to finite cardinals, and only to them, it seems obvious that there can only be finite cardinals. A cardinal number, for him, is arrived at by counting; and the very definition of an infinite totality is that it is impossible to count it. This is not a stupid prejudice. The scholastics favoured an argument to show that the human race could not always have existed, on the ground that, if it had, there would be no number that would be the number of all the human beings there had ever been, whereas for every concept there must be a number which is that of the objects falling under it. All the same, the prejudice is one that can be overcome: the beginner can be persuaded that it makes sense, after all, to speak of the number of natural numbers. Once his initial prejudice has been overcome, the next stage is to convince the beginner that there are distinct infinite cardinals: not all infinite totalities have as many members as each other. When he has become accustomed to this idea, he is extremely likely to ask, "How many transfinite cardinals are there?" How should he be answered? He is very likely to be answered by being told, "You must not ask that question". But why should he not? If it was, after all, all right to ask, "How many numbers are there?", in the sense in which "number" meant 'finite cardinal', how can it be wrong to ask the same question when "number" means 'finite or transfinite cardinal'? A mere prohibition leaves the matter a mystery. It gives no help to say that there are some totalities so large that no number can be assigned to them. We can gain some grasp on the idea of a totality too big to be counted, even at the stage when we think that, if it cannot be counted, it does not have a number; but, once we have accepted that totalities too big to be counted may yet have numbers, the idea of one too big even to have a number conveys nothing at all. And merely to say, "If you persist in talking about the number of all cardinal numbers, you will run into contradiction", is to wield the big stick, not to offer an explanation.

The fact revealed by the set-theoretic paradoxes was the existence of indefinitely extensible concepts—a fact of which Frege did not dream and even Cantor perceived only obscurely. An indefinitely extensible concept is one such that, if we can form a definite conception of a totality all of whose members fall under that concept, we can, by reference to that totality, characterize a larger totality all of whose members fall under it. Russell's concept *class not a member of itself* provides a beautiful example of an indefinitely extensible concept. Suppose that we have conceived of a class *C* all of whose members fall under the concept. Then it would certainly involve a contradiction to suppose *C* to be a member of itself. Hence, by considering the totality consisting of the members of *C* together with *C* itself, we have specified a more inclusive totality than *C* all of whose members fall under the concept *class not a member of itself*. Are we to say, then, that the concept *class not a member of itself* does not have an extension? We must indeed say that, by the nature of the case, we can form no conception of the totality of all objects falling under that concept, even of the totality of all objects of which we can conceive and which we should recognize as falling under that concept. On the other hand, to the question whether it is wrong to suppose that every concept defined over a determinate domain of distinguishable objects has an extension we must answer, "Surely not". Suppose that we have succeeded in specifying, or in clearly conceiving, some determinate domain of distinguishable objects, some or all of which are classes, and over which the membership relation is well defined. Then we must regard it as determinate, for any element of that domain, whether or not it is a class and, if so, whether or not it is a member of itself. A concept whose application to a determinate totality is itself determinate must pick out a determinate subtotality of elements that fall under it; and so the concept *class not a member of itself* must have a definite extension within that domain. All that we are forbidden to suppose is that any class belonging to the domain coincides with the extension of that concept. Frege's mistake thus did not lie in taking the notion of a class, or, more exactly, his notion of a value-range (the extension of a function), to be a logical rather than a mathematical one, as is sometimes said, nor even, in any straightforward sense, in supposing every function to have an extension; it lay in failing to perceive the notion to be an indefinitely extensible one, or, more generally, in failing to allow for indefinitely extensible concepts at all.

There can be no objection to quantifying over all objects falling under some indefinitely extensible concept, say over everything we should, given an intelligible description of it, recognize as an ordinal number, provided that we do not think of the statements formed by means of such quantification as having determinate truth-conditions; we can understand them only as making claims of the kind already sketched. They will not then satisfy the laws of classical logic, but only the weaker laws of intuitionistic logic. Abandoning classical logic will not, indeed, by itself preserve us from contradiction if we maintain the same assumptions as before; but, since we no longer conceive ourselves to be quantifying over a fully determinate totality, we shall have no motive to do so.

Cantor's celebrated diagonal argument to show that the totality of real numbers is not denumerable has precisely the form of a principle of extension for an indefinitely extensible concept: given any denumerable totality of real numbers, we can define, *in terms of that totality*, a real number that does not belong to it. The argument does not show that the real numbers form a non-denumerable totality unless we assume at the outset that they form a determinate totality comprising all that we shall ever recognize as a real number: the alternative is to regard the concept *real number* as an indefinitely extensible one. It might be objected that no contradiction results from taking the real numbers to form a determinate totality. There is, however, no ground to suppose that treating an indefinitely extensible concept as a definite one will always lead to inconsistency; it may merely lead to our supposing ourselves to have a definite idea when we do not. This hypothesis explains the lameness of our attempts at a characterization of the supposed determinate totality of all real numbers, and relieves us of the embarrassment resulting from the apparent need for such a characterization; for the characterization of an indefinitely extensible concept demands much less than the once-for-all characterization of a determinate totality.

The adoption of this solution has a steep price, which most mathematicians would be unwilling to pay: the rejection of classical methods of argument in mathematics in favour of constructive ones. The prejudices of mathematicians do not constitute an argument, however: the important question for us is whether constructive mathematics is adequate for applications. We have so far assumed a realist view of the physical universe: would this be compatible with a less than fully realist view of mathematics? Not on the face of it; but, having taken the concept *real number*, but not yet that of *natural number*, to be indefinitely extensible, we have not yet attained a fully constructive conception of the real numbers, since they are essentially infinite objects, involving some notion such as that of an infinite sequence. By contrast, each natural number is a finite, that is, finitely describable, object: the totality of natural numbers is therefore of a radically different kind from the totality of real numbers. It does not follow that we may call it a determinate totality. Consider Frege's 'proof' that every natural number has a successor: given any initial segment of the natural numbers, from 0 to n, the number of terms of that segment is again a natural number, but one larger than any term of the segment. As Frege presents it, the proof begs the question, since it rests on the assumption that we already have a domain containing the cardinal number of any subset of that domain; but the striking resemblance between this argument and that which showed the indefinite extensibility of the concept *set not a member of itself* suggests a reinterpretation of it as showing the indefinite extensibility of the concept *natural number*. The natural objection is that, when we attain the totality of all natural numbers, the supposed principle of extension ceases to apply, since the number of natural numbers is not itself a natural number. This, however, is again to assume that we have a grasp of the totality of natural numbers: but do we? Certainly we have a clear grasp of the step from any natural number to its successor: but this is merely the essential principle of extension. The totality of natural numbers contains what, from our standpoint, are enormous numbers, and yet others relatively to which those are minute, and so on indefinitely; do we really have a grasp of such a totality?

A natural response is to claim that the question has been begged. In classing *real number* as an indefinitely extensible concept, we have *assumed* that any totality of which we can have a definite conception is at most denumerable; in classing *natural number* as one, we have assumed that such a totality will be finite. Burden-of-proof controversies are always difficult to resolve; but, in this instance, it is surely clear that it is the other side that has begged the question. It is claiming to be able to convey a conception of the totality of real numbers, without circularity, to one who does not yet have it. We are assuming that the latter does not have, either, a conception of any other totality of the power of the continuum. He therefore does not *assume* as a principle that any totality of which it is possible to form a definite conception is at most denumerable: he merely has as yet no conception of any totality of higher cardinality. Likewise, a conception of the totality of the natural numbers is supposed to be conveyed to one as yet unaware of any but finite totalities; but all that he is given is a principle of extension for passing from any finite totality to a larger one. The fact is that a concept determining an intrinsically infinite totality—one whose infinity follows from the concept itself—simply *is* an indefinitely extensible one; in the long history of mankind's grappling with the notion of infinity, this fact could not be clearly perceived until the set-theoretic paradoxes forced us to recognize the existence of indefinitely extensible concepts. Not all indefinitely extensible concepts are equally exorbitant, indeed; we have been long familiar, from the work initiated by Cantor, with the fact that there is not just one uniform notion of infinity, but a variety of them: but this should not hinder us from acknowledging that every concept with an intrinsically infinite extension belongs to one or another type of indefinitely extensible one.

The recognition of this fact compels us to adopt a thoroughly constructive version of analysis: we cannot fully grasp any one real number, but only to an approximation, although there are important differences in the extent to which we can grasp them, for example between those for which we have an effective method of finding their decimal expansions and those for which we do not. This strongly suggests that the constructive theory of real numbers is *better* adapted to their applications than its classical counterpart; for, although the realist assumption is that every quantity has some determinate magnitude, represented, relatively to some unit, by a real number, it is a commonplace that we can never arrive at that magnitude save to within an approximation.

This partly answers our question how far a realist view of the physical universe could survive the replacement of classical by constructive analysis. On a constructive view of the matter, the magnitude of any quantity, relatively to a unit, may be taken to be given by a particular real number, which we may at any stage determine to a closer approximation by refinement of the measurement process; but no precise determination of it will ever be warranted, nor presumed to obtain independently of our incapacity to determine it. The assumption that it has a precise value, standing in determinate order relations to all rational numbers and known to God if not to us, stems from the realist metaphysics that informs much of our physical theory. This observation does not, however, settle whether the assumption is integral to those theories or a piece of metaphysics detachable from them; and this question cannot be answered without detailed investigation. If it should prove that the applications of any mathematical theory to physics can be adequately effected by a constructive version of that theory, it would follow that realist assumptions play no role in physical theory as such, but merely govern the interpretation we put upon our physical theories; and, in this case, physics itself might for practical purposes remain aloof from metaphysics. If, on the other hand, it were to prove that constructive mathematics is inadequate to yield the applications of mathematics that we actually make, and that classical mathematics is strictly required for them, it would follow that those realist assumptions do play a significant role in physics as presently understood. That would not settle the matter, of course. There would then be a metaphysical question whether the realist assumptions could be justified; if not, our physics as well as our mathematics would call for revision along constructive lines.

But would it not be better to adopt Field's approach, rather than one calling for a revision of practice on the part of the majority of mathematicians? What the answer ought to be if there were any real promise of success for Field's enterprise is hard to say; but there is a simple reason why he has provided none. He proposes to infer the conservativeness of a given mathematical theory with respect to a given physical theory from the relevant representation theorem by means of a uniform argument resting upon the consistency of a version of ZF with Urelemente. Why, then, does he believe ZF to be consistent? Most people do, indeed: but then most people are not nominalists. They believe ZF to be consistent because they suppose themselves in possession of a perhaps hazily conceived intuitive model of the theory; but Field can have no such reason. Any such intuitive model must involve a conception of the totality of ordinals less than the first strongly inaccessible one; and no explanation of the term 'model' has been offered according to which the elements of a model need not be supposed to exist. The reason offered by Field himself for believing in the consistency of ZF is that "if it weren't consistent someone would have probably discovered an inconsistency in it by now"; and he refers to this as inductive knowledge. To have an inductive basis for the conviction, it is not enough to observe that some theories have been discovered to be inconsistent in a relatively short time; it would be necessary also to know, of some theories not discovered to be inconsistent within around three-quarters of a century, that they *are* consistent. Without non-inductive knowledge of the consistency of some comparable mathematical theories there can be no inductive knowledge of the consistency of any mathematical theory. Field's proof of conservativeness therefore rests upon a conviction for which he can claim no ground whatever; one far more extravagant than any belief in the totality of real numbers.

I have argued that it is useless to cast around for new answers to the question what mathematics is about: the logicists already had essentially the correct answer. They were defeated by the problem of mathematical objects because they had incompatible aims: to represent mathematics as a genuine science, that is, as a body of *truths*, and not a mere auxiliary of other sciences; to keep it uncontaminated from empirical notions; and to justify classical mathematics in its entirety, and, in particular, the untrammelled use of classical logic in mathematical proofs. Field wishes to abandon the first, and others argue for abandoning the second: I have urged the abandonment of the third. On some conceptions of logic, it may be protested that this is not a purely logicist account, on the ground that mathematical objects still do not qualify to be called logical objects; but this is little more than a boundary dispute. If the domains of the fundamental mathematical theories are taken to be given by indefinitely extensible concepts, then we have what Frege sought and failed to find: a way of characterizing them that renders our right to refer to them unproblematic while yet leaving the existence of their elements independent of any contingent states of affairs. If the price of this solution to the problem of the basis of those theories is that argumentation within mathematics is compelled to become more cautious than that which classical mathematicians have been accustomed to use, and more sensitive to distinctions to which they have been accustomed to be indifferent, it is a price worth paying, especially if the resulting versions of the theories indeed prove more apt for their applications.

19

Wittgenstein on Necessity: Some Reflections

A realist believes that there are, or at any rate may be, true statements that it is beyond our capacity to recognize as true: for instance, statements about the remote past, or number-theoretic statements no proof of which is possible by means of any resources we have or ever will have. A moderate constructivist will deny that there are any true statements whose truth we *could not* have recognized, had we been suitably placed; and a more radical constructivist will deny that there are any true statements whose truth we *can never come* to recognize. But constructivists of both persuasions are likely to agree that there are true statements whose truth we do not at present recognize and *shall not in fact ever* recognize; to deny this would appear to be to espouse a constructivism altogether too extreme. One surely cannot crudely equate truth with being recognized, or with being treated, as true.

It is otherwise with necessity; or, at least, it appears that necessity and truth differ in this regard. A long time ago, I attributed to Wittgenstein the thesis that for a statement to be necessarily true is simply for it to be *treated* as being necessarily true, that is, as being unassailable or as providing a standard by means of which other statements, at best contingently true, may be judged. The effect of a mathematical proof, on this account, is to induce us to treat the theorem as unassailable—to 'put it in the archives'. Having done so, we have a new criterion for the application of some mathematical concept. For instance, when we first encounter the proof that a cylinder intersects a plane in an ellipse, we acquire, provided that we accept the proof, a new criterion for the application of the term "ellipse"; we might, for example, appeal to the theorem in a particular case to establish that a certain figure, which, perhaps, did not look quite like an ellipse, *must be* one.

It can be objected that we do not, in fact, treat as unassailable whatever has been accepted as having been proved. There are actual cases of putative theorems having been acknowledged as such over many years, from which other putative theorems have been derived, only to be eventually confronted by a counter-example, leading to the detection of an error in the original proof; whereas, if our behaviour matched the account of it Wittgenstein frequently gives, we should have ruled out the apparent counter-example a priori,

Delivered as a talk at a conference on the philosophy of Hilary Putnam held at St Andrews in November 1990. Forthcoming in Bob Hale and Peter Clark (eds.), *Reading Putnam* (Oxford).

declaring that there must be a mistake in the characterization of it as one. This may lead one to suspect that Wittgenstein confused necessity with certainty; whether we reject the counter-example or the theorem, in advance of locating a specific mistake in the description of the former or the proof of the latter, depends upon which we are more certain of. The thesis can, however, be formulated so as to allow for revisions in what we take as having been proved, by admitting proofs, in general, to be only *provisionally* compelling. A counter-proof of the same general character, or even an apparent empirical counter-example, will threaten the status of the theorem, although a failure then to locate a mistake either in its proof or in its purported refutation will provoke a crisis demanding resolution. What is necessary is what we treat as such and will continue to do so. But the Wittgensteinian account will not tolerate the introduction of the *ideal*. We must not say that the necessary is what the ideally competent mathematician *would* treat as such, for that invokes the conception of an external standard of correct judgement—one perhaps formulated by us, but certainly not applied by us—and there is none on this account. According to it, there is not in general any truth of the matter concerning what the ideally competent mathematician would and would not do or acknowledge, or even concerning what should count as ideal competence.

Hilary Putnam and I are agreed that the radical conventionalism about necessary truth which I attributed to Wittgenstein evades a fatal objection to the more restrained conventionalism advocated by the logical positivists and their fellow travellers. According to restrained conventionalism, all necessary truth derives, immediately or remotely, from linguistic stipulations we have tacitly made, linguistic conventions we are trained to observe. Some necessarily true statements, such as "There are seven days in a week" or "April comes after March", are the direct subjects of such stipulations; learning to treat them as true is expressly required for learning the use of the word "week" or the names "March" and "April". Other necessarily true statements, however, do not directly reflect conventions we consciously follow, but are *consequences* of more basic conventions. This prompts the objection that it leaves the necessity of the consequences unaccounted for: what makes it the case that, if we observe such-and-such conventions, which require us to treat such-and-such statements as true, we *must* accept such-and-such other statements as true? Radical conventionalism escapes this objection by treating *every* necessary truth as the direct expression of a linguistic convention. It does not, indeed, obliterate the distinction between basic necessary truths, in defence of which we can say no more than "That's what the word *means*", or something of that order, and consequences of those basic truths, for which we can offer a proof: but the latter are consequences solely because we count them as being consequences, which is to say that we accept their proofs as compelling; there is no sense in which they would be consequences whether we recognized them as such or not.

Hilary Putnam's comment on my proposed interpretation of Wittgenstein runs as follows:[1]

Michael Dummett suggested a daring possibility:[2] namely, that Wittgenstein was a *radical conventionalist*. That is, Wittgenstein was a conventionalist who held not just that some finite set of meaning postulates is true by convention, but that whenever we accept what we call a 'proof' in logic or mathematics, an *act of decision* is involved: a decision to *accept* the proof. This decision, on Dummett's reading, is never *forced* on us by some prior thing called the 'concepts' or 'the meaning of the words'; even given these *as they have previously been specified*, it is still *up to us* whether we shall accept the proof as a valid deployment of those concepts or not. The decision to accept the proof is a *further* meaning stipulation: the 'theorems of mathematics and logic' that we actually prove and accept are not just *consequences* of conventions, but *individually* conventional. Such a 'radical' conventionalism, Dummett pointed out, would be immune to the Quine–Wittgenstein objection to the Ayer–Carnap sort of conventionalism.

In response, Barry Stroud pointed out[3] that the position Dummett calls 'radical conventionalism' cannot possibly be Wittgenstein's. A convention, in the literal sense, is something we can legislate either way. Wittgenstein does not anywhere say or suggest that the mathematician proving a theorem is *legislating* that it shall be a theorem (and the mathematician would get into a lot of trouble, to put it mildly, if he tried to 'legislate' it the opposite way).

Basing himself on a good deal of textual evidence, Stroud suggested that Wittgenstein's position was that it is not *convention* or *legislation* but our *forms of life* (i.e., our human nature as determined by our biology-plus-cultural-history) that cause us to accept certain proofs *as* proofs. And Stroud's reply to Dummett's interpretation appears to have been generally accepted by Wittgenstein scholars.

It appears to me that Stroud's reply, while correct as a response to Dummett's interpretation, does not speak to the real philosophical point Dummett was making. The real point is that if *either* Dummett *or* Stroud is right, then Wittgenstein is claiming that mathematical truth and necessity *arise in us*, that it is human nature and forms of life that *explain* mathematical truth and necessity. If this is right, then it is the greatest philosophical discovery of all time. Even if it is wrong, it is an astounding philosophical claim. If Stroud does not dispute that Wittgenstein advanced this claim—and he does not seem to dispute it—then *his* interpretation of Wittgenstein is a revision of Dummett's rather than a total rejection of it.

It is clear that Putnam is right to say that even Stroud's Wittgenstein is propounding a thesis that goes against the common opinion; but, at the risk of appearing obstinate, I do not think he is right to accept Stroud's emendation of my interpretation. For it is really a version of moderate conventionalism, in that it acknowledges something—namely human nature or our form of life—

[1] In 'Analyticity and Apriority: Beyond Wittgenstein and Quine', in P. French (ed.), *Midwest Studies in Philosophy*, iv (Notre Dame, Ind., 1979); repr. in H. Putnam, *Realism and Reason*, iii (Cambridge, 1983), 116–17.

[2] The reference is to my 'Wittgenstein's Philosophy of Mathematics', *Philosophical Review*, 68 (1959), 324–48; repr. in M. Dummett, *Truth and Other Enigmas* (London, 1978).

[3] The reference is to Barry Stroud, 'Wittgenstein and Logical Necessity', *Philosophical Review*, 74 (1965), 504–18.

that *determines* the consequences of the basic necessary truths, or of the conventions that directly confer necessity upon them. Admittedly, as Putnam remarks, it locates what determines that within us; it is not an external necessity. Nevertheless, if Stroud is really propounding an interpretation that conflicts with mine, it must involve that, given the basic necessary truths, or, equivalently, the basic linguistic conventions, human nature, or our form of life, determines what we shall take as their consequences: granted what we are like, we cannot but draw from our basic conventions the consequences we in fact draw.

Well, it may be said, that is just as Stroud intended: he meant to present Wittgenstein's view as less radical than I had done. It seems to me, however, that such an interpretation misses Wittgenstein's primary contention. Certainly we do, by and large, agree on what the consequences are, what follows from what, what is a valid proof and what is not. This is a fact of our existence—our form of life, if you wish to use that phrase—and, without it, mathematics, as we practise it, could not exist. But, on Wittgenstein's view, it is a *brute* fact: nothing explains it. It cannot be accounted for by appeal to any general feature of our nature; and so no general feature of our nature suffices to determine what, specifically, we take to be consequences of the truths whose necessity springs from our basic linguistic conventions—the 'grammatical' remarks that register our conformity to those conventions. If our nature did determine what, for us, would constitute a consequence of them, then there would be necessary truths that were, by our lights, consequences of the fundamental conventions even though we had not yet recognized them as such; indeed, there might be such necessary truths that we should never recognize. A conventionalist of what Putnam calls the Ayer–Carnap type thinks that the conventions we have adopted for the use of the words "cylinder", "intersection", "plane", and "ellipse" of themselves determine the inescapable truth of the theorem connecting them, by an ineluctable metanecessity. Wittgenstein, as interpreted by Stroud, thinks that they do so in virtue of our human nature, or our form of life. But Wittgenstein himself thought that *nothing* determines it in advance: only when we have accepted the proof and put the theorem in the archives does it *become* a consequence of the initial conventions.

The phenomenology of mathematical proof is, indeed, quite different from that of taking a decision or of making a stipulation. We do not, in the normal case, see ourselves as having any other option than to accept the proof; we cannot think of anything we can say to resist it. Wittgenstein is well aware of this obvious feature, and indeed emphasizes it. It is part of the brute fact: but, as I understand him, he thought that we should not be seduced by it into supposing there to have been anything which determined in advance that such a proof was waiting to be discovered, or that, once given, it would strike us as compelling.

The core of Wittgenstein's argument is the observation that the proof provides us with a new criterion. This observation is, however, susceptible of a wholly banal construction. When we know the theorem, our accepting that *this* is a cylinder and *that* a plane gives us a reason for saying that the figure determined by their intersection is an ellipse; and this is a reason that we did not have before. If this is all that is meant by saying that we have a new criterion, it is indisputable; but it tells us nothing about what a mathematical proof is, or about the status of the theorem that it proves.

Now Wittgenstein's official description of his method in philosophy is that it consists in assembling truths that no one could dispute; if we believe that this is a true description, we may be inclined to suppose that the banal interpretation of the observation about the new criterion is the intended one. But, if so, the observation tells us precisely nothing; if, so understood, it is an example of Wittgenstein's philosophy, then that philosophy is incapable of throwing any light on anything. It seems, therefore, that the official description of Wittgenstein's philosophical method cannot be the true one, and that, in particular, the observation about new criteria cannot be meant to be understood as a mere platitude.

If it is not a platitude, what is its content? It is a platitude if it is construed as compatible with assuming that the new criterion will always agree with the old criteria, when these are correctly applied in accordance with our original standards for applying them correctly; that is, with the assumption that, whenever we apply the new criterion correctly, we should have been justified by the original criteria in making the assertion that we do, even if we had failed to notice the fact. For instance, whenever we rightly judge, by the old criteria, that this is a cylinder and that a plane, and, applying the new criterion, judge their intersection to be an ellipse, we should have been justified by the old criteria in declaring it to be an ellipse, even though, had we not known the theorem, we might not have noticed that it was or even, as the result of some mistake, have judged it not to be one.

That, however, is precisely what we take the force of the proof to be. We normally take the proof to show that whatever is judged by the new criterion to be an ellipse *must* be an ellipse by the old criterion, rightly applied, provided that we have also rightly applied the terms "cylinder" and "plane". Seeking a more than banal interpretation of the central observation about new criteria therefore appears to be a hopeless task: to all appearance, it is not merely a delicate matter to state the Wittgensteinian alternative, but an impossibility. We might try the following: if the observation that the proof supplies a new criterion is not to be a platitude, then it must be possible for there to be an apparent counter-example to the theorem whose description as being a counter-example involves no specifiable mistake in the application of the original criteria for applying the terms "ellipse", "cylinder", and "plane". But to say that there cannot be a counter-example, and hence that any description of something as one must involve a mistake, is an expression of our acceptance of the theorem; and, since we do accept it, we do say that, and there is no questioning our correctness in saying it. It is useless to retort that it does not follow that there must be some *specifiable* mistake. There may obviously be a mistake that we are unable to specify, not having spotted it; but this is, once more, banal. It remains that every mistake must be intrinsically capable of being specified; there can be no such thing as a mistake that is in itself unspecifiable.

In order to arrive at a robust interpretation of the thesis about new criteria which will give some substance to Wittgenstein's view of mathematical necessity, we might try saying that we are not entitled to claim that, in arriving at a judgement in conflict with the theorem, any *particular* mistake will in all cases come to light. That, however, is again banal: what is needed is a claim that there need *be* no particular mistake to come to light. Such a claim would be incoherent: there cannot be a mistake that is not a particular mistake, any more than there can be a donkey that is not a particular donkey.

Must we conclude, therefore, that there is no admissible interpretation of the thesis that the proof supplies a new criterion other than the banal one? That appears to land us back in moderate conventionalism: the validity of the new criterion is a consequence of our adoption of the original criteria, a consequence that holds whether we recognize it or not. That certainly does not represent Wittgenstein's view, at least as I am interpreting him: according to him, its being a consequence depends wholly upon our recognizing it as a consequence. But it seems that can be maintained only if we put a more than banal construction upon the thesis about new criteria: and we have seen that it appears impossible to arrive at any coherent formulation of any such construction.

Where have we gone wrong? I believe that the fact is that Wittgenstein does not want us to attempt to imagine the circumstances as from a superhuman viewpoint. We strive to differentiate the banal from the robust interpretation of the thesis about new criteria by talking about mistakes that we might in fact make, although we neither detect them nor currently possess any reason for supposing them to have occurred; in general, by talking about what would have been *true* even though we had not recognized it as true. But this is to adopt the externalist standpoint that it was the whole point of Wittgenstein's account to repudiate: to attempt to step outside the situation in which we are placed, and thus to pass beyond the limits of language and say what can only be shown. We possess certain criteria for the application of our words; we make, and detect, mistakes in applying those criteria; and, since our criteria overlap, we also declare that a mistake must have occurred in cases in which we have not detected any. And all that can be done, according to the view I am attributing to Wittgenstein, is to describe those criteria and their interaction.

We want to say that, if we have an apparent counter-example to the theorem, God must be able to see what mistake we have made in the application of our own criteria, even if we cannot. It seems that, if we say this, we shall have reduced the thesis about the new criterion to banality. In reaction, we may attempt to formulate our internalist thesis, defending the conception that our acceptance of the theorem constitutes the whole substance of the proposition that we must have made a mistake by saying that, on the contrary, there need not have been any specific mistake for God to notice. But if we choose this option, we shall have been unfaithful to our acceptance of the theorem. This is, essentially, the core of Putnam's refutation of relativism and allied heresies: any attempt to state the general thesis must run foul of that actual practice which it claims to be the source of necessity and truth, and hence be self-refuting: it is an attempt to view our language and our thought from that external vantage-point which it declares to be inaccessible.

The resolution of the difficulty lies in our acquiescing in the impossibility of our so much as talking intelligibly about how things are in themselves—how they are as God apprehends them—independently of what we treat ourselves as having reason to say. If we acquiesce in this, then there are no two distinct interpretations of the thesis about new criteria to put in contrast with one another. It can be admitted to be banal, thus vindicating Wittgenstein's description of his philosophical method; but, because it uses the only resources that we have, it also constitutes the account that has to be given of the character of mathematical proof and the source of mathematical necessity. It is vain and presumptuous to attempt to see reality through God's eyes: all we can do is to describe our own practices as we can view them through our own eyes. Considered as a constituent of those practices, what a mathematical proof does is to induce us to accept a new criterion as being justified by the criteria we already had. That, therefore, is the sole and sufficient account of mathematical proof and of the necessity of mathematical theorems. We are not to ask whether the new criterion is *really* so justified: justification is whatever we *count* as justification.

If I have interpreted Wittgenstein aright, his doctrine is internalism with a vengeance; it could hardly be called internal *realism*. To say that we cannot intelligibly talk about what is true independently of what we recognize as true is, in effect, to hold that there is no admissible notion of truth other than that of being accepted as true. The internalist thesis that necessity attaches to a statement only in virtue of its being treated as necessary proves to require holding also that truth can attach to a statement only in virtue of *its* being treated as true. The claim that there are true statements whose truth we do not at present recognize can be admitted only in so far as it relates to those we shall come to recognize as true. Truth *is* to be equated with being recognized, or, better, with being treated, as true.

On reflection, it is evident that the internalist thesis about necessity *must* imply the internalist thesis about truth. For we are not here concerned with the, to my mind misbegotten, concept of metaphysical necessity, and logically necessary statements interest us only in so far as they encapsulate principles of inference, fundamental or derived. The disagreement between defenders and opponents of the law of excluded middle, for example, is about the validity of certain forms of reasoning such as the dilemma. A defender of the law who had some ingenious means of recognizing every instance of it as a logical truth, while rejecting as invalid all those rules of inference ordinarily thought of as standing or falling with it, would be occupying a position indistinguishable in substance from that of an opponent of the law: it is deductive validity that concerns us for its own sake, and necessary truth only as an instrument in securing that. The whole point of establishing a logically necessary truth is to provide us with a more streamlined means of arriving at contingent truths; so, if the necessity of the necessary truth depends solely upon our according it that status, the truth of contingent truths arrived at by its means must also depend in part on that. It might be retorted that mathematicians value theorems for their own sake; but Wittgenstein, at least, appears to have held that they have no value save in so far as they can be applied.

The difficulty with externalism—with purporting to say how things are in themselves, independently of how they appear to us—is that it soon presents itself as an attempt to say the unsayable. It is of little use to console ourselves with the reflection that there nevertheless *is* the unsayable, and that its only disadvantage is that we cannot say it; to say that is to pretend that the unsayable is nevertheless thinkable, whereas, if it cannot be said, it cannot be thought either. It is at this point that realism and idealism seem to coincide: once you have recognized that what you were attempting to say was unsayable, and have abandoned the attempt to say it, then there is nothing that cannot be said. How do we know that things exist when we do not perceive them? Well, we apply certain criteria for something's having existed during an interval within which we were not perceiving it; and so, if it satisfies those criteria, it *did* exist during that interval, which is to say that we are right to say that it did—according to *our* criteria. But, to the externalist, internalism appears to be one of those traps from which it is, unfairly but undeniably, impossible to escape. How do I know that I am not dreaming, or mad? It seems that I can, in principle, offer no reply: for anything I might adduce might merely be part of my dream or a product of my madness. So here. I cannot, by the nature of the case, cite an instance of a true statement that we have no ground to recognize as true. I can, of course, claim that the statement "There are true statements that we have no ground to recognize as true" would be generally recognized as true; but all this does is to display the internalist thesis, in the strong form in which I am discussing it, as itself unsayable. But that is not to refute it. It does not show that we can ever do more than describe what our practice is; and any consequence I draw from supposing some particular statement to be true although unacknowledged will still be the apodosis of a conditional that I have shown that we have good reason, by our existing criteria, to accept.

Still, if realism and idealism, or, as I am here preferring to say, externalism and internalism, coincide, there can be no harm in being an externalist. The externalist has an advantage over the internalist, in that, of certain things that we say, it is our practice to claim that they represent how things are in themselves, independently of how we apprehend them. Granted, we can have no grounds for asserting anything that, according to our linguistic conventions, we do not have a ground for asserting; but, when we assert something as representing how things are in themselves, the internalist's objection is stifled, since he has no means of expressing his thought that it does not *really* so represent them, but merely accords with a linguistic convention allowing, or requiring, us to *say* that it does.

It seems that neither the externalist nor the internalist view can be estalished, since to establish either would require us to say the unsayable; both sides may comfort themselves that there still *is* the unsayable, but it will be a different unsayable that each is constrained to refrain from attempting to say. Putnam nevertheless argues that it is possible to demonstrate the externalist view to be incoherent. From the side of physics quantum mechanics makes it impossible to maintain that we are able to say how things are quite independently of our observation of them, unless we are prepared to adopt the metaphysical extravagances of the many-worlds interpretation; and, from the side of logic, the paradoxes block us from supposing that we can devise a language in which everything can be expressed.

The paradoxes—both the set-theoretic and the semantic paradoxes—result from our possessing indefinitely extensible concepts; the concepts of set, ordinal number, and cardinal number are all indefinitely extensible, as is the concept of a statement. An indefinitely extensible concept is one for which, together with some determinate range or ranges of objects falling under it, we are given an intuitive principle whereby, if we have a sufficiently definite grasp of any one such range of objects, we can form, in terms of it, a conception of a more inclusive such range. A sufficiently definite grasp of a language, for example, is for this purpose one yielding an intuitive conception of the notion of truth as applying to the assertoric statements of that language. Given this, we may always frame a richer language in which we can talk about the first language, in the sense of formulating semantic properties of it, and also say anything that we could say in that language. Hence there can be for us no all-inclusive language, any more than we can talk simultaneously about all ordinal numbers in the sense of all objects that we could ever recognize as falling under the intuitive concept *ordinal number*.

By the nature of the case, we can form no clear conception of the extension of an indefinitely extensible concept; any attempt to do so is liable to lead us into contradiction. Is it intelligible to suppose that a superhuman intelligence could form such a conception? The concept could not be given to that intelligence as indefinitely extensible; but might it not have a concept whose extension covered all and only those objects we are capable of coming to recognize as ordinal numbers? The question seems unanswerable; but we should be cautions in formulating the proposition that we cannot talk simultaneously about all objects falling under an intuitive concept given to us as indefinitely extensible. We can obviously frame some incontestably true statements about all such objects, for example, "Every ordinal number has a successor". What we cannot do is to suppose that a language admitting such statements obeys a two-valued semantics; but there is no difficulty in envisaging such a language as obeying intuitionistic logic. That will not, of course, satisfy the externalist, because the statements of such a language will not all be determinately true or false, and for the most elementary reason, namely that the quantification they involve is not over a determinate domain (or at least over one of which we can attain a definite conception). We here come upon a link between externalism, as I have been discussing it, and realism, in the sense in which I have frequently discussed it and in which it crucially involves the principle of bivalence, a link that justifies Hilary Putnam's use of the phrase 'external realism'. Since the focus is different, however, I shall continue to use the term 'externalism'.

We may thus accept that full-blown externalism is incoherent. That does not vindicate full-blown internalism, however, since it, too, is incoherent. Of the two, externalism is definitely the more congenial to common sense; but from where do we get so much as the idea of a distinction between how things are in themselves and how they appear to us? We get it from our own linguistic practices, that is, the practices in which we learn to engage in the course of becoming masters of our mother tongues. I am not meaning here to allude to the contrast between delusive and veridical appearances, or between carrying out a procedure incorrectly and carying it out correctly, since those, in general, are just matters of rectifying one observation or procedure in the light of others; they are distinctions *within* the realm of the way things appear. What we need to fasten on are those practices which induce us, or compel us, to form a conception of how things are independently of any observations we make; and that on which I wish to concentrate is that of deductive inference. If we spoke a language devoid of all inferential practices whatever, then there would be nothing to debar us from equating the truth of a statement with its having been directly verified; more properly expressed, the speakers of such a language would have no need of, and would not in fact possess, any notion of truth for which they could conceive that it might apply to any statements they had not directly verified. There would be for them no distinction between the world as it is and the world as it impinged on them. The introduction of deductive inference into the practice of the speakers of such a language would immediately compel them to frame a broader conception of truth. Perhaps "truth" is too strong a term for the notion they would have to have, for they would not need, simply in view of their admission of inferential procedures, to differentiate between it and the notion of what may justifiably be asserted; but they would certainly need a conception of what can be *indirectly* established as assertable, even though it has not been *directly* so established, just because that is what, in any interesting case, inference does, namely to establish its conclusion indirectly.

I hope I may be forgiven for using an example I have used before, that of Euler's proof concerning the bridges at Königsberg. This proof certainly does not show that, whenever we have verified that someone followed a connected course involving his crossing every bridge, we shall thereby have verified that he crossed at least one bridge more than once, for this is by no means so. What it establishes, rather, is that any sufficiently detailed observations that serve to verify the former can be so arranged as simultaneously to verify the latter; more exactly, that, when we have so arranged our observations, we have an effective means whereby we can locate an error whenever our observations appear to verify the former and to falsify the latter. In any specific case, the opportunity to carry out such detailed observations may have irretrievably passed; we may have verified that the walker crossed every bridge, without having the detail to transform this into an observation that he crossed some bridge twice. In the light of Euler's proof, we nevertheless take the observations we have made as entitling us to assert that he (must have) crossed some bridge twice.

In so doing—more exactly, in coming to engage in the practice of accepting and applying such proofs—we *extend* our notion of what justifies the assertion of such a statement; the proof really does induce us to adopt a new criterion. Well, it may be said, internalism can take that in its stride. This just is one of our practices: we have the custom of taking such a thing as justifying the assertion; and the statement is true precisely inasmuch as we have that practice, and the circumstances which it requires us to take as justifying the assertion do in fact obtain. But that is too glib: the question is whether we should maintain the practice if we believed the claims of the internalist. It is like Cantor's paradise: Wittgenstein does not drive us out of it, but, if we believe him, it will cease to appear a paradise and we shall see no reason for remaining. Our criterion for the validity of a proof of this kind is that it provides an effective method for transforming a sufficiently detailed current observation that verifies a statement of a certain form into a verification of a related statement of a different form. The practice of making inferences on the basis of proofs valid by this criterion involves our willingness, when we have verified a statement of the first form, to assert one of the second form, even though we have not verified it and can no longer do so; that is why we have in such a case an *indirect* justification. Our having learned to engage in this practice has induced in us a conception of how things are—must have been—

even when we have not observed them to be so. Once we have this conception, it is integral to our perceiving the practice we learned as a sound one; we have a conception of the truth of a statement in terms of which an argument which invokes the theorem is to be seen as transmitting truth from premiss to conclusion. We are entitled to assert that the walker crossed at least one bridge twice because the proof shows that that is how it must have been; we did not, but we *could have*, observed it to be so at the time. But full-blown internalism repudiates this conception of truth. According to it, it is our practice of applying proofs of this kind that *constitutes* the truth of the statement we infer. And, once we believe that, why should we continue to apply them? Doubtless, when we first adopted the practice of inferential reasoning, there was little choice in the matter; we were simply trained to do so. But we do not maintain it simply because it is what society expects us to do: we do so because it appears to us to have a rationale, that is, to be a method of ascertaining how things in fact are. The full-blown internalist would have us think that rationale an illusion; if we believe him, only inertia can make us go on reasoning as before. Better to strive to eradicate within ourselves the delusive distinction between the world as it is and the world as it impinges on us.

Thus full-blown internalism can make our linguistic practices the whole source of necessity and of truth only by discrediting those practices, and, indeed, the concepts of necessity and truth themselves: that is *its* incoherence. Logic and physics bar us from being full-blown externalists; but full-blown internalism will lead us to dismiss as pointless the practices on which it so heavily insists. It thus appears that a reasonable position must lie between the two extremes; but where? Hilary Putnam has attacked externalism in its full-blown form, but opposes to it a rather moderate internalism; full-blown internalism he equally repudiates. One temperamentally disposed towards externalism might aim at being as much of an externalist as possible, while shunning the untenable full-blown version; but, conversely, one temperamentally disposed towards internalism might wish to remain as internalist as possible, without going to the extreme in *that* direction.

This presents us with three problems. Is there a coherent moderate externalism? Is there a coherent moderate internalism? And do they coincide?

Unquestionably there have been philosophers whose views have embodied both externalist and internalist doctrines, held in apparent harmony. Frege is a clear example. His celebrated principle that a term has meaning only in the context of a sentence is a strongly internalist one. It involves a rejection of the conception whereby to treat a term as referring to some particular object is to make a mental association between the term and the object, considered as directly apprehended by the mind from a standpoint outside our language and our thought. According to the context principle, nothing can be picked out as an object of thought save in some particular way, which will in principle be expressible in language. Hence the determination of the reference of a term must reduce to fixing the conditions for the truth or falsity of identity-statements connecting it with other terms: grasping which object the term refers to is nothing more than knowing the conditions under which statements purporting to identify it in other ways are true.

Equally internalist is the corollary derived by Frege from the context principle, that with any term there must be associated a criterion of identity. This says, essentially, that the world does not come to us already dissected into discrete objects; rather, it is we who, by adopting particular criteria for what is to count as being presented with the same object as before, slice it up into objects in one manner rather than another.

Despite his propounding these internalist theses, Frege was, notoriously, a staunch realist. The mathematician's task is to discover what is there; truth is to be utterly distinguished from what is taken to be true; the sun is what it is, regardless of what we think it to be. We express our thoughts in language, but, in grasping those thoughts, recognize them as being determined as true or as false in virtue of how things are and independently of whether we do or can judge of their truth or falsity. The conception that reconciles the internalist and externalist components of Frege's philosophy is expressed in the *Tractatus* in the metaphor of the grid. To describe the world at all, we need a grid, and might use one or another; but, given the grid, what constitutes a correct description is wholly independent of us.

Kant and Putnam are agreed that the grid does not resemble one of the projections by means of which we draw a flat map of part of the surface of the earth; for there, by representing it upon a sphere, we can get to the reality we project in different ways. Frege, for all his realism, was also in agreement with this; we cannot think about any object save in some particular way, and we cannot think about the world save within the framework of a system of senses expressed by a particular language. But that is only the first surrender externalism is called upon to make to internalism. Internalism contests Frege's unargued externalist assumption that the grasp we have of the thoughts we express entitles us to regard the world as determining each of them either as true or as false independently of our ability to decide its truth-value, as if we were able in thought to stand outside our means of arriving at judgements and envisage reality as rendering our thoughts true or false independently of those means. (I remain somewhat uncertain where Putnam stands on this question.) But, once the internalist has abandoned the firm ground of the realist conception of truth, he is in some embarrassment over just what he wants to replace it by. This is because, as argued earlier, the extreme internalist conception, which would simply identify the truth of a statement with our eventual sustained acceptance of it, while perhaps not actually incoherent, would render uninteresting and pointless a great deal that we regard as interesting and full of point. It would, in fact, ride roughshod over all that prompts us to strain after a full-fledged realist and externalist conception, whereas there is much in our 'form of life' that does so prompt us and which it is nihilist to treat with scorn. The internalist's problem is how to arrive at a conception of truth which does justice to these constituents of our form of life without allowing them to push him back into externalism. In particular, we need to acknowledge the degree to which the desire to attain a description of the physical world as it is in itself has motivated a good deal of science, even if it is in principle impossible to atain or even conceive of such a description and even if the aim has had to be forsworn at the most fundamental level. The completely objective may be unattainable, perhaps unimaginable, perhaps even nonsensical; but our drive to approximate to it is not to be dismissed as a mere product of a metaphysical error.

It is not merely that our means of determining truth are circumscribed; we also commit constant errors in applying them. To accommodate *this* feature of our form of life, Putnam's moderate internalist notion of truth invokes both the ideal and the subjunctive conditional; truth is what we should eventually arrive at were we to commit nothing that was a mistake by our own lights. This appeal is difficult to resist; yet it embodies a substantial externalist component. For it assumes that there is a fact of the matter concerning what we should do were we ideal human beings, rather than the imperfect ones that we are; what we should do were we to make no mistakes. By the nature of the matter, this is something that we cannot in all cases know: what justifies us in assuming that there is some specific thing that we should in those ideal circumstances do? Indeed, to put the question in this epistemological form is to make it too weak; it should be a metaphysical question, namely: if there *is* some specific thing that we should do, *what makes it the case that we should do that*, even though we cannot be sure what it is?

Wittgenstein was resolute in refusing to take an externalist view of subjunctive conditionals. A passage in the *Lectures on the Foundations of Mathematics* illustrates this vividly, and is the clearest evidence in favour of my interpretation of him. Wittgenstein says, of a calculation that we have not made and will never make, that it is wrong to say that God knows what its result would have been had we made it, for "there is nothing for God to know". What is the difference between a calculation and an experiment? According to Wittgenstein, it is simply that, having once made and checked the calculation, we treat its result as a criterion for our repeating the calculation correctly. It is only our doing the calculation and "putting it in the archives" that constitutes its result as being that obtained by doing it correctly; so, if we never do that calculation, there *is* no one correct result, and hence God cannot be said to know what that result is. There is, in other words, no determinate result which is that which we should get if we were to perform the calculation correctly according to our criteria for correctness.

This conclusion is the outcome of an unflinching application of Wittgenstein's ideas about rules; and it leads to a thoroughgoing internalism. He was certainly right to observe that, for the most fundamental of the rules that we follow, there is nothing *by which* we judge something to be a correct application of them. It certainly does not follow from this that, if we never do make such a judgement in some particular instance, there is no specific thing that would have been a correct application: to draw that inference, you need a general internalist premiss, that there is nothing to truth beyond our acknowledgement of truth. This premiss is totally implausible: and the conclusion induces a scepticism so profound that few can swallow it. Suppose the calculation in question is an ordinary addition. One of the rules that make up the computation procedure is that, if one of the two final digits is 7 and the other 8, you write 5 in the digits column of the sum and carry 1 to the tens column. To maintain that there is no determinately correct result of the calculation, you must say one of two incredible things. Either you must say that, until someone has done it, it is not determinate what would count as writing down 5 and carrying 1; or you must say that, although it is determinate what the outcome of each application of one of the constituent rules would be, it is not determinate what would be the outcome of a large but finite number of such applications. I do not know how many of the followers of Wittgenstein *really* believe either of these things; for myself, I cannot, and conclude that the celebrated 'rule-following considerations' embody a huge mistake. If they do not, then, if no one judges the position of the door, there will be no fact of the matter concerning whether, if someone had judged it to be shut, he would have been right; there will be no truth that we have not expressly acknowledged as such. But I have suggested that the argument begs the question: global internalism is required as a premiss to take us from the epistemology of rules to their metaphysical standing.

The moderate conventionalist view was never a solution to the problem of logical necessity at all, because, by invoking the notion of consequence, it appealed to what it ought to have been explaining; that is why it appears to call for a metanecessity beyond the necessity it purported to account for. The conventionalists were led astray by the example of the founders of modern logic into concentrating on the notion of logical or analytic *truth*, whereas precisely what they needed to fasten on was that of deductive *consequence*, which it is helpful to think of in terms of the metaphor of patterns. Even the simplest judgement imposes a pattern upon reality, a pattern in common between the variegated circumstances which would verify it. To make the judgement requires us not merely to attend passively to the relevant circumstances, but, deploying the concepts involved in the judgement, to discern the appropriate pattern in them. A deductive step brings about a small shift in the pattern apprehended; a series of such steps brings us to discern a pattern previously quite unexpected. When the step requires two premisses, we first superimpose two patterns on one another, to extract a third. The discernment of a new pattern is not merely compatible with, but *requires*, a recognition that that in which it is discerned has not itself changed; it is this which renders the deductive argument valid, while the novelty of the pattern represents the epistemic advance. The rules of inference which govern the deductive transitions themselves consist in the recognition of a pattern; not of a pattern in reality, but of one in a set of judgements, which mediates the passage from the discernment of one simple or complex pattern in reality to the discernment of another. Certainly our ability to discern patterns depends upon the stock of concepts available to us, which we acquire with our language and to which to a very limited extent we ourselves add; but we do not *impose* the patterns, but *discern* them, and the capacity of one pattern to be transformed into another is intrinsic, not created by our ability to perform the transformation.

This externalist account of deductive reasoning says nothing about the nature of the reality in which the patterns are discerned. I have argued that the admission of the practice of deductive inference requires a notion of truth not grossly internalist, but in some degree differentiated from the occurrence of a direct verification. On how great the distance is between the two will depend which rules of inference are to be recognized as valid, and how much compromise the internalist is compelled to make with externalism. But that is a further question, not to be enquired into here.

20

Realism and Anti-Realism

I begin by performing a duty, pleasant in itself, that I ought to have performed thirteen years ago, and one that I deeply regret having failed to perform at that time, that of celebrating the contribution of my predecessor Sir Alfred Ayer to philosophy in general and to Oxford philosophy in particular. During my year as Wykeham Professor-elect, I looked forward with great pleasure to the prospect of paying such a tribute, not only because it was his due and would give him pleasure, but because I owed him a debt of gratitude for the support he had given me over the years. The tribute was never paid, because I failed, through inefficiency in organizing the disposition of my time, to deliver an inaugural. When I succeeded to the Chair, I was in what has been a virtually permanent state for at least the past two decades of being in arrears with multiple obligations to compose contributions to collections, lectures for conferences, etc. By the time I had shaken these off, it was almost too late to give an inaugural without appearing ridiculous, but I began to write one all the same. It does not often happen to me that something I have started to write falls to pieces half-way through, but it happens to all of us sometimes, and it happened to me then. By this time, it was irrevocably too late to begin anything new, and so I resigned myself to giving no inaugural, consoling myself that I could include an encomium of Freddie in my valedictory. It was a particular pain to me that he died before he could hear what I said in praise of him.

What was, academically, the interlude of the Second World War imposed on Freddie very early in his life the awkward transition from being an *enfant terrible* to being the defender of tradition. He had come of age philosophically in an Oxford in which a band of younger men, the oldest still in their thirties, were in revolt against an old-fashioned style of philosophy divided between idealism and a realism that spurned modern logic and, indeed, all movements of thought not originating in Oxford. Celebrated at the age of 26 as the British exponent of the threatening doctrine of logical positivism, he returned from the army to find that the younger generation had captured almost all the strategic positions, but were by no means all his allies. They thought of themselves as revolutionaries, indeed, who had carried out a revolution and had now to consolidate it; but their attitude to logical positivism was that it was *passé*. Freddie himself was no longer a logical positivist, but he was

Delivered as a valedictory lecture in Oxford in Trinity Term, 1992.

faithful to its spirit, and far from sympathetic to the 'ordinary language' school which seemed to him brash; he therefore saw himself as an upholder of traditional philosophical virtues of rigorous argument and precise formulation. After a successful tenure of the Grote Chair at University College, London, he returned to a still somewhat hostile Oxford environment as Wykeham Professor; in that role, he rendered an indispensable service to Oxford philosophy. He always craved being well regarded, but differed from certain of the leaders of the 'ordinary language' school in never demanding discipleship or assessing others by their agreement with him. During his long tenure of the Chair, he succeeded in what he most wanted to do, to maintain the intellectual virtues he saw as essential in philosophy and to instil them in the embryo philosophers he taught. Ready to recognize those virtues in those whose opinions differed sharply from his own, he was generous in encouraging young philosophers who had not yet made their mark; ever patient and courteous, he brought his sharp intellect and quick responses to bear on whatever was placed before him, without ever discouraging, let alone humiliating, those to whose mistakes he drew attention. As a friend and colleague, he was charming, and always a gentleman in an age which has accorded ever less respect for the qualities that phrase connotes; as a colleague and a teacher, his influence was wholly benign, a devotee of rationality in a subject which, for all it purports to be, does not always exemplify that virtue.

Nearly thirty years ago, I first made a proposal concerning realism that took some time to evoke a response. The response, when it came, initially surprised me. My original intention had been to prompt what is called a 'research programme' in the form of a comparative study of disputes over realism. It had struck me that a variety of different traditional disputes within philosophy took the form of an opposition between a realist view of some particular subject-matter and a rejection of realism concerning that subject-matter; often one side in the dispute was conventionally labelled 'realist', though in other cases not. It appeared to me that no agreed method of settling these disputes was available, and that philosophers picked sides in them on the basis of predilection, not because they had discovered a means of resolving them. It further appeared to me that there was a striking parallelism in the arguments used on both sides in each of these disputes, so that, if one prescinded from the particular subject-matter, one could exhibit the abstract structure of the dispute. No two of the disputes seemed to me to be completely isomorphic, so as to have an identical abstract structure in common; but the structures were so similar that it seemed to me fruitful to propose that we should make a comparative study of them, from which, I hoped, principles would emerge for deciding in which cases the realist was in the right and in which cases his opponent.

I was understood, however, not as proposing a research programme, but as putting forward a specific philosophical thesis of great generality: not as suggesting a comparative study of a range of structurally similar problems case by case, but as advancing a single unitary thesis.

On reflection, I concluded that this response was not wholly mistaken, but not wholly right, either. It was not wholly right, in that I viewed it, and still continue to view it, as a research programme, not the platform of a new philosophical party; I thus regarded the adversarial stance adopted by many who discussed the topic as inappropriate. That was precisely because I did not conceive myself as proposing for consideration, let alone sustaining, any precise thesis, to be accepted or rejected. I saw the matter, rather, as the posing of a question how far, and in what contexts, a certain generic line of argument could be pushed, where the answers "No distance at all" and "In no context whatever" could not be credibly entertained, and the answers "To the bitter end" and "In all conceivable contexts" were almost as unlikely to be right. Nevertheless, the common response was not wholly incorrect, either. What principally interested me, if it did not amount to a single overall thesis, was a fairly uniform *line* of argument, not a mere clutch of distinct theses about disparate subject-matters, united only by bearing a certain structural similarity to one another. I will try in this lecture to explain in more detail why the common response to my proposal strikes me as neither wholly right nor wholly wrong.

In attempting to delineate the common framework of the various disputes, I naturally labelled one side "realist"; for the other, I chose the deliberately colourless term "anti-realist". This was for two reasons. First, although in many cases the opponent of realism could be regarded as a species of idealist, this was not always so. For instance, one dispute that plainly exhibited the characteristic features common to others was that between realists about mental states and processes and behaviourists; and behaviourists are not naturally included under the generic characterization "idealists". Secondly, the term "idealism" carried too many specific connotations, some of them irrelevant to the issue of realism, for my purpose. There is a sense of "idealism" in which it denotes the mirror-image of materialism: the doctrine that every truth is either included in, entailed by, or supervenient upon the totality of truths concerning what is immaterial. An idealist in this sense would be likely to reject a realist view of the physical universe, but would not be logically constrained to do so. If he did not, he would be a sophisticated, not a naïve, realist about it, just as, in the end, Berkeley was; but he would still be a realist. The term "idealist" was therefore unsuitable as a *general* label for the opponent of realism in each of these disputes. Moreover, I aimed at generality: I did not want to tie opposition to realism to any specific doctrine, but to consider any form that a rejection of realism might take.

In trying to describe the general form of disputes of the kind in which I was interested, I needed some generic means of referring to the particular subject-matter of any one such dispute. Very often, realism of a particular variety is referred to as realism about some particular class of putative entities—mental events, for example, or mathematical objects. I chose to speak instead of the "disputed class of statements", rather than of the "disputed class of objects". The motive was twofold.

1. In some cases—e.g. the dispute over realism concerning the future and that over realism concerning the past—there did not seem to be any objects in question; to count states of affairs as objects for this purpose would be mere sophistry, like the man imagined by Wittgenstein as saying that a ruler modifies our knowledge of length.

2. To characterize a type of realism as a thesis about (putative) objects of some kind focused attention, I thought, on the wrong issue. For example, a neo-Fregean platonist about mathematical objects, such as Wright or Hale, could still deny that they have any properties other than those we are capable of recognizing, whereas, conversely, a Dedekindian who maintained that mathematical objects are free creations of the human mind might nevertheless insist that, once created, they have properties independently of our capacity to recognize them. It appeared to me evident, and still appears to me evident, that, interesting as the questions about the nature of mathematical objects, and the ground of their existence, may be, the significant difference lies between those who consider all mathematical statements whose meaning is determinate to possess a definite truth-value independently of our capacity to discover it, and those who think that their truth or falsity consists in our ability to recognize it. Hence, from my standpoint, the Dedekindian would be a species of realist, and the neo-Fregean a species of constructivist. Put more generally, what reality consists in is not determined just by what objects there are, but by what propositions hold good: the world is the totality of facts, not of things. This was the reason for the concentration on acceptance or rejection of the principle of bivalence.

The formulation in terms of a class of statements, rather than of putative entities, and the emphasis on the underpinning of the logic that ought to be taken as governing those statements, made more plausible the strategy I recommended, of starting, not with the metaphysical status of the entities, but with the account to be given of the meanings of the statements. That was not the ground of the recommendation, however. Rather, since these metaphysical disagreements embodied divergent pictures of the reality to which the statements in question related, it seemed to me apparent that what underlay them were divergent pictures of the meanings of those statements. Since no means offered itself for deciding which picture of reality was correct, the more fruitful approach lay in determining which picture of meaning was, since in this case there was a theory of meaning to be constructed and a linguistic practice against which to check it.

What is a dispute of the relevant kind? A frequent philosophical move is to deny the status of statement to any member of a certain class of apparent assertables: on the one side, moral utterances (expressivists), and on the other conditionals (Ryle) and laws of nature (Ramsey). There is an important distinction between the two types. For expressivists, moral utterances express *attitudes* incapable of objective justification; but the proposal concerning conditionals and laws was that their content depended on what was required to justify them. Hilbert's account of unrestricted quantification over natural numbers provides the archetype of such a proposal: the speaker does not assert a state of affairs to obtain, but makes a *claim*, whose justification is perfectly objective; for instance, an unrestricted existential statement is justified if the one who makes it can produce an instance. The difference between utterances understood as embodying claims and statements proper is, on this view, that the latter have truth-conditions independent of the knowledge or abilities of the speaker, whereas the condition for a claim to be justified relates to what the speaker can do to vindicate his claim. The justification nevertheless concerns his *epistemic*, not his *affective* state; it is therefore wholly objective—he was right or wrong to make the claim.

Hilbert argued that, since utterances construed as making claims, such as arithmetical statements with unbounded quantifiers, are not understood as having truth-conditions, the sentential operators (Wittgenstein's 'calculus of truth-functions') could not be applied to them. The intuitionists denied this, however, proposing that all logical constants should be explained in terms of justification-conditions rather than truth-functionally. They thus rejected Hilbert's view that utterances embodying objectively assessable claims, but not possessing independent truth-conditions, could not qualify as statements; on the contrary, they proposed to interpret all mathematical statements in the former way, as embodying claims but not having independent truth-conditions. We need some terminology to distinguish these two types, or two interpretations, of assertoric utterances: let us call one embodying an objective claim a 'declaration', and one with independent truth-conditions an 'affirmation', using the term "statement" to cover both.

Would a parallel reinterpretation of the logical constants be possible for expressivistically interpreted utterances? Peter Geach is famous for having argued that an expressivist interpretation of moral statements rules out the application to them of the sentential operators such as "if . . . then", and hence cannot account for such reasoning as "If telling lies is wrong, getting your little brother to tell lies must be wrong, too"; the argument is conclusive unless a suitable non-truth-functional reinterpretation of the sentential operators is to be found. Discussing the general category of what I called 'quasi-assertions', I once suggested that such a reinterpretation would be possible, a suggestion followed up by Blackburn. Even if it be so, the distinction between the subjectivist denial of statementhood to some utterance and the objectivist denial of the status of an affirmation to some statement would remain; all that would be gone is a simple knock-down argument against expressivism.

In the disputes about realism that interested me, the opponent of realism did not question fundamental objectivity: it has been common to both disputants that statements of the kind in dispute can, in favourable circumstances, be objectively established as true. Controversy between subjectivists and objectivists in ethics was therefore not an example of that kind of dispute. Crispin Wright, in recent lectures in Oxford, repudiated the strategy of declaring certain forms of utterance not to be genuine statements, maintaining that, in a thin sense of "statement", even expressivists, if they are to formulate their view correctly, ought to allow that moral utterances make statements. However this may be, the dispute between the subjectivist and the 'moral realist' is not one of those to which my comparative method was meant to apply: the issues in that dispute are different and *prior* to it.

Locating disputes over realism in the choice of a model for the meanings of statements of the disputed class tends to make the acceptance of bivalence a criterion for being a realist. More accurately, the criterion for having an anti-realist view becomes that of occupying a position that undercuts the ground for accepting bivalence. Phenomenalism is a case in point. Phenomenalists have not traditionally made any great objection to bivalence for material-object statements, and have sometimes overtly accepted it. I nevertheless wished to classify them as anti-realists, on the ground that their doctrine removed any rationale for accepting bivalence for such statements, and that, if they were consistent, they would reject it.

For all that, acceptance of bivalence should *not* be taken as a sufficient condition for realism: a generalization is required. For some time, I struggled to find a principled distinction between deep and shallow grounds for rejecting bivalence, the latter being compatible with realism and exemplified by the truth-value gap recognized, in different ways, by Frege and by Strawson, as induced by empty subject-terms. A plausible suggestion to this effect would be to make it a mark of the realist that he accepted, not bivalence, but the weaker principle that every unambiguous statement must be determinately either true or not true; let me dub this the principle of valence. This would allow the realist to favour a many-valued semantics which classified as false only a statement the application to which of what was recognized as a negation operator was true, and thereby flouted bivalence; for, after all, the use of more than two truth-values would merely systematize the effect of the sentential operators, and it would remain that the assertoric content of any statement was determined by the condition for it to be true. Moreover, the principle of valence would *allow* of the application of two-valued sentential operators, even if those actually existing in the language required a non-classical interpretation. A deep rejection of realism, by contrast, must have it that the classical logical constants would not even make sense.

It is undoubtedly correct that the distinction between one who accepts the principle of valence and one who rejects it is more profound than that between those who disagree about bivalence proper. Nevertheless, I came to think it mistaken to draw the line between realists and anti-realists at the former place rather than the latter. The admission of truth-value gaps in order to handle empty terms *was* a form of anti-realism—a rejection of Meinong's ultra-realism concerning possible objects. Russell indeed avoided being a realist about possible objects without impugning bivalence in the least degree. He did so by not countenancing definite descriptions as genuine singular terms, i.e. by interpreting sentences containing them otherwise than at face-value. I concluded that the true criterion for a realist interpretation of any given class of statements is an acceptance of classical two-valued semantics as applying to them in its entirety, where this includes construing apparent singular terms occurring in them at face-value, to be explained in terms of their referring to elements of the domain of quantification. This has the advantage of doing better justice to the intuition that realism has to do with the existence of objects, while retaining the insight, as I hope it to be, that rejection of bivalence is a salient feature of the deepest and most interesting forms of anti-realism.

The example shows that anti-realism can be manifested by a reinterpretation of statements of the disputed class, construing them not at face-value but as having a structure belied by their surface appearance; and this reinterpretation may serve to salvage bivalence. We should be aware that the descriptions 'realist' and 'anti-realist' are relative to what the philosophers to whom they are applied are being said to be, or not to be, realist about. Out of context, it would be wrong to deny that Frege, or Russell in 1905, was a realist: but, compared to Meinong, they were certainly both anti-realists concerning possible objects.

A formulation of bivalence must allow for vagueness. The thesis that every statement is determinately either true or false, even if it is vague, can be sustained only on the implausible supposition that our use of vague expressions confers on them meanings which determine precise applications for them that we ourselves do not know. A realist must therefore hold that, for every vague statement, there is a range of statements giving more precise information of which a determinate one is true and the rest false. An anti-realist may deny this, holding that reality may itself be vague, whereas, for the realist, vagueness inheres only in our forms of description.

The opinion is sometimes expressed that I succeeded in opening up a genuine philosophical problem, or range of problems, but that the resulting topic has little to do with traditional disputes concerning realism. That was certainly not my intention: I meant to apply a new technique to such wholly traditional questions as realism about the external world and about the mental, questions which I continue to believe I characterized correctly. One immediately striking feature common to many traditional anti-realist arguments has been a reductionist account of statements of the disputed class. The anti-realist accuses the realist of interpreting those statements in the light of a conception of mythical states of affairs, not directly observable by us, rendering them true or false. According to the anti-realist, what makes them true or false are the observable states of affairs on the basis of which we judge of their truth-value. On the realist's interpretation, these merely provide *evidence* for the truth or falsity of the statements, or constitute an *indirect* means of judging them true or false; the anti-realist retorts that they are the most direct means there could be.

Behaviourism is typical. As Wittgenstein describes it, the realist conceives of mental events and mental processes on the analogy of physical events and processes, but in an immaterial medium, the individual's words and behaviour being evidence for these inner transactions; the behaviourist maintains that there is no such immaterial medium, and that the subject's words and behaviour, and, in certain cases, his physical condition, are what render our statements about his mental processes true.

Instrumentalism, the traditional alternative to a realist interpretation of the theoretical statements of science, likewise proposed to reduce them to statements about the grossly observable, such as readings of measuring devices. The same held good of radical formalism in mathematics, which proposed to reduce statements about mathematical entities such as real numbers, differential manifolds, groups, etc. to ones stating the derivability of individual formulae in a formal calculus—a reduction evidently vitiating bivalence whenever the calculus was incomplete. Phenomenalism, the traditional form of opposition to realism about the physical world, was equally obviously reductionist; but did it fit my characterization of the kind of anti-realism of which I proposed a comparative study? The issue of bivalence, for me central in all interesting cases, historically played little role in the debate over phenomenalism. To show that that debate nevertheless fitted my characterization, I argued that bivalence *ought* to have been an issue, since the phenomenalist had no principled reason to accept it; if he did so, that was mere logical inertia. Any reductionist thesis will lead to a repudiation of bivalence for statements of the disputed class, if there are occasions on which the (reductive) criterion for the truth neither of a given such statement nor of its negation is satisfied.

Philosophy abounds in anti-realist theses of this general form. It was the reductionist character of their traditional versions that made them so easy for the realists to refute. Phenomenalism proposed a reduction to a sense-datum language whose very intelligibility was shown by Wittgenstein's attack on the private ostensive definition to be unsustainable. The intelligibility of statements about behaviour and about formal calculi is not open to question; but, in both these cases, the proposed reduction showed itself implausible. Instrumentalism is the most interesting example. "The Sun" is not an indexical term in the ordinary sense: its denotation is constant from speaker to speaker. But it is indexical in an extended sense, in that its reference is fixed in terms of *our* position in the universe: it is the star that gives *us* light and heat. There is, at least as an ideal, a level of objectivity deeper than intersubjectivity: a form of description involving concepts that are not essentially dependent upon our perceptual abilities, position in space and time, and the like. The attainment of such a level of objectivity is the endeavour to describe the world as it is in itself; scientific realism credits science with striving for such an ideal, one to which it believes that we can approximate. The instrumentalist effort to repudiate this conception of the scientific endeavour is hampered, not merely by the gradual permeation of our 'common-sense' picture of the world by scientific concepts, but by the continuity of the striving of the scientist for an objective description with pre-scientific attempts to achieve greater objectivity in which we all engage—for example, with the transition from the concepts possessed by a child and their counterparts in an adult's understanding. This placed instrumentalists who were not, like Mach, also phenomenalists, in a delicate position; their problem was to discern where they must draw the line between what is unproblematically true and what, as purely theoretical, is a mere device for summarizing regularities exhibited by what is unproblematically true. No clear line presents itself between what they are proposing to reduce and what they are hoping to reduce it to; and so the reduction forfeits credibility.

This threatened that all the contests would end in victory for the realist before the comparative study had begin. There was, however, one form of anti-realism about mathematics, quite different from formalism, that was not reductionist: intuitionism (or, equally, the less adventurous version of constructivism advocated by Errett Bishop). Although intuitionists denied that we have any conception of truth for mathematical statements other than our possessing proofs of them, they did not postulate any language for describing proofs, to which the language of mathematics, taken as disjoint from it, could be reduced: they accepted mathematical concepts as indispensable, neither to be eliminated nor to be explained away. Instead, they propounded a new conception of what it is to understand a mathematical statement: not to know what it is for it to be true, independently of whether we are able to recognize its truth or falsity, but to know what is required to prove it. In the terms we used earlier, mathematical statements were to be interpreted as declarations, not as affirmations.

This means of rejecting a realist conception of mathematics appeared to me a prototype for a sustainable version of anti-realism in all other cases. The traditional anti-realist theories failed because of their reductionist form: but realism (including scientific realism) scored too easy a victory, because the reductive thesis was not essential to challenging realism. What was needed, therefore, was to undertake a comparative study, not of the disputes in their historical forms, but of versions of them in which the anti-realist view followed the intuitionist prototype in resting, not on a reduction of the disputed class of statements to those of some disjoint class, but on a non-realist, that is, non-truth-conditional, theory of meaning for them. It is a far from trivial matter to rebut the anti-realist arguments when divested of their reductionist guise, because it is at least highly plausible that a mastery of the use in practice of statements of the disputed class can be explained in terms of a grasp of what we take as establishing the truth of those statements; and since we accept mastery of use as confirming grasp of meaning, how can grasp of meaning involve more than mastery of use? The realist picture, though possibly faithful to our unreflective impression of what our understanding of statements of the disputed class consists in, will then fall away as superfluous, unless the anti-realist's challenge can be met; indignant expostulation is an inadequate response.

The charge that my enquiry did not concern realism as traditionally understood is thus mistaken: it concerned realism in precisely its traditional sense, but considered as facing, not the theories traditionally opposed to it, but emended versions of them.

Objectivity is an ingredient in the concept of truth, but does not of itself amount to it. An exponent of a sustainable anti-realism must have taken many strides in the direction of objectivity before his dispute with the realist begins; one reason why the traditional versions failed was their insufficient acknowledgement of this objectivity. The sense-datum language of the phenomenalists was an illusion because it was a solipsistic language, whereas human language, and hence the capacity for thoughts expressible in human language, is essentially communal, because essentially apt for communication. Thoughts are of their essence communicable; whether or not more than the most rudimentary thoughts are possible for those without language, *our* thought is shaped by the means for communicating it that we start to acquire in infancy. This means, not only that the experiential basis of knowledge must consist in *our* experience, not in *my* experience, but that experience can be characterized only as the experience of a common world inhabited by others as well as me; it is intrinsic to our grasp of our language that we take testimony as contributing to our stock of information.

Mathematics was the most propitious field for the development of an anti-realist theory of meaning precisely because the gap between the subjective and the objective is there at its narrowest. Brouwer was, notoriously, a solipsist, or something very close to one; but that did not vitiate his development of a theory of meaning for mathematical statements, and a consequent revisionist programme for mathematical practice. The reason is precisely the flagrant untruth of his solipsism. Far from its being the case, as Brouwer maintained, that mathematical constructions are only imperfectly communicable, the very opposite is true: they are *perfectly* communicable. Individual mathematicians may have different aptitudes, angles of attack, ranges of knowledge, etc., but they do not have different viewpoints on mathematical reality: whatever construction one mathematician discovers, any other is in a position to carry out. Just for this reason, it did not matter that Brouwer was conceiving his mathematical language solipsistically, as the analogue of a sense-datum language: by simply reversing the principle that mathematical language can only imperfectly convey mental constructions carried out by any one mathematician, it could without modification be interpreted as a language common to all mathematicians, and his theory of meaning understood in terms, not of individual mental constructions, but of constructions available to all.

As long as the disputes over realism concerning different subject-matters are treated as distinct, there is no reason to presume that all are to be resolved in the same sense: a realist about the physical world is under no compulsion to be a realist about mathematics or about mental events and states. The most a *general* argument for realism can do is to demonstrate its possibility in principle, never to show it to be correct in any particular case. By contrast, treating the topic as at bottom an issue about the representation of meaning does make possible a general argument for anti-realism, on the ground that a theory of meaning in terms of truth-conditions is never tenable.

This appears to yield a global form of anti-realism, of which the revised local anti-realisms would be merely particular applications. It would require displacing the notion of truth—of a statement's being true independently of our knowledge—from its central role in the explanation of meaning, substituting that of what we take as establishing truth: we should thus no longer be concerned with the criterion for the *truth* of a statement, but with the criterion for our recognizing it as true. That criterion would not be characterized as if each sentence had a meaning independently of the rest of the language: rather, a weak holism must be admitted, in accordance with Wittgenstein's dictum that to understand a sentence is to understand a language. The holism would only be weak, in that the language in question would not, in general, be the entire language to which the sentence belongs, but, rather, some fragment of it which could be, but was not, an entire language. The criterion for recognizing a statement as true would thus be whatever we actually count as establishing its truth, with no presumption that the process must be independent of language: it may well, and in general will, include inferences carried out in language.

The interpretation according to which I have been propounding a single philosophical thesis of very high generality seems thus to be vindicated. We appear to have arrived at a global anti-realism posing a challenge to realists as strong as, and more general than, those posed by the local anti-realisms, and rendering it unnecessary to pay any further attention to the purely local anti-realisms. This global anti-realism appears as a single unitary thesis, to the effect that a justificationist theory of meaning should supplant the generally received truth-conditional theory, on the ground that the obscurity of the general notion of a grasp of the condition for a statement to be true inhibits the received theory from yielding a plausible account of our understanding of language and our mastery of its use. The matter is then to be resolved by face-to-face combat between this general anti-realist theory of meaning and the truth-conditional theory, based on two-valued classical semantics, espoused by realists.

I have now to explain why this way of viewing the matter seems to me seriously mistaken. First, the thesis of global anti-realism has not merely to be *applied* to particular areas of language: it is no more than programmatic, and has to be *worked out* for different ranges of statement. Even a generalization of the constructive interpretation of the logical constants is far from straightforward. Ramsey long ago proposed an interpretation of conditionals as declarations rather than affirmations, virtually identical with the intuitionist understanding of them, and this is highly plausible as a representation of our use of conditionals in natural language. Negation, on the other hand, is highly problematic. In mathematics, given the meaning of "if . . . then", it is trivial to explain "Not A" as meaning "If A, then $0 = 1$"; by contrast, a satisfactory explanation of "not", as applied to empirical statements for which bivalence is not, in general, taken as holding, is very difficult to arrive at. Given that the sentential operators cannot be thought of as explained by means of the two-valued truth-tables, the possibility that the laws of classical logic will fail is evidently open: but it is far from evident that the correct logical laws will always be the intuitionistic ones. More generally, it is by no means easy to determine what should serve as the analogue, for empirical statements, of the notion of proof as it figures in intuitionist semantics for mathematical statements. In mathematics, we may take as the property which a constructively valid proof is required to preserve from premisses to conclusion that of our having an effective means of devising a canonical proof. In the empirical case, however, a wholly constructive proof may lead from premisses that have been verified to a conclusion that cannot be directly verified, because its subject-matter is no longer accessible to observation. So, even where it makes sense to speak of a statement as having been conclusively established by direct means, we cannot without more ado take that property as the analogue of canonical proof for mathematical statements; and it is commonplace to observe that not all empirical statements can be conclusively established, even on the most generous reading of the term "conclusively".

A hostile critic might conclude from all this that the anti-realist theory of meaning is in at least as bad shape as the realist one, and hence that realism has nothing to fear until its opponents have clarified their views. This, however, is to insist on viewing the matter adversarially, to be fought out between two well-defined theories, whereas it remains, for me, a research programme.

Justificationist and truth-conditional meaning-theories do not stand opposed to one another as rivals. Neither is a worked-out theory: the justificationist principle is an unavoidable starting-point, the truth-conditional one no more than a hoped-for goal. Present-day truth-conditional meaning-theorists simply help themselves to what they have not earned. They ask neither what conception of truth is forced on us by the need to make sense of our linguistic practice—the practice we acquire as we grow to adulthood—nor what conception yields a credible account of that understanding which underlies our mastery of the practice. Their theories have the advantage that Russell famously called that of theft over honest toil, but make no serious contribution to philosophical comprehension of the functioning of language. We cannot hope to achieve any illumination by taking the notion of truth as given: we have to *win through* to that notion if we can, and in what form we can.

The notion of truth is not immediately given by the mere existence of a linguistic practice involving utterances of an assertoric character. That is sufficiently shown by the possibility, demonstrated by the intuitionists' way of construing mathematical statements in general, of interpreting a large range of statements, including ones of unlimited logical complexity, as declarations, rather than affirmations, that is, as embodying objective claims but not having independent truth-conditions. It is, indeed, open to doubt whether such an interpretation can be extended to non-mathematical statements; but it is a matter for investigation how far this can be done, and, if it cannot, what the obstacles are and just what notion of truth-conditions is called for.

A salutary lesson is provided by the controversy that has continued to surround indicative conditionals of natural language. Philosophers have continued to dispute what we should take the truth-conditions of such conditionals to be: in just which cases should an indicative conditional be considered true, and in which false? They asked this question because they were in the grip of a truth-conditional conception of meaning; and, if asked what they were investigating, they would have replied that it was the exact meaning of the indicative conditional form, as revealed by its truth-conditions. The fact was, however, that they were not in practice in the least doubt of its meaning. Philosophers who disagreed about the truth-conditions to be assigned to indicative conditionals did not, in ordinary converse, diverge in their understanding of particular conditional statements: they understood them in exactly the same way. The reason was that their understanding did not consist in any grasp of truth-conditions: in our terminology, they understood such utterances as declarations, embodying a certain claim on the part of the speaker, not as affirmations. Nothing in our use of indicative conditionals requires us to ascribe comprehensive truth-conditions to them; they therefore cannot be said to have truth-conditions, and any enquiry into what their truth-conditions are is doomed to futility.

We have therefore to start with an interpretation of the statements of our language as declarations, and enquire where and to what degree it falls short of being adequate. It is in this sense that a justificationist meaning-theory is an unavoidable starting-point. I am using the term "justificationist", which, to avoid misunderstanding, I have substituted for the word "verificationist" I have been accustomed to use, in the sense in which the intuitionist interpretation of mathematical statements may be termed 'justificationist': the meaning of a statement, on such a theory, is determined by what has to be done by a speaker to vindicate the claim that he makes by means of that statement.

We have, then, to start from that point and enquire how far it is necessary to move from it. To move from it can only mean that, in order to explain the meanings we attach to many of the forms of statement we employ, we find ourselves forced to adopt some notion of truth for them in terms of which we account for the principles underlying our use of them. The phrase "some notion of truth" is obviously exceedingly vague, and so I must provide some explanation of how I am understanding it. A stymie is laid by proponents of the minimalist theory of truth, who maintain that the sole notion of truth we have or can have is that for which the *whole* content of the term "true" is given by the fundamental equivalence between a statement A and the statement that A is true. Certainly, for any language that we already understand, it will almost always be possible to introduce a truth-predicate explained in this way; there is, for example, no difficulty about doing so for statements of intuitionistic mathematics. But such an explanation of "true" is plainly intended only for those who already know the language; unless I already understand the statement A, I cannot derive from the explanation the condition for it to be true, since that condition is stated by means of A itself. It follows at once that, if my grasp of the notion of truth had really been obtained in this way alone, my understanding of the language could not be explained in any manner that relied upon my grasp of it. That fits the language of intuitionistic mathematics very well, since it has a semantics not appealing to the notion of truth which can serve to explain the understanding of it I had before I was introduced to the truth-predicate as applying to it. It does not fit our ordinary employment of "true", however, for it fails to explain our knowledge that true statements can be made in every natural language (and many others), although we do not know all those languages. Paul Horwich, for example, refers, in a footnote, to someone ignorant of German who is told the condition for a certain German sentence to be true:[1] evidently, his understanding of the word "true", as applied to German sentences, cannot consist merely in his knowledge of the fundamental equivalence for English sentences. However this may be, in the present context we are concerned with notions that can be used to explain in what the meanings of statements framed in a natural language consist, and

---

[1] P. Horwich, *Truth* (Oxford, 1990), 73.

what constitutes a speaker's understanding of them; to such an explanation, the truth-predicate as interpreted by the minimalist is irrelevant.

What is at issue is the conception common to the speakers of a language of the contents of statements that can be made in it. The primary content of a statement is what is conveyed to a hearer who accepts an assertion of it as correct. We can also characterize it by what counts as the *ultimate* warrant for someone's assertion of it, that is, the ground of his knowledge when he first acquired it or the ground of the knowledge of the initiator of the information transmitted from one speaker to another (his *immediate* warrant may be merely that he remembers things as having been so or that he was told that things are so). Probably the best means of characterizing it is by appeal to that feature of statements which we require a valid argument to preserve from premises to conclusion. Inferential reasoning (including non-deductive reasoning) may be direct or indirect. It is direct when it would be a step in the simplest means of warranting an assertion of the conclusion that accords with its composition out of its constituent words. For instance, the simplest means of warranting the assertion of a disjunctive statement is by whatever would warrant the assertion of one of its two clauses, followed by an application of the standard rule of "or"-introduction, which allows us to infer the statement "*A* or *B*" from the statement *A* or from the statement *B*. If we engaged only in direct inferential reasoning, then the property of a statement that a valid argument must preserve could be taken to be simply the existence of a direct warrant for asserting it; and the only notion of content it would be necessary to attribute to the statements of our language would be that determined by what we treated as such a warrant. In such a case, we should have a language whose statements could all be construed as declarations, in our sense: a theory of meaning for it would no more need any notion of truth going beyond that of the existence of a warrant for assertion than does the theory of meaning for intuitionistic mathematics.

Inferential reasoning has the value that it does, however, because it is usually indirect: a more direct warrant for the conclusion is conceivable, but not to hand. This has the effect that the property preserved by valid argument cannot be simply the existence of an ultimate warrant, since we draw conclusions for which there is in fact no such warrant from premises that have them. Now is our practice justifiable, or is it simply what we do, without the need for any rationale? If it is simply what we do, then we need no notion of truth distinguishable from that of what, in accordance with our established practices, we treat as true; but we do not normally think in this nihilistic way. We take for granted that, in default of any demonstration that they are unreliable, our practices are faithful guides in a sense of "faithful" explicable without appeal to our engaging in them. In forming some conception of a property, weaker than our having a direct warrant, that a valid argument must preserve, we acquire an implicit grasp of a notion of truth.

This is not at all to say that the notion of truth required to account for our linguistic practice will be the full-blown realist conception. The realist helps himself to that conception by presuming that he has the right to use the notion of knowing what it is for something to be so without further explanation but, rather, as part of an explanation of what a speaker's understanding of a statement consists in; for instance, an understanding of the statement "There were once intelligent beings on Mars" will rest upon a knowledge of what it is for there once to have been intelligent beings on Mars. It is true that in everyday contexts we use the phrase "know what it is for . . .", but here the direction of explanation is the opposite: "Don't you know what it is for *A* to be the case?" is simply a way of asking, "Don't you know what *A* means?" When it is required, conversely, as part of an explanation of understanding, however, the notion is *not* self-explanatory, and especially not in the context of a theory of meaning intended to explain in what our understanding of our mother tongue consists, so that the knowledge in question cannot be *verbalized* knowledge: if the notion is to be used at all, an account is required of what it is to have such knowledge, and it is quite obscure whether any can be given. Yet all proponents of a truth-conditional theory of meaning appeal to the notion of knowing what it is for . . . , save those who purport to explain meaning without attempting to explain understanding.

We cannot leap from a recognition that *some* notion of truth is needed for an account of our use of many of our statements to an embrace of full-fledged realism: rather, we have to undertake a research programme. We have to examine piecemeal which features of our linguistic practice call for a notion of truth, and what notion they call for, which is to say, how far that notion goes beyond the simple conception of the existence of a direct warrant. In the course of this investigation, we have, at each stage, to consider whether it is plausible to attribute to a speaker a grasp of such a notion of truth, and how his grasp of it is to be explained. All this is what I meant by saying that we have to *win through* to a notion of truth.

There is here a delicate balance to be maintained. Our object is to achieve a theory of meaning that accounts for our linguistic practice; but that practice is not sacrosanct when that object proves unattainable. Classical logic can be underpinned by other semantic theories than that which forms the base of truth-conditional meaning-theories, classical two-valued semantics: but such meaning-theories provide the most natural justification for our use of classical modes of reasoning that are not intuitionistically valid. Anyone who is prepared to say, "That is simply what we do", rejects all need for justification; and speaking of the complex web of theory and practice, within which neither can be distinguished from the other, is little more than a grandiose way of saying, "That is simply what we do". But one who cannot adopt this attitude, as I cannot, and who believes what I strongly suspect, that such meaning-theories are incapable of supplying a viable account of linguistic

478 *Realism and Anti-Realism*

understanding, must either find an alternative semantics to justify our use of those modes of reasoning or declare our practice in this respect erroneous. I do not claim to have taken more than a few first steps in this research programme; my principal aim has been to convince my philosophical colleagues that such a programme is called for. That aim is frustrated when it is mistaken as the advocacy of a large and sharply defined philosophy.

Index

abilities 53–4, 60
abstract objects 430–5, 437–9
affirmations 466, 470, 473–4
analytical philosophy 97, 171
Anscombe, G. E. M. 216, 276, 415
anti-realism about the past 244, 246–7, 249–50
Aquinas, St Thomas 366–7
argument from illusion 377
articulated character of language 71
assertion 40–1, 76, 89, 122, 124–5, 153–4, 157–60, 171–2, 207, 214, 216–17, 220–1
  correct or incorrect 48–51
atomism, linguistic 22, 25–6, 38, 41–2, 65–6
Austin, J. L. 213
Ayer, A. J. 244, 274, 376–8, 380–3, 386–7, 389, 392–4, 401–3, 406–7, 448–9, 462–3

backwards causation 362–5, 415
bare truth 53–7, 62, 66–7
Bar-Hillel, Y. 371–3, 375
behaviourism 247, 249, 260, 263, 464, 469
Bell, D. 224–9
Bergson, H. 386–7
Berkeley, G. 394, 464
Bishop, E. 470
bivalence 54, 56, 62–4, 71, 73, 75, 80, 112, 116, 230–1, 235, 237–8, 239, 241, 246, 250–3, 256, 258, 264–6, 269, 271, 379, 455, 465, 467–9
Blackburn, S. 466
Bolzano, B. 153
Boolean algebra 64, 267, 328, 330
Brentano, F. 224
bringing about the past 359–63
Brouwer, L. E. J. 78, 471–2

cancelling an utterance 48
Cantor, G. 440–3, 456
Carnap, R. 448–9
Cartesian doubt 274–6, 381
causal theory of names 24
causal theory of perception 406–7
central-state materialism 245–7
Chakrabarti, A. 277 n.
Chomsky, N. xi, 173–4, 176–7, 184–5

claims 189–91, 438–9, 441
classical logic 64, 73, 75, 107, 194–5, 241, 267, 442, 445, 477
cluster theory of names 26
code conception of language 97–8, 149–51, 166–7, 169, 170, 172–3, 183
colour 274–5, 377, 378, 384–5, 386, 389–90, 393–5, 397–402, 405–6, 407
command 40, 82, 123–4, 207, 208, 213–14
communication 89, 91, 102, 151, 165, 166–87
concepts viii, 4–5, 97–8
conceptual change ·315
conditionals:
  counterfactual 49, 53–5, 62, 65–6, 375
  indicative 49–50, 81, 188, 191–2, 196–8, 199, 343, 355, 356–7, 473, 474
  subjunctive 46, 53–5, 60, 248–53, 258, 264, 343, 355, 356–7, 378, 380–1, 459
context principle 239–40, 434–5, 457–8
conventionalism:
  radical 447–9
  restrained (moderate) 447–9, 451, 460
conservational implicature 52, 110

Davidson, D. vii–ix, 5–7, 11–13, 14, 16–20, 23, 25–9, 32, 34, 36, 67, 69, 87, 114, 130, 140, 178–9, 188, 197, 202–23, 245, 380, 426
decidable statements 45–6, 52, 83
declarations 466, 470, 473–5, 476
Dedekind, R. 465
deductive consequence 460–1
Descartes, R. 274
description theory of names 24, 31
direct verification 74–5, 88, 142–3, 145, 456, 461
dominance 370–2, 374
Duhem, P. 408
Dunne, J. W. 350

epistemology 270–1
equivalence principle 42–5, 107, 111, 181–2, 199, 475
Euler, L. 456
Evans, G. ix–x, 34 n., 169, 281, 298–307, 333
expression 152, 173
externalism 451–61

fatalism 352–8
Field, H. 433–4, 435–7, 444–5
finitism 199
force 38–41, 47, 51, 65, 72, 76, 84, 87, 88–9, 100, 110, 113, 122–4, 125, 135–6, 153–4, 159, 173–4, 202–23
Foster, J. 406
free will 358, 372–3
Frege, G. xiv, 12, 23–5, 34–5, 38, 47, 65, 85–6, 89–91, 97, 99–100, 101–2, 108, 112, 113, 125–30, 135, 147, 148, 150, 153–7, 161–4, 168, 169–71, 172, 174–6, 177–8, 187, 188, 195, 202–8, 210, 211, 222, 224–9, 232–3, 236, 240–1, 269–70, 277–8, 280–6, 288–9, 293–5, 298–9, 306, 318, 319, 383, 430, 432–5, 437, 439–42, 445, 457–8, 465, 467, 468
Freud, S. 386–7
future tense 50, 52

Geach, P. T. vii, 196, 255–6, 281, 308, 310–27, 466
Gettier's paradox 9, 416
Gödel's incompleteness theorem xii–xiv
Goodman, Nelson 385
Greek Colonels' régime 423
Grice, P. 23, 52, 110, 171–4
Griffin, N. 327
grounds for assertion 48–51
Guttenplan, S. viii, 18 n.

Hale, Bob 465
harmony 142–3, 162–3
Heyting, A. 234–5, 259
Hilbert, D. 188–91, 436, 466
Hintikka, J. 84
holism, linguistic 16–17, 19–20, 21, 25–33, 44, 66, 99, 139, 162, 472
Horwich, P. 475
Hume, D. 406
Husserl, E. 177, 224–9

idealism 453–4
idiolects 30–1
immediate awareness 401–2, 407, 410
indefinitely extensible concepts 441–3, 454–5
indirect verification 456–7
indiscernibility 383–7
inference and truth 74–5, 107, 144–5, 455–7, 476
infinity 200, 440, 442–3
information 85–6, 89–90, 425–6
instrumentalism 376, 381, 408–10, 469–70
internalism 452–61

intuitionist logic and semantics 66, 69–70, 190–1, 194–5, 199–201, 234–5, 259, 328–9, 441, 445, 455, 466, 472, 473–4, 475
irreducibility thesis 247–8, 270, 378

Kant, I. 156, 227, 277–8, 458
knowledge 411–26
    explicit x, 44–6, 63, 95, 101, 133
    of the future 412–17
    immediate 274–6
    implicit xi, 36–8, 46, 96, 101, 105, 131–3, 218–20
    of language x–xi, 3–4, 7–8, 23–5, 27–9, 33, 36, 94–105, 131–4, 218–19
    practical x–xi, 36
    propositional 36
    theoretical x–xi
Köhler, W. 149
Kripke, S. xv–xvi, 9, 284–6, 298–9, 305, 307, 329, 331–2, 339, 341

law of excluded middle 74, 92, 106–9, 210, 231, 237, 267, 354, 453
Leibniz, G. W. xvi, 329–30
Lewis, C. I. 244
Lewis, D. 268, 348
linguistic convention 39–40, 51, 89, 104, 152, 204, 209, 211–13, 216, 221–3
linguistic revision 64–6, 75, 142, 162–3, 200
Locke, J. 274–5, 394, 401–2, 404
Łukasiewicz, J. 244

McDowell, J. x, 21, 25, 34 n., 171–3, 281 n.
Mach, E. 470
Mackie, J. L. 356, 371–4
Malebranche, N. 406
manifestation of understanding xii–xv, 16, 37–8, 46–7, 52, 91, 92, 162
many-valued logic and semantics 63, 68, 72–3, 79, 81 n., 264–5, 467
Margalit, A. 371–3, 375
mathematics:
    application of 430, 432, 433–8, 443–4
    empiricist account of 430, 432
    formalist account of 469
    intuitionist (constructivist) account of 200–1, 241, 248, 249, 258–61, 267, 465, 470–2
    logicist account of 432–45
    Platonist account of 230–1, 248, 258, 267, 430–2, 465
    as a science 429–30
meaning as use 38–9, 91, 94–116, 181–3, 209

Meinong, A. 269–70, 468
metaphysical necessity and possibility xv, 307, 331–47
metaphysics vii, xvi, 56–7, 59, 116, 263–4, 268–9, 271, 274, 277, 281, 353, 361, 377–8, 454, 459, 460, 465
Mill, J. S. 148, 430
Miller, B. 290–1
mistakes 18–20
modal logic xv–xvi
molecular view of language 17, 19, 22, 26, 38, 42, 44, 65–6
mood 202–16, 221–3
Moore, G. E. 214, 298
M-sentences 7–11

negation 71–2, 264, 293, 379, 467, 473
neutralism about the future 241, 254–7, 267, 353
Newcomb's paradox 355–6, 370–5
nominalism 434–5
Noonan, H. W. 327
normal conditions 396–8, 400–2, 405

ontological argument 278–80

paradigm-case argument 390
past, the 46, 60–1, 244, 246–7, 249–50, 258
phenomenalism 241, 250–4, 263, 467, 469–71
philosophy of language vii, xvi
point of an utterance 106–10, 174, 209–11, 221–3
Polya, G. 51
Popper, K. 84
possible-worlds semantics xv–xvi, 268, 280–1, 284, 307, 329–31
practical abilities x–xi, 36, 94–6, 101, 132
pragmatic/semantic distinction 51
primacy of sentences 100
priority of language over thought 147–53, 217
proto-thoughts 148–9
psychologism xiv, 102, 177
Putnam, H. 31, 188, 446 n., 447–9, 452, 454–5, 457–9

quantum mechanics 454
Quine, W. V. O. 18, 71, 104, 110, 114, 115, 138–9, 140–1, 276, 295–6, 308–10, 315, 327, 331, 353

Ramsey, F. P. 181–2, 376, 389, 466, 473
realism 56–7, 61–2, 62–3, 73–4, 75, 83, 91, 199–201, 230–76, 378–81, 389–90, 408–10, 439, 443–4, 453–4, 455, 458–9, 463–78
  external 455
  internal 452
  naïve 57, 59–60, 248, 253, 263, 270–3, 377, 378, 379, 381, 464
  semi-naïve 273–4, 276
  sophisticated 247, 253, 263, 276, 379, 380–1, 464
reductionism 56–7, 63, 239, 242–6, 259–60, 262, 469
redundancy (minimalist) theory of truth 107, 111, 181–2, 475–6
regulative principles 52, 61
relativism 452
remote, the 46, 60
reports of observation 57–8, 61
request 40, 211, 213–14, 216–17
Russell, B. 61, 269–70, 276, 432–3, 441, 468, 474
Ryle, G. 188, 466

scepticism 425–8
scientia media 53
Scroggs, S. J. xvi
secondary qualities 275
semantic theory 130–1, 135, 234–6, 242, 270, 283
sense and reference 23–6, 85–7, 92, 155–6, 174, 176, 204, 210, 224–9, 236, 270, 283, 286–90
speech as a rational activity 104
stability 163
Strawson, P. F. 23, 171–3, 176, 185–6, 269–70, 467
Stroud, B. 448–9
superhuman observers 60–2, 64
syntax 154–5

Tarski, A. 5, 34–5, 43, 65, 67, 178, 197, 204, 232–4
testimony 158–9, 272–3, 411–28, 471
theories of meaning viii–ix, 1–93, 100–1, 114, 115, 130–1, 133, 135–7, 144, 152, 154–5, 158, 162–5, 176–81, 186, 209–10, 218–20, 234, 235–7, 241, 260, 262–3, 265–6, 269, 270–1, 409, 465, 471–2, 477
  atomistic, *see* atomism, linguistic
  austere 21–2
  falsificationist 82–4, 91–2, 93
  full-blooded viii–ix, 5, 6, 21–2, 25

theories of meaning (*cont.*)
  justificationist 473–5
  modest viii–ix, 5–6, 20, 22, 25–6
  molecular, *see* molecular view of
    language
  pragmatist 137, 139–43, 163–5
  rich 21–2
  as theories of understanding 3–4, 14,
    35–6, 89, 218–19, 234, 270–1, 473,
    477–8
  truth-conditional xii, 18–20, 21–2,
    34–6, 39–41, 57–8, 60–2, 65–6, 74,
    77, 88, 91, 92–3, 100, 111–13,
    115–16, 143–6, 163–5, 176–81, 199,
    218, 237, 241–2, 254, 263–5, 471,
    473–4, 477
  verificationist 22, 41, 70–4, 143–4,
    163–5, 199–201, 471, 475
theory of truth 5–6, 11, 12, 14, 17,
  19–20
time travel 349–52, 364–5
translation manual 2–3, 6, 13, 15, 20, 97,
  114, 130, 134
true in virtue of 52–3, 60–1, 66–7, 248,
  378
truth and meaning 118, 147–65
truth as correspondence 52, 117, 178

truth, concept of 39–40, 42, 47–52, 56,
  109, 117–19, 157–9, 161–2, 164, 178,
  182–3, 188–201, 217, 219–21,
  259–61, 476–7
truth-definition 5, 178, 197, 204
T-sentences 5, 9, 16, 57, 67–8, 197

unbounded quantification 46, 60, 61
undecidable statements 46, 60–1, 63,
  69–70

vagueness 468
vehicle of thought 99, 149, 151, 156,
  166–87

Wells, H. G. 349
what "true" is a predicate of 125–8
Whitehead, A. N. 432–3
Williamson, T. 416
Wittgenstein, L. xii, xv, 26–31, 34, 38, 66,
  91, 97, 99, 108–9, 111–14, 116, 121,
  123, 151, 167–8, 173, 181–7, 188,
  204, 210, 216, 237–8, 241, 263, 276,
  367, 377, 423, 425, 432, 446–53,
  456, 459–60, 465, 466, 469, 472
Wodehouse, P. G. 94
Wright, C. 465, 467